RETAIL MANAGEMENT

RETAIL MANAGEMENT
Satisfaction of Consumer Needs

Raymond A. Marquardt
University of Wyoming

James C. Makens
University of Dallas

Robert G. Roe
University of Wyoming

The Dryden Press
Hinsdale, Illinois

COVER: Model of "City of the Future", conceived by a planning and design team of EW DIRECTIONS, INC., Stroudsburg, Pa., store development firm. Originally proposed in 1972, the plan was a pioneer effort to foster recognition of the vital need to utilize natural land contours in ecologically sound development of organic living, shopping and working environments.

CONTENTS

PREFACE

APPROACH

"Retailing," as used in this book, refers to all the business activities that are concerned with selling goods and services directly to ultimate consumers. This definition includes all forms of selling to the ultimate consumer: direct-to-consumer sales activities made through store outlets, by house-to-house canvass, or by mail order—including the selling of services as well as goods. This broad definition of retailing is important because the annual growth in consumer demand for services is expanding faster than the demand for many merchandise items.

A retailer cannot be limited by a narrow definition of his business. His very existence depends upon his ability to satisfy consumer wants. This cannot always be accomplished if a retailer retains his traditional product/service offering. The rising level of competition offered by other retailers, increasing disposable personal income, increased consumer mobility, and the psychological need of consumers for more individualized, personal service have made it imperative that a retailer truly satisfy consumers' needs whether he intends to grow or merely remain in the retailing business.

Thus the retailer must first determine what the consumer wants. Then he can use all the elements in the "marketing mix" (such as price, promotion, service, merchandise selection, location, etc.) to satisfy these consumer needs. This is not an easy task. It requires a great deal of ingenuity and creativity to be able to meet the ever-changing needs of consumers.

Any change in his merchandise selection, prices, promotion, location, or service involves the consideration of many alternatives. To further complicate matters, a change in any one element may affect all other elements the retailer uses to sell his merchandise. For example, changing from a high-price policy to a low-price policy must also necessarily affect the quality of merchandise carried, the merchandise assortment carried, the level of service provided, and the type of promotion used. Although a retailer may not be able to investigate every interrelationship in detail, he must be able to determine which interactions are significant and must investigate the consequences of these significant interactions.

This book presents a discussion of the process of the continuous choice of appropriate alternatives. It provides the reader with more than a descriptive view of retailing by using marketing analysis to obtain the "why" and "how," in addition to the "what," of retailing. The retail manager is treated as the decision maker who determines goals and objectives, defines problems needing attention, and generates and evaluates alternative courses of action. This approach will, hopefully, provide the reader with a deeper and longer lasting understanding of retailing fundamentals. The emphasis is placed upon the development of a process that can be used to think through and solve retail problems.

Retailing is influenced by many external factors besides consumer preferences. The legal system prevents the retailer from having complete control over most of the elements of the marketing mix. Increased governmental regulation over pricing, advertising, and mergers illustrates the trend toward more restrictions on retailers. This book will attempt to explain the more important current legislation that influences retailing because in some areas (pricing, in particular) the restrictions may become so severe that firms will spend most of their time and effort in merely complying with the law.

AUDIENCE

This book is written for several types of prospective readers. The person who is investigating retailing because of an interest in retailing as a career will find a comprehensive treatment of the more important retailing principles. The more casual reader, who is reading the book to see what "goes on" in a retail store, will find a discussion of the actions that take place in the entire retailing system. Such a reader will also find that the economic, social, and legal environments affect retailing greatly.

An effort is made to integrate some of the newer retail concepts derived from the fields of marketing, finance, economics, statistics, and the behavioral sciences. This has been done at a relatively low level of sophistication, so that the reader benefits by the exposure to new ideas. Thus the book contains material that will be useful to persons presently engaged in retailing.

It is hoped that this book will be stimulating and appealing to any undergraduate student who wants to investigate retailing. It is written in a manner that requires no prerequisite courses. The contributions of the behavioral sciences, management, and marketing are discussed in Chapters 2 and 3.

The primary concern of the first three chapters is to build the analysis of retailing on a sound foundation—not to repeat material taught in these courses. Contributions of other academic fields, such as economics and statistics, are presented when appropriate in the discussion of the retail topic—where the outside field makes a significant contribution. A knowledge of any of these outside fields might speed up the learning process. However, the presentation is simple and it assumes no prior knowledge of the outside areas.

ORGANIZATION

This book is organized to proceed from the general to the specific. The general retailing environment is discussed in the first three chapters, which provide the foundation for retail decision making. They also emphasize the dependence of retailing upon the consumer, who is influenced by many factors. Chapter 1 consists of an overview of the retail environment, including a presentation of current retailing trends and some of the alternatives available to would-be retailers. Contributions that the fields of consumer behavior, management, and marketing make to retailing are discussed in Chapters 2 and 3.

Part 2 consists of four chapters that identify the retailing opportunities available by using proper procedures in product planning (Chapter 4), store location (Chapters 5 and 6), and store layout (Chapter 7). These three opportunities require careful planning before the outlet is opened because they involve fairly long-term commitments which cannot be changed overnight. The merchandise assortment is probably determined first because it is usually dependent upon specialized managerial skills or particular market demands.

The most appropriate store location may then be selected—in a manner that will indicate that there is a sufficient market volume to profitably support a retail outlet of the selected type. Store layout can then be determined so that it will provide compatible physical and psychological support for the product line and the site used by the retailer.

Part 3 contains a discussion of sales stimulation policies, such as pricing (Chapter 8) and promotion (Chapters 9, 10, and 11). Policies are required in these areas as they identify basic courses of action to guide the business toward the attainment of its objectives. If policies are not developed, the retailer is likely to become so occupied with routine operating details that major decisions are not given sufficient consideration.

Operation policies, practices, and controls are discussed in Part 4, which consists of four chapters. Merchandise management is discussed in Chapter 12. Physical distribution, handling, and buying considerations are presented in Chapter 13. Other topics included in this section are personnel (Chapter 14) and financial control (Chapter 15). This section deals with the organization of the work that must be done to accomplish the firm's objectives. Successful store operation requires that a large number of tasks be performed by the store's personnel, who use its equipment and labor-saving techniques to effectively accomplish the firm's objectives. Financial control involves the task of seeing that the performance of the firm conforms to the company plans. It consists of establishing desired standards of financial performance, providing for periodic information that will reveal if the plan is or is not being carried out, and taking appropriate corrective action to bring activities back in line with the plan.

Part 5 consists of a one-chapter presentation of some of the peculiarities that retail service firms incur in their effort to serve customer needs at a profit.

The concluding three chapters (17, 18, and 19) are concerned with planning for the future and evaluating the effectiveness of the retailer's current activities. Chapter 17 contains a discussion of the planning and research efforts needed to prepare for changes that are likely to occur in the future. Chapter 18—"putting it all together": the retailing audit—attempts to pull all the concepts together in the form of a retailing audit. This chapter considers the retailing audit as something separate and more comprehensive than other control efforts. This retailing audit chapter provides an opportunity to review the major concepts in effective contemporary retailing as they have been presented in this book.

Each chapter concludes with a carefully prepared summary and several short cases. These cases are designed to illustrate the principles developed in that chapter. A glossary of definitions of the more important terms in retailing is presented at the end of the book, in Appendix A.

ACKNOWLEDGMENTS

Unfortunately, it is impossible to enumerate all the persons who contributed to the preparation of the book. Especially helpful criticisms and comments were made by Dr. Paul E. Green of the University of Pennsylvania, Dr. Philip Kotler of Northwestern University, and Dr. Anthony F. McGann, Dr. Jack C. Routson, and Mr. Robert Frahme of the University of Wyoming. Many other professional retailers provided material, cases, and helpful suggestions on specialized topics. To all of these individuals, and also to our students, who have criticized and made comments on the original manuscript, we are most grateful.

We are also very indebted to Mrs. Eileen Routson and Mrs. Charlette Donelson, who provided invaluable editorial assistance, and for the exceptional typing and organizational assistance performed by Mrs. Lucille Roehrkasse, Mrs. Joey Smith, Mrs. Evelyn Smith, Mrs. Pamela Seeman, Mrs. Margaret Boevers, Ms. Laurie Bath, and Mrs. Pat McDowell.

Last, but not least, we must thank our wives—Alberta, Kay, and Suzanne —for considerable patience and assitance under sometimes chaotic conditions.

To all of these people we are deeply grateful. Responsibility for any errors or omissions is certainly ours, but the book would not have been possible without the help of these people.

PART ONE

General Retailing Environment

CHAPTER 1

Photo courtesy of EW Directions, Inc.

An Overview
of the Retail Environment

The retail system plays an important role in our lives because retailing involves all of the business activities that are concerned with selling goods and services directly to ultimate consumers. Thus our definition of retailing consists of all the processes in selling *goods and services to the ultimate consumer*, including direct-to-consumer sales activities made through store outlets, house-to-house canvass, and mail order.

This chapter examines the role that retailing plays in the American economic system. Specifically, the significant retail institutions will be identified and the future prospects for the growth and development of the retail industry will be assessed.

ROLE OF RETAILING IN THE U.S. ECONOMY

The three basic types of economic activity in our economy are the extractive and manufacturing, the marketing, and the consumption activities. Extractive activities are exemplified by mining, fishing, and agriculture. Manufacturing processes change the form of the physical or chemical composition of materials by assembling, processing, fabricating, and the like.

Marketing activities move and store merchandise so that the consumer can purchase goods *when* and *where* he wants to buy them. Marketing also informs the prospective buyer of the attributes, capabilities, and usefulness of goods and services. Retailers are the final unit in the chain that links extractive and manufacturing firms with the ultimate consumer. Wholesalers and other middlemen assist the manufacturing and extractive institutions by making the latter's products and materials available to retailers at the time and in the place desired by the retailer. The retailer, in turn, must satisfy consumer needs by offering goods and services in the form and at the time and place desired by the consumer. The consumption activities use the output of extractive, manufacturing, and marketing activities to satisfy individual human desires.

The collective consumption activities of the population have demonstrated that the human desire for a state of well-being is insatiable. Thus new and modified products are introduced each year by firm after firm in an attempt to meet these individual human needs. Figure 1–1 illustrates this cycle of events.

Retailing exists in many forms because each form is part of the most efficient distribution system currently available to meet differing consumer demands. Several factors necessitate a strong retail system.

First, the American economy relies upon mass production and labor specialization to achieve economies or lower unit costs in the production process, which increases the standard of living. The specialization within the production process tends to separate production from the distributive activities (such as retailing and wholesaling) that take place outside the factory. Specialization in the production process results in large quantities of goods being produced by few firms on an irregular timetable and at a few locations (Figure 1–1).

Manufacturers then turn to distribution specialists (wholesalers and retailers) to convert their production into cash. Manufacturers and producers continue to use each distribution specialist until he is no longer the most efficient means for reaching the ultimate consumer. Changes in the distribution system are necessitated because the ultimate consumer, who is highly mobile, continuously demands small quantities of goods near his place of consumption.

The retailer partially justifies his existence by providing the consumer with the opportunity to make transactions conveniently. Consider the alternative in our economy, composed of production specialists. If each specialist

Figure 1–1 *Marketing in the United States: A Macro View*

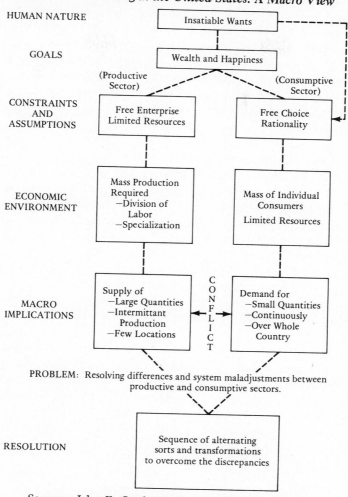

SOURCE John F. Grashof and Alan P. Kelman, *Introduction to Macro-Marketing* (Columbus, O.: Grid, Inc., 1973), p. 75.

had to exchange his specialized product with other specialists for all of the other products he wishes to consume, he would spend most of his time making transactions. Therefore retail outlets provide transaction convenience because they collect many different items that the consumer can purchase in one *place* and in one *transaction.*

Retailers also provide consumers with "place convenience." Although manufacturers may be located many miles from the consumer's residence, retailers and other middlemen help bridge this geographical gap by providing outlets that are near the consumers' homes.

The retailer also performs a useful function by helping other middlemen break the large-volume shipments from specialized manufacturers and producers into smaller units that consumers can use most efficiently. The necessity for "breaking of bulk" is illustrated by the supermarket, which receives "case lots" of fresh produce but sells small quantities to meet individual consumer's needs. A typical sorting and transformation process is shown in Figure 1–2. The raw material may be sorted before manufacturing, transformed into a consumer product, and shipped to a warehouse where it is stored until it is needed. After different styles, sizes, and colors are ordered, they are displayed by the retailer so that the consumer will know of their availability and can purchase the merchandise in the form and at the place and time he desires.

Retailers also function as an informational source to both the manufacturers and the consumers. Moreover, retailers, the mass media, and fellow consumers are the main sources of product and/or service information available to consumers. In many cases, cooperative advertising programs between a manufacturer and retailers are used to provide consumers with information. The trend toward consumerism has placed more emphasis upon the presentation of factual information by retail sales people and retail advertisements. Another phase of the information transmittal process provided by retailers is the feedback of consumer preference and reactions to manufacturing firms, which is needed if production firms are to respond to changes in consumer demand. Retailers communicate consumer information to manufacturers by their order levels, buyers' comments, refunds on inferior merchandise, and the like.

All of these marketing functions must be performed if the *desired* goods and services are to reach the consumer at a convenient *place* and *time* and in the *quantities* demanded by the *consumer*. Individual retailers survive and grow if they perform these functions efficiently. Certainly manufacturers can eliminate all middlemen, including retailers, and sell directly to the consumer, but in this case the manufacturer also becomes a retailer because he is selling directly to consumers.

Figure 1–2   *Typical Resource-Creation Process: Sorts and Transformations*

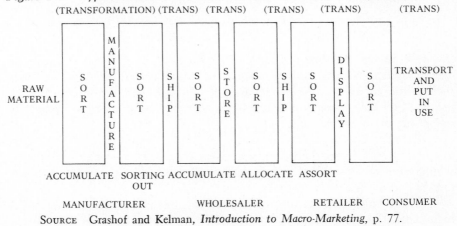

SOURCE   Grashof and Kelman, *Introduction to Macro-Marketing,* p. 77.

SIZE OF RETAILING IN THE U.S. ECONOMY

The importance of retailing is evident from many perspectives. From an employment point of view, approximately 8.3 million individuals, or 15.5 percent of all American employees, are employed in the retailing industry.[1] From a monetary point of view, about 1.8 million retail outlets generate annual sales of over $300 billion.[2] In addition, retailing offers the qualitative advantage of obtaining independence by being one's own boss. Retailing is one of the few remaining business alternatives that requires a relatively modest investment of private capital. Some of the opportunities offered in retailing are presented in Appendix B.

STRUCTURE OF RETAILING IN THE U.S. ECONOMY

The structure of retailing also can be analyzed from several points of view, but space limitations confine our discussion to legal forms of retail organizations and to the classification systems used to describe retail stores.

Classification of Retail Stores

Four retail classification systems will be used to describe retailing from alternative viewpoints: the type of merchandise or service offered, the number of outlets owned or controlled by a single firm, the relative emphasis on prices, and the number and nature of surrounding stores.

By Merchandise Offered

This classification groups retail establishments according to the types of merchandise offered for sale. A wide offering of different types of products to meet a wide range of consumer needs would be classed, on one end of a scale, as a "general store." Many large-scale mass merchandisers, such as K Mart, offer "one-stop shopping"—which is reminiscent of the earlier general store. Admittedly, the variety of goods has been significantly expanded, but so have consumer needs.

On the other end of the spectrum are "specialty stores," which appeal with a narrow range of merchandise to a specific segment of the market. Thom McAn shoe stores, Mrs. Steven's candy shops, and travel agencies all exhibit a narrow line or assortment of merchandise and service. Their competitive advantage lies in their *depth* of assortment. They usually operate under the motto, "If we don't have it, or can't get it, you don't need it."

The nation is currently experiencing a significant increase in the number of specialty stores because the consuming public has more money available for increasingly differentiated needs. Paradoxically, general stores that offer place convenience are also growing to meet the needs of individuals who prefer to save time and energy by shopping closer to home. The consuming public seems to be shopping for everyday needs in general stores and expressing a desire for individuality by patronizing specialty shops.

By Service Offered

In these days of relative consumer affluence the services that a retail firm offers may determine its survival. As noted at greater length in Chapter 16, the American consumer appears to be willing to spend more of his disposable income on the purchase of services for shelter and household operations, arrangement of travel and vacations, medical care, education, and the like. Thus the product offered for sale today tends to be a product-service mixture that will yield satisfaction to the consumer.

In general stores, the consumer expects little or no service beyond credit. Conversely, in specialty stores the potential customer expects to be greeted and professionally assisted in his purchase decision. Thus the breadth of merchandise is generally inversely related to the amount of service provided. Department stores, having made a point of recognizing the differing needs of various consumer groups, provide both minimum-service "bargain basements–general stores" and upper floors that stress boutique or specialty shops. (The boutique effect can be achieved by erecting temporary internal walls to segregate the floor space.) Considerable personal and customer services are also provided.

By Number of Outlets

Another method of classifying retail activity is by the number of outlets owned by a retail organization. "Chain store" refers to the common ownership of multiple units. Such stores have grown because of economies of scale that can be effected through more efficient advertising exposure and the centralized buying of goods. All units within the chain generally exhibit uniform architectural motif, pricing, and availability of credit. Such firms as J. C. Penney and Montgomery Ward attempt to centralize all their purchasing and credit operations so that consistent prices and credit policies are presented to customers everywhere in the nation. Regional grocery chains will often attempt to accomplish similar objectives with regard to price, product assortment, and store decor.

Another aspect of classification by number of outlets is the branch or catalog store. In both cases, firms attempt to establish a presence in a suburban or rural community. They rely on central or main store stocks and expeditious merchandise interchange and delivery to meet the customer's need. This practice makes it unnecessary for such stores to carry duplicate or complete assortments of merchandise and it limits the amount of fixed overhead in numerous buildings. Recent renewed consumer interest in catalog sales, if not discouraged by costly and ineffective delivery systems, may reduce the need for numerous outlets while still producing additional sales revenues.

By Relative Emphasis on Price

A close relationship exists between classifying a store according to merchandise diversity and according to relative emphasis on price. There are no "free services." Every activity performed by a retailer costs money that must be recouped either by lower laid-in costs or by higher prices charged to the consumer. Thus we find that retail establishments that emphasize relatively lower prices either perform fewer customer services than competitors or use a variable markup strategy to achieve "higher than normal" markups on noncomparable or luxury items. The point is that retailers tend to differentiate themselves on the basis of initial markup on the merchandise they offer. Suffice it to say, retail organizations generally can be categorized by their relative emphasis on markups, which results in varying price lines and price images in the mind of the consumer.

By Nature of Neighborhood

Lastly, under the conventional classification system it is possible to group retail establishments according to the number and nature of neighboring stores. Historically, retailers have gathered together at convenient points of travel. Early settlements were usually placed at the convergence of rivers, land trails, or transportation intersections. Today this same tendency can be observed in (a) central business districts, (b) regional shopping centers, (c) community shopping centers, and (d) neighborhood shopping centers. The specific characteristics of each retailing cluster will be presented in Chapter 5.

It is important to note that certain types of retail stores require more "aggregate convenience" than others to prosper and grow.[3] Here again the assortment of offered goods becomes important when viewed in the light of consumer shopping habits. For example, when consumers want to do comparative shopping for apparel, they may frequent a regional shopping center because the central business district, containing the "main" stores, no longer has complete assortments or depth of stock. Many small retailers offer consumer goods to shoppers as they travel by car to the major chain and department stores that are the mainstay of the regional shopping center.

Similarly, it is quite common for neighborhood shopping center clusters to contain supermarkets, drug centers, hardware stores, and service stations because they complement each other's merchandise assortments and are convenient for customers. If properly located, merchandised, and managed, these complementary stores should succeed as a collective unit.

Legal Forms of Retail Establishments

Retail organizations may take one of three common legal forms: sole proprietorship, partnership, or incorporation.

Sole Proprietorship

The single proprietorship continues to be the most popular form of legal organization in the nation (see Figure 1–3). The qualifications for membership are minimal: personal incentive, relatively small initial capital investment, and compliance with local licensing and ordinances. The owner-

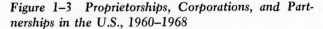

Figure 1–3 Proprietorships, Corporations, and Partnerships in the U.S., 1960–1968

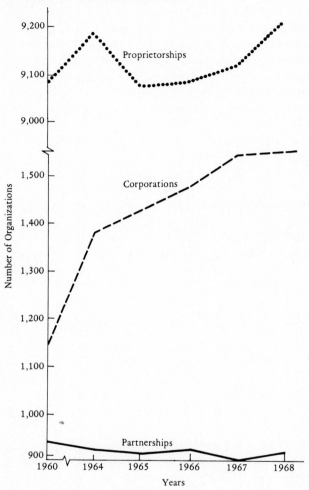

SOURCE   U.S. Department of the Treasury, Internal Revenue Service, *Statistics of Income, Business Income Tax Returns* (publication series number 438) (Washington, D.C., 1963, 1967, 1968, 1969, 1970, and 1972).

manager goes into business simply by opening the door. While the initiation "dues" are deceptively low, the attending risks of failure are high. Some of the primary causes of retail failures are discussed in Chapter 19.

Partnership (Creative Combination of Talents)

Partnerships are created to overcome some of the inherent disadvantages in sole proprietorships. A partnership really represents an agreement of co-ownership, usually among individuals who have complementary business or production skills, some venture capital, confidence in the joint effort, and personal compatibility. While this form of legal organization would appear to be a near optimum arrangement, a partnership is not without potential problems.

Each partner can make a decision without necessarily consulting the other partners and can commit the firm to contract obligations. If a partner decides to withdraw from the arrangement, the partnership ceases to exist (a partner's interest is nontransferable) and a new legal organization must be formed. Even though its access to capital and capacity to borrow increase, the partnership still experiences limited financial capability. In short, there is a wide range of potential conflicts among the partners that may result in a short life for the firm. One should not conclude, however, that a partnership arrangement is unworkable but rather that a partnership provides a vehicle for a joint effort in certain appropriate situations.

Corporation (Legal Depersonalization of an Organization)

When confronted with starting a new business venture, many individuals automatically think of the corporate form of organization, which is exceeded only by sole proprietorships in popularity. The corporate form provides these advantages:

1. Limited liability of stockholders
2. The life of the firm is limited only by managerial effectiveness and economic conditions
3. Virtually unlimited access to a wide range of talents and the abilities of specialists, including professional management
4. Technically better access to sources of equity capital and a wide variety of debt instruments that are attractive to lending institutions because of the potential permanence of the organization.

The potential entrepreneur should be cautioned that while the seeming advantages of incoporation make this form of legal organization most attractive, it has its limitations. For the small business that is just beginning, incorporation is appropriate only when some potential investors have access to significant quantities of venture capital and are looking for capital appreciation through company growth and development rather than income from their investments.

Other disadvantages of incorporation include (1) double taxation of profits, (2) greater state and federal regulation, (3) difficulty of maintaining personal control of the firm, due to the separation of ownership and management, and the conflicting goals of operating management and stockholders, and (4) the general depersonalization of the organization.

In summary, the appropriate use of the corporate form would appear to be after the firm has successfully evolved into an ongoing business. One authority advises that a retail firm should not incorporate until its profits continually exceed $25,000 (in 1966 constant dollars) per year. Even then, such action has marginal economic value, and may be deferred until profits can consistently be projected at over $100,000 per year.[4] The risks of failure are too great to attract investor participation until such conditions are reached.

FACTORS ENCOURAGING EXPANSION OF RETAIL INSTITUTIONS

Every prospective retail career specialist should have a general knowledge of how environmental influences affect the growth and development, or the demise, of retail institutions. While the retailer may not be able to control these influences, he may have an opportunity to influence certain outcomes that will assure the survival of his retail institution.

Population Trends

Without doubt, the most important variable in the success or failure of retail institutions in general is the absolute growth or decline in the population. More people mean more opportunities to attempt to satisfy more consumer needs. The level of need satisfaction, both in terms of type of goods (food, clothing, shelter versus luxury items) and the quantity of merchandise sold, will vary with the individual's life cycle and the relative economic environmental conditions. Such changes in economic conditions spawned the supermarket concept during the Great Depression of the 1930s. The significant inflation period after World War II encouraged the development of the "discount store." Some retail authorities feel that the low rate of births in the 1960s, combined with women's desires for more personal freedom and autonomy, helped spur the development and adoption of fast-food franchising. The harried mother, with her typical 2.5 children, under pressure to fulfill many different roles in her home, job, and community, welcomed the convenience of the limited-menu, fast-food service.

Population movements can have significant impact on retail institutions as well as individual stores. The mass movement of a major portion of affluent America to the suburbs contributed to the demise of the central business district as a center for consumer shopping. Severe traffic congestion and increased street crime in most large cities have reduced the consumer traffic to individuals who could not afford to move out of the inner city and to office employees who spend part of their lunch hour in impulse buying.

Similarly, many small retailers who once thrived on the business generated by people who travel to and from central work areas along major arterials have gone broke. The shopping habits of the American family have been changed by the movement to the suburbs and by the high-speed expressways that connect downtown business centers and suburbia. Shopping centers are "in," major arterial and intersection shopping clusters are "out."

Transportation

The nation has experienced significant transportation changes within the last generation. We moved from the horse and buggy to limited car ownership and mass transportation provided by street cars and commuter trains. Then came the present situation of mass automobile ownership and jet air travel. Convenient and relatively cheap transportation by personal automobiles has assisted in the development of such retail institutions as the "drive-ins," including convenience food merchandisers (such as "7–11" stores), and mass merchandisers of furniture and home furnishings (such as Levitz or Mangurian). Free-standing "one-stop shopping centers" (such as K Mart, Woolco, and Target Stores) and the entire shopping center cluster also owe their development to mass automobile ownership.

Technological Development

The retail community has progressed very far from the days when business was conducted in multiple-purpose buildings with drop-cord incandescent lights where merchandise was sacked in reused paper bags. The introduction of elevators and escalators, pneumatic tube cash systems, glass-front display cases, open displays, computer-linked cash registers, and other physical changes have played a major role in changing the image of retail institutions. Currently, large retailers are adopting electronic transaction centers capable not only of handling the economic exchange but also of recording merchandise movements for inventory management, fashion trend analysis, consumer credit validation, and other valuable information for managerial decision making. Such innovations have made possible mass merchandising and have heralded the long-anticipated (but yet to be realized) "cashless society."

Retailers' Traditionalism

Established retail institutions sometimes resist any change that might better meet the needs of the consumer if they also threaten a loss of patronage to their establishments. One might call such retailers protectionists or micro-oriented merchandisers. Philosophically, the average retailer takes the present retail system as given and attempts to "fine tune" the system by maximizing internal efficiencies, but such preoccupation with detail encourages non-retailers to innovate and carve out new structural niches for themselves. For example, why did the low-price restaurants not recognize and respond to the need for fast-service, limited-menu outlets? They were too busy serving food and competing with each other. Such conservative traditionalism serves as an invitation for the development of new forms of institutional competition by nontraditional, retail-oriented enterprises.

Environmental Factors

Much speculation has been advanced as to why and how retail institutions either fail or adapt and change.

The "natural selection" or "survival of the fittest" concept maintains that the retail institution that most effectively adapts to its environment is the one most likely to survive and grow. A firm must have the ability to adjust to changes in technology, competition, consumer demographics, economic conditions, and social and cultural attitudes on relatively short notice if it is going to survive in the competitive business world. Retail organizations must be flexible enough to make needed responses quickly.

The "wheel of retailing" or life cycle concept explains the evolution of retail institutions. The basic premise, developed by Professor Malcolm P. McNair, is that a new retail institution first appears with low-margin, low-price, and minimum-service offerings. As time passes, these establishments add more service and upgrade their facilities and offerings, which requires higher margins and higher prices. The process continues until these firms eventually become high-cost, high-price retailers that are therefore vulnerable to the next innovator.

An "accordian theory" is frequently used by retailers to explain changes in merchandise assortments. This explanation involves the historical tendency for retail business to become dominated (in an alternating pattern) by general stores, and then by specialty stores, and again by general stores. This concept suggests that merchandise balance is yet another element that influences retail institutional change. A new institution would probably begin as a specialty store because of limited capital and managerial knowledge. Gradually, as it became more successful, it would tend to expand offerings until it eventually became a general store.

A common thread runs through these three explanations: inappropriate cost management. In each case, a new institution is launched with a limited selection, deliberately chosen for a specific customer group that purchases on the basis of price. It is located in a simple facility, which results in lower overhead costs. Combined, all these factors permit the new retailer to offer relatively low-price products and/or services. If the firm is successful, it is emulated by other competitors, each trying to win a share of the relevant market segment.

If one asumes that, for all practical purposes, prices cannot be significantly lowered, then the emulators practice "one-upmanship" by adding "free services," broader assortments, credit, and even trading stamps to hold or increase their share of the market. As the services become institutionalized by this steady, incremental, spiral process, the affected retail institutions become "fat," traditional, and generally locked into a higher cost level of operation due to consumer expectations. In the meantime, prices have been gradually and selectively raised—and are usually publicly justified on the basis of increased manufacturing costs—until the very thing that gave the institution its start, low price, has been lost.

Astute marketeers detect periodic consumer dissatisfaction with relatively high prices, particularly during periods of significant recession or inflation, and rush in with the original low-price concept, and the cycle repeats itself.

Some retailers justify adding "frills" by saying that, as their target market's income is increased, they must tradeup or lose the market because the consumer wants to shed his "poor" image and buy products and services that carry more status. This may be an appropriate strategy for some merchandise, but it has been overused.

Institutional failure also may be hastened by transportation system changes. These are the same forces that encouraged shopping center development and spelled the demise of small, independent, local neighborhood retailers unless they relocated in other, appropriate locations.

In summary, environmental factors can significantly affect the growth and development, or the demise, of selected retail institutions. The successful retailer anticipates such events and forecasts their impact on his operation so that he can take innovative or adaptive action instead of some form of defensive reaction.

RETAILING TRENDS

The number of U.S. retail establishments has increased slightly since 1954. This increase, however, has been confined to growth in the number of multi-unit (chain and franchise) stores (see Table 1–1). The number of independent, single-unit retail outlets has actually declined slightly since 1954. This same trend toward multi-unit organizations exists in an even more pronounced sense for retail sales volume. Multi-unit retail organizations accounted for only 30 percent of total retail sales in 1954, but they now account for 40 percent (Table 1–1).

Table 1–1   U.S. Retail Trends

ITEM	1954	1958	1963	1967
Retail Trade				
Total establishments (thousands)	1,722	1,795	1,708	1,763
Multi-unit organizations (thousands)	167	183	220	220
Total sales ($ billion)	170	200	244	310
By multi-units	30.1%	33.5%	36.6%	39.8%
Per capita	$1,055	$1,152	$1,294	$1,567
Payroll ($ billion)	18	22	28	36
Paid employees, Nov. 15 work week (thousands)	7,124	7,942	8,410	9,381*
Proprietors of unincorporated businesses (thousands)	1,766	1,825	1,546	1,624
Selected Services				
Total establishments (thousands)	786	979	1,062	1,188
Receipts ($ billion)	23	33	45	61
Payroll ($ billion)	7	9	12	18
Paid employees, Nov. 15 work week (thousands)	2,362	2,904	3,262	3,841*

* Data for week including March 12.
SOURCE   U.S. Department of Commerce, Bureau of the Census, *Pocket Data Book, USA 1971* (Washington, D.C.: U.S. Government Printing Office, 1971), p. 319.

The overall increase in retail sales has taken some of the sting out of the increased competition that multi-unit organizations are giving independent, single-outlet operators. Retail sales have increased from $170 billion in 1954 to $310 billion in 1967 (Table 1–1). Thus, although single-unit retailers have been losing their share of the total business to multi-unit organizations, the total retail market has expanded so rapidly that the sales of single-unit outlets have increased from about $12 billion in 1954 to about $19 billion in 1967. This pattern does not exist in all types of retailing. For example, multi-unit stores accounted for about 81 percent of all department store sales in 1970.[5]

The trend in services has been for an even faster rate of growth both in number of firms and sales (Table 1–1). Sales have more than doubled since 1954, while the number of firms has increased by over 50 percent.

Retail executives believe that trends are now developing that will exert a considerable impact upon future retail operations.[6] These projected trends now will be discussed.

Economic Trends

The data in Table 1–1 indicate that retail sales have increased because of increases in both population and per capita sales. Despite the declining birth rate, the U.S. population is not expected to stop growing until the year 2020.[7] In addition, family incomes are expected to increase substantially, to the point where three out of five American families will have incomes of $15,000 or more (in 1972 dollars) by about 1990.[8] Currently, only one family in four has an income of $15,000 or more. Retail executives believe that this increase in income will upgrade the demand for quality and specialty merchandise, better customer service, and better retail personnel. Increasingly limited natural resources may cause an even greater demand for skilled repair service and services such as leasing.

A sharp expansion of government controls over business is likely to result in antitrust actions, limitations on corporate growth, and environmental regulations. Retail executives foresee an increase in the price of most goods to cover the cost of proper disposal.[9] Most retailers believe that this cost will result in a price increase paid by the consumer, and don't believe that the added cost will be paid in the form of a reduced retail profit margin.

Employment Patterns

Retail executives believe that the four-day, 32-hour work week will become common by the late 1980s.[10] The increased leisure time presented by this factor is believed to call for a 365-day, 24-hour-a-day opening for many retail outlets. This would result in higher in-store labor costs, and would also increase the market for leisure merchandise. The increase in women who work outside the home is another factor that would encourage the extension of store opening hours. Fifty-one percent of all women in the 18–64 age group were employed in 1971, and this is expected to increase to 65 percent by 1987.[11] This increase in the number of working women will enhance the sales of women's fashions and convenience goods and services.

Technological Innovations

New advances in technology are expected to have an important effect on the retailing structure. Retail executives believe that in ten years better in-store use of computerized information will reverse the present trend for tactical decisions to be centralized in chain store operations (even though they accept a trend toward centralized buying).[12] Between 50 and 60 percent of the general merchandise purchasing is now handled through general buying facilities or cooperative central buying offices, and this figure is expected to rise to 75 percent by 1986.[13] A nationwide computerized credit and banking system is expected to be in operation by 1989.[14] Such a system will eliminate many customer service problems that result from a lack of coordination among the numerous retail credit cards and accounts. It will reduce operating expenses, but it may also reduce store loyalty.

Cable television is likely to revolutionize promotion and sales methods by the early 1990s, when cable television is expected to be in 50 percent of American households.[15] It will be designed so that consumers may use it to order merchandise that has been displayed on their television set.

Future Trends

Retail executives believe that—besides cable television—catalog stores, discount houses, direct mail, and telephone selling are likely to offer the most growth possibilities in the future. Discounters accounted for 15 percent of the total general merchandise sales volumes (excluding groceries) in 1971.[16] The growth in discounting is expected to continue until discounters obtain 25 percent of the general merchandise sales volume.[17] The furniture warehouse retailer (such as Levitz and Wickes) is regarded as a major threat to established furniture outlets. In addition, grocery, drug, and other specialty retailers are likely to generate new competition for the consumers' general merchandise business.

A renewed emphasis upon the pleasurable aspects of shopping is another trend that should accelerate in the next few years. In an attempt to reestablish excitement in the marketplace, retailers are expected to locate their stores close to a variety of competitors in a single suburban shopping complex. New department stores may "be located in geographical clusters, each within a few miles of other units of the same chain, and almost never located as single operating units."[18] These department stores are expected to place increased emphasis on boutiques and specialty shops within the department store itself. This will allow them to provide more individualized service and to appeal to specific kinds of consumers.

The future of the specialty stores appears bright. They accounted for

40 percent of the general merchandise market in 1971, and their share is expected to increase to 48 percent by the mid-1980s, although the *number* of small, independent specialty stores is expected to continue to decline. Those that survive will become stronger and will generate the increase in sales volume.

Retail changes may be explained and predicted by using the matrix presented in Figure 1–4, where the major problems that households face in their shopping tasks are listed vertically. Each retailer must solve most, if not all, of these problems for the consumer if he is to prosper, or even survive. The retailer is also faced with major constraints (listed horizontally in Figure 1–4) that limit his ability to solve these household problems. The consumer is anxious to get the greatest gains from shopping with the least investment of money, time, and energy. He also wishes to avoid any tension that may be associated with uncertainty over product/service performance and with being offended in the process of shopping.

The retailer must have a profit to grow or even to survive. Obviously, this limits the ability of retailers to solve all the consumer problems. Prices cannot be reduced below a level that will allow them to meet all of their expenses. The second constraint indicates that the retailer will not be innovative unless the innovation will allow him to achieve some differential advantage over his competitors. Any change (such as a price reduction) that can be easily copied will be effective only in the short run. The fact that one outlet cannot satisfy all consumer needs is presented as the third constraint. Every household is unique, so that store offerings that appeal to some consumer groups do not appeal to others. For example, minimum service may attract economy-oriented customers but alienate those who want personal attention.

Retailers are also limited by the need to service an adequately sized market if they are to be profitable. Thus small communities are not able to attract discount or department stores because these institutions require large clusters of people. Technology and the government also place restraints on the retailer's ability to solve consumer problems, but technological improvements can ease retailing constraints by:

1. Reducing the cost of handling merchandise and servicing shoppers
2. Providing a wider variety of goods and services
3. Providing more adequate knowledge of consumer needs and the retailers' operations
4. Improving communication to consumers and employees.

One can use the matrix framework presented in Figure 1–4 to predict the effect that sociological and technological changes will have upon retailing in the 1980s.

> In view of possible decline of convenience stores (such as supermarkets) and the rise, in their place, of large-scale warehouses offering direct delivery to homes, and of a probable increase in the importance of certain specialty

Figure 1–4   *A Matrix for Explaining and Predicting Change in Retailing*

HOUSEHOLD PROBLEMS TO GET THESE GAINS FROM SHOPPING:	RETAILER CONSTRAINTS ON MEETING HOUSEHOLD PROBLEMS					LIMITS OF TECHNOLOGY			
	1. Need for Profits to survive and grow	2. Need for differential advantage to achieve profits	3. Diversity Among Shoppers	4. Size of Market	5. Government Interventions	6. For low cost handling of merchandise–shoppers	7. For production of goods and services wanted	8. Inadequate Knowledge	9. Communicating effectively to relevant audiences
1. Product or Services needed or wanted	●	●	●	●	●	●	●	●	●
2. At time wanted	●	●	●	●	●	●	●	●	●
3. If possible with immediate gratification or pleasure	●	●	●	●	●	●	●	●	●
4. And feeling of oneness (sense of belonging) with seller	●	●	●	●	●	●	●	●	●
AND TO GET GAINS WITH THE LEAST POSSIBLE INVESTMENT OF:									
5. Money	●	●	●	●	●		●	●	●
6. Time	●	●	●	●	●		●	●	●
7. Energy	●	●	●	●	●		●	●	●
8. Psychological Pain (such as uncertainty)	●	●	●	●	●		●	●	●

SOURCE   Eugene R. Beem, "Retailing in the 1980's," *Marketing Insights*, November 18, 1968, p. 10.

stores, the matrix shows that there are only six reasons why consumers would prefer going to a store to make their purchases rather than having the merchandise delivered to their homes with virtually no investment of shopping time and money:

1. A few stores are able to provide that sense of belonging that causes shoppers to talk about "our store."
2. Some kinds of shopping provide immediate gratification, for instance, the buying of apparel and certain home furnishings.
3. The store will offer more choices to the shopper.
4. The difficulty of deciding what merchandise will be needed, which is solved by a quick trip to the store to procure the item as soon as the need for it arises.
5. Less uncertainty or psychological pain, because merchandise of questionable quality or appropriateness can be personally scrutinized. (Tomatoes can be pinched and the fat in the steaks shrewdly evaluated.)
6. To save money. So long as store operation is cheaper than home delivery, many shoppers will invest the time and energy to make the trip.[19]

Changes in consumer values may lead to tomorrow's shoppers searching mostly for immediate gratification. They may avoid the time and energy investments needed for shopping at stores. The increasing concentration of population, the proliferation of the automobile, limited fuel supplies, and the growing affluence of our society are likely to stimulate non-store shopping, even if in-store shopping could offer a moderate savings in money.[20]

Other pertinent elements in the sociological stream are steadily rising labor costs, the resulting escalation of store operating expenses, the increased cost of space, and the impracticality of having idle store space except during the relatively few hours of the week when the great mass of customers appears. Greater affluence is also creating greater diversity among shoppers, which makes it increasingly difficult for stores to maintain sufficiently large stocks of the unique product assortments wanted by each shopper.[21]

However, the future is also likely to bring an increase in the importance of outlets where shopping is fun or where shopper uncertainty is high. For example, interior decorator shops may employ expert counselors who have access to an almost infinite variety of decorator items. Picture slides could be used to allow shoppers to put together varieties of colors and styles of furnishings and view them as they would look when installed in the home. This would reduce uncertainty and be an enjoyable experience for most shoppers.

Retail outlets are likely to be hooked into an electronic complex. Indeed, the increase in total retail selling space may level off, and perhaps decrease, as electronic in-home shopping grows.[22] The remaining outlets may be quite different in location, architecture and fixtures, and service. A proposed design for the store of the future (Figure 1–5) incorporates the concept of spiral outside walls that expand with seasonal selling needs or for permanent expansion. The central core of service facilities and the restaurant are the

Figure 1–5 "Store of the Future," As Designed by Edinger-Wyckoff, Inc., May Be an Ascending Spiral, with Walls That Expand or Contract at Will

focal points for people using the spiral walkway and moving ramp, which give a panorama of the entire store.

Cities of the future may well consist of circular stores with concentric transportation beltways encircling the city's core (Figure 1–6). The core would be composed of apartment dwellings, banks, hospitals, schools, commercial businesses, and the central shopping center. Underground are parking lots, offices, and public utilities and services.

SUMMARY

In this chapter we have attempted to identify the significant retail institutions and to examine the future of the retail industry. We found that the general trend of retail growth is healthy.

Significant changes are taking place among the various retail institutions. Large, multi-unit organizations are growing at the most rapid rate. Catalog stores, discount stores, furniture warehouse retailers, supermarkets, drug store chains, franchises, and carefully managed specialty stores are expanding their sales volume. However, the number of small, independent retailers has declined.

These changes have resulted from environmental influences (such as increased incomes, population increases, movement to the suburbs, increased mobility, and technological changes) and the resulting managerial responses to these changes.

Figure 1–6   "New Town," Proposed by Edinger-Wyckoff, Would Provide a Total Environment for a Population of 125,000

Products and services must continue to reach the consumer in the form and at the time and place that he or she desires. The retailing industry plays an important role in this process, but individual retailers will continue to be successful only if they are the most efficient means by which manufacturers and producers can reach the ultimate consumer.

QUESTIONS

1. Why is retailing important in the U.S. economy?
2. What basic economic law dictates whether an individual retailer can stay in business?
3. Discuss the effects of consumer preference on retailing.
4. Considering the movement toward general, emporium-type retailing, what competitive advantage is held by specialty stores, if any?
5. How would you explain the rapid growth of chain stores?
6. Distinguish between sole proprietorship, partnership, and corporate forms of retail establishments. What are the advantages and disadvantages of each?
7. What is the primary factor that determines the success or failure of retail institutions?
8. What factors have influenced the development of discount stores and fast-food franchising?
9. How has transportation influenced the development of retailing since World War II?

10. How would the anticipated "cashless society" affect retailing? What problems might be anticipated?
11. How has "conservative traditionalism" contributed to the demise of some retail establishments?
12. Since population growth is important in the development of retailing, why has the growth in the number of retail establishments been only modest in the last twenty years?
13. Considering population and labor trends, what areas of retailing do you think will experience the best growth between now and 2000?

FOOTNOTES

[1] Percent figure represents wage and salary employment as covered by the Bureau of Labor Statistics monthly survey of nonagricultural payroll employment.

[2] U.S. Bureau of the Census, *Census of Business 1967, Retail Trade Sales Size,* Bc67–RS2 (Washington, D.C.: U.S. Government Printing Office, 1970), pp. 1–2.

[3] Reavis Cox, "Consumer Convenience–Retail Structure of Cities," *Journal of Marketing* (April 1959), pp. 355–362.

[4] Robert D. Entenberg, *Effective Retail and Market Distribution: A Managerial Economic Approach* (New York: World Publishing Co., 1966), p. 189.

[5] U.S. Department of Commerce, Bureau of the Census, *Pocket Data Book, USA 1971* (Washington, D.C.: U.S. Government Printing Office, 1971), p. 321.

[6] *The Future of Retailing* (Bryn Mawr, Pa.: Robinson Associates, 1973).

[7] Ibid., p. 4.

[8] Ibid.

[9] Ibid., p. 7.

[10] Ibid., p. 11.

[11] Ibid., p. 11.

[12] Ibid., p. 14.

[13] Ibid., p. 15.

[14] Ibid.

[15] Ibid., p. 14.

[16] Ibid., p. 20.

[17] Ibid.

[18] Ibid.

[19] Adapted from Eugene R. Beem, "Retailing in the 1980's," *Marketing Insights,* November 18, 1968, pp. 10–11.

[20] Ibid.

[21] Ibid., p. 11.

[22] E. B. Weiss, "The Retail Store Won't Last Forever," *Marketing Insights,* November 18, 1968, pp. 12–13.

CHAPTER 2

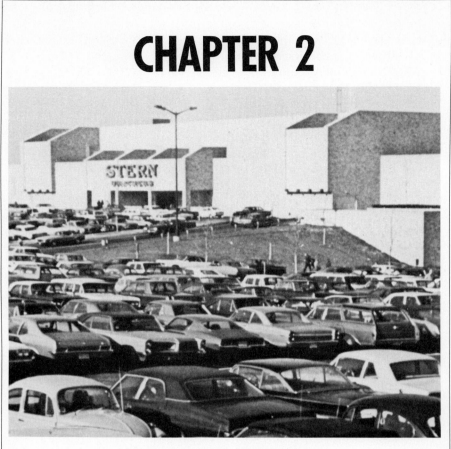

Photo courtesy of Allied Stores Corporation.

Application of the Marketing Concept: Developing a Marketing Strategy

Chapter 1 concluded that retailing is the most important institution in the process of distributing goods and services in the American economy. Retailing represents the ultimate link in the channel of distribution of a complex production and marketing system that has been created to meet consumer needs. This chapter is devoted to linking the marketing process and the contribution of the marketing concept and marketing mix to improve retailing efforts. Although the retail process has succeeded in assembling vast assortments of merchandise to meet client needs, it has yet to totally implement a true marketing concept. The retail process, as practiced by a significant sector of the economy, is a relic of a past production orientation that is in need of innovation and change.

A brief review of economic history reveals that prior to the 1950s the nation was operating on an economic philosophy of scarcity; that is, not enough goods and services were produced at low enough prices for mass consumption and mass consumer satisfaction. Particularly during the depression years of the 1930s, people were concerned with meeting their basic needs for food, clothing, and shelter.

A subtle but profound change in the nation's economic system occurred following the end of the Korean War. The period from 1946 to 1950 was marked by a change from the production of war material to the production of consumer goods and services. The long drought of consumer goods generated consumer acceptance of any physical product that would meet their needs. Once the pent-up consumer needs were satisfied, the nation's manufacturing and distribution system needed a new method of tapping the relative affluence of consumers. A new, more appropriate concern for individual consumers was required to encourage consumption. The marketing concept was formulated to meet this challenge.

THE MARKETING CONCEPT

The essence of this change in thinking is expressed in the definition of marketing, which is "the performance of business activities which direct the flow of goods and services from producer to consumer or user in order to satisfy customers and accomplish the company's objectives."[1] Instead of centering on inventing, producing, and selling a generalized product, the emphasis shifted to determining the consumer's needs and wants first. Using these findings, the firm can then attempt to develop, produce, and make available the best product and/or service to meet perceived consumer needs.

When a firm adopts this philosophy, "the consumer is king." All company efforts are focused on having the right product at the right place, at the right time, at the right price, and in the right quantity to capture the consumer's dollars—profitably.

How does the marketing concept facilitate the meeting of consumer needs? The implementation of the marketing concept rests upon three pillars: genuine consumer orientation, an integrated marketing approach, and the generation of customer satisfaction.[2]

Consumer orientation is implemented by the firm's (1) adopting a definition of the basic *needs* that it intends to serve, (2) identifying the target group(s) of customers it wants to serve, and (3) meeting the varying needs of its target group(s) by using a differentiated product/service offering.

Integrated marketing means that each of the firm's various departments must recognize that its actions will have an effect upon the company's ability to attract and retain customers. Integrated marketing also means that the firm's entire effort can be coordinated to build a strong, positive, consistent image in the minds of consumers. To achieve such integration, many com-

Figure 2–1   A Corporate Structure for Implementing a Marketing Plan

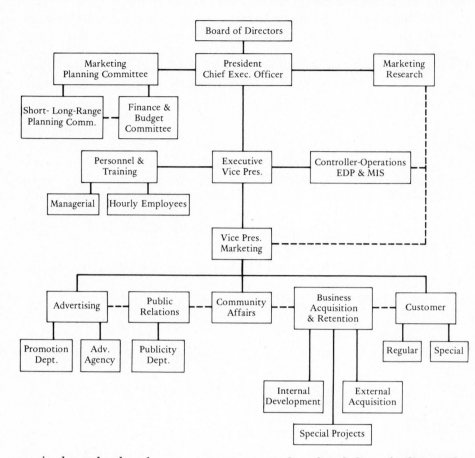

panies have developed a corporate structure that they believe facilitates the implementation of an active marketing plan (Figure 2–1).

The third pillar of the marketing concept involves the recognition that the firm's long-run welfare is dependent upon the amount of customer satisfaction it is able to provide. A firm can utilize its sales people and/or conduct studies to analyze consumer repeat-purchase patterns and attitudes and to obtain other measures of consumer satisfaction. The employees' manual of Marshall Field and Company illustrates how important a concept customer satisfaction is to one large department store. It reads:

The customer is always right if she thinks she is right.

We are more interested in pleasing a customer than in making a sale.

Every sale of merchandise or services includes the obligation to accept the article for credit, refund, exchange or adjustment promptly and courteously to the customer's satisfaction.

We sell only merchandise of the best quality obtainable at the price.

We offer merchandise in a broad assortment from lowest to the highest price at which the quality, fashion and value measure up to our store's standards.

We strive to give completely satisfactory service to every customer.[3]

The sales person serves as the last vital link in the marketing chain. Customers often make long-term patronage decisions on the basis of limited encounters with retailers' sales personnel. The quality of the personal interaction often can be traced to profits or losses on year-end financial statements.

Sales personnel are also helpful in supplementing research efforts to analyze consumer repeat-purchase patterns, attitudes toward merchandise selection, store image, and other measures of customer satisfaction.

TARGET MARKET: APPROPRIATE CONSUMER WITH BUYING POWER

A retailer's most fundamental task is to identify and satisfy a profitable target market. The wide diversity of consumers with individual, unique, personal needs, combined with intensive competition from other retailers for their patronage, mandates that a single retailer can't be "all things to all people." The effective retailer concentrates on satisfying a profitable set of needs commonly held by a certain group of consumers within a reasonable geographic proximity to his activities.

Consumers with unmet needs do not automatically become a profitable target market. Experience has amply demonstrated that individuals are never able to satisfy all of their personal needs because of limited financial resources. Therefore the retailer should concentrate on identifying consumers who have similar needs and the economic ability (money and credit) to purchase the need-satisfying goods or services. Thus the retailer's target market becomes qualified buyers with inadequately satisfied needs.

MARKET SEGMENTATION: CHARACTERISTICS OF QUALIFIED BUYERS

Qualified buyers can be classified on the basis of demographic characteristics such as sex, age, marital status, gross income, geographical location, and so on. A second, and more comprehensive, categorization may be made on the basis of personal behavorial characteristics, such as social values, biases, or prejudices that affect individual purchase decisions. The actual process of market segmentation is explored more completely in Chapter 3.

PRODUCT DIFFERENTIATION: A UNIQUE TOTAL OFFERING

A fundamental but often obscure concept of the total product will be foremost in the mind of an effective retailer. Often retailers lose sight of the fact that products alone do not yield customer satisfaction, that products or services are means to an end. Mere possession of a product doesn't accomplish any goal in and of itself. The perceived usefulness that the product or service will provide in the hands of the owner is the reason the customer wants to acquire it. The retailer must remember that his ultimate goal is customer need satisfaction, not just the sale of goods or services.

Such need satisfaction may be achieved in three ways. First, the product or service may, in the act of being consumed, serve some physical need, such as a cold beer on a hot day. Secondly, the possession or use of a product or service may serve to meet psychological needs—say a large diamond engagement ring. Lastly, a combination of physical and psychological needs may be met by the acquisition and use of products or services—perhaps a mink coat at Christmas for a woman in Minneapolis. In each case the retailer sold a physical product/service, but in reality he also sold human need satisfaction.

Consumer satisfaction is affected by the concept of relative value derived over time. The product may perform perfectly and reliably but yet not be perceived by the purchaser as meeting his or her needs, and hence dissatisfaction will be felt. For example, a housewife and mother returned a pair of boy's blue jeans after six weeks of use to a large department store, claiming that the garment "did not hold up well enough." Even though the lady admitted that the jeans had been worn daily, she felt that they should "wear longer." One may question the woman's motives, but she was discontented and was demanding satisfaction.

Product differentiation may be achieved by artfully blending the four marketing variables of product, place, price, and promotion, resulting in a "marketing mix"[4] (which is discussed at length in later chapters). Suffice it to say, each of these variables can be combined in almost infinite sets to generate a wide range of consumer need-satisfying products and services. The question for the retailer is how to combine these variables into a unique, dynamic package to meet the needs of his chosen target market better than any other current and potential competitor.

PRODUCT/SERVICE OFFERING: A MEANS TO HUMAN SATISFACTION

The selection of product/service assortments represents the toughest and least well-performed function in retailing. Retailers typically identify a target market, then search out the various goods being produced, and purchase items that they feel will appeal to their customers. Generalizations are always dangerous, because not all situations are appropriately described, but most small retailers go to merchandise shows or "markets" semiannually and make purchase decisions based solely on past personal experience and some vague, rough summary of sales records.

Through a combination of economies of scale, large concentrations of capital, and intensive and extensive consumer research through advertising agencies, the producers or manufacturers more or less dictate what products will be available in the retail marketplace. Retailing—the very institution that deals most directly with the consumer—has generally poorly performed the pre-production consumer-information gathering and product-shaping functions. With some marked exceptions, most retailers view their task in product management as determining the location and arrangement of goods that are demanded by their patrons, who have been pre-sold by mass media techniques.

Some notable exceptions are large retail chains, such as J. C. Penney, Sears Roebuck and Company, Safeway, and A & P, which have products manufactured or processed to their specifications to be sold under their own brand labels. Such product-shaping decisions are possible only through some degree of vertical integration or the capture of large segments of the target market.

What product variables can be used to tailor products to a target market's need satisfaction? The physical product can vary in quality or workmanship, type and quality of materials used, or design and manufacture.

The concept of multiple usage seems to be assuming more importance in the products sold in retail markets today, particularly appliances. More and more radios, stereos, and television sets are being produced that use conventional alternating current or may be powered by batteries. Small imported trucks, such as Toyota, Datsun, and Chevrolet's "Luv," are being purchased as multiple-use vehicles, such as commuting vehicles, camping units, and general-purpose runabouts.

Similarly, products are being produced that have wide product adaptability to individual requirements. Such items as men's and women's stretch hosiery reduce the breadth of assortment necessary to meet customer needs.

Another aspect of product determination that may often be overlooked is the package in which a product is presented to the customer. With heavy emphasis on pre-selling merchandise by mass media and with self-service facilities, the package becomes the point-of-purchase sales agent. For example, a retailer, faced with a decision of stocking shampoo in glass or nonbreakable plastic containers, in the past chose the product packaged in plastic. Today, because of ecological considerations and the recycling of materials, the retailer may select glass containers if his target market is ecologically oriented.

A package may enhance the use or encourage appropriate use of a product. The widespread prescription of birth control pills, for example, was delayed until a suitable package could be perfected that would assist the user in maintaining daily usage of the product. A whole range of products has been introduced into mass markets since the widespread adoption of "plastic bubble" packaging. Such packaging not only protects the merchandise but also permits the potential user to see the product without opening or destroying the package.

Another aspect of packaging is providing the appropriate quantity for convenience of purchase and consumption. For example, the Coors Brewing Company of Golden, Colorado, spent considerable sums of money on research to determine the average beer consumption by women at one sitting. The results indicated that women prefer smaller quantities at one sitting than men. Coors developed a 7-ounce aluminum can for the female market, and subsequently has enjoyed great success in tapping that market.

Similar decisions, made by manufacturers of hundreds of items, have allowed retailers to better satisfy consumer preferences. As a result, more pressure is placed on stores to offer a greater assortment of different quantities of goods. If the retailer agrees, he encounters shelf-space limitations that may force him to reduce his merchandise assortment or ultimately move to a larger facility. This is just one example of the interrelatedness of the variables in the marketing mix. Just one change in a small basic decision has its effect throughout the operation.

As noted earlier, branding may play a large part in a product's success and hence affect the retailer's degree of success. Branding becomes particularly important to retailers when national producers develop consumer confidence in their branded product to the point that a significant segment of the population will not accept a substitute. Such customer loyalty is often associated with products that are distributed through exclusive dealerships. For many years, the California Packing Company built and established such a reputation for quality that the retailer was able to charge premium prices for Del Monte foods. More recently, an exclusive franchise for Mazda automobiles was valued at an additional premium of $100,000 to $200,000 because of the national acceptance of the product. Thus, whenever the consumer cannot determine value/price/quality comparisions readily by inspection, branding may become a valuable part of product satisfaction for him.

In addition to the physical aspects of products, the retailer can differentiate his product assortment for his target market by varying the amount, kind, and quality of supporting services he provides. Such services may include the installation of major appliances, education in the use of certain products (such as microwave ovens), the repair of products, the delivery of goods (either free or for a minimum charge), gift wrapping, clothing alterations, return of merchandise privileges, and credit. Each of these services may enhance the attractiveness of a product or the patronage of an establishment because the combined product package provides better customer need satisfaction. A more complete treatment of this subject will be found in Chapter 11. (However, one point should be clear: there are no "free" services. Every added service should either be covered by higher gross margins or be recoverable in increased volume at normal markups on the products.) Accurate retailer perception of his target market's needs will determine the composition of the total product he should attempt to profitably provide.

PROPER PRODUCT PLACEMENT: LOCATION

The one market variable that cannot be duplicated is place. Only one store can occupy a prescribed space at one time. One example of an attempt to reduce the competitive impact of location has been the placement of petroleum retailers (service stations) on all four corners of an intersection of major arterial streets. Despite this attempt at place equalization, each corner has its own set of unique advantages and disadvantages.

For all practical purposes, the place variable can be thought of as yielding convenience satisfaction for the customer. The degree of convenience is closely related to the type of product(s) currently needed by the customer to meet his perceived wants. Entire retail businesses, such as the 7–11 Stores, have been based on merchandising a limited assortment of convenience merchandise in high-population densities and operating from 7 a.m. to 11 p.m. daily. Conversely, a Denver metropolitan area retailer is quite successful in specializing in "rockhound" and lapidary supplies by being open only in the evenings and on weekends. The specific location of a retail establishment has been the subject of considerable research, and will be discussed at length in Chapters 5 and 6.

Store location is doubly important in these times when great consumer mobility is an integral part of the American life style. The automobile can be a curse to a retailer if too many are driven on poorly designed highway systems, which results in serious traffic jams and hinders store access. On the other hand, if adequate entries and exits are available to and from a spacious, amply lighted parking lot, additional customers may be encouraged to shop in the shopping center, thereby increasing customer density for most resident stores.

With increased pressure on people to become involved in more activities, both business and leisure, time has become a scarce commodity and convenience a necessity. Thus retail chains have followed the bulk of the affluent population to the suburbs, where they have become the "drawing stores" of large shopping centers. In well-designed shopping centers, such major stores have generated customer traffic that has given the small retailer opportunities to capture impulse buyers. New shopping centers in prosperous subdivisions do not spell instant success for all retailers, but they enhance the concentration of consumers with wants to be met.

One word of caution should be noted concerning significant common ownership of the same kind of retail establishment in the same general place. According to the Clayton Act and the subsequent legal cases concerning the reduction of competition, competitors at the same level of competition cannot "buy out" or acquire competitors and thereby significantly reduce competition. Thus a large retail chain can be prevented from purchasing other retail outlets that sell similar merchandise in the same geographical area if such action is interpreted to significantly reduce competition.

Place considerations should not be limited to external or geographic alternatives in isolation. Interior design or store layout constitutes a vital consideration in conducting the ongoing business of the retail firm. A potential retail lessee may be offered a location in a shopping center that is quite attractive in terms of pedestrian traffic density but may find the interior space is unsuitable for his purpose. One national chain store accepted an "anchor" position at one end of a medium-size shopping center, only to find that there was no way of utilizing the irregularly shaped space. Departmental isolation and poor traffic circulation resulted in substantially less sales than had been projected, based on the given characteristics of the target market.

Another interior layout problem may result from the critical placement of supporting structural members or columns. As noted earlier, customers' needs are relatively infinite, and they are constantly on the alert for new modes of need satisfaction. Thus they shop "where the action is" or "where things are happening." Innovative retailers should constantly consider interior store rearrangement, as well as frequent changes of merchandise displays, to create customer interest. Store layout will be explored in depth in Chapter 7, but it is important to note that the placement of a department's merchandise and its periodic rearrangement can serve a vital function in generating customer interest. Such changes also serve an important supporting role in an effective interior promotion program.

CHANNELS OF DISTRIBUTION: TAPPING DIFFERING TARGET MARKETS

A classic case of using different channels of distribution to tap differing consumer markets is that of the F. W. Woolworth Company, which operates variety stores under its own name and discount department stores under the name of Woolco. A similar example is the Kresge Company and its K Mart stores. In each case the parent firm's stores have established an image of acceptable quality at a low price and are primarily located in low-income neighborhoods. The discount units were established to tap the middle-class suburban market, using free-standing units and merchandising a higher-quality, higher-price, wider variety of goods, and in some locations offering one-stop shopping. Thus the target market may dictate not only the place but also the channel of distribution.

PRICE: RELATIVE VALUE

Most consumers are concerned with one question when it comes to price: "How much does it cost?" The usual clerical reply is some dollar figure, which doesn't answer the full implication of the question. What the consumer is actually requesting is information with which to make a comparative decision. The complex question in the mind of the consumer is, "Are the benefits promised by this product or service worth the expenditure relative to other possible purchase choices?" The actual total cost, in dollar terms, is not generally considered in isolation, as the original question would imply. The price question is just the top of a complex economic iceberg.

At this introductory point it would seem appropriate for students of retailing to note that the price variable is the least effective long-term competitive tool of the four Ps (product, place, price, promotion) available to the marketer. Any retailer can buy merchandise and "give it away." Additionally, any competitor can duplicate any other competitor's price policy in the short run to attract patronage. An excellent example of the marketing effectiveness of price competition among retailers is a gasoline price war. Research has shown that the absolute gallonage purchased by the customers in the immediate vicinity rarely increases during a local price war. In short, consumers have come to view gasoline as a homogeneous product delivered by indifferent attendants in service stations offering equal credit; so price becomes the decision criterion. The retailer is well advised to avoid price competition as his prime competitive strategy.

The classic presentation of price determination is usually based on such concepts of supply and demand. Retailers will supply goods and services only as long as they can recover their costs and make an acceptable return on their investment of time and money. This was graphically demonstrated during the late stages of Phase III economic controls in 1973. Consumers, similarly, will buy the goods and services only when they have resources (money and future-income credit) and are willing to trade their scarce resources for goods and services that provide greater need satisfaction than retaining money or a line of credit.

Mutual agreement in a free market establishes "the price." But this is an ideal relationship, and rarely explains retail pricing behavior accurately. Prices are actually set at "what the traffic will bear." (Chapter 8 will discuss at length the interactive variables of price determination.) Suffice it to say here that the typical small retailer goes to the market and selects merchandise that he thinks will be attractive to his customers. He is quoted a list price by the supplier (less any applicable quantity and cash discounts), adds in freight and overhead costs, and adds a markup of 30 to 50 percent so that he can "price line" his merchandise. Such items as shrinkage, theft, and markdowns are supposedly considered in the overhead costs.

Some manufacturers who encourage resale price maintenance may even pre-ticket the merchandise with the suggested retail price. In such a situation the retailer's pricing problem is reduced to haggling over the "laid in" cost. This is, unfortunately, a description of what happens quite often, but should not be construed as the way prices should be established. Chapter 8 will provide a more effective and profitable approach to price management.

In summary, price is a very relative concept that assists the consumer in establishing his priorities and levels of acceptable need satisfaction. Many different price strategies are available to the retailer, but ultimately he must decide which strategy best fits his firm's image and his ability to best meet the needs of his target market.

PROMOTION: PROVIDING MARKET KNOWLEDGE

"Promotion" is an all-encompassing term for all the processes of telling the consumer what products and/or services are being offered for his need satisfactions. In addition, promotions may inform the consumer of related product attributes, prices, and location of goods and services, and may attempt to persuade the consumer to take purchase action. The promotion process is perhaps the most researched and yet least understood aspect of marketing.

Certain aspects of promotion, particularly advertising, have been—and are—under attack for creating or uncovering latent consumer needs that lead to "wasteful use of the nation's resources." Conversely, without advertising and other promotional processes the consumer would not be aware of need-satisfying products unless he undertook a personal search of retail establishments. Most consumers have neither the time nor inclination for such activities. Complete discussions of the social benefits and liabilities of the use of promotion can be found elsewhere; the task here is to discuss promotion as a retailing competitive strategy.

Retailers can use the promotional process in a variety of ways, but it is useful to separate promotional efforts into two classes. Those communicative efforts that are directed at a broad general class or target market by impersonal means—through such mass media as magazines, newspapers, radio, television, billboards, car cards, handbills or circulars, point-of-purchase displays, window displays, and the like—make up the first category. A second type, personal promotional effort, is directed toward a single individual, such as personal selling in a store, or via telephone, or door-to-door or in-home presentations such as "Tupperware parties."

Regardless of the type or combination of types of promotion a retailer may choose to use, it is vitally important that he use a "rifle" instead of a "shotgun" approach to get the most effective return on his promotional investment. Zero in on the promotional tasks to be performed, establish priorities for each task, select the most appropriate promotional tool, allocate adequate funds to do an adequate job, and then implement the plan. Follow through with evaluative techniques to determine the effectiveness of the firm's promotional strategy. Learn from past mistakes by keeping a daily diary of promotional efforts and those of competitors. One might even keep an annual scrapbook of advertisements, both the firm's and those of its relevant competition, and perform a sales analysis correlating promotional efforts and gross sales. Admittedly, one cannot say with absolute assurance that an advertisement resulted in X dollars of sales, but some inferences may be made and insights gained about future promotional efforts of the competitors.

It is important at this point to establish connective links between the promotional tools. Retail advertising should be focused on generating traffic. This can be accomplished by providing information on seasonal, consumer-wanted products or by reducing prices on regular merchandise for limited periods. Other techniques include purchasing special merchandise or using "give away" contests or drawings for prizes or cash. The essential point of retail promotions is to get people to frequent the establishment so that they may be exposed to merchandise the retailer has acquired for their need satisfactions. Additionally, sales personnel are given an opportunity to encourage, persuade, and convince the potential customer that the firm's products best meet his needs. It is important to note that retail mass media promotions are aimed not only at retaining present patrons but also at attracting new customers. This latter function is particularly important when the selected target market includes young adults who display high geographic and economic mobility.

Personal promotion in retailing is primarily limited to big-ticket or high-profit-margin items that require personal instruction, persuasion, or advice. Unfortunately, the "salesman stereotype" is not held in high regard by the general public due to past unpleasant experiences. Paradoxically, retail salesmen are both the lowest- and the highest-paid employees in business. Many retail clerks earn minimum hourly wages while life insurance salesmen make thousands of dollars per year. The retailer must decide, in light of his target market's need characteristics, what balance of mass media and personal selling will best inform and motivate his potential clientele to patronize his establishment. A complete examination of promotional strategies and implementation will be presented in Chapters 9, 10, and 11.

DEVELOPING AN APPROPRIATE MARKETING MIX

The selection of a unique set of relationships between price, product, place, and promotion results in a market mix that creates and sets that firm apart from the other competitors by creating a unique instrument of need satisfaction.

A retail store may compete on the basis of its unique combination of location, store layout, organization, promotion, pricing, service, merchandise assortment, and buying to create its own "retailing mix."[5] The integrated decisions reached among each of the competitive areas will collectively paint the store image in the minds of the customers. Consumers consider patronizing that establishment which appears to be capable of most completely satisfying their needs. If the firm has anticipated the needs of the consumer in the past, a patronage motive or connective link has been made for associating need satisfaction with that particular store. Thus an appropriate retail marketing mix creates a retail personality that will generate seller-buyer trust, loyalty, and good will.

In order to anticipate the target market's collective needs, a retailer must engage in market planning and research. Each one must segment his market and focus his efforts on a profitable but limited target market. However, even within this target market he may discover varying degrees of heterogeneity among his potential customers. While the major attribute of the target market will be the degree of common needs among these potential customers, selected individuals will have unique needs that the retailer cannot afford to meet.

For example, suppose a man's retail clothing boutique finds it has two potential customers out of 4,000 possible customers that require a 15½–36 dress shirt. The source supplies these shirts packaged and prices them by the dozen in assorted colors, with each shirt retailing for $10. Should the boutique attempt to meet such customer needs? The answer, obviously, is no, because the cost of inventory maintenance and alternative use of shelf space and its associated costs, plus the ordinary fashion obsolescence of a single body style, color, or collar style, would make such a decision unprofitable.

Such decisions may appear clear cut, but as the number of such customers increases or the various needs begin to be more commonly shared (homogeneous), the more difficult the decision becomes. This is the point where market planning really pays off. Instead of reacting to an individual and immediate customer demand and later regretting it, the effective retailer delimits his market mix and *profitably adheres to it*.

However, such lack of response to market requests cannot be absolutely and blindly observed or the firm will not adapt to the changing market needs. This is where constant market awareness through research begins to pay dividends in return for its costs. Properly designed and implemented market research will alert a retailer to secular and fad trends that must be recognized and merchandised if he is to be competitive and profitable.

MARKETING RESEARCH: DEFINING THE ENVIRONMENT

Marketing research, as it is generally applied, had its origin in the early 1900s when marketers began to apply the principles of scientific investigation to marketing unknowns. The application of the techniques of observing, formulating hypotheses, testing hypotheses, and predicting the future has led to considerable insight into a more effective functioning of the marketing system.[6] Such important areas of investigation have included (1) target market segmentation, (2) market forecasting and analysis, (3) market investment considerations, (4) customer behavior, (5) product development, (6) merchandising, (7) advertising, (8) pricing, (9) personal selling, and (10) physical distribution.[7]

This partial list of marketing research efforts gives some feeling of the complexity of the marketing process. While retailing is a terminal system of the marketing process, it contains micro examples of similar macro-marketing problems. The same techniques that are used to solve macro-marketing problems can be applied to similar retail situations. Territory decisions become location decisions; product development questions become assortment decisions; and so on.

Perhaps the most concentrated marketing research effort during the last decade has been focused on consumer behavior, and is done primarily by advertising agencies and producer-sponsored university research. Generally, the retail industry has been reluctant to encourage, or even permit, experimentation in its stores. Actually, the store represents an ideal laboratory for the study of consumer purchase behavior, yet in order to do such research the investigator must simulate the environment. More test stores should be made available and active support of research should be given by the retail industry to find out what the consumer needs are, rather than going to market and taking what the producers offer. Retailers should take a more active part in product development and hence better represent their customer clients.

MARKETING MANAGEMENT: EFFECTIVE MERCHANDISING

The term "merchandising" means many things to different marketing practitioners. The American Marketing Association defines merchandising as the planning and supervision involved in marketing the particular merchandise or service at the places, times, prices, and in the quantities that best serve to realize the marketing objective of the business.[8] For the purposes of this text, we will consider the concept of merchandising as the internal coordinative effort to meet the customers' needs. Admittedly, external environmental conditions, influenced by suppliers, competitors, economic conditions, governmental regulations, product development, and consumer demands, will condition the merchandising effort. However, it is important to stress that just as no single customer will determine consumer demand, no single product or department will determine, in isolation, the viability of a retail operation.

As noted earlier, the consumer has a mental image of a firm or its store, and this conditions his/her behavior. A retail operation is a composite blend of goods, services, prices, promotion, and personnel with certain personality characteristics. Merchandising ties these various qualities together to form a retail business. As Wingate et al. note, differences in merchandising methods are not simply the result of outside factors affecting customer demand; they grow out of differences in the thinking of each store's management team and its degree of willingness to plan ahead in a systematic way.[9] That is, simply stated, the difference between a true merchandiser and a store owner.

The merchandiser fits complementary assortments of goods together in logically grouped categories in attractive store layouts. His prices provide quality satisfaction for the customer at a reasonable profit for the service provided, and he anticipates customer needs of tomorrow. Store owners buy goods for people to buy today, based on their own personal choices and experience. Market management through merchandising is the route to retailing growth and survival.

LEGISLATION AFFECTING RETAILERS

In his efforts to serve consumers the retailer is restricted by the existing legal environment which has developed in response to attitudes of the public as expressed through legislation and interpretive court decisions. The common thread has been that economic competition, as expressed by small competitors, must be preserved at all cost. Bigness is, *prima facie*, suspect.

Specifically, the Sherman Act of 1890 was intended to deal with monopoly practices that resulted in unlawful restraint of trade. This act set the stage for an era of trust busting and a continued campaign against the concentration of economic power. The Clayton Act (1914) was passed in an attempt to specifically define certain acts that were then considered unlawful restraints of trade. The accompanying Federal Trade Commission Act set up the implementing machinery to handle the enforcement of the Sherman Act, the Clayton Act, and subsequent related legislation.

While these acts were used to regulate competition in the general economic arena, other attempts were being made to control retail competition. Small, independent retailers attempted, at the state level, to tax department stores out of existence. Only one state, Missouri, actually passed such a law, which was in effect from 1899 until 1909, when it was declared unconstitional by the supreme court of Missouri, and was later repealed.[10] Some thirty years later, this same sentiment was expressed in resale price-maintenance laws directed at the abolition of discounters.

During this same period, an investigation of internal trade and commerce was conducted by the U.S. Industrial Commission, specifically examing the competitive effect of the mail-order system.

> There can be no doubt that the establishment of the mail-order system tends to decrease sales of the local dealer, and that he has reason to view its growth with a certain degree of apprehension. . . . In so far as the mail-order system exists, however, it must exist because the people in the small towns can not be served so satisfactorily by their home stores as they can by the department stores in the large cities. The first consideration is doubtless the greatest good to the greatest number, and if customers find the mail-order system of advantage there is every reason for its continuance.[11]

Even though the commission laid to rest the attacks against the mail-order system, the anti-competitor spirit was reborn in the 1920s by passage of chain store regulatory legislation in various states. The attack was mounted in the form of a graduated license fee based on the number of stores operated by the chain in the state. Some state legislatures even considered taxing the chain stores on the number of stores nationwide, but abandoned this proposal as unenforceable.

An examination of the history of retailing seems to indicate that whenever an innovative idea to reduce retail costs and prices is introduced it is immediately subject to competitor litigation. While some states were busy attempting to curb chain store growth, other coordinated attacks were being directed at supermarkets. Local ordinances concerning zoning, public parking in front of the stores, special taxes, and license fees created impediments to the introduction of new forms of retail competition.

Such "grass roots" concern inevitably resulted in "anti-competition" legislation at the federal level in the form of the Robinson-Patman Act (1936), the Miller-Tydings Act (1937), and later the McGuire Act (1952).

In order to fully appreciate the impact of the various laws it is necessary to consider the environment of the times when such legislation was passed. After eight years of severe economic depression, many small businessmen were fighting for their economic lives. The basic issue was the size of discounts, such as quantity discounts, promotion discounts, and the like, to be given to various retailers. From the evidence presented to Congress, it appeared that certain producers gave "extraordinary" discounts to large-volume purchasers or retailers, hence putting the small merchant at a competitive disadvantage. Much controversy still shrouds the Robinson-Patman Act, but it went far in the regulation of discounts offered to differentiated retailers.

Following closely on the heels of the Robinson-Patman Act, the passage of the Miller-Tydings Act permitted states to enact so-called fair trade laws or, more appropriately, resale price maintenance laws. Briefly, such laws are designed to permit a manufacturer of a product to set the price of the product in the marketplace. While the Miller-Tydings Act did not impose such a philosophy nationwide, it was permissive legislation that shielded such restrictive laws from being in violation of previous anti-monopoly legislation. The specific laws varied from state to state, but a general feature in most state statutes was the "non-signers' clause." If a manufacturer could "encourage" any retailer in the appropriate state to sign such a contract, then all other retailers were bound to observe the same resale price agreement when notified by the manufacturer.

Such legislation proved so politically popular that by 1941 some forty-five out of forty-eight had passed similar laws. Even the declaration of nonconstitutionality by the Supreme Court in 1951 did not signify the death knell of the non-signers' clause. In 1952 Congress passed the McGuire Act, which contained another version of the infamous non-signers' clause.

State constitutional attacks, combined with manufacturers' indifference due to prohibitive enforcement costs, have reduced the number of effective resale price maintenance laws to about twenty. Today, although these laws are still in effect, most manufacturers do not avail themselves of such protection because they are interested in volume, regardless of retail price. A more detailed discussion of resale price maintenance laws is presented in Chapter 8.

Perhaps of most interest are the unfair practices acts or minimum markup laws now in effect in some thirty-two states. Technically, these laws require retailers to maintain a stated markup of 6 to 12 percent on invoiced cost, although retailers are permitted to lower such markups to meet competition. Most of these laws are not vigorously enforced, but they still remain a potential anti-competitive restriction on retailers.

Although not specifically directed at the creation or maintenance of a competitive environment for retailing, several other related pieces of federal legislation have had a considerable impact on retailers. Among these are the Wheeler-Lea Act (1938), dealing with truth in advertising; the Antimerger Act of 1950 (an amendment to the Clayton Act); and the Fair Labor Standards Act of 1938 (amended in 1966), which sets the current minimum wage of certain hourly employees (with attendant overtime provisions).

Without doubt, the most costly and significant related legislation in recent years is the Consumer Credit Protection Act, generally known as the Truth in Lending Act of 1968; and the Fair Credit Reporting Act of 1970. In the first case, the intent of the law was to provide retail purchasers with factual, comparable costs of credit through the use of a "full disclosure statement" on all merchandise offered for sale or sold on credit. The statements must contain, on a simple interest per annum basis, any interest or service charge, the number of payments, the size of the down payment, and the basis for calculating interest on "revolving credit accounts." Retailers' compliance with this law has been rather costly, with seemingly marginal benefits realized by the consumer.

The Fair Credit Reporting Act permits any credit applicant who is rejected for credit on the basis of adverse information supplied by a credit bureau to be notified of such rejection and the basis for it. He must be notified of the location of the bureau so that he may examine his own file and prepare a rebuttal statement (to be included in his personal file) or have the file corrected. Since credit is so vitally important in the American life style, such legislation was needed to protect the innocent victim from inaccurate credit information reporting and compilation.

In addition to the aforementioned laws, the local retailer is restricted in his activities by local building codes, fire regulations, traffic regulations, and public health laws, all of which go to make up the legal environment in which the retailer is asked to provide consumer satisfaction.

SUMMARY

The marketing concept represents a fundamental reorientation in the economic systems of the world. The industrial revolution emphasized mass production of uniform goods at prices that a wide segment of the population could afford. An age of relative scarcity in the World War II years gave way to an age of relative affluence that demanded new methods of product and service distribution.

The marketing concept was born in the mid-1950s, and continues to gain acceptance in enlightened business centers around the world. The marketing concept stresses consumer need satisfaction through the possession and/or use of goods and services. Instead of designing a car body based on aerodynamic characteristics or an automotive engineer's calculations, the Japanese automakers surveyed American consumer tastes and designed automobiles to sell in America. Their success speaks for itself.

Through the skillful blending of various combinations of product, place, promotion, and price, marketers everywhere are devising an almost infinite series of total need-satisfying packages to vie for the customer's dollar vote in the retail marketplace. Thus the retailer, the ultimate bridge between producer and consumer, bears the heavy burden of anticipating consumer needs and buying, transporting, financing, promoting, merchandising, and pricing goods and services. All of this is done in competition with other retailers in an attempt to serve the consumer better and transform him into a repetitive customer who will assure the businessman of continued survival. The effective modern retail merchandiser is truly a servant of the consuming public.

QUESTIONS

1. Discuss the meaning of the marketing concept. Can you anticipate any future limits on the implementation of this concept?
2. How would you determine how far a retailer should go in satisfying consumer needs?
3. What factors determine whether a retailer has an effective marketing mix?
4. How does promotion serve consumers?
5. Why do retailers generally prefer non-price competition in their long-run pricing plans?
6. What variables are at a retailer's disposal in deciding on a product mix? Using a systems approach, trace the effects on the organization of manipulating these variables. Consider both short- and long-run effects.
7. Cite some examples of product differentiation for various target markets.
8. Pick a consumer product that might be sold by a retailer and suggest a method of segmenting the market for that product.
9. What major interpretation of the Sherman Act has changed since its enactment? How does public opinion run today regarding this interpretation?
10. How would you explain the development of "anti-competition" legislation such as the Robinson-Patman Act?
11. What is a full disclosure statement? What consumer benefits can you see in requiring a full disclosure statement? Do you think that this statement has made consumers more reluctant to make purchases on time?
12. What recourse does a consumer have if he is rejected for credit?

FOOTNOTES

[1] E. Jerome McCarthy, *Basic Marketing: A Managerial Approach* (Homewood, Ill.: Richard D. Irwin, 1971), p. 19.

[2] Philip Kotler, *Marketing Management* (2d ed.; Englewood Cliffs, N.J.: Prentice-Hall, 1972), p. 18.

[3] Ibid., p. 24.

[4] McCarthy, *Basic Marketing*, p. 44.

[5] Ronald R. Gist, *Basic Retailing: Text and Cases* (New York: John Wiley & Sons, 1971), pp. 65–66.

[6] McCarthy, *Basic Marketing*, p. 77.

[7] Joseph C. Seibert, *Concepts of Marketing Management* (New York: Harper & Row, 1973).

[8] Ralph S. Alexander, ed., *Marketing Definitions: A Glossary of Marketing Terms* (Chicago: American Marketing Association, 1960), p. 17.

[9] John W. Wingate, Elmer O. Schaller, and F. Leonard Miller, *Retail Merchandise Management* (Englewood Cliffs, N.J.: Prentice-Hall, 1972), p. 16.

[10] *Laws of Missouri*, H.B. 384, passed at the session of the 39th Assembly, January 4, 1899 (Jefferson City: Tribune Printing Co., 1899), p. 72.

[11] U.S. Industrial Commission, *Final Report of the Industrial Commission* (Washington, D.C.: Government Printing Office, 1902), 19: 548.

INTERNATIONAL HARVESTER
Intensified Dealer Support
by a Manufacturer

The management of International Harvester was seriously planning a totally new marketing organization for the purpose of better serving their dealers and customers. The key man in the new structure was J. P. Kaine, who had formerly served as farm equipment sales manager.

According to Mr. Kaine, several forces had been responsible for the change from the traditional system of a line-field sales approach common throughout most industries. "International Harvester had been consolidating personnel and management down to the bare bones. This didn't allow time for critical planning. Our dealers had been telling us they needed more help with the expanding problems of a modern retail farm dealership, but we simply couldn't give them the assistance they needed. The changing character of agriculture was also affecting our dealers. Farms were getting bigger and the remaining farmers wanted more assistance with their equipment needs."

International Harvester and their dealers realized that farmers needed assistance in scientifically selecting the best fleet of machinery to match their needs. As Mr. Kaine stated, "We needed to change from a traditional production-sales orientation to a true marketing concept with customers and our dealers as the focal point."

Several dealers had adopted sophisticated sales marketing systems, including such advances as radio-dispatched service trucks to aid customers with repair needs in the field. Yet, with a retail sales force of 2,800 dealers, there was still a great deal of work to be done among the bulk of the dealer system.

The problem of rural migration had also affected the dealer organization. In many cases the sons of International Harvester dealers had chosen to leave the town and the business upon graduation from school. This often left the dealerships without a clear succession of interested and qualified managers.

A recent example of the problem of succession had occurred in Illinois, where one of the top dealers in the country had suddenly died of a heart attack. This left the dealership strangled for management talent and cash, as the widow wanted to sell the business.

Overall, the major problem facing farm equipment dealers was that of planning and control. Experience had shown that most dealers did not plan and budget. Only a handful attempted to describe their objectives and then match these against accomplishments.

The new organization plan envisioned by International Harvester called for a greatly expanded dealer support system, as demonstrated by the organization chart. The sales staff was left intact, but would now be aided by new support areas. As an example, the marketing program managers for the midwest, south, west, and northeast were entirely new functions.

The new plan called for a horizontal dissemination of information within the company, and with everyone working together, rather than strictly the old vertical line systems. Such a system would be new to the industry and to International Harvester, and it was admitted that "problem areas" would have to be worked out over time.

The new system first called for a scientific planning of regions by dealer strength and potential. This fell under the responsibilities of the Marketing Services Department, headed by Dr. L. S. Fife. Dr. Fife held a Ph.D. in agricultural economics from Cornell University and had several years of experience in the farm equipment industry.

A research audit had been designed and was being used to classify dealers into four groups, depending upon their relative strengths. This audit had been completed by an in-field research staff, which had surveyed the entire United States as to the market potential and dealer strength within each region. Although the detailed plan was regarded as proprietary information, it was known that it took into consideration such factors as farm size, type of crops, and past sales performances.

Once the dealers had been grouped, the overall plan called for first working with dealers in the "A" market classification or "Best" market, and eventually including all dealers.

The new dealer support program included business management consulting, computerized accounting packages, and other tools designed to appreciate the value of the dealership. It would also include special attention to the problem of parts inventory, as this was a common problem shared by dealers. Many overstocked and, eventually, were stuck with obsolete parts, while others understocked and then could not satisfy the customers' needs. A new computerized parts ordering and inventory system has been developed and is now in use with selected dealers.

The new plan called for greater use of marketing research in identifying consumer needs. The results of a recent market study on combines had shown that International Harvester was not reaching the younger farmers in the proportion it should. As a result, new programs were being directed to this market target. It was felt that the increased use of marketing research, combined with the Geographical Marketing Program managers, would result in new machinery to better meet the needs of farmers in particular regions. Under the new program, large agricultural customers would also be given sales engineering assistance by International Harvester.

International Harvester believed that the future for farm equipment dealers was strong, but that many changes were coming. The trend in the leasing of farm equipment was increasing, and it was felt that this could be an important supplement to equipment sales in the foreseeable future.

Certain areas of the nation were continuing to witness a decline in farm population and several dealers would have to be informed that, in the best judgment of the company, their business very likely would not survive the years ahead.

It was also felt that the role of customer financing might change under the new system. International Harvester had a strong financing plan for dealers and had instituted a "waiver of finance charges" program for customers. This, essentially, allowed customers to purchase machinery considerably ahead of the date of use without paying interest charges. It was also creating additional business for the International Harvester Credit Corporation since the customer now financed his equipment through the company rather than a local bank, and many continued the contracts after the interest-free period.

Future finance programs could conceivably include an International Harvester credit card, to be used by customers for the purchase of small equipment, service, and parts.

At the present time, approximately 5 percent of the dealer network consists of company-owned and -operated stores. The new plan called for intensified use of these stores as training grounds for future management or as experimental models for other dealers. New merchandising, parts inventory, and other programs would first be tried in these stores before extending them to the other dealers.

DISCUSSION QUESTIONS

1. Why should a national manufacturer, such as International Harvester, have to go to the expense and trouble of initiating a complex dealer support system? Isn't it the responsibility of each dealer to conduct his business in the most professional manner? Is the situation facing International Harvester unique to this company?

2. What is your opinion of the new marketing organization? Does it appear as though it can accomplish the objectives in an efficient manner? Do you see any weaknesses?

3. What additional steps should International Harvester undertake to ensure the perpetuity of its independent dealers?

4. If possible, visit a nearby farm equipment dealer. What are the differences (besides merchandise assortment and customer profile, if any) between his business and other retailers, such as a hardware store, a car dealer, or a yard goods retailer?

5. Do the changes facing International Harvester dealers signal the beginning of similar changes that will occur in other retailing areas?

6. Would International Harvester be better advised to expand their system of company-owned stores rather than place so much emphasis on strengthening independents?

7. "The best laid plans of mice and men ofttimes go astray." Isn't the weak link in this new plan the individual dealer's willingness to accept and implement the changes? What, if anything, can International Harvester do to ensure that independent dealers implement new programs?

ENERSYST INC.
Influence of Technology on Retailing:
Vertical Integration and Consumer Behavior

The president of Enersyst Inc. and the Associated Food Equipment Company division of Dallas, Texas, Mr. Don P. Smith, was developing plans for the best method of marketing a new automated system in the vending of ready-to-eat foods. The automatic equipment had been developed by Enersyst under a contract with the owner of a marina and diner on the inland waterway canals. The concept was also applied to studies for the U.S. Air Force.

The air force had been seeking a means of serving hot meals to officers, staff, and enlisted men at sites where a commissary was uneconomical to operate due to the small number of people involved. Mr. Smith was widely recognized throughout the food equipment industry as one of the most creative minds in the business, and had pioneered in the development of new equipment, packaging, and food products. The end product of the development was an automated system that stored frozen food and automatically retrieved and served the hot food. The food server cooked it in a microwave oven and, if desired, added a crisp golden crust through a "finisher" that had been developed and patented by Mr. Smith.

Selection of entrees for separate portions or a complete meal could be performed simply by pushing buttons on the outside of the machine, much as record selections are made on a juke box.

Although Enersyst was not the first company to think of the idea, Mr. Smith believed it was the first to produce a workable machine of this nature. The Swedes had been early pioneers in this field, but their machines were best adapted to the mass feeding of single items and were not set up for automatic smaller operations offering a variety of dishes. The addition of the crisper was also unique to Smith's system, and happened to be a breakthrough in microwave cooking to permit serving freshly crisped and browned foods.

Enersyst had not done any advertising of the machine, nor had it released any P.R. material, and yet several prospective customers had already called on Mr. Smith. They represented a variety of industries, but it was interesting to note the enthusiasm among large agricultural producers, including large corporate farms and cooperatives.

The agri-businessmen stated that they were interested in finding a means of bypassing traditional marketing channels for their products and selling direct to the consumer. As an example, one thought was to establish a chain of quick-food retail outlets along major interstate highways. These would sell such staple foods as fried chicken and french fries or a small steak.

The use of a system such as that of Enersyst would allow a firm to offer quality food at a reasonable price and would eliminate a great deal of the help presently needed in retail fast-food operations.

The possibility of having large agricultural producers as a market target was intriguing, yet Mr. Smith also recognized that existing caterers, contract feeders, and vending companies, as well as retailers of convenience foods and fast-food chains, could also be excellent markets. Thus Mr. Smith was faced with the need to develop a marketing plan, select market targets, and market his invention as a new retailing concept.

DISCUSSION QUESTIONS

1. Who do you believe is the most appropriate market target for the Enersyst system? Would you view a firm such as Monfort of Colorado (over-the-counter stock) or Ralston Purina as a logical customer?
2. Is there evidence today that large agri-business firms are ready to enter direct-to-the-consumer retailing? Who owns the Jack-in-the-Box system or the Betty Crocker Tree House?
3. In your opinion, what degree of interest would established retailers such as Stuckeys, Horn and Hardt (a New York City food vending firm), Kentucky Fried Chicken, Holiday Inns, and others have in such a system?
4. Looking back historically, who seems to be the first to accept dramatic new technology: existing retailers with established patterns of doing busibusiness or new firms with little or no retailing experience?
5. Is the consumer ready for this concept of food merchandising? What steps would a firm need to take to ensure consumer acceptance of this method?
6. Examine available statistics concerning the growth of food retailing through traditional channels and the growth of institutional and fast-food retailing in the past few years. Which has demonstrated the greatest gain? Is this trend likely to continue?

CHAPTER 3

Photo courtesy of J. C. Penney Company, Inc.

Consumer Behavior

Chapter 2 stressed the need for retail managers to study consumer behavior to obtain an understanding of consumer habits and motivations. An improved understanding of the reasons consumers behave as they do can enable management to predict changes in tastes, behavior, and attitudes. These predictions can be used to plan a retail strategy that will reach the consumer more effectively and more efficiently. Indeed, the success of the retailing effort depends upon an understanding of consumer behavior. The effectiveness of retail merchandise assortments, price and promotion policies, and even the selection of store location(s) depends on how well management understands the needs, motivation, and habits of its potential customers.

This chapter is devoted to the task of identifying some basic explanations for consumer behavior. It is concerned with the question, "Why do consumers behave as they do? How do consumers learn? How can consumers' impressions and opinions be modified?" Many large retail managers no longer have the time to interact with many of their retail customers on a face-to-face basis; nevertheless, these managers must understand consumer behavior by being aware of the general concepts and by undertaking specific marketing research projects (such as those described in Chapter 17). Management can then use its understanding of consumer behavior as a basis for building a retail strategy that will better meet the needs of the consumer group(s) the outlet is attempting to serve. The different methods of communicating with and selling to the consumer groups are discussed in the remaining chapters of this book.

GENERAL APPROACHES TO UNDERSTANDING CONSUMER BEHAVIOR

The study of consumer behavior will now be examined from four different approaches. Unfortunately, none of these approaches offers a complete explanation of consumer behavior, but each approach provides a partial explanation of consumer behavior in the retail environment.

Economic Aspects of Consumer Behavior

The economic aspects of behavior involve those elements of consumer behavior that are influenced by income or purchasing power.

Maximizing Satisfaction

Traditional economic theory has focused on the belief that a consumer acts to maximize the satisfaction that he purchases with his available monetary resources.[1] Despite some limiting assumptions, this theory suggests several useful behavioral explanations of consumer buying behavior.

First—other things being equal—the lower the price of the merchandise, the higher the sales level on that product. For most items, a price reduction increases the consumer's perception of the relative value of the item and thereby generates increased sales. This is a general rule, which does not apply to all people or all merchandise items. If some consumers buy a smaller quantity as a result of a price decrease, they may believe that the quality has deteriorated or that ownership of the item has less status value as a result of the price decrease. Some items (diamonds, jewelry, furs, boats, campers, etc.) are used as status symbols and are displayed to gain and maintain esteem. Severe price reductions on these items may not stimulate sales but merely reduce the value of the items in the minds of the consumer. In this case the consumer may not believe that the actual quality of the item has declined, but the display or status value has declined. It is important that retailers identify purchases made for purposes of conspicuous consumption because their pricing, advertising, merchandise selection, and packaging can be used to appeal to this consumer motivation.

A second implication of the economic model involves the interrelationship of merchandise items. Other things being equal, a lowering of the price on *substitute* (or similar) items will lower the sales of the item being observed. For example, a price reduction on the retailer's house brand of clock radios will likely cause an increase in the sales of that item but reduce the sales of the other brands of clock radios the store carries. Some items tend to generate sales for companion merchandise or *complementary* items, and the economic model predicts that lowering the price on one item will stimulate additional sales of its complementary products. For example, retailers may reduce the price and/or increase the promotion of a card table in the hope of stimulating the sales of card tables *and* folding chairs.

The third implication of the economic model is that higher real personal income tends to result in higher sales of goods and services. The amount of the increase, however, varies among specific items and services, and two basic consumer expenditure patterns have implications for retailers. These patterns are the nondiscretionary and the discretionary patterns of income allocation.

The nondiscretionary pattern concentrates upon the consumer's monetary outlays on contractual, necessary, and habitual expenditures.[2] Mortgage payments, installment debt, and insurance premiums are examples of contractual expenditures for which the consumer's commitment cannot be changed unless he wishes to lose some or all of the value of his past payments. Necessary expenditures are those life-sustaining purchases that are made mostly for food, clothing, and medical care. Habitual expenditures are the purchases made so frequently that the consumer develops a regular purchasing plan to acquire them. Daily newspapers, cigarettes, and beer are examples of habitual outlays of a relatively low unit value.

Discretionary income expenditures are made for those purchases in which the consumer is not motivated by a compelling need, and is not generally governed by habit, and which entail some deliberation prior to purchase.[3] Many retailers depend upon discretionary consumer expenditures for their main source of business. Rising consumer income and increased consumer willingness to use credit has caused some retailers to concentrate on product and service offerings that capitalize on these trends.

Certainly the proportion of income spent for nondiscretionary goods and services tends to decrease as consumer income increases. Similarly, Engel's laws and the income elasticity concept can be used to identify those products and services that respond best to increases in consumer income. These concepts are explained and their use is illustrated in Chapter 5.

Expected Changes in Income

Another aspect of income that influences consumer behavior is expected changes in the consumer's income. Income expectations depend upon the percent of chance that the consumer attaches to the likelihood that his income will change in the near future. Expectations also depend upon *how much* the consumer believes his income will increase or decrease in the near future. Finally, expectations depend upon whether the consumer views the anticipated change in income as a *permanent* or simply a *temporary* change.

Consumers who expect a temporary decrease in income usually do not immediately adapt their purchases to this reduced income level.

As income declines, expenditures decline, but at a much slower rate than the decline in income would suggest. On the other hand, unexpected income (which the consumer didn't believe he would receive in the near future) is usually spent fairly quickly. For example, 63 percent of a group of consumers who did not intend to buy a new car actually bought a new car soon after they received an unexpectedly large income.[4]

Social Aspects of Consumer Behavior

Social dimensions of consumer behavior are implicit in those consumer actions that are related either to demographic matters or to reference-group considerations. A demographic study of a population involves an analysis of the effect that age, social class, education, geographical density characteristics, occupation, marriage status and sex have upon purchase behavior. The term "reference group" refers to any group of people that is capable of influencing the behavior of an individual.[5]

Demographic Characteristics

Demographic characteristics that are particularly critical to retailers are population size, geographical distribution of the population, and the social class concept.

The upward trend in the U.S. population, its current and projected geographical distribution, and the effect that these factors have upon retailing are discussed in Chapter 5 (Store Location Considerations). Suffice it to say that retailers have learned that they must serve consumers from a location that is conveniently reached by the consumer. For example, the suburban shopping centers are an outgrowth of population movements to the suburbs.

Social Role

A consumer's social position and the perceptions of his role in society also exert an influence upon retail buying habits. For example, isolated urban dwellers have been found to prefer to make purchases in small stores because the small store provides them with personal contacts.[6]

The *conspicuous consumption* process, whereby the consumer buys and uses goods and services primarily to raise his prestige rather than to satisfy his material needs, is designed to gain for him acceptance by his reference group. Thus the newly rich minority-group member may be in a market group that is especially likely to buy large diamonds or fashion clothing because they offer visual proof that the individual "has arrived."

The individual's role in the family also has important implications for retailers. Some retailers' merchandising strategy may be oriented exclusively toward the actual buyer of the merchandise. Others may orient their merchandising toward the users of the item. For example, a supermarket's breakfast cereal assortment may reflect the preference of children rather than the preference of the adult buyer.

Housewives have historically performed the role of the family purchasing agent, but about 40 percent of the housewives now work outside the home. This additional demand on the housewife's time, combined with lengthened store hours (which allow the husband to assist in the shopping effort at night and on Saturdays and Sundays), has reduced the dominance of the wife in making purchase decisions on many goods and services. One study indicated that 80 percent of the women check with their husbands before making a purchase on an item costing more than $50.[7]

The where, when, what, and how-much-to-spend decisions are not always made by the same individual. For example, Table 3–1 indicates that the husband may have more influence than the wife on when an automobile should be purchased, where it should be purchased, how much should be spent on it, but the color, model, and make may be decided by mutual agreement between husband and wife. Similarly, the wife may have more influence in determining the style, color, and fabric of furniture purchases, but the how-much-to-spend, when to buy, and where to buy decisions may be made jointly by husband and wife (Table 3–1).

It is important for retailers to realize who is buying and to identify the degree of influence the buyer is receiving from within or outside the family. If the influences can be identified, the firm's promotion and merchandise assortment can be shaped to appeal to both the buyer and the influencing reference group.

It is also important to realize that consumers may identify negatively with particular reference groups. That is, they avoid the unique behavioral traits of such a group.[8] Thus a store may have considerable difficulty appealing to two widely different consumer groups simply because members of each group perceive the store to be catering to the other group.

Social Class

The social class concept is another sociological consideration that has helped retailers better understand consumer behavior. All U.S. citizens do not have the same power and prestige. They are engaged in different occupations that are not equally prestigious. They do not have similar possessions or value systems. Thus there is an informal ordering of individuals into relatively similar groupings in terms of social status. A social class is a group of many people who are about equal to one another in prestige and community status. People within a social class regularly interact among members of their group and share the same general goals and philosophy of life.

Professor W. Lloyd Warner is largely responsible for the development of a system of social stratification that divides U.S. society into six social classes (which are described in Figure 3–1). The major contribution of the study of social classes to a retailer's understanding of consumer behavior is

Table 3–1   Marital Roles in Selected Automobile and Furniture Purchase Decisions as Perceived by Wives and Husbands

(N = 97)

Who Decided:	PATTERNS OF INFLUENCE (%) AS PERCEIVED BY WIVES			PATTERNS OF INFLUENCE (%) AS PERCEIVED BY HUSBANDS		
	Husband Has More Influence Than Wife	*Husband and Wife Have Equal Influence*	*Wife Has More Influence Than Husband*	*Husband Has More Influence Than Wife*	*Husband and Wife Have Equal Influence*	*Wife Has More Influence Than Husband*
When to buy the automobile?	68	30	2	68	29	3
Where to buy the automobile?	59	39	2	62	35	3
How much to spend for the automobile?	62	34	4	62	37	1
What make of automobile to buy?	50	50	—	60	32	8
What model of automobile to buy?	47	52	1	41	50	9
What color of automobile to buy?	25	63	12	25	50	25
How much to spend for furniture?	17	63	20	22	47	31
When to buy the furniture?	18	52	30	16	45	39
Where to buy the furniture?	6	61	33	7	53	40
What furniture to buy?	4	52	44	3	33	64
What style of furniture to buy?	2	45	53	2	26	72
What color and fabric to select?	2	24	74	2	16	82

SOURCE   Harry L. Davis, "Dimensions of Marital Roles in Consumer Decision-Making," *Journal of Marketing Research*, 7 (May 1970): 169, 170.

that it provides a useful tool with which to segment the market into meaningful consumer groups.

Shoppers in the various social classes seek out retail outlets that make them feel most comfortable and that cater to their particular class. The lower-status woman has been found to believe that if she enters high-status department stores, the clerks and the other customers will make her wait or will punish her in some other subtle way.[9] This belief causes lower-status people to avoid the upper-class stores. The result is retail institutions that convey a sense of different levels of social class and social prestige to their customers.

Figure 3–1 A Description of Warner's Six Commonly Used Social Classes

1—UPPER-UPPER or "Social Register" consists of locally prominent families, usually with at least second or third generation wealth. Basic Values: living graciously, upholding family reputation, reflecting the excellence of one's breeding, and displaying a sense of community responsibility. About ½ of 1% of the population.

2—LOWER-UPPER or "Nouveau Riche" consists of the more recently arrived and never-quite-accepted wealthy families. Goals: blend of Upper-Upper pursuit of gracious living and the Upper-Middle drive for success. About 1½% of the population.

3—UPPER-MIDDLE are moderately successful professional men and women, owners of medium-sized businesses, young people in their twenties and early thirties who are expected to arrive at the managerial level by their middle or late thirties. Motivations: success at a career, cultivating charm and polish. About 10% of the population.

4—LOWER-MIDDLE are mostly non-managerial office workers, small business owners, highly paid blue-collar families. Goals: Respectability, and Striving to live in well-maintained homes, neatly furnished in more-or-less "right" neighborhoods, and to do a good job at their work. They will save for a college education for their children. Top of the "Average Man World." About 30%– 35% of the population.

5—UPPER-LOWER or "Ordinary Working Class" consists of semi-skilled workers. Although many make high pay, they are not particularly interested in respectability. Goals: enjoying life and living well from day to day, to be at least Modern, and to work hard enough to keep safely away from the slum level. About 40% of the population.

6—LOWER-LOWER are unskilled workers, unassimilated ethnics, and the sporadically employed. Outlooks: apathy, fatalism, "get your kicks whenever you can." About 15% of the population, but have less than half of the purchasing power.

Source Irving J. Shapiro, *Marketing Terms: Explanations, Definitions, and/or Aspects* (West Long Branch, N.J.: S-M-C Publishing Company, 1973), pp. 156–157.

Such differences are more noticeable with some merchandise lines than others. The middle-class shopper may patronize relatively low-status discount stores to buy large items (such as refrigerators, color television, washing machines, etc.) whose quality is "assured" by the brand name of a national manufacturer. The selection of the "right" store is much more important for items (such as clothing or furniture) whose style or taste is important to the consumer, because these items convey social awareness and values.[10]

Preferences for different types of retail outlets are also related to social class membership. The lower-level working class tends to prefer the neighborhood store because they fear being snubbed or ignored if they go outside the neighborhood to a downtown merchant or large shopping center. Middle-class housewives are more confident in their shopping ability and are more willing to seek out new stores and new shopping experiences. Lower-status consumers appear to prefer face-to-face contact with friendly local clerks whom they know and believe can be trusted to assist them in making purchase decisons. They also prefer to shop in stores that extend credit.

The difference in store choice by members of different social classes can be illustrated by consumer behavior in buying cosmetics. Upper middle-class women buy their cosmetics in department stores while lower-class women prefer to buy cosmetics in variety stores. Drug stores appear to be equally suitable to all classes.[11] When consumers from several different social strata buy in the same store, they are likely to purchase different items or to buy the same items for different reasons. For example, when the lower-class woman shops in a store patronized by middle-class women, she may be interested only in buying gifts for others and not in making purchases for herself.

The social class concept is also useful in selecting media that can be used to reach the various market segments because corresponding differences occur in the exposure to media. The following quotation summarizes some of the differences in media reaction or behavior among classes.

> The different meanings of media have been explored in many studies. The media function in varied ways, and each also fits differentially into the lives of the social classes. There are (sometimes sharp) class preferences among the newspapers available in a community, in evaluating magazines, in select-ing television shows, in listening to the radio, in how newspapers are read, in receipt and meaning of direct mail; and, in general, in the total volume of materials to which people are exposed and to which they attend in one or another of the media. Higher status people see more magazines, read more of the newspaper, and buy more newspapers. Lower class people tend to prefer the afternoon paper, middle class people tend to prefer the morning paper. Studies in the past three years of television in fifteen major cities show that upper middle class people consistently prefer the NBC channel, while lower middles prefer the CBS; and these preferences are in keeping with the images of the networks, and the characteristics of the social classes.[12]

Family Life Cycle

The family life cycle concept, which divides the population into dif-ferent age groups, is also used to segment markets and identify market tar-gets. Expenditure patterns and purchase motivations change over a consumer's lifetime (Figure 3–2 contains a general description of such changes). Market targets, revealed by the family life cycle concept and identified in Figure 3–2, include clothing for the fashion-conscious singles. The young-married, no-children family is a good market for consumer durable goods. The change toward more youth-oriented products is apparent for the full-nest stages. The empty-nest stages are identified as good markets for luxury goods and services and other quality merchandise. Some of the families in the empty-nest stages are now moving to exclusive apartment dwellings or condominiums that require little upkeep and are convenient to their places of work. This group of people represents a new market segment with new needs and purchase motivations. Alert retailers will respond to meet these needs and increase profits by recognizing this shift in consumer behavior.

Psychological Aspects of Consumer Behavior

Several psychological concepts make important contributions to the study of consumer behavior.[13]

Pavlovian Learning Model

The Pavlovian learning model, as it has been modified over the years, is based on the four central concepts of drive, cue, response, and reinforcement.[14]

Drives are an individual's strong internal stimuli that impel him to action. Drives, or needs, may be either physiological (hunger, thirst, cold, pain, and sex) or socially derived motives (cooperation, fear, and acquisitiveness), which are learned.

Cues are weaker stimuli in the individual and/or environment that influence the consumer's response. For example, a McDonald's hamburger advertisement can serve as a cue that stimulates the hunger drive in a child. His response will depend upon the advertisement cue and other cues, such as the time of day, the relative availability of other hunger-satisfying alternatives, and the like. A change in the relative intensity can frequently be more forceful than the absolute level of the cue. For example, a child who has only a small amount of money may be more motivated by a special price offer that is good for one day only than by the fact that the hamburger is usually low priced.

The *response* is the individual's reaction to all of the cues. The same relative arrangement of cues will not always produce the same response each time in the individual because the earlier experience may or may not have been rewarding. If the response generates a favorable experience, that response is strengthened or *reinforced* and the response will probably be repeated when and if the same arrangement of cues reappears.

The Pavlovian model does not adequately treat concepts such as perceptions, the subconscious, and interpersonal influence. It does, however, offer some useful insight into consumer behavior. It provides guidelines in developing advertising strategy by suggesting that a single exposure to an advertisement is too weak a cue to stimulate a strong, favorable response. Thus it is desirable to repeat advertisements because repetition reduces forgetting on the part of the consumer. The absence of a message would tend to result in a weakened learned response, according to the Pavlovian model.

In addition, repetitive advertising provides reinforcement as the consumer becomes selectively exposed to the advertisement after he has made the purchase. The Pavlovian model also indicates that copy strategy must

Figure 3–2 *An Overview of the Family Life Cycle*

Bachelor Stage Young Single Not Living at Home	Newly Married Couples: Young, No Children	Full Nest I; Youngest Child under Six	Full Nest II; Youngest Child Six or over Six	Full Nest III; Older Married Couples with Dependent Children	Empty Nest I; Older Married Couples, No Children Living with Them, Head in Labor Force	Empty Nest II; Older Married Couples, No Children Living at Home, Head Retired	Solitary Survivor, in Labor	Solitary Survivor, Retired
Few financial burdens.	Better off financially than they will be in near future.	Home purchasing at peak.	Financial position better.	Financial position still better.	Home ownership at peak.	Drastic cut in income.	Income still good but likely to sell home.	Same medical and product needs as other retired group; drastic cut in income. Special need for attention, affection, and security.
Fashion opinion leaders.	Highest purchase rate and highest average purchase of durables.	Liquid assets low.	Some wives work.	More wives work.	Most satisfied with financial position and money saved.	Keep home.		
Recreation oriented.	Buy: Cars, refrigerators, stoves, sensible and dura-bles.	Dissatisfied with financial position and amount of money	Less influenced by advertising.	Some children get jobs.	Interested in travel, recreation, self-education.	Buy: Medical appliances, medical care, products which aid health, sleep, and digestion.		

ble furniture, vacations.	saved. Interested in new products.	
Buy: Basic kitchen equipment, basic furniture, cars, equipment for the mating game, vacations.	Buy: Washers, dryers, TV, baby food, chest rubs and cough medicine, vitamins, dolls, wagons, sleds, skates.	Like advertised products.
	Buy: Many foods, cleaning materials, bicycles, music lessons, pianos.	Buy larger sized packages, multiple-unit deals.
	Hard to influence with advertising.	Make gifts and contributions.
	High average purchase of durables.	Not interested in new products.
	Buy: New, more tasteful furniture, auto travel, non-necessary appliances, boats, dental services, magazines.	Buy: Vacations, luxuries, home improvements.

Source William D. Wells and George Gubar, "Life Cycle Concept in Marketing Research," *Journal of Marketing Research* (November 1966), p. 362.

arouse strong drives in the individual if it is to be effective as a cue. The strongest item- or service-related drives must be identified and presented with the right words, colors, and photos to provide the strongest stimulus to these drives.

Maslow's Hierarchy of Motives

Maslow's hierarchy of motives offers a good perspective for better understanding of consumer behavior. Maslow believed that a man is a perpetually wanting individual. As certain needs are satisfied, the next most important need tends to dominate the individual's conscious life.[15] Maslow considers *physiological needs* (hunger, sex, thirst, etc.) to be the most basic type of needs, which must be satisfied before an individual can be concerned about other needs. When these physiological needs are satisfied, the buyer proceeds to the second-level needs, which are *safety needs*. Safety needs consist of the desire for security, protection, and order or routine. Consumers satisfy their safety needs by means of savings accounts, insurance, pension plans, refrigerators, home freezers, and the like.

After the physiological and safety needs are satisfied, individuals become concerned about *social needs*, such as love needs, or the need for affection and belonging. To satisfy love needs, the individual strives to be accepted by the members of his family and to be an important person to them and to others who are close friends. Different status groups and symbols emerge as a way of satisfying this level of need satisfaction. The fourth need level, *esteem needs*, emerges as soon as the love needs are satisfied. The esteem needs are those demanded for reputation, self-respect, prestige, success, and achievement.

The fifth and last basic need is the desire to know, understand, organize, and construct a system of values that can be used to develop one's desire for self-fulfillment. These needs, called the *self-actualization needs*, consist of developing one's self to the fullest.

Maslow's theory is based on the concept that people have these five basic goals or needs. They are motivated to achieve various conditions that provide satisfaction for these needs. The needs are related in order of importance in such a way that the most powerful need will monopolize the conscious thought process of the individual, who will minimize the less prepotent needs. When that need is satisfied, the next most powerful need emerges to dominate the individual's conscious reactions. Thus a starving person (need 1) is not likely to be interested in whether he is breathing unpolluted air (need 2), or in how he is seen by others (need 3 or 4), or in a travel tour of Europe (need 5).

Social-Psychological Aspects of Consumer Behavior

The social-psychological concept of consumer behavior views behavior as depending mostly upon four factors: cognition, perception, motivation, and learning.[16]

Cognition

Cognition is a process an individual uses to make sense out of what he sees or perceives. It is the individual's total belief system, consisting of his values, ideas, and attitudes. Cognitive processes assist the person in his attempts to satisfactorily achieve his needs and determine the direction to take in his attempts to attain satisfaction of the initiating need.

Perception

Perception is what an individual "sees" as a result of complex patterns of stimulation filtered through his own unique cognitive processes. Perception reflects the person's past experience, present attitudes, and inclinations. For example, a customer entering a store "perceives" things that he does not "see." He "sees" the physical items, such as the building, fixtures, merchandise, people; his "perception," however, is influenced by previous experience in shopping in the store, by conversations with friends, and the like. Thus he may perceive the outlet to be a warm, friendly atmosphere, conducive to shopping and lingering, if his predispositions have been pleasant.

No two people perceive a situation in exactly the same terms, because people have a different view of the world. Each person's view, or total belief system, is formed over time as a result of his physiological abilities (his eyesight, sense of smell, intelligence level, etc.), his psychological characteristics (his personality and need-value systems), and the nature of his past experiences.

The consumer's total belief system, or cognitive set, predisposes him to receive and retain perceptions that he wants to see. Thus the consumer is a decision maker in his communications process. He decides what messages to receive by his exposure to different kinds of media. He also decides what messages to perceive and retain on the basis of his attitudes, culture, and past experiences.

Risk is one element of perception that deserves further discussion. Any consumer action can produce consequences that cannot be anticipated by the consumer with 100 percent certainty.[17] Any purchase competes with alternative uses of the same money, and any purchase involves a risk that the product will not work properly, that the consumer's friends may not approve of his selection, that the service was performed improperly, and the like. The concept of *perceived risk* may exist when the consumer is not able to define his buying goals and/or there are some unknown consequences that relate to the quality of the product or service and the ability of the purchase to fulfill the consumer's psychological and social needs. Thus the consumer may perceive risk to be the result of one or more of the following factors:

1. *She may be uncertain as to what the buying goals are.* Would she rather have an outrageously expensive new cocktail dress or a new piece of furniture? If a dress, should it be the cocktail dress she has always wanted or a more functional wool suit?
2. *The consumer may be uncertain as to which purchase (product, brand,*

model, etc.) will best match or satisfy acceptance level of buying goals. Should the suit be purchased at Lord and Taylor's or the local discount house? Will she really be more satisfied with a modern styling or a more conservative basic cut?

3. *The consumer may perceive possible adverse consequences if the purchase is made (or not made) and the result is a failure to satisfy her buying goals.* For example, she may suffer intense embarrassment if she buys her cocktail dress and it is much too risque at a party, or she looks fat, or it fits poorly.[18]

Consumer risk can be reduced by either decreasing the possible consequences or increasing the certainty of the possible outcome. Consumers read advertisements and *Consumer Reports,* examine merchandise, talk to friends, purchase items that have performed well for them in the past, buy advertised products, and buy at familiar stores to increase the certainty of the outcome of their purchases. Retailers can assist the consumer in reducing uncertainty by refusing to handle items that have not performed well for their customers. The rate of product returns and the frequency of consumer complaints will quickly identify these inferior-quality items that may have slipped through a buyer's careful selection process.

In addition, retailers can reduce consumer's perception of risk by providing a good warranty policy, complemented by a good public relations policy, in the consumer complaint or refunds and exchange departments. Retail advertising can also reduce consumer uncertainty by truthfully emphasizing the styling, function, and performance attributes of merchandise or service. Retail sales people can reduce the consumer's perception of risk by assisting the individual in defining his buying goals or identifying his problem(s) and then providing the best available solution. Handling nationally advertised, familiar brand-name products also results in a reduction of the consumer's perceived risk.

Motivation

Motivation, the driving force behind consumer behavior, is aimed at attaining protection, satisfaction, and self-enhancement. Motives are the impulses or desires that initiate behavior. The major motives can be divided into physiological and psychological or social forces.

MASLOW'S CONTRIBUTIONS   Maslow's hierarchy of needs concept (discussed previously) reveals that man first satisfies his physiological needs. The major motivating force is then channeled to satisfy the individual's next highest order need, according to Maslow's listing.

Retailing is a means by which a consumer can reach his goals. In other words, retailing assists the consumer in satisfying the range of needs contained in Maslow's list. Maslow's ranking also indicates that a satisfied need is no longer an important consumer motive. Because most American consumers are able to satisfy their basic physiological desires, retailers should concentrate on strategies that satisfy consumers' social needs (love and belongingness), esteem needs, and self-actualization needs. Indeed, most consumers in American society appear to make discretionary purchases to satisfy social or esteem needs.[19] For example, advertising does not emphasize the nutritional content of food items but concentrates on social messages that illustrate how well various products will be enjoyed at parties, by friends, and so on.

FREUD'S CONTRIBUTIONS   Sigmund Freud organized motivation into three main systems of psychological forces: the *id*, the *ego*, and the *superego*.[20] Behavior is a function of the interaction of these three systems, according to Freud.

The *id* is the aggressive, destructive, and pleasure-seeking impulses that are present at birth. The *superego* consists of the moralistic inhibitions placed on the *id* by society. The conflict between the *id* and the *superego* results in a compromise action arbitrated by the *ego*, whose goal is integrated action and rational behavior. This conflict between the *id* and *superego* and the particular balance struck by the *ego* can lead to frustration and anxiety. The *ego* has several ways of reducing this anxiety. It uses both rational methods (reasoning and problem solving) and defense mechanisms that distort reality in such a way that internal conflicts and frustrations are resolved. Similarly, the consumer may use four major types of defense—identification, projection, displacement, and rationalization—to resolve conflict and protect his *self-concept*.

Identification   This is the mechanism whereby consumers copy and imitate others whom they admire. "Opinion leaders," whose purchase and display behavior is copied by consumers wishing to identify with them, play an important role in the retailing of fashion clothing, automobiles, recreation equipment, and many other items. Even store patronage can be used to give the consumer identification. The "in" entertainment place is patronized by consumers who wish to be identified with its target group.

Projection   Projection consists of the individual's attributing to other people those motives and actions he unconsciously recognizes as undesirable in himself. Advertisements may feature unattractive models whose undesirable appearance and actions are conveyed to be a consequence of not using the advertised product, service, or method of shopping.

Displacement   Displacement substitutes or transfers energy from one object to another. Purchases of certain products or services are made because they are a subconscious substitute for some alternative motive. For example, the purchase of a sports car is claimed by some motivation researchers to be a substitute for sex. One of the main contributions of Freud is the recognition that much behavior is motivated in the subconscious level.

Rationalization   The rationalization process provides the individual with acceptable reasons for his actions. A basic sales principle consists of offering the consumer economic, quality, or functional reasons for purchasing merchandise.

Learning

Finally, the social-psychological concept views behavior as depending upon learning in addition to the cognition, perception, and motivation factors just discussed. Learning is the change in the individual's response tendencies due to the effects of his insight and experience.[21] The experience may be a previous visit he made to a particular retail outlet, a promotional message sent by a retailer, or merely a suggestion made by a friend. His response may be a strong inclination to return to the store the next time he needs the merchandise and/or service it offers, a weak inclination to return, or a strong inclination to avoid the outlet if at all possible.

The learning process involves the four concepts discussed previously in the Pavlovian learning model: drives, cues, responses, and reinforcement. In addition, learning involves the restructuring of the individual's attitudes and beliefs about his environment. A consumer's response is thus based on his insight and his past experiences. He has the capacity to solve problems involving the selection of the response that is most appropriate to the situation, although he may not have previously encountered an identical situation. The various aspects of learning that affect buyer behavior are illustrated in the following observation:

> The first time a man looks at an advertisement, he does not see it.
> The second time he does not notice it.
> The third time he is conscious of its existence.
> The fourth time he faintly remembers having seen it before.
> The fifth time he reads it.
> The sixth time he turns up his nose at it.
> The seventh time he reads it through and says, "Oh brother!"
> The eighth time he says, "Here's that confounded thing again!"
> The ninth time he wonders if it amounts to anything.
> The tenth time he thinks he will ask his neighbor if he has tried it.
> The eleventh time he wonders how the advertiser makes it pay.
> The twelfth time he thinks perhaps it may be worth something.
> The thirteenth time he thinks it must be a good thing.
> The fourteenth time he remembers that he has wanted such a thing for a long time.
> The fifteenth time he is tantalized because he cannot afford to buy it.
> The sixteenth time he thinks he will buy it some day.
> The seventeenth time he makes a memorandum of it.
> The eighteenth time he swears at his poverty.
> The nineteenth time he counts his money carefully.
> The twentieth time he sees it, he buys the article, or instructs his wife to do so.[22]

Generalizations about Consumer Behavior

Many of the concepts discussed above can be incorporated into the model of buyer behavior presented in Figure 3–3, which consists of four "fields." *Field one* includes the retailer's attributes (such as location, interior and exterior appearance, merchandise offering, price levels, etc.) and his promotional message (such as advertising, personal selling, displays, consumer services, etc.). As the total attribute and promotional message reaches the consumer it becomes an input into *subfield two*, which is the consumer's psychological attributes and inclinations. The total message is received and acted upon in light of the individual's psychological orientation, to form an attitude toward the retail outlet's total offering.

This attitude then serves as the input for *field two*, which consists of the consumer's search and evaluation of that outlet's offerings and the total offerings of alternative outlets. The output from field two may be a motivation to buy a particular product and/or service in that outlet. If so, the motivation is an input for *field three* because it transforms the motivation into

Figure 3–3 **Summary of the Nicosia Model of Buyer Behavior**

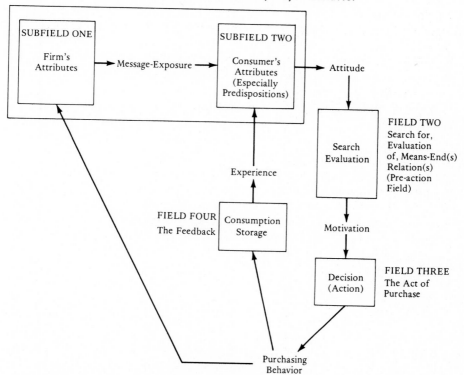

SOURCE Francesco M. Nicosia, *Consumer Decision Processes: Marketing and Advertising Implications* (Englewood Cliffs, N.J.: Prentice-Hall, 1966), p. 156.

purchasing action. The retail sales person is an especially important factor in instilling in the consumer the motivation needed to make the purchase. Finally, *field four* is the feedback of the sales information to the retailer and the retention of the consequences of the purchase in the consumer's memory.

This model and our previous discussion indicate that consumers make rational efforts toward problem solving. Rational motives originate by a process of conscious deliberation and are aroused by appeals to reason. Buying motives generally belong to two groups: operational buying motives and sociopsychological buying motives.[23] Operational buying motives are directly related to the physical performance characteristics of the merchandise and service. Sociopsychological buying motives are more related to the consumer's social-psychological interpretation of the merchandise and/or service.

The consumer's efforts are considered to be rational if they fit his own goal-oriented behavior pattern. His needs—whatever they might be—lead to drives. As these drives to satisfy these needs are intensified, the consumer tends toward a state of tension or disequilibrium. Cues (the retailers' attributes and promotional efforts) provide the consumer with a means of differentiating between retail merchandise/service offerings.

Part of the consumer's behavior is occupied with search activity, which may consist of straight data gathering or a preference for receiving information presented in the form of semi-entertainment. In either case, the consumer's behavior is rational in light of the goals he is seeking. If the search activity leads to a purchase, that need, at least temporarily, is satisfied and the original causes for behavior tend to be removed. The consumer learns from his experience in making the purchase and in searching for and evaluating alternative solutions to his problem.

Some consumer purchase decisions are sufficiently repetitive and routine so that a definite purchase procedure is developed and is repeated until some strong change occurs in purchase motivation or by presentation of a strong cue by a retailer. A retailer's ability to change the consumer's purchase behavior for these types of purchases may be very slight. Convenience products, such as cigarettes, newspapers, headache remedies, or toothpaste, are examples of routinely purchased merchandise. Retailers of these types of merchandise generally sell via self-service, as retail sales people are not needed except to indicate where the merchandise is located. Similar layouts and merchandise arrangement in all outlets of a chain allow the consumer to develop a constant shopping routine for these types of merchandise.

Other purchasing decisions are sufficiently novel, complex, or important to the consumer to warrant renewed search and evaluation efforts. In this case, because consumers are more open minded about the decision and want to receive information on several alternatives, they investigate merchandise and store attributes and match these images with their own *self-images* and life styles. (It should be emphasized that the consumer's self-image—the impression that he forms of himself—is likely to be a little different from the way he appears to other people. The consumer is striving to purchase goods or services that enhance, increase, or change his self-image. His purchases are made so he might see himself becoming bolder, smarter, richer, more secure, and more socially acceptable.) To make these nonroutine purchase decisions, the consumer is searching for detailed information on merchandise, services, and/or outlets. Retailers that provide such information will appeal favorably to him. In addition, because he has an open mind, he is more receptive to personal sales efforts that attempt to identify and solve his problems.

Field four in the buyer behavior model (the feedback process occurring after the purchase) contains some important implications for retailers. There is frequently a lack of harmony (dissonance) among the buyer's various cognitions about the product and/or service purchased and the alternatives he has "passed by." Dissonance occurs as a result of the consumer's having made a decision that he may doubt is the right choice.[24] The magnitude of post-purchase dissonance is believed to be an increasing function of the general importance of the decision to the consumer and of the relative attractiveness of the unpurchased alternatives.[25] Thus post-purchase dissonance may be common among buyers of a foreign travel tour, automobiles, major appliances, homes, and the like.

Consumer behavior that is influenced by dissonance may lead to sufficient guilt feelings that the purchase is returned, or it may simply lead the customer to achieve internal harmony by intensifying his search for additional information that will support his original decision. The retailer can attack dissonance by emphasizing personal selling, by advertising, warranties and return policies, and by not offering too many similar product choices. The personal selling and advertising, warranty, and return programs should be designed to thoroughly convince the customer of the worth of the store and its merchandise/service offering.

Customers who are presented with adequate information experience less dissonance, but the retail communications process must be truthful and consistent if consumer post-purchase dissonance is to be decreased. Consumers who receive conflicting information about an item will experience more dissonance, so the firm's advertising, sales, and warranty and return policies must be consistent and each sales person must be informed of their content. Retailers may want to consider showing or carrying fewer similar product choices as the presentation of many close alternatives can lead to increased dissonance. Shoe salesmen, for example, may limit the number of shoes they present to the customer at any one time.

Conclusion

The consumer is constantly changing. As his habits, attitudes, and life style change, his preferences for retail stores and merchandise/service also change. Retailers who do not keep abreast of these changes can easily lose out to firms that research the consumer to determine which merchandise strategies will best meet the consumers' needs. The research tools used to gain insight into consumer behavior are presented in Chapter 17.

SUMMARY

Consumer behavior is subject to many influences. Consumers attempt to satisfy a variety of needs—physiological, safety, belongingness, status, and self-actualization—with the financial resources available to them. There are different explanations of how they pursue these objectives.

The Nicosia buyer behavior model, presented in Figure 3–3, is a summary explanation of the activities in the consumer's decision-making process. This model reflects the nearly boundless aspects of consumer behavior. Thus the retail manager must be aware of the consumer's psychological attributes, his self-image of himself, how he interprets the retailer's attributes and messages, the resulting consumer attitude, the way that the consumer approaches the search and evaluation process, the motivation that may result in a purchase, and even the post-purchase feeling of the customer.

Keeping abreast of changes in consumer attitudes and motivations is absolutely mandatory if a retailer is to conceive effective merchandising strategies.

QUESTIONS

1. Distinguish between complementary and substitute items in terms of price and demand changes. What relationship (if any) would you expect between an increase in the price of gasoline and the price of motor oil? Between a decrease in the price of butter and the demand for margarine?
2. What is meant by real personal income? How does real personal income affect the discretionary and nondiscretionary patterns of consumer spending?
3. Of what importance are reference groups in retailing?
4. What is conspicuous consumption and why is it important in retailing?
5. What social classes are most likely to patronize a store that is designed to attract members of some other social class? Which classes are least likely to make this changeover? What types of merchandise would you expect to sell to these changeover customers?
6. How would you use the concepts covered in question 5 to design a sales promotion plan for high-quality suits to be sold in a discount store in a major metropolitan area?
7. How does the concept of the family life cycle influence retailing decisions and long-range plans?
8. Discuss the practical applications of Pavlov's learning theory to retailing. Considerable criticism has been directed at the private sector for the use of psychological techniques to promote sales. Briefly discuss and comment on the validity of some of these criticisms.
9. Consider each level of Maslow's hierarchy as a market segment and describe how you would go about marketing some product or line of products to each segment.

10. Describe some of the techniques currently in use to reduce real and perceived buyer risk and post-purchase dissonance. What tends to increase post-purchase dissonance? Can you suggest any other measures to reduce consumer dissonance?

11. Describe the four defense mechanisms commonly used by individuals to protect the self-concept and cite an example of each as it might be used by a consumer (other than those examples in the text).

12. What is meant by rational behavior on the part of a consumer?

FOOTNOTES

[1] Philip Kotler, *Marketing Management Analysis Planning and Control* (2d ed.; Englewood Cliffs, N.J.: Prentice-Hall, 1972), pp. 102–204.

[2] George Katona, *The Powerful Consumer: Psychological Studies of the American Economy* (New York: McGraw-Hill, 1960), pp. 14–15.

[3] Ibid., pp. 11–12.

[4] Ibid., pp. 150–151.

[5] T. M. Newcomb, *Social Psychology* (New York: Dryden Press, 1950), pp. 225–232.

[6] Gregory Stone, "City Shoppers and Urban Identification," *American Journal of Sociology*, 55 (July 1954): 36–45.

[7] "Queen of the Family Purse—Or Is She?" *Business Week*, August 10, 1963, pp. 26–27.

[8] James E. Stafford, "Effects of Group Influence on Consumer Brand Preferences," *Journal of Marketing Research* (February 1966), p. 69.

[9] Pierre Martineau, "Social Classes and Spending Behavior," *Journal of Marketing*, 23 (October 1958): 121–130.

[10] Peter D. Bennett and Harold H. Kassarjian, *Consumer Behavior* (Englewood Cliffs, N.J.: Prentice-Hall, 1972), p. 119.

[11] Sidney J. Levy, "Social Class and Consumer Behavior," in J. W. Newman, ed., *On Knowing the Consumer* (New York: John Wiley & Sons, 1966), p. 154.

[12] Ibid., pp. 155–156.

[13] Kotler, *Marketing Management Analysis Planning and Control*, pp. 104–108.

[14] John Dollard and Neal E. Miller, *Personality and Psychotherapy* (New York: McGraw-Hill, 1950), chap. 3.

[15] A. H. Maslow, "A Theory of Human Motivation," *Psychological Review*, 50 (1943): 370–396.

[16] Rom J. Markin, Jr., *Retailing Management, a Systems Approach* (New York: Macmillan, 1971), pp. 152–157.

[17] Raymond A. Bauer, "Consumer Behavior as Risk Taking," in Robert S. Hancock, ed., *Dynamic Marketing for a Changing World* (Chicago: American Marketing Association, 1960), pp. 389–398.

[18] Adapted from Donald F. Cox, ed., *Risk Taking and Information Handling in Consumer Behavior* (Boston: Harvard University Division of Research, Graduate School of Business Administration, 1967), pp. 5–6.

[19] Thomas S. Robertson, *Consumer Behavior* (Glenview, Ill.: Scott, Foresman, 1970), pp. 33–34.

[20] Ibid., p. 34.

[21] James F. Engel, David T. Kollat, and Roger D. Blackwell, *Consumer Behavior* (New York: Holt, Rinehart and Winston, 1968), p. 140.

[22] Thomas Smith, *Hints to Intended Advertisers* (London, 1885), quoted in Herbert E. Krugman, "An Application of Learning Theory to TV Copy Testing," *Public Opinion Quarterly*, 26 (1962): 626–634.

[23] John G. Udell, "A New Approach to Consumer Motivation," *Journal of Retailing*, 40 (Winter 1964/65): 9.

[24] Leon Festinger, *A Theory of Cognitive Dissonance* (Stanford, Calif.: Stanford University Press, 1957), p. 13.

[25] Ibid., p. 262.

NATIONAL SHIRT SHOPS
Stocking to Match Fashion Trends in the Black Market

National Shirt Shops Inc. operates a chain of 225 men's clothing stores throughout the United States. These stores are located in downtown and suburban shopping centers in cities with a population base of 100,000 or more.

The chain is independent, although it has had a history of ownership by the McCrory Corporation, BVD, and Glen Alden.

Throughout the years, National Shirt Shops has stressed fashionable merchandise at reasonable prices. This was the key to the growth and success of the chain, according to Mr. Dave Hamner, district manager for the Dallas region. A specific example cited by Mr. Hamner was that of a doctor who recently discovered that he had paid three times the price in an exclusive men's shop for the same shirt marked at $4.59 in a National Shirt Shop.

The company spent very little on advertising as it relied upon the image of National Shirt Shops, plus word-of-mouth advertising and good locations.

Mr. Hamner joined National Shirt Shops in 1930 as a part-time employee and now has responsibility for eleven stores in the Dallas–Fort Worth area. As district manager, he has responsibility for the overall operation of all eleven stores, including employment, personnel administration, assistance in selecting new store sites, and merchandise selection.

Merchandise selection had been growing in importance for district managers due to the new awareness in men's fashion, and appeared likely to become more complex in the future. Each district manager was sent, on a seasonal basis, computer printouts of merchandise sales trends by product and by each store over the past two years. A comparison with the national average was also included in this analysis, plus a printout of forecasted sales versus actual sales. Although these were helpful in ordering standard items, they were of limited value in ordering new, fad-type merchandise.

Buying for the chain was handled by professional buyers out of New York. They kept track of the latest styles and negotiated contracts with factories for production.

However, it was an impossible task for the New York buyers to accurately determine the particular needs of each of the 225 stores. The exact merchandise selection for each store varied according to climate, local buying habits, consumer income levels, and the profile of the store's customers. As an example, style changes in Southern California tended to be accepted quite rapidly while changes in Shreveport, Louisiana, were not as well accepted until several months later. Some areas, such as Memphis or St. Louis, were more price conscious than others.

Variations within a region could also be extreme. This was the case in Mr. Hamner's district. The Main Street (downtown) store was even different from the Elm Street store, only a block and a half away. Approximately 75 percent of the customers of the Main Street store were fashion-conscious young black men who put style before price in their purchase requirements. The fashion need of this market varied considerably from the Caucasian markets.

Although some fashion spillover occurred, it was generally confined to one market or the other for several months or longer. The Levi or blue-jean look, which originated in the white market, had spilled over somewhat into the black segment but had not reached great popularity there, according to Mr. Hamner.

The latest trend affecting the Main Street store had originated among black students at the University of Houston. This was the "elephant ear" collars or extra long button-down collars. Mr. Hamner had written to New York requesting aid in securing these, although he knew it would require special orders.

Several times in the past, Mr. Hamner had written to New York concerning emerging trends. In some cases, New York had been slow to respond, giving competition a lead over his store.

This had been the case with "banana skin" pants, named by black customers for their resemblance to the color of bananas. Many of the Main Street customers had requested banana pants but Mr. Hamner had been unable to secure them, and in fact New York said that Dallas was an isolated case. The pants had proved quite popular in Dallas, and sold for $25 to $30 a pair by other retailers.

In the case of men's jump suits, Mr. Hamner had convinced New York of the need for stocking these and had been allowed to purchase them from a local manufacturer. As a result, his stores carried this item early and made a good profit.

Mr. Hamner knew the value of fads, and in fact stated that they were the lifeblood of his industry. He realized that a retailer could enter a fad too early but also felt that, once the merchandise became easy to obtain from manufacturers, "the bloom was off the rose" and it was too late to do well with the item.

The Main Street store employed two black men and a Mexican American as clerks, and Mr. Hamner believed these employees assisted greatly in spotting early fads. He also called district meetings with his store managers to discuss what the consumer was looking for. In addition, he personally tried to keep track of the consumer pulse and asked that any information on new trends be phoned in to him. If he saw a customer leave one of his stores without buying, he would often stop the customer and ask him if there was anything he had been looking for but hadn't seen in the store. Mr. Hamner attended clothing shows at the Apparel Mart in Dallas, where he talked with vendors and also with competitors concerning emerging trends. Even so, Mr.

Hamner expressed concern at continuing to meet the rapidly changing needs of all his customers, and in particular the black customer.

DISCUSSION QUESTIONS

1. What other practical means are available to help Mr. Hamner keep ahead of trends, particularly those among black customers?
2. Can a nationwide system be developed to help district managers such as Mr. Hamner keep ahead of trends?
3. What action (if any) should the New York buyers take when they receive information from district managers such as that concerning banana skin pants?
4. Is Mr. Hamner correct in believing that there are many local differences in consumer buying preferences? If regional differences exist, are they likely to increase in number and complexity?

TOWN & COUNTRY MOBILE HOMES, INC.
Reentry in Retailing—Associated Problems with Finance, Personnel, and Corporate Structure

The management of Town & Country Mobile Homes Inc. was seriously considering reestablishing company-owned retail outlets throughout its market area. Nearly fifteen years had passed since the early '60s, when the company decided to sell its company-owned and -operated lots.

At that time, repossession rates for mobile homes were high and commercial acceptance of mobile home credit paper was low. According to Mr. Barry Donnel, president, several significant changes had occurred in the intervening year that prompted the company to take a second look at entering this phase of the business.

Town & Country is a public stock corporation (AMEX) with headquarters in Wichita Falls, Texas, and with annual sales around $30 million. The company specializes in the manufacture and distribution of mobile homes. These are produced in modern production facilities in Texas, Oklahoma, Mississippi, South Carolina, and South Dakota. It is vertically integrated backward through a timber processing division known as Fry Forest Products.

The marketing system used by the company consists of 220 independent dealers. Unlike most competitors, Town & Country likes brand exclusivity in its dealers. This program reflects the training and philosophy of Mr. Donnel's father and uncle, who founded the company. Both men had spent the greatest part of their business careers as dealers for General Motors and believed strongly in the retail marketing methods used by GM.

The possible reentry of Town & Country into company-owned lots had several serious ramifications that were being considered by management.

All available evidence from company records and industry research had shown that the profile of the mobile home owner had changed since the late '50s and early '60s. The present buyer was less transient than the earlier buyer. He was also better educated, had a higher income, and in general represented a considerably higher class individual.

At the same time, the financial community had changed its opinion of mobile-home loans and actively sought their paper.

The industry had also become more sophisticated and competitive as the "fly by night" manufacturers and dealers disappeared. The larger manufacturers continued to increase their percentage of the market.

In addition, management also believed that company-owned outlets would permit Town & Country to crack markets where prior success had been limited or nonexistent. In some cases this would mean entering a market presently served by weak dealers.

It was also well known that the percentage return per mobile home from retail sales was higher than that from manufacturing.

A successful company-owned lot would permit much greater control of the market than through independents. It was also felt that the ever present possibility of the company's establishing its own outlets would cause its dealers to work harder to prevent this from happening in their territory.

In examining the possible problems in such a move, the earlier experience in this form of forward vertical integration was remembered. Another consideration was the initial effects upon cash flow and corporate profits.

Mobile home stocks in general had suffered serious setbacks in the past few years and Town & Country was no exception. If company-owned retail lots were opened, they would have to be stocked with fifteen to twenty homes averaging between $7,000 and $10,000 each, depending upon the part of the country. These would not be immediately sold, and would temporarily reduce profits as a percentage of goods manufactured. Other costs would also be incurred, such as the approximate $25,000 in variable costs simply to prepare a sales lot.

All advertising and sales promotion would now have to be borne by the company instead of the dealers, as well as salaries and commissions for sales and service personnel.

Rather than establish a complex and costly new marketing division to oversee retail sales, it was felt that this responsibility would be given to each of the five plant managers. Thus each manager would have the added responsibility for establishing retail sales lots, hiring personnel, and overseeing them during the initial stages.

Mr. Donnel had also been exploring the idea of establishing a GMAC-type program with the cooperation of a large financial group, but knew that it would not be ready by the time the new program was initiated.

The management had earlier considered entering the mobile home park business but felt this was far less critical in the marketing program than sales outlets. In a few areas such as Boulder, Colorado, or Corpus Christi, Texas, the availability of parking space was a critical problem. In these cases, mobile home retailers were forced to lease any available space in parks and to retain them as inventory so that they could offer their customers a place to park their new homes. However, these areas were the exception, as others had the problem of too much space.

DISCUSSION QUESTIONS

1. Should Town & Country again establish company-owned retail outlets? Discuss the pros and cons.
2. What potential problems and advantages (other than those mentioned) do you foresee in the proposed move?
3. Discuss the proposed use of plant managers to oversee company-owned retail operations in their area in both the short and the long run. What type of a permanent, internal retail marketing structure should the company plan to establish if it goes ahead with the proposed program?
4. What economic, political, or social conditions caused the change in the consumer profile of mobile-home owners in only a few years? Is the profile of the buyer likely to change greatly in the years ahead? If so, what effect will this have on the proposed program?

PART TWO

Identification of Retailing
Opportunities

CHAPTER 4

Photo courtesy of Allied Stores Corporation.

The Product
and Product Planning

A successful retail outlet must stock goods of a type and a price level that are consistent with the target consumer's needs and the store's location and image. The discussion in the present chapter will concentrate on the importance of stocking a product line that will meet the needs of the retailer's potential or actual customers. It will examine the major merchandise policy decisions faced by retailers—those relating to the question, "What products should we stock?" The first section presents some basic product concepts. The second section examines the merchandise assortment decision—the range, kind, and brands of products the retailer should stock. This second section also examines the product elimination decision.

The interrelationship between location and product decisions is presented in Chapter 5. The importance of maintaining an appropriate store image is presented in Chapter 7. Related major merchandising issues—how much to buy, how to buy, and when to buy—will be discussed in Chapters 12 and 13.

TOTAL PRODUCT CONCEPT

The idea of a product seems to be simple and easily defined. However, as noted before, a product consists of more than the tangible, physical "thing" that is offered to consumers. The *extended product* is the tangible item combined with the whole set of services that accompany it when it is sold to the consumer.[1]

The term "systems selling" is used to convey the idea of selling a total product. Additional elements of customer satisfaction may include a formal, written guarantee and assistance in full utilization of the product or in its proper care and maintenance. When retailers fully appreciate the extended product concept, they profitably consider their potential customer's total consumption system. The consumption system describes the way a purchaser of a product performs the total task of whatever it is that he or she is trying to accomplish when using the product.[2]

An illustration of the extended product system is an observed reaction to a recent announcement of stricter enforcement of a local ordinance requiring each person to use covered metal garbage cans when he disposes of his trash. All retailers—except one—stocked many pairs of garbage cans and lids to sell to the consumers who would be "forced" to buy their product at a combined price of about $5. The astute exception stocked some matched garbage cans and lids, but fully recognized that the main consumer need was not for more cans but only for lids to cover their old garbage cans. He therefore stocked and sold lids separately (at about $1.19) to a volume market. Of course, this retailer did not make a fortune from the sale of lids, but through suggestive selling, he sold chains to fasten the lids to the garbage cans so they could not be lost again. The profits derived from the combined sales were not large, but his recognition of this consumer need attracted several hundred new customers into his store for the first time.

This kind of creative merchandising can have a tremendous long-run impact upon business. Satisfied consumers who give word-of-mouth reference for a retailer can influence more consumers to shop at that store than any single expenditure in the mass media.

A product can also be viewed as a *generic product*, which involves the essential benefit that the buyer expects to get from the product. Consumers will be looking for different benefits, depending upon their needs. The generic product idea implies that benefits, not product features, should guide the retailer's strategy.

The retailing of cosmetics can be used to illustrate the function of the different product concepts. In this case, the tangible product, the cosmetic, is viewed in the strictly physical sense as a product possessing a specified set of chemical and physical attributes. But the *tangible* product is not what the consumer is buying; she is buying beauty. Thus retailing the *generic* product involves selling beauty—not lipstick or eye shadow—to provide the essential benefit expected by the potential customer. Once retailers recognize this, they begin to provide beauty counselors to assist women in their search to become (or remain) beautiful by suggesting the purchase and use of certain cosmetics that would "go well together" and be individually tailored to suit one's needs.

Clothing retailers can use the same reasoning to sell color-coordinated ties, suits, shoes, and socks.

In summary, the total product concept involves using the whole product—tangible product, service, warranty, and psychological contributions—to coincide with the benefits that a group of potential consumers expects to receive from a product.

MERCHANDISE LINE DECISIONS

Particular lines of merchandise used to be considered the exclusive property of particular types of retail stores. The trend toward scrambled merchandising—where the store carries merchandise that is unrelated to the regular lines of the store—has tended to make it extremely difficult to distinguish retail outlets solely in terms of the merchandise they carry. The so-called grocery store now stocks many non-food items. Discount and department stores sell nearly every kind of merchandise. Nearly all of the product line tradition has been abandoned in favor of using different merchandise assortments to compete in the retail arena.

Current Customer Need Satisfaction

Consumer needs are the most basic considerations in establishing a retailer's product line policy. Customers' preferences with regard to the price class of goods, quality, styles, colors, and the like determine if products will sell well or will not sell at all. In an economy where discretionary consumption is quite prevalent, the task of anticipating consumer preferences successfully is quite difficult. Information on consumer preferences can be obtained through research conducted within the company and from outside sources.

Data from Company Sources

An analysis of past sales records provides one of the best estimates of consumer preferences for all items, including those that are subject to changes in demand because of preference switches made on the basis of fashion, style, or whatever. Analysis of a retailer's past sales data, adjusted for seasonal fluctuations, indicates consumer preferences for size, color, style, quality, brand labels, etc. This information allows the retailer to identify those items that are most likely to be "best sellers."

Returned goods and adjustment data also contain information pertaining to product line decisions. Frequent consumer complaints and/or frequent returns of an item indicate some fundamental weakness in that item's ability to give satisfaction under normal use conditions. Such negative feedback is even more serious than it might initially appear to be because only a few of the dissatisfied customers will make the effort to complain and/or return merchandise. Severely dissatisfied consumers are also likely to classify all of the store's merchandise in the same category as the inferior items. This can lead to a switch in store patronage and cause the store to lose many previously loyal customers. Thus products made of inferior material or with poor workmanship should be eliminated from the product line as soon as their inferior qualities are discovered.

A record of items requested by potential customers but not carried by the store is an excellent source of new product ideas. This record could be maintained on a form located near the cash register. The request record or "want slip" should be sufficiently detailed to include a description of the items desired, plus other consumer-provided information on color, size, style, price, etc. (Figure 4–1).

Sales people may be encouraged by certain incentives and regular super-

Figure   4–1   Sample   "Want   Slip" Form

Lost ... a Sale!

Because we were out of:

_____

_____

_____

Remember:

• A sale lost is money lost in commission.

• We don't know you're out of something 'til you tell us.

• Don't wait . . . tell us now before you lose another sale.

Name	Dept.	Sales No.	Date

• If no sales were lost, please so indicate by checking here . . . ☐

704113R   The Baltimore Business Forms Co., Atlanta, Ga. BUY-38

SOURCE   The Baltimore Business Forms Company, Atlanta, Ga.

vision to suggest alternative merchandise that is currently in stock. If such substitutes are not acceptable, the originally requested item should be reported. Usually sales clerks are also able to make good suggestions on the types of products that should be stocked. Because sales people have the most direct contact with customers, they are good sources of product ideas.

Careful consideration should be given to "want slip" information. Requests for fad and/or fashion items require an immediate, decisive response. The greatest risk is getting too much merchandise too late to profitably capitalize on the item. Timing, such as 24- to 48-hour delivery, and a "leader" store image spell success in these situations.

Customer inquiries for additional staple items require a different retailer response. The danger in meeting isolated, individual requests is accumulating slow-moving inventories and "overstock." Most merchandise is packaged in multiple units that require special orders and entail delays. Unless the customer makes a significant deposit, he may be tempted to purchase elsewhere, leaving the merchant with excessive stock.

Remember, the retailer must be responsive to his target market needs but cannot be "all things to all people."

Information from Outside Sources

Retailers can obtain estimates of consumer demand from the wholesalers, manufacturers, jobbers, and others who sell merchandise to the store. The accuracy of such estimates is dependent upon the amount of consumer research conducted by these sellers. Some vendors (as these sellers are commonly called) provide bulletins or computer reports that indicate past sales for items they are selling. Franchise vendors usually provide sales estimate data to their outlets to assist their "client-partners" in maximizing their profitability.

Retailers may observe the product lines offered by other retailers with the idea that successful outlets have already identified the items that are selling well. Such visits to other local stores and similar stores in other areas are made by retail management personnel, who may even purchase merchandise for the purpose of making a detailed comparison with their store's offerings. These visits also provide the retailer with an estimate of the intensity of the competition he is likely to encounter on each item.

Many retailers are successful because they offer a unique product line. "Shopping the competition" is frequently done by small retailers who cannot afford more costly methods of demand estimation. These smaller retailers are also more likely to be able to carry unique merchandise because they are not bound by established product line policies as are some large chain stores.

The store visits are also used by retailers who are opening a new outlet in the area and lack past sales records for the target area.

Trade magazines, newspapers, and other publications also contain information on the items, styles, colors, etc. that consumers appear to prefer or are likely to prefer in the near future.

Consumer surveys can be used by large retailers to provide preference information on fashion or fad items. Such surveys could be conducted either by telephoning or by mailing questionnaires to the store's current or potential customers. The store's credit and customer records could serve as a mailing or telephone listing. These surveys should be designed and analyzed by knowledgeable persons who are familiar with proper survey procedures, as the use of improper survey techniques can lead to incorrect decisions.

Several "outside" agencies conduct customer surveys that provide retailers with information on consumer purchasing habits. The A .C. Nielsen Company and the R. L. Polk Company supply consumer buying data. Newspapers such as the *Denver Post*, the *Chicago Tribune*, and the *New York Times* also sponsor periodic research on consumer buying patterns.

Interest Arousal with Merchandise Assortment

Retail competition frequently involves the use of market segmentation based on merchandise assortment. Retailers use market segmentation by planning their merchandise assortment to meet the demands of some particular subgroup of consumers who have similar motivations. One of the first requirements for successful use of the market segmentation concept is to identify the consumer group or groups that appear to offer the best potential market. The retail merchandise assortment can then be altered to meet the needs and preferences of these target market groups.

Merchandise assortment based upon quality, style, color, size, etc. can then be selected so that it will reflect the needs of the people who represent the target market. Very seldom, if ever, can the retailer satisfy the wants of *all* people. Instead, he must determine which consumers will be included in the target market to be served.

Stores selling "shopping goods" (goods the consumer usually purchases only after he makes several comparisons on quality, price, and style) usually make the most distinct segmentation appeals. The merchandise assortment in stores selling mainly shopping goods such as furniture, used automobiles, and major appliances may be selected to appeal to a specific market target, which may be the youth market, a specific ethnic group, an extremely high income group, and the like.

Stores selling "specialty goods" (goods that are sufficiently unique or have a strong enough brand identification to entice a significant group of buyers to habitually make a special purchasing effort) can also benefit by developing a merchandise assortment to reach one or more market segments. Some retailers of photographic equipment, hi-fi components, sporting goods, and men's suits, for example, carry only exclusive, high-quality brands to cater to the very quality-conscious segment of the market.

Another—often overlooked—specialty merchant is the farm cooperative, serving the agricultural and farm needs of the nation. Farmland Industries, located in mid-America, has built a progressive, diversified firm that offers the rural consumer a wide range of retail products and services to meet his unique needs.

Segmentation is used to a lesser extent by stores that primarily sell "convenience goods" (goods the consumer usually purchases with minimum effort at the most convenient and accessible place). Stores stocking only well-known branded merchandise appeal to a different market group than do stores that stock mostly unadvertised brand items or private brand items that are associated with the retailer or some wholesaler instead of with a nationally known manufacturer. Soap, personal care items, packaged food items, other staple items, and impulse goods are examples of convenience goods.

Retailers who sell convenience goods must place emphasis upon the proper location of their outlets. Consumers of convenience goods generally spend only a minimum amount of effort on making their purchases. Thus they are likely to make most of their purchases of convenience goods at the nearest outlet that sells acceptable merchandise.

Advertising and promotional efforts on convenience goods will not be as likely to lure customers from long distance as similar efforts featuring shopping goods. Retailers who offer mostly shopping goods may therefore be better able to use promotional appeals to overcome a less than optimal location.

Merchandise Assortment

The merchandise assortment decision involves three dimensions: width, depth, and consistency. The *width* or *breadth* of a merchandise assortment refers to the number of different merchandise lines a store may carry. "Merchandise line" refers to a group of products that are closely related because they satisfy a class of needs, are used together, or are sold to the same consumer groups. A "merchandise assortment" is composed of a series of demand-related merchandise items that is unique and distinguishable as a separate entity. A supermarket's merchandise assortment typically consists of hundreds of merchandise lines (soft drinks, for example). However, a supermarket generally carries over 10,000 different merchandise items (such as Coke, merchandised in 16-ounce bottles in a carton consisting of eight bottles).

Stores offering many merchandise lines (supermarkets, for example) are said to offer a *wide* line of goods. Stores selling only one line, such as Shakey's Pizza, are said to offer a *narrow*, specialized line.

Merchandise assortments also differ in respect to their *depth*. "Depth of assortment" refers to the number of items offered within each merchandise line. A *shallow* assortment is an offering of several items within a product line. A *deep* assortment involves the stocking of many different items within a merchandise line.

The *consistency* of the merchandise assortment (the degree of relationship of various merchandise lines in terms of consumer end use) is also an important aspect of merchandise assortment planning. Merchandise assortments that are very closely related in use are said to be *highly consistent*. Liquor stores that sell only liquor and mix items offer a highly consistent merchandise assortment. An *inconsistent merchandise assortment* exists when the merchandise lines offered are not related to one another in terms of consumer usage. The proper grouping of related merchandise within departments, as well as physical arrangement in a store layout, enhances the possibility of additional, impulse purchases by customers.

The appropriate assortment is affected by the estimate of the marketing opportunity and by the image the store wishes to project. A store that emphasizes "one-stop shopping" or "full-service merchandise" advertising themes is likely to offer complete merchandising assortments—wide merchandising lines, with deep assortments of goods and services that complement each other. Other retailers, who find a small market segment to serve, usually offer more narrow merchandise lines and more shallow merchandise assortments because their offering is reduced to the most popular items that appeal to their target market.

For example, if a retail manager of such a store finds that three-fourths of his store's sales in a certain merchandise line originate from only four of the fifteen items carried, he is likely to decide that it is not worth the extra effort and expense to stock and maintain eleven extra items. On the other hand, a store that has a "one-stop shopping" or "full service" theme is more likely to carry all fifteen items because of its different management philosophy. Neither policy is incorrect, because merchandise assortments must be based on company goals and objectives and on consumer preferences.

Adding and Dropping Merchandise Lines

Retailers are continually besieged with offers of "new" merchandise. This merchandise may be considered "new" because it is an entirely new technological development or merely because it is a substitute "me too" product (one that is similar to those already on the market) being offered for the first time by a particular manufacturer. This continuous stream of new product offerings and a rapid decline in the popularity of some current product offerings forces the retailer to develop a system that will assist him in identifying the products that should be discontinued. The same system could be used in the selection of new merchandise lines. Some large firms have developed elaborate point systems, based on projected volume, gross margin, turnover, etc., which they effectively use to make their product line decisions.

GROWTH POTENTIAL   The growth potential of the new merchandise line should be evaluated to determine how the proposed line compares to other lines in terms of expected performance. Some products' sales (those with high income elasticities, as outlined in Chapter 5) respond better to increases in consumer incomes than do other products (those with low income elasticities). Accelerated growth potential is indicated on merchandise lines having a high income elasticity (those products for which a relatively higher percentage of income is spent as consumers' incomes increase).

Radios, television sets, foreign travel, sporting goods, and toys have responded very favorably to the income increases that occurred between 1948 and 1965. Items that are associated with the rise of leisure time have recently experienced relatively significant growth. The most spectacular increase is in the purchase of products used in the pursuit of pleasure and relaxation. Items such as bowling balls, color television sets, camping vehicles, cameras, and boats are faring quite well in this boom. Dollar totals in sales of leisure equipment have increased 52 percent over the five-year period 1967 to 1972.[3] Expenditures related to the use of these goods, such as traveling and vacationing, also are increasing rapidly.

Merchandise line growth is also affected by the age of the product line being considered. Products age and their sales decline over time. The product life cycle concept can be used to provide some insight and guidelines to assist the retailer in making his merchandise assortment decisions. The *product life cycle* concept suggests that products move through four stages of sales and profit conditions: introduction, growth, maturity, and decline. Figure 4–2 is a graph of the product life cycle concept.

This life cycle concept implies that retailers frequently incur losses in the *introduction* phase because many risks are associated with products positioned in this stage. Generally, the price is relatively high and the item may be merchandised only by exclusive outlets. Sales volume is normally low. The low sales volume and the high degree of risk influence the retailer to carry only a relatively low level of inventory for the product positioned in the introduction phase.

The *growth* phase begins when sales start to rise rapidly. The retail merchandise assortment usually increases as more models, styles, colors, sizes, etc. are manufactured to meet increased consumer demands. A buildup of larger retail inventories is needed to lessen the possibility of being out of stock.

The *rate* of growth begins to decline at the start of the *maturity* phase. Sales continue to increase, but at a decreasing rate. Competition also begins to intensify as more "me too" products are introduced. This causes a decline

Figure 4–2   Typical Product Life Cycle

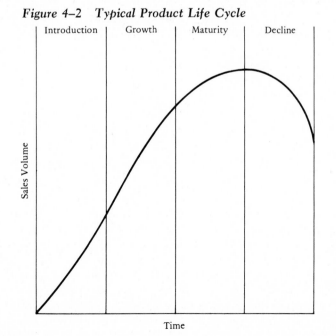

in prices, which requires a more careful balancing of retail inventories. Retailers may also attempt to capitalize on the product differentiation and packaging innovations offered by the leading suppliers during this maturity stage of the cycle.

Sales of merchandise start to turn downward at the beginning of the *decline* stage. The product is making continually smaller contributions to retail profit primarily because of lower sales volume. The retailer's responses made at this stage include the reexamination of required inventory levels and a decision on the appropriate time to close out the remaining product stock.

The *fashion cycle* concept is also important to retailing, as the fashion-minded consumer is a prime market target for the retail industry. *Fashion items* are associated with frequent changes in style, color, and/or design. The other class of merchandise, *staple goods*, refers to standardized items that change slowly over time. The increasing emphasis on new products, colors, and unique designs is making it more difficult to distinguish staple goods from fashion goods. However, staple goods are the necessity items. As incomes increased, the relative importance of fashion goods increased.

The length of the fashion cycle is affected by the same factors that affect the product life cycle, and the same four stages can be defined. However, the fashion cycle can repeat itself continuously over time, because the decline phase is temporary. It is followed by an upswing and a new cycle. A successful fad product may also follow the typical product life cycle, but its sales usually rise faster, reach a peak (as opposed to a plateau), and then fall more abruptly (Figure 4–3).

Figure 4–3   Life Cycle for Fad Product

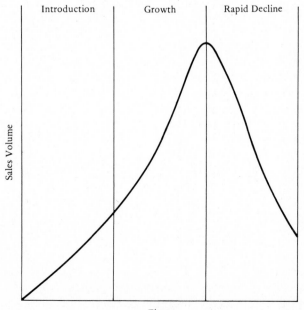

As noted earlier, retail managers should consider the fashion cycle concept when they are planning their merchandise assortment. And certain types of stores are more appropriate than others for merchandising a given fashion through each of its four stages. If the store is to project its desired image, its management should balance the store's merchandise assortment of fashion items with its customers' shopping attitudes and practices.

COMPATIBILITY WITH OTHER MERCHANDISE LINES   Compatibility of product lines refers to the degree that either current or planned lines meet the needs of the market segments being served by the store. The trend toward "scrambled" merchandising (unrelated merchandise is sold by the same store) may have decreased the relative importance of this compatibility consideration. However, merchandise lines must agree (in terms of quality, style, color, size, etc.) with the preferences of the target market customers.

Some of the merchandise lines available to the store are simply consumer substitutes for one or more of the store's existing lines; that is, the consumers use several products for the same purpose. The products may be identical (except for the brand name or color), or they may differ in some slight way. Stocking similar or "me too" merchandise lines usually causes most sales to originate from the brand that is considered to be superior by the store's consumers. One brand begins to divert sales from the others.

Because a store's selling space is limited, each item's sales must be evaluated to determine if it is worth handling. In cases where one item is superior to other similar items, the inferior items may be pared from the offering.

In some instances, however, consumers do not consider one item to have a market superiority over other so-called substitute items. If this is the case, total store sales volume can increase because the consumer responds favorably to a wider merchandise selection.

Merchandise lines can also complement one another. Perfectly complementary items are usually sold together because the sale of one necessitates the sale of the other if the first item is to be used immediately. For example, the sale of a camera necessitates the sale of the appropriate film before the consumer is able to take pictures. The sale of a fishing pole can be combined with the sales of a reel, fishing line, and lures because the customer ultimately will need to acquire these items before he or she can use the fishing pole.

Stocking complementary merchandise lines is usually desirable because the sale of one item can stimulate the unplanned purchase of several complementary or accessory items. Moreover, the customer is likely to be less sensitive to higher price tags on smaller complementary items, such as film, fishing lines, and lures. Ties, belts, and shoes that are color coordinated with a sport coat that has just been purchased are also examples of accessory items that can be merchandised successfully because of their complementarity to a larger item.

Other merchandise lines that are neither substitutes nor complements for existing merchandise lines should generate sufficient sales to be profitable by themselves. In other words, items that are unrelated to the rest of the merchandise assortment can increase store profits and remain in the merchandise line only if they make a positive contribution to overhead. If such products do not generate traffic for complementary, accessory, or substitute products, the stocking decision must be based solely on the items' own merits.

COMPETITIVE CONDITIONS   Competition is another consideration in the task of evaluating the worth of a new merchandise line. If a retail outlet can obtain an exclusive geographical right to carry an item, this agreement would minimize direct competition with other local retailers. A retailer may also prefer to handle such an item if the estimated sales volume appears to justify its addition to his line and if the manufacturer is going to spend a considerable amount of money promoting the item. It is a risky practice not to handle popular, well-promoted new items, because consumers will be drawn into stores by national advertising, and it is difficult to tell these customers (who may be regular customers) that such an item is not carried by the store. They will probably go to a competitor to make that purchase. Once they enter a competitor's store, they may make price, merchandise, and service comparisons that may result in the loss of their patronage.

PROFITABILITY OF MERCHANDISE LINES   Profitability is one of the most important considerations in merchandise planning. Evaluating the profitability of a proposed merchandise line generally involves the use of some estimated elements. Manufacturers may offer retailer clients test market results that estimate dollar sales based on store size or volume. The estimated unit sales can be multiplied by the gross margin percentage to obtain estimates of future total receipts. The expenses associated with the item can be subtracted from total receipts to obtain the item's contribution to overhead.

Retailing expenses vary from item to item, depending on how much time is required for their sale, the amount of service they require, the amount of money required to carry an inventory, and the amount of shelf or floor space required to stock the items. However, from the store management point of view, the profitability resulting from the addition or deletion of an item is the change in contribution to store profit resulting from the decision to stock or not stock the item.

The more conventional ways of determining an item's profitability involve a series of techniques such as indices of turnover rates, gross margin dollars, return on investment, and dollar margins per linear or cubic foot of shelf space.

Turnover is usually obtained by dividing total dollar sales volume by the average value of inventory in retail prices. "Gross margin dollars" refers to the dollar difference between per unit selling price (retail) and purchase price (wholesale). Both turnover and margin influence a good's profitability.

Return on investment is an important measure of effective capital utilization. It indicates profitability as a percentage of the amount of money invested in the store. The margin and turnover values (mentioned above) are components of the return on investment (ROI) figure:

ROI = Margin times turnover

$$= \frac{\text{Profit \$}}{\text{Gross sales \$}} \times \frac{\text{Gross sales \$}}{\text{Tangible assets \$}}$$

$$= \frac{\text{Profits \$}}{\text{Tangible assets \$}}.$$

"Tangible assets" includes the value of the store building and equipment (counters, cash registers, etc.), the amount of money owed the store on credit sales (accounts receivable), and the store's investment in inventory.

The "net space yield" concept is a more complete approach in determining product profit. It takes handling costs, space costs, and margins into account. The concept is based on the fact that the exposure area of a store (the area exposed to the shopper) must be used in the most productive way.

Under the net space yield concept, the space dimension is considered in exposure area terms because:

1. Different stores use different shelf depths. Exposure (facing) area is more likely to be uniform.
2. Exposure area can be studied from photographs and easily charted on graph paper.
3. Manufacturers can compute the necessary exposure area for their own products. All they need know is the number of facings required.
4. Store personnel think in terms of facing or exposure.
5. Companies using computers can determine exposure area by item and insure adequate shelf allocation from store to store.[4]

Table 4–1 shows the necessary measurements that must be completed so that space yield can be calculated for three merchandise categories. The handling cost per case is the cost of handling from warehouse through checkout. The amount of handling cost can be estimated by retail management or it can be obtained by using secondary estimates available from management consulting firms such as McKinsey and Company, Price Waterhouse and Company, Arthur Anderson Company, etc.

In the example in Table 4–1, the handling cost for vegetables is estimated to be 42 cents per case. This figure, multiplied by the number of cases sold per week, gives the total weekly handling cost. The linear display of vegetables is measured as 32 feet long and 5 feet high, so that the total exposure and display in square feet is 160. The shelf depth is 1½ feet, so that the exposure area is 240 cubic feet. The "occupancy" cost for vegetables is estimated to be $16, based on a 10 cents per square foot occupancy cost. The occupancy cost is derived by adding the estimated annual cost for rent, utilities, and depreciation, and dividing the result by the square feet of exposure area in the store.

The gross margin percentage obtained by merchandising vegetables is 25 percent and weekly sales have averaged about $1,000, so the gross profit for vegetables is $250 (gross margin percentage × dollar sales). The net gain is the sum of the total handling cost and the occupancy cost, subtracted from

Table 4–1   *Illustrative Net Space Yield Calculations for Three Merchandise Categories*

(A) HANDLING COST PER CASE (¢)	(B) CASES SOLD	(C) TOTAL HANDLING COST $ EQUALS (A) × (B)	(D) LINEAR DISPLAY FEET	(E) EXPOSURE AREA DISPLAY (SQ. FT.)	(F) OCCUPANCY COST $ EQUALS (10¢) × (E)	MERCHANDISE CATEGORY	(G) GROSS MARGIN (%)	(H) WEEKLY DOLLAR SALES	(I) GROSS MARGIN DOLLARS EQUALS (G) × (H)	(J) NET GAIN $ EQUALS (I) MINUS (C + F)	(K) NET SPACE YIELD $ EQUALS (J)/(E)
42	170	72	32	160	16	Vegetables	25	1000	250	162	1.01
24	112	27	18	90	9	Baby food	13.2	360	47	11	0.12
37	95	35	30	150	15	Health and beauty aids	38	1000	380	330	2.20

SOURCE   Paul J. Cifrino, "Cifrino's Space Yield Formula," *Chain Store Age* (November 1963), pp. 32–34.

the gross profit: $250 − ($16 + $72) = $162. To obtain the net space yield, the net gain is divided by exposure area display in square feet, giving a value of ($162 / 160 ft. = $1.01), the net profit yield per square foot in the area occupied by vegetables.

This procedure is repeated for all of the merchandise lines the store carries. In this example, baby food items contributed only 12 cents per square foot of exposure area—considerably less than the $1.01 yield on vegetables and the $2.20 on health and beauty items. Thus the health and beauty line appears to be the most profitable. The high gross margin percentage (38%) obtained on the health and beauty line combined with a good weekly sales level ($1,000) to make this a very profitable line. Baby items, on the other hand, have a low gross margin percentage (13.2%), combined with low weekly sales ($360), to considerably reduce their profitability.

The net space yield concept is the basis of the following recommendations:

1. Give profitable categories more display space.
2. Give them more desirable locations.
3. Prune variety in low-yield categories.
4. Enrich variety in high-yield categories. Retailers will want to consider doing something even more basic. They will want to set in motion a dialogue with suppliers to learn what can be done with low-yields. Together with suppliers, they will try among other things:
   a. To reduce handling costs.
   b. To reduce bulk wherever possible and urge redesign of hard-to-handle packages.
   c. To shed more light on the relative impact of couponing and deal promotions.[5]

Thus, in our three-category example, the health and beauty aid line could be expanded by adding more items that provide the consumer with more variety. The display space could also be increased for health and beauty items, and they should be given a desirable, high-traffic location in the store. If possible, some items might be pruned from the baby food category.

However, even a low profitability does not automatically indicate that those lines should be severely reduced or eliminated. Baby food is an essential product that will be purchased *somewhere* by a specific segment of the market. A severe reduction in item variety could easily result in a loss of sales for other items, or even store patronage. The more practical alternative would be to reduce the display space devoted to baby food and place this category in a less desirable location, which will raise the net space yield and redistribute customer traffic past impulse items.

MERCHANDISE LINES MUST CHANGE OVER TIME

Consumers' desires and needs change not only seasonally but also over long terms of five- to ten-year cycles. For example, Scandinavian modern furniture was quite popular in the early 1960s, but this preference gave way to the massive Mediterranean decor of the late 1960s.

Another example that demonstrates the point is the automobile preferences of Americans over the last decade. The '60s began with great consumer interest in foreign and American compact cars, but gradually the consuming public expressed its preference for larger, better-equipped, full-size units. With the advent of pollution controls and fuel shortages, the current auto buyer is showing great interest in subcompact cars loaded with luxury accessories (power steering, air conditioning, etc.).

Particular note should be made that even though a cycle has seemed to repeat itself, there have been subtle but profound changes in the merchandise offerings that reflect the needs and preferences of today's consumer. Every retailer must be aware of these attitudinal changes and make appropriate adjustments in his merchandise offering.

Many of these attitudinal changes are traceable to changing demographic characteristics of the consumer. For example, the characteristics of variety store customers are shifting to a younger group. In 1963, 50 percent of all variety store customers were in the 30 to 45 age group.[6] By 1968, this 30 to 45 age group comprised only 33.5 percent of the shoppers, and the under-20 age group made up almost 20 percent of all variety store shoppers. Another 25 percent of the shoppers were in the 20 to 29 age group.

The younger customers, particularly teenagers, were also found to have more money to spend, as over 50 percent of the teenage girls had from $5 to $10 available for spending each week. Teenage boys were also found to be increasingly good customers. Other market segments that accounted for an increasing amount of the variety store sales were senior citizens, young married couples, and minority groups.

Changes of this magnitude indicate the need for a continual reevaluation of the merchandise assortment to ensure that the store is stocking items that satisfy consumer demand.

FRANCHISING

Franchising represents one instance when the merchandise line decision is usually accepted in its entirety or rejected. The current popularity of franchising warrants a detailed discussion of this important product decision. Franchising is a joint venture or cooperative agreement between an owner of a product/service and a dealer—a form of licensing by which the owner (the franchisor of a product or service or method) obtains distribution at the retail level through retail distributors (franchisees). The product, service, or method to be marketed is usually identified by a brand name and associated trademarks, uniform symbols, standardized equipment, common storefronts, and stores that operate under a set of standardized policies and procedures. While the franchisee is usually given exclusive access to a relevant target market, the franchisor maintains some degree of control over the operational aspects of marketing the product or service.[7]

Franchise agreements exhibit a wide range of permissions, prohibitions, and statements of duties and responsibilities on the part of both the franchisor and the franchisee. In many cases the relationship extends beyond mere licensing—as is noted by the International Franchise Association when it defines franchising as "a continuing relationship in which the franchisor provides a licensee the privilege to do business, plus assistance in organizing, training, merchandising, and management in return for a consideration from the franchisee."[8]

Basic Franchise Forms

Franchise agreements can be divided into two fundamental types: those that are based on territorial considerations and those concerned with operating aspects.[9]

A territorial franchise provides the franchisee with the exclusive right to develop the market potential in a given area, with the expectation that the individual or firm already possesses the necessary skill and resources to proceed on its own with the development of that area for that product or service, bound only by certain basic policies and understandings. Such territorial franchises may encompass a country, a state or region, a city, or a section of a community. Quite often, such firms or individuals subfranchise their region and act as the resident management for the parent franchisor.

The more popular operating franchise agreement concentrates on attracting individuals who qualify for franchisee training and have access to sufficient investment or risk capital. In this case the franchisee receives training, guidance, and assistance from the parent franchisor in return for his own work and a share of the *gross sales*. Franchisors consider their fees as operating expenses of the franchisee and thus receive their remittance on gross sales whether the outlet is profitable or not.

Historical Perspective of Franchising

Even though the current interest in the franchise industry and its expansion might lead one to believe that franchising is a twentieth-century innovation, historical evidence indicates that limited franchising was practiced in the early 1800s.[10] Modern franchising, as practiced today, really dates back to 1898, when it was introduced by General Motors. This pioneering effort was followed by Rexall (1902), Western Auto (1909), A & W Root Beer(1919), and Howard Johnson (1926), plus innumerable petroleum, soft-drink bottling, variety, grocery, drug, hardware, motel, and fast-food merchandisers through the intervening years.[11] The growth of the franchise industry has demonstrated considerable expansion in both the types of retail products and services offered and the absolute increase in sales.

Franchising Trends

In the last two years alone, franchise sales of goods and services have increased some 21 percent, and they are expected to reach an all-time high of $156 billion in 1973. Not only have sales increased, but so has the number of franchised businesses. In 1971 some 431,000 franchisors were engaged in a wide variety of business activities, and their number has continued to increase since 1971.[12]

While the spotlight of public attention has focused on the newer methods of franchising, the traditional forms (such as automobile dealers, service stations, etc.) still represent the backbone of the industry, with some 255,703 outlets generating an estimated $126.2 billion in sales in 1973. Admittedly, these traditional franchisees seem to have reached a maturity plateau, but they still serve a vital retail function.

Franchising's hopes for future growth would seem to lie in the areas of recreation, entertainment, and travel, all of which utilize the newer methods of retail merchandising. Gross sales from this sector alone are expected to increase in 1973 some 86 percent over 1972, which was a banner year of $91 million in sales. Substantial increases are expected in campground franchises, construction sales, home improvements, home and office maintenance and cleaning services, and educational products and services.

Some of the underlying reasons for this phenomenal increase in franchise growth are:

1. Technological advances—equipment and systems have been perfected that reduce product variability and provide uniform products/services. Also certain products can more effectively be merchandised as a product group rather than in combination with other products. (Example: Amway, Avon, Tupperware, etc.)

2. Businessmen realize that national saturation of product/service potentially produces better profit returns but the cost of creating and maintaining the necessary nationwide network of outlets is prohibitive. Thus, through franchising they can tap the savings and credit capacity of small investors who may want to be "independent" but lack the proven product/service or the demonstrated managerial skill to pursue an entrepreneurial career. Such an arrangement assists the producer in reaching his goal while maintaining some degree of control over the distribution of his product/service.

3. The American Dream of independence through "owning your own business" supplies motivation for many people who actually work harder for themselves than for an employer. Such perceived "independence" is economically and psychologically rewarding to the franchisee while providing the franchisor with, perhaps, the best sales force available, provided of course that appropriate selection procedures are followed and adequate training and support are continually supplied.

4. Recent economic reverses have resulted in selective massive layoffs creating doubt in the minds of the affected employees about the future

security "in working for someone else." Unfortunately some unscrupulous franchise promoters have capitalized on such fears and promised financial security for a relatively worthless franchise opportunity. Be that as it may, many professional and skilled employees have sought personal security in the perceived independence of becoming a franchisee.

5. Urban "sprawl" or decentralization has created a need for more small retail establishments, particularly those specializing in convenience goods and services which franchising is well adapted to market effectively.

6. Lastly, as our population has increased its geographical mobility, it has created some psychological uncertainty about meeting everyday, basic needs of food and shelter while traveling. Creative, modern franchising has met this need by providing a certain level of homogeneous quality in its product or service so a traveler (or newcomer to the community) can depend on, with some degree of certainty, these retail merchants to meet his needs. For seasoned travelers, this "sameness" of Holiday Inns or McDonald's while reassuring for others may be dissatisfying. Which target market do you wish to please? At the moment, gross sales figures would indicate the former represent the majority of the consuming public.[13]

Products and Services That Breed Franchise Success

Significant product characteristics that best lend themselves to distribution through franchising are:

1. The product is sufficiently distinctive and identifiable by brand or trademark and consumer acceptance has reached a point where he will search out the product when it is needed.

2. The product cannot be offered along with similar products and still have public acceptance, i.e., prepared foods, rug and upholstery cleaning services.

3. The product has unique qualities that require special handling or preparation for proper product consistency and satisfaction when sold to the consumer. (Example: Shakey's Pizzas, Coca-Cola, etc.)

4. The product-service requires installation, periodic service, and a stock of locally available parts such as automobile repair services.[14]

Franchisor-Franchisee Qualifications

Specific qualities that are desirable for potential franchisees are good health, an outgoing personality, good credit and financial standing, a sufficient education level, stable and productive work experience, and an ability to manage people and operations.

A potential franchisor should be evaluated on the basis of his knowledge of financial requirements, fairness, expected profitability, the training programs provided, the reputation and progressiveness of the firm, and consumers' demand for the product or service.

The Other Side of Franchising: Disadvantages

Without a doubt, one of the most discouraging influences on the growth of franchising has been the problem of "exclusive dealing arrangements" or "tying contracts," which are expressly prohibited by the Clayton Act. Franchisors argue, and with some justification, that such contracts can *potentially* result in cost savings to their franchisees due to bulk purchases and resulting quantity discounts. Secondly, and particularly in the fast-food segment of the industry, in order to maintain consistent product quality throughout a wide geographic area a franchisor should be able to control the quality of the raw material and supply inputs by supplying all these items and assuring their proper use through frequent visitations to the various locations.[15]

From the franchisee point of view, such an argument represents a two-edged sword. If indeed the franchisor really had the best interest of the franchisee at heart and attempted to maximize the gross profits through such suggested economies of scale, then such practices should be encouraged. However, in most situations under such tying contractual arrangements, the franchisor negotiates the price of the raw materials and supplies with outside vendors, adds his expenses of handling and distribution, *plus a profit margin for his "managerial" activities,* and then charges the entire cost to "his" franchisees. In short, the franchisees represent a captive market that the franchisor can monopolize. The franchisor is free to charge virtually any price he wants for the basic ingredients that the franchisee must have to operate. From a macro point of view, such exclusive agreements would preclude local competition for the franchisee's purchases, which is anti-competitive. This issue, particularly in fast-food franchise arrangements, has yet to be clearly resolved.[16]

Another problem pertains to the right of the franchisor to repurchase the franchise after the franchisee has made the outlet successful. Many franchise agreements have guaranteed-repurchase clauses, permitting the franchisor to repurchase the outlet after some period of time, say two to five years. At first glance, a potential franchisee might view such a provision as being to his benefit if he should want to sell out or the business turns out to be less profitable than anticipated. Actually, the guarantee is exercisable only by the franchisor, at his option, which he will exercise only if the guaranteed price is less than the value of the going business.

Another problem is the maintenance of exclusivity in a geographical area. Many franchisees have found that their "exclusive territories" shrink in size or are "carved up" by the franchisor so as to increase the level of product or service saturation. The franchisor will not suffer, because he still reaps his collective share of the gross sales, but the franchisee may find his market too small to sustain the needed profit levels for his personal independence.

A serious problem that seems to be a major point of contention in most modern franchise relationships is the matter of initial and continuing managerial training and assistance. Many potential franchisees have little or no business or managerial experience. (If they had such abilities and capital, they would have their *own* retail operations.) While most franchise agreements provide for some initial managerial training, they do not guarantee success—or, for that matter, make any statement about the quality of the training or continuing assistance. If the franchisor is primarily interested in making his money by charging a sizable fee for setting up franchise outlets and using the franchisees' capital and borrowing ability, little or no assistance may be expected after the "grand opening." Alternatively, a change in the franchisor ownership or top management may result in a deemphasis on training and development. In any event, the potential franchisee should be aware of these and other pitfalls before he becomes an "instant entrepreneur."

One should not take the previous comments as a blanket indictment of *all* franchisors or the franchise concept. Reputable firms and viable products and services exist in all types of franchising, both modern and traditional. Voluntary chain associations of independent retailers (usually sponsored by wholesalers) serve the vital functions of providing lower costs for goods due to economies of scale for the retailer and assured outlets for the wholesalers' products. For example, in the food field the Independent Grocers' Alliance (IGA) will grant a franchise to a wholesaler, who in turn licenses member stores to participate in the collective group.

Other examples of wholesaler-sponsored retail franchise outlets are Western Auto Stores, Radio Shack, Coast-to-Coast Stores, and some small, relatively isolated Sears and Montgomery Ward mail-order catalog-retail stores.

Sometimes retailers come together and form a franchise cooperative by setting up a wholesale operation (or retail cooperative chain) for their mutual benefit. Such chains as Associated Grocers (AG) and Certified Grocers represent such franchising arrangements.

Some franchise agreements may take the form of franchised departments in discount centers, where the grocery operation, the shoe department, the optical department, and others are operated by independent retailers under terms of a franchise-lease agreement. The more popular, modern form of producer-sponsored franchise usually covers the entire operation of a particular physical plant and/or service, such as Dairy Queen, Colonel Sanders Kentucky Fried Chicken, and Holiday Inns.

The Future of Franchising

The future of franchising seems bright and promising. It is generally agreed that the modern forms of franchising have grown, and continue to grow, in number and sales volume at a remarkable rate. Some segments of the industry have yet to experience the "shake out" of marginal product/service ideas and selling firms that will inevitably occur as this form of franchising matures. Cyclical economic events may take their toll as rising prices make consumers more aware of the costs of specialized services and pre-prepared foods. The same effect may result during a significant economic slowdown, when every consumer's pennies count.

Another conditioning element in the prediction of franchise growth is the pending legislative backlash, particularly against "pyramiding" types of franchises. "Franchise fair dealing" legislation has been introduced in Massachusetts, New York, California, Texas, and Colorado. This same concern was embodied in Senator Harrison A. Williams' Senate bill (The Franchise Full Disclosure Act of 1970) and similar federal legislative proposals.[17] Such nationwide concern is not unexpected in light of a 1966 study that revealed that 38 percent of the franchisor respondents had been involved in legal disputes with their franchisees.[18]

Successful franchisee recruitment and the establishment of appropriate (continuing) franchisor-franchisee relationships are vital if the franchising industry is to enjoy continued public confidence and support. Individuals who contemplate participating in the franchising field should be fully aware that this is not a short cut to retail success, but it may provide an opportunity for entrepreneurs to partially realize their dreams of independence and success.

SUMMARY

A retailer's merchandise/service offering must meet the needs of his target market consumers. His goods/service offering mix should reflect consumer demand by analyzing the way potential consumers use the merchandise. This can be accomplished if the offering is evaluated in terms of the benefits offered to the consumer, and this should not be limited to tangible products. Thus the offering should provide assistance to the consumer in using the item, maintenance and repair service, and warranties. Delivery and credit also should be provided, but only if the consumers want and are willing to pay for these extended versions of the product. The merchandise assortment must provide the quality, style, color, size, and variety that the target consumer groups demand.

Store-shelf and floor space limit the width and depth of the merchandise assortment an outlet can offer. Outlets that sell shopping and specialty goods may benefit by using their limited selling space to concentrate on meeting the needs of a single, narrowly defined target group. Stores that sell convenience goods generally define their target market in broader terms, to include numerous market segments.

Each merchandise line should be evaluated on the basis of its current sales, growth potential, compatibility with other merchandise offered, profitability per unit of selling space, and its availability in competitive stores. The profitability criterion indicates that the more profitable merchandise lines should be given relatively more display space in the more desirable locations. This will allow retailers to enrich the variety of their offering in the higher-profit categories.

Finally, franchising represents a rather unique product decision because in many cases the retailer is under contract to sell only products associated with a particular franchise. Persons considering the purchase of a franchise outlet should make a thorough investigation of contract terms, market potential, cost structure, and payback period before they make any commitment.

Failures occur in franchise outlets despite the current increase in the number of franchise outlets in operation. The franchise concept perhaps exemplifies the ultimate in a total product designed for a narrowly defined market.

This chapter has discussed the product decision in considerable detail. One should realize that the other variables in the retail mix are equally as important as the product. However, the appropriate product decisions in retailing follow the identification of a target market and set the stage for the effective placing, pricing, and promotion of products and services to meet the needs of the target market.

QUESTIONS

1. What internal and external sources of information are available to retailers to help in making product line decisions?
2. Briefly segment the market for tooth brushes and stereo systems. For which of these two products does segmentation seem most effective? Why? What are the implications of this phenomenon for promotion and store location?
3. What is meant by a wide line of goods? A narrow line? A deep line? A shallow line? Cite real or hypothetical examples of each.
4. Discuss the concept "consistency of merchandise assortment." In what types of retailing would you expect the assortment to be consistent?
5. What factors would you consider in deciding whether to add a new product line to your merchandise? Why would you expect the margin to be high on a new product?
6. List some products for which the income elasticity is low. Why is the elasticity for these products low?
7. Discuss the concept of complementary goods and cite examples of such goods. Discuss and cite examples of substitute goods. What are the retailing implications of these concepts?
8. A company has a $100,000 inventory and sales of $10,000 per month.
   a. Find the turnover.
   b. If inventory is increased by 20 percent and turnover remains constant, what is the new sales volume?
   c. Assuming the same turnover rate, which margin is required if management decides it must have a 20 percent return on investment?
   d. If management finds that it must maintain a 5 percent margin on a certain product line, and turnover is 50, what is the ROI for this product line? What would you recommend to management in this situation?
9. Why is the measure of gross margin dollars usually a poor method of measuring the profitability of a product line? In what cases would this criterion be an adequate measure of profitability?
10. Why is net space yield considered to be the most reliable measure of product line profitability?
11. What characteristics would you look for in a franchisor if you were con-

sidering the franchise business as a career or investment? If you were the franchisor, what characteristics would be important in the franchisee?

FOOTNOTES

[1] Philip Kotler, *Marketing Management: Analysis, Planning and Control* (2d ed.; Englewood Cliffs, N.J.: Prentice-Hall, 1972), pp. 424–425.

[2] Harper W. Boyd, Jr., and Sidney J. Levy, "New Dimensions in Consumer Analysis," *Harvard Business Review* (November–December 1963), pp. 129–140.

[3] "Leisure Boom: Biggest Ever and Still Growing," *Business Week*, April 17, 1972, pp. 42–45.

[4] Paul J. Cifrino, "Cifrino's Space Yield Formula," *Chain Store Age* (November 1963), pp. 32–34.

[5] Ibid.

[6] "Variety Store Shopper Is Changing," *Marketing Insights*, March 18, 1968, p. 16.

[7] *Franchise Company Data: For Equal Opportunity in Business*, U.S. Department of Commerce, Bureau of Domestic Commerce, Washington, D.C., December 1970, p. xi.

[8] Ibid.

[9] Harry Kursh, *The Franchise Boom* (rev. ed.; Englewood Cliffs, N.J.: Prentice-Hall, 1968), pp. 30–40.

[10] Ibid., p. 5.

[11] Aaron M. Rothenberg, "A Fresh Look at Franchising," *Journal of Marketing*, 31 (July 1967): 52–53.

[12] U.S. Department of Commerce, *Franchise Company Data*, p. xi.

[13] Jack M. Starling, "Franchising," *Business Studies* (North Texas State University) (Fall 1970), pp. 10–16.

[14] Robert J. Mockler and Harrison Easop, "Guidelines for More Effective Planning and Management of Franchise Systems," Research Paper 42, Bureau of Business and Economic Research, Georgia State College, Atlanta, May 1968, pp. 14–16.

[15] *Red Rock Bottlers Inc.* v. *Red Rock Cola Company*, 195 F.2d 406 (CA-5, 1952).

[16] *Sigel* v. *Chicken Delight*, CCH 73, 703 (CA-9, September 1971); *Cartrade Inc.* v. *Ford Dealer's Advertising Association et al.*, CCH 73, 760 (CA-9, August 1971); *England* v. *Chrysler Corporation*, CCH 73, 668 (D.C. N. Cal., August 1971).

[17] Starling, "Franchising," p. 14.

[18] J. A. H. Curry and others, *Partners for Profit: A Study of Franchising* (New York: American Management Association, 1966), p. 107.

"THE RANCH" STORES
Changing the Image and Product Line

The Wiener Corporation of New Orleans was undergoing a shift in the product line and image of a division of stores known as "The Ranch." The first pilot Ranch store had been opened two years before in New Orleans under the name "Wrangler Wranch." This store was opened under franchise agreements with Blue Bell Inc. and carried a line of genuine western clothing and accessories, such as saddles and tack.

Initially, these stores were located in free-standing locations or in strip shopping centers. The target market for the original stores was the western-oriented individual who wore western clothes as standard dress or on weekends.

The pleasure horse population in the U.S. had been growing dramatically, particularly among upper-income suburban residents. In addition, there was a market segment of rodeo goers and gentleman cowboys, as well as the genuine thing. These facts and other considerations led the Wiener Corporation into this market.

After a year of operation, the corporation decided that the western market in the company's area of southern and southwestern states surrounding Louisiana was not large enough.

A decision was made to drop the line of western clothes and to change the name to "The Ranch."

Management also decided to change from free-standing or strip shopping locations to regional shopping centers.

The product line was changed to branded medium-priced casual wear for both sexes, catering to age groups from 12 to 40.

These are not discount shops, nor are they expensive boutiques. Name brands include Haggar, Levi, Van Heusen, Arrow, Garland, Lady Wrangler, Bobbie Brooks, A-1, Farah, and Mr. California, as well as many other well-known brand-lines for men and women. Specialty shoe departments have replaced the area formerly occupied by Western Boots.

The new Ranch stores require an initial per store investment of approximately $200,000. Of this, $55,000 is for fixtures and leasehold improvement, $125,000 is for inventory, and $20,000 is for pre-opening expense. Locations usually are leased for twenty years.

Normally, new units begin contributing to profits within 120 days, and management projects $500,000 in sales during the first year of operation—with a breakeven of approximately $300,000 to $325,000 in sales.

At the present time there are eleven Ranch stores and ten more are planned for the near future. In addition to Louisiana, the stores are located in Dallas and Lubbock, Texas; Mobile, Alabama; Fort Smith, Arkansas; Nashville, Tennessee; and Biloxi, Mississippi. Medium-range future plans call for Ranch stores as far north as Ohio and throughout the south and west to New Mexico.

The philosophy behind the Ranch stores is to provide an atmosphere that will appeal to a large cross-section of the youth-oriented casual wear market. All decor and advertising are designed to attract youth without offending older customers or becoming "trendy." Management decided not to allow the use of peace symbols, teen talk, black-light posters, and other youth symbols in decor and advertising.

It was the feeling that in the long run it is impossible to keep abreast of the latest youth fad and that the use of such material could offend many potential customers.

The Wiener Corporation did not want to encourage undesirable patrons to shop in their stores, such as dirty, unkempt persons. It was management's belief that the western motif and the low-key advertising would help to discourage such customers.

After a "wrong track" start with the western apparel and accessory stores, the Wiener Corporation believed it had now developed a merchandising concept to appeal to a moneyed and growing market target.

DISCUSSION QUESTIONS

1. What steps can retailers take to prevent mistakes such as the "Wrangler Wranch"?
2. Do you believe the Wiener Corporation is on the right track with its Ranch stores?
3. What is your opinion of management's decision to retain the western motif and name for the new casual wear shops? Consider your answer in view of the present market area and potential new market areas such as Ohio and Indiana.
4. Do you agree with the philosophy of not trying to talk to the youth market in their idiom and with their symbols?

QUEEN'S STORES, INC.
General Management—
Small Town Retailer

As described by the owner, Mr. Arlie H. Queen, his store is somewhere between a junior department store and a super variety store. The 3,000 items stocked in his store are located over 18,500 square feet of selling space throughout a two-story building in the small town of Wayne, West Virginia. In addition to him and his wife, there are twelve employees, including a full-time assistant manager who came to him from the W. T. Grant Company. Besides the bank, courthouse, two cafes, and a few smaller retail stores, there aren't many more commercial buildings in this town of 1,800 people. The total trading area has a 5-mile radius and encompasses approximately 7,000 persons, including those in the town. The majority of these people receive their income from small farms, "wagon mines" (small coal mines), welfare, and state and county government positions.

The area makes heavy use of food stamps and is a section of the United States that has generally been bypassed by the economic growth of the nation. Nevertheless, the owner, Mr. Arlie H. Queen, receives yearly returns of 10 to 10.6 percent on sales.

Mr. Queen describes himself as extremely cost conscious in every area of his business, and personally keeps track of every phase of the operation. He expressed a belief that most retailers do not concentrate enough on cost-saving ideas but tend to buy expensive new equipment instead of working with what is already available.

As an example of this, Mr. Queen recently received a bid for a new freight elevator and was told it would cost $4,000. Instead of buying it, he personally built one (using a chain and electric motor) for less than $400. Instead of expensive carpeting, linoleum is used. Counter displays are also home made—of pegboard and heavy window glass. Manufacturers' displays are also widely used, even though they may not always be used for the manufacturers' brands.

In sections of the store, such as work clothes, heavy stocking of merchandise is needed. In these sections it is not uncommon to find four or even five pine board shelves, one on top of the other along the wall. Pipe racks are also utilized, using plumber's pipe that has been cut and fitted to serve as racks.

Fitting rooms consist of unpretentious curtained cubicles. These are carefully watched by the sales personnel, to see that only one set of clothing is taken in at a time. Mr. Queen related the story of once catching a customer with six pairs of new Levis underneath his old work clothes. He let the customer go—after he purchased all six pairs—but in general, Mr. Queen said, he turns every shoplifter over to the sheriff regardless of the size of the offense and thus has a very low loss rate.

In addition, his office in the back of the store is elevated and open, which permits constant inspection of half the store. Another, glassed-in office, occupied by his wife, is situated near the center of the store, where she can observe daily operations.

Throughout the years, Mr. Queen has modified or improved several areas to improve efficiency. Instead of reading the cash registers daily, they are now read once a week, but cash pickup is made daily. The lay-away system was also changed—from placing all stored merchandise under the twenty-six alphabet letters to only ten sections.

Another development is the placement of counter displays around the front cash register in a fashion similar to the spokes of a wheel, rather than in the conventional parallel or 40-degree-angle arrangement of displays. This permits closer examination of the merchandise by the sales clerks, particularly those at the front of the store, and is credited with reducing shoplifting losses. Mr. Queen indicated that this and the lay-away system had been carefully inspected by a major variety chain, and the chain planned to implement both innovations.

Although Mr. Queen is the largest advertiser in Wayne County, very little of this is done through conventional mass media. Instead, handbills are mailed eleven times a year to every postal patron in his market area. These are typically 6-page advertisements in the form of a newspaper, with pictures and prices of sales merchandise.

The majority of the buying is done through the Kling Company of Louisville, Kentucky, a large wholesale corporation. It is Mr. Queen's feeling that without the benefit of such a company, the small independent retailer would be doomed.

All orders are sent from Mr. Queen on IBM cards rather than on an order blank. Over the years, the wholesaler has learned the needs of Mr. Queen's store and has been given authority by Mr. Queen to send him one dozen, or one packing, of any new item he feels is appropriate for his store.

The wholesaler also sends him a newsletter from his New York buying office that briefly explains new retailing techniques and products.

Approximately 70 percent of the merchandise comes from the wholesaler, while the remainder comes from manufacturers and is solicited by salesmen from companies such as Blue Bell.

The extension of credit is extremely small, as Mr. Queen believes in cash and carry. In the few instances where, for extenuating circumstances, credit is extended, a very careful watch is kept of each account. If the customer lags in payment, he is informed of this and is not allowed to purchase additional merchandise.

Neither does he believe in clearance sales. The advertised sales are on merchandise that is specifically bought for this purpose. Mr. Queen believes that clearance sales can be avoided by careful buying and by dating each item in the store. The sales clerks are then told to watch the dates on the merchandise and to offer a special reduced price to a customer on a personal basis if the items show wear, damage, or slow turnover. Mr. Queen also believes it is his duty to watch the sales force to see that they do not abuse this by granting special prices to friends and relatives.

Mr. Queen believes there is no substitute for personal involvement in every phase of the company's operations and for continually stressing cost savings. As a result, both he and his wife often work on company records and planning late into the evening after a full day of work in the store. He is also convinced that small-town retailers do not need to close their doors, but that they cannot make it on their own without the benefit of a buying group such as Kling. He is also convinced that a small-town retailer must be innovative by experimenting with new merchandising concepts, but at the same time avoid expensive new systems and equipment.

DISCUSSION QUESTIONS

1. Do you believe that Mr. Queen could operate his store in the same manner if it was located in a city of 100,000 or 1 million or more population?
2. Are basic differences in management necessary for a small-town retail store and one in a large city? If so, what?
3. In a few years Mr. Queen may wish to retire. What steps should he take to ensure the continuation of his business in a successful way after his retirement?

4. What are the possibilities that a retail chain might wish to purchase his business?

5. Discuss, in general, the management practices followed by Mr. Queen. Do you believe they are applicable to other small and medium-size towns, or is Wayne, West Virginia, a unique case?

CHAPTER 5

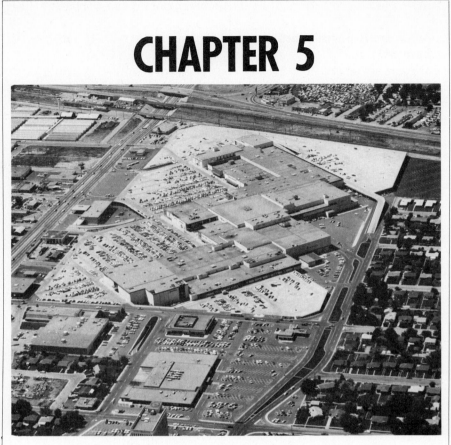

Photo courtesy of New Englewood, Ltd., Cinderella City, Englewood, Colo.

Store Location Considerations

A retailer's merchandise may be easily duplicated. His promotions can be imitated. His prices can be matched. But through a good location the retailer achieves a unique advantage. Once the site has been selected and secured, the space cannot be occupied by a competitive retailer. This chapter examines the factors that retailers should consider when choosing a general trade area in which they may locate an outlet. The process for selecting a specific site within the general trade area is discussed in Chapter 6.

Location has an influence upon all the other elements which the retailer uses to attract customers. In a poor location, a retailer will have to spend additional effort persuading people to seek out his store. This may simply mean that he will spend more on advertising and promotion. However, added drawing power might also be obtained by lowering prices or increasing service —all of which costs money. Thus a good location can save future expenditures that might otherwise be needed to attract customers to the store.

Most site evaluation work consists of a careful investigation of a location for a new store. However, changes in consumer behavior may make a once suitable site suddenly unprofitable. For example, the deterioration of a neighborhood or the opening of a new freeway often causes a change in consumer demand that calls for a site (or at least a consumer target) reevaluation. Therefore, present sites must be continually reevaluated.

A particularly crucial location decision arises every time a retailer signs a new lease. By signing a lease, he commits the store to continue operations from that same location for a specific period, usually six months to twenty-five years. It is advisable to analyze the current location every year or two with the same care as if a new store location decision were being made.

These periodic analyses allow the retailer to spot current or potential deficiencies in market saturation and thereby anticipate the need to change the location to meet changing consumer demands. Although the following discussion is conducted in terms of a new store, the factors involved are also applicable to the appraisal of an established store.

GENERAL TRADING AREA EVALUATION

An evaluation of the general trading area is needed before the specific site is selected. Often, however, this evaluation of the city or trading area is omitted because the retailer believes that it is convenient to locate in a certain area. This can be a tragic mistake, as competitive or environmental conditions may cause the business to fail even if the best site is chosen. Thus the evaluation must be objective and include an analysis of the general trading area as well as the specific site. The profit potential in different areas can be compared. The retailer can then choose the opportunity that appears to offer the best potential in terms of profit for his operation.

Selection of a City or Town

Population

The number of people in the general trading area and the age distribution of this population determine the number of potential customers of retail stores of a particular type. Generally, the purchase of most retail products responds favorably to population increases.

The average population served by retailers has been increasing during the past twenty years as annual sales volume has increased for the stores that have remained in business (Table 5–1). However, the total number of retail establishments has declined slightly since 1948. These trends would indicate that a retailer would want to locate in areas where the average population served per store was (or will be) above the national average population served per store, as reported in Table 5–1.

City and town population data are available from the U.S. Census Bureau. Detailed demographic data are collected every ten years and are available

Table 5–1 *Comparison of Number of Retail Stores, Sales, Average Population Served, and Average Annual Sales Volume for Selected Retail Outlets: 1948 and 1967*

TYPE OF RETAIL OUTLET	NUMBER OF STORES (IN 1,000's)		SALES (IN MILLIONS $)		AVERAGE POPULATION SERVED PER STORE*		AVERAGE ANNUAL SALES PER STORE†	
	1948	1967	1948	1967	1948	1967	1948	1967
Retail trade, total	1,773	1,763	130,521	310,214	82	113	74	176
Hardware stores	35	27	2,494	2,813	4,213	7,330	72	104
Farm equipment dealers	18	17	2,386	4,832	8,294	11,894	135	289
Department stores (including mail-order sales)	3	6	10,645	32,344	56,125	34,375	4,125	5,584
Variety stores	20	21	2,507	5,407	7,229	9,460	124	257
Grocery stores	378	218	24,774	65,074	386	913	125	298
Meat and fish markets	30	18	1,776	1,831	4,958	11,096	60	102
Motor vehicle dealers (new and used cars)	66	62	18,744	48,636	2,230	3,210	286	784
Gasoline service stations	188	216	6,483	22,709	776	921	34	105
Total apparel and accessory stores	115	110	9,803	16,672	1,268	1,807	85	151
Furniture, home furnishing and appliance stores	86	99	6,914	14,542	1,707	2,015	81	147
Eating and drinking places	347	348	10,683	23,842	422	572	31	69
Drug and proprietary stores	56	54	4,013	10,930	2,618	3,706	72	203
Sporting goods stores and bicycle shops	9	16	549	1,173	21,057	12,410	79	73
Jewelry stores	21	24	1,225	2,207	6,869	8,405	58	93

* Average population served per store is total U.S. population divided by the number of stores; population figures used were 1948—146.1 million, 1967—199.1 million.

† Obtained by dividing total sales by number of stores. Sales are reported in $1,000.

SOURCE U.S. Census of Business, Retail Trade, U.S. Department of Commerce, Washington, D.C., 1948 and 1967.

by state, county, and city in the *County and City Data Book: A Statistical Abstract Supplement*. This supplement is published by the U.S. Department of Commerce every five years. *The Editor & Publisher Market Guide* also provides annual population estimates by town and county. An example of the type of data provided is presented in Table 5–2.

The data provided by most sources do not account for seasonal shifts in population. Some trading areas gain people during the summer and lose them during the winter. Some communities, located in states such as Colorado, Wyoming and Michigan, have a large influx of tourists and summer residents who increase the potential number of customers for the summer months. Other communities, in Arizona, California, and Florida, obtain temporary population gains during the winter months. In some locations tourists and temporary residents may arrive at a fairly constant rate throughout the year. College and university towns benefit from the increased population of students during the September to June period. Whatever the seasonal pattern may be, the amount of business generated by these people must be added to the resident business potential to obtain a valid estimate of potential business for the general trade area.

Long-term trends in population growth must also be considered because the store is expected to generate sales and profits far into the future. The U.S. population is expected to grow from 195.9 million in 1966 to 234.5 million in 1980.[1] This represents a 25 percent growth over a fourteen-year period.

Not all areas will grow during the next ten years. Between 1950 and 1966, metropolitan dwellers increased from 56.1 percent to 67.3 percent of the U.S. population.[2] During the same period a large segment of the central-city population moved to the suburbs. In 1969, 45 percent of the metropolitan dwellers lived in the central city and 55 percent lived in the suburbs.

The rate of population growth has not been equivalent for all areas of the United States. Population in the Pacific Coast area has increased most rapidly during the 1960–1969 period. The South Atlantic, West South Central, and Mountain areas have also increased at a rapid rate during this period (Table 5–3). Detailed state-by-state population increases and five-year projections and retail sale estimates are available from *Sales Management*. An example of the data provided by *Sales Management's Survey of Buying Power* is presented in Table 5–4.

Of course, some towns and cities within the same state will grow faster than others. The proximity to a large population center will encourage growth in the nearby towns. The attractiveness of the city or town is enhanced by good schools and churches, health facilities, parking, shopping, and entertainment facilities. A positive attitude of the town leaders toward attracting new industry is also a must if an area is to achieve its share of population growth.

An increased trading area may be obtained by sponsoring civic and merchant events, conventions, and the like that draw people from the fringe of the trading area into town. Improved public transportation and good highway and street systems can increase the size of the trading area by reducing the time required to reach the shopping area. As traffic becomes more con-

Table 5-2 Population, Income, Household, Colorado

	POPULATION		TOTAL PERSONAL INCOME			1971 Number of Households	Editor & Publisher '71 Estimate Income per Household*
	1960 U.S. Census	Editor & Publisher Estimate* Jan. 1, 1971	Editor & Publisher '60 Estimate* (in $1,000)	Editor & Publisher '71 Estimate* (in $1,000)	Editor & Publisher '71 Estimate* (in $1,000)		
State totals	1,753,947	2,173,140	4,039,000	8,170,897		655,956	12,456
Standard Metropolitan Statistical Areas							
Colorado Springs	143,742	208,713	320,688	797,551		61,203	13,031
Denver	929,383	1,152,027	2,457,227	4,563,557		348,537	13,093
Pueblo	118,707	119,538	226,730	350,751		32,543	10,778
Counties, Cities							
Adams	120,296	175,993	248,772	517,695		44,968	11,512
Alamosa	10,000	11,240	17,070	30,094		3,163	9,514
Alamosa	6,205	6,466	13,639	26,514		1,842	14,394
Arapahoe	113,426	145,752	308,519	584,027		40,102	14,563
Archuleta	2,629	2,695	3,657	6,169		760	8,118
Baca	6,310	5,774	12,191	17,775		1,800	9,875
Bent	7,419	6,492	12,189	16,370		1,772	9,238
Boulder	74,254	119,846	176,799	417,246		35,878	11,629
Boulder	37,718	61,594	96,294	263,364		17,803	14,793
Longmont	11,489	17,463	25,437	70,232		6,044	11,620
Washington	6,625	5,466	12,100	15,235		1,649	9,603
Weld	72,344	82,689	132,836	234,581		24,231	9,680
Greeley	26,314	40,418	53,522	111,836		12,933	8,647
Yuma	3,912	7,887	17,066	21,810		2,563	8,509

* Editor & Publisher refers to VI-2 Editor & Publisher.
Source Editor & Publisher Market Guide, 1971 edition, p. 80.

Table 5–3   Residential Population by Regions (In Millions, Including Armed Forces)

	1960	1969 (EST.)	% GAIN FROM 1960–1969
New England	10.5	11.5	10
Middle Atlantic	34.2	37.3	9
East North Central	36.2	39.9	10
West North Central	15.4	16.2	5
South Atlantic	26.0	30.5	17
East South Central	12.1	13.1	8
West South Central	17.0	19.5	15
Mountain	6.9	8.0	16
Pacific	21.2	26.0	23

SOURCE   U.S. Department of Commerce and The Conference Board.

gested, consumers tend to think more in terms of the additional driving time required to reach their destinations than in the actual distance involved. Population changes and accessibility to population have a great influence upon retailing as people tend to shop at the nearest, most convenient location.

Income or Purchasing Power

Population influences the sales of all products and services, but it relates more directly to sales of products that are frequently purchased, such as groceries, than to seldom purchased durables (autos), semi-durables (clothing or small appliances), or services (insurance, for example). Spending on all but the first group is influenced by the level of disposable income, which is the money that families have available to them to spend. So population, while still important, may not be *the* dominant factor affecting sales.

As family income increases, there are pronounced shifts in the relative demand for different categories of goods and services. Ernst Engel, in 1857, observed that although rising family income tended to be accompanied by increased spending in all product and service categories, the percentage spent on housing and household operations remained constant, and the percentage spent on clothing, transportation, recreation, health, education, and savings tended to increase. These findings have been validated in budget studies conducted by *Life* magazine.[3]

The increases in income that have occurred in the United States from 1948 to 1965 have resulted in proportionately higher per capita sales for radios, television sets, foreign travel, sporting goods, and toys. These product lines have demonstrated the highest income elasticities during this eighteen-year period (Tables 5–5 and 5–6).[4]

Product lines that benefited least from the increases in disposable income include footwear, restaurant meals, transportation services, alcoholic beverages, apparel, china, glassware, utensils, tobacco, food consumed at home, furniture, and semi-durable household furnishings. Because of their low

Table 5–4   Summary of Data Available from Sales Management, Inc.

CAL. (CONT.) ESTIMATES — Counties Cities	Met Area Code	Total (thousands)	% of U.S.A.	Households (thousands)	Net Dollars (000)	Median Hsld. Cash Income	A	B	C	D	E	F
△Oakland		367.7	.1756	147.2	1,617,921	8,237	19.0	10.5	19.0	14.0	20.4	17.1
San Leandro		70.9	.0339	26.0	354,041	11,100	9.3	4.4	12.1	17.0	32.2	25.0
Alpine		.5	.0002	.3	2,583	7,630	19.6	18.0	18.0	18.3	20.8	5.3
Amador		12.7	.0061	4.5	43,441	7,540	18.9	11.3	24.6	16.2	17.7	11.3
Butte		108.0	.0516	38.1	350,505	7,071	20.6	14.3	23.4	14.8	16.5	10.4
Calaveras		13.9	.0066	4.9	48,731	7,884	20.5	10.2	20.3	17.4	19.1	12.5
Colusa		12.7	.0061	4.5	49,608	7,690	18.7	11.5	22.4	13.4	18.6	15.4
Contra Costa	240	587.6	.2805	189.6	2,839,147	11,341	10.1	5.4	12.3	14.5	28.7	29.0
Concord		97.2	.0464	29.3	419,244	11,669	8.1	3.9	10.8	15.6	34.4	27.2
Richmond		79.0	.0377	27.1	317,459	9,675	13.6	7.3	15.8	15.9	28.2	19.2
Del Norte		15.1	.0072	5.1	47,002	7,307	16.8	12.2	27.2	18.9	15.6	9.3
El Dorado		47.7	.0228	17.1	187,711	8,588	17.6	9.4	18.9	14.1	23.1	16.9
Fresno	94	434.7	.2075	138.6	1,401,636	7,589	18.7	12.9	21.6	14.4	18.9	13.5
△Fresno		178.2	.0851	61.6	595,441	7,526	21.8	11.8	19.8	14.2	19.8	12.6
Glenn		16.4	.0078	5.6	52,007	7,069	20.2	14.6	23.1	14.1	17.2	10.8
Humboldt		101.7	.0486	34.0	352,543	7,692	16.3	10.5	26.3	16.2	17.8	12.9
Imperial		79.3	.0379	23.3	231,326	7,346	20.5	12.2	22.5	14.4	16.7	13.7
Inyo		15.5	.0074	5.7	58,330	8,183	18.8	10.9	18.6	17.1	20.9	13.7
Kern	24	344.0	.1642	110.6	1,099,654	7,872	19.3	11.7	19.9	14.9	20.9	13.3
△Bakersfield		73.9	.0353	25.5	263,085	8,051	21.7	10.6	17.4	13.3	21.6	15.4
Kings*		68.0	.0325	20.1	182,472	6,613	23.9	14.0	22.6	12.9	16.2	10.4
Lake		22.8	.0109	9.4	81,776	5,924	25.0	17.7	22.7	11.5	12.6	10.5
Lassen		15.7	.0075	5.5	51,687	7,773	17.7	9.4	25.4	17.2	19.9	10.4
Los Angeles	150	6,983.4	3.3314	2,516.9	31,384,661	9,354	13.4	8.9	17.9	14.4	24.5	20.9
Alhambra		61.1	.0292	25.7	292,413	8,994	15.5	9.2	18.2	14.2	23.7	19.2
Arcadia		43.2	.0206	15.7	277,781	12,325	10.7	6.8	12.3	9.9	22.2	38.1
Baldwin Park		48.7	.0233	14.3	147,102	8,722	11.8	9.9	21.4	18.8	25.5	12.6
Bellflower		50.8	.0243	19.2	210,394	9,163	12.8	8.4	18.8	17.3	26.6	16.1
Burbank		88.7	.0423	36.1	445,904	9,695	13.6	8.0	16.4	14.1	25.3	22.6
Compton		77.7	.0371	21.1	203,245	8,098	16.5	10.3	22.3	17.2	21.7	12.0
Downey		85.9	.0410	31.2	437,207	10,753	11.1	6.2	14.3	14.2	27.9	26.3
El Monte		70.9	.0339	24.3	235,903	7,744	22.2	10.8	18.9	14.3	20.5	13.3
Gardena		50.9	.0243	18.3	225,459	9,951	12.6	7.5	16.4	14.0	27.9	21.6
Glendale		130.5	.0623	55.8	691,193	9,059	16.2	9.6	17.5	12.8	21.8	22.1
Hawthorne		55.5	.0265	20.4	242,938	10,072	11.7	7.2	15.6	15.2	29.3	21.0
Inglewood		93.3	.0445	39.6	452,003	8,802	19.3	8.9	16.6	12.9	22.4	19.9

% HSLDS. BY CASH INCOME GROUPS: (A) $0–2,999 (B) $3,000–4,999 (C) $5,000–7,999 (D) $8,000–9,999 (E) $10,000–14,999 (F) $15,000 AND OVER

POPULATION 12/31/72 — EBI 1972

* Military sales of $12,206,000 are not included in the totals above.

RETAIL SALES—1972

Total Retail Sales ($000)	% of U.S.A.	Food ($000)	General Mdse. ($000)	Furn. House Appli. ($000)	Auto-motive ($000)	Drug ($000)	Buying Power Index
855,498	.1928	155,981	171,227	45,425	165,516	28,312	.1952
248,746	.0561	42,101	66,516	8,494	52,962	11,037	.0460
127	.0000		25				.0002
26,911	.0061	8,686	1,295	172	5,201	608	.0058
237,181	.0535	53,409	26,318	10,460	50,698	8,644	.0485
22,836	.0051	6,601	2,853	211	3,810	716	.0060
26,872	.0061	5,064	888	519	4,801	792	.0062
1,250,871	.2819	319,911	231,366	49,906	250,349	63,319	.3200
312,054	.0703	67,258	75,860	13,328	81,476	13,115	.0569
150,587	.0339	29,104	29,484	8,991	43,746	3,330	.0378
28,285	.0064	7,836	2,127	1,082	3,519	1,275	.0063
106,032	.0239	34,297	4,815	1,368	16,005	7,615	.0236
1,036,763	.2337	204,672	144,100	57,733	195,415	46,169	.2002
637,024	.1436	105,943	124,580	46,011	126,950	30,967	.0977
38,826	.0088	9,390	2,809	788	7,036	1,033	.0075
219,954	.0496	55,673	31,816	7,673	42,569	5,399	.0469
213,329	.0481	47,831	32,956	8,127	34,815	6,220	.0366
52,716	.0119	10,642	4,571	979	12,830	1,423	.0088
730,437	.1646	143,189	107,353	30,868	144,192	25,654	.1517
372,849	.0840	41,047	81,248	20,819	89,300	11,585	.0489
134,782	.0304	21,075	15,254	5,615	21,636	4,586	.0272
40,993	.0092	14,342	1,605	1,264	6,009	1,214	.0101
36,951	.0083	10,023	3,479	782	6,752	1,053	.0072
16,200,055	3.6506	3,321,876	2,977,013	796,744	3,306,763	616,888	3.7249
156,615	.0353	26,164	20,229	8,123	60,391	6,596	.0349
119,632	.0270	26,490	30,361	4,127	14,010	7,584	.0298
59,150	.0133	20,898	1,473	3,758	3,625	2,685	.0180
114,723	.0259	23,151	9,038	10,298	35,847	2,878	.0259
222,969	.0503	47,972	37,829	8,225	51,177	8,470	.0517
153,881	.0347	34,200	38,521	7,362	36,074	7,140	.0307
318,461	.0718	41,618	69,153	12,676	108,497	10,232	.0573
185,654	.0418	29,686	62,101	6,403	42,709	3,726	.0342
162,813	.0367	37,510	12,479	6,021	40,610	10,701	.0301
334,672	.0754	60,600	56,533	20,098	98,839	11,051	.0787
105,247	.0237	27,033	6,000	4,787	24,994	9,834	.0278
249,720	.0563	41,683	43,110	15,344	69,486	8,787	.0543

SOURCE "1973 Survey of Buying Power," *Sales Management*, July 23, 1973, p. D10. Copyright, Sales Management, Inc., 1973.

Table 5–5   The Diversity of Real Growth (Average annual growth rates, 1948–1965, based on constant dollars)

ITEM	AVERAGE ANNUAL GROWTH RATE	ITEM	AVERAGE ANNUAL GROWTH RATE
Disposable Personal Income	3.6	China, glassware, utensils	2.1
Total Expenditures*	3.6	Semi-durable house	
Food at home	3.1	furnishings	3.0
Restaurant meals	1.1	Household supplies	4.8
Alcoholic beverages	1.7	Personal care services	4.5
Tobacco	2.1	Toilet articles, preparations	6.5
Women's, children's			
apparel	3.3	Medical care services	4.6
Men's, Boys' apparel	2.0	Drugs, supplies	5.8
Footwear	1.1	Automobile purchases	5.0
Jewelry, watches	5.2	Tires, tubes, accessories	5.4
Shelter	5.1	Gasoline and oil	5.4
Household operation		Transportation services	1.3
services	4.8	Sporting goods, toys	7.2
Furniture	3.4	Foreign travel	7.7
Household appliances	4.8	Higher education	5.5
Radio, TV, etc.	7.6	Personal business	3.5

* Personal consumption expenditures.
SOURCE   U.S. Department of Commerce and The Conference Board.

response to increases in disposable income, sales of these items may be more dependent upon population growth than upon increases in income. Thus the demand for these products is not likely to increase as rapidly as sales of products that are favorably related to higher incomes.

There is no simple measure of income or purchasing power that can completely describe the consumer's ability to buy merchandise. The average family income and per capita income are provided in several sources, such as the *Editor & Publisher Market Guide* and *Sales Management* (see Tables 5–2 and 5–4). The buying power index in Table 5–4 provides an approximate value for the ability of an area to purchase consumer goods. For example, Table 5–4 indicates that Butte County, California, had a buying power index of 0.0485 in 1972. The projected buying power index for El Dorado County, California, was 0.0236. Thus the market potential in Butte County is estimated to be approximately double the market potential in El Dorado County. This index is most applicable to mass market products (as contrasted with items not sold on the mass market) that are sold at "popular" prices. These index calculations provide a good estimate of the level of income available for spending, but they do not take into consideration the following factors:

1. *Distribution of income.* The distribution of income is important because average per capita income can be distorted by a few individuals with very high or very low incomes. More importantly, the dispersion of income can be estimated from the proportion of families that are homeowners, the average value of the single-unit dwellings, the educational level of the people in the area, the number and make of automobiles registered in the area, and per capita retail sales.

2. *Stability of income.* Income is generally more stable in areas with diversified industries than in areas dominated by one industry. Of course, *some* areas that are dominated by one employer offer a strong but stable economy. Washington, D.C., and the small-town location of large colleges and universities are examples of areas that usually have relatively strong but seasonally stable retail sales. Retail sales in areas dominated by employers whose sales are affected by seasonal or economic conditions are likely to fluctuate with the decline and expansion of these industries.

   The quality of the labor-management relationship also affects stability of income and hence retail purchases. Constant labor strife and

Table 5–6   The Discretionary Effects of Rising Income (Income sensitivity ratios, based on years 1948–1965)

ITEM	INCOME ELAS-TICITY*	ITEM	INCOME ELAS-TICITY
Total Expenditures†	1.00	China, glassware, utensils	.59
Food at home	.86	Semi-durable house furnishings	.83
Restaurant meals	.32	Household supplies	1.36
Alcoholic beverages	.49		
Tobacco	.60	Personal care services	1.25
		Toilet articles, preparations	1.84
Women's, children's apparel	.92	Medical care services	1.29
Men's, boys' apparel	.57	Drugs, supplies	1.63
Footwear	.31		
Jewelry, watches	1.46	Automobile purchases	1.40
		Tires, tubes, accessories	1.51
Shelter	1.44	Gasoline and oil	1.52
Household operation services	1.34	Transportation services	.38
Furniture	.95	Sporting goods, toys	2.01
Household appliances	1.34	Foreign travel	2.11
Radio, TV, etc.	2.13	Higher education	1.52
		Personal business	.98

* Percentage change in personal consumption expenditures for each 1 percent rise in disposable personal income.

† Personal consumption expenditures.

SOURCE   U.S. Department of Commerce and The Conference Board.

periodic strikes may result in violent fluctuations in retail sales, and also require merchants to overextend credit during strikes.

3. *Trend of income* in a particular area. For most retailers it is desirable to be located in areas where consumers' incomes are growing at a faster rate than the national average annual increase in income. However, some retailers prefer to appeal to the low-income market segment and thus locate stores in low-income areas offering a narrow merchandise assortment and high-risk credit terms.

Purchasing Habits of Potential Customers

Purchasing habits must be investigated to determine if the potential customers are likely to do their buying at the most accessible locations. If the majority of the people rely mostly upon mail-order purchasing or like to combine a shopping trip with a pleasure trip and travel many miles, it will take some additional advertising and promotional expenditures, or price reductions, to influence these consumers to change their buying habits. These differences in purchasing patterns may correspond to group differences in social class, age, race, nationality, or religion.

Better estimates of an area's sales are obtained if the prospective retailer is personally familiar with the buying habits, preferences, and prejudices of the people residing in the trading area. Familiarity with potential consumers' purchasing patterns will also make it easier for the prospective retailer to estimate the importance that consumers give to services and wide and deep merchandise assortments. This knowledge is useful not only in the site selection process but also when the retailer decides what products and services he will offer.

Legislative Restrictions

The legal environment influences the profitability, and may determine the existence or nonexistence, of any store. Local zoning ordinances limit the number of sites that are suitable for retailing. Municipal or state regulations relative to the hours of business may limit night and Sunday openings for many types of retail outlets. The decision on location is also influenced by the tax and license structure in the particular area. The relative level of sales tax charged in nearby areas is particularly important to retailers who sell shopping goods. For example, the difference between a 3 and a 6 percent sales tax on a $1,000 stereo system is $30. Such marked differences can influence consumer buying habits toward making purchases in the lower tax area. Fair trade laws and unfair trade practices acts must also be considered because they have a noticeable effect on retail prices.

Competition in the Area

The choice of a location is also influenced by the number, type, location, and floor space of competing stores. The competition should be evaluated to determine to what extent its merchandise and service mix meet the desires of the prospective consumers.

The trend toward "scrambled merchandising"—selling many unrelated lines in a single outlet—has made this evaluation more difficult. Today, much of the competition for items that used to be sold in specialty stores is not derived from other specialty stores but from chain, department, discount, grocery, drug, or hardware stores. Thus the study of competitors must be based on a realistic estimate of the share of the total market that can be obtained when one faces this vigorous competition.

Store Saturation

Preliminary estimates of the extent to which the competition has already obtained the retailing opportunities in the trade area can be obtained from several sources.

County Business Patterns, which is published annually by the U.S. Department of Commerce, uses a classification system called the Standard Industrial Classification (SIC) to classify most manufacturers, wholesalers, and retailers into designated categories for each geographical area. Using this information, one can determine the number of retailers doing business in the trade area. State sales tax revenue offices sometimes summarize and make public the number of retail outlets doing business in each county, and also provide the volume of business obtained by each type of outlet (as defined by the SIC code system).

No matter which source is used, the SIC system of trade area appraisal has several weaknesses. It is difficult to identify the precise activities of a particular firm because some retail outlets sell wide assortments of merchandise. Then, too, the mere number of a specific type of store in an area does not give an evaluation of the aggressiveness of the outlets.

A more precise measurement tool, called an *index of retail saturation*, can be used to determine if the stores in a trade area adequately or inadequately supply consumer needs. When an area has too few stores to meet the needs of the consumer community satisfactorily, an *"under*stored" condition exists. This situation presents the best retailing opportunity for new stores to satisfy consumer needs.

If an area is *"over*stored," it has more stores than are needed to satisfy consumer demand. This situation would probably result in a low return on investment for the retail outlets operating in the area. It would not represent an opportunity for a new store unless the new store could serve the consumer needs much more effectively than the current outlets. In such a case, some of the current outlets would probably be driven out of business.

The index of retail saturation can be calculated by dividing estimated consumption by the ability of current retailers to satisfy consumer needs. In formula terms, that calculation could be obtained as follows:[5]

$$\text{Saturation Index} = \frac{(C)(RE)}{RF}$$

where C is the number of prospective consumers of the proposed product, RE is the average expenditure for the proposed product line for a selected period of time, and RF is a measurement of competing (and planned) retailing facilities in the trade area, measured in square feet of space devoted to the proposed lines of merchandise.

The use of this index may be illustrated by the following example. Saturation index calculations could be made for several different areas to indicate which area offers the most potential for a proposed supermarket. There are 50,000 consumers in area A. The average consumer in the area spends $6 per week in supermarkets. The six supermarkets serving area A have a total of 60,000 square feet of selling area. The index calculation is:

$$\text{Saturation Index} = \frac{(50,000)\,(\$6)}{60,000} = \frac{\$300,000}{60,000} = \$5$$

The $5 sales per square foot of selling area can be measured against the sales needed per square foot if the business is to just "break even." The $5 calculated sales per square foot could also be compared with the index figure for other possible location areas. The highest index would indicate the area with the best potential. It does not indicate that the area will be a profitable location unless the highest index is higher than the break-even sales needed per square foot, and even then it does not "guarantee" success because the outlet must be well-managed, competition may change, and so on.

This index of saturation is an excellent measure of potential sales (per square foot) because it uses both consumer demand and competitive supply to evaluate the trading area. However, the index does not reflect the quality of the competition in each trade area. Some areas may have more progressive merchandisers than others, and this difference may not appear in the square footage measurement of competitive strength used in the denominator of the formula. Thus qualitative evaluation of competition should also be made to determine if (and to what degree) competitive strength differs from the assumed power made on the basis of square feet of selling space.

Type of Location Considerations

Every retail outlet can be classified according to its type of location. More importantly, a retail outlet's type of location has a strong influence upon the size and shape of the trading area that the store is able to serve. The type of location also determines the degree to which a store is able to penetrate its market area.

Classification of Location Types

Locations may be either free-standing (no other retailing businesses are adjacent to the site) or business-associated sites. Most locations are business associated as a part of either a planned shopping center or an unplanned shopping district. Characteristics of store location types are:

1. Free-standing see Figure [5–1]
   a. Neighborhood—an isolated retail outlet which serves the needs of a a small portion of the town
   b. Highway—an isolated oulet located on a highway

Figure 5–1   "K Mart," an Example of a Freestanding, One-Stop Shopping Retail Outlet

SOURCE   S. S. Kresge Company.

2. Business-associated
   a. Unplanned
      1) Downtown—the traditional commercial core of the town. It may contain department, variety, apparel, and food stores plus many offices and service shops.
      2) Edge of downtown—the area located at the edge of the downtown area.
      3) Neighborhood business district—neighborhoods are small parts of a town that are usually defined by social, economic, or geographic boundaries. A neighborhood business district contains small stores with nothing larger than a supermarket or variety store.
      4) Secondary business district—a small-scale downtown area usually bounded by major street intersections. It must contain at least a junior or general merchandise department store and a variety store and some smaller retail and service shops.
      5) Highway business string—an elongated area which contains several retail businesses. Extensions of the string down perpendicular streets are very shallow.[6]
   b. Planned shopping center—its location, size, type of tenants, and park-

ing space are the result of conscious planning by the developers. The expansion of this type of retailing has been continuing. Retail shopping center sales expanded from $68 billion and less than 25 percent of total retail sales in 1965 to $117 billion or 33 percent of all retail sales in 1970.[7] The three major types of planned shopping centers are:

1) Neighborhood shopping centers—oriented toward convenience shopping so they contain nothing larger than supermarkets, variety, or small department stores. Total (gross area) store space in the center should range from 25,000 to 75,000 square feet. The supermarket or the drug store is the leading tenant in a neighborhood shopping center.

2) Community shopping centers—can serve both the convenience and shopping goods needs of a city and a few of its suburbs through its larger junior department stores, smaller branch stores and specialty shops. The community shopping center offers wider style assortments, wider price ranges and more stores designed to attract more impulse sales than stores located in the neighborhood shopping center. Total store space in a community shopping center usually ranges from 75,000 square feet to 300,000 square feet.

3) Regional shopping centers—are larger centers which contain over 300,000 square feet of gross store area. Regional centers feature at least one full-line department store and a wide range of junior department, variety, apparel and miscellaneous stores. The smaller tenants are selected to offer a range of complementary goods and services formerly found only in the downtown area. Many regional centers are now featuring an enclosed mall for year-round shopping comfort. This type is designed not only to shut out the weather but also to provide psychological integration. Such climate-controlled malls give the impression of one giant store with individual shops. As a result it often serves an even larger trade area than other regional centers.

A few new shopping centers are conceived as integral parts of new developments and are becoming the hubs of community social activities. The centers may include as many as five department stores, many smaller stores and services, plus hotels, apartment houses, office buildings, cultural centers, churches, and theaters. This type of center is also made more attractive by using fountains, waterfalls, and landscaping. The size of such centers is also becoming larger. Woodfield Shopping Center, located in Schaumburg, Illinois, 25 miles northwest of Chicago, claims to be the world's largest enclosed, multi-level shopping center. It contains 2 million square feet of space, 215 shops and services, and three major department stores. Other new centers such as North Park in Dallas, Texas; Newport Center in the Los An-

geles area; South Hills Village in the Pittsburgh area; and East-
ridge in the San Jose area are also considered shopping cities.

The expanded form of a regional shopping center integrates
all of the retail and commercial functions plus activities in the
areas of entertainment, health, shopping, eating, and education.
These larger regional shopping cities are growing in importance,
although only a few of the 12,000 United States shopping centers
could currently be classified as shopping city centers. Such large
centers have an added impact beyond their numerical importance
because large city centers outdraw smaller centers and can pull
shoppers from much longer distances.

The trading area differs for each of these location types and
even for each store in the center. Store size and operating procedures differ markedly from one company to another, so it is
impossible to make accurate statements about trading areas for
all companies. The experiences of two eastern companies provide
an example of the drawing power of each location type for a
supermarket [Table 5–7].[8]

Shopping Center Location Considerations

The shopping center's characteristics attract customers who like the
convenience, parking facilities, and variety offered by the wide assortment of
stores located in the center. Some large shopping centers also provide social
drawing power. Teenagers, particularly, are drawn to these centers on Saturday; not to shop, but to socialize. Some centers sponsor community activities
such as dog shows, flower shows, and art and other special exhibits to increase
their appeal to all age groups. The merchant who is deciding if he should
locate in a center must weigh these positive characteristics against the higher
rental costs in such centers and the limitations placed upon him as a center

Table 5–7 *Comparison of Trading Areas for a Supermarket Situated in Different Location Types*

LOCATION TYPE	PRIMARY TRADING AREA SIZE (RADIAL DIMENSION)		% OF TOTAL SALES 0–1 MILE AREA
Neighborhood free-standing	½–¾	mile	65–70
Central business district	½–¾	"	70–75
Neighborhood business district	¾–1	"	60–65
Secondary business district	¾–1	"	60–65
Highway business string	1–1¼	miles	60–65
Highway free-standing	1–2	"	55–60
Edge of downtown	1½–2	"	40–45
Community shopping center	1½–2	"	50–55
Regional shopping center	1½–2½	"	35–40

SOURCE Bernard Kane, Jr., *A Systematic Guide to Supermarket Location Analysis*
(New York: Fairchild Publications, 1966), p. 91.

tenant. The shopping center tenant must pay his prorated share of all joint center promotion efforts. The shopping center retailer must also keep store hours, light his windows, and place signs in accordance with center regulations.

Developers and owners of shopping centers want to attract a wide assortment of successful retailers. Their initial selections are likely to include one or two prestige merchants (usually large chain stores or large department stores) as their lead tenants. Then at least one day-time restaurant and other complementary types of stores (usually small, independent retailers) are selected so that the center achieves a "tenant mix" and offers a varied array of merchandise. The developer needs leases from companies with strong credit ratings to be able to obtain his financing prior to construction, and most lenders favor tenant rosters that include the best of the national chains. However, the average developer also prefers to devote at least 40 percent of his store space to specialty or other shops on short-term leases.[9] This provides the developer with some protection against inflation because many specialty shops pay a percentage of their sales as rental. Big chains usually will not agree to share a percentage of their sales with a developer. Specialty shops also carry a wide merchandise assortment, which can be adjusted to draw additional customer traffic. Also, an overbalance of major chain stores can be detrimental to small merchants' sales because of their rather complete merchandise assortments.

The retailer who is considering locating in a shopping center has several major items to investigate.[10] First, an objective trading area analysis (including an evaluation of competitive outlets analysis) must be performed. Second, an analysis of the merchandising characteristics of the stores must be conducted. The selection of stores should be sufficient to meet the needs of the area's customers. The arrangement of the stores should give the retailer's store at least an equal chance of obtaining passerby pedestrian traffic. Ideally, every retailer would like to be located between the stores with the greatest "customer pull." Third, "total rent" should be evaluated in making the decision, and this includes the maintenance of common areas, the dues paid to the center's merchants' association, and the minimum lease guarantees—typically 5 to 7 percent of gross sales.

The retailer must evaluate these costs with the additional profits he believes he can obtain by locating in a center. He would choose the center location if he could reasonably project that the added profits would be greater than the added costs.

A fairly comprehensive list of the factors that should be investigated by a retailer who is considering a shopping center location is presented in Figure 5–2.

Figure 5–2 Factors to Consider when Evaluating Shopping Center Locations

1. Who is the shopping center developer?
2. How long has he been in the business of developing real estate?
3. What are his financial resources?
4. With whom has he arranged for the financing of the center?

Figure 5–2 *(Continued)*

5. What is his reputation for integrity?
6. Who performed the economic analysis? Does the report cover both favorable and unfavorable factors?
7. What experience has the economic consultant had?
8. Has an architectural firm been retained to plan the center?
9. Has the architect designed other centers? Have they been successful from a retailing standpoint?
10. Who will build the center? The developer? An experienced contractor? An inexperienced contractor?
11. Has the developer had experience with other centers?
12. What is, or will be, the quality of management for the center?
13. Will the management have merchandising and promotion experience? (Some developers are large retailers rather than real estate operators.)
14. What percent of the leases have been signed? Are they on a contingent basis?
15. Has every facet of the lease been carefully studied?
16. Is the ratio of parking area to selling area 3–1 or more?
17. Has sufficient space (400 feet) been assigned to each car?
18. Is the parking space designed so that the shopper does not walk more than 300 to 350 feet from the farthest spot to the store?
19. What is the angle of parking space? (Ninety degrees provides the best capacity and circulation.)
20. What is the planned or actual car turnover? (3.3 cars per parking space per day is the average.)
21. Is the number of total spaces adequate for the planned business volume? (Too many spaces make the center look dead; too few openly invite competition around the center.)
22. Does the parking scheme distribute the cars so as to favor no one area?
23. Is there an adequate number of ingress/egress roads in proper relationship with the arrangement of parking spaces?
24. For the larger centers, a ring road is preferable. Is this the case?
25. Is the site large enough for the type of center?
26. Is the size sufficiently dominant to forestall the construction of similar shopping centers nearby?
27. Is the center of regular shape? If not, does the location of the buildings minimize the disadvantage of the site's shape?
28. Is the site sufficiently deep? (A depth of at least 400 feet is preferred; if less, the center may look like a strip development.)
29. Is the site level? Is it on well-drained land?
30. Can the center be seen from a distance?
31. Are any structures, such as a service station, located in the parking area? (If so, do they impede the site's visibility?)
32. Is the site a complete unit? (A road should not pass through the site.)
33. Are the buildings set far enough back on the site that the entire area may be seen?
34. Are all the stores readily accessible to each other, with none having an advantage?

SOURCE J. F. Mertes, "Site Opportunities for the Small Retailer," *Journal of Retailing* (Fall 1963), p. 44.

SUMMARY

Considerable care must be used to select and review the general area where a retailer could locate a store. The population must be sufficient to support a new store which carries the proposed merchandise assortment. Thus competition must also be evaluated to determine if an area has too few stores to meet the needs of the community's consumers satisfactorily.

If the current or projected population is not large enough to support an additional store, a new or proposed store will have to rely upon other elements of the marketing mix (such as low price, heavy promotion and advertising outlays, better service, a larger merchandise assortment, etc.) to drive current competition out of business. This could result in continual low-profit margins, even if the new entry is successful in eliminating an established outlet.

The income level of the people living in the area will also influence retail sales. Retailers who stock shopping goods such as radios, TVs, sporting goods, and other items that are extremely sensitive to changes in income must place relatively more emphasis upon the area's income level than retailers who carry merchandise that does not appear to respond much to income changes. Other factors that must be considered are the purchasing habits of potential consumers, the legal environment, and the progressiveness of the community in attracting customers.

Type of location must also be evaluated because stores located in shopping centers may have a much different trading area than stores that are located downtown or in neighborhood business districts. The trend is toward extremely large shopping centers which draw customers from a large trading area for entertainment, health, education, eating, and shopping purposes.

Each retailer must make an independent judgment, weighing all the variables, and then select the type of location that will provide him with the best possible chance of success.

QUESTIONS

1. Based on Tables 5–3, 5–4, and 5–6, what types of retail establishments would you recommend starting and where would you recommend starting them (city or region)? Once you have decided on cities and regions for these establishments, how would you go about finding the exact locations of the establishments in these cities or regions? Give your reasons for making these choices.

2. What strategies are available to retailers who find themselves in an *over*stored area? Would you expect an *under*stored situation to continue in the long run? Why?

3. Suggest several reasons why retail shopping center sales have expanded since 1965. Would you expect this trend to continue? If so, for how long? Why?

4. Since lead tenants are considered so important in drawing customers to

a shopping center, why would a shopping center developer want to devote at least 40 percent of his floor space to specialty shops?

5. Suggest a retailing mix for the following:
   a. A retail hardware/appliance dealer in a middle-class suburb
   b. Similar-type store in a small rural community approximately 200 miles from the nearest metropolitan area
   c. A large, very exclusive haberdashery store, for example, Brooks Brothers
   d. A mobile-home dealer.

6. If you were offered very low-cost financing to open a retail store in Watts, Harlem, or some similar inner-city ghetto area, how would you decide exactly where to locate and what to sell? Develop a complete retailing mix for whatever type of establishment you would suggest and give your reasons. What major problems would you anticipate in the first year of operation?

7. Some cities and states (Boulder, Colorado, and the state of Oregon, for example) have made deliberate attempts to limit population and/or economic growth. Considering the retailing industry as a whole, what are the implications of these limits? What line of merchandise and what retailing mix would you suggest for a potential retailer in these areas?

FOOTNOTES

[1] *Economic and Demographic Projections for States and Metropolitan Areas*, Regional Projection Series (Washington, D.C.: National Planning Association, Center for Economic Projections, 1966), Report 68-R-1.

[2] Ibid.

[3] *Study of Consumer Expenditures* (New York: Time, Inc., 1957), vol. 1.

[4] Income elasticity is measured by the percentage change in personal consumption expenditures for each 1 percent change in disposable income. Thus an elasticity value of more than 1.0 indicates that a larger percentage of a person's rising disposable income is being spent on items with income elasticities above 1.0.

[5] B. J. LaLonde, "New Frontiers in Store Location," *Super Market Merchandising* (February 1963), p. 110.

[6] This classification was obtained from J. Ross McKeever, *Factors in Considering a Shopping Center Location* (Washington, D.C.: Small Business Administration), Aids No. 143.

[7] "Shopping Centers Grow into Shopping Cities," *Business Week*, September 4, 1971, pp. 34–38.

[8] McKeever, *Factors in Considering a Shopping Center Location*, pp. 6–7.

[9] "Shopping Centers Grow into Shopping Cities," p. 37.

[10] John Mertes, *Site Evaluation for Small Retailers* (Washington, D.C.: Small Business Administration, 1966), pp. 1–4.

DOLLAR GENERAL STORES
Store Location

The Dollar Stores Corporation of Huntington, West Virginia, operates a chain of cash-and-carry soft goods discount stores called Dollar General Stores throughout West Virginia. The location strategy has been to locate a store in each county seat.

At the present time the corporation operates 30 stores, with plans for a total of 43 in West Virginia. Future expansion plans call for locations throughout Pennsylvania.

The Dollar Stores Corporation is an independent corporation but is affiliated with Dollar General Corporation of Scottsville, Kentucky. The parent-affiliate has 500 stores throughout 17 southeastern states and has been highly successful. This success pattern has been followed by the Huntington-based corporation.

According to Mr. Earle S. Dillard, president and treasurer of Dollar Stores Corporation, the company began making a profit in the first three months of operation. By the end of the first sixteen months, it had produced net profits of $113,000 on sales of $1,784,790. Mr. Dillard attributes this success to the pattern of store selection and merchandising.

He stated that an even more important reason was the management team that was attracted to the idea and the corporation. These included Paul Hampton, chairman of the board; Milton Utley, vice-president of operations; and Jimmie D. Cox, comptroller. Although the idea originated with Mr. Dillard and Mr. Hampton, they stated that the accomplishment would have been impossible without this management team.

Small towns are the target market where competition is less intense and there is a reservoir of consumer desire for a discount operation.

A typical Dollar General Store has free-standing displays where merchandise is displayed in a dump-bin fashion. All prices are in even-dollar amounts, as opposed to conventional pricing. Printed signs, very much like those in many food stores, are hung from the ceiling, along the wall, or on stands in the merchandise. Examples are: "Rugs—$1," "Aprons 2 for $1," "Shirts 2 for $3."

All of the buildings are leased, some for as low as $95 per month. A Spartan atmosphere prevails, with uncovered fluorescent lighting, floors of cement or linoleum, a cash register and counter in front, and a complete absence of frills—such as carry-out service, music, electric doors, and interior decorating.

The merchandise consists primarily of American-made soft goods acquired from the manufacturer as irregulars or overruns. Each store receives its deliveries on a drop ship basis, thus avoiding the necessity for a warehouse and a delivery system.

Among all the stores in West Virginia, only one is managed by a man; the others are typically managed by middle-aged women from the local area. "We average two and a half employees per store," said Dillard: "the manager, a clerk, and a part-timer to help out at peak periods."

The location strategy followed by the Dollar Stores Corporation has been to locate a store in every county seat since these are regarded as natural market areas. Other store locations are determined with the aid of insurance agents throughout West Virginia. Since Mr. Dillard also owns an insurance management company, he is in contact with agents throughout the state. These men are consulted about future locations, as it is believed that their knowledge of local conditions is as good as that of anyone in the town—or better.

If the most desired store site in a town is not available, a less-desired building is leased, with plans to move to a better site at the first opportunity.

According to Mr. Dillard, "We like to go into an area where another retailer has gone bankrupt or moved out and lease that building." As an example, in Logan, West Virginia, a Dollar General Store was placed in a building that had previously been a Sears Catalog Store. In the first year of operation this Dollar General Store accounted for nearly $300,000 in sales.

The distance from one town to another seems to have little importance in the success of a Dollar General Store. For example, the stores in War and Mann, West Virginia, are separated from the larger shopping areas of Welch and Logan (with large discount operations) by only 12 miles, yet both these stores generate sales of approximately $8,000 per week.

Mr. Dillard believes that the narrow mountain roads between towns in West Virginia account for the willingness of residents to shop in their home town.

He also related several stories of customer reaction at the grand opening of new Dollar General stores. In many cases, customers would seek out the store manager or Mr. Dillard to express their gratitude for the opening of this new store in their shopping area.

According to Mr. Dillard, "West Virginia residents of small towns and rural areas such as the hollows and hills are honest and proud people who are glad to see improvements in their local area. They demonstrate this through a low incidence of shoplifting and by trading at the local store."

Due to the success of the West Virginia operation, the Dollar Stores Corporation was planning to establish retail operations in Pennsylvania.

DISCUSSION QUESTIONS

1. Do you believe the Dollar Stores Corporation should use the same location strategy in Pennsylvania? Remember, this will be the northernmost location for any Dollar General store. Is there any reason to believe Pennsylvania will be different?

2. Is the logic for situating stores in the county seat a reasonable approach, or was the Dollar Stores Corporation just lucky? Is it possible that the

residents of small West Virginia areas were so hungry for a discount-type operation that any location would have been successful?

3. In your estimation, could a competitive chain, using a similar merchandising approach, successfully enter the same market area as the Dollar Stores Corporation? What criteria should a potential competitor use in selecting towns in which to compete with Dollar General?

4. Is it possible that the Dollar General system could be equally successful in such other states as California, Michigan, New York, and South Dakota? Use the *Sales Management Survey of Buying Power* to determine the profile of West Virginia towns and counties and compare this to other states. Is this a meaningful guide in this case?

LOCATING A MOBILE-HOME PARK

A group of Wyoming businessmen is interested in establishing a mobile-home court in either Lander or Worland, Wyoming. They have collected the following data from the U.S. Bureau of the Census and other governmental agencies:

Population Trends	LANDER	WORLAND
1970	7,125	5,055
1975 estimate	9,011	8,166
1980 estimate	10,171	9,119

Resident Income Levels		
1970 median family income	$8,932	$8,354
1970 mean family income	$9,542	$8,940
1970 per capita income	$2,483	$2,576
Percent of families with income less than poverty level in 1970	12	12
Percent of families with incomes of $15,000 or more in 1970	12	10

Type of Housing Occupancy		
Total housing units	2,094	1,750
Owner-occupied housing units	1,389	1,091
Renter-occupied housing units	626	547
Median value of owner-occupied units	$16,200	$14,400
Median monthly contract rent of renter-occupied units	$76	$65
Vacant homes for sale or rent in 1970	79	106
Vacant homes for sale only	21	12

Median asking price	$17,200	$12,500
Number of units for rent	36	65
Number of units for rent that have been vacant for less		
than two months	24	41
Median rent asked	$69	$47
Units in housing structure in 1970:		
One	1,523	1,454
Two	169	79
Three and four	52	84
Five to 19	117	72
20 or more	9	0
Mobile home or trailer	208	64

They know that the national market for mobile homes is growing at a 15 percent annual rate. They also believe that many mobile-home owners in both Lander and Worland are forced to buy a lot in which to park their mobile homes. Competition from mobile-home parks comes from several small lots which do not offer many services or improvements.

The businessmen would like to provide the following facilities for each lot: grass yard area, storage space, paved streets, concrete sidewalks, underground utilities, concrete patio, clothes line, and fenced yard. In addition, a central playground, grocery store, laundry, and community hall facilities would be provided. They anticipate charging $50 per month rent for each mobile-home lot. In addition, they hope to make a profit from the laundry and grocery store.

DISCUSSION QUESTIONS

1. What other data do you think these businessmen need before they make their decision? Where would they obtain these data?
2. Use the information given, and other information you believe to be relevant, to analyze the course of action you think should be taken.

CHAPTER 6

Photo courtesy of J. C. Penney Company, Inc.

Factors in Retail Site Evaluation

The selection of the specific site must be made after the general trade area has been evaluated. The discussion in this chapter will therefore concentrate on this process, which is critical to the successful operation of a retail business.

Although no standard evaluation procedure is used by all retail firms, the selection of a specific location within the chosen trading area can be determined by considering the following location principles.

DEFINING THE TRADING AREA

Measuring the trade boundaries for *existing* retailing facilities is much easier than estimating the trade area for *proposed* stores. However, studies of the trading area for similar existing stores can provide an excellent measure of the probable trading area for a proposed store. Chain retailers who must use more than one outlet to reach most of a city's population utilize trading area "overlays" to determine how well their stores are serving the consumers (Figure 6–1). Each store's trading area is plotted on a transparent plastic sheet and placed over a city map to spot geographical areas from which the chain is not drawing customers. A new store that is located in such an area could be a profitable addition to the chain's current list of outlets.

Figure 6–1   *Example Illustrating the Use of Trade Area Analysis to Identify Store Coverage in a Specified Market Area*

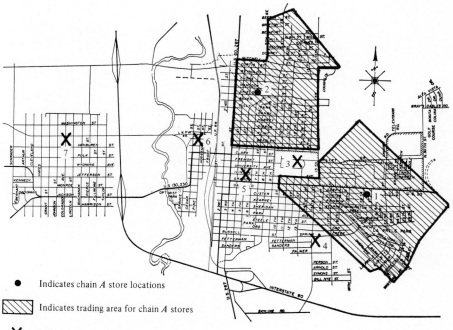

●   Indicates chain *A* store locations

▨   Indicates trading area for chain *A* stores

✗   Indicates competitive store locations

Trading area analysis also allows the firm to prevent trading area overlap, which results in higher retailing costs by having an excessive number of small higher-cost, lower-volume outlets. In this case, the less profitable stores may be eliminated by building larger stores with more complete merchandise assortments which better serve most of the customers. This type of trade area analysis offers more benefits to chain retailers whose outlets have a relatively small trading area. Grocery stores are examples of stores whose trade areas are relatively small.

The hypothetical trade area analysis in Figure 6–1 contains the trade areas for the two chain A stores which are numbered 1 and 2 on the map. The trading area for each store (1 and 2) would be drawn independently so that about 80 percent of each store's customers reside within the outlined trade area designated for that store. This analysis indicates that the two chain A stores are not drawing customers from the extreme west side of the city (from the area surrounding competitor store number 7) or from the south central part of the city in the area surrounding competitor stores numbers 4, 5, and 6. Chain A would be able to expand its sales if it would locate a new store in each of these areas. However, this is only the preliminary step in retail site evaluation. It must be determined if either of the new stores could generate enough sales to operate on a profitable basis.

The following techniques can be used to measure the boundaries of the trading area for existing outlets.

Store Credit Record Analysis

The observational technique of store credit record analysis consists of examining store credit records for data on the residences of the store consumers. It is relatively inexpensive, and can produce acceptable results if the credit customers' store patronage patterns do not differ from the store-selection habits of non-credit-using customers. The use of credit may vary among different consumer groups residing in an area, and in these cases the addresses of cash customers must be obtained if the trade area is to be accurately defined. Addresses of cash customers may be obtained by analyzing the addresses on checks written by cash customers. Addresses of cash customers may also be obtained from delivery tickets or cash sales slips. After a representative sampling of the store's customers has been made, the addresses of the clientele are plotted on an area map with dots or pins.

The trading area is then determined and area boundaries are defined. The intensity of a store's penetration within its trading area usually diminishes with increased distance, measured in travel time, from the store. The entire trading area can then be divided into primary, secondary, and fringe trading areas. All three areas should be defined in statistical and geographical terms. The primary trade area is usually determined on a population basis. For example, the area could be defined so that 55 to 70 percent of the customers reside within its boundaries. The secondary trade area could contain about 70 to 90 percent of the customers, and the fringe area, which will probably be widely dispersed, will contain the remaining customers.

License Plate Analysis

License plate analysis, another observational technique, consists of inconspicuously recording the license numbers of cars in the store's (or shopping center's) parking lot. The county treasurer's office (or some other appropriate county office) is then contacted to learn the addresses of the owners of the automobiles. The addresses of these "customers" are then plotted on an area map to define the trade area.

This is a fairly inexpensive technique if license numbers are recorded during peak business hours. The technique (as does the credit record analysis) also yields a list of "customer" names which can be used for other research purposes, such as determining store image, improving store service, etc.

The person who records the license numbers should be certain that the person is a customer and not a store clerk or a patron of a different store in the same area. This may be done if the recorder watches the entrance and exit doors and records *only* the license numbers of persons passing through these doors during business hours.

Another precaution is that license numbers should not be collected during times when an atypical representation of consumers might be chosen. For example, large conventions, sporting events, or special sales could temporarily overstate the actual trading area.

Customer Interview

Interviews with people residing in an area can also be used to identify the trading area. These interviews can be conducted by mail questionnaire, personal interview in the respondent's home, or telephone. Cross-reference books provide listings of telephone numbers by address, so that persons in any selected area may be interviewed. These data collection techniques are discussed in detail in Chapter 17.

In addition, a *short* questionnaire may be placed in customers' shopping bags. A high percentage of the customers will return these questionnaires if the return postage is prepaid and if there is some incentive to return them. A contest or offer of a small prize is usually a sufficient stimulus to induce a good return rate of 60 to 70 percent of the customers receiving the questionnaire. This approach allows the store to obtain additional information on demographic characteristics such as age, family size, educational background, and the like.

The chief disadvantage is that the sample selected in this manner may not be representative of all customers. The middle-income customer is likely to be overrepresented among those who respond to the questionnaire. In general, higher-income customers don't like to take the time to complete and return questionnaires. Lower-class customers are sometimes afraid to cooperate because of fear that a hidden commitment is involved or because of fear of revealing their lower level of formal education. The extent to which these types of biases occur should be determined carefully by examining the response rate. Lastly, many shoppers don't inspect the bags at home but simply remove the merchandise and discard the bags.

Household shopping surveys are also used to estimate trade areas for proposed outlets. They can provide detailed insight into consumer purchasing patterns. However, caution must be used when analyzing the results as about 30 percent of all people will say yes to anything.[1]

DETERMINING THE TOTAL POPULATION OF THE TRADING AREA

The total population residing in the primary trading area may be estimated by taking a personal survey of the area and counting all the dwellings.

If the proposed site is located within a standard metropolitan area, the U.S. Bureau of the Census provides detailed population and demographic data by census tract. Municipal agencies are usually able to provide an estimate of the number of water hookups in an area, which gives a rough estimate of the number of families residing within an area. Local utilities (power, gas, telephone) might be able to provide a more reliable estimate of the number of families residing within an area because each family is more likely to be billed separately for these items than for water and sewage.

DETERMINING PER CAPITA PRODUCT LINE PURCHASES IN THE TRADING AREA

Per capita purchases are usually available from trade sources or from publications such as *Sales Management's Survey of Buying Power, Editor & Publisher Market Guide,* and other secondary sources. The latest *Census of Business* provides data on sales made by various types of retail outlets in standard metropolitan areas. The annual total sales made by different types of retailers may also be available from the state department of revenue. Whatever secondary source is used, the total sales may be divided by population to obtain an estimate of per capita expenditures on the proposed line of merchandise (or service).

Consumer surveys or "diary" studies may be used to estimate per capita expenditures if the data are not available from secondary sources. (A "diary" study consists of a sample of typical consumers who record all their purchases for a week or month in a diary, which is then returned to the researcher for analysis.) A "crisscross" directory can be used to select the sample of "typical consumers" residing within a specified area, and the selection of an area can be based upon differences in consumer income, age, education, and the like.

The crisscross directory, which is usually available from a city office or public utility company, lists all the "active" addresses in an area. It also provides the names of the persons residing at each address. (A diary study is a fairly expensive method unless purchases of several product lines are observed simultaneously, which allows the cost to be shared by several retailers.)

The chief difficulty associated with consumer surveys that rely on querying consumers on past purchases is the inability of respondents to recall all the purchases they made during the previous month. Thus the best estimates of purchases are sometimes made when the respondents are asked to recall last week's purchases with the aid of a prepared list of possible purchases. The short time period and the memory-enhancing list are especially important if consumers are asked to recall purchases of lower-price items. Of course expenditures on major items, such as autos, furniture, and appliances, are remembered for a much longer period of time.

DETERMINING TOTAL PRODUCT LINE PURCHASES
MADE IN THE TRADING AREA

Total purchases can be obtained simply by multiplying the population by per capita consumption of the product line. This step answers the question, "If we obtain all the business available in this trading area, how large would our sales volume be?" The remainder of the volume estimation analysis has to determine how much of the total business can be obtained by the proposed outlet.

Both the volume of total sales and sales by type of outlet obtainable in a shopping center can be determined by the following analysis:

1. Establishment a priori of a tentative trade area for analysis. 2. Creation of a conceptual image of the completed shopping center in order to determine the strength of attraction which would be exerted by the envisaged facilities. 3. Determination of the gross personal consumption expenditures of the residents of this area through population tabulation, income analysis, and consumer expenditure studies. 4. Study of consumer movements, characteristics, and attitudes—both within and outside of competitive centers—to determine the probability of patronage from various segments of the subject trade area. 5. Derivation of quantitative sales expectancies and spatial requirements for specific retail facilities within the subject center.[2]

DETERMINING THE SHARE OF TOTAL TRADING
AREA PURCHASES
Evaluation of Site Accessibility for Residents
of the Trading Area

Accessibility to a site can be categorized according to the type of business.[3] *Generative* business, which is produced by the store itself through an effective promotion and merchandising effort, can be calculated for each segment of the trading area. Retail outlets that must generate all of their own business should be located in the most accessible location, commensurate with cost.

Shared business, which is secured by a retailer as the result of the generative pulling power of nearby retailers, can also be isolated. This business is represented by customers who are in the area primarily because they want to visit a neighboring store or service agency. Much of the prescription business of a drug store located near prescribing doctors' offices will be a shared business.

Suscipient business comes from people whose principal purpose for being near the retail outlet is *not* because the store or its neighbors attracted them; thus a newsstand at a commuter railroad station or an airport does mostly suscipient business. It does not generate any of its own business but merely offers a service to people who are at the location for another purpose—transportation to another destination. Some downtown stores specifically serve people working in the area. Because these stores do not attract people directly from their homes, the accessibility requirements can be so specific that they can be satisfied only by an outlet located within walking distance of the work area.

The volume of business done by most retailers and service suppliers is composed of all three types of business; thus the evaluation of a site's accessibility must take all three business types into account. Estimates of the amount of business that is believed to be available from each source can later serve as a checkpoint to determine if a store is realizing its full potential.

Passing foot and car traffic can be counted to determine how accessible the site is to a potential customer. A foot and car traffic count (which shows the number of passersby during a given period) can be made several times at the proposed location and at successfully operating stores. The comparative passerby traffic count at successfully established stores and proposed new sites provides a relative measure of accessibility. Both passing foot and car traffic offer customer potential that a good promotional merchandising effort can turn into business.

The minimum traffic count needed to indicate that the site has substantial potential will depend upon what type of retail or service outlet is being proposed. Outlets which depend upon shared or suscipient business will require a higher traffic count than outlets which depend upon generative business. Passing traffic must also be evaluated on a qualitative basis. Daily commuters going to and from work are much less valuable than passing pedestrian traffic.

Ease of ingress to and egress from the site must also be evaluated. Passing auto traffic offers no potential if it cannot enter the retailer's location with a minimum degree of accident risk and with little effort and time.

Evaluation of the Compatibility of Nearby Businesses

Retailing outlets are said to be compatible when two businesses, because of their adjacency, have a larger sales volume together than they would have if they were located in separate areas. Compatibility may be caused by the two firms selling complementary product lines or services. For example, a prescribing doctor's office and a pharmacy offer complementary services. Compatibility also occurs when firms sell competitive goods of different styles, lines, and prices. A drug store and a supermarket, for example, may benefit by being located next to one another, even though they carry many of the same product lines.

In addition to business interchange, a group of negative factors can be used in measuring compatibility. These variables tend to reduce the business of nearby retailers. Interruptions in pedestrian traffic flow can reduce business interchange with adjacent stores. Interruptions may be caused by "dead" frontage spots which cause a shopper to lose interest in continuing to walk farther in the same direction. Driveways and other physical disruptions in the sidewalk and heavy vehicular or pedestrian cross traffic that tends to create congestion[4] also cause interruptions. Other items that interfere with traffic flow are associated with hazard, noise, unpleasant odors, unsightliness, or other inhibiting qualities. Nearby businesses whose customers require an extremely long parking period will also minimize traffic flow.

It is extremely important that the layout of the shopping area ensures that consumers pass the specialty outlets on their way to the chief drawing attractions, which usually are major deparment stores. In the layout of a regional shopping center in Figure 6–2, note that the focal or anchor spot in the main center is a three-level Macy's department store (location *AA*). Macy's utilizes about 38 percent of the 408,000 total square feet available. Other major retail magnets in the main center are Hastings (location *FF*) and Roos/Atkins (location *BB*), both of which feature men's and women's wear, and Bank of America (location *DD*). The convenience shopping-type stores (supermarket, drug store, bakery, delicatessen, liquor store, etc.) are located separately (in sections *8, 9,* and *10*) from the comparison shopper-type outlets such as the department store, clothing, shoe, jewelry stores, etc. The major retail attractions in the convenience shopping area are Thrifty Drugs and Lucky Supermarket.

A customer survey revealed that Macy's, Hastings, and Thrifty Drugs have relatively stronger customer drawing power (they attract consumers from farther geographical distance) than Roos/Atkins and Lucky Supermarkets. This survey also indicated that half of the customers in the "drawing stores" also shopped in one or more of eleven other stores.[5]

Evaluation of the Physical Characteristics of Location

The size, shape, and frontage of a building can increase its visibility and thereby have a significant influence upon drawing traffic into the store. Also, proper interior layout can stimulate impulse sales after potential customers have entered the store. (A detailed discussion of store layout is presented in Chapter 7.) Parking space must also be analyzed to determine if it is sufficient to provide customers with parking near enough to the store so that it will be more convenient to stop and shop than to go to the next trading area.

Modern shopping centers provide a minimum of about four times as much parking space as store floor space to ensure adequate nearby parking facilities. A lower ratio is usually found in downtown shopping locations, as shoppers are expected to park in some commercial facility and shop at several stores on foot. Observation of parking opportunities and shopping patterns can indicate if there is likely to be a parking problem near a new store.

Evaluation of Competition

Other things being equal, people will seldom pass by a store to get exactly the same product at a more distant location. Thus the location of

Figure 6–2   Del Monte Shopping Center: Tenant Mix (May 1968)

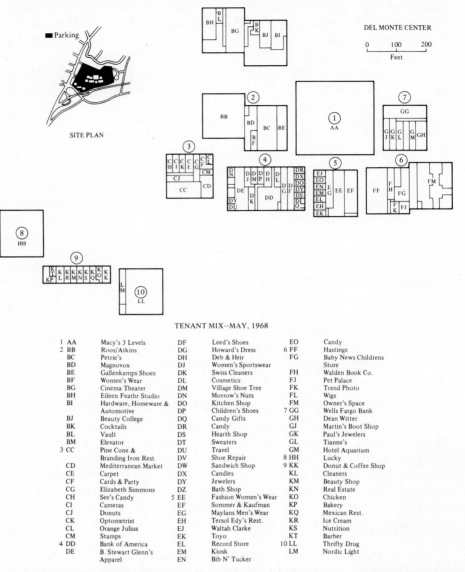

TENANT MIX—MAY, 1968

1	AA	Macy's 3 Levels	DF	Leed's Shoes	EO	Candy
2	BB	Roos/Atkins	DG	Howard's Dress	6 FF	Hastings
	BC	Petrie's	DH	Deb & Heir	FG	Baby News Childrens
	BD	Magnovox	DJ	Women's Sportswear		Store
	BE	Gallenkamps Shoes	DK	Swiss Cleaners	FH	Walden Book Co.
	BF	Women's Wear	DL	Cosmetics	FJ	Pet Palace
	BG	Cinema Theater	DM	Village Shoe Tree	FK	Trend Photo
	BH	Eileen Feathr Studio	DN	Morrow's Nuts	FL	Wigs
	BI	Hardware, Homeware &	DO	Kitchen Shop	FM	Owner's Space
		Automotive	DP	Children's Shoes	7 GG	Wells Fargo Bank
	BJ	Beauty College	DQ	Candy Gifts	GH	Dean Witter
	BK	Cocktails	DR	Candy	GJ	Martin's Boot Shop
	BL	Vault	DS	Hearth Shop	GK	Paul's Jewelers
	BM	Elevator	DT	Sweaters	GL	Tianne's
3	CC	Pine Cone &	DU	Travel	GM	Hotel Aquarium
		Branding Iron Rest.	DV	Shoe Repair	8 HH	Lucky
	CD	Mediterranean Market	DW	Sandwich Shop	9 KK	Donut & Coffee Shop
	CE	Carpet	DX	Candles	KL	Cleaners
	CF	Cards & Party	DY	Jewelers	KM	Beauty Shop
	CG	Elizabeth Simmons	DZ	Bath Shop	KN	Real Estate
	CH	See's Candy	5 EE	Fashion Women's Wear	KO	Chicken
	CI	Cameras	EF	Sommer & Kaufman	KP	Bakery
	CJ	Donuts	EG	Maylans Men's Wear	KQ	Mexican Rest.
	CK	Optometrist	EH	Tersol Edy's Rest.	KR	Ice Cream
	CL	Orange Julius	EJ	Waltah Clarke	KS	Nutrition
	CM	Stamps	EK	Toyo	KT	Barber
4	DD	Bank of America	EL	Record Store	10 LL	Thrifty Drug
	DE	B. Stewart Glenn's	EM	Kiosk	LM	Nordic Light
		Apparel	EN	Bib N' Tucker		

the new store relative to the population density of the trading area and to competitive locations has a very significant influence upon what share of business can be obtained by the new store. It is easier to stop potential consumers en route than to pull them away from their normal traffic patterns.

The prospective retailer can improve his position relative to competitors by selecting a location near most of the potential customers (or their normal traffic routes) but near as few competitive sites as possible. He may also be able to protect his location in the future by gaining control or by designating the use of unoccupied sites for noncompetitive purposes through restrictive lease provisions.

A key factor to consider in selecting shopping center sites is the tenant mix, which is the combination of business firms that occupy selling space in the shopping center. If a large center is properly planned, its tenant mix should satisfy the needs of the consumers in the trading area with no duplication of offerings. The factors to be considered by shopping center developers in relation to the tenant mix include:

1. The total amount of space allocated to each major line of trade within a shopping center. This should bear a reasonable relationship to the amount of space allocated to every other major line of trade. These relationships are established after analysis of consumer needs in the trade area, competitive facilities existing or anticipated for the future, and the availability of tenants acceptable to financing institutions, the developer, and the community. 2. The relationship that space allocated to an individual merchant bears to the total space allocated to his specific line of trade and to closely related lines of trade. This relationship in a tenant mix must consider the requirements of the various prospective tenants and the limitations in accommodating all competitive merchants within the shopping center. 3. The exact location of each retail store in relation to every other retail store within a shopping center. This is closely tied to shopper convenience and shopper traffic patterns, and hence to the objective of optimizing sales for all merchants. 4. The minimum rent and the average rent, year by year, projected for each merchant. Rent projections, however, must also consider financing requirements, since tenants from whom high rents might be obtained may not be acceptable to financing institutions. Thus, the amount and proportion of retail space allocated to prospective tenants in relation to their financial standing must be balanced to optimize rent, without impairing the ability of the developer to borrow funds with which to construct and operate the center. 5. The retail sales projected for each line of trade and for each individual merchant. This provides a basis for projecting revenues. Total revenues, of course, also take into consideration projected average rentals.[6]

The center's projected sales for each retail line are useful when one is forecasting future sales for an outlet located in a center. Most shopping center planners conduct surveys of consumers' purchasing patterns for those people residing in the center's defined trading area. The findings are presented by the center's developers to financial institutions for projections upon which loans are obtained. Thus these forecasts are likely to be optimistic but fairly reliable.

Conditions change, however, and the final tenant mix can deviate from the original or "ideal" tenant-mix plan. Although the number of competitors may vary, the total amount of space allocated to each major retail line usually

Table 6–1   Del Monte Center: Projected and Actual Tenant Mix, Gross Leasable Area, Average Rent per Square Foot, and Average Guaranteed Annual Rent

TENANTS	STORES Actual	GLA—SQ. FT. (000) Projected	Actual	RENT/SQUARE FEET Projected	Actual
Department store	1	150.0	158.0	—	—
Supermarket	1	20.0	19.6	$2.00	$2.00
Drug store	1	18.0	18.1	2.00	2.00
Bank	2	6.0	12.8	4.00	4.08
Family wear	3	30.0	38.1	2.50	2.54
Shoes	5	19.2	18.0	3.80	3.76
Men's store	1	14.5	2.9	3.28	5.00
Women's store	7	25.0	25.4	3.90	3.67
Children's wear	3	6.0	6.1	3.00	4.24
Jewelers	2	5.0	2.4	6.00	5.72
Restaurants	7	12.0	15.3	3.84	4.72
Service stores	11	15.0	20.9	4.00	4.22
All other*	35	79.3	51.8	4.45	5.03
Total	79	400.0	389.4	$3.55†	$3.87†
Space to lease			18.6		
Total			408.0		

* Includes 11 food stores (specialties like candy, nuts, bakery, ice cream, health foods, etc.), 4 gift shops, a movie theater (nearly 10,000 square feet), a hardware store (over 5,000 square feet), a TV store (over 3,000 square feet), and 17 other specialty stores.

† Excludes department store, but includes the anticipated guaranteed annual rent from the space still to be let, as of May 1968.

SOURCE   Copyright 1970 by International Council of Shopping Centers. Reprinted by permission of the copyright owner from Applebaum, *Shopping Center Strategy, A Case Study of the Planning, Location and Development of the Del Monte Center, Monterey, California* (1970).

departs relatively little from the original plan. The deviation that occurred during the first five years of operation for one regional shopping center is presented in Table 6–1.

Estimation of Market Share

The amount of business that a store obtains from a given area can be divided by the total amount of business conducted in the area in the specified category. The result, multiplied by 100, equals the percentage share of market obtained by the store. The estimate of the market share must be made after all of the previously discussed factors have been evaluated. Subjective judgment and experience can then be used to determine the share estimate.

The ratio of market sales share to selling space share can be used to estimate the market share that a new store can obtain, provided additional information is available from stores currently operating in other areas. If the new store is affiliated with a chain, or if it can obtain information from similar independent stores, this same ratio can be used. This ratio provides a measure that is most useful in forecasting shares for new stores.

The share of market sales volume is usually measured by dollar sales; the share of selling space is usually calculated on a square footage basis. The reliability of this ratio has been proved over years of research in the grocery industry.[7] If a store obtains a 25 percent share of market in an area and has a 40 percent share of the total selling space for the product line in the area, then the ratio of the market share to selling space share is 25/40, or 0.625. The average ratio for similar existing stores and the share of selling space to be occupied by the proposed store can be used to forecast the market share that a proposed store can obtain. Both figures can be inserted into the ratio formula to obtain this estimate of market share.

For example, if the average market share to selling space share ratio is 0.625 for similar stores and the proposed new store will occupy 20 percent of the selling space in the area, its estimated market share (X) would be $X / 20 = 0.625/100$, or X equals 12.5 percent of the forecast market share. The estimated share projected from this ratio can then be adjusted to reflect the deviations from the average in regard to the quality of competition, the physical characteristics of the location, the compatibility of nearby businesses, and the accessibility of the site to the trading area.

Table 6–2 contains a format for tabulating some of the most important information used in evaluating a supermarket location.

ESTIMATING THE SALES VOLUME OF THE PROPOSED STORE

The estimated sales volume that can be obtained by the new store is found by multiplying its estimated market share by the total product line purchases made in the trading area.

Determining if Estimated Volume Will Be Sufficient to Support a New Store

Costs must be examined and compared to expected profits to determine which proposed site will yield the most profit. Industry sources will usually provide estimates of the average rent expense for leased stores. For example, average rent expense for new supermarkets was 1.5 percent of sales in 1964.[8] If the estimated weekly sales volume is $32,000, then 32,000 times 0.015, or $480 per week, could be spent on the site if the store wanted to pay no more than average leasing rates for its facilities.

If the building and land price (or leasing) cost (not including equity buildup in land and buildings) is less than $480 per month, the proposed store should be more profitable than the average supermarket. If the cost exceeds $480, these extra costs must be overcome by reduction in other costs, such as labor, transportation, etc. If these costs are not reduced, the profit margin will be below the industry average.

The payback period—the estimated period of time in which a project will generate cash equal to its cost—should also be calculated if the store

Table 6–2 Summary of Information Used in Evaluating Supermarket Locations

SUPERMARKETS IN CITIES OF 25,000 OR MORE

Store	Weekly Sales	Location Type	Adjusted Weekly per Capita Sales by Mileage Zone				Population and % of Sales within 1 Mile	PRIMARY TRADING AREA					
			0–¼	¼–½	½–¾	¾–1		Population	Adjusted Weekly per Capita Sales	% of Total Sales	Share of Market	Share of Space	Ratio: Share of Market to Share of Space
Bellville	$22,000	Neighborhood	$1.75	$0.90	$ .40	$ .15	24,000–75%	8,000	$1.50	62	11%	23%	48%
Riverview	28,000	Neighborhood	1.90	1.10	.40	.20	26,000–78%	10,500	1.65	67	14	27	52%
Willsboro	30,000	Edge of downtown	2.00	1.40	.60	.20	22,500–70%	12,200	1.30	55	15	30	50%
Newtown	28,000	Edge of downtown	2.00	1.00	.50	.15	19,000–65%	11,400	1.20	53	18	34	53%

SUPERMARKETS IN CITIES UNDER 25,000

PRIMARY AND SECONDARY TRADING AREAS COMBINED

Store	Weekly Sales	Location Type	Population, Store-Town	% of Sales, Store-Town	Adjusted Weekly per Capita Sales, Store-Town	Share of Market	Share of Space	Ratio: Share of Market to Share of Space
Weston	$31,000	Edge of downtown	14,000	60	$1.20	16%	34%	47%
Hillboro	20,000	Edge of downtown	9,500	66	1.25	19%	44%	43%
Milburn	45,000	CSC*	18,000	48	1.10	18%	32%	56%
Bristow	35,000	CSC	16,000	45	.90	15%	30%	50%

* CSC is an abbreviation for "Community Shopping Center."
SOURCE: Bernard Kane, Jr., A Systematic Guide to Supermarket Location Analysis (New York: Fairchild Publications, 1966), p. 105.

owners are going to buy the land and building.[9] If the annual cash inflow is estimated to be received in equal annual amounts, the payback period (in years) equals the cost of the project divided by annual net income after taxes and depreciation. For example, if a retail building project costs $100,000 and is expected to yield an annual net income after taxes and depreciation of $10,000, the payback period would be $100,000 divided by $10,000, or ten years.

There is no common agreement on how many years it should take a building and land to pay for themselves from the revenues generated from the store. The selection of the appropriate payback period is influenced by the cost of obtaining money (interest rates) and alternative uses of the investor's money. Most realtor investors say that a building should receive 1 percent of its cost per month as a payment for its rental (or lease) value. The land should receive 0.5 percent of its appraised value as its monthly payment. This means that the building should pay for itself in 100 months, or 8⅓ years.

In speculative types of retailing where market and environmental changes occur quite rapidly, the desired payback period might be much less—say five years. The higher the degree of uncertainty and the cost of obtaining money, the lower the desired payback period will be.

Of course the site evaluation analysis must also project the potential sales and profits into the future. A growth area will be much more attractive than a declining area. A growing profit trend can legitimately be incorporated into the payback period analysis because, hopefully, the store will be generating profits over at least a five- to ten-year period. If the annual cash inflow generated by the building is not received in equal amounts, one may compile a list of cumulative cash gains expected to originate from the project until the year in which the running income total is equal to the amount of the expenditure.

BUY, LEASE, OR BUILD?

Another important aspect of the site selection problem is to determine if the firm should buy the property outright or if it should lease the facility. As noted earlier, some retailers prefer not to own property because of the high fixed cost involved and the uncertainty of future market potential. If the dollar return in inventory investment is greater than the dollar invested in real estate, it is usually desirable to lease instead of purchase.

Leasing terms vary by location, type of store, and numerous other considerations. Supermarkets usually generate an annual sales volume of from $1 million to $3 million. Because of their low profit margin, supermarket rents are generally comparatively inexpensive on both a percentage of sales (1.5 percent) and square footage ($1.50 to $4) basis. Large, full-line department stores have a higher profit margin, but they also have a great deal of bargaining power. This usually results in a rent of 2.5 percent of gross sales.[10] Specialty stores, which have the highest markups and the least bargaining power, usually pay from 5 to 8 percent of their gross sales, or about $2.50 to $5 per square foot of space, as rent. A summary of rental rates for space in new shopping center locations is presented in Table 6–3.

Table 6–3   National Terms of Lease for Space in New Shopping Centers

TYPE OF STORE	ESTI- MATED SALES $ PER SQ. FT. FOR NEW STORES	ESTI- MATED SALES $ PER SQ. FT. FOR PRESENT STORES	RENTAL RATE	% OF TOTAL SPACE USED FOR SELLING PURPOSES
Drug	94.00	59.00	From 2.0 to 4.5% of sales	79.0
Variety store	41.80	27.50	58% of stores will pay more than min. rate of $1.69/sq. ft.	83.5
Supermarket	136.00	100.00	50% of stores will pay more than min. rate of $1.69/sq. ft.	75.0
Department store	55.13	53.00	57% of stores will pay more than min. rate of $1.21/sq. ft.	75.7
Women's apparel	71.00	51.00	$4 to $6/sq. ft.	74.0
Men's wear	76.13	57.00	All but 5% of new stores will pay more than min. rate of 3.67% of sales	76.3
Women's shoes	66.08		5.03% of sales	78.7
Family shoes	66.84		41% of stores will pay more than min. rate of $2.17/sq. ft.	77.4

SOURCE   S. O. Kaylin, "Terms of Leases for Space in Centers," *Chain Store Age* (May 1968), pp. E42–E77.

The rental policy of shopping center developers is designed so that operating expenses (mostly maintenance, utilities, and upkeep) are only 15 to 18 percent of total gross rental income.[11]

Some land developers and some retailers are now using a philosophy of "storing land." This involves the purchase of vacant land in the development path of a city or suburb on which low-cost business structures are erected. Taxes and interest payments can be made from the income generated by these buildings; and the buildings are constructed so that they can easily be torn down when the land becomes a desirable site for a major retail development.

This practice is based on the belief that development land values will rise faster than interest costs and taxes. Site selection that is based upon projected population movements involves the additional risks associated with imperfect foresight. It also involves a high fixed cost. However, retailers should plan ahead so that consumers can be served near their places of residence. Storing land can be a part of expansion planning as it can guarantee a location in areas where real estate is expected to become difficult to acquire.

Generally, developers have only a small percentage of equity in a shopping center or large retail building. Lending institutions usually mortgage up to 75 percent of the "economic value" (the value of the project based upon future estimated earnings) of a shopping center. Typically, the economic value of a well-planned center will be 25 to 33 percent higher than total building costs.

For example, the developers of Willowbrook Center in New Jersey were able to build their $23 million center by using only $500,000 as their own cash equity.[12] The other $22.5 million came from an insurance company that made a twenty-nine year loan at 7½ percent interest. An estimated net economic value of nearly $32 million was calculated by capitalizing on an estimated annual net profit of $2.7 million at the going interest rate of 8½ percent. The insurance company loaned about 70 percent of the estimated economic value ($32 million), but the loan ($22.5 million) amounted to nearly 98 percent of the total project cost ($23 million) in this case.

Unless individual stores develop their own centers or build their own large stores, they will not be able to obtain such low equity financing. Instead, they will have to pay rental fees similar to those in Table 6–3.

Despite the availability of low equity financing, retail developers are finding that storing land is appealing because of increasing costs for land, construction, and money. For example, land could be purchased for $20,000 an acre in the metropolitan New York area in 1966, whereas similar land cost from $40,000 to $80,000 an acre in 1971.[13] Construction costs in the New York area for the shell of a shopping center, exclusive of department stores, have increased from about $10 per square foot in 1966 to about $17.50 in 1971. The interest costs in the area also increased substantially, from about 8 percent in 1966 to about 10 percent in 1971. Of course increasing construction and financing costs could not be avoided by storing land; however, the increase in land costs and some interest costs can be avoided if the land-storing policy is used.

Such factors as the financial condition of the company, the profitability of the business, and the degree of growth orientation in company philosophy determine the proper investment that should be made in buildings and real estate. Thus each retailer must make commitments based upon his own financial and marketing situation at the time a site is available.

SUMMARY

A more detailed analysis of population, trading area, per capita purchases, and competition is needed for the evaluation of a specific site within the general area that has previously been selected as the location of a new store. In addition, factors such as accessibility to consumers, compatibility of nearby businesses, and the physical characteristics of the site must be analyzed in the site selection process.

Firms use site evaluation to obtain estimates of a site's sales potential and the probability of the store's long-term success. A thorough site evaluation program provides the firm with a profit estimate for each site, sales volume estimates, and an estimate of the degree of risk involved in locating a store at each site. These data can be used to establish expansion priorities for a firm considering building several new stores in the near future. Finally, these same data can be used in the firm's critical decision to buy or lease a new building on a selected site.

QUESTIONS

1. Discuss the concept of trade area and describe how it is used.
2. How would you suggest defining the trade area for a discount store? Explain your reasoning.
3. Distinguish between generative, shared, and subscipient businesses. Can you suggest ways a retailer might estimate the relative effects of each type of business?
4. How can two adjacent stores, selling goods competitively, be considered compatible?
5. What is the value of the ratio of market share to selling space share? If a retailer estimates he must have 18 percent of the market to break even and the ratio is 0.5, what percent of the selling space must he have if all other variables are held constant? What other factors must be considered in reality?
6. If the average rent paid out in an area is 3 percent of sales and estimated annual sales are $1,600,000, how much monthly rent can a retailer with these sales expect to pay? If rent is expected to increase at 5 percent per year (i.e., 5 percent of the previous year's rent), what level of sales would be required for the first three years? (Assume all other variables to be held constant.)
7. What factors influence the payback period? What other factors must be considered in purchasing a store? Why should the payback period be shorter for high-risk locations?
8. Discuss the concept of "storing land." How would you suggest determining the proper payback period for such land?
9. How does "economic value" differ from building cost?

FOOTNOTES

[1] David K. Hardin, president of Market Facts Inc., Chicago, Ill., as reported by Edwin Darby in the *Chicago Sun-Times* (March 24, 1971).

[2] William Applebaum, *Shopping Center Strategy* (New York: International Council of Shopping Centers, 1970), p. 74.

[3] Richard L. Nelson, *The Selection of Retail Locations* (New York: McGraw Hill, 1958), pp. 51–56, 63–68.

[4] Ibid., pp. 51–55, 65–68.

[5] Applebaum, *Shopping Center Strategy*, pp. 135–136.

[6] Ibid., pp. 111, 113.

[7] Bernard Kane, Jr., *A Systematic Guide to Supermarket Location Analysis* (New York: Fairchild Publications, 1966), pp. 103–105.

[8] *Facts about New Supermarkets Opened in 1964* (Chicago: Super Market Institute, 1965), p. 13.

[9] Joseph F. Bradley, *Administrative Financial Management* (2d ed.; New York: Holt, Rinehart and Winston, 1969), pp. 140–141.

[10] "Shopping Centers Grow into Shopping Cities," *Business Week*, September 4, 1971, p. 37.

[11] Ibid.

[12] Ibid.

[13] Ibid.

S. S. KRESGE CO.
Store Location—K Mart Stores

The S. S. Kresge Company of Troy, Michigan, is one of the largest retailers in the world, ranking as the third largest non-food retailer in the United States. The company began as a five-and-dime store, and still operates over 500 Kresge variety stores. However, its real growth in recent years has been due to the company's expansion in discounting through its 117 Jupiter discount stores and, in particular, through the network of over 600 K Mart discount stores. In total, sales for S. S. Kresge exceed $3.5 billion, and are expected to exceed $5 billion by 1975.

The typical K Mart store is a free-standing one-level structure with 94,500 square feet. Recently, a few have been located in small shopping centers, where this was the only choice, but the preference is for free-standing units. In areas where the market will not support the largest K Mart, an 84,000 square foot building is erected. Construction of a 65,000 square foot unit has been confined to smaller towns with good market potential, such as the one recently opened in Victoria, Texas.

Each K Mart has over fifty departments and stocks 65,000 items, of which approximately 20 percent carry a private K Mart label.

The fact that most K Mart stores are free-standing is no accident. The management's philosophy has been that when a K Mart is located on a good site, it will pull its own customers, independently of other retailers. Also, the size of the store permits an advertising budget sufficient to generate its own traffic.

It is interesting to note that, in this same time period, several traditional free-standing retailers, such as Robert Hall clothing stores, announced they would locate future stores in shopping centers.

The K Mart stores have contributed substantially to the growth of Kresge and are expected to become even more important in the future. Reasons given by management for the success of K Mart are many and include low retail prices, in-store merchandising, and well-trained, loyal employees. In addition, proper store location is listed as being of paramount importance.

Since the beginning of K Mart in 1962, the company has never closed a K Mart store. Throughout this period a system of determining store location was developed that is followed for each proposed site. This system is as follows:

1. Possible future site locations are suggested by land developers, farmers with land to sell, real estate agents, stockholders, and employees, and internally from the K Mart real estate division.
2. The appropriate K Mart real estate area manager inspects the proposed site. If he believes it would make a good site, he completes a report and asks for the regional vice-president to inspect the site. (There are five regional vice-presidents throughout the United States.)
3. If the regional vice-president approves the site, he completes a report and sends it to the corporate head of the real estate division in the home office.
4. The corporate head of real estate reviews the site recommendation with a small "directional committee."
5. If recommended by the directional committee, the recommendation moves to the Corporate Development Committee. This group meets once a week, and includes Mr. R. E. Dewar, chairman of the board of S. S. Kresge and chief executive officer, and Mr. H. B. Cunningham, past chairman and chief executive officer. It also includes fourteen top executives who represent a variety of corporate areas, such as legal, food operations, personnel and employee relations, K Mart operations, and many others.
6. If the proposed site meets with this group's approval, it is inspected by one or more members of the group with an executive rank of vice-president or greater.
7. The results of this inspection trip are reported back to the Corporate Development Committee, where a final decision is made.

Although the research department is asked to examine the early reports and to add fresh inputs, its function is strictly one of staff support. This department does not have "go" or "no go" authority at any stage.

Each site is evaluated on the basis of the following factors: growth possibilities, type of population, accessibility, topography, competition, estimated volume by the end of the third full year, costs, and zoning.

Other factors include the type of local media and their circulation, the amount of advertising done by competitors, traffic count on access roads, and other miscellaneous inputs.

At times, the miscellaneous factors assume particular importance. The owner of a very desirable tract of land in a midwest city agreed to sell to K Mart's developer only if his dog, Fred, could remain on the land until its death. The owner was afraid that any change in scenery would be too much for Fred—even though the dog's house was in the center of the proposed parking lot. This detail had not been passed on to the Corporate Development Committee, as everyone was sure that Fred would depart before the store opened. In the end, Fred outlived the grand opening, which meant that a small section of the central parking lot could not be used.

Although Fred-type problems occasionally occur, the overall consideration in evaluating the feasibility of a proposed location is return on investment. A proposed site must offer a pre-tax return on investment of 25 percent or more after three full years of operation. There have been occasions where store locations were accepted even though this figure did not appear feasible during the three-year period. These involved such considerations as future growth rate for the area or other overriding factors, but the case for each must be extremely strong to override the return on investment goal.

In its eastward expansion, K Mart had selected Philadelphia as the next market area. Among the sites selected was one in a suburban fringe area that appeared to be a growing residential area. The required information was compiled and passed on to the Corporate Development Committee. Unfortunately, the calculated return on investment fell 4 percentage points under the determined goal. In other words, it did not appear that the store could realize the required return on investment in the next three years. Nevertheless, the area looked good to those who had examined the site. An example of this enthusiasm was demonstrated in one of the reports for the Corporate Development Committee, which stated: "This is a virtually untapped market as far as discount competition is concerned. Road patterns and heavy traffic make it difficult to drive to competition. A store on this site just could not miss. It would make an excellent addition to the Philadelphia program to give us saturation in this growing area."

The area was developing with middle-income housing and it appeared that the growth would continue. However, there was no knowledge of when the area would be completely developed. It was clear to some that a K Mart should be here in the foreseeable future, and with land values and construction costs going up, it could be advantageous to get in early and benefit from lower occupancy costs in later years. Typically, a twenty-five-year lease is taken, with several options to renew. Other sections of the city were also developing, and it was unknown what effect they might have upon the growth of the proposed site location.

There was also talk of a possible mortgage credit crunch such as that in the late '60s, when tight money forced housing starts to dwindle. Some economists were quoted as saying this was inevitable, while others expressed opposite opinions.

Rumors had been heard that another major discount competitor had expressed serious interest in this area to local real estate people and developers, but there was no confirmation of this.

Locations were available in other cities that would meet the return on investment goal, but the Philadelphia site in question would give K Mart the market exposure it desired in the important projected growth areas and would help share the advertising burden with other area stores.

DISCUSSION QUESTIONS

1. Do you believe the Corporate Development Committee should accept the proposed site even though it does not meet the return on investment criteria? Present a logical case for whatever decision you elect.
2. Obviously a great deal of top-management time is involved in the selection of new K Mart locations. Do you believe this is the best way to perform this function?
3. If possible, visit a nearby K Mart and compare its layout, location, access routes, parking, and prices with other discount stores. After comparing the stores, what do you believe are the most important factors in the success of this chain? In your opinion, could the K Mart that you examined do just as well in other locations?
4. How does the location planning system used by K Mart compare to that used by other retail chain operations? Could the K Mart system be used equally well by a chain of convenience food stores, a major oil and gasoline retailer, a chain of supermarkets, and a chain of drug stores?

NEIGHBORHOOD GROCERY CO.

Mr. Kent, owner of Neighborhood Grocery Company, is considering building a new store one block from his present site. Neighborhood Grocery Company is not affiliated with any grocery chain organization. It has been operating from a leased building in a neighborhood shopping center that contains a drug store, doctors' offices, a restaurant, and a barber shop. The center is four years old and is located near a new upper middle-class residential area. Sufficient parking space has been provided in the center's parking lot. Auto traffic appears to flow smoothly in and out of the lot.

Mr. Kent is not satisfied with his present weekly sales of $22,000. He believes that sales could be increased if he built a larger store. The present store contains 4,700 square feet of selling space in a brick building of 7,000 square feet. The new outlet would contain 10,200 square feet of selling space in a 15,000 square foot building. Mr. Kent can renew the lease on the old building for the next five years at the present rate of $11,000 per year. The cost of the land for the new location is $144,000; the construction cost is estimated to be $300,000.

Neighborhood Grocery Company's trading area is believed to be centered in the 10 square block area surrounding the store. The nearest competitive store is run by a small, independent grocer who operates in a 2,500 square foot building with no off-street parking. The main competitor is a supermarket 15 blocks away. However, another chain supermarket is building a new outlet 10 blocks away from the present Neighborhood Grocery Company location.

What action do you recommend Mr. Kent take?

CHAPTER 7

Photo courtesy of Joseph Magnin.

Attracting with Atmosphere

After the site has been selected, the retail building must be constructed or remodeled and fixtures and equipment purchased and arranged so customers may be attracted to the store, stimulated to make purchases, and served promptly with minimum cost. This chapter is devoted to a discussion of the factors that retailers should consider when they build, remodel, or rearrange their outlets.

PSYCHOLOGICAL IMPACT AND STORE IMAGE

The image a store projects to its customers is one of the most important influences contributing to a retailer's success. It is also the most difficult variable to control, to measure, and, indeed, to define. If *image* may be defined as "the aggregate stimulus value the company, store brand or product has for a particular individual or group,"[1] it is obvious that a store's image may be seen somewhat differently by each person. Nevertheless, for a particular group of like customers, or market segment, a store's image may be fairly similar. A store such as Saks Fifth Avenue or Tiffany and Company may be thought of as ultraexpensive and out of reach by low-income persons, while more affluent individuals may think of them as stores with excellent quality products and service to match a sophisticated taste.

Another way of looking at image is to view it as the overall personality of the store. This personality is always present, regardless of whether or not it was planned by the management. Just as the personality of an individual attracts or repels certain types of people, so too does that of a store.

This is not to imply that a store's personality or image remains the same over time. It is often a shock for us to encounter a high school classmate several years after graduation and to witness the change in his or her personality. Some grow old before their time; others seem to develop a wit and charm they never had in school. For this reason it is not uncommon for old friends to discover at a class reunion that they no longer have much in common and that others, whom they scarcely knew, have become interesting and attractive individuals.

This analogy also holds true for retail stores. A store always has a personality, even if that personality reflects blandness, a lack of creativity, and general sterility. A store manager who feels that a store's image is a concern only for the supersophisticated, or who says, "I only worry about price and quality," is naive. Whether he knows it or not, he is developing an image for his store.

Major renovations, usually performed every five to ten years, require the purchase of new, modern, and flexible store fixtures. Such costly events provide an excellent opportunity for redefining the target market and creating a place the customers can call "their store."

The target market should be defined in terms of such factors as income level, race, price consciousness for the products to be sold, geographical location, seasonality, age, and other important variables.

Recall, for a moment, the notion of image and note that it is defined as the aggregate stimulus value the store has for an individual or group. It is apparent from this definition that image is a result of all our sensory reactions. Thus each reaction should be considered in the image-planning process.

Scent Considerations

Retail stores that sell food, flowers, perfumes, soaps, candles, and even automobiles need to be constantly aware of the effect that odor has upon overall image. Anyone who has passed a Karmel Korn store or a fresh roasted nut and coffee establishment in the heart of a city can attest to the value of smell. Fans that are placed to whiff the aroma of these products to the sidewalk are not accidentally placed. Used-car dealers sometimes have been accused of spraying their near-new automobiles with a heavy spray to represent the odor of new cars in an attempt to change consumer images. Imagine the negative effect that stale cigar smoke would have in a dress shop, or even in a shoe store. New cars and new-car showrooms are expected to have a new-car smell. Strong disinfectants, greasy smells, and other foreign odors can adversely affect the image of many establishments.

Sound Considerations

The tinkling of Chinese wind chimes in an import store immediately sets the stage for image creation. Even the background noise of elevated trains, freight trains, or shopper congestion can add a vital ingredient to the image of a store. The "believability" of a freight salvage store may be enhanced if the sounds of switching trains and semi-trailer trucks are audible to shoppers.

Other stores depend upon the almost total absence of extraneous sounds. Many exclusive dress and fur shops eliminate unwanted sounds through heavy carpeting, multiple partitions, low ceilings, and the low-key, hushed tone of sales personnel. Yet only a short distance away, on the same shopping mall, other retailers such as "teen shops" depend upon loud noises, including recordings of the latest "hit group."

It is a costly mistake for a retailer to overlook the effect of sounds on the success of his store. Appropriate background sounds or music convey the message that "things are happening here. Stop, look, see what's going on." In fact, many stores deliberately start a retail day by eliminating the "dead store" silence when they turn on lively music. Activity generates customer interest.

Touch Considerations

We tend to say, "Let me see that, please," when we really mean, "Let me touch that, please." Many objects are *meant* to be touched, and can best be sold after they *have* been touched. Imagine the success an automobile dealer or furrier might have if no one were allowed to touch their products until after the purchase. Furs are irresistibly touchable. Toys are meant to be handled, books to be looked through, and cars to be sat in—with doors to slam and tires to kick.

As important as touch is, far too many retailers place artificial barriers in the path of the natural and desirable reaction of the customer to touch the merchandise. It is highly probable that the "Do Not Touch" or "Touch at Your Own Risk" signs in tourist and curio shops have caused lost sales far in excess of the breakage they have prevented. Small children cannot read these signs, so they touch anyway, but shoppers—with dollars to spend— may be frightened away. The recent practice of covering books with cellophane or plastic may also be questioned, particularly if no sample books are provided.

Certainly there are times when touching must be prevented, as in art galleries featuring original oils, but in many other cases the touching of merchandise may be desirable and profitable. Displays and samples may be arranged within a store to invite touch. In these cases, only the samples may be soiled or damaged, and they can be inexpensively replaced.

Although the term "sensuous" is generally applied to a beautiful woman, it is also applicable to some retail stores or sections within stores. The products sold within these stores appeal to our needs for love, affection, sex, and perhaps even religion. These stores should be designed to promote a feeling of sensuality within the customer. The proper use of touch in these stores can add to the desired image. There's an old saying that sums up the discussion: "Put the merchandise out where the customers can feel it and steal it so they will try it and buy it."

Sight Considerations

Only a blind man can deny the importance of sight, yet thousands of retail stores each year are established almost as if by the blind. The visual impression that is imposed upon customers by signs, sidewalks, window displays, awnings, parking lots, and every nut and bolt of the building is of the utmost importance.

"Visual merchandising" is a combination of every factor which can affect the consumer's visual perception of the store. Moreover, visual merchandising is the utilization of every square inch of the building, inside and out, to "sell" the company and its products.

Visual merchandising is more than image building; it is the conscious recognition of the fact that a consumer is in one's store to buy goods and services. Therefore each moment that a consumer is the guest of a retailer, he or she should be exposed to planned visual merchandising. The same retailers who spends hundreds of thousands of dollars a year on advertising, catalogs, and other material designed to bring the customer to them often neglect the importance of a total selling environment once the customer is in their store.

Because store layout usually concentrates on developing optimum traffic patterns, important areas are planned with total disregard for visual merchandising. Elevators and escalators are planned only for the function of hauling bodies from one floor to another. Yet in each case the customer is in a captive position for several seconds to several minutes. Why shouldn't this time and space be utilized to sell the products and services of the store? It would not be difficult to line the walls of the elevators with samples of carpet, wall paper, fabrics, or other goods sold in the store.

Many other store areas are traditionally treated as nonselling areas. These include the credit department, the employment and personnel department, and the rest rooms. Is it really too extreme to consider visual merchandising of toiletries, cosmetics, facial tissues, and other products in the rest rooms?

Today, companies such as Susan Crane Packaging are entering the field of visual merchandising. These companies manufacture and sell an integrated program to aid in visual merchandising. Such firms are able to provide supporting assistance with visuals from window dressing to tote bags. However, their effectiveness is limited by a store's commitment to visual merchandising as a concept and as a continuing program.

Each year department stores are opened that, at best, resemble mausoleums. Mexican import stores suddenly appear without even a sombrero in the window and restaurants appear and disappear within buildings that never change in appearance save for the occasional "For Rent" signs.

The appearance of the store can seldom be divorced from that of its neighbors. It might be impossible for a retailer of high-quality jewelry to convey such an image, regardless of his creativity in design, if his store is surrounded by discount record shops, fast-food drive-ins, and a pawnshop or two. It might be equally difficult for a low-margin retailer to establish an appropriate image in an area known for its appeal to the affluent "carriage trade," which is conscious of good taste and proper style regardless of cost.

In most cases, errors in location and their effect upon image are not as extreme as those described in these examples. Exorbitantly high rents, zoning restrictions, shopping center restrictions, and common sense prevent such glaring errors. Nevertheless, errors are made. This can be easily proved simply by observing the variety of stores in one's area. It is highly probable that among these will be at least one store that seems to have no personality at all. Such stores seem to say: "I'm here and open for business; come in at your own risk."

Small-town department and clothing stores sometimes feel compelled to try to be all things to all people. A department store in a small Michigan town was once observed to feature in its front window men's work overalls *and* women's formal dress. The end result of such image building is often a loss of customers to the nearest metropolitan shopping center.

Of course image impression through sight extends beyond the appearance and location of the building, equipment, and signs. The dress, personal grooming, and composition of the labor force are equally important. It is not enough to consider simply the sales force, as the appearance of delivery men, credit personnel, and many others leaves strong impressions upon customers and potential customers. The fact that a particular store employs members of minority groups only as janitors and shipping clerks can be a strong negative factor for customers from these racial groups.

Employees' mode of dress is of particular importance in the case of high-quality merchandise as the total image of the store can be lowered by even one employee. While the problem of dressing "below" the image of the store appears to be most common, the reverse situation can also be true. Stores that specialize in products such as feed, fertilizer, auto parts, and plumbing supplies generally expect their sales personnel to dress in work clothes for practical as well as image-building purposes. Individuals in these types of retail establishments often perform laborious and dirty tasks.

The wearing of a coat and tie may also place a barrier between the customer and the retailer, for it is not uncommon to find among middle-class consumers a distrust of those who wear a suit and tie. As retailers grow larger, they often hire salesmen and troubleshooters to call on their customers in the field, and when these persons are hired they sometimes assume that a coat and tie is the proper dress. This, however, is usually incorrect as they will be calling upon contractors, farmers, ranchers, and others who are seldom dressed in suits and ties and who often resent such attire in the salesmen who call on them. Thus the sight-image impression that customers hold of a retailer extends well beyond the confines of the retail store.

Image Control

The development and control of image creation cannot be planned for a store opening and then forgotten. It is an ongoing and everyday function of retail management. It requires a coordinated effort between all areas of the promotional mix, personnel policy, pricing, location, and indeed every function of retailing.

In a very true sense, image creation and control is what retailing is all about. It has allowed retailers such as Abercrombie and Fitch, Saks Fifth Avenue, Tiffany's, Neiman Marcus, and other firms that are known for their quality and high prices to grow in the face of discount houses and other mass merchandisers.

RETAIL LAND, BUILDINGS, FIXTURES, AND EQUIPMENT

It has previously been demonstrated that the outlet, its fixtures, and its equipment influence the store's image. A more detailed discussion of the way each factor is viewed by retailers is now warranted.

Land Utilization Considerations

Choice pieces of land are valued at a high rate; therefore the retailer must decide carefully how much space should be allocated to the building and how much to parking and other open, landscaped space. Although the cost of providing a one-car parking space may amount to $2,000 in downtown areas and about $50 in suburban shopping centers, consumers may demand the convenience associated with the availability of a nearby parking space.

The amount of land required for a parking area varies by the type of retail outlet. Shopping centers usually provide four square feet of parking space for every square foot of selling space. Outlets that cater to consumers who spend only a short amount of time in the store can provide less parking space. However, stores such as supermarkets, whose customers typically spend about twenty minutes per store visit, must provide more parking space if a large volume of consumers is to be served.

Outlets that wish to create a more prestigious image will probably need to allocate more space to open, landscaped areas, fountains, etc., than will discount or bargain-image retailers (see Figure 7–1).

Figure 7–1   *Shopping Center Focal Point*

This fountain serves as a focal point for a shopping center. Such a focal point and the open-space surroundings create a prestigious image for all of the stores in the center.

Building Exteriors

High interest rates, rising construction costs, new construction materials and techniques, and rising crime rates have caused numerous changes in the type of buildings used as retail outlets. Retailers have attempted to reduce building costs by using more multistory outlets, some of which are windowless, at least in the upper-floor levels (Figure 7–2). The absence of windows also improves security in case of civil disorders and reduces heating and air conditioning costs.

The storefront should convey the impression that the outlet is permanent, stable, and progressive. It should also clearly identify the store. Customer entrances should be wide enough to prevent consumer congestion and inviting enough to attract walk-in trade. Curtains of warm or cold air may serve as doors during store hours, and this increased ease of entering may attract some consumers who might otherwise hesitate to enter through a revolving or regular door (Figure 7–3).

Figure 7–2 **Example of Windowless Exterior**

This Joseph Magnin Store in San Diego provides an attractive appearance and reduces air conditioning and heating costs.

Figure 7–3 **Illustration of Doorless Design**

Source Photo courtesy of National Shirt Shops.

Despite their cost, display windows continue to be used to attract consumers into stores. In fact, many stores use an open or all-glass store front through which the consumer can see even the store's interior displays (Figure 7–4). The visual storefront allows the consumer to view most of the store's merchandise offering at a glance. Other stores may use a closed-back-

Figure 7–4   Illustration of an Open Store Front

At Stage's in the Cinderella City Shopping Center in Englewood, Colorado, an open store front allows the customer to view the store's interior displays.

SOURCE   Photo courtesy of STAGE, a division of Fashion Bar, Colorado.

ground show window display which lets the consumer see only the specially prepared window display and shuts off the interior view of the store completely (Figures 7–5 and 7–6). This practice allows merchants to focus consumer attention on displays which can convey either a quality or a popular-price image.

Higher building and land costs and effective display techniques have caused more retailers to use inexpensive out-of-door merchandise displays. These displays may be erected in the parking lot or in a specially designated space that is incorporated into the building and landscape design plans. The displays are generally crude in construction, so care should be taken that they do not detract from the permanent exterior appearance. The merchandise that is sold from these exterior displays is usually bulky, seasonal merchandise, such as lawn and garden-care products in the spring, boats in the summer, Christmas trees in December, and so on.

Building Interiors

The interior of a building must be attractive to the consumer. This may be accomplished by providing good lighting, colorful walls, attractive floors, colorful displays, and ceilings of a proper height and by arranging store fixtures and equipment in a manner that will accommodate the anticipated consumer traffic.

The color of a store's interior can enhance the store's appearance and

Figure 7–5 Illustration of Closed-Background Window Display Featuring Quality Image

emphasize its individuality. Color and design patterns can be used to direct consumers to specific areas and to put them in a buying mood. The effect that different colors have upon consumers is discussed in detail in Chapter 10, where it is noted that a different color scheme is likely to be most appropriate for each department, or perhaps even for each merchandise line. The men's section of Neiman Marcus reflects a man's color preference, with a com-

Figure 7–6   Illustration of Closed-Background Window Display Emphasizing Popular-Price Appeal

bination of deep blue and oak wood. Only a few feet away, the children's section offers a contrast in light pastels and designs that incorporate movement. Even different floor tile designs can be used to differentiate departments.

Every retail facility must be properly lighted to direct or attract the consumer's attention to the desired areas of the building. Lighting can be an effective sales tool if it is used to highlight different types of merchandise. A qualified lighting engineer can provide suggestions on the use of colored lights, as well as on the physical arrangement of lighting fixtures. Lighting can also be used to increase employee productivity by properly illuminating the checkout, storage, receiving, and other work areas.

Interior Layout

The layout of a retail store refers to the plan that designates the specific location and arrangement of equipment, fixtures, merchandise, aisles, and checkout facilities. Store layout automatically—and instantly—invites or repels a customer—the moment the customer looks through the window or passes through an entry. This may be the most crucial moment in consumer shopping behavior, particularly in modern shopping center malls where dozens of stores stand one against the other.

There is only one universal law in layout that applies to all retail stores: each store must have a *distinctive* layout. Plan it with the store's clientele in mind, and make certain it reflects the desired image and personality of the store.

Retailers have discovered that it is impossible to design a general layout that works for all types of retail stores in all areas. A certain degree of uniformity is possible within a single chain or a single industry, but strict adherence to a generalized model even within a single chain usually leads to disaster. The layout that is best suited for a store in Skokie, Illinois, may be completely out of character in Honolulu.

In a few cases, store layout is planned to detract rather than attract. A regional chain of exclusive dress shops uses this approach to invite only the clientele it has determined it wants. Its layout consists of a few extremely expensive fashions displayed near the front window. Behind this is a "no man's land" of plush rug nearly twenty feet in width. There is nothing but open space in this section, through which all customers must pass. They are then met by a stately and stiff-looking sales clerk, and behind her are the racks of clothes and the dressing rooms. Such a layout is scarcely designed to attract the casual shopper.

Although the above system seems to work for the retailer, it has inherent disadvantages. It may repel customers who could afford the merchandise but simply do not have the courage to walk the obstacle course. It may also offend the daughters of the store's adult clientele. In an age of casualness and informality, the future clientele may easily develop shopping habits that are different from this style and are not easily broken later in life.

There is a basic conflict in all mass merchandising layouts, for which a compromise must be reached. The customer wants a layout that does not cause undue inconvenience, or take added time, or tend to hinder shopping. The retailer wants a plan that exposes the shopper to the maximum amount of merchandise.

In the case of existing stores, traffic pattern studies should be conducted before remodeling to determine the natural flow of customers. In such studies, the percentage of consumers who pass—or buy from—each merchandise area is recorded by interviewers, who plot the paths of a sample of consumers on a floor plan similar to the one in Figure 7–7. Retailers believe that those merchandise lines which have high passing or buying percentages should be dispersed about the store so that consumers are exposed to more merchandise lines.

A scientific study of this nature usually is not available to new retailers, but observation of the patterns followed by shoppers in similar and competing stores is possible and desirable. Although the layout requirements facing retailers tend to vary, there are basic and common considerations.

Planning Layouts with Customers in Mind
Various social, age, and race segments exhibit different shopping habits and have individualized needs. This must be recognized before any layouts are planned.

Figure 7–7   Percent of Consumers Passing by Different Sections of a Super-market

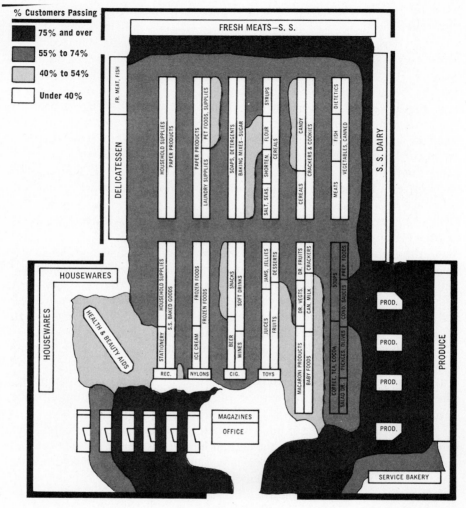

Source   "Colonial Study," *Progressive Grocer* (1964), p. C90.

Establishing a Friendly, Informal Atmosphere

Establish a friendly, informal atmosphere to make the consumers feel comfortable and at home. This is not solely the function of the sales force, as the entire surroundings should provide an aura of friendliness.

Promoting a Buying Mood

It is important to establish a buying mood. This is the sum total of what layout is all about. The most creative designs and best research are valueless unless an effective environment for buying can be created.

Using a Simple Layout

In general, the more simple and natural the layout, the more likelihood of success. Consumers object to being treated like mice in a laboratory maze. They express their objections in a silent but forceful manner: they don't return to the store! Have a well-defined entrance to the sales area. Again, this goes hand in hand with a simple layout (Figure 7–8).

Figure 7–8   *Illustration of a Well-Defined Entrance to Sales Area*

Note the different floor pattern.

Using Color, Design, and Lighting

Design patterns and color combinations should be planned on the layout so that they can effectively direct the attention of consumers to a particular location in subtle and attractive ways. Color and lighting can be used to create the effect of a separate department without using permanent walls or fixtures. Built-in fixtures and permanent walls are difficult to change if remodeling becomes necessary.[2] An illustration of the use of portable designs and fixtures is presented in Figure 7–9.

Lighting should also be planned as part of the layout. Lights are not simply fixtures that provide illumination; they create moods and atmospheres. Only certain types of lighting are appropriate for particular retail stores. Neglect of this results in consumer fatigue, improper reflection, and shadows on merchandise. Additionally, the shade of fluorescent lights must be considered, particularly in apparel shops. In artificial lighting, a beautiful blue sweater may appear to be purple. Lighting, in both quantity and quality, is of paramount importance.

Figure 7–9   Illustration of Use of Flexible Fixtures

S<small>OURCE</small>   *Chain Store Age* (October 1972), pp. E28–E29.

Planning Definite Themes

The layout and decor should not be simply brought together in a haphazard fashion. A definite theme is more effective. A central theme, such as a North Woods, Mexican, or Hawaiian setting, helps give the store a personality and helps set the pace for departments within the store.

There are mixed feelings as to whether the theme of the store should follow the general theme of the shopping center. In general, if acceptance of the shopping center theme will tend to make the store another "me too" retailer, it is wise to select something else. In many cases a slight variation from the central theme can achieve the desired results without a "sore thumb" effect. An overall North Woods shopping center theme might be varied by using a ghost town or Alpine village theme. Such a change is different, yet it complements the overall theme.

Avoiding Natural Shoplifting Areas

Avoid natural shoplifting areas. Secluded areas or areas that do not lend themselves to observation by store personnel are open invitations to shoplifters. Store fixtures and related displays should be kept low so that maximum customer visibility is maintained.

Capitalizing on the Flow of Traffic

The entire display area should be designed to follow the natural flow of traffic, rather than in a random or forced manner, and two major patterns are used in planning store layouts. The grid pattern routes consumer traffic in a manner similar to the rectangular street plan of a city (Figure 7–10) and

Figure 7–10 *Illustration of Grid Layout Pattern in a Super-market*

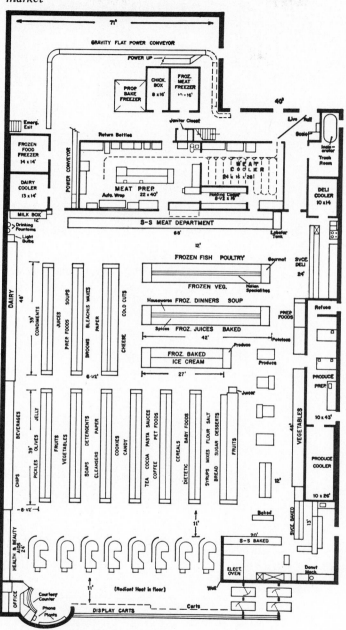

SOURCE *Progressive Grocer.*

creates a series of aisles similar to those found in most supermarkets, where customers' movements are directed by the aisles and fixtures. A "warehouse" image may also be created by the grid layout pattern unless colorful walls and fixtures are used to enhance its appearance.

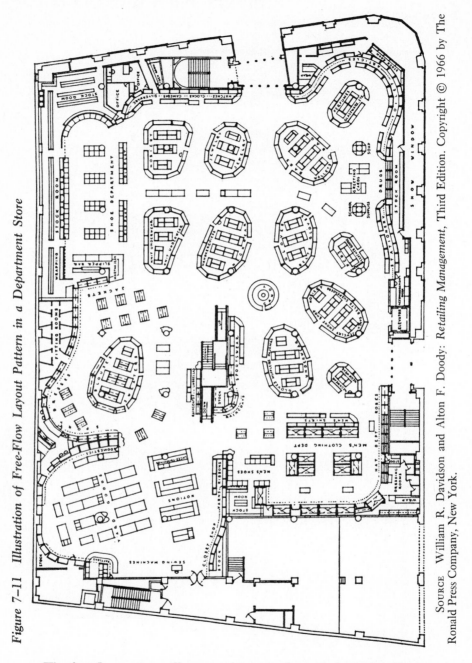

Figure 7–11 Illustration of Free-Flow Layout Pattern in a Department Store

SOURCE: William R. Davidson and Alton F. Doody: *Retailing Management*, Third Edition. Copyright © 1966 by The Ronald Press Company, New York.

The free-flow pattern allows consumers to form their own traffic patterns and browse within the outlet. It is a more casual pattern, as right angles are eliminated (Figure 7–11). It is most appropriate for shopping goods and specialty stores, in which the customer wishes to compare and evaluate products in a relaxed atmosphere. Less merchandise and fewer fixtures can be placed per square foot of space under the free-flow pattern than under the grid pattern; however, the more favorable consumer impression generated by the free-flow pattern offsets the higher display costs in stores where relaxed shopping is important.

Supermarkets and other outlets where customers make frequent repurchases of the same items can use the grid pattern more effectively. In these stores, consumers follow the same traffic pattern regularly and become familiar with the location of the various products. The customers want to make their purchases with a minimum amount of time and effort, and the grid pattern layout is both efficient in displaying products and convenient for consumers with these shopping motives.

Most stores use some combination of these two basic layout patterns to better display various types of merchandise and serve the different target market customers. The "shoppe" or boutique concept utilizes the free-flow pattern within a department that sells related merchandise. In effect, these boutiques become small specialty stores within a large store.

Some retailers are using curved layouts to increase the consumer's view of goods (Figures 7–12 and 7–13). The curved or radial floor plans are also easier to observe and police for security reasons.

Grouping Merchandise

Assemble items of merchandise that fit together with a natural association. Hammers and nails, syrup and pancake mixes are examples. A close examination of merchandise may reveal some previously unthought of related items and chances for extra sales. Studies by *Progressive Grocer* have demonstrated that sales were nearly twice as great for pretzels and potato chips when these items were displayed near complementary products such as soft drinks, compared to noncomplementary items such as milk and cheese.[3]

Departmentalize when possible. Form sections of the store into departments such as shoes, men's clothes, bakery goods, and auto parts. Departmentalization personalizes the store and tends to reduce the feeling of both consumers and store personnel that they are numbers in a vast wilderness of merchandise (Figure 7–14). Also, management planning and control are facilitated if operating expenses and receipts are maintained separately on a departmental basis. However, due to increased labor costs and computerized merchandise control, central "cash-wrap" stations on the floor are diminishing the importance of departmental considerations.

Several criteria can be used to group merchandise into departments. The generic or functional kind of merchandise (such as footwear, health and beauty aids, etc.) is one criterion. Others are target market groups (economy-minded consumers might be served from a bargain basement), trade practices used in the industry, and the method used to display the merchandise.

The location of the various departments depends on such considerations as the size and shape of the building, the type of customer clientele, the nature of the merchandise, and the value of the floor space. In a single-floor outlet, the most valuable space is the area nearest the store entrance. This is the area with the heaviest consumer traffic. Floor space decreases in value

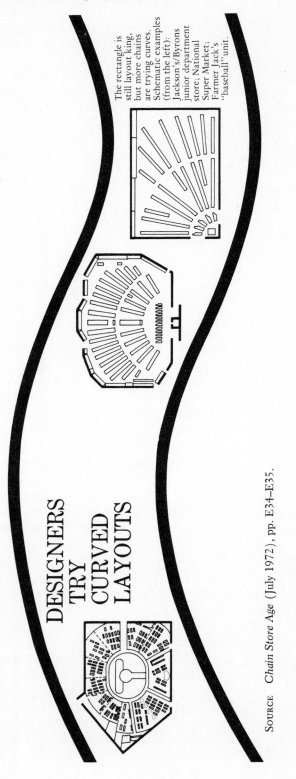

The rectangle is still layout king, but more chains are trying curves. Schematic examples (from the left): Jackson's/Byrons junior department store; National Super Market; Farmer Jack's "baseball" unit.

DESIGNERS TRY CURVED LAYOUTS

Figure 7–12   Illustration of Curved Layouts

SOURCE   *Chain Store Age* (July 1972), pp. E34–E35.

Figure 7–13   Curved Layouts Give a Wide View of the Merchandise

SOURCE   *Chain Store Age* (July 1972), p. E36.

Figure 7–14   Illustration of Departmentalization to Personalize a Store's Offering

Note how the Denver Dry has separated a merchandise department, The Place, by using a different floor covering and a mobile divider.

as one moves from the entrance to the rear of the building. In a multifloor building, the space decreases in value as one moves up or down from the main floor.

Merchandise departments usually are located according to their sales-generating capacity relative to the value of the space occupied. Frequently purchased items usually are given the most favored space allocations. However, the nature of the merchandise also must be considered. Impulse items, high-rate replacement items, and convenience goods (such as cigarettes) should be located in the heaviest traffic areas because consumers will not search them out. Shopping goods (such as furniture) and specialty goods (such as sporting goods) can be located in less heavily traveled areas because they will pull traffic to the outer locations. Bulky merchandise, such as large appliances, boats, etc., generally are located in less heavy consumer traffic areas.

If possible, it is advisable to locate departments with different seasonal sales patterns adjacent to each other. An exchange of selling space among adjacent departments can provide a more efficient use of space if the departments have different seasonal selling peaks.

A store that merchandises on many levels may display a portion of its offerings on the main floor. Impulse items and a small sample of the type of merchandise that a consumer can expect to see in the primary location are also usually displayed on the main floor. This main-floor display can encourage consumers to make a trip to the primary department location.

Planning Perimeters and Crosswalks

Perimeters are the heaviest customer traffic area in the store and should be planned to accommodate those items that account for a store's major

Figure 7–15   Illustration of Display at Escalator Exit

revenue. Aisles within perimeters that are unduly wide can create consumer dissatisfaction by the need to continually cross from one side to the other. Narrow aisles create a feeling of claustrophobia in many consumers, particularly when merchandise is stored above eye level.

Crosswalks are often considered poor merchandising areas, but they can break up the "canyon" effect of long perimeters. Crosswalks and escalator exits also are effective locations for end-of-the-aisle displays of weekend specials and so-called impulse items (Figure 7–15).

Planning Midstore Sales Appeal

Plan midstore sales appeal. Many retailers have found that the midstore is a poor merchandising area. As a result, it is necessary to examine carefully and relist the type of merchandise that sells best in this area rather than to stock indiscriminately. In the case of supermarket items, the following were found to be the best customer attractors for a midstore location.[4]

PRODUCT GROUP	PERCENT OF TOTAL STORE TRAFFIC ATTRACTED
Coffee	66
Cookies and crackers	65
Canned vegetables	62
Baking needs	60
Paper products	59
Canned soup	58
Laundry supplies	55
Cereal	55
Sugar	55
Salad dressing and oils	53

Designing "Eyeball" Merchandising

Studies and experience have demonstrated that merchandise displayed at eye level sells better than merchandise at either a very low or high level. Eye-level merchandising should be planned for the "bread and butter" lines of a retailer. Retailers can locate brands and items within a merchandise category to maximize profitability. Per unit margins, sales volume, and the sales sensitivity of each brand and/or item must be considered. Brands and/or items providing the highest profit contribution as measured by a margin times volume divided by space-used calculation should usually be given the eye-level shelf space.[5] An exception to this rule would be an item whose popularity is so strong that consumers will search for the item no matter what height level it occupies.

Shelves should not be more than 54 to 60 inches high or they will block the view of consumers. And, of course, sales will suffer if the consumer cannot see the merchandise. In the case of mass merchandising displays, consideration should also be given to peripheral vision (as few consumers walk sideways down a shopping aisle).

Planning Return per Square, Linear, or Cubic Foot

Plan the return per square foot of selling space. A dollar return per some measurable unit of space is the most common measurement used by retailers to establish rental rates and to gauge merchandising success (this concept is discussed in detail in Chapter 4). While it should always remain in the back of the retailer's mind, it should not be given an overemphasis in the planning of layout.

If a retailer finds that men's undershirts return more per square foot than any other product, should he stock his store with nothing but this item? Unless there is sufficient demand for a specialty retail store of this nature, the answer is obviously no. Yet if reliance upon return per measurable unit of space is the sole consideration, dangerous merchandising errors such as this can occur.

Likewise, complete dependence upon other considerations involved in layout can result in stores that are works of art but have a very low dollar return.

Planning Locations of Sales-supporting Areas

Plan the locations and space occupied by sales-supporting and sales-generating equipment. Multifloor outlets require stairways, elevators, or escalators to move customers from one floor to another. Stores that merchandise from the ground level, basement, and only one floor above the ground level can often provide only a stationary stairway. Larger stores must provide some more elaborate system. Customers do not like to wait for elevators or escalators or to climb steps; so adequate facilities must be provided if consumers are to be attracted to another floor.

Sales-supporting equipment and space must be arranged so goods can be received, inspected, marked, and placed on the shelves with minimum effort. Mechanical handling equipment, communication devices, and other labor-saving equipment should be considered, and incorporated into the store layout if economically feasible. The storage and work areas should be located in low consumer traffic areas, but they should be easily accessible to the selling areas. These storage and work areas are generally located at the rear of single-floor outlets, and not on the ground floor of multifloor outlets.

Higher retail land values and increased building costs have caused some retailers to reduce the amount of nonselling space in the retail outlet or to move the nonselling area to less valuable space, such as mezzanines.[6] Faster and more frequent delivery and labor-saving techniques, such as pre-packaged and pre-marked merchandise that is ready for display when it arrives at the store, are being used to reduce the amount of space devoted to nonselling activities. (The handling of merchandise is discussed in Chapter 13.)

Planning Checkout Areas

Plan the placement and size of checkout areas. There is no other single area in a store more important than the checkout counter. Once a customer has decided upon her purchases, she wants to make the purchase transaction as quickly as possible.

Most of the problems at the checkout counter can be controlled only by providing adequate checkout facilities and by careful scheduling of clerks, but the location can have important bearings on the efficiency of operation. If the checkout stand is designed so that incoming and outgoing customers mingle in traffic jams, customers will be dissatisfied—and there is a good chance that shoplifting will increase.

At best, a checkout counter necessitates a short wait. The checkout area should be planned with a layout that incorporates attractive impulse-type items in point-of-purchase displays. One mass retailing chain has deliberately engineered a five-minute wait per customer by designing the checkout system to generate an average waiting line of three people. This retailer has determined the average time (and deviation from the average time) that each checkout activity (sorting, "ringing," and bagging) requires. The three-customer-average wait line was selected because it makes better use of the cashiers' time. In addition, the retailer may encourage impulse buying at the checkout stands by placing last-minute convenience items in the checkout area.

The wisdom of such a plan depends on how dissatisfied consumers become over the wait. The consumer is likely to react negatively when the line happens to be a little longer than planned. If this happens, the loss in patronage could easily amount to a loss in future profits that will exceed the savings in cashier wages and the extra margin generated by the impulse items purchased because of the long wait.

Planning Dressing Rooms and Rest Rooms

Incorporate dressing rooms and rest rooms in the plan. Unless they are incorporated in the original layout and overall theme, they tend to become conspicuous boxes and can easily detract from the overall purpose of creating a favorable buying mood. For security reasons, only one entrance should be provided to the dressing room. This entrance should not be located near a stockroom, stairwell, rest room, or outside exit.

The overall store theme should give the planner many ideas for creative design for the dressing room and rest room areas. In a circus theme, the dressing rooms might be identified and designed as the "magic show." These areas should be used to sell merchandise, but the dressing rooms in most stores are hardly designed to encourage purchases. It is difficult for the most expensive suit or dress to complement the wearer in a coffin-like upright rectangle complete with faded mirror and unpainted walls. A dirty, unkept, barren rest room can suddenly reduce the image of any store to little more than a backwoods filling station.

Planning Uses for Dead Areas

Regardless of the best planning, "dead spaces" are likely to occur within the store. Such areas as corners often become dead areas. These can be utilized for vending machines, a play area for children (complete with toys), or for other functions that attract customers and add directly or indirectly to sales.

SUMMARY

Retailers should consult the Small Business Administration, industry trade associations, and similar stores in other locations when they begin to plan a layout. The entire physical project (including outside surroundings, parking lot, exterior building appearance, and interior layout and appearance) creates an overall store personality for consumers. Each consumer will perceive the store image differently, so the entire project should be designed to appeal to the store's selected target market group.

QUESTIONS

1. How is the concept of image related to the wheel of retailing?
2. What factors might cause a retailer to want to change his image? How would a retailer go about deciding whether it would be beneficial for him to do so?
3. In what types of retail establishments would you expect the "sensual approach" to selling to be most effective? Can you make any generalizations about types of products and demand for those products which are sold by using a highly sensual approach?
4. In what types of stores is the free-flow traffic pattern most useful? Why?
5. In what types of stores is the grid pattern most useful? Why?
6. Considering as many variables as you have studied (i.e., location, layout, risk, retailing mix, etc.), suggest a store design, given the following parameters: supermarket in a middle-class suburb; private bookstore in a college town; sporting goods store in a wealthy suburb.
7. Discuss your own opinion of the ethics of making a used car "smell new," as mentioned in this chapter. Retailers often practice other similar techniques, such as bakeries blowing baking smells to the sidewalk and record stores playing loud music. Briefly comment on the social desirability of these and similar practices. Is it ethical to "display" private merchandise on a public sidewalk? Is it good business?
8. Considering the current anti-materialistic trends in our society, what would you say lies in the future for traditional upper-class establishments such as Brooks Brothers, Saks, Abercrombie and Fitch, Gumps, Hastings of San Francisco, and similar stores? Do you think these stores should adapt to the current trends or should they increase their uniqueness by not changing?

FOOTNOTES

[1] William J. E. Crissy, "Image: What Is It?," *M.S.U. Business Topics* (East Lansing, Mich.) (Winter 1971), pp. 77–80.

[2] "Kennedy's Uses Lights Instead of Walls," *Chain Store Age* (September 1971), pp. E46–E49 (executive's ed.).

[3] *Consumer Dynamics in the Super Market* (New York: Progressive Grocer, n.d.).

[4] Ibid.

[5] James F. Engel, David T. Kollat, and Roger D. Blackwell, *Consumer Behavior* (New York: Holt, Rinehart and Winston, 1968), p. 485.

[6] "Double-Deck Saves SCOA Backroom," *Chain Store Age* (March 1970), p. E20 (executive's ed.).

DANNY'S MEN'S STORES

Danny's Men's Stores are owned by the Wiener Corporation of New Orleans. The original Danny's store is located in New Orleans and does approximately $1 million in sales volume per year.

The store carries medium-price branded wearing apparel for men and boys. This line of merchandise is designed to appeal to the "young of all ages." These styles were described by a member of management as "traditional, but with a flair of what's-going-on." Way-out fashion boutique and formal men's attire are excluded from the product line.

Several new Danny's stores are scheduled in the company's expansion program in metropolitan areas such as Dallas. These new stores are planned around the merchandising concept of selling men's wear to the wife or mother, along with the male consumer.

Mr. Sidney Wiener, executive vice-president, expressed the belief that it is difficult to motivate men to buy new wearing apparel and that women buy around 60 percent of men's clothes, especially accessories.

With this philosophy in mind, the advertising sales personnel and in-store decor were planned with women in mind.

Advertising would be pointed toward the wife or mother, and suggestions had been made about a series of "witty ads" such as "Bring your best friend's husband." A free bottle of perfume for women shoppers was also considered as an incentive.

Store location was also an important factor, and it was felt that new regional shopping centers would be the future sites.

With the large numbers of men's wear shops in existence, management was convinced that a new merchandising strategy was essential, and believed it had hit upon a sound approach.

DISCUSSION QUESTIONS

1. Do you agree that men cannot be motivated to buy men's wear except in small numbers?

2. What do you think of the strategy being planned for new Danny's stores?
3. Would you advise the Wiener Corporation to seek out locations near women's wear shops?
4. What type of in-store decor and sales personnel would you suggest as most likely to appeal to women customers?

CITIES SERVICE OIL COMPANY

In the fall of 1971 the Cities Service Oil Company initiated a test market in LaCrosse, Wisconsin, involving fourteen self-service gasoline stations. The results of this test were very encouraging, according to Mr. R. C. Moore, vice-president of marketing for CITGO. "We have been highly pleased with the sales results," he said. With decreased overhead, our prices have been attractive to customers, and gallonage has moved up sharply. Acceptance of self-service has been excellent."

Based on the results of the LaCrosse market, CITGO decided to move into self-service at other stations in selected markets.

According to a *Wall Street Journal* article of April 4, 1972, the total number of self-service stations of all brands in the United States had nearly quintupled in the last three years, to about 12,000 stations. These accounted for approximately 5 percent of the gasoline sales in the United States, but expectation for further dramatic increases was widespread within the industry.

CITGO had also been experimenting with the operation of three convenience stores in Arkansas and six large ones in Charlotte, North Carolina. These were free-standing buildings that stocked convenience goods such as cigarettes, health needs, mouth washes, and bread. The Charlotte stores also sold gasoline through self-service pumps.

"Again, we're pleased with results," stated Mr. Moore. "Sale of convenience items and gasoline has exceeded our first projections. All of this experience, coupled with that in LaCrosse and a few other places, has made us more and more at home in this new field. The typical petroleum company has much to learn as it wades into the convenience store waters. Without merchandising savvy, an operation of this kind won't pan out, and most oil companies have few people with this type of knowledge. Fortunately, we're learning a lot, and this could be a double payoff—not only in successful convenience stores but in the adaptation of these techniques to regular service stations to improve tire, battery, and accessory merchandising."

After viewing the entire test results, CITGO entered into an agreement with Munford Inc. of Atlanta. With over a thousand convenience food stores, Munford was one of the leading convenience food store chains in the nation.

This agreement meant that CITGO would be merchandising gasoline through self-service pumps at Munford stores. It also meant that Munford would be building new stores at appropriate CITGO locations.

At the same time, CITGO was working with two smaller convenience store organizations, Job Enterprises and Time Saver Stores.

Convenience stores had been growing rapidly, and by 1970 more than 13,000 such stores accounted for $2.6 billion, or three percent of total grocery store revenue. An estimate by *Progressive Grocer* envisioned 25,000 stores by the end of 1975, accounting for 5 to 7 percent of grocery sales, and 35,000 stores by 1980.

In viewing the recent moves, CITGO management realized there was a possibility of petroleum companies' establishing extensive convenience store empires. It also realized that risks were involved, due to the growth rate of convenience stores.

DISCUSSION QUESTIONS

1. In view of an almost certain future saturation in the convenience store field, should CITGO continue to expand in this area?
2. What competitive moves should other convenience food chains and other petroleum companies undertake?
3. What do you believe has caused the simultaneous growth of self-service gasoline stations and convenience food stores? Keep in mind that convenience food stores generally sell their items at a higher price than other stores while self-service stations sell gasoline at cut rates.
4. Are there other logical retail outlets for self-service gasoline sales not presently used by major petroleum companies? If so, what are they, and why do you believe they are logical outlets?

PART THREE

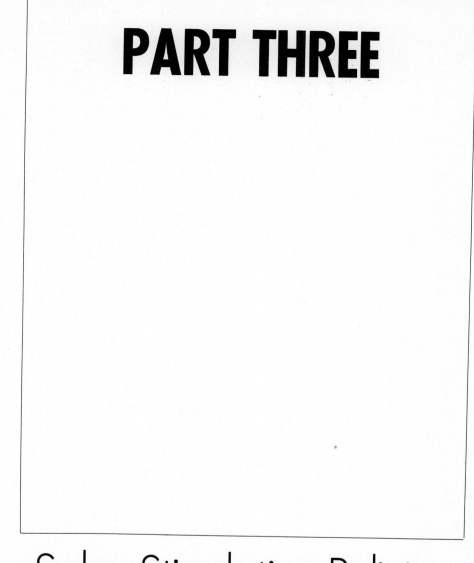

Sales Stimulation Policies

CHAPTER 8

Photo courtesy of Howell's Department Stores, Denver, Colo.

Pricing for Profit

The heart of an effective retail operation is pricing the goods or services so that the customer sincerely believes that he or she has received fair value. This is accomplished by using an appropriate pricing strategy, and is implemented through aggressive pricing tactics. This chapter examines the proper use of long-term pricing strategies, such as initial markons and pricing elasticity, price lining, and the overall psychology of pricing. The chapter closes with an examination of such tactical pricing practices as markdowns and promotional pricing and, finally, the legal aspects of proper pricing.

PRICING STRATEGY

Pricing decisions are important because they can nullify the effect of intelligently conceived product, location, and communication programs. The retailer's pricing strategy is a form of market cultivation, but it is also a reflection of all the firm's actions. Pricing is symbolic of the kind of product strategy used by the retailer because the price tag conveys a mental image about product quality to the customer. Pricing may be used as a store location substitute in an effort to attract customers from greater distances.

Pricing strategy must be consistent with the retailer's communication appeal. Generally, a retailer who uses a low-price appeal must sacrifice some methods of demand stimulation, such as advertising. Rarely can large sums be spent on advertising and promotion if low price is the dominant appeal. Discount retailers may initially appear to be the exception. However, if advertising and promotion budgets are considered as a percentage of sales volume, most discounters spend relatively less on advertising.

Price is the dominant factor that directly influences the retailer's profit or loss. Other things being equal, price can be lowered to increase sales. However, the increase in unit volume may not be sufficient to generate a higher level of profit. Thus retailers must review price changes with regard to their effects upon both sales and profits.

Markup Pricing

Most retail prices are determined by a cost-oriented markup. Markup means the difference between the cost of an item and its retail price. Cost, in this case, usually refers to the invoice cost of the merchandise, minus trade discounts, plus inbound freight paid by the retailer. Markup is generally expressed as a percent of the retail price. In formula form, markup percent = retail price per unit minus per unit cost, divided by retail price per unit, times 100. If, for example, an item costs a retailer $50 but he retails it at $75, the markup percent is ($25 / $75) × 100, or 33⅓.

Markup can also be defined by using the cost as a base. Markup on cost is calculated by dividing the margin by the cost to the retailer. In formula form, markup percent of cost = [(retail price per unit minus per unit cost) / per unit cost] × 100. In this example the markup on cost percent would be $25 / $50, or 50 percent. In this text the term "markup percent of cost" will always be differentiated from markup as a percent of price.

One important point should be stressed when considering markups using both cost and selling prices as bases. A markup percent based on the retail or selling price will always be smaller than an equivalent dollar margin based on the cost of an item. A conversion from a given markup percent on cost to an equivalent markup on retail can be made by using the following formula: markup percent = [markup percent of cost / (100 plus markup percent of cost)] × 100. If the markup percent of cost is 20 percent, the comparable markup percent is equal to [20/(100 + 20)] × 100, or 16.7 percent. Table 8–1 contains equivalent markups, and may be used to convert markup percent into markup percent of cost.

Retailers frequently want to determine what price must be charged on

Table 8–1   *Markup Table*

To use this table find the desired percentage in the left-hand column. Multiply the cost of the article by the corresponding percentage in the "markup percent of cost" column. The result, added to the cost, gives the correct selling price.

MARKUP PERCENT OF SELLING PRICE	MARKUP PERCENT OF COST	MARKUP PERCENT OF SELLING PRICE	MARKUP PERCENT OF COST	MARKUP PERCENT OF SELLING PRICE	MARKUP PERCENT OF COST
4.8	5.0	18.0	22.0	32.0	47.1
5.0	5.3	18.5	22.7	33.3	50.0
6.0	6.4	19.0	23.5	34.0	51.5
7.0	7.5	20.0	25.0	35.0	53.9
8.0	8.7	21.0	26.6	35.5	55.0
9.0	10.0	22.0	28.2	36.0	56.3
10.0	11.1	22.5	29.0	37.0	58.8
10.7	12.0	23.0	29.9	37.5	60.0
11.0	12.4	23.1	30.0	38.0	61.3
11.1	12.5	24.0	31.6	39.0	64.0
12.0	13.6	25.0	33.3	39.5	65.5
12.5	14.3	26.0	35.0	40.0	66.7
13.0	15.0	27.0	37.0	41.0	70.0
14.0	16.3	27.3	37.5	42.0	72.4
15.0	17.7	28.0	39.0	42.8	75.0
16.0	19.1	28.5	40.0	44.4	80.0
16.7	20.0	29.0	40.9	46.1	85.0
17.0	20.5	30.0	42.9	47.5	90.0
17.5	21.2	31.0	45.0	48.7	95.0
				50.0	100.0

SOURCE   National Cash Register Company, *Expenses in Retail Businesses* (Dayton: N.C.R., n.d.), p. 45.

an item to yield a desired markup. The following formula makes this conversion.

$$\text{Retail price} = \frac{(\text{cost in dollars})}{(100 \text{ minus desired markup percent})} \times 100$$

Thus if an item were purchased by the retailer for $10 and he wished to obtain a markup of 50 percent, the calculation would be

$$\frac{\$10}{(100 - 50)} \times 100,$$

or $20.

Markup pricing is also used to ensure that planned gross margin percentages exceed expenses. The gross margin percent is obtained by subtracting the cost of goods sold from gross sales volume. The resulting number (gross margin dollars) is divided by the sales dollar volume and multiplied by 100 to give the gross margin percent. In formula form:

$$\text{Gross margin percent} = \frac{(\text{gross margin dollars})}{(\text{sales in dollars})} \times 100.$$

Thus the difference between markup and gross margin is that markup is the initially planned margin, while the gross margin is the realized margin *after* reductions for markdowns, discounts, shrinkage, pilferage, etc.

For example, a retail store may have an average markup of 40 percent but produce a gross margin of only 35 percent. If expenses were 30 percent of sales dollar receipts, the store would *obtain* a net profit margin of 5 percent.

Retailers must be aware of the amount of *shrinkage* that occurs between markup percent and gross margin percent. If the usual deviation between the two measures is known, and the expenses can be estimated, markup pricing can be used to reach a pre-specified net profit percent.

Maintaining a Minimum Markup

Retailers use markup pricing because it is a convenient method of pricing the very large number of items they stock. The retailer generally cannot afford to spend the time and effort to determine the best price to charge on *every* item, although few retailers use the same markup for all of their goods. In fact, some retailers use different markup percentages for each merchandise department and key each item's markup percentage into checkout facilities, thereby identifying sales by department and maintaining a perpetual inventory in the process.

Retail merchants also use markup percentages as a negotiation tool and as a control and planning device.[1] The retailer can gain significant benefits by using markup as a commitment to a specific minimum markup policy of X percent on all lines stocked in the store. The success of the commitment will depend upon the ability of the buyer to communicate this commitment to the supplier. A rigid markup schedule, if used by a retail outlet that dominates the trade in a locality, can help counteract the advantages otherwise held by a powerful supplier. Particular note should be made that such practices set only the *minimum* markup and still leave the retailer the option of increasing the markup.

Retail management can also use markup as a control and planning tool if it controls the level of markup required in each department. Markup pressures could induce department merchandise buyers to make purchases at the lowest possible price or to discover new products which yield more than the minimum markup. Management pressure for a minimum markup could also help top retail management protect the firm against a continually low sale-price policy that might injure the long-run image of a store selling high-quality merchandise. However, retail management should also realize that rigid adherence to a high markup percentage will not necessarily maximize store profits. At a lower markup, sales volume may increase enough to generate more profits than the firm obtained when a higher markup was used.

Factors Affecting Markup

The rate of markup percentage is influenced by many factors, including rate of turnover, product cost, branding policies, and the degree of retail competition.

Generally, the retail markup varies inversely with merchandise turnover.[2] A higher markup is usually placed on products that sell less frequently. Slow-moving products generally occupy the same amount of selling space and require the same investment as fast-selling items. Thus a higher margin is required on slow-moving items if these items are going to contribute an equivalent share to the retailer's profits.

This can be demonstrated by calculating the margin needed to return an equivalent profit on both fast- and slow-selling items. An item's gross profit margin can be determined by multiplying its per unit margin by its turnover. Suppose two products, A and B, both cost the retailer $500 and require about the same amount of shelf space, sales time, and investment. Suppose, further, that the retailer desires to obtain $1,000 annual gross profit margin from each product. The annual merchandise turnover is estimated to be 20 for product A and 4 for B. The per unit margins needed if each product is to contribute $1,000 gross margin can be calculated by using the following formula:

Annual gross profit margin equals per unit margin $\times$ annual turnover.

The calculations for product A are:

$1,000 = \text{(required per unit margin)} \times 20$, or $\dfrac{\$1,000}{20}$;
so per unit margin is $50.

For product B:

$1,000 = \text{(required per unit margin)} \times 4$, or $\dfrac{\$1,000}{4}$;
so per unit margin is $250.

Therefore, to obtain an equivalent $1,000 gross profit margin, the per unit margin would have to be $50 on fast-moving item A, compared to $250 on slow-moving item B. The gross margin percent required would be (50 / 550) (100), or 9 percent for A, and (250 / 750) (100), or 33 percent for B.

The markup percent needed to obtain an equivalent $1,000 gross profit margin can also be calculated. For example, if total retail reductions (markdowns, discounts, shrinkage, pilferage, etc.) are estimated to be 5 percent of sales, the following formula can be used to determine the required initial markup percent:

$$\text{Initial markup percent} = \frac{\text{(gross margin + retail reductions)}}{\text{(100\% + retail reductions)}}$$

The calculations for product A are:

$$\text{Initial markup percent} = \frac{(9\% + 5\%)}{(100\% + 5\%)},$$

or 13 percent.

For Product B:

$$\text{Initial markup percent} = \frac{(33\% + 5\%)}{(100\% + 5\%)},$$

or 36 percent.

In this example, an initial markup of 13 percent is required to yield a gross margin of 9 percent on A. The initial markup of 36 percent would result in a gross margin of 33 percent for B.

In summary, per unit gross margin, gross margin percent, and markup percent must all be higher on the slow-moving item B if the item is going to generate the same annual gross profit margin as the fast-selling (high turnover) item A.

Higher-price items normally carry a lower markup percent than lower-price items. A study, conducted by Holden, indicates that this relationship holds at the retail level.[3] Consumers are likely to notice similar percentage price differences on higher-priced items; so competitive pressure may partially explain the lower markup percent on higher-priced items. For example, a 10 percent price difference (amounting to 3 cents) between two stores on a 30 cent item is less likely to be noticed by customers than a 10 percent difference (amounting to $600) on a new car selling for $6,000. Customers are likely to spend more time making purchase decisions (and to make more comparisons on prices and quality) on major items than on lower-price items which are purchased infrequently.

Branding policies also affect the level of markup. Higher markups are usually applied to private label brand items which a retail chain prices below the price for similar national brand items.[4] Higher markups can be applied to private label items because their acquisition, distribution, advertising, and promotion costs are usually lower than comparable costs for national branded items. Thus the private label items are usually priced lower than national brand items, but still provide the retailer with a product line that has a higher markup percent.

Retailers may change their regular markup policy to meet a competitor's price, but few retailers meet all prices of all competitors. However, most stores compare merchandise and prices in competing stores. Thus the degree of retail competition in an area determines the markup level charged by its stores.

Other things being equal, more stores and more aggressive competition tend to produce lower markups. Larger stores generally use a slightly lower markup (and hence receive a slightly lower gross margin percent) on their merchandise than similar smaller stores.[5] Average gross margin percent data for forty types of retail outlets are presented in Table 8–2.

Price Elasticity and Markup

Most of the factors that influence markup are considered in the calculation of the price elasticity of the demand coefficient, hereafter referred to as E_d. The value of E_d indicates the percentage change in sales per 1 percent

Table 8–2 Gross Profit Margin Percent for Different Types of Retail Outlets, 1971

TYPE OF RETAILER	GROSS MARGIN PERCENTAGE*
Family clothing	36
Furs	42
Infants' clothing	40
Men's and boys' clothing	40
Shoes	40
Women's ready-to-wear	34
Books and stationery	37
Office supplies and equipment	33
Building materials	25
Hardware	29
Heating and plumbing equipment	22
Lumber	25
Paint, glass, and wall paper	35
Cameras and photographic supplies	30
Department stores	34
Dry goods and general merchandise	36
Drugs	39
Farm equipment	21
Farm and garden supply	29
Flowers	32
Dairy product—milk dealers	17
Groceries and meats	21
Restaurants	45
Floor coverings	30
Furniture	40
Household appliances	35
Radios, TV, and record players	28
Jewelry	44
Liquor	22
Luggage and gifts	45

* *Disclaimer statement:* Robert Morris Associates cannot emphasize too strongly that their composite figures for each industry may *not* be representative of that entire industry (except by coincidence), for the following reasons: (1) The only companies with a chance of being included in their study in the first place are those for whom their submitting banks have recent figures. (2) Even from this restricted group of potentially includable companies, those which are chosen, and the total number chosen, are not determined in any random or otherwise statistically reliable manner. (3) Many companies in their study have *varied* product lines; they are "mini-conglomerates," if you will. All they can do in these cases is categorize them by their *primary* product line, and be willing to tolerate any "impurity" thereby introduced.

SOURCE *Annual Statement Studies*, the Robert Morris Associates, the National Association of Bank Loan and Credit Officers, Philadelphia National Bank Building, Philadelphia, Pennsylvania, 1972 Edition, pp. 98–119. The copyright is held by the Robert Morris Associates.

Table 8–2   (Continued)

TYPE OF RETAILER	GROSS MARGIN PERCENTAGE*
Marine hardware, boats and supply	21
Autos—new and used	15
Gasoline service stations	19
House trailers	18
Tire, battery, and accessories	31
Musical instruments and supplies	38
Sporting goods	31
Vending machine operators, merchandise	29

change in price, other things being held constant. The value of E_d, if known, can be used as a guide to determine the markup for an item, group of items, or even a department in a store.

The price elasticity of the demand coefficient, E_d, may be calculated by using the formula:

$$E_d = \frac{(Q_1 - Q_2)/(Q_1 + Q_2)}{(P_1 - P_2)/(P_1 + P_2)},$$

where Q_1 is the quantity sold when the price is P_1 and Q_2 is the quantity sold when the price is P_2. The value of the calculated coefficient is nearly always negative because of the inverse relationship between price and quantity (i.e., an increase in price generally causes a decrease in the number of units sold).

The calculated value of the coefficient indicates if the price elasticity of demand is inelastic, elastic, or of unitary elasticity. If the calculated coefficient, E_d, has an absolute value of less than 1.0, the demand is said to be inelastic.[6] The price increase (to the higher of the two prices—P_1 and P_2) will increase both total revenue (sales dollars) and profit if the demand is inelastic. If demand is found to be inelastic, then a new, higher price level should be tested in the next time period to determine if demand is still inelastic at a higher price level. Any calculated inelastic E_d indicates that prices must be increased even further to maximize profit. Thus retail markups can be higher on products which have few substitutes, as indicated by an inelastic E_d. Stocking exclusive brands, obtaining a regional dealer franchise, and keeping the store open when other stores are closed are several ways of reducing the competition from substitute products or retail outlets.

Unitary elasticity is indicated when the calculated value of E_d is −1.0. Unitary elasticity maximizes total revenue but not profits. Thus a price increase to the higher of the prices P_1 and P_2 would *reduce* total gross receipts, but would *increase* profit unless production and marketing costs are zero or there is a large difference between P_1 and P_2.

An elastic demand occurs when the percentage change in quantity is relatively greater than the percentage change in price. In this case, the calculated value of E_d has an absolute value greater than 1.0. A price *decrease* in the elastic section of the demand curve will result in an *increase* in the total revenue. Profit at the lower price may be *either* increased or decreased, depending upon margin and product marketing costs. One must analyze the costs and total revenue obtained under the two price levels before one can determine the effect a price change will have on profit in the elastic section of the demand curve. A very elastic E_d indicates that there are many close substitutes for the product; so the markup must be low to allow the retailer to remain competitive.

Retail markups should vary inversely with the price elasticity of demand if profits are to be maximized. High-profit stores have been found to price competitively on readily identifiable items with a high turnover rate and "known" prices.[7] However, the high-profit stores also have used higher margins on less important merchandise. Thus they could charge relatively high average prices but still give the appearance of competitiveness. In this same study, stores receiving lower profits tended to charge a higher price on items with a fast turnover and to charge a lower price on items with a low turnover. This pricing strategy can give the consumer the incorrect impression that the store charges high average prices.

Estimating Price Elasticity

Estimates of retail price elasticity of demand usually are based upon the experience of the retailer or upon representative markups charged by competitors or quoted by trade associations. There is no guarantee that any of these approaches will provide a reliable estimate of price elasticity for a specific product category sold by a specific store. Years of experience can provide the retailer with an approximate estimate of E_d, but it is a costly and time-consuming process. Several research techniques can be used to reduce the cost of making serious long-term pricing errors by analyzing sales data.

One way to measure price elasticity at the retail level is to change price and observe what happens to sales. However, care must be taken when interpreting the resulting sales since other factors, such as advertising, competitive actions, or seasonal fluctuations, may distort the sales data. A retailer should be able to control his advertising and promotion, or at least know that a promotion is planned, so that he can select a product line and time period when little abnormal promotional activity will be going on. Of course, retailers are not able to control competitive promotions. However, sales data obtained during weeks of abnormally heavy competitive promotion can be deleted from the analysis.

The effect that seasonal fluctuations have upon sales can be eliminated by comparing the weekly sales of a product during price changes with its weekly sales during previous years (Table 8–3). Other factors, such as shelf

Table 8–3   Determining Price Elasticity for a Product Line (or Department) by Changing Prices in 1974 and Comparing Sales with Previous Sales Levels

			SALES IN UNITS		
Product Line (or Department)	Week of	Price Level	1974	1970–1973 Average	Index or Percent 1974 Sales Are of 1970–73 Average
Meat	May 1	No change	1,210	1,100	Plus 10
	May 8	No change	1,080	1,000	Plus 8
	May 15	No change	1,120	1,000	Plus 12
	May 22	No change	990	900	Plus 10
Pre-price change average			1,100	1,000	Plus 10
	May 22	Lowered by 10%	1,500	1,100	Plus 36
	May 29	Lowered by 10%	1,536	1,200	Plus 28
	June 5	Lowered by 10%	1,703	1,300	Plus 31
	June 12	Lowered by 10%	1,501	1,200	Plus 25
Post-price change average			1,560	1,200	Plus 30

$$\text{Calculation of } E_d = \frac{\text{Percent change in quantity}}{\text{Percent change in price}}$$

$$S_o \, E_d = \frac{(\text{Post-price change average index sales}) \text{ minus (Pre-price change average index sales})}{\text{Percentage change in price}}$$

$$\text{Or } E_d = \frac{(\text{Plus } 30) \text{ minus (plus } 10)}{(\text{Minus } 10)} = \frac{(\text{Plus } 20)}{(\text{Minus } 10)}, \quad \text{or } -2.0$$

space devoted to the test products, sales personnel attention, shelf inventory on the test products, etc., also influence sales and should be controlled.

If a chain has several stores in similar areas, it can use several different experimental designs to obtain an estimate of price elasticity. A Latin square design statistical procedure may be applied. It involves the use of the same number of time periods, store groups, and price levels (Figure 8–1). Products priced at each level appear in each store group and in each time period. Data obtained from the Latin square design and subjected to an analysis of variance statistical test allow price effects to be separated from sales variation caused by store groups, time, and other random elements.[8] The chief disadvantage of the Latin square design is that the price labels must be changed every time period. This is not only a costly process, but each time period must allow the consumer to follow a normal purchasing pattern on the product(s) whose price is being changed. If the time periods are too short,

Figure 8–1   Example Illustrating the Use of the Latin Square Design to Estimate Price Elasticity

	FIRST SIX-WEEK PERIOD	SECOND SIX-WEEK PERIOD	THIRD SIX-WEEK PERIOD
Store Group A (10 Stores)	Product(s) Price 79¢	Product(s) Price 99¢	Product(s) Price 119¢
Store Group B (10 Stores)	Product(s) Price 99¢	Product(s) Price 119¢	Product(s) Price 79¢
Store Group C (10 Stores)	Product(s) Price 119¢	Product(s) Price 79¢	Product(s) Price 99¢

the estimate of sales obtained at low prices will be inflated because the consumer is just "stocking up" at bargain prices. Such a purchase pattern does not represent long-run behavior.

A less costly store testing procedure for retailers is the *before-and-after design*. This method uses several matched groups of stores. Sales are measured in each group during a pre-test (base) period. Then price changes are made in all but one group (called the "control group") of stores (Figure 8–2). Test product sales in each store are then recorded as a share of each store's total sales. The effects of the price change are measured by comparing the shares obtained by each group of stores.

Any estimation procedure is costly and time consuming, so retailers are likely to estimate the values of E_d for only their most important products.

Figure 8–2   Example Illustrating the Use of the Before-and-After Design to Estimate Price Elasticity

FOUR WEEKS PRE-TEST PERIOD	TWELVE WEEKS TEST PERIOD
Product(s) Priced at Regular Price—99¢— in All Stores	Store Group A—10 Stores Product(s) Price—79¢
	Store Group B—10 Stores Product(s) Price—99¢ (Control Group)
	Store Group C—10 Stores Product(s) Price—119¢

Price Lining

Price lining involves the search for merchandise that can be sold at previously determined retail price levels. It is contrary to markup pricing, which involves the purchase of merchandise and adding a markup to arrive at the retail price. Price lining results in selling merchandise at only a few (generally three to five) price levels. For example, men's sport coats could be separated into $69, $59, $49, $39, and $29 classes.

Price lining is said to offer an advantage to the consumer. It reduces the number of product classes and thereby simplifies comparison shopping. If the consumer's decision-making process is simplified, sales might be increased on both the main item (men's sport coats) and on complementary items (ties, shoes, slacks, belts, socks, etc.).

Retail price lining simplifies accounting and pricing procedures for the retailer because it reduces the number of price levels. Price lining makes it easier for the retail salesmen to convince the customers they should purchase the highest-quality line they can afford. The limited number of price lines can easily be associated with different levels of quality by the consumer. The different price classes may also provide convenient steps for making a price markdown if the merchandise does not sell. Care must be taken to ensure that the consumer actually perceives that the price has been reduced.

For example, men's sport coats that have been priced at $59 could simply be moved into the $49 line without advertising the price reduction. Price lining would make this more convenient. However, the advertising of a price decrease might be communicated more easily if the price were *not* reduced to exactly the level of the next price line ($49 in the case of a $59 sport coat). The full reduction to the next price level might confuse potential customers, who might think that the store is merely trying to advertise the $49 line and sell it at the regular price. Pricing the coat at $53 and/or careful advertisement writing could reduce this confusion.

The merchandise buyer may also encounter problems associated with price lining. Products must not only be selected on the basis of style, color, quality, price, etc., but they must also fit into the previously determined price lines. Price lines must be upgraded continually to reflect increases in wholesale purchase prices and increasing preferences by consumers for items possessing more quality. If the price lines are not upgraded by introducing a "new" top line and/or abandoning the lowest price line, markups will decline or quality must be reduced as wholesale prices increase.

Price lining is widely used despite the difficulties associated with it. However, the principles established in the discussion on markup pricing should be used to establish the price lines that best meet consumer needs.

Consumer Knowledge of Retail Prices

Reliable knowledge about consumers' price awareness is needed if an appropriate pricing strategy is to be established. If consumers don't know the price of any products, the price elasticity of demand is likely to be more inelastic, as they are not aware that identical or close substitute items are available at different prices in other outlets. High markups would maximize profits in this case.

If consumers have a great deal of knowledge about prices on many products, the price elasticity is likely to be elastic, since consumers are aware of the existence of substitute products. Relatively low markups would result in maximum profits for those products.

Consumers' knowledge of prices is more likely to fall somewhere between the two extremes. They may know only the prices of a small number of frequently purchased items. In such cases it is even more important to determine which items' prices are known by consumers. These items could be priced lower to give a low-price or discount image. The items whose prices are well known are also items that would respond best to advertised, temporary price reductions.

Studies of consumers' knowledge of prices must be conducted separately for each type of retail outlet. Published results from such studies are very limited. A study of consumers' awareness of fifty-nine highly competitive and frequently advertised grocery items revealed that 71 percent of the consumers were unable to estimate within 5 percent of the actual price.[9] The responses—from about 2,000 customers—were obtained by placing unpriced products on tables in the store and asking the consumers what prices the products sold for. This study revealed that consumers were not aware of highly competitive and frequently advertised products. They were probably less aware of the prices of other items sold in a supermarket. Consumer awareness can change over time and distance, so there is a need to conduct similar studies every two to three years.

Psychology of Retail Pricing

Markup pricing and/or price lining strategies can be used to establish a general price level. However, attention must be given to the psychological aspects of price when the specific price is established.

"Odd pricing," which uses prices like 39 cents and $4.95 rather than the nearly equivalent even prices of 40 cents and $5, is frequently practiced. A study of all products advertised by supermarkets in newspapers in twenty-three metropolitan areas revealed that 57 percent of all advertised prices ended in 9.[10] Another 15 percent of the prices ended in 5.

The practice of using odd pricing probably began as a safeguard against petty theft.[11] Even-price items tend to be paid for with the exact amount of cash, and the clerk can then serve other customers before ringing up a sale. This provides an opportunity for pocketing a portion of the proceeds. If every shopper demands a receipt, this type of theft can be prevented; but there are always a few customers—small children, for example—who don't obtain a sales slip. When odd prices are used, the customer is likely not to have the exact amount of cash, so the clerk must make change from the cash register. Some of the advantages of odd pricing have been lost by the universal adoption of local sales taxes, which tend to create similar change situations.

The actual impact of odd retail price endings on sales and profits is not determined in the published marketing literature. Experimentation is needed to determine if odd prices really promote sales. If they don't promote sales, they could be abandoned because they are "sticky" prices that could hinder profit-maximizing pricing decisions.

Multiple-unit prices are also used in selling frequently purchased items. The "Two for 50¢" or "Five for $1" multiple prices convey the impression of potential savings to the consumer. Generally, the multiple price ends in 9 (e.g., two for 39 cents), so the consumer saves 1 cent by buying two items simultaneously instead of one unit at 20 cents on two different trips. The savings may be sufficient to persuade the customer to buy a larger quantity. However, the psychological aspect of buying a larger quantity may give the impression of additional savings.

There appear to be several different types of psychological reactions to price. A *quantum effect*[12] occurs when a certain price is the maximum price that consumers will pay for any quantity of a product. For example, a product may not sell well at $1.05, but a package containing only four-fifths as much, clearly labeled as to quantity content, will sell well at 98 cents. In this case, $1 is a quantum point from the consumer viewpoint. This quantum psychological reaction may partially explain the popularity of using odd prices which are established just below the quantum point.

Consumers may also develop some idea of a fair price for many items. This results in a "best" price that will actually generate more sales than either a lower or higher price. A major retail chain discovered that a common hardware item sold better at $1.09 than it did at either 89 cents or $1.29.[13] Consumers apparently considered the 89 cents price too low to be attached to a quality item. The $1.09 price apparently reflected the image of a quality product to consumers.

Frequently, consumers think they can judge the cost of production. In this case their fair price standard is based upon the allowance of a modest profit, but no more. For example, many consumers may react negatively to a restaurant's pricing a cup of coffee at 25 cents because they know the approximate cost of the coffee used is about 4 cents. Few consumers will complain about paying 40 to 50 cents for a loaf of bread that contains only 6 cents worth of wheat or other ingredients. They are not able to judge the cost of materials that are used in bread making but can easily judge the cost of the materials used to make a cup of coffee. A lower markup usually must be charged when most consumers can accurately evaluate the production cost of an item.

DYNAMIC AND TACTICAL ASPECTS OF PRICING

Retail pricing strategies function as planned only when they are implemented effectively. Many decisions have to be made during these implementation efforts. These tactical decisions are concerned with day-to-day decisions which should be made within the guidelines established when the pricing strategy was determined. Tactical decisions are therefore the short-run decisions needed to carry out the basic pricing policy.

Many day-to-day pricing decisions are either passive responses to cost squeezes or estimated adaptations to what seem to be competitive requirements of the market. Many different price tactics can be utilized to make these day-to-day decisions more profitable. Familiarity with the different kinds of tactical price movements provides the background necessary if the retailer is going to expand or hold profitable markets.

Markdowns

Markdowns consist of a decrease from the original price of an item. The markdown percentage is usually stated as a percentage of the reduced selling price. In formula form,

$$\text{Markdown percentage} = \frac{\begin{pmatrix}\text{per unit original retail price}\end{pmatrix} - \begin{pmatrix}\text{per unit reduced retail price}\end{pmatrix}}{\text{per unit reduced price}} \times 100.$$

For example, the markdown percentage on a sport coat originally selling at \$49 but reduced to \$40 would be (\$9 / \$40) $\times$ 100, or 22½ percent.

One objective of markdown pricing is to convert surplus merchandise into cash that can be reinvested in faster-moving merchandise or in some other demand-stimulating activity. Some markdowns are caused by an oversupply of merchandise, which must be sold to reduce the store's inventory level. Oversupply may result from errors in purchasing merchandise, which can be "overbought" by an overly enthusiastic purchasing agent. Overbuying of an item can arise because of overly optimistic sales forecasting or because of an inappropriate merchandise assortment which does not meet consumers' needs or likes. Thus overbuying is likely to occur with any merchandise that goes out of fashion (or never becomes stylish) because of preferences for different styles, color, size, etc.

Poor timing in the arrival of merchandise can also result in the oversupply of merchandise. This is especially true of seasonal merchandise, which consumers buy only once a year to meet a specific need. If the store's supply has not arrived at the time of peak consumer demand, sales are likely to be lost. Anti-freeze and winter overshoes are examples of products that are likely to be purchased over a short period of time.

Markdowns may also be necessary when the correct quantity and quality merchandise is purchased but the selling and/or promotion efforts are deficient. Selling errors can originate from poor department management, a weak sales force, or a poor promotion program. Poor management may be revealed by a failure to interpret sales records early enough to spot items that are not selling well. Some retailers are now using computer systems to provide reliable inventory and sales data quickly. The sales force may contribute to the overstock problem by not exposing all of the products in the category, so that some items are unexposed until it is too late to sell them at regular prices.

Markdowns are required even in cases where proper purchasing and selling procedures are used. Odds and ends merchandise gradually accumulates over time, so most retailers use markdowns to unload the least desirable merchandise from their shelves.

Many markdowns are deliberately planned price reductions, designed to assist in sales promotion and in generating an image of meeting competition.

"Leader prices" are relatively low (or negative) markups on items that attract customers to the store, where, hopefully, they will also purchase other, regular-priced merchandise. Leader prices contribute little, if any, per unit profit, but may make substantial contributions to total dollar profits by generating added sales of products at regular prices. Leader items must be recognized as good values by customers, as their principal aim is to draw customer traffic. Good leader items are products whose normal price is known by most potential customers. A good leader item is usually purchased frequently by a large number of consumers.

The use of price leaders for a limited, specified time as a promotional device appears to create less disturbance among competition than general price reductions. General price reductions are likely to initiate a price war because they offer the threat of a permanent price cut. Leader prices are more acceptable to competition because the prices are viewed as only temporary reductions and hence are considered part of the normal pricing routine.

Leader prices are generally used on high-frequency purchase products, and a good price leader is:

1. Well known, widely used, and appealing to many customers
2. Priced low enough so that many people can buy it
3. Not so low in price that price cuts will generate no interest
4. Not generally bought in large quantities and stored
5. Likely to have a high price elasticity of demand
6. Not in close competition with other products in the retailer's merchandise assortment.[14]

Types of Markdown

Leader prices can be classified by the degree of markdown and the purpose of the promotion.

LOW-PRICE LEADERS   Low-price leaders are products whose prices represent bargain prices. Low-price leader items are not priced below the actual cost to the retailer but merely represent a reduced markup percentage. The low-price leader does not violate the intent of most unfair trade practices acts, which usually prohibit sales of merchandise at less than cost when the intent is to injure competition. Often, large chains are able to make "special purchases" of seasonal merchandise at reduced costs which serve as excellent low-price traffic generators.

LOSS-LEADER PRICING   Loss-leader pricing involves sales of an item at a price below the actual cost to the retailer. The objective of loss-leader pricing is to attract customers to the store. A good merchandising program can then be used to stimulate consumers to make additional purchases of other regular-price items. The profit obtained from sales of the regular-price items must overcome the loss incurred on the loss-leader items. Proper placement of loss-leader merchandise within a department can encourage such additional purchases. Thus loss-leader pricing is really a form of promotion, because loss-leader pricing costs the retailer money in the same manner as additional advertising.

The legality of loss-leader pricing must be established before it is used by retailers. Most states have passed laws prohibiting "sales below cost" and/or laws that establish a minimum markup if the intent of the pricing practice is to injure or extinguish competition. Exceptions are usually provided for specific merchandise which is sold for (1) clearance or close out, (2) charitable purposes, (3) liquidation of a business, or (4) liquidation of perishable, seasonal, or damaged goods.[15]

BAIT-LEADER PRICING   Bait-leader pricing involves the use of an advertised price on an item that is not intended to be sold. It represents a very low price on a well-known item which is found by the customer to be relatively unattractive after he arrives at the store. Bait-leader pricing could involve the advertising of a very low price on a relatively low quality (or small) item that is not likely to be purchased by a large percentage of the potential customers. After the consumer arrives at the store, the sales clerk uses persuasion to upgrade the consumer's purchase (at unreduced prices) to a better quality than was originally advertised. For example, USDA standard-grade beef may be advertised at 79 cents per pound, but the sales clerk would suggest that the good, choice, or prime grades are better-quality meats and would be better accepted by other family members.

Another version of bait-leader pricing involves the advertisement of some central component item (e.g., a new-model car) at an extremely low price. However, the price is quoted on only a portion of the total merchandise that is likely to be purchased. Accessory items are sold at the regular price; so the total "package" purchase price may not be lower than competitive prices. Accessory items may take the form of both supplementary and complementary items.

The use of bait-leader pricing could also involve advertising an item which is in very short supply at a very low price and telling the customers who rush to the store that the last unit of the advertised item has just been sold. However, this practice has been made illegal and is policed by the Federal Trade Commission (hereafter referred to as the FTC). The FTC watches over deceptive acts by firms that do a substantial share of their business in interstate commerce. All firms may be required to make good on all offers made in advertisements, according to current legislation. The FTC publishes guides for businessmen who want clarification of the legality of related practices. Examples are *Guides against Deceptive Pricing, Guides against Bait Advertising,* and *Guides against Deceptive Advertising of Guarantees.*

Firms should exercise care when any of the leader-pricing techniques are used. Low-price leaders and some forms of loss-leader and bait-leader pricing may be legal pricing practices, but they may strengthen customer support for the consumerism movement. However, long-run businesses must be based upon providing consumer satisfaction. A poor post-purchase feeling, generated by a consumer belief of having "been taken," will not promote future patronage. Thus leader pricing must be used in a way that will not offend or mislead consumers. The low-price leader and the loss-leader are not likely to offend consumers if the featured items are always available for purchase in quantity and quality without special qualifications (coupon clipping, etc.). The consumerism movement is here, and—like it or not—the trend is toward more consumer protection from deceptive pricing of all kinds.

OFF-SEASON PRICING   Off-season pricing is another form of markdown. Firms engaged in the more seasonal service or retail businesses (e.g., travel, resort, and tourist service) use off-season and special group-pricing practices to reach a different market segment than their regular-season customer. The off-season business may be promoted at the partial expense of the regular-season business, but the increased business volume may result in lower year-round average costs that justify price reductions.

Retail firms use special advertisements, mailings, and reduced off-season prices to generate a more constant sales level than they would otherwise attain. The more constant sales level reduces cost by better use of the somewhat fixed level of personnel who are needed to operate a retail outlet.

Farm machinery retailers have been using off-season price reductions during the fall and winter months to provide a more reliable sales forecast, which results in a more constant work load over the year. Sales are also promoted by offering a cash discount and delaying the payment until spring (the normal purchase period), with little or no interest charges being assessed.

Timing of Markdowns

The appropriate time to mark down the price on merchandise depends on many factors. Stores catering to the same clientele on a frequent basis will want to mark down prices early on items that are not selling well. Stores relying on sales made to different transient customers may delay the price reductions and hope to make additional sales at regular prices.

Earlier markdowns are more likely to be taken on fashionable and/or perishable merchandise than on items that are not subject to sudden changes in fashion or spoilage. Taking early markdowns keep a retailer's stock fresh and more in tune with the latest fashion preferences. Retailers may mark down a fashion item when its sales begin to decline if the outlet is estimated to be in an oversupplied condition. Seasonal items whose sales are dependent upon fashionability are usually reduced in price as soon as the rush of seasonal buying is completed and excess stock is estimated to be held in inventory. For example, ski equipment prices may be reduced in January, although sales are still made during February and March.

Staple goods prices are usually reduced if the supply is excessive or if the products have been on the shelf long enough that their appearance and/or quality is about to decline. Staple items whose demand fluctuates seasonally are usually marked down if the store does not have sufficient low-cost storage space to carry them until next year. An evaluation of the costs incurred in placing these items in inventory is needed before seasonal items are stored for nearly one year.

Fashion merchandise is not carried over, no matter how costly the markdown. If it didn't sell now, it will not sell next year. "Recognize the mistake, mark it down, take the bath, and get merchandise that will sell' is a maxim of the trade.

Mass merchandisers are also more likely to use earlier markdowns than are exclusive outlets. Exclusive shops prefer to delay price reductions to discourage bargain hunters (sometimes referred to as "cherry pickers") who select only markdown items and thereby detract from the stores' class appeal. If price lining is used, exclusive outlets can move slow-selling items into the next lower price line without advertising the price reductions. This practice is less likely to attract "cherry pickers," and could increase sales to their normal market segment.

Pricing for Special Sales

Pricing for special sales poses particular problems of pricing for the retail operator. The amount of the markdown is not easily determined. The markdown level must be sufficient to generate sales on items that were not selling well. Department stores have been found to reduce the retail price by about a third on the first markdown.[16] The retailer must consider the quality of the merchandise and its sales relative to other items sold in his store.

For example, a retail store carried two major price lines of women's hosiery; one line was priced at $1 and the other at $2. A special purchase was made on the $2 line at a cost of 65 cents. Sales were poor when the better line was offered as a special at $1 per pair. When they were marked up to $1.14 a pair and could be more easily differentiated from the lower-priced line, they sold quite well. The higher price represented a higher value to consumers, and this increased sales.[17] However, reactions of competitors, and of consumers who bought the merchandise at the regular price, also must be considered.

The retailer must evaluate the effect that advertising and sales effort have upon sales. Other things being equal, a large promotional effort can stimulate as many sales at a moderate markdown as a larger markdown promoted on a small scale.

The language used to advertise special sale items usually involves hoopla and sensational-type advertising. Words and phrases such as "incredible," "unbelievable," "fantastic," "free," "2 for 1 sale," "1¢ sale," etc. are frequently used to describe promotional sales, but indiscriminate use of such terms has been overdone by too many retailers. The FTC has been increasing its regulation activity by forbidding the use of deliberately deceptive language in the promotion of price specials.

This increased level of regulatory activity, plus the consumerism movement, are likely to result in a continual growth of informational advertisements. Such advertisements clearly state all the terms and conditions of the sale. The advertisements would answer such questions as, "What is the product? How can it be used? What does the price tag include and what's extra? Does it come fully assembled?" These important questions are being asked by both consumers and the government.

Pricing Restrictions

The retailer is not entirely free to set any price that he may believe will maximize sales and/or profits. A manufacturer or distributor of a well-known branded product can strongly influence the retail price if he threatens to withhold the product from retail outlets that do not comply with the manufacturer's pricing suggestions. Manufacturers and distributors control much of the marketing effort of franchised dealers (retailers), who represent the manufacturer or distributor in the market. Franchising allows the manufacturer to restrict his product to a few outlets which he expects to price his products according to his suggestions.

In nonfranchising situations, manufacturers sometimes pre-ticket their products with "suggested retail prices." The retailer does not *have* to sell the item at the supplier's suggested price, but it is inconvenient to re-price the merchandise. In some cases, the re-marking of "suggested retail price" items can lead to strained dealer-supplier relationships. Alternatively, re-ticketing to a lower price has been used by discount retailers to reinforce a "low price" image.

The structure (number and size) of the local retail competition can influence a retailer to stress other, non-price sales stimulating devices. In some cases, smaller, less powerful retailers may simply price their goods according to the price used by the dominant firm. The prevalence of price leadership of this type certainly impairs the effectiveness of the individual's price-setting policy, which should be designed to maximize long-run profits. In other instances, several retailers of equal power may recognize that a reduction in price by any one of them will result in a retaliatory price reduction by the others. Such firms would probably attempt to prevent price wars by emphasizing non-price competition. Non-price competition has two general benefits: it may be longer lasting and it is more difficult to imitate. For the retailer attempting to build a distinct store image, both benefits are important. However, low profits by any of the current retailers or the entry of a new competitor will usually disturb static pricing after a period of time.

A retailer's freedom to establish prices is also limited by governmental authority at many different levels—local, state, and national. States and the federal government limit a retailer's price-setting power by preventing the maintenance of high prices if retailers get together and make price-fixing agreements. Governmental authority can also impose minimum price levels which prevent a retailer from cutting prices too drastically.

Fair Trade Laws (Resale Price Maintenance)

Federal and some state laws sanction resale price maintenance agreements which allow the seller of a brand name or trademark item to set a minimum price which the retailer must charge his customers. Of course, this reduces the retailer's price-setting freedom. The Miller-Tydings Act (1937) and the McGuire Act (1952) allow manufacturers to establish the resale prices of brand name merchandise in states whose legislatures have authorized such price fixing. However, manufacturers cannot legally establish the resale prices of brand name merchandise for all retailers in states whose legislatures have not passed acts containing a "non-signer" clause.

A non-signer clause enables a manufacturer who is engaged in interstate commerce to sign a resale price-maintenance agreement with *one* retailer in a state on the retail price of a branded item and thereby bind all other retailers in that state to the price agreement. As a result of this legal authority, it is possible for a manufacturer of a branded good, which is in competition with other goods, to fix the retail price of his item within any of the seventeen states which have passed legislation containing a non-signer clause.

The states where retail price maintenance is legal because of the non-signer clause are Arizona, California, Connecticut, Delaware, Illinois, Maine, Maryland, Massachusetts, New Hampshire, New Jersey, New York, North Carolina, North Dakota, Ohio, Tennessee, Virginia, and Wisconsin.[18]

Nineteen states operate under a "signer-only" clause. These fair trade states have passed laws that require only the actual signers of fair trade contracts to adhere to the suggested manufacturers' prices.[19] The laws of these states permit non-signer retailers to resell fair traded goods at prices of their own choosing. These laws also prohibit any agreements by which a retailer refuses to deal with any non-signer retailer.[20]

There are fourteen states that have no fair trade laws. Retailers in these states do not have to use the price that is fixed by manufacturers or wholesalers who use fair trade laws in the seventeen states where the non-signer clause is in effect. Thus federal fair trade laws do not inhibit a retailer's pricing freedom in the states where there are no local fair trade laws. A recent FTC complaint alleges that Corning Glass Works, in establishing its fair trade programs, has entered illegally into contracts with wholesalers and retailers in these fourteen states where there are no local fair trade laws. These contracts allegedly are written primarily to prevent Corning's goods from being sold to discounters in the nineteen signer-only states.

> By a provision in which non–fair trade state resellers agree "not to sell or transfer" Corning's "products to any reseller unless such reseller has agreed with Corning to maintain Corning's fair trade prices." Corning's standard form contracts are said to prevent "free trade state wholesalers and retailers from making sales of Respondent's goods in interstate commerce to all non-signer retailers . . . in the signer-only states." As so written, the complaint alleges that Corning's agreements with non–fair trade state resellers are outside the McGuire Act's exemption from federal antitrust attack.
>
> In another count, the complaint asserts that although Corning's boycott contracts may have once been lawful in the nineteen signer-only states, they are today illegal. The laws of these states, the complaint alleges, "not only permit non-signers to resell fair traded commodities at prices of their own choosing, they also prohibit or render unenforceable any agreements by which a reseller is bound to refuse to deal with any non-signer."[21]

In general, the use of retail price maintenance has been declining because of legal difficulties and a changed attitude on the part of manufacturers. Apparently, most manufacturers believe that the volume sales made by discount sellers offer more of a market opportunity than a market threat. Stiff competition from similar products, manufactured by companies that use discount oulets, has forced some manufacturing firms to abandon their practice of resale price maintenance.

Today the major advocates of fair trade laws are small-scale independent merchants who prefer to compete on the basis of product selection and service instead of using any form of price competition. Retail price maintenance penalizes the low-cost retailer who wants to sell his goods below the fair traded minimum price. In general, the fair trade laws also result in a higher level of retail prices that consumers have to pay for fair trade merchandise.[22]

The recent consumerism trend is likely to result in a continued decline in the use of resale price maintenance.

Unfair Sales and Unfair Trade Practices Acts

Unfair sales and unfair trade practices acts establish a mandatory minimum price for all goods sold in states where "unfair sales practices," "unfair trade practices," "minimum price laws," "minimum markup laws," or sales-below-cost laws (known by some other name) are on the books. The unfair sales act in some states defines the minimum price as the cost of merchandise without the addition of markup. Other states require retailers to add at least a specified percent of their invoice cost of goods. Usually the minimum retailing costs exceed the specified legal minimum markup percentage. Thus unfair sales acts normally prevent the practice of drastic price cutting. However, the unfair sales acts do not generally force an efficient retailer to raise his prices above a low price level, based upon his low cost of operation, low merchandise costs, and/or a low profit margin percentage on a large sales volume. This would not be true if the minimum specified legal markup is higher than the markup required for profitably marketing some items. In this case, the unfair sales act can result in consumers' paying higher prices than they would pay if this type of act were not law.

There are about twenty-five states that use unfair sales acts to establish a minimum price on retail goods. These acts are usually supported by small-scale, independent retailers who wish to prevent or inhibit the establishment of large-scale retailers. Minimum markup laws are designed to prevent predatory price cutting, which a large, powerful retailer could use to drive small retailers out of business. The large retailer may then increase his prices above the original price level, as soon as the competition is eliminated.

Predatory pricing of this kind is most likely to occur in areas where the retail competition is already weak. To be successful, this type of predatory pricing would not only have to eliminate current retailers but also discourage potential competitors from establishing a new outlet in the area. New retailers are likely to move into the area if the original predator uses an abnormally high pricing policy after he has eliminated all competition.

Unfair sales practices acts are also supported because they curb the use of loss-leader pricing, which may deceive customers into patronizing the store with drastically reduced prices on only a few items to which the consumer is price sensitive.

DECEPTIVE PRICING The FTC regulates deceptive pricing which may mislead the consumer into believing that he is getting a bargain.

FORMER-PRICE COMPARISONS Retailers can use *former-price comparisons,* which indicate that an item was formerly priced at a higher level but is now reduced to a new price level. To do so, however, they must be certain that the former price has been regularly used in sales during the recent course of business.[23]

COMPARABLE-PRICE COMPARISONS Bargain advertising that offers a reduction from the price charged by other local retailers for either the *identical* or *comparable* merchandise is legitimate if the higher price is a genuine price, regularly charged by merchants in the local trade area.[24] Thus the advertisement of brand X cameras, "Price Elsewhere $75; Our Price $50," is legitimate if the higher price is truly established and if brand X cameras are made available to the customers.

This type of price advertising has several advantages. The retailer does not have to establish the higher comparative price in his own store, so he may introduce the article to his customers at the lower price and maintain the lower price on a permanent basis or raise the price later. This type of comparative pricing also combines the pull of a brand name product with the lure of a bargain to generate additional sales.

Use of *comparable* merchandise pricing is allowed if it is made clear to the consumer that a comparison is being made with other merchandise of essentially similar quality that is regularly available in the local market area. The terms "comparable value $75" or "comparable retail $75" can be used if the comparable merchandise is "competing merchandise" of "like grade and quality."[25] The FTC also permits the retailer to relate a bargain price to one "being charged" by him for other merchandise of like grade and quality. Thus a retailer may compare the price of his private label brand with a higher-priced nationally advertised brand that he also carries, provided the private label product is of the same quality or quantity as that of the national brand.

Under revised FTC guides, a retailer is permitted to rely on a "good-faith estimate" (possibly obtained by a market survey) of the higher price that he advertises. A retailer operating on a regional or nationwide scale need not investigate all prices *throughout* his market area if he determines the price at which substantial sales are made by principal retail outlets in *representative* communities. However, if such information is not available, the FTC advises that price-comparison claims not be made.[26]

FREE OFFERS   Offering and giving free goods is a very effective merchandising and advertising method for attracting customers. The word "free" usually refers to an offer involving *something other* than an unconditional gift the consumer can receive without doing something or paying something. The "free" offer usually is an offer to give something if the customer purchases other goods or services for a stated price. In reality, most of these offers are merely price reductions, which are legal if the word "free" is not used in a deceptive manner.

Practices that are condemned by the FTC are:

1. Failure to fully disclose the terms and conditions of the bargain offer "at the outset"
2. Increasing the usual and regular price of the article to be purchased
3. Reducing the quality of the article to be purchased
4. Reducing the quantity or size of the article to be purchased.[27]

All bargain offers that are based upon the purchase of other items are judged on the basis of these four recommendations. The designation of the offer as "free," "buy one, get one free," "two for one sale," "half-price sale," "1 cent sale" or "50 percent off" does not influence the fact that the offer will be judged according to its adherence to the four guidelines.

An unconditional gift is not in violation of the FTC Act if it is truly a gratuity. Examples of such gifts are product samples received in the mail or distributed door to door, balloons and lollipops given to children who shop with their parents at a retail outlet, and coupons which must be mailed to a place of business. The inclusion in a "mail in" offer of a request for a small sum to cover handling and mailing costs is legitimate if the amount is no more than the actual cost to the distributor.[28]

CENTS-OFF PRICING   The FTC is also involved in ensuring honesty in "cents off" promotion pricing. Under current regulations, the manufacturer must print the amount of "cents off" on the label and the retailer must stamp the resulting price on the box. In addition, the store must post a shelf placard that contains the product's regular price in that store.[29] For example, a can of corn might be labeled "10 Cents Off Regular Price." The store would stamp the can lid with the resulting price—say 20 cents—and also post a shelf placard saying "Regular Price 30 cents."

Price Ceiling Regulations

All deceptive pricing, fair trade, and minimum markup laws restrict the pricing freedom of the retailers, but the other restrictions are associated with price freezes. During some of the various phases of 1971–1973, retailers' prices were both frozen at base period prices and controlled on the basis of customary percentage markups that were added to the cost of the merchandise or service. The absolute prices or the customary percentage markups were not allowed to exceed those prices or markups used during the various base periods.

Price ceiling regulations provide another illustration of the trend toward more legal restriction on a retailer's freedom to determine his own price levels. The additional time and effort required to comply with price freeze regulations results in extra cost. If similar profit margins are maintained, this added cost eventually must be passed on to the consumer through higher prices. Apparently, governmental officials believed that price increases would be greater if free pricing prevailed than under controlled pricing, which requires more record keeping and new placard-posting costs.

Effects of Price Restrictions upon Retailers

The main feature of our free-enterprise economy has been competitive pricing. A major unanswered question now is, "How much can a distributor's pricing freedom be limited if he is still expected to provide for an easy transfer of goods, service, and manpower?" On one hand, fair trade and minimum markup laws may prevent a retailer from being too competitive on the price variable. On the other hand, price ceiling restrictions limit the upward movement retail prices. Considerable time must be spent making sure that the prices and the communication of the price level to consumers are permissible according to the latest legal interpretation. These additional costs will eventually be passed on to consumers in the form of higher prices, unless profit margins are allowed to decline. The consumer is paying for more information, which will presumably allow him to make more intelligent purchasing decisions.

These pressures result in a preference, on the part of most retailers, to concentrate on non-price competition instead of outright price competition. Thus we are likely to continue to see more examples of Professor Malcolm

McNair's wheel of retailing. The new retail firms are likely to appear as low-margin, low-price establishments, but they will gradually upgrade their facilities and services and thus join the majority retailers by shifting to non-price competition. The retail environment is again appropriate for the entry of new low-price retailers. (One of the major elements of non-price competition—promotion—will be discussed in the next three chapters.)

SUMMARY

Generally, retailers use markup pricing because it is a convenient method of pricing the very large number of items they stock. Retailers cannot afford to spend the time and effort needed to determine the best price to charge on every item. However, few retailers use the same markup for all items. The markup percentage that is generally used varies inversely with merchandise turnover and the price of the item.

For maximum profits, retailer markups should also vary inversely with the value of the price elasticity of the demand coefficient. Estimates of retail elasticity of demand are usually based upon the experience of the retailer or upon representative markups charged by similar outlets.

Experimental techniques can also be used to obtain elasticity estimates. Retailers can use the estimates to identify items whose sales are greatly influenced by price. Lower markups can generally stimulate greater profits on these items, besides drawing additional consumers to the outlet.

Consumers do not always perceive prices from an objective, mathematical viewpoint, so the general price level must be "fine tuned" to be compatible with consumer psychology. Multiple-unit pricing and odd pricing are two pricing techniques that might satisfy consumer preferences for certain exact prices.

Retailers use markdowns to stimulate purchases of items that (1) have not been selling well, (2) are overstocked, or (3) will draw potential consumers into the store, where—hopefully—they will purchase other, regular-price merchandise.

Firms should use only pricing techniques that provide long-run consumer satisfaction. A post-purchase feeling of having "been taken" will not promote long-run purchases.

A price markdown is not likely to offend customers if the featured items are always available for purchase in the same quantity and quality, and without the consumer's having to meet special qualifications which are not clearly defined in the retailer's advertisements or price labels.

Some retailers are pressured by fair trade and minimum markup laws to maintain their prices at high levels. Price ceiling legislation limits the amount of price increases that can be made by retailers. So, despite the apparent price-conscious mood of consumers, these legal pressures could cause well-established retailers to continue to rely upon non-price elements of the marketing mix (such as advertising, service, etc.) to attract consumers.

QUESTIONS

1. If a decrease in price will generate higher sales, why will it not necessarily generate higher profits? What factors other than price must be considered?

2. Why do slower-moving items usually have a higher markup?

3. If a retailer requires an annual gross profit margin of $500 and he knows (from studying the competition) that he can obtain an $80 per unit margin, what turnover must he have to carry this product? If a 10 percent reduction in per unit profit margin results in a 15 percent increase in turnover, what are the new values for turnover, per unit profit, and gross profit margin? Discuss the total effect of such a price cut.

4. If a retailer finds that in the first quarter he sells 1,000 units at $5 and in the second quarter he sells 1,200 units at $4.75, what would you recommend that he do in the third quarter, assuming no correction for seasonality and assuming constant costs?

5. What factors, other than turnover, influence retail markup? How might a retailer use these factors to increase his gross per unit profit? If a retailer used these factors to increase gross per unit profit, what other factors would tend to limit net profit?

6. Define price lining. Why would a retailer want to use this practice? What is meant by upgrading a price line?

7. What is the effect of consumer knowledge of retail prices on price elasticity? How can a retailer obtain information about this knowledge? Do you think it is ethical for a retailer to take advantage of a lack of this knowledge on the part of consumers by using a higher markup? What are the implications of consumer price knowledge in maximizing the benefits of advertising expenditures?

8. Why is odd pricing used frequently in retailing? Why are multiple-unit prices also used?

9. List as many factors as you can that determine the amount of markup a retailer can use. Briefly discuss how each of these factors affects markup. Pick several high, low, and intermediate markup goods and show how these factors affect the markups.

10. What items would you suggest as leader price items in a:
    a. Supermarket?
    b. Sporting goods store?
    c. Men's clothing store?
    d. Ladies' boutique?
    e. Hardware/appliance store?
    What characteristics do your leader-price items have in common?

11. What precautions must a retailer take when practicing leader pricing? Which of the various leader-pricing techniques is least likely to injure repeat business and customer relations?

12. What types of goods are likely to be marked down quickly? Why? What types of retailers are likely to mark down their merchandise quickly? Why?

13. Why do retailers frequently prefer non-price competition over price competition?

14. If a tire dealer advertises that his customers receive one tire free for each tire purchased at the regular price, what FTC regulations must the tire dealer meet? Could a retailer use this approach continuously as part of his long-run promotion scheme?

15. What recourse do retailers have if prices are controlled to the extent that they cannot be used as a competitive device? Do you think that price ceilings and minimum price levels are in the public interest? What market distortions would you expect if these measures are carried to the extreme?

FOOTNOTES

[1] Roger Dickinson, "Markup in Department Store Management," *Journal of Marketing* (January 1967), pp. 32–34.

[2] Turnover is usually measured by dividing total sales by the average level of inventory valued at selling prices.

[3] Bob R. Holden, *The Structure of a Retail Market and the Market Behavior of Retail Units* (Englewood Cliffs, N.J.: Prentice-Hall, 1960), p. 72.

[4] Private label brands are brand names that are owned by a wholesaler or retailer.

[5] *Annual Statement Studies* (Philadelphia: Robert Morris Associates, 1970), pp. 98–119.

[6] The "absolute" value indicates that any value of E_d from 0 to minus 0.99 falls in the inelastic section of the demand curve. The demand curve indicates the quantity of an item that will be purchased, other things being equal, at various price levels during a particular time period. In graphic form, the demand curve generally appears as a downward-sloping curve.

A more detailed explanation of the elasticity concept can be found in Richard H. Leftwich, *Introduction to Microeconomics* (New York: Holt, Rinehart and Winston, 1970), pp. 62–68.

[7] Holden, *Structure of a Retail Market*, p. 72.

[8] Seymour Banks, *Experimentation in Marketing* (New York: McGraw-Hill, 1965), chap. 5.

[9] *Colonial Study* (New York: Progressive Grocer, 1962), p. C105.

[10] Dik Warren Twedt, "Does the '9 Fixation' in Retail Pricing Really Promote Sales?" *Journal of Marketing* (October 1965), pp. 54–55.

[11] Ibid., p. 55.

[12] Chester R. Wasson, *Managerial Economics* (New York: Appleton-Century-Crofts, 1966), p. 222.

[13] Ibid., p. 223.

[14] Roland S. Vaile, E. T. Grether, and Reavis Cox, *Marketing in the American Economy* (New York: Ronald Press, 1952), p. 447.

[15] Marshall C. Howard, *Legal Aspects of Marketing* (New York: McGraw-Hill, 1964), pp. 44–45.

[16] Richard M. Cyert and James G. March, *A Behavioral Theory of the Firm* (Englewood Cliffs, N.J.: Prentice-Hall, 1963), pp. 139–140.

[17] Oswald Knauth, "Considerations in the Selling of Retail Prices," *Journal of Marketing*, 14 (July 1949): 8.

[18] *Federal Trade Commission News*, Federal Trade Commission, Washington D.C., October 8, 1971, p. 3.

[19] Ibid., p. 1.

[20] Ibid., p. 2.

[21] Ibid., p. 3.

[22] Jerome C. Darnell, "The Impact of Quality Stabilization," *Journal of Marketing Research* (August 1965), pp. 274–282.

[23] Earl W. Kintner, *A Primer on the Law of Deceptive Practices* (New York: Macmillan, 1971), p. 157.

[24] Ibid., pp. 161–162.

[25] Ibid.

[26] Ibid.

[27] Ibid., p. 171.

[28] Ibid., p. 187.

[29] "Cents Off Rules Demanded," *Laramie* (Wyoming) *Boomerang*, November 26, 1971, p. 1.

LIGHTHOUSE FOR THE BLIND
Retail Pricing

The Lighthouse for the Blind is a national organization devoted to providing meaningful employment and work training opportunities for persons classified as legally blind.

The Lighthouse for the Blind is a name or identity that has been used by several workshops throughout the nation. The different shops are identified by many names, but all are dedicated to providing meaningful employment and work training opportunities for persons classified as legally blind. There are eighty shops throughout the United States and Puerto Rico that contribute to and participate in a coordinated effort of government sales and research into new products. This organization is known as the National Industries for the Blind, and it oversees the use of the Skilcraft trademark.

The Lighthouse for the Blind manufacturers a variety of products for use by industry, government, and the consumer. The consumer items manufactured in its factories consist primarily of household cleaning hand tools, such as mops, plastic dust pans, and several types of brooms. Although the complete line includes other items, such as pants hangers, the largest dollar volume of sales in the consumer products division comes from the major household cleaning tools.

The products produced in a particular Lighthouse for the Blind factory are often shipped to other affiliate plants, where they are used to complete the retail line of the local Lighthouse plant. There is a standing national rule that the product line sold by any Lighthouse affiliate must consist of at least 75 percent "blind made" labor.

The Dallas office, like other plants, has traditionally employed a sales force of blind salesmen to sell its products on a house-to-house basis. Over the years, this sales force had stabilized at around six full-time men.

A continuous recruiting program is in force for new salesmen, but they are difficult to locate. The requirement of being legally blind automatically narrows the field. In addition, the salesmen are paid on a commission basis. The work itself is physically demanding as it requires continuous walking in all types of weather with a sales kit of items that weighs approximately 60 pounds.

The sales force assembles at the plant before 8 a.m. each morning and is driven by Andy, the sales supervisor, to the neighborhood to be canvassed that day. Andy remains with them in the truck throughout the day. An inventory of products is carried in the truck so that sales can be made on a one-call basis.

Throughout the years, Andy and his crew have discovered that sales to middle-income homes are the most productive. Apartments often have restrictions against door-to-door sales, the steps are difficult for blind people to climb, and many residents are not home during the day. Low-income areas have never been productive, nor have the very wealthy areas.

Nevertheless, Mr. Doug Johanning, sales manager, and Mr. Austin G. Scott, executive director, were convinced that a large sales potential existed in this market. They also agreed that it could best be reached through displays in neighborhood supermarkets.

Discussions had been held with the buying committees and managers of supermarket chains and there was genuine interest in handling the Lighthouse line in special rack displays. These items would be sold under the national Skilcraft tradename, the same name under which the products are sold door to door. The line carried in the supermarkets would not be exactly the same as that sold by the blind salesmen.

Lighthouse for the Blind products had traditionally been sold at a premium price at the door. The products were well known for their high quality, but in addition there was a strong element of "sentiment" in the consumer's purchase decision. Market research studies and experience had demonstrated that a heavy percentage of housewives felt sorry for the salesmen and were willing to pay higher prices than for competitive products in the store.

For the most part, supermarkets were interested in carrying the line, but only if the prices were lowered. They did not believe that the sympathy motive would have a carryover to an unmanned display in the supermarket. In addition, they did not want to carry lines that would be noncompetitive with other food chains.

Mr. Scott and Mr. Johanning realized this might cause embarrassment to their sales crew, and could result in lower morale and possibly in reduced sales. At the same time, they believed the market potential through supermarket sales might be double the present volume sold on a door-to-door basis.

Apartment growth in Dallas had been phenomenal, as well as the increase in working mothers. These developments constituted a reduced possible-market penetration for the sales force.

Although the possibility of supermarket sales excited the management, it had absolutely no intention of eliminating or reducing the activity of the salesmen. In fact, the opposite was true. The Lighthouse was actively engaged in a sales training program for its salesmen with the volunteer help of top sales marketing executives from the Dallas Sales Marketing Executives' Organization.

DISCUSSION QUESTIONS

1. Is the Lighthouse faced with an "either-or" situation between supermarket trade and its salesmen? If not, what alternatives do you see?
2. Would you recommend lowering the door-to-door prices to make the products competitive with those in the supermarket?
3. Is it possible that supermarket business and door-to-door business are noncompetitive?
4. Do you believe that the average housewife is aware of the price for a broom or mop? Would she be likely to notice a difference in price between the store and the door?

HANS AUTO PARTS
Pricing and Promotion

Hans Auto Parts is located in a small neighborhood shopping center known as Northgate Mall in the suburb of Irving, Texas, northwest of Dallas. For years Irving was one of the fastest growing cities in the U.S.A., and grew from a sleepy town to a city of over 100,000. The growth has continued as old homes and vacant lots give way to apartment complexes.

Northgate Mall has only five or six small specialty shops, a short-order cafe, and a medium-size independent supermarket. The local office of the state drivers' license bureau is also located in the center. Hans Auto Parts is located in a corner of the L-shape center and is near a barbershop, the license bureau, and a teenage billiard-recreation center.

A sign painted on the window and a plastic "Auto Parts and Supplies" sign above the door serve as means of identification.

Although the store has been in that location for two and a half years, it has been operated by the new owner, Mr. Paul Collingsworth, for only five months. The interior layout is similar to most auto part stores, with a large counter separating the parts section from the front, where auto accessories are displayed for customer shopping.

Parts and accessories for most American cars and many foreign makes, particularly Volkswagen, are carried at "discount" prices—that is, prices below those charged by auto dealers. Although prices and parts availability are good, business could be better.

The problem, according to Mr. Collingsworth, seems to be that "most people just don't know we exist." People who have lived in Irving for years, and drive by the shopping center regularly, don't seem to know about Hans Auto Parts.

During his five months of operation, Mr. Collingsworth has tried hand-bills but has received a very low response from them. He questioned whether they had all been delivered. Yellow Page advertising was also used, and the local paper was being considered. However, it is uncertain how much of the potential market could be reached with the local paper. It is felt by Mr. Collingsworth that the apartment complexes, with younger residents, are probably good market targets, but the paper seems to be subscribed to primarily by homeowners.

One of the promotional techniques used by Hans Auto Parts is the sale of well-known brands of motor oil at discount prices. Approximately 8 percent of the total floor space in front of the counter is occupied by open cases of motor oil. These sell at prices considerably below the prices in filling stations. For example, one of the top brands sells for 65 cents a can, as opposed to 90 or 95 cents at nearby filling stations.

There are three discount houses and a freight salvage store within a 5-minute driving radius that undersell Hans Auto Parts, and Mr. Collingsworth said he simply cannot match their prices. In the case of the discount store, oil seems to be used as a loss leader.

As a rule of thumb, all items sold by Mr. Collingsworth have to bring a 30 percent minimum margin, yet motor oil brings only 15 to 20 percent. For that reason, most other discount auto parts stores in the area refuse to carry oil. Instead, they place higher-margin items in the space that would otherwise be occupied by motor oil. Mr. Collingsworth has considered doing the same, yet he knows that motor oil customers often buy other items, such as filters and spark plugs, at the same time.

It is not known how many of their customers would continue to patronize the store if motor oil was not available. Each of the discount stores carries a limited line of plugs, tune-up kits, and filters for popular U.S. makes, although the assortments cannot compare with Hans Auto Parts.

Wholesale prices of motor oil have been climbing in the past weeks and a decision has to be made whether to raise retail prices or drop the entire line. The distributor will not give even a 2 percent discount for cash, and he delivers only once per week. This means that Mr. Collingsworth or his help often have to travel to the distributor's warehouse to pick up additional cases, or run out.

DISCUSSION QUESTIONS

1. What types of advertising and promotion should Hans Auto Parts try to attract additional customers?

2. Who do you believe is the major market segment for discount auto parts such as those carried by Mr. Collingsworth? How far will a customer travel to trade at a store such as Hans Auto Parts?
3. Would you advise Mr. Collingsworth to discontinue selling motor oil? If so, what item should replace the oil?
4. Should the price of motor oil be increased to keep up with the wholesale increases or would it be better to take an even smaller retail margin just to attract customers?

CHAPTER 9

Chateau Pyrenees

Dining Magnificence
at its most Magnificent

*7 course GOURMET
dinners with complete
selections each course.*

*$19.00 per person —
by reservation ONLY
770-6660*

*Listen and dance to the
captivating Pyrenees
Strings.*
*Relax amid the elegance
of the Andorra Room
with after dinner
cocktails*

*Enjoy fine art from
some of the world's
most renown masters.*

*Descend the circular
staircase — visit our
wine cellar*

Chateau Pyrenees

*I-25 & Arapahoe Rd...Exit 89
770-6660*

Elegant Continental Dining that defies definition.

Photo courtesy of Dunshee and Company of Denver, Colorado.

Promotional Strategy

The discussion in this chapter is limited to the development of a retail promotional strategy. Promotional budget size, the scheduling of promotional expenditures over time, and the allocation of expenditures to the various promotional alternatives are the strategical promotional concepts covered in this presentation.

Retailers exert considerable effort to persuade prospective buyers that their merchandise or service offering is "right," that it is attractively priced, and that the circumstances surrounding its presentation will lead to purchase. It is the function of promotion to stimulate transactions by making a retailer's marketing inputs more attractive to potential customers who are currently engaged in the negotiation process. Attracting consumers to a store by advertising is one function of this type of promotion. Another example involves a consumer who has visited a store in order to replenish his stock of groceries and personal care items and who encounters a display of toothpaste which reminds him that his supply of toothpaste is low.

Promotion may also generate an attitude among consumers that will be conducive to making future transactions. A consumer's purchase of larger, durable goods (such as furniture) may, for example, be the result of the cumulative effect of years of retail advertising. Even then, the advertising may not have been received directly by the purchasing consumer. Instead, he may have received the message from others, who by word of mouth passed the information along.

Thus promotion facilitates the flow of information from the retailer to the consumer concerning such bargaining issues as product features, price, service aspects, warranties, etc. A promotion program must make a retailer's goods and service offering meaningful to potential buyers. After all, the consumer must see how a product or service can be useful to him in achieving some personal or social goal before he will make the purchase.

In recent years the term "promotional mix" has been used to describe the combination of tools used to promote business firms, products, or services. The promotional vehicles available to retailers can be classified into advertising, personal selling, sales promotion, and publicity categories.[1] The promotional mix concept emphasizes the belief that each promotional vehicle more effectively persuades consumers if it is accompanied by some combination of the other methods. In other words, a retailer is not likely to be effective in his promotional efforts if he concentrates on advertising, personal selling, or any other single method. Instead, a combination of promotional methods is used because one method frequently complements another.

Before we proceed to a discussion of the promotional decisions facing a retail firm, it is essential to understand the definitions used to categorize the various promotional vehicles.

Advertising may be defined as:

. . . any paid form of nonpersonal presentation and promotion of ideas, goods, or services by an identified sponsor. It involves the use of such media as the following:

    Magazine and newspaper space
    Motion pictures
    Outdoor (posters, signs, skywriting, etc.)
    Direct mail
    Novelties (calendars, blotters, etc.)
    Radio and television
    Cards (car, bus, etc.)
    Catalogs
    Directories and reference
    Programs and menus
    Circulars

This list is intended to be illustrative, not inclusive. . . . Advertising is generally but not necessarily carried on through mass media.[2]

Personal Selling involves:

. . . oral presentation in a conversation with one or more prospective purchasers for the purpose of making sales.[3]

Sales Promotion includes:

. . . those marketing activities, other than personal selling, advertising, and publicity, that stimulate consumer purchasing and dealer effectiveness, such as display, shows and exhibitions, demonstrations, and various non-recurrent selling efforts not in the ordinary routine.[4]

Publicity involves:

. . . non-personal stimulation of demand for a product, service, or business unit by planting commercially significant news about it in a published medium or obtaining favorable presentation of it upon radio, television, or stage that is not paid for by the sponsor.[5]

The combination and volume of the various promotional vehicles are problems that must be continually coordinated by retail management. Maximum returns from promotional efforts will not be achieved unless the purpose of the promotional mix is kept in focus constantly.

The promotional mix is used to achieve the overall corporate goals and objectives of the retail enterprise. Its purpose is not simply to serve as an outlet for creative talents, nor should it be viewed simply as a means to attract added customers for a "sale." If promotional goals and objectives have not been defined by management, the promotional efforts of the firm cannot be expected to serve at maximum efficiency or in a coordinated and meaningful pattern. They will, instead, tend to reflect either a "stone statue" or a "reed in the wind" position. On the one hand, promotional policies may become so rigid and unbending that it virtually takes a hurricane-force wind to change their direction. Or, like a reed in the wind, they may move in first one direction and then another at the slightest reason for change. Either position is damaging to the retailer and results in lost promotional opportunities and wasted dollars.

The retail firm's advertising objectives depend on the nature of the firm itself, the market opportunity represented by its potential customers, the overall retail store image desired by retail management, and the nature of the goods and service assortment offered by the retailer.

A sound promotional policy must consider the correct proportion of each element in the promotional mix in view of the objectives to be met. Retailers should have realistic and specific ideas concerning the image they want to project to the consumers. (The components of retail image were discussed in detail in Chapter 7.)

The first step involved in determining what image is best consists of an analysis of the outlet's target market consumers. Retailers need to identify their target market consumers by age, income, sex, family size, tastes, life style, place of residence, pay periods, etc. Only after the retailer has decided who his customers should be can he effectively decide what kind of image he is going to present in his promotional activities and how he can reach the target consumers.

The next step involved in determining the appropriate image for the individual retail firm consists of making a thorough self-analysis. This analysis might consist of a complete retail audit (which is discussed in Chapter 18) or a comparison with competitive retailers in terms of (1) price policy, (2) merchandise quality, (3) brands of merchandise offered, (4) employees' attitudes, (5) employees' appearance, (6) store layout, (7) store fixtures and display, (8) store windows, (9) customer services, (10) advertising layout, (11) advertised price level, and (12) type of clientele.[6]

The self-analysis or retail audit allows retail management to identify and remedy the things that appear to be inconsistent with the desired store image. The self-analysis also provides an analysis of the reasons why regular consumers continue to make purchases at that outlet. These same shopping motivations may then be featured in the retailer's general promotional effort.

A brief discussion of the promotional factors that influence the store image is required to illustrate how each factor can be used to create the desired image. The relative price level can reflect a bargain basement or discount impression by using a "we will not be undersold" pricing policy. At the other extreme, a "you get what you pay for" impression may be achieved by using a relatively high price policy, combined with relatively high quality merchandise.

Employee attitude and appearance are important factors in establishing a store image. Retailers who attempt to build a bargain basement or discount image may successfully use employees who have gruff attitudes and overworked appearances.[7] On the other hand, retailers who desire to maintain a quality merchandise image must employ helpful, neat-appearing personnel because the personalities of the employees influence the consumer's perception of the personality of the store.[8]

The kind and quality of services offered influence the impression consumers get of the store. Few or no services suggests a bargain image. Offering many services, such as delivery, easy merchandise return, credit, carry-out service, etc., usually is associated with a prestige image.

Advertisements themselves can be prepared in such a way as to generate either a discount image or a high-quality, prestigious impression. Product display and advertising that are crowded and cluttered tend to make people think that the store is of the low-quality, bargain basement type. On the other hand, a clean, well-balanced advertisement, with considerable white space, can convey the opposite impression.[9] Cost considerations also enter into the layout decision, as the more white space an advertiser uses, the less he can say about the products he is selling.

A store's image is also influenced by its clientele. If the store's customers belong to one social group, the general population will tend to think that it is catering to that group. Thus retail management must consider how the reputation of servicing its present customers will affect any new target market segment it may wish to cultivate.[10]

PROMOTIONAL EXPENDITURES

Retailers can begin planning their promotional program after they have determined what their message is and who should receive it. The planning generally begins with a determination of how much to spend on promotion, when to spend the promotional funds, what merchandise to promote, and which promotional vehicles to use.

Promotional Budgets

Advertising must be considered as a prime ingredient in the process of image building and control. This is true even when advertising is seldom or never used by a retailer. Retailers who can afford to commit promotional dollars to advertising but elect to spend little or none may pursue this strategy for any or all of the following reasons:

1. They feel that their ad would be lost in the mass of ads by other retailers in the mass media—principally newspapers.
2. They believe that their customers represent a different type of person, one who seeks out special values in particular quality, and may not even read the daily newspapers, listen to radio, or watch much television.
3. They believe that their customer's shopping behavior is a result of his peer group association and that his shopping habits are directed by his social standing. It is felt he is more apt to be affected by word of mouth and shopping patterns developed over years, or even generations, than by advertising.
4. They feel that their regular customers will be offended by advertising, since it might cheapen the store's image and place it in the class of all other retailers.
5. They are afraid that advertising might draw a different type of customer than their old customers and that this mixing of different social classes could cause their established clientele to shop elsewhere.
6. They believe the community they serve is so small that advertising is simply repeating things that people already know.

While any or all of these arguments may be valid for a particular retailer, they may prove to be dangerous myths in the long run. New generations within the old social class of dependable customers may change their shopping habits. They may become ardent television viewers. They may wish to break from tradition simply because they do not wish to follow exactly in the family footsteps. In addition, new social groups, armed with considerable purchasing power, may emerge as "turned off" to the image and messages they receive from these retailers.

In addition, a policy of complete avoidance of advertising will cause retailers to overlook the growing segmentation of media. Thus they may miss excellent opportunities to relate their message in specialized media directed specifically to their target market.

Marginal Analysis

Several different techniques are used by retail management to determine how much should be spent on retail promotion, and marginal analysis considers the additional increment of return which is earned as an additional increment of expenditure. This method is appropriate for determining the impact of hiring additional salesmen (permanent or temporary), using additional promotional expenditures, extending credit, etc. Marginal analysis is accomplished by comparing the change in store *profit* which may be attributed *directly* to a change in the expense item being considered, other things being equal. In formula form, marginal return ratio equals the change in store profits resulting from the addition of the last unit of input divided by the change in store expenses resulting from the addition of the last unit of input.

For example, increasing the number of permanent salesmen by one may increase store expenses by $520 per month. If this change *alone* increases store profits by $1,060, the marginal return ratio for the added salesman is $1,060 / $520, or 2.04, and the store earns $2.04 per $1 of increased expenditure. A margin return ratio of less than 1 indicates that the increased expenditure was not "covered" by the increased return. A ratio greater than 1 suggests there is "money to be made" through still greater expenditures. Promotional expenditures should be increased until the margin return ratio is "unity." In other words, retailers should continue to make additional promotional expenditures until the last marginal dollar spent generates one additional dollar of profit.

Use of the marginal analysis rule requires accurate estimates of the sales-to-promotional-expenditure relationship. The character or shape of the sales-response-to-promotion curve is likely to conform with the "law of diminishing returns." This law indicates that as equal, additional promotional expenditures are added, while all other retail factors are held constant, the additional sales generated by each additional promotional expenditure will eventually be smaller than the sales response generated by the preceding unit. Thus the sales response function is likely to follow the pattern in Figure 9–1. Sales, in this figure, expand at an increasing rate until point A, then at a decreasing rate until point B, when additional promotional expenditures do not influence sales at all.

Experimental Approach

Retail management can experiment with different advertising expenditures—in the same way prices were changed in Chapter 8. Latin square and before-and-after designs can be used and sales comparisons can be made with previous sales levels, as already indicated. These methods of estimating sales

Figure 9–1 Response of General Sales to Promotional Expenditure, Illustrating the Law of Diminishing Returns

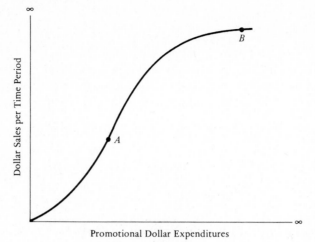

response to promotional expenditures are likely to yield satisfactory results for "promotional–direct-action" efforts. In this case, promotion attempts to sell specific products or services by making a direct appeal to consumers to (1) come into the store and buy the product, (2) fill out a coupon and purchase the product by mail, or (3) purchase the product immediately by phoning the retail outlet.

Mail-order advertisers can measure the short-run effect of their advertising by "keying" their ads so that each customer can be attributed to a particular advertisement. The short-run effect of changes in promotional–direct action retail expenditures can be obtained by comparing the sales level in the days following the appearance of a given promotional campaign with the sales level in previous periods when different promotional expenditures were made.

Long-run-effect measurement may not be necessary for a retailer because most of the value of retail advertising is received within a few days.[11]

Long-run "institutional" advertising does not make a bid for direct consumer action. Instead, it uses the "soft sell" approach to stress the retailer's advantage in areas such as convenience of store location, the general high quality of his merchandise, the wide range of goods and services offered, the friendliness and knowledgeability of personnel, and the like. Thus institutional advertising attempts to build good will and create a favorable image. The lag between expenditure and eventual sales stimulation makes it considerably more difficult to estimate the sales response to this long-run type of advertising than that of promotional–direct action. For this reason, the objective-and-task method may be used to evaluate the contribution of institutional advertising.

Objective-and-Task Approach

Under the objective-and-task method, retail management defines the promotional objectives as specifically as possible. For example, an objective in institutional advertising may be to make 40 percent of the general population in the trading area aware of the fact that only XYZ Furniture Company carries brand X furniture. The tasks needed to be performed to achieve each objective are then listed and management estimates the cost of performing these tasks. The promotional budget is then established by adding the costs of performing the necessary tasks for all of the objectives that are deemed worthy of pursuing on the basis of benefits derived from costs incurred. The method allows management to concentrate on achieving only those objectives which are most productive relative to their associated cost.

Percentage-of-Sales Approach

Many retailers use a percentage-of-sales method to determine the level of promotional expenditures. Using this method, retailers budget their promotional expenditures at a pre-specified percentage of current or anticipated dollar sales volume. For example, a retail firm may budget 2 percent of its forecasted sales of $1 million ($20,000) for promotional purposes.

This method of determining the level of promotional expenditures considers advertising to be a necessary cost, but it is difficult to support on the basis of logic. The percentage-of-sales technique lets the sales level determine the amount of money spent on promotion; however, the relationship should be reversed, as the level of promotion is supposed to influence sales. If promotion does not influence sales, there is no reason to make promotional expenditures. Using the volume of retail sales to determine the size of the promotional budget also ignores the marginal relationship of added promotional expenditures to added sales. The cost or worth of obtaining added sales is not considered under the percentage-of-sales approach. Nevertheless, the approach is widely used because many retailers are not able to estimate the sales-response-to-promotion relationship.

Competitive Parity Approach

The competitive parity method involves establishing a promotional budget that will match competitors' outlays for promotion. Industry figures are frequently available to indicate the percentage of gross dollar sales volume that similar retailers use in their promotional efforts (Table 9–1), and knowing the level of promotional expenditure that competitors are using is helpful in establishing the promotional budget. However, it should not be followed blindly, as it does not account for differences in location, reputation, opportunities, or company objectives. In addition, there is no reason to believe that competition uses any logical method for determining promotional outlays.

Thus the competitive parity approach can indicate only a starting point for determining the level of the budget. Changes in the budget can then be

Table 9–1   Percentage of Sales Invested in Advertising in 1969–70

INDUSTRY	PERCENT
Retail Trade	
General merchandise stores	2.60
Food stores	1.10
Automotive dealers and service stations	0.91
Gasoline service stations	0.81
Apparel and accessory stores	2.12
Furniture, home furnishings, and equipment stores	3.13
Eating and drinking places	1.50
Drug stores and proprietary stores	1.27
Liquor stores	0.43
Other retail stores	1.26
Banking	1.24
Insurance agents, brokers, and service	1.79
Services	1.61
Hotels and other lodging places	2.02
Personal services	1.62
Automobile services and miscellaneous repair services	0.87
Repair services except auto	0.70
Amusements and recreation services	3.31
Motion pictures	5.51
Other amusement and recreation services	2.68

SOURCE "Percentage of Sales Invested in Advertising in 1969–70," *Advertising Age*, July 16, 1973, p. 24.

made and the resulting influence on sales observed to determine if promotional expenditures should be raised or lowered.

Return-on-Investment Approach

The return-on-investment method is another method for determining the size of the promotional budget. This approach treats promotion primarily as a capital investment rather than a current expense. Determination of the amount of promotional spending then becomes a problem of capital expenditure budgeting, and the promotional budget must compete for funds with other kinds of internal investment on the basis of prospective rate of return. Each piece of promotion affects current sales and also builds good will to increase sales at a later date.

The relative importance of the two effects can vary tremendously, according to the type of promotion used. At one end of the spectrum is institutional advertising, with its long-term orientation, which reflects an almost pure capital investment. At the other end are promotional–direct-action efforts, such as advertising a special sales event. This type of promotional expenditure usually represents only a small portion of capital investment.

Isolating the portion of the promotional budget that can be considered a capital expenditure and then estimating the rate of return that can be obtained on the capital expenditure are difficult tasks, but perhaps not impossible.[12]

Concluding Remarks

The previous discussion has centered on the various methods used to determine the size of the retail promotional budget. Deciding how much to spend on promotion is a continual problem because none of the approaches discussed is likely to yield an exact estimate of sales response to promotional efforts. Many factors, such as media effectiveness, the effectiveness of the promotional appeal, competitors' promotions, consumer attitudes, etc., affect the sales-to-promotional-expenditures ratio. These factors are considered to be important to many retailers, who believe that either the percentage-of-sales or the competitive parity approach provides an acceptable way of determining the level of the promotional budget. These retailers believe that attempting to measure the response of sales to promotional expenditures requires too much time, expense, and mathematical proficiency.

There are several fundamental considerations no matter what method is used. The level of promotional expenditure will need to be higher for outlets that operate from less favorable locations. In addition, stores that operate in areas of exceptionally strong competition are likely to use higher promotional expenditures to combat the promotional efforts of the competitors. New and expanding retail firms must use larger promotional expenditures to make consumers *aware* of their existence and merchandise offering. Higher advertising expenditure may also be required by stores which continually stress low price in their campaigns.

The list could continue, but the point of this discussion is to indicate that each retailer operates under unique conditions. Thus his promotional expenditures must be tailored to fit the situation. If the promotional expenditure appears to be low, it might be raised a little at a time and the results observed to see if added sales contributed enough profit to more than cover the added promotional expense.

The essential steps used in planning and evaluating the retail promotional budget are summarized in Figure 9–2.

Scheduling Promotional Expenditures over Time

The timing of promotional expenditures over seasons, months, weeks, and days must be determined after the level of the promotional budget has been established. Some components of the promotional mix, such as personal sales, require fairly constant expenditures throughout the year. Certainly part-time sales people can be added during the extremely busy sales periods, such as the Christmas season. Overtime payments can be paid to regular employees during these peak periods, but otherwise the level of expenditure for personal sales is likely to remain fairly constant throughout the year.

It is much easier to change the level of retail spending for advertising and sales promotion because advertising media and printing companies do

Figure 9–2   *Planning and Evaluating the Advertising Budget*

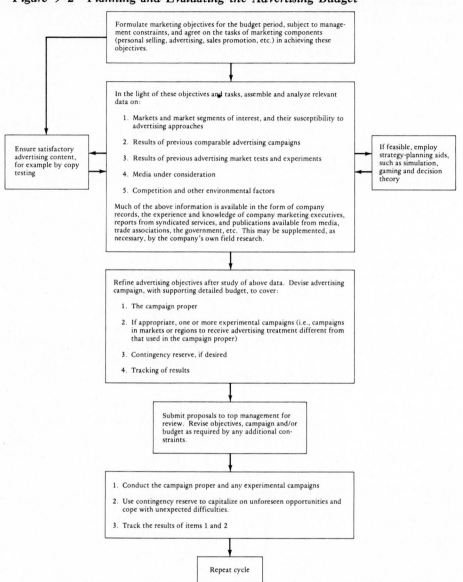

SOURCE   *Some Guidelines for Advertising Budgeting* (New York: The Conference Board, Inc., 1972), p. 38.

not require a constant expenditure, as do store salesmen. Some media contracts contain cancelable clauses that may be used if it is necessary to reduce expenditures. Media options may be passed up to provide additional flexibility. Finally, a portion of the annual advertising and sales promotion budget is not contractually committed and hence can be shifted to a cash account if this is necessary to improve the short-run financial condition of the firm.

On the other hand, when an unanticipated competitive threat develops, intensification of the advertising effort may be the easiest method of retaliation. Thus it may be argued that advertising and sales promotion are the most flexible retail marketing factors.

Despite the flexibility, retailers are likely to benefit more from spending smaller amounts of promotional money on a frequent basis than from spending a considerable amount on promotion for just infrequent, special occasions. Consistency of the promotional effort reinforces the store's image in the minds of consumers. It also reminds consumers of the outlet's advantages and merchandise/service offerings.

This is not to say that the advertising and sales promotional budgets should be the same for all months of the year; it merely suggests that some minimal promotional expenditure be made each month. The level of the total advertising and sales promotion budget will probably vary from month to month because of holiday, seasonal, and other special promotions, and it is a common practice for retailers to divide their monthly advertising and sales promotion expenditures into amounts that parallel expected sales patterns.[13] The actual promotional advertisements may be placed just before the expected peak in sales. For example, supermarkets spend a large percentage of their advertising budgets on Wednesday advertisements, which influence shopping on the high-volume days of Thursday, Friday, and Saturday.

Allocating promotional expenditures in this manner allows the retail firm's communication to reach the consumer when he is beginning to make purchasing decisions. Heavier promotion can also be scheduled to reach the consumer when he will be able to react to the promotional activity. For example, response to an advertisement placed just prior to pay day may be considerably better than the response obtained from an advertisement placed just after pay day.

Promotional plans are generally made on a planning form or promotional calendar, such as the ones in Figures 9–3 and 9–4. Such planning must be coordinated with merchandise planning (which is discussed in Chapter 12). Normally, retailers prepare the promotional budget, promotional calendar, and merchandise budget simultaneously because of their interrelatedness. The distribution of promotional expenditures during each month should be scheduled to take advantage of the payroll days of important area firms, days of the week in which sales and traffic are normally highest, national and local events, night openings, and seasonal merchandise sales patterns. These calendars can be used when one is planning future promotional expenditures, provided such factors as last year's sales figures, this year's sales figures, weather conditions, unusual competitor promotions, etc. are recorded.

Allocating Promotional Expenditures to Departments and Merchandise Lines

Another important decision involves the determination of how much should be spent promoting each merchandise line and each department. One

Figure 9–3 *Worksheet for Preparing Monthly Promotional Budget*

	SALES VOLUME						PROMOTIONAL EXPENDITURES					
	In Dollars			Percent of Total Annual Sales			In Dollars			Percent Cent of Total Promotional Expenditures		
Month	Two Years Ago	Last Year	Estimate For This Year	Two Years Ago	Last Year	Estimate For This Year	Two Years Ago	Last Year	This Year	Two Years Ago	Last Year	This Year
January												
February												
March												
April												
May												
June												
July												
August												
September												
October												
November												
December												

method of attacking this problem is simply to allocate promotional expenditures to the departments in proportion to their contributions to total sales. For example, if the hardware department is expected to generate 9 percent of the store's total sales volume next month, about 9 percent of next month's promotional budget is allocated for promotion of the hardware department. Another approach is to allocate promotional expenditures in proportion to the department's contribution to total profit.

Either approach is insensitive to the fact that promotion of some departments and merchandise lines creates more store traffic than others. Since the main purpose of promotion is to attract consumers to the store, the heavy traffic-generating departments should have a more than proportional share of the promotional budget. For example, many supermarkets allocate more than proportional advertising funds to the meat and produce departments. Since the same brands of canned, frozen, and packaged goods are available in most outlets, management believes that these perishable commodities give the outlets a unique chance to differentiate themselves from their competitors. Intensive promotion of these perishable items also is defensible on grounds that the consumer is likely to plan menus around the meat and produce items that are featured in the advertisements. Consumers are likely to purchase (at regular prices) the staple items that are used with the featured meat and produce items during their visit to the outlet. Other departments that frequently are believed to be heavy traffic generators are ready-to-wear apparel, furniture, and appliances.

Thus the allocation of promotional expenditures to the various departments should promote the heavy traffic-generating departments by granting them a more than proportional allotment of the budget. Another consideration in the allocation process involves the relationship between each department's inventory level and its expected near-term sales. Some departments may require heavier promotional expenditure to clear overstocked merchandise because its selling season is nearly over or it is in danger of going out of style. New products and new or expanding departments may also require a more than proportionate share of the promotional budget to make consumers aware of their existence.

It is important to realize that specific merchandise lines and departments benefit most from promotion during times when consumer demand is at its peak. Past sales patterns can be used to make allocations to departments in a way that will better balance departmental promotional expenditures with expected departmental sales. A special effort might be made to identify the best traffic pullers for each month. Promotion of these "hot items" attempts to match promotional expenditures with expected sales volume. The promotional campaign then tells customers that the store is offering those items that the consumer is seeking.

Another important consideration in deciding what items to promote involves the effect the promoted item will have upon the store's image. Is the promoted item consistent with the desired price and quality image? Is the promoted item likely to appeal to a desired group of consumers? Do

Figure 9–4 Sample Promotional Calendar

Planned Promotional Expenditures: During Week _____
During Month _____

Week of _____

SALES VOLUME DATA

	In Dollars				Per Cent of Annual Sales			
	Two Years Ago	Last Year	Estimate For This Year	Actual This Year	Two Years Ago	Last Year	Estimate For This Year	Actual This Year

PROMOTIONAL EXPENDITURES

	In Dollars				Per Cent of Total Promotional Expenditures			
	Two Years Ago	Last Year	Estimate For This Year	Actual This Year	Two Years Ago	Last Year	Estimate For This Year	Actual This Year

Type of Promotion	Date Used	Merchandise or Theme Featured	Cost		Less Discounts and Co-op Funds Reimbursed	Actual Promotional Cost	
			Last Year	This Year		Last Year	This Year
(1) Advertising							
Newspaper							
Radio							
Television							

Outdoor
Direct Mail
Circulars
Other Advertising
(List Type Used)
    Total Advertising

(2) Personal Selling

(3) Sales Promotion

Displays
Demonstrations
Other Sales Promotions
(List Type Used)
    Total Sales Promotion

(4) Publicity
    (List Type Used)

(5) Weekly Totals

Planned Promotional Expense for Week
Actual Promotional Expense for Week
Deviation From Promotional Expenditure Plan

we have an adequate quantity on hand to meet anticipated consumer demand? These questions should be considered when items are selected and promotions are prepared.

The promoted items should also represent a good value from the consumer's point of view. It may not be the lowest priced, but by offering better quality, guarantees, service, advice, etc. the consumer should see the total product/service package as the best buy among the alternatives. Efficient use of this concept requires consumer knowledge of prices on different items. Price reduction advertising is likely to be more effective if it features an item whose price is known by most consumers. This simply makes the advertising more believable, as consumers can verify from their own experience that the price has been reduced.

Some retailers rely heavily upon manufacturers to assist them in their promotional efforts. These retailers advertise only those items whose manufacturing companies provide cooperative allowances. This practice, known as "cooperative advertising," reduces the cost considerably, but it needs to be combined with advertisements on known traffic-pulling items to provide consistent results. Although the rate varies, the manufacturer most commonly pays 50 percent of the local advertising expenditure used to promote the specified items. (The contract usually states that any promotion must have the prior approval of the manufacturer.) These cooperative allowances let the retailer maintain a more consistent promotional effort over time. It also allows a retailer to use larger advertisements, thereby attracting more attention to the advertisements. Another benefit is the synergistic effect of national advertising and national brand names, which complements local promotional efforts and enhances the prestige of the local outlet. The manufacturer also benefits by paying lower local ad rates than if he advertised alone.

A new development in cooperative advertising is "in-ad couponing." "In-ad" coupons are authorized and paid for by the manufacturer; however, these coupons are distributed in the context of the retailer's own weekly newspaper ads. In-ad couponing has been successful in moving large amounts of merchandise. Retailers like these coupons because they can cooperate in the actual merchandising of the product—and because the redemption rate of coupons is increasing.[14] The need for more couponing stems from strong customer acceptance of coupons which are used to reduce household expenditures. Departments which can take advantage of cooperative allowances are frequently promoted more heavily because of the reduced cost to the retailer.

Departmental managers may be asked to prepare their own promotional plan on the basis of their knowledge of monthly promotional requirements. The budget amount, the media usage, and the general theme may be worked out with the store manager, merchandise manager, or sales promotion director and may reflect the planning done on the promotional calendars. The decision as to which products and merchandise lines to promote within a department is likely to be made by the department head, who may be better informed on inventory levels, consumer preferences, seasonal patterns, and the like.

Allocating Expenditures to Promotional Alternatives

Ideally, the promotional budget should be allocated among advertising, personal selling, sales promotion, and publicity in a manner that yields equivalent marginal profits on the last dollar spent in each of these four areas. To implement this principle, a retailer has to determine the dollar sales and profit response obtained by each promotional method. He then selects the alternatives that give the highest marginal return ratio, until all the ratios for all methods are equivalent at the value of 1.0. At this point he is maximizing profits by using each type of promotion until the last expenditure is just covered by the increase in profits that it generated.

This reasoning simply involves the use of the marginal analysis approach to budgeting (which was discussed earlier in the chapter) for each individual type of promotion. The same reasoning can also be used when allocating expenditures within media—by choosing the vehicles which generate the largest marginal profits per added dollar expenditure until marginal profits no longer cover marginal costs for each vehicle. This marginal analysis principle must be continually followed in making allocation decisions if unprofitable promotions are to be avoided. Measurement of the marginal sales and profit response to each alternative promotional vehicle is a complex and time-consuming procedure. Therefore the use of the marginal analysis principle is likely to consist of a managerial judgment as to whether the added benefits derived from the additional promotion exceed the added promotional costs.

The marginal effects of each vehicle depend upon the retailer's objectives, opportunities, and the constraints he faces. Different promotional mixes may be used successfully by similar retailing organizations; different tasks must be accomplished before sales can be generated; and each promotional tool differs in its ability to perform these tasks. The selling process may be considered to follow four steps: creating *awareness*; developing customer *comprehension* of the product/service offer; producing customer *conviction* that the offer is a good offer; and encouraging customer investigation that leads to *purchase*.[15]

Awareness is probably obtained most efficiently through publicity and advertising. For example, the opening of a new retail outlet or the handling of a new line of merchandise will likely require heavy advertising and publicity to make consumers aware of the change.

Developing customer comprehension of the product/service offer may require the use of a combination of all four types of promotion. The most effective techniques would probably vary from one retailer to another, depending upon the quality of the sales personnel used and the complexity of the product/service offering. Retailers who sell complex merchandise and services will have to place more reliance on sales persons to explain the advantages of their offering.

Personal selling is usually more effective in instilling consumer conviction of a good offer, especially for technical goods. However, extensive low-price advertising of national brand or private-label items may be the most efficient method of establishing conviction among a price-conscious segment of consumers.

Personal contact of some type is also influential in triggering the purchase act, even in self-service outlets where clerks may only provide information on merchandise location and availability.

The extent to which retailers should use each promotional vehicle depends on the target customer's reading, listening, watching, and shopping habits. The selected vehicles should reach the target customers at the lowest possible cost per potential customer. In addition, the vehicles' effectiveness for presenting the merchandise/service offering must be considered. The various media provide different opportunities for presenting demonstrations, conveying visual descriptions and impressions, providing explanations, etc.

The problem of allocation among various advertising media is complicated by the fact that they have overlapping audiences. Therefore it is difficult to determine which sales are attributable to each method. For this reason, allocation among promotional vehicles is usually based upon a judgment of the media believed to reach the largest number of target customers, as many times as possible, as steadily over time as possible, and with the minimum cost.

At this point the retail promotional planner begins to investigate specific alternatives in terms of which programs, newspapers, etc. offer the best promotional purchase. The analysis will center on the characteristics of each vehicle, its coverage, the nature of its audience, and how these factors relate to the outlet's promotional objectives.

The *cost-per-thousand-potential-customers criterion* is frequently used to compare the effectiveness of the numerous vehicles in reaching the target market consumer. Under this approach, retail promotional planners calculate the cost per 1,000 potential customers reached by each vehicle. For example, suppose a retailer could reach 100,000 potential target market customers with a full-page newspaper advertisement costing $2,000. The cost per 1,000 target market consumers reached would be $2,000 divided by 100, or $20, because 100,000 target market customers are contacted with the $2,000 expenditure. The promotional planner would make similar calculations for each vehicle and rank them according to the lowest cost per thousand. Advertisements would be placed in those vehicles with the lowest cost per thousand target market homes reached. It is important to use the target market concept in making cost per thousand calculations because total readership, viewership, and/or listenership does not represent only potential consumers. The exposure value of each vehicle depends upon how closely the audience's characteristics match those of the target market. The cost per thousand in the target market calculation takes this into account.

Table 9–2 Example of Detailed Local Newspaper Readership Data Available

PHOENIX NEWSPAPER STUDY   MIDWEEK (DAILY)   MAR–APR, 1972

Total Household Annual Income

Newspapers	Income Male under $5,000 (00)	Income Male $5,000–$7,999 (00)	Income Male $8,000–$9,999 (00)	Income Male $10,000–$14,999 (00)	Income Male $15,000 & Over (00)	Income Female under $5,000 (00)	Income Female $5,000–$7,999 (00)	Income Female $8,000–$9,999 (00)	Income Female $10,000–$14,999 (00)	Income Female $15,000 & Over (00)
Arizona Republic (Morn)	108	130	227	299	396	229	219	162	293	336
Mesa Tribune (Eve)	14	9	40	21	80	20	11	19	21	68
Phoenix Gazette (Eve)	83	165	121	184	359	128	220	87	273	265
Miscellaneous				23	77	24	7	9	52	49

Age & Sex

Newspapers	Men 18–24 (00)	Men 25–34 (00)	Men 35–49 (00)	Men 50–64 (00)	Men Total (00)	Women 18–24 (00)	Women 25–34 (00)	Women 35–49 (00)	Women 50–64 (00)	Women Total (00)
Arizona Republic (Morn)	183	276	267	253	1160	217	145	313	370	1239
Mesa Tribune (Eve)	9	12	60	45	164	44	20	39	21	140
Phoenix Gazette (Eve)	214	123	247	263	912	97	239	297	284	974
Miscellaneous		16	60	24	100	28	10	46	24	141
Total	308	399	499	492	1962	314	389	603	578	2166

SOURCE Newspaper Pulse, Inc., 730 Fifth Avenue, New York, N.Y. 10019.

The use of the cost per thousand in the target market concept requires the use of data containing detailed demographic and geographic breakdowns. Pulse Inc. provides detailed newspaper readership information for 157 cities (Table 9–2). In addition, Standard Rate and Data Service publishes *Newspaper Rates and Data* and *Weekly Newspaper Rates and Data*, which provide six-month average summary circulation information. In the daily publication, circulation is divided into "city zone," "trading zone," and "other." In the

Table 9–3   *Example of Radio Listenership Data Available*

AVERAGE ¼-HOUR AUDIENCE ESTIMATES IN HOME & OUT OF HOME

THE PULSE, INC.
PHOENIX CENTRAL ZONE

6 A.M.–10 A.M.

| | Persons Reached Estimates | | | | | | | |
| | Men | | Women | | Teens | | Total | |
Stations	RTG*	(00)	RTG	(00)	RTG	(00)	RTG	(00)
KBUZ	1.3	42	.7	24	.1	1	.9	67
KDKB	1.6	49	.9	32	.1	1	1.0	82
KDKB-FM	.1	2	.1	2			.1	4
KDOT	.1	4	.3	9			.2	13
KHAT	.6	20	.4	15			.4	35
KHEP-FM				1				1
KIFN	1.9	59	3.1	108	2.1	26	2.5	193
KJJJ	3.4	107	3.3	112	.5	6	2.9	225
KMEO	1.1	33	1.2	41	.1	1	1.0	75
KNIX		1		1	.1	1		3
KOOL	3.9	123	4.1	140	.5	6	3.4	269
KOOL-FM	.1	2	.3	11	.2	3	.2	16
KOY	4.0	124	3.2	109	.6	8	3.1	241
KRDS	.9	28	.9	32	.2	2	.8	62
KRFM	2.0	64	.9	30			1.2	94
KRIZ	1.6	50	1.5	52	5.9	74	2.2	176
KRUX	1.2	37	1.7	60	3.8	47	1.8	144
KTAR	.5	15	.4	15	.6	7	.5	37
KTAR-FM	.4	11	.6	20	.1	1	.4	32
KTUF	.7	21	.8	28	.3	4	.7	53
KUPD	2.0	64	1.5	52	2.1	26	1.8	142
KXIV	.6	19	.4	14			.4	33
Total	28.4	891	27.6	949	16.7	209	26.2	2049

* +RTG indicates the estimated audience size. It is the average ¼-hour rating of the total listening audience (in home and one of home combined) for each station as the percentage of all persons interviewed.

weekly publication, circulation data are separated only into "paid" and "non-paid." *Newspaper Circulation Analysis* breaks down the circulation of daily papers by county of distribution and makes a report for each county wherein a newspaper achieves more than a 5 percent penetration of households.

Both Radio Advertising Bureau and Pulse Inc. provide detailed audience listenership data, as illustrated in Table 9–3.[16] The *Nielsen Station Index* contains detailed viewer profiles for television audiences in over 200

AVERAGE ¼-HOUR AUDIENCE ESTIMATES IN HOME & OUT OF HOME

MONDAY–FRIDAY
SEPT–OCT, 1972

6 A.M.–10 A.M.

Persons Reached Estimates by Age

Men 18–24 (00)	Men 25–34 (00)	Men 35–49 (00)	Men 50–64 (00)	Women 18–24 (00)	Women 25–34 (00)	Women 35–49 (00)	Women 50–64 (00)
	16	22	4	1	12	11	
23	26			27	3	2	
	2			2			
		4		2	6	1	
2	4	5	9	3	5	7	
						1	
9	21	16	4	23	33	28	11
	17	29	42	2	9	38	31
2		22	9	10	4	19	8
	1				1		
1	1	45	62		12	23	84
1		1		6		4	1
14	46	50	12	13	45	32	14
	5	20	3	2	8	22	
	8	39	17		8	6	16
27	9	4	10	13	14	22	3
16	10	11		23	11	15	7
1	3	3		2	3	5	1
6	5			10	3	7	
6	15			3	20		5
9	15	31	9	38	6	6	2
	1	16	2			7	7
119	207	320	185	180	197	268	208

SOURCE   *Pulse Radio Station Report*, Pulse, Inc., 730 Fifth Avenue, New York, N.Y. 10019.

markets.[17] Estimating the cost per thousand potential customers appears to be most appropriate when comparing two or more vehicles in the same medium (e.g., several newspapers which claim to serve the trading area).

Estimating Relative Media Efficiency

The larger problem of determining allocation to each medium (e.g., radio versus newspaper) is a more complex decision, involving considerations beyond the cost per thousand potential customers. The following factors, not considered in the cost per potential customer calculations, should be analyzed.

(1) Lead time, which is the length of time between submission of the finished advertisement to the medium and the time when the advertisement will appear. (2) Life of the advertisement, which is the length of time that a consumer will be exposed to an advertisement. (3) Intimacy, which describes the consumer's degree of confidence in the medium which is being used. (4) Editorial climate, which refers to the degree that articles or programs are used to support the advertisements. (5) Repeat or multiple exposures to the advertisement, which is the number of times that a consumer may be exposed to the same advertisement. (6) Type of advertisement, which refers to product or promotional direct action advertising versus institutional advertising. (7) Competitor's use of the medium. (8) Availability or appropriateness of the medium.[18]

Analysis of all these factors and a review of the calculations of the cost per thousand potential consumers reached is time consuming, but the results can be rewarding.

Another measure of the relative efficiency of each advertising media can be obtained by determining which media attract customers to the store.[19] These data can be obtained simply by asking each customer (or a random sample of customers if the number is large) how he or she happened to come into the store. A summary of their responses can be recorded for each type of advertising. Weekly records can be kept to indicate the number of people attracted to the store by each type of advertising. Sales slips can also contain sales volume for each consumer and can be totaled by category. The week's results can then be compared with costs, as indicated in Table 9–4. If the relative amount spent on each medium is not changed for several months, a retailer should have a fairly good estimate of how much it costs him to attract a customer by using each medium. Then expenditures can be changed on one medium for about a month and the results observed.

By carefully changing expenditures and analyzing the results, the retailer is able to judge the relative efficiency of each medium. He may also be able to determine if there is a significant carryover of his advertising in each medium. Most retail advertising does not generate a significant carryover effect because sale or promotion–direct-action advertising is remembered for only a short time and does not generate a continual purchasing habit.

Both the cost-per-thousand-potential-customers approach and the analysis of relative media efficiency provide estimates that should be used with

Table 9–4   *Analysis of Relative Media Efficiency*

MEDIA CATEGORY (1)	NUMBER OF CUSTOMERS ATTRACTED BY EACH MEDIUM (2)	$ PURCHASES MADE BY CUSTOMERS ATTRACTED BY EACH MEDIUM (3)	ADVER- TISING EXPENDI- TURE IN MEDIUM (4)	NUMBER OF CUSTOMERS ATTRACTED PER ADVERTISING DOLLAR (5) = (2)/(4)	SALES PER ADVERTISING DOLLAR EXPENDED (6) = (3)/(4)
Referred by friend	200	$1,000	—	—	—
Regular customer	400	1,600	—	—	—
Newspaper	150	500	50	3.0	$10.00
Radio	80	400	40	2.0	10.00
Television	50	250	100	0.5	2.50
Magazines	—	—	—	—	—
Yellow Pages	5	25	5	5.0	5.00
Special window displays	3	30	100	.03	0.30
Direct mail	—	—	—	—	—
Other	10	50	—	—	—
Total	898	$3,855	$295		

caution. These methods should be used to assist retailers in making allocations to the various promotional media and vehicles. They do not provide absolute answers on media effectiveness. It may take a considerable length of time to develop the skill needed to interpret the data. In addition, data provided by asking consumers why they came into the store may not reveal the true reasons. People are influenced by a combination of factors, but they tend to mention only the ones to which they have been most recently exposed. Despite these limitations, retailers can benefit by using all or portions of both techniques when they plan their promotional expenditures.

SUMMARY

A retailer's promotional mix must be used to achieve the firm's unified goals. Thus the promotional mix will depend upon the nature of the firm's merchandise/service offering, the needs of its target consumers, and the overall retail image desired by management. Promotion can generate either a quality image or a discount image, whichever is desired.

The level of promotional expenditures can be determined by using marginal analysis, experimentation, the objective-and-task approach, the percent-of-sales method, the competitive parity, or the return-on-investment techniques.

Marginal analysis and the experimental approach appear to offer the most logical approach to the problem, but both require considerable time, effort, and expertise. Thus many retailers use either the percent-of-sales method or the competitive parity technique.

It is common for retailers to divide their promotional expenditures into amounts that parallel but precede expected sales patterns. This allows the firm to send more of its message to the consumer when he is beginning to make the purchase decision.

The cost-per-thousand-potential-customers approach is one method that can be used to guide expenditures to vehicles within any promotional medium. Other considerations, such as the permanence of the advertisment, the need for the merchandise to be displayed visually or demonstrated, etc., also must be made when allocating expenditures between media.

In conclusion, promotion is an inexact science which is highly dependent on the situation, personal experience, and proper timing. Ultimately, each promotion program must be tailored to each retail unit in order to reflect the uniqueness of the relevant target market.

QUESTIONS

1. What is the reasoning used by some retailers for avoiding advertising? Can this reasoning be justified?
2. Why is marginal analysis difficult to implement in determining the effectiveness of an advertising campaign?
3. Why is it difficult to determine the sales response to the long-run types of advertising? What would you suggest to overcome this problem?
4. Why is percent-of-sales a poor method for determining an advertising budget? Why is it used so frequently?
5. What are the disadvantages of the competitive parity approach to determining advertising budgets? Can any use be made of the knowledge of a competitor's advertising budget?
6. What is the fundamental difference between the return-on-investment approach and the methods discussed in questions 4 and 5?
7. Why is it generally a good practice to maintain a relatively steady and consistent advertising effort rather than advertising heavily during some periods and not at all during others? What events might cause justifiable "spurts" in advertising expenditures?
8. Since advertising is supposed to increase sales, why do many retailers advertise merchandise lines at peak demand periods when a high sales volume can be expected without advertising? Why not concentrate on merchandise that needs advertising and promotion?

FOOTNOTES

[1] Jerome B. Kernan, William P. Dommermuth, and Montrose S. Sommers, *Promotion: An Introductory Analysis* (New York: McGraw-Hill, 1970), pp. 11–13.
[2] Ralph S. Alexander et al., *Marketing Definitions: A Glossary of Marketing Terms* (Chicago: American Marketing Association, 1960), p. 9.
[3] Ibid., p. 18.
[4] Ibid., p. 20.
[5] Ibid., p. 19.

[6] Laurence W. Jacobs, *Advertising and Promotion for Retailing* (Glenview, Ill.: Scott, Foresman, 1972), pp. 6–15.

[7] Ibid., p. 7.

[8] Ibid.

[9] Ibid., p. 10.

[10] Ibid., p. 13.

[11] Julian L. Simon, *The Management of Advertising* (Englewood Cliffs, N.J.: Prentice-Hall, 1971), pp. 14–15.

[12] Joel Dean, "Does Advertising Belong in the Capital Budget?" *Journal of Marketing*, 30 (October 1966): 15–21.

[13] Jacobs, *Advertising and Promotion*, pp. 88–97.

[14] *Editor and Publisher*, March 6, 1971.

[15] Philip Kotler, *Marketing Management, Analysis, Planning, and Control* (Englewood Cliffs, N.J.: Prentice-Hall, 1967), p. 453.

[16] The address of the Radio Advertising Bureau is 555 Madison Avenue, New York, N.Y. 10022.

[17] The address of the A. C. Nielsen Company is 2101 Howard Street, Chicago, Ill. 60645.

[18] Jacobs, *Advertising and Promotion*, p. 128.

[19] Ibid., pp. 132–133.

DAVIS BROTHERS FLORISTS

Dramatic changes in the retail distribution of fresh-cut carnations were causing Davis Brothers Florists of Wheatridge, Colorado to seriously evaluate present and future marketing channels. For years, the marketing of cut flowers had been accomplished through a traditional wholesaler and retailer system.

The system began to show signs of changing in 1959, but the most important distribution shifts had occurred since 1965. At that time a California wholesaler began selling potted plants to mass merchandisers. This was followed by sales of cut flowers in the same manner, which amounted to nearly $14 million per year.

These sales were being accomplished by three methods: bucket sales, satellite stores, and flower shops within mass merchandising outlets.

As the name implies, "bucket sales" consist of buckets of fresh-cut flowers placed at convenient locations inside or outside stores. Satellite stores were designed for customers to pass through them before entering a supermarket. These were staffed with professional florists who sell a product line ranging from simple bouquets to complex and expensive arrangements. The in-store shops are simply sections within a supermarket. These are not staffed by professionals; instead, a clerk waters the flowers and removes any wilted or dead items.

In recent years the number of ways of marketing cut flowers has continued to increase, and Mr. Kent Davis of Davis Brothers estimated there are at least ten systems in use. In addition, he stated that large corporations, such as Pillsbury, Alcoa Aluminum, and United Fruit, were entering the business.

Davis Brothers Florists has operated as a wholesaler for over fifty years. Although Davis Brothers sells many types of flowers, its primary business remains the marketing of cut Colorado carnations to retailers throughout the United States.

The firm ships by refrigerated semi-trucks to retail florists, particularly those to the east and south of Colorado, with truck deliveries as far as Alabama. In addition, retailers throughout the rest of the nation are served by air freight.

Each year the company sells over 40,000,000 cut carnations, of which only about 9 percent are grown by Davis Brothers. The remainder are provided by approximately forty growers who sell to Davis Brothers.

Throughout the years Davis Brothers has established a core of retail florists, ranging in size from small "mom and pop" operations to modern floral chains. These continue to constitute the backbone of the company's distribution system.

Four salesmen are hired to travel the market area served by Davis Brothers to service existing retailers and seek new ones. A sales staff of five sells daily—via phone—to all areas of the country.

The management of the company consists of three brothers in their thirties, Ron, Keith and Kent, who were raised in the business and left it only to complete college and satisfy their military requirements.

Although Davis Brothers is not the largest wholesaler of Colorado carnations, the Davis brothers are quick to point out that it is one of the most modern and aggressive firms. As Ken Davis stated, "I have been in hundreds of other plants and can truthfully say there aren't any that are better set up than this one."

The plant reflects modernity, with well-planned loading docks, controlled-temperature storage units, a testing lab, a computer room, and paneled offices.

During the last few years Davis Brothers has begun to sell through completely new retail outlets, as well as established florists. However, recent events have caused it to reexamine a newly emerged and important retailing system. This is the "hippie" salesman system.

In many parts of the nation, including Davis Brothers' traditional market area, large numbers of so-called hippies or flower children have been organized to sell flowers on street corners.

The original organization was well planned and quickly grew throughout large sections of the United States. The organizers first incorporated, and then sought a peddler's license in each locality. Their technique was to sit in the public office responsible for granting licenses until one was given. In many cases this meant staying overnight and literally camping in the office. They had found that if they once left the office to return later, their request for a permit would normally be denied.

Normally this license covered all the company's salesmen, but in one state it was necessary to pay $50 for each salesman to be placed on street corners.

The organizers established a branch manager in each city and determined sales locations by obtaining traffic flow figures. Once these figures were obtained, a specific site was located in income areas of $7,000 to $12,000.

Recruiting hippie salesmen was never done through advertising but simply by the hippie underground. It was claimed that, once the word was out, as many as thirty hippies might show up to ask about selling on a corner.

Each salesman was told he could not smoke pot on the job or violate other laws. Afterward he could do whatever he wanted, as he no longer represented the company. In most cases the selling days were Friday, Saturday, and Sunday. During this time, several of hippie salesmen indicated, it was quite possible to make $30 to $40 per day on a commission rate of 50 cents per dozen carnations.

In summer the hippies would move north, and in the winter would return to places such as Texas, New Mexico, and Arizona, all the time selling flowers at each location.

The selling company bought the flowers for 7 or 8 cents each and sold them for 25 cents each. The city manager distributed flowers to his salesmen and picked up the receipts several times during the day. Thus the company had no overhead and no accounts receivable.

Mr. Davis stated that it was possible for a firm selling carnations in this manner to sell $150,000 gross per month. He also stated that a street corner in Dallas had been so successful that it was named "Mother Alpha" by the hippies, who sold 15,000 to 20,000 carnations on that corner on a weekend.

The hippie salesmen proved to be very aggressive and would rush out to cars with a bouquet of flowers. At first, people seemed to be reticent about buying from them, but after a few weeks it was normal for customers to seek out these street-corner vendors.

As the hippies' sales volume grew, the traditional florists began complaining, and some threatened to quit buying from Davis Brothers. In reply, Davis Brothers stated that the hippie organization bought at the same price schedule available to the florists and that they sold to a different customer. Prices in retail florist shops for a dozen carnations traditionally ran from $7.50 to $12 per dozen, as opposed to $3 from the hippies. Moreover, it was felt that the reason a customer enters a florist shop is different from the reason a motorist stops at a hippie's corner.

As an example, Mr. Davis stated the case of a florist who had gone to court to prevent a flower peddler from selling in front of his shop—the peddler won the case and continued to sell in front of the florist. However, the florist experienced a sales increase as long as the peddler was in front. It seemed that people could not always find what they wanted from the peddler and therefore came into the store.

Eventually, the peddler died and the store owner offered a $10,000 salary to a man to continue to run the peddler's stall in front of his store.

When Davis Brothers began to deal with the hippie groups, it demanded

C.O.D. Later it sold on a 30-day basis, and all went well for a year. Then checks began to bounce, and eventually a lawsuit was filed.

Although Mr. Davis was uncertain as to all the causes, he believed that improper management of the hippies' selling organization had been the major cause for these defaults.

Even though this group failed, new hippie sales organizations were being formed. The Davises knew that there was a tremendous market potential in this type of retail organization, and wanted to continue selling through them. At the same time, they were cautious of default payments by these groups.

While they did not believe that the hippies' sales of carnations hurt their established dealers, they were cognizant of the psychological effect it had on them. Consequently, the Davis brothers were meeting to discuss the situation and decide on future courses of action.

DISCUSSION QUESTIONS

1. Do you believe that Davis Brothers Florists should continue to sell through hippies' sales organizations? Can it successfully sell to both florists and hippies at the same time?
2. Is the hippie life style a temporary social phenomenon or is it likely to continue for several years?
3. Discuss the consumer motivation involved in buying flowers from a hippie on the street corner as opposed to buying from a florist.
4. Are there other types of products that could successfully be sold through a hippie-type sales force? If so, how would you organize it?
5. What marketing changes can you visualize in the cut-flower business, regardless of the permanence of hippies? Discuss the implications to a firm such as Davis Brothers and the possible future moves that may be necessary for management.
6. What methods could best be used to educate those florists who feel the hippie marketing methods are hurting them?
7. What method could be used to stimulate more retail florists to sell through nontraditional outlets?
8. What do you feel is the future of the mass marketing of fresh-cut flowers through the produce departments of large chain grocery stores?
9. Would the involvement of large corporate organizations increase the potential and latitude of the flower industry, so as to benefit all distributors (grower, wholesaler, and retailer)?

KING SOOPERS DISCOUNT STORES
Promotion

After several months of study the management of King Soopers Discount Stores decided to activate two new programs in all of its thirty-three stores. While these were not to be initiated concurrently, they placed additional responsibility on the advertising department.

The advertising department, under the direction of Mr. Marl Shanahan, advertising director, was assigned the task of explaining and promoting both programs to the general public and to all King Soopers employees.

The assignment given the ad department was to promote "unit pricing" and a "personalized" check-cashing card. In both cases, these were new programs for the company and the Denver area.

Unit pricing consisted of determining a price per ounce, pound, or other commonly used unit of measure for each of the 12,000 items sold in a typical King Soopers store. This system would allow a customer to compare prices for a similar item (such as coffee) per unit of measure. Although a few other retailers in the United States had instituted this system for selected items, King Soopers was the first to do it for all items in the store.

Once the unit price was determined, it would be fed into a computer and IBM shelf markers would be printed to appear below each item on the shelf.

Since the concept was new, it was felt that the customer might need special help and information to understand the system. A random survey of King Sooper shoppers had also shown that the low-income consumer seemed to have special problems in understanding or appreciating the value of unit pricing.

The management directed that it was not enough to simply inform the consumers. In addition, every store employee was to be instructed as to the purpose and working of unit pricing so that he or she could explain them to the consumer. This task was also assigned to the advertising department.

Prior to the decision to use unit pricing there had been considerable discussion of the pros and cons of such a system by government officials and consumer groups. Although King Soopers had been attuned to this, it had not been forced to adopt unit pricing by any group. The decision was voluntary, and the company did not wish the public to feel that it had been pressured into this move.

Nevertheless, the decision seemed to fit the current mood of the consumer, and King Soopers was anxious to obtain as much favorable publicity from the move as possible.

The second new program to be introduced was that of a personalized check-cashing card. Consumers who held this card would be allowed to pay for their purchases with a personal check. The check could be written for $10 more than the cost of the products.

Previous to the check-cashing card, King Soopers had tried several systems, including the manager's okay on all checks, and even a rather complicated system of photographing each customer at the time he cashed a check. In spite of these systems, the company had continued to experience losses through bad checks.

The new system would require that customers first complete an application form. The information given by the customer would then be checked for accuracy by King Soopers—much the same as any credit card company checks credit risks.

The King Soopers card was not a credit card, and the management did not wish that there be any misunderstanding of its proper role.

Since it was necessary to ask for personal information about consumers, the advertising department was faced with the need to "sell" the program to the consumers in a clear, concise manner that would avoid confusion or hard feelings.

As in the case of unit pricing, it was also necessary to design a program to ensure that all employees were familiar with the new program and could explain it to consumers.

A strict budget allocation was not made for the promotion of either program, but Mr. Shanahan knew that the costs would have to be reasonable.

With a department of twelve people, he believed the task could be completed internally without the need for additional full-time employees. It was highly possible, however, that part-time employees might be needed for in-store distribution of literature if that course of action were decided upon.

The ad department of King Soopers had equipment and facilities to do printing, photography, layout, and copyrighting.

King Soopers also had the advantage of years of experience and good will in the Denver market. According to a *Denver Post* survey, the chain had 37 percent of the grocery business in Denver.

Throughout the years the company had been an innovator in the introduction of many new merchandising concepts, and it was felt that the public recognized this. One of the most dramatic new changes was the move from strictly supermarket merchandising to discount merchandising. New King Soopers stores were being built to encompass 40,000 square feet—with departments such as a pharmacy, general merchandise, a delicatessen, and an in-store bakery in addition to the supermarket.

As he began to plan the introduction and promotion of each program, Mr. Shanahan envisaged a four- to six-week planning and preparation deadline for each one. The success or failure of each now rested in his department.

DISCUSSION QUESTIONS

1. Design a realistic promotion-publicity program for both of the new King Soopers plans (unit pricing and the personalized check-cashing card). Be certain to include time sequences.

2. What is your opinion of the concept of unit pricing? Do you believe it should be initiated by all food retailers, including specialty houses such as delicatessens? Who do you believe is most likely to use such a system while shopping: middle-income, upper-income, or low-income groups? Why?

3. Do you feel that the idea of a personalized check-cashing card will solve the problems of bad checks faced by retailers? What is the next probable step?

CHAPTER 10

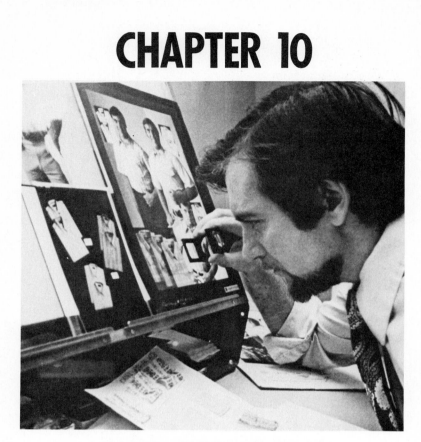

Photo courtesy of J. C. Penney Company, Inc.

The Promotional Mix

The discussion in Chapter 9 centered on the financial aspects to consider in developing a promotional strategy: level of expenditure, proper scheduling, in-store allocation, and appropriate media. Chapter 10 looks more closely at each promotional medium and focuses upon the considerations necessary to establish a promotional mix that will be consistent with the retailer's objectives and effective in reaching his target market customers.

ADVERTISING

Perhaps the most difficult advertising task in all marketing is the continuous problem of advertising faced by retailers. In most cases, stores are too small to purchase large amounts of advertising in any media. In addition, they usually serve a relatively small area, such as a suburb of 50,000 persons.

There may not be a good local paper serving their trade area, and if there is, it may have a small readership. Persons who live in the store's trading area subscribe to major newspapers and listen to the major radio stations. A small retailer usually cannot afford to buy time and space in these media, since he will be paying for coverage in areas outside his market perimeter.

Faced with these problems, a retailer should be aware of the characteristics of each medium so that he can make appropriate promotional appeals and audience and cost comparisons.

Printed Media

Because they are durable, all print media vehicles allow the consumer more freedom in translating the meaning of advertisements into something that is meaningful to him personally. A consumer can read and look at the advertisement at his own pace. If necessary, he can reread the advertisement to understand its message more clearly. In general, print media, because of their durable nature:

> (1) Provide greater opportunity for the consumer to translate the advertisement's message with more careful thought. (2) Allow for group participation in translating the advertisement's message. Members of a family can study a print advertisement together in a way that is not possible for radio or television advertisements. (3) Offer increased opportunity for consumers to make comparisons, by looking back and forth between pages, of the product-service offerings made by various retailers.[1]

The various kinds of print media possess different characteristics from a consumer viewpoint. Therefore each will be discussed separately.

Newspapers

Although retailers may use all forms of mass media advertising, the primary promotional tool used by most retailers is the local newspaper and its supplements. The local newspaper offers retailers the opportunity to reach a large percentage of their customers at a comparatively low cost with an extremely short lead-lag time between preparation of the ad and exposure to the customer. It also allows customers the opportunity to compare prices, shopping hours, and other differences between competitive retailers, if that is desired. Newspapers are sufficiently timely that the retailer can tie his advertisements to current events, such as a forecast of the first freeze of the year.

Newspapers appeal to a broad range of customers, and local newspapers are perceived by the consumers as factual.[2] Newspaper advertisers regard newspaper advertising as being easily understood. It is believed that advertisements are read most closely by consumers who are in the process of making a purchase decision.[3] Another advantage of newspaper advertising is that the makeup of a typical advertisement requires less technical skill than the creation of advertisements for most other media.[4]

The short life of a newspaper is one of the disadvantages of newspaper advertising; consumers tend to spend only a little time reading each issue, and then they discard it. Another disadvantage for retailers who serve a small area is the wasted circulation resulting from the wide geographical distribution of the large-city papers. Finally, the quality of reproduction in newspapers is generally low because they must be printed at high speed.

The type of newspaper can be selected for effectiveness in reaching the target market customer. The morning papers in most cities have a masculine image, with emphasis on sports and business. The advertisements in the morning paper frequently are read shortly before the consumer makes the purchase (later in the day).[5] The evening paper may be read more carefully, in a more relaxed environment, but is likely to be larger in size than typical morning papers. Sunday papers are read in an even more thorough manner, but are even larger in size than evening papers. The circulation is also expanded on Sundays, so that retailers may be able to place their advertisements in a specialized section of the paper. The disadvantages of the Sunday paper are the increased competition from rival retailers and the larger circulation, which may raise advertising costs. It is easy for an advertisement to become practically unavailable to the reader when the paper is very large and a particular location within it cannot be specified. This is the case when run-of-the-press rates are obtained.[6]

Specialized papers, with relatively small circulation, are increasing in popularity because they reduce waste circulation by aiming at a specific group of people. Such a paper may limit circulation to only a small geographical area, or reach only a specific religious or occupational group. The cost per potential customer is frequently lower on specialized papers because wasted circulation is reduced.

Magazines

Magazine advertisements have a longer life and better-quality reproduction than newspapers. Consumers are likely to read and reread the copy at a leisurely pace and examine the pictures in more detail in magazine advertisements. This repeated exposure is a unique feature of magazine advertising. As such, magazines are well suited for the creation of the desired store image or institutional type of advertising. Because different moods are created by the content of each magazine, advertisements can illustrate how the outlet or selected merchandise fits this consumer mood.

Despite these desirable characteristics, magazines are not used extensively by retailers because even specialized magazines are likely to have a high level of wasted circulation. Specialized magazines appeal to a specific group, but their per square inch advertising rates are usually higher than newspaper rates.[7] In addition, magazine editors require a much longer lead time for an advertisement to be included in a particular edition.

Direct Mail

Direct-mail promotion includes any literature that is sent to customers or prospective customers through either the U.S. or a private mail system. Although the cost of postage and handling has increased markedly in recent years, so too have the possibilities for effectively using direct mail. This may be attributed to the growth of credit sales, the increased use of the computer, and zip code mailing.

Direct mail can be used most effectively when the retailer is catering to a small, well-defined segment of the market. In this case the cost per potential customer reached may be lower with direct mail than with other media. The success of direct-mail advertising depends on the quality of the mailing list, which should be selective, so all names should be potential customers for the product/service being offered. Mailing lists may be developed by a retailer from the records of his credit department. These can be further segmented, through the development of a computer program, to group customers on the basis of similar characteristics. Although the initial development of this system may be expensive, it allows a retailer to pinpoint his market and thus save on future promotions.

The use of zip code data and a "crisscross" directory enables the retailer to stratify mailings by income area and by areas of high social or ethnic concentration. Direct-mail promotion can then be employed in using a rifle method of hitting a target market, rather than a shotgun approach.

Advances in printing have allowed the retailer a great deal of flexibility and much room for imagination. Samples of products (such as fabrics) have long been sent to prospective customers. Now it is also possible to appeal to the customer's sense of smell through direct mail. New perfumes and colognes may be introduced through a process that impregnates the scent in the direct-mail piece.

The nature of the sample must, however, be carefully considered in any direct-mailing piece. A manufacturer of razor blades included a new blade in the evening edition of urban newspapers, only to get a rash of serious complaints by homeowners—children and dogs discovered the blades before the adults. It is a dangerous—and sometimes unlawful—practice to distribute samples of many products in a direct-mail campaign. Premium coupons, rather than the sample product itself, should be used for products such as razor blades, medicines, and other potentially dangerous products.

Another advantage of the direct-mail approach is that the advertisement does not compete directly for attention with other advertisements, as most mail is opened and at least scanned by the consumer. Thus consumers may pay more attention to direct-mail advertisements than to other forms of advertisements. Retailers should nevertheless be aware that consumers frequently discard third class "occupant" mail without opening it. Personalized, first class mail increases attention, but costs more than third class mail.[8]

Several different forms of direct-mail advertising are used by retailers. *Personalized letters* are designed to be similar in appearance to personal correspondence; and the more personalized the letter, the higher the readership—and the cost.[9] *Cards* are frequently sent out to introduce a sale; although the cost of mailing them is relatively inexpensive, they do not have a confidential or impressive appearance. *Circulars, leaflets,* and *folders* can be used to reach the audience at a low cost, but they suffer because they are not personalized. *Catalogs* and *coupons* are other forms of direct mail that, because of their importance, deserve a more detailed discussion.

The first thing that probably comes to mind when catalogs are mentioned is Sears and Montgomery Ward, yet the use of catalogs as a promotion and sales tool is by no means limited to the giants of retailing. Nor is it strictly limited to mass merchandise–type items. Thousands of firms rely heavily upon their catalogs for promotion and for direct sales. Moreover, the use of catalogs is increasing rather than declining, in spite of bigger and better shopping centers. Catalogs are usually quite expensive to produce and mail, but they have an extremely long life.

The expansion of catalog advertising is particularly noticeable in industries that sell specialized products to a particular market segment. The leisure industry is indicative of this increase. There has been a growth of specialty retailers selling items such as back-packing equipment and pre-cut vacation homes.

Catalogs are also important promotional tools for "carriage trade" retailers, such as Neiman Marcus. Customers look forward to viewing the Christmas catalog of Neiman Marcus to discover what exotic new "his and her" gifts are being offered for sale. These have included Egyptian mummy cases for "him and her" and his-and-her Chinese junks. Neiman Marcus has been able to develop a suspense buildup in the introduction of these gifts, complete with all the secrecy that automobile manufacturers use with yearly model changes. At the correct moment, the catalogs are released and the press is informed of the his-and-her gifts for the coming Christmas. This promotional technique dramatically ties together the use of catalogs and publicity to enhance the overall image of Neiman Marcus.

An entire mailing program could easily be a disaster if the tone of the catalog does not meet the image goals of the retailer. As a result, special attention is paid to layout, copy, color, and the overall esthetic appeal of the catalog. It is not simply a directory of products and prices but a carefully planned promotional arm for the company. Unfortunately, the catalogs of many retailers are poorly planned and do not reflect an image consistent with that desired by the retailer. This is often true with small retailers who sell high-quality merchandise but feel they cannot afford the services of professionals in the design and layout of their catalogs. As a result, most of the planning is left to the sales manager and printer, who may only incidentally possess artistic talents.

Small retailers who are faced with this problem should give special thought to the possibility of *selling* their catalogs. Pre-cut home manufacturers, and many other retailers, have demonstrated that consumers will pay over $1 for professionally designed catalogs. Such a program will enable a retailer to hire the services of professionals to produce a catalog consistent with the corporate image. The catalog must appear to be worth the charge. If it does not, customers will feel they have been taken and that the products sold by this retailer must also be overpriced. Retailers who sell their catalogs also believe that this policy results in a more careful reading of their information and a longer "shelf life"; that is, the customer is reluctant to dispose of the catalog. He may also be more prone to show it to his friends than if it were acquired free.

Coupons

Coupons are a promotional tool that is widely used throughout the nation by manufacturers and retailers of supermarket items. Coupons are small cards or cutouts that are found in magazines, newspapers, direct-mail envelopes, and retail outlets. Coupons offer the consumer a savings on a particular product or service when they are redeemed at the cash register. They may be valued at as little as a few cents to as much as two items for the price of one.

Although coupons have been used for a variety of products, they are used predominately by manufacturers of branded products with a nature of frequent repeat purchase, such as detergents, personal care products, and foods. Coupons are also a popular promotional tool of local retailers of services and prepared foods. Even the smallest pizza shop or beauty parlor generally can afford the costs of printing and distributing coupons door to door. Retailers and manufacturers have discovered that coupons are effective marketing tools when used in the following ways:

(1) In the introduction of a new or improved product; (2) Introducing a product into a new market; (3) In obtaining broader distribution of a product by using the coupon program as an inducement for more stores to carry the product; (4) Reducing excessive inventories of a product; (5) Equipping salesmen with an additional sales tool; (6) As a marketing research tool.[10]

The use of coupons as a marketing research tool is a side benefit that has been discovered and used by marketing executives. Since coupons can be coded by area, it is possible to derive such information as trading patterns, the effect of different types and values of coupons upon sales, generalized consumer profiles, and other important data.

It is obvious that a coupon is valuable as a promotional medium only if it is redeemed. In a study of coupons by the A. C. Nielsen Clearing House, five factors appeared to influence the redemption rate of coupons:

(1) Method used to distribute the coupon. The use of direct mail and in-product coupons resulted in a higher redemption than magazines or newspapers.
(2) Size of the product class. As the rate of sale per $1000 increased, the redemption rate of coupons also increased.
(3) Rate of discount. The rate of discount relative to the price of the product also seemed to affect redemption rate. Although the consumer may not know or calculate the exact percentage, she apparently did recognize better discount values.
(4) Face value of the coupon. Consumers were influenced by high face values on the card, particularly when these reflected high discount values.
(5) Brand distribution. As can logically be expected, redemption rate in-

creased as the distribution of the brand increased. A housewife can't buy a product if she can't find it.[11]

Although couponing can be an effective promotional tool for retailers and manufacturers, it is not without problems for both. Retailers often find it difficult or impossible to check purchases against coupon redemption. As a result, the manufacturer may redeem coupons for cash when in reality his product was never purchased. In addition, the sheer volume of coupons creates additional work and control problems for both parties.

In recent years a problem of counterfeiting has occurred in some areas. This is not a problem as long as the coupon is redeemed upon purchase of the specific product or service; it becomes a problem when coupons are redeemed for cash without proof of purchase.

The Yellow Pages

One of the best advertising media available to small retailers is the Yellow Pages of the local phone book. Because the vast majority of American homes now have a telephone, most retailers can be assured that their advertising message is present in their customers' homes. The only exception is in extremely low-income areas.

If a phone book serves an entire area of suburbs and city, the retailer may be forced to pay higher rates than he wishes, since the market area served by this medium is extensive. Nevertheless, the cost may still be worthwhile, and this method should not be automatically dismissed as an advertising possibility. Retailers in suburban areas are often faced with the question of placing an advertisement in the local phone book and another one in the larger metropolitan directory.

Retailers with limited lines may also use the Yellow Pages as a catalog. A scaffolding rental and sales company discovered the Yellow Pages worked well as a catalog. As the number of do-it-yourself homeowners increased, the company owner found that he and his staff were spending many hours on the phone trying to explain the different equipment to nonprofessionals. To correct this situation, illustrations of the major types of scaffolding were pictured in the Yellow Page ad. The owner and his staff were then able to ask a telephone customer to turn to the Yellow Pages and select the type of scaffold needed.[12]

Statistics by American Telephone and Telegraph Company have shown that, during a 12-month period, 76 percent of the adult population 20 years and older turned to the Yellow Pages to locate a product or service. Of the total references to the Yellow Pages, 89 percent were followed up with a telephone call, personal visit, or letter to the advertiser.[13] A more detailed analysis of a national study of Yellow Page usage is presented in Table 10–1.

Broadcast Media

Retailers use both radio and television advertising to relay their messages to consumers. Both media reach a large number of people at a low cost as

Table 10–1 *National Consumer Usage of "Yellow Pages"*

ALL PRODUCTS AND SERVICES COMBINED		Adult Population	PENETRATION OF MARKET		EXTENT AND NATURE OF YELLOW PAGES USAGE	
			Yellow Pages Users	*% of Market*	*Total References*	*Average Reference per User*
Sex	Men	55,917,000	41,685,000	75	1,883,142,000	45.2
	Women	63,960,000	50,417,000	79	1,809,628,000	35.9
Age	20–39	49,856,000	42,605,000	86	2,205,196,000	51.8
	40 & over	70,021,000	49,497,000	71	1,487,574,000	30.1
Family Income	Under 5,000	32,166,000	19,050,000	59	395,662,000	20.8
	$5,000–$10,000	50,426,000	40,269,000	80	1,587,492,000	39.4
	$10,000 & over	37,285,000	32,783,000	88	1,709,616,000	52.2
Family Size	1 or 2 persons	45,723,000	31,675,000	69	781,095,000	24.7
	3 or 4 persons	43,593,000	34,902,000	80	1,607,465,000	46.1
	5 or more persons	30,561,000	25,525,000	84	1,304,210,000	51.1
City Size	Metropolitan areas	77,444,000	62,150,000	80	2,659,825,000	42.8
	Non-metro areas	42,433,000	29,952,000	71	1,032,945,000	34.5
Residential Mobility	Moved less than 2 years ago	28,836,000	24,522,000	85	1,197,010,000	48.8
	Moved 2 years ago or more	91,041,000	67,580,000	74	2,495,760,000	36.9
Home Ownership	Rent	37,119,000	27,398,000	74	1,110,326,000	40.5
	Own	82,758,000	64,704,000	78	2,582,444,000	39.9

SOURCE *The Yellow Pages in Marketing and Advertising* (New York: American Telephone and Telegraph Company, 1970), pp. 50–51. Data are based on a study conducted by Audits and Surveys Inc. in 1966. Copyright © American Telephone and Telegraph Company, 1970.

nearly every home has at least one radio and one television set. But the amount of wasted circulation is also high for both media, unless the retailer is large enough to serve the entire broadcast area. If the retailer serves only a small segment of the population reached by the broadcasts, the waste circulation problem could be serious enough to make the use of broadcast media uneconomical. Some radio or television stations counteract this objection by scheduling programs that appeal to specific consumer groups. Retailers who cater to these groups can then advertise on these programs at a lower cost per potential customer simply because waste circulation has been reduced.

Another problem, shared by both radio and television, is that each medium presents many advertisements which are unrelated to the purpose for which the consumer is tuned to the medium. Television and radio audiences are normally in a mood for diversion, but unfortunately that mood usually has only a slight connection to the accompanying promotional message.[14] Despite the fact that consumers do not appear to give radio and television advertisements as much attention as they do to advertisements in print media, it appears that they remember a surprisingly large part of the former's commercial messages.[15] In general, the length of time that a television commercial is remembered is longer than that of a radio commercial, but shorter than that of a newspaper advertisement.[16]

One of the largest problems associated with radio and television advertising is that consumers frequently use these media as "background noise" and may not hear or see the presentations. A high level of creativity in advertisement writing and preparation and considerable repetition of these advertisements may be required to reach the consumer effectively.

Radio

As radio is one of the most flexible media, a retailer can usually find a radio station, program, and broadcast time that will appeal to his target market. The commuting hours are generally the peak listening hours, and radio reaches most automobile drivers exceptionally well because they can simultaneously drive and listen to their preferred programs. Radio can become a companion to drivers and to people spending time at home reading or relaxing. As a result, radio's personalities frequently are perceived as personal friends by the listener. This intimate relationship is an advantage because these listeners place more trust in an endorsement when they believe they hear it from a friend.[17]

The per minute cost of advertising is much lower over radio than on television. A retailer can take advantage of this relatively low cost and combine it with an advertising schedule that is designed to reach the target market group in an effective promotional campaign.

Television

Television advertisement uses both sight and sound to take the retailer's appeal to the consumer. Indeed, its ability to show certain products that require demonstration may necessitate the use of television advertising. Because consumers spend many evening hours relaxing before a television set, advertisements reach these people when they are more susceptible to new ideas.[18]

The disadvantages of television include a high cost for advertising time and the relatively high cost required to prepare a good television advertisement. In addition, small retailers encounter much waste circulation because television does not generally offer as selective an appeal as radio. The total television audience in any area is also likely to be less segmented than the radio audience because there are fewer television stations. For these reasons, it is difficult for a small retailer to reach his target market through television.

Creating Print and Broadcast Advertisements

Although advertising creativity is not likely to be programmable, there are certain ideas that can be used by people who are responsible for preparing retail advertisements. First, the message must speak for the retailer in tone and content that match his objectives. Thus the retailer must:

(1) Identify his target market customers.

(2) Identify the reasons for advertising, be they: stimulation of immediate purchases, changing of consumers' shopping habits, enhancing the store's image, informing consumers about the store's continued existence, the merchandise [and/or] service offerings, etc.

(3) Determine the unique selling features that are most likely to appeal to his target market group. Seeing things from the point of view of the target market customers can generate unique selling features. Talking to customers, and surveying consumers by the use of questionnaires can give retailers ideas on the desires of [their] target group.

(4) List the benefits that should be featured in his advertisements. Consumers want to know "what does this advertisement offer me?" Facts (such as a large number of automobiles on hand) mean little to the consumer until they are turned into benefits for him by emphasizing that he can choose from a large selection of automobiles.

(5) Develop the theme for the advertisement by taking the above factors into consideration.[19]

Converting the theme into an advertisement should follow the AIDCA process. This consists of attracting *attention*, stimulating *interest*, creating *desire*, *convincing* the consumer that the merchandise/service offering will provide the best solution to his problem, and, finally, suggesting that the consumer take *action*. The different ways of using print and radio advertising to take the consumer through the AIDCA process will now be discussed.

Print Media

Headlines are used to capture the reader's attention. On the average, five times as many people read the headline of an advertisement as read the body.[20] Therefore, if retailers don't "sell" a benefit in a short, simple headline, they waste 80 percent of their money. "Benefit headlines" are designed to answer the target consumer's question, "What does this advertisement offer me?"

Illustrations, if used, should reinforce headlines to capture the reader's attention. Usually photographs attract more readers, are more believable, and are better remembered than drawings.[21] Captions should be placed below a photograph because, in general, twice as many people read the captions as read the body of the advertisement.[22] More awareness can be obtained if each caption is considered to be a miniature advertisement containing brand names and benefits.

The headline and illustration should capture the *attention* and stimulate the *interest* of the reader. The text, or copy, is used to *create* the *desire* for the product or service and to *convince* the reader that the advertised merchandise/service offering is best in light of *his* needs.

Copywriting is truly a creative process, but several concepts may be of assistance. First, the message should include the benefits that are likely to appeal to the target group. Second, the writing should be phrased in the type of language that is most familiar to the people in the target group. The arguments should be presented in terms to which target consumers can relate. Third, the benefits should be presented in simple words and short sentences that get the ideas across quickly and clearly. The creative element is involved in using words which arouse interest and encourage people to read an advertisement to its conclusion. Readership falls off rapidly up to 50 words, but it drops off only slightly between 50 and 500 words if the copy is well written.[23] The decline in readership means that the most important ideas should be presented first in copy.

The layout of an advertisement involves visually fitting together the lead line, illustration, copy, and a signature or logotype, which may include the store name, location, store hours, and phone number. Whenever printed advertisements are used, special care should be given to the mechanics of producing the best layout for the money. For an advertisement of a given size, this involves careful consideration of the following details.[24]

AMOUNT OF WHITE SPACE   The retailer should consider the image that he wants to project and allocate more white space to expensive, quality merchandise if he wishes to project a prestige image (Figure 10–1). If he wishes to project a discount-price image, he will want to reduce the white space and use a more crowded, cluttered layout, similar to Figure 10–2.

PLACEMENT   Regular advertisers will find that newspapers are generally willing to place their ads on desired pages or sections. Retailers should give serious consideration to the correct area even if a small premium is required to reserve space in this area. Many small retailers sell specialized products, such as women's wear, wigs, sporting goods, and pet supplies, that coincide well with such special areas as the sports or the women's section.

*Figure 10–1   Example of "Sale" Advertisement
Conveying Prestige Image by Using White Space*

——— MONTALDO'S ———

1632 California Street

Fall Clearance

Special Groupings

¼ to ⅓ off

SOURCE   Montaldo's, Denver.

THE BORDER   A border can help to establish the desired image, set a retailer apart from others, and eventually act almost as a logo.

PRINT STYLE   A retailer may wish to purchase a print type not carried by the local newspaper. This can be kept on stock at the newspaper and used only by the retailer. Although difference is desired, an extreme can actually work to the detriment of the retailer.

THE SLOGAN   A good slogan can aid in establishing an image and in repeating a message to the customer. It should contain the name of the firm and/or the merchandise or service offered. It should also have recall value, may arouse curiosity, and should serve as a focus point for the advertising policy of the firm.

SPONSOR IDENTIFICATION   A signature in the form of a logo or distinctive design can help improve identification. It does no good to advertise if the reader cannot remember later which store it was that was having the sale or confuses it with a competitor. Signature "cuts" may be purchased through engraving companies and stored with the local newspaper or printer.

Figure 10–2   Example of "Discount Price" Advertising

SOURCE   Bill Crouch Chrysler-Plymouth, Denver

HUMAN INTEREST ILLUSTRATION   Illustration can add to the interest in the ad if well done. Newspapers carry a catalog of illustrations which may have applicability. A special illustration, to be used in a recurring theme, should be custom made and kept on file with the newspaper or printer.

CHECK THE ADVERTISEMENT BEFORE PRINTING   Each advertiser should check the advertisement to be certain that (1) the advertisement is easily recognizable; (2) a simple layout has been used; (3) a dominant element, such as a headline or illustration, has been used to present a benefit to the consumer; (4) the amount of white space is consistent with the store image; (5) the copy is complete, including the store name; (6) possibly related items are included in the advertisement; (7) wording is simple and excessive claims are not used; (8) the advertisement urges readers to buy now.

Broadcast Media

Broadcast media present difficult creative problems because consumers must understand the message the first time. They cannot go back and reread the message, as they can in print advertisements. Only a very short message can be communicated because the consumer's attention is not completely focused on the advertising presentation. Both television and radio commercials can suffer from wordiness. One-minute radio commercials should present between 120 and 150 words.[25]

There are different types of radio commercials.[26] A *straight announcement* involves an announcer's delivering the commercial without the use of music or any backup noise. The personality of a regular announcer is used to attempt to make the commercial more believable. Use of irrelevant celebrities, who are not connected with the offering, may only steal attention from the message.

A *dramatization* is a commercial playlet, which is a good attention getter but is also expensive to produce. Normally a realistic consumer problem is posed and the sponsoring store eventually solves the problem in a believable way. The problem that is selected should be based upon some unique merchandise/service offering available at the store. A good *dialogue* commercial involves a realistic conversation between several announcers.

Good *jingle* or *singing commercials* are quite effective in gaining a listener's attention. However, they should be well done or they may irritate the listener and adversely affect the store's image.

Television commercials use the same techniques as radio, but also allow the use of *visual demonstrations*. If they are honest and believable, these demonstrations are quite effective ways to communicate with customers. *Animated* and *cartoon commercials* can be used effectively to reach children. They are less persuasive than live commercials in reaching adults who cannot identify themselves with the character in the cartoon.[27]

Broadcast advertisements require the use of a natural, simple language that will appeal to the target group of consumers. The desired store image and its merchandise/service offering must then be turned into consumer benefits and presented in a short amount of time. Generally this means that the advertiser should try to communicate only one idea during a commercial. The more ideas presented, the less consumers remember about the content of the commercial. The name and address of the store should be repeated several times during the commercial. Musical jingles or spoken slogans that rhyme with the name of the store can be used to assist the memory of consumers. A strong windup, calling for consumer action, is also desirable.

Position Media

Position media include all types of signs, posters, programs, menus, directories, sky writing, and transportation advertising, such as the signs that appear on the back of taxicabs or inside public vehicles.

Figure 10–3   Example of Sign Advertising
Outdoor advertising delivers imagery. Dan
Howells, Marketing Director, Six Flags over
Texas, states, "Advertising for Six Flags over
Texas must communicate the fun and fan-
tasy of a visit to this family amusement
center. Outdoor advertising gave us the visibility and impact necessary to deliver these
'one liner' opinions of Six Flags by historical
and storybook characters."

SOURCE   *Advertising Age* (July 2, 1973),
p. 42. This is a reproduction of an advertisement
prepared by Foster and Kleiser, a Metromedia
Company.

Signs

Advertising by means of signs is more suitable for institutional image
promotion than for product–direction-action promotion because it is difficult
and expensive to change the message continually. Thus position media are
generally used to reinforce the messages presented in other media or other
signs (Figure 10–3). The content of the former generally consists of no
more than 8 words, unless the sign is presented on the inside of a bus or
train.[28] In the latter cases, the sign may contain up to 15 words, as a consumer frequently has nothing better to do than read the advertisement.

It is becoming increasingly clear that decisions concerning outdoor
signs are no longer strictly the province of the retailer. Legislation regulating
outdoor signs is almost certain to increase in amount and severity. The more

vociferous anti-sign groups argue that if all signs were removed, no single company would have an advantage. Unless this viewpoint gains more support, the argument will remain academic. In the meantime, retailers will continue to utilize signs.

In recent years, corporations have placed increasing importance upon their images and logos. Retailers of gasoline have been particularly concerned with the image portrayed through these signs. This reflects the fact that a logo must give quick and positive identification to the viewer, and means that every aspect of such signs must be given careful consideration. The color, shape, size, and type of illustration also have taken on increased importance. For this reason, it is advisable to use the services of professional design firms. Although the design and planning of signs should be assigned to professionals, it is well for retailers to be aware of some of the considerations in design.

Color

The role of color in our lives has taken on increased importance. As a result, many variables should be considered in the selection of colors.

VISIBILITY Yellow can be seen from a greater distance than other colors when placed on painted or printed surfaces. Red and blue follow next in order of visibility from distances. Even though yellow exhibits greater visibility, it may not be selected because of other overriding considerations. Color combinations give maximum legibility and visibility in the following order:

1. Black on yellow
2. Black on orange
3. Orange on navy blue
4. Green on white
5. Scarlet red on white
6. Black on white
7. Navy blue on white
8. White on navy blue
9. Orange on black
10. White on black
11. White on bottle green
12. White on scarlet red
13. White on purple
14. Purple on white
15. Navy blue on yellow
16. Navy blue on orange
17. Yellow on black
18. Scarlet red on yellow
19. Yellow on navy blue
20. Purple on yellow

SYMBOLISM AND TRADITION Certain colors traditionally have had specific images and meaning. Purple has long been associated with royalty, red with danger, green with safety, blue with first place, gold with richness, pastels with spring, and on and on. The symbols and traditions associated with colors are overlooked by retailers only at their loss.

Reference to the colors black and white and their symbolism can be extremely dangerous for today's retailer. White has long been used to designate cleanliness, virginity, goodness, wholesomeness, the "good guy," etc. Black has been associated with quite the opposite, and today the traditional use of black as a negative symbol is at best a risky undertaking. In an era of

"Black is beautiful" and "Black Power," only the most "tuned out" will elect to represent the bad guy as the one in black.

Color may be used as a replacement for certain signs. The skillful use of colors in interior design can help to direct the consumer's eye to key spots within the store, thus avoiding the use of potentially objectionable signs. A chain of retail candy stores is credited with the use of color to eliminate the need for signs inside its phone booths to remind customers to keep conversations short. Since man cannot remain long in a pure red environment, the insides of problem phone booths were painted red. This action was credited with the elimination of long phone conversations, and the store was able to remove its unsightly signs.[29]

SENSORY EFFECTS   Hues of brown and gold are appetite-stimulating colors and should be considered in connection with food products and areas of the store that sell these items. Yellow, orange, and red are generally classified as stimulating colors. Blue, green, and violet are sedative or "cold" colors. The stimulating or action colors may be used in an environment in which things are done quickly. Red is the most volatile, following by orange and yellow. These colors cause farsightedness in large areas; they cause the colors to "come closer." Small rooms seem to close in psychologically when these colors are used.

POINT-OF-PURCHASE PROMOTIONS

Point-of-purchase promotions (P.O.P.) range from a simple counter display with a sign to free samples distributed by girls in bikinis accompanied by a brass band. Point-of-purchase advertising

> sells both by reminder and by impulse. When selling by reminder it utilizes the impact already made by other advertising media, serving as a link between them and the place where sales are made. When selling by impulse it also appeals independently. In either case, it is a potent instrument in clinching the sale. It asks for the order.[30]

Point-of-purchase promotions exist to strengthen overall retail promotional strategy. A great quantity of the point-of-purchase material available to retailers is furnished by the manufacturer. These displays may have been designed to tie in with a current promotional theme by the manufacturer, but may be completely out of place in the retail store. Retailers have both the right and the responsibility to reject any P.O.P. material they feel is damaging to the store's image. Unless P.O.P. material is planned around the habits, needs, problems, and fears of the retailer, it is almost assuredly headed for the trash can.

Even the best planned and most creative P.O.P. display is destined for a short life. This is the very nature of P.O.P. material. Since the marketing and creative staffs of manufacturers and retailers continually create obsolescence in P.O.P. material, a precise classification is impossible. However, certain types of P.O.P. displays have emerged over time. These should not be considered totally independent classifications. Creative P.O.P. designers purposely blend one type with another to create hybrid displays.

Cut-Case Displays

The simplest type of P.O.P. display is made from the shipping container. The carton is designed to be cut along dotted lines to form a display case. "Cut case" displays have widest application in the mass merchandising field, particularly in food stores, variety stores, and discount houses. In addition, they are often used by liquor stores. Other retailers, including department stores, use these displays during heavy buying periods, such as Christmas.

This type of display is simple to assemble, and often comes with a "riser" card to be attached as a poster. Cut-case displays fit in nicely as end-of-aisle displays, and may be used to form temporary partitions to direct shopper traffic patterns. They are also used as displays near cash registers for so-called impulse items.

Dump-Bin Displays

As the name implies, dump bins are tubs, boxes, wire baskets, or any other container in which products are dumped in a random method. Although brands and varieties may be mixed, the dump bins furnished by manufacturers usually lend themselves to a particular brand. Dump bins are used in the same way as cut-case displays.

Mobile Displays

One definition of a mobile is a sign or figure that is generally suspended from the ceiling. It is widely used by supermarkets to direct customers to a specific brand. Another definition refers to any movable P.O.P. display.

Counter Displays

The checkout counter represents the last selling opportunity in the store and is an excellent location for "impulse" or "unplanned purchase" items. As a result, many manufacturers supply special racks or other display units specifically designed to be used at the counter. Items commonly sold at this counter range from penny mints in restaurants to expensive hosiery in women's style shops. Although items such as gum and cigarettes "sell themselves" in this manner, the sale of many others should be helped by suggestions from the cashier.

The old question, "Will there be anything else?" is practically useless as it is sure to be followed by the programmed response, "No, I don't think so." However, if a salesman suggests that a new pair of shoes needs the protection of wax or that a new pair of hose would complement the shoes, the chances for success are infinitely greater. This last-minute selling effort is made considerably easier by the careful placement of a counter display to remind both the salesman and the customer.

Permanent P.O.P. Displays

The term "permanent display" should not be taken literally. Unless the life of the retail store is extremely short, virtually no display is permanent. "Permanent" is used to express a relative measure, compared to many dump bins and other P.O.P. displays that exist only a few weeks. Most of the so-called permanent P.O.P. displays are furnished by manufacturers in an attempt to gain more shelf space. Over the years, three common types of P.O.P. units for displaying merchandise on a shelf have emerged. These are "shelf dividers," "shelf extenders," and "spring loaders."

Shelf Dividers

This device usually sits on the shelf and contains notches into which the merchandise is placed. They are usually designed to display merchandise at an angle most appropriate for lateral vision.

Shelf Extenders

This is a small tray that is fastened to the shelf and extends beyond it to give additional shelf space.

Spring Loader

A spring loader is simply a special tray or double-deck tray with a spring attached to the rear. As items are loaded into this tray, they are continually held tight by the push of the spring from behind. This device is widely used as a counter display at the checkout stand.

Posters

Posters are undoubtedly the most common form of P.O.P. material used in retail stores. They can be printed on an infinite variety of material and sizes. They may take the form of a banner or (as it is sometimes called) streamer. The low cost and storewide applicability of posters ensure their popularity with retailers. Posters may also take the form of counter cards when mounted on a paperboard back. These are generally placed in store windows or on the counter.

Traditional rules for the design of posters have called for a clear style with easy-to-read numbers and letters, combined with an easy-to-understand message and illustration. It has also been felt traditionally that a poster should not attempt to relay more than a single message, such as "Fire Sale," "Vacation in Hawaii," "Fresh Peaches," or other simple messages.[31]

In recent years the growth of pop art, black-light posters, soul messages, and similar forms of expression has shown that traditional rules may be broken with success. This is not to say that overnight acceptance of such P.O.P. material is a wise policy for the retailer. However, if the retailer sells pop records, or clothing oriented to a young black customer, these posters may be absolute necessities.

WINDOW DISPLAYS

Windows, which represent the face of a store, must be viewed as a reflection of what is inside. For this reason, most large retail chains refuse to leave window dressing to chance. Instead, store managers are sent packaged store dressings complete with instructions and a photograph demonstrating how the window is to look. Manufacturers also realize the value of window displays, and may provide professionally created displays for a retailer's window.

Many retailers have found that they can create special buying moods by using a promotion aimed at a particular country or event. For example, a week aimed at featuring the goods and services of Mexico can produce sales for Mexican goods, and may include a special section in which tours are sold. In cases such as this, the window display should feature a Mexican decor. The cost of such a program can be minimized by cooperation or "tie in" promotion with other firms or organizations interested in promoting Mexico. Airline companies, national tourist promotion bureaus, etc. are usually anxious to supply material and labor to assist in window displays. These types of promotions can be used in slump buying periods to create new customer interest and to attract new customers to a store.

Retailers are often asked to display posters for neighborhood clubs, high schools, and other groups. Unless prior planning is given to these requests, a retailer can easily find his windows filled with a variety of signs which detract from the overall appearance of the window and the store. Rather than either accept or reject all posters, a display policy can be used to the benefit of all.

Many retailers let it be known that their windows are available at certain times of the year at no cost to local groups. Schools, in particular, are encouraged to develop a window display for their homecoming, spring prom, or other events. These are particularly effective when a professional display person from the retail store helps coordinate the activity. Fall and winter sports wear may be featured along with the homecoming decorations. Spring formal wear can be arranged with posters and other information concerning the prom. These traditional displays generate a great deal of interest from sidewalk viewers and can have a strong appeal for teenage target markets.

SPECIALTY ADVERTISING

Matchbooks, calendars, blotters, paper clips, and other novelty items are frequently used to keep the name of the retailer in front of consumers. This type of reminder advertising is best suited for outlets where consumers shop infrequently. The institutional message, of no more than five to ten words, should be used to communicate that the outlet is ready to meet consumer needs in specific merchandise/service areas.[32] This type of reminder message can usually indicate only who the retailer is, where his outlets are located, and what he sells. Short reminder messages of this type are usually supplemented with other forms of promotion which contain a more detailed message.

Specialties are generally more effective in keeping customers than in attracting new customers. These specialty items represent an invitation to continue to buy and a token of appreciation for the consumer's patronage. The effectiveness of a specialty item depends upon the attractiveness of the item to the consumer and upon its distribution to him. Items that are unusual but that can help solve small customer problems are likely to be used, and valued more, by the consumer. Because the message is presented each time the item is used, retailers should give items that will be used more often than those that are given away by their competitors. The items may also be associated with the business. For example, a gasoline service station may give away a free ice scraper imprinted with its name, address, telephone number, and store hours.

Matchbooks, calendars, pens, and pencils are the most frequently used specialties. Specially designed covers on book matches and calendars can increase the exposure of a retailer's advertisement by being used and displayed by consumers instead of being discarded. The effectiveness of such calendars, pens, and pencils is likely to depend on who receives them. A housewife will probably use these items because she is seldom oversupplied with them. Businessmen probably receive many of these items from other sources and may not use them unless they possess some unique feature. A calendar, if displayed in a popular place of business not inconsistent with the retailer's image, can be an effective but inexpensive type of advertising. The trick is to get the calendar displayed in other places of business that serve your target customers.

THEATER SCREEN ADVERTISING

Movie watchers are a fairly captive audience, so 40- to 60-second theater screen advertisements can be used to disseminate the retailer's message. The advertisement may consist of either slide or film presentations that are inserted between feature movies, news, and shorts. The rates are usually based on theater attendance. The retailer will want to consider how well the characteristics of the audience match those of his target market consumers before he commits himself to a long-run contract. Contracts are usually issued on a weekly basis, so a retailer may benefit by advertising only during those weeks when the featured movie appeals to his target market.

SALES PROMOTION

It should be recalled that sales promotions are different from advertising in that mass media are not used. Sales promotions include the use of premiums, such as stamps, free gifts, contests, etc. Sales promotions also include consumer services, such as packaging, alterations, wrapping, delivery, refunds and exchanges, and credit. The various types of sales promotion are designed to encourage the immediate sale of merchandise or service and to keep customers loyal to the store.

Premiums

The major appeal of premiums is that the customer believes he is getting something for nothing. Stamps and small gifts are thought of as being free. Even contests and sweepstakes give the consumer a chance to win something for nothing. Some of the more frequently used gifts include the following.

Giveaways or Traffic Builders

These are small items, such as a piece of candy or gum, a trash bag, etc., which are given away with each purchase.[33]

Referrals

"Thank you" gifts are given to customers who send their friends to your outlet.

New-Customer Gift

These are small, free gifts that are given to new customers the first time they enter the outlet.

Continuity Program

Given one at a time, matched glasses, chinaware, towels, etc. keep customers coming back to complete the set.

Trading Card

Customers can collect a free gift when their card is completely punched out—after making the necessary amount of purchases. If the free gift is some service—say a free car wash by an automatic machine—it can be a real benefit to the customer and still increase retail costs only slightly.

Trading Stamps and Games

Trading stamps and games, which are also used to promote retail sales, have been historically linked to supermarkets, service stations, and an assortment of small retailers, including a few small, independent department stores. These promotional techniques were never adopted in significant numbers by large department stores, discount houses, car dealers, furniture outlets, and many other types of retailers. There have been a few exceptions in almost every retail category, but they are the exception rather than the rule.

History shows that national diffusion occurred in the period 1951–1962 for trading stamps and in the period 1962–1966 for games. After these periods, the popularity and use of both methods declined.[34] The decline in the use of both promotional techniques may be traced to several developments.

1. The industry became saturated with both techniques. As a result, little or no competitive advantage was left.
2. Discount houses and other retailers who had not accepted stamps offered increasingly heavy competition to those with stamps. In fact, advertising campaigns were built around the fact that a particular store did not give stamps and thus offered consumers a savings.
3. In some areas, retailers were forced into stamp wars, in which a significant number of extra stamps were given for purchases.
4. The attitude of shoppers changed. Housewives actually formed protest movements in certain areas against stamps, games, and other promotional techniques.
5. Stores that had dropped stamps and games reported initial losses, but then reported profit gains without giving stamps. Stamp companies charge the retailer between 1.5 and 3 percent of sales volume.[35] For many retailers, the expense associated with stamps is greater than their entire advertising expenditure.

The history of these promotional techniques offers retailers several important lessons concerning these and other new promotional techniques which may occur in the future. These may be summarized as follows:

1. The use of promotional techniques that are readily available to other retailers cannot replace sound retailing/merchandising strategies and planning.
2. Consumer preferences and response to promotional techniques may shift in short periods of time, so that what was in vogue last year is the villain the next.
3. The first retailers to use new promotional techniques may easily capture larger market sales and gain greater profits in the short run; however, once the technique becomes widespread, they may easily be in a worse competitive condition than other, more powerful retailers who adopt the same technique.
4. Dependency upon a promotional technique overlooks the fact that strong new retailers and retailing concepts may emerge while the older retailers are engaged in a competitive promotional battle.
5. It is evident that a particular market segment is attracted to stores that offer particular promotional techniques such as stamps and games. As a result, it may be possible for certain retailers, particularly independent stores and chains, to use these techniques as long as large competitors

do not adopt the practices. This is particularly true after larger competitors have tried and discontinued the techniques.

Publicity

Unique approaches are required to get favorable publicity for retail outlets. Since the retailer does not have to pay for the coverage, the media programmers and writers must believe that the item appeals to the general population. Consumerism and ecological and minority-opportunity program campaigns may be used to bring the retailer's name before the public. No matter what the appeal is, a skilled writer and speaker is usually required to place the item in the media.[36]

Many retailers seem to feel that by hiring a specialist in publicity, or a P.R. director, they have satisfied the need to "do something" about publicity. Publicity extends well beyond placing free articles in newspapers. In fact, the values to be obtained extend beyond those of the promotional mix. They have a direct bearing upon employee morale, motivation, and education.

A large department store is faced with an abundance of publicity opportunities. Nearly every department will find there are clubs, fraternal organizations, and consumer groups that are interested in knowing more about their particular products. Art groups and garden clubs are examples of types of organizations with special interest in particular products. Yet all too often the only contact a retailer of garden supplies or art goods has with these groups consists of sending a $10 item to the yearly benefit auction.

The growing interest among American consumers in wines and specialty foods provides invaluable publicity opportunities. Retailers have found they can sponsor wine-tasting parties at a cost to the customer. These are excellent opportunities to educate the customer concerning wines—at his cost—and at the same time subtly sell one's products. Retailers who sell baby goods might profit through infant-care sessions for expectant mothers. Auto supply stores might find a full house for a profitable evening on the need for high-quality motor lubricants.

We are an affluent nation—a nation of consumers—in which one of the most popular pastimes is shopping. In this environment, there is little reason to believe that consumers will not respond to well-planned informative sessions on the products retailers sell. The success of many retailers in this area has proved that the problem is not lack of consumer interest but, rather, lack of employee time to honor all the speaking opportunities they would receive.

SUMMARY

Selection of the media that will most effectively reach the retailer's target market consumers must include consideration of the characteristics of each media. Retailers rely heavily upon printed media and radio for their promotional efforts. Some newspapers have the advantage of serving a specific geographical group of people, so they can be used to reach the local target market with minimal waste circulation. Direct mail, including catalog mailings, can be used to reach a specifically defined target group if a good mailing list is available. Coupons are frequently used to promote sales of special items that are designed to draw customers to the store. The Yellow Pages serve as reminder advertising and provide a listing to attract new customers. The chief advantage of Yellow Page advertising is the continuous exposure offered for a long-life period of one year.

Radio is one of the most flexible media in that many different stations offer many different programs at any time of day. Also, its per minute cost of advertising is relatively inexpensive. Thus retailers can use radio to reach their target market at a fairly low cost. Repeated radio advertisements may be required to be effective, however, as listenership changes nearly every hour and the message is presented for only a few seconds at a time. Television is a useful medium for large retailers who serve most, if not all, of the area reached by the television station.

Advertising by signs is more suitable for institutional image promotion than for product–direct-action promotion because it is expensive to change the message. Point-of-purchase (P.O.P.) promotions are used to create a buying mood after the consumer reaches the outlet.

Sales promotions use the appeal that the consumer believes he is getting something for nothing. The first retailers to use new promotional techniques can gain short-run sales increases until competitive outlets adopt similar techniques and a promotional war begins.

QUESTIONS

1. What media would you recommend in the following situations (state your reasons):
    a. Pre-Christmas at Neiman Marcus or Abercrombie and Fitch?
    b. A suburban FM radio station, specializing in "easy listening," that needs advertising revenue?
    c. A grand opening of a small-city discount store?
    d. A supermarket in a major urban area opening a kosher delicatessen section?
    e. A grand opening of a year-round resort 80 miles from a major metropolitan area?
    f. A county-supported technical trade school that will open in six months with various one- and two-year trade programs?
2. Design an ad for each situation in problem 1 and for each medium you have recommended.
3. How would a counter display be used in a retail liquor store? In a bookstore?
4. Suggest a point-of-purchase display mix for the coming year for:
    a. A travel agent in Chicago

b. A suburban gift shop

c. A farm implement dealer in the midwest.

5. Explain the decline in the use of trading stamps and games in recent years. In order for any premium to be effective, what characteristics must it have?

6. Outline a 1-year promotional mix for a large department store such as Macy's and justify each suggestion in terms of the store's overall goal. Start by stating a set of hypothetical goals for the coming year.

7. What promotional tools would you recommend for the following situations, and how would you use them?

a. A new furniture department in a discount store

b. A moderately priced luncheon special at a restaurant in a midtown business section

c. The addition of sports wear to a ladies' boutique that formerly specialized in formal apparel.

FOOTNOTES

[1] Jerome B. Kernan, William P. Dommermuth, and Montrose S. Sommers, *Promotion: An Introductory Analysis* (New York: McGraw-Hill, 1970), pp. 11–13.

[2] Ibid., p. 203.

[3] Ibid.

[4] Laurence W. Jacobs, *Advertising and Promotion for Retailing* (Glenview, Ill.: Scott, Foresman, 1972), pp. 6–15.

[5] Ibid.

[6] Ibid., p. 118.

[7] Ibid., p. 124.

[8] Ibid., p. 119.

[9] Ibid., p. 120.

[10] A. C. Nielsen, Jr., "The Impact of Retail Coupons," *Journal of Marketing* (October 1965), pp. 11–15.

[11] Ibid.

[12] *The Yellow Pages in Marketing and Advertising* (New York: American Telephone and Telegraph Co., 1970), p. 17.

[13] Ibid.

[14] Kernan et al., *Promotion*, p. 205.

[15] Ibid., p. 207.

[16] Jacobs, *Advertising and Promotion*, p. 123.

[17] Ibid., p. 121.

[18] Ibid., p. 123.

[19] Ibid., p. 156.

[20] David Ogilvy, *How to Create Advertising that Sells* (New York: Ogilvy and Mather Advertising Agency, n.d.), p .1.

[21] Ibid.

[22] Ibid

[23] Ibid.

[24] Adapted from Jacobs, *Advertising and Promotion*, p. 161; Carl W. Birchard, "Distinctive Advertising for Small Stores," *Journal of Retailing* (Spring 1964), pp. 23–29, 50; Harry W. Hepner, *Effective Advertising* (New York: McGraw-Hill, 1949), pp. 558–560.

[25] Jacobs, *Advertising and Promotion*, p. 174.

[26] Ibid., p. 174.

[27] Ogilvy, *How to Create Advertising that Sells*, p. 1.

[28] Jacobs, *Advertising and Promotion*, p. 125.

[29] Kurt H. Vahle, *The Importance of Color in Advertising* (New York: Direct Mail Advertising Association, n.d.), p. 3.

[30] Association of National Advertisers, *Advertising at the Point of Purchase* (New York: McGraw-Hill, 1957), p. 1.

[31] Harvey Offenhartz, *Point of Purchase Design* (New York: Reinhold Book Corp., 1968), p. 111.

[32] Jacobs, *Advertising and Promotion*, p. 126.

[33] William C. Battle, "Attract—and Hold—Customers with Premiums," *Motor* (September 1967), pp. 80–81.

[34] Fred C. Allvine, "The Future for Trading Stamps and Games," *Journal of Marketing*, 33 (January 1969): 45–52.

[35] Jacobs, *Advertising and Promotion*, p. 187.

[36] A list of dos and don'ts that can guide the nonprofessional in preparing publicity releases is presented in Harold L. Jenkins, *Action Marketing for Savings Institutions* (Chicago: Savings Institutions Marketing Society of America, 1972), pp. 168–169.

THE PALMER HARDWARE STORE*

The Palmer Hardware Store is a family-owned operation in the Old Town area of Chicago. The store operated from the same location for 60 years, during which the neighborhood steadily deteriorated. Like most small businessmen in this community, the store's owner did no advertising whatever—except the single-line Yellow Pages listing (under the "hardware retail" heading) that was furnished with his business telephone service. His clientele, along with that of his competitors, consisted exclusively of nearby residents.

Then, in a period of about five years, many of the old neighborhood families sold their homes to developers. A younger group, which had no ties to stores such as Palmer Hardware, moved into the area.

With the new residents involved in restoring apartments and homes to their earlier elegance, Joel Palmer sensed that there was great potential for hardware sales. The problem was that newcomers weren't aware of Palmer and purchased their supplies from the large hardware outlets outside the neighborhood. Palmer decided that the cost of a larger Yellow Pages ad would be slight compared with the new business it might generate.

Palmer's new ad gave the location of the store, mentioned prominently that Palmer's had been "serving Old Town for over 60 years," and promised "complete supplies for apartments and home renovation."

DISCUSSION QUESTIONS

1. What other types of advertising could Mr. Palmer effectively employ?
2. What is your opinion of the type of ad selected for use in the Yellow

Pages? In particular, what do you think of the statement "serving Old Town for over 60 years"?

3. Do you believe the Yellow Pages are the best advertising medium to reach this new market?

THRIFTY RENT-A-CAR SYSTEM
Advertising-Promotion of a Service Retailer

Thrifty Rent-a-Car System has a continuing need to tell the "Thrifty" story to potential customers in the face of heavy promotional expenditures by larger corporations. This is complicated by the fact that Thrifty service desks are located away from the airport, as opposed to the larger competition with service desks inside the terminal.

In spite of heavy competition, the growth of Thrifty has been very impressive. The Thrifty operation was acquired by Mr. W. F. Stemmons in 1962. Mr. Stemmons had served as vice-president of Avis Rent-a-Car System prior to that date.

Prior to the acquisition of Thrifty by Mr. Stemmons, the company was a small rental firm operating strictly in Tulsa, Oklahoma. Today, Thrifty operates more than 275 offices in all fifty states, plus others in Canada, Puerto Rico, and Europe. Negotiations for locations in Africa, South America, Australia, and other parts of the world are in process.

The Thrifty chain is a franchised operation, although seven offices are company owned and operated. This permits Thrifty to have a working knowledge of day-to-day operations and set the standards for the entire system. The parent company provides its licensees with continuous guidance and assistance in system operations as well as promotions. It also provides national advertising in segmented print media such as *Business Week, U.S. News and World Report,* and *Newsweek,* as well as in the in-flight magazines of the nation's principal airlines.

According to Mr. John Stemmons, division manager and son of W. F. Stemmons, these ads are often superior to those of competition (based on Starch ratings), but the total space and broadcast time purchased by Thrifty is much less than that of major competition.

The company is opposed to changing ads simply to get a new creative tack. Instead, if an ad receives a good Starch rating, it is used over and over again.

The primary theme in all Thrifty locations and promotions is "service and savings." Consistent with costs, Thrifty rates are generally $3 a day, and

3 cents a mile less than the major competition for the same, or superior equipment, including insurance second to none in the industry.

In accord with the Thrifty theme, female rental agents wear an attractive scotch plaid uniform. Thrifty's offices are clean and functional, but also reflect an air of frugality. This extends to the home office in Tulsa, which consists of a one-story masonry building with small and unpretentious offices.

The extra service offered by Thrifty consists, in part, of prompt customer pickup at the airport baggage exit. When a customer phones for service, "Miss Thrifty" is there in minutes, usually before the customer has obtained his baggage. She then drives him to the nearby Thrifty office and assigns him the car of his choice. Upon his return, he simply stops in front of the Thrifty office and "Miss Thrifty" immediately drives him to the terminal entrance opposite the airline of his choice. Mr. Stemmons stated that the cars offered by Thrifty are top-of-the-line, fully equipped models, as opposed to the stripped-down versions offered by some of its competition, and that the cars are excellently maintained.

Thrifty also offers a "customer hospitality office" for customers, where they are provided with free coffee and a desk and telephone for local calls. Advance reservation service for Thrifty rent-a-car locations in other cities is always available. Other services offered by Thrifty include free maps, reservation service at local motels and restaurants, and directions for various customer destinations. The prime market target selected by Thrifty is the businessman-professional traveler who arrives by commercial or private airplane.

Instead of maintaining a national corporate sales force to call on corporate accounts, Thrifty's local managers call on the corporations in their areas. If a corporation qualifies, it is given a special discount for its traveling personnel. Corporate and individual credit cards are also issued. In addition, if a company needs a special billing plan or other individualized car rental program, Thrifty will accommodate these needs.

Local managers also follow a point-of-purchase program that works well in many locations. This program calls for the manager to visit local travel agencies, motels, and restaurants to ask for their literature to display in the Thrifty rental office. In turn, these managers of motels, restaurants, etc. normally reciprocate by displaying "Thrifty" brochures.

The company has not conducted research to determine Thrifty's brand awareness in the minds of potential customers, but the management generally believes there is much more work to do in the area of brand awareness. A related problem facing the company is the reluctance of some traveling businessmen to seek out a less expensive rental firm. Since most businessmen travel on a corporate expense account, many choose what seems to be the easiest course—walking to the nearest car rental booth in the airport.

Mr. Stemmons believes that this is usually more time consuming than calling Thrifty, but many travelers do not realize this. Accordingly, a continuing "public education" program is promoted by Thrifty to reach these people with the message that they really *can* save money without sacrificing service.

Only a few corporate travel managers tell the employees of the companies what rental firm to use. As a result, even though a company may prefer that its employees use Thrifty, it is not always done.

Although Thrifty could rent space in airports, it prohibits all licensees from doing this. It is felt that the added cost of in-terminal service will eliminate the savings that are now passed on to the customer. This, in turn, would make Thrifty just another car rental firm. Thus management is faced with the task of more effectively telling the Thrifty story without engaging in the costly location and promotion programs used by competitors.

DISCUSSION QUESTIONS

1. What additional promotional techniques do you believe could be effectively employed by Thrifty without huge expenditures of money?
2. Is it possible that the total "thrift-conscious" market segment of travelers has already been reached by Thrifty through its promotion and by word of mouth?
3. How important is word-of-mouth advertising to a retailer such as Thrifty? How can it be increased?
4. Where do you believe the traveler generally makes his decision to use a particular car rental firm—in the plane, at the airport, in his office, etc.?
5. Check with a few local businessmen who do a great deal of traveling by air and ask them how they select a car rental firm. Do you detect a strong brand preference or a habitual process of renting cars? Are they interested in savings? If so, are they members of a large corporation or do they own their own company?

WALL DRUG
Promotion

Without advertising, Wall Drug would probably still be that little drug store with the curtain separating the living quarters and the store. That's the way it was in 1931, when the young pharmacist Ted Hustead and his wife and son moved to Wall, South Dakota.

The thirties were depression years everywhere, and in Wall the depression was made even gloomier by years of drought. Those were the "dirty thirties," when the only feed that was available for cattle was thistle.

Even in the best years, a druggist in Wall could hardly expect to do the kind of business a comparable store might do in Chicago or St. Louis. After all, Wall has only 800 residents, plus the ranchers who live on mesas and run cattle in the draws and plain nearby.

Not many folks have chosen to live in the Badlands, yet that gigantic chunk of real estate, with 10,000 prairie dogs for every human resident, serves as Wall's market area to the south.

It couldn't happen but it did! Today Wall Drug has 6,000 to 8,000 customers each and every day of the tourist season. About 30 to 50 percent of these are repeat customers, who were so happy with Wall Drug the first time that they came back again, and have told their friends to do the same.

Traffic jams are commonplace in Wall now, and the streets and parking lots are filled with cars, campers, and motorcycles from every state and province in the United States and Canada, plus a good number of visitors from all parts of the world.

Promotion did it, and it all began with a brainstorm by Mrs. Hustead. Business had been slow that hot summer day in the '30s; in fact it was just plain dead. The combination of heat and no business was enough to give anyone a headache, and Mrs. Hustead left the store to recover from hers.

A short time later she came back, full of enthusiasm and an idea. She had watched the highway outside of town and had seen dozens of cars pass by in that terrific Badlands heat. "Those people just had to be suffering from the heat and I was sure they would appreciate a free glass of ice water," thought Mrs. Hustead. She also remembered those Burma Shave signs, and figured that if signs could sell shaving cream they could also bring folks to a drug store for free ice water.

The idea worked so well that customers almost beat the Husteads back to the store. The Husteads' signs have continued working ever since, and still serve as the backbone of the store's promotion.

Ted wasn't content to place just a few signs outside of Wall. He kept thinking up new slogans and planting the signs farther from town. Finally they reached such unlikely spots as Greece, North Africa, Korea, Vietnam, and even the South Pole.

Friends of Wall Drug seemed to enjoy carrying those signs with them wherever they traveled, and that meant everywhere. Three generations of foot soldiers in the Second World War, Korea, and Vietnam found Wall Drug signs in the most unlikely spots in the world. After the war they remembered and paid a visit to Wall.

Those were rent-free locations, but Ted also placed Wall Drug signs on some that he had rented. As an example, there are signs on a lamp post in Amsterdam and in the subways of London and Paris.

Anyone from Wall, South Dakota, who advertises his drug store in those kinds of places has got to be worth a story. More than one reporter felt this was the case, and stories of Wall Drug have since appeared in the

Reader's Digest, the *New York Times Magazine, Newsweek, Coronet, Good Housekeeping,* and dozens of other U.S. publications.

American reporters weren't the only ones to see the material for a story. Stories about Wall Drug have also been printed in Holland, England, Australia, and many other parts of the globe.

Television wasn't to be outdone, and Gary Moore asked Bill Hustead to appear on his show "To Tell the Truth." The BBC also got into the act with a taped interview of Ted.

What's it done for Wall Drug? Visit Wall and you'll find a store that serves 100 to 150 dozen eggs each day to customers for breakfast. Don't be surprised if four busloads of people stop at the same time.

Within that block area of stores, you'll find 120 employees, among whom are fifty college women and fifteen college men who work there for the summer. Ted will point out ten homes he has purchased just to house the part-time help and a company swimming pool to offer escape in the evening from the heat and crowds.

You'll also find the largest bookstore in the 366 miles between Rapid City and Madison, as well as a clothing store and pottery ranging from typical tourist stuff to expensive collector's items. Order a stuffed buffalo head, if that's your thing, or enjoy a cup of coffee or mug of beer and listen to a live combo.

If you prefer animated musicians, listen to the cowboy band. Pose with a giant jack rabbit or a miniature of Mount Rushmore.

Tourists are big business for Wall Drug, but it still remains a drug store for the natives. Since there is no veterinarian in town, Wall Drug sells vet supplies—and lots of them. Ask Ted what to do for worms or foot rot, and he'll tell you. That's the reason why real cowboys mix with the animated kind and the New York City type in the same store.

Advertising and publicity built Wall Drug, and the Husteads know it can't stop. Sure, a lot of people know about Wall Drug, but a lot more still don't, and there are all those new generations to come who won't know about signs in Korea and Vietnam or past articles in famous magazines.

To keep it all going, Wall Drug distributes thousands of bumper stickers to its customers each year. Wall Drug store signs are also given to anyone who will take them along to place on their farms, factories, etc.

The highway sign program hasn't stopped either. Signs such as "You'll be Walleyed at Wall Drug" or "Have you dug Wall Drug?" still face the motorist in such numbers that anyone with half an ounce of curiosity is compelled to stop in Wall.

Yet Wall Drug isn't the only store to give out bumper stickers and signs. At the same time, the "Lady Bird Bill" (the Highway Beautification Act of 1965) threatens to make things considerably tougher for all roadside advertisers. Ted feels that the real pressures from this act are only beginning to be felt. Miles of interstate highway are not zoned for commercial use, and land can't be bought or leased for the use of sign display.

The Hustead's son, Bill, joined the firm in 1951 and has been in charge of the roadside advertising program for the past ten years. Under his supervision, business has continued to be great at Wall Drug. The impossible has been accomplished. Now it is a matter of making sure it grows.

DISCUSSION QUESTIONS

1. Do you believe that Ted Hustead's ideas have application for other small retailers or is Wall Drug a special case?
2. Design a promotion program that will ensure the growth of Wall Drug. Remember that Wall Drug grew because of an "unconventional" approach, using a centuries-old medium.
3. What social, political, and economic factors might affect Wall Drug in the next few years? What, if anything, can the Husteads do to plan to meet them?

CHAPTER 11

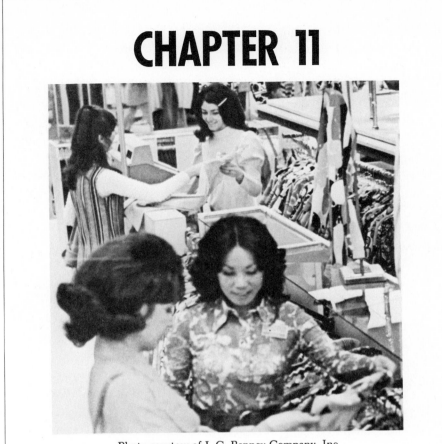

Photo courtesy of J. C. Penney Company, Inc.

Personal Selling
and Consumer Services

This chapter focuses on two of the most important elements of the retailer's promotional mix: personal selling and consumer services.

PERSONAL SELLING

Personal selling is the heart of all retailing. Advertising can attract consumers to the store, but the face-to-face communication that occurs in personal selling provides unique opportunities. As sales persons talk with customers they can read the customers' reactions and identify the *individual* consumer's needs. Sales people then can tailor their message to meet the specific needs of that customer. The face-to-face communication also allows sales people to provide information that will reduce consumers' uncertainties about the product/service offering. Only through personal selling can the customers receive individualized feedback from the retailer. The importance of personal selling is summarized in the following poem.

IF I POSSESSED A STORE

If I possessed a shop or store
I'd drive the grouchers off my floor.
I'd never let some gloomy guy
Offend the folks who come to buy.

I'd never keep the boy or clerk
With mental toothache at his work.
Nor let the man who draws my pay
Drive customers of mine away.

I'd treat the man who takes my time
And spends a nickel or a dime
With courtesy and make him feel
That I was glad to close the deal.

Because tomorrow (who can tell?)
He may want the things I have to sell.
And in that case how glad he'll be
To spend his dollars all with me.

The reason people pass one door
To patronize another store,
Is not because the busier place
Has better shoes, or gloves, or lace.

Or lower prices, but it lies
In pleasant words or smiling eyes.
The greatest difference, I believe,
Is in the treatment folks receive.

—Anonymous

Retail Selling Environment

The major elements involved in a retail sale are the outlet and its policies, its merchandise, its promotion policies, its customers, and its sales people. Sales people need to be familiar with the *store* and its policies before they can offer the customer any reliable advice. First, the sales person must know the types, price ranges, and quality of *merchandise* that the outlet stocks. Second, he (or she) must know what services the store makes available to its customers. A sales person must be knowledgeable about the firm's delivery, credit, adjustment, and product/service offerings if he is to serve his customers effectively. A sales person should also know the layout of the entire store well enough to locate merchandise for consumers who have difficulty finding specific items.

The store's promotion policy is the third vital area of which he must be aware. The promotion mix concept should be understood by the sales person so he knows that advertising, sales promotion, and personal selling require coordinated teamwork to communicate with consumers successfully. Sales people should keep informed of the store's promotional activities by reading its advertisements, looking at its displays, attending sales meetings, and the like.

Customers expect retail sales people to have a thorough knowledge of the store's *merchandise*. The amount of information needed varies with the type of merchandise sold and the clientele served. High-price products generally require the sales person to be more knowledgeable. The sales person should know the identity of the manufacturer, the ingredients or raw materials in the merchandise, its construction, color, size, model, etc. In addition, he should know what the product is used for, how it should be used, how it performs, how much care and service it requires, etc. Sufficient knowledge is required to be able to compare any product with its closest competitor and to highlight its superior points.

Merchandise information is found on the label, tag, or package of the product and in wholesale or retail catalogs. Salesmen who represent manufacturers and wholesalers also are sources of information. Independent testing bureaus are another good source because their findings can be quoted to customers to enhance the credibility of the presentation.

The *customer* is the heart of every sale, so the sales person must try to satisfy her. The customer who enters a store is probably in a buying mood and therefore interested in some merchandise to satisfy some need or desire. The sales person should realize that even if a sale is made, the consumer must be pleased with her reception and completely satisfied with the outlet's merchandise and services if the sale is going to be of long-run benefit to the store. Thus sales people need to sell from the consumer viewpoint. To do this, the sales person must be aware of consumer psychology and buying motives. Merchandise is purchased because it satisfies some consumer need for beauty, pride, romance, feeling important, comfort, convenience, durability, safety, health, or economy. Sales people should attempt to identify each consumer's primary buying motives and determine what pleases or irritates him.

The *sales person* is the final element in the retail sale. The characteristics that are associated with successful retail sales people may be discussed under five categories: objectivity, personal appearance, sociability, maturity, and mental alertness.[1]

Objectivity refers to the ability of sales people to understand consumers from the individual consumer's point of view. By being objective, the sales person can put himself in the customer's place and then interpret the consumer's needs. A nonobjective or subjective sales person is more concerned with forcing his own values and solutions on consumers than with solving the consumers' problems. Thus subjective sales people are not likely to be successful retail sales generators.

A good personal appearance is required to make a good initial impression on the consumer. The sales person who is well groomed and poised, and who expresses himself with correct speech and in a pleasant tone of voice, creates a good impression and gains the respect of consumers.

Sociability—the traits required to create an atmosphere in which consumers enjoy making purchases—includes the enthusiasm displayed by sales people and the ability to deal tactfully and courteously with consumers, without offending them. Friendly retail sales people make consumers feel welcome, and greet them by name if possible. Sales people who are confident of themselves give consumers the impression that they are receiving worthwhile opinions.

Emotionally mature sales people handle unpleasant situations smoothly because they are more understanding. They listen better and are better able to interpret the consumer's needs. Mature sales people are also more dependable and industrious in being on the job and working hard to generate sales.

Mentally alert sales people help make a sale by remembering customers and being knowledgeable about the features of the product/service offering that would best meet their demands and purchase capabilities. Sales persons must also use their imagination to interpret customers' needs in terms of the available merchandise/service opportunities. Retail sales people must also be accurate in their handling of countless details and still remain *courteous to all customers.*

The Selling Process

After the sales person has an understanding of the retail selling environment, he or she can proceed to the selling process.

Greeting the Customer

The sales person's manner is more important than the particular opening words he uses. Customers want sales peoples to be alert and prompt so that quick service may be obtained. In addition, the sales person's appearance and actions should generate a friendly and pleasant feeling. The customer must be welcomed with a *genuine* smile and made to realize that the sales person wants to be of service.

The opening greeting may be "May I help you?" "Good morning." "Are you being served?" etc. In many stores, customers are greeted by name (if at all possible) to give them recognition and indicate that their patronage is appreciated. If the customer is already looking at merchandise, the sales person may remain silent and wait for the customer's comment or use a merchandise type of opener, such as "Pretty, aren't they?" "That is one of our new models." or whatever is appropriate.

Determining the Customer's Wants

A consumer's needs should be defined as quickly as possible by *observing* his interest in various products and by *listening* to his comments. Placing merchandise in the consumer's hands starts him thinking and quickly generates reactions that can be observed and heard. *Questioning* the consumer in a tactful way can reveal his problem. Questions about material, uses, interests, purposes, and style can be used effectively, but questions on size and price may offend the consumer.

The above process should allow the sales person to determine if the consumer (1) knows exactly what he wants, (2) wants something but doesn't know precisely what, or (3) is a "looker" who doesn't want anything particularly. If the consumer knows what he wants, the sales person should quickly place the merchandise before the customer with a short sales story. A consumer who falls in the second category needs more assistance in identifying his problems. Some merchandise can be shown immediately and the consumer's reaction observed. From the moment he sees the merchandise, the typical customer starts asking information about prices, colors, styles, etc. The sales person can then show additional merchandise of the type preferred by the customer. However, the sales person should be careful not to show too much merchandise and confuse the customer but enough to convince her that she has seen all the items that are suitable for her needs.

The "looker" presents a challenge because frequently he will not reveal his desires. One solution is to leave the customer and the merchandise together, hoping the display will sell him. Another course of action is to offer to escort the looker on a guided tour of the merchandise. Or the salesman may indicate the general location of the merchandise, invite him to feel completely at home, and assure him prompt and interested service as soon as he wishes. Regardless of the method used, the sales person should watch closely so that the looker may be served when he needs assistance.

Presenting the Merchandise

The sales person should present merchandise that reflects what he believes will satisfy the customer's needs. A request to see a certain item simplifies the interpretation process as the sales person can immediately show the desired item. In most cases the consumer may be a little vague. If this is the case, the sales person must present merchandise that he believes will satisfy the consumer's desires. The first merchandise shown is usually medium-price items.

Then the sales person must decide whether to attempt *trading up*. Trading up consists of selling either a better-quality item or a larger quantity than the consumer intended to buy. Frequently, better-quality merchandise will last longer and/or need less service and thus generate more long-run consumer satisfaction than the lower-quality item requested by the customer. To use trading-up selling, a sales person must know his goods and be able to point out the benefits of buying better merchandise. The approach should not be misleading or dishonest but an objective evaluation of the item's benefit for the customer.

When the store is out of stock on the item requested, the consumer should be informed of the unavailability of the item immediately. If the outlet has something in that line which will satisfy the consumer, that item should be presented to the consumer at the same time he is informed of the out-of-stock condition. The requested product should not be criticized but the benefits of the in-stock item should be pointed out.

Demonstrating or showing merchandise involves several considerations. First, it is desirable to obtain consumer participation by asking him to handle or operate it just as he would in normal use. Second, the way the sales person handles the merchandise must show that he has respect for the item. The demonstration should also show the advantages promised by the sales person.

Selling Techniques

The sales person's job is to identify the consumer's wants. After the consumer's needs have been identified, the sales person can emphasize the features of the product/service offering that will meet the consumer's needs. The sales person's role consists of translating the merchandise/service features into individualized consumer benefits and advantages. The sales person must be able to talk well and listen well in this consumer problem-solving approach. The sales presentation should be short enough to make shopping a pleasant but businesslike experience. Naturally, arguments should be avoided and the consumer's feeling of risk in buying reduced by assurances that the store is reliable, the brand is dependable, and the sales person has a personal interest in seeing that the customer is properly served. It is the sales person's job to make the customer feel important. The consumer must believe that he is *buying*, not *being sold*.

The value of the item should be discussed before the price is quoted. If the consumer asks for the price, he should be told immediately, but the accompanying story should stress product advantages and customer benefits that justify the price.

Meeting Objections

Consumer uncertainty in areas of *product, price,* and *time* give rise to most buying resistance. Thus the sales person is frequently dealing with a customer who is not completely certain that the product under consideration is the best buy for him.

Good sales people learn to anticipate consumer objections and incorporate answers to the objections into the presentation of the merchandise. By presenting the most appropriate items from a consumer viewpoint, the sales person reduces the amount of product objections he must handle. By pointing out all the benefits offered by the item, the sales person reduces the importance of the price objections by emphasizing *value* instead of cost.

Time objections usually come in the form of a customer's saying "I'll have to think it over." The sales person might agree that some thought is desirable before making the purchase, and then point out that the store allows merchandise to be taken home "on approval" or on credit with a liberal return policy.

Frequently, time objections are used as excuses which are supposed to conceal the real reason the consumer doesn't want to make the purchase. Such excuses are more difficult to handle than real objections because they don't reflect the honest opinion of the customer. Thus the real objection is not defined so that the sales person can meet it. Further questions may be asked in an attempt to identify the objection. If this fails, the sales person should not argue with or belittle the customer's opinion.

The entire process of meeting objections should inspire consumer confidence in the quality of the merchandise and the knowledgeability of the sales person.

Closing the Sale

Closing the sale is simply following through with the right remark at the right time. Questions such as "Can I wrap it for you?" and "Which color (size or style) do you want?" can be used for a closing. Getting the customer in a "yes habit" can make the closing easier. This can be done by using easy questions to get the consumer to agree with the sales person throughout the sales presentation.

Sales people can also benefit by analyzing the reasons for losing a sale. Sales people can lose sales if they hurry the customer and try to get him to buy before he is ready to make the decision. Attempts to force action by using high-pressure methods, failure to meet objections directly, discourteous behavior, and stressing unimportant points in the sales presentation can also result in lost sales.[2]

Suggestion Selling

The sales person has an opportunity to increase sales by using suggestion selling after the sale has been closed on the initial purchase. Trading up could be used to increase sales by suggesting the purchase of better-quality merchandise or larger-volume purchases. Suggestion selling also emphasizes sales of companion items, bargain items being promoted by the store, new merchandise just received, and other items that the sales person believes the customer might need. The sale of companion items is usually the easiest to promote. A man who has just purchased a sport coat is likely to appreciate advice on coordinated apparel such as slacks, shirts, ties, and socks.

Suggestion selling must not be undertaken too aggressively or it will build customer resentment. Instead, it must be a personalized, natural presentation that points out the benefit of the added item to the consumer.

Developing Customer Good Will

A sincere expression of gratitude for the purchase is required before the consumer departs. In addition to indicating it was a pleasure to serve each consumer, the customer might be sent away by name. Attempts should be made to follow up on major purchases to determine if the customer was really satisfied, and why or why not. Consumers should be thanked for their interest even though they may not have made a purchase. Such actions promote customer good will that has a long-lasting effect.

Customer good will may also be accomplished by using "gimmicks" to provide an additional benefit to the consumer. An example is the "Snowjob" offered by one Chicago restaurant, which works this way:

> The customer phones in, orders the Snowjob and tells the restaurant exactly when he and his date or client will arrive. When the customer does arrive, he is greeted effusively. "So nice to see you again, Mr. _____!" the head waiter exclaims, although he probably has never seen the man before in his life.
>
> Two menus are used, with the one presented to the date or client having prices three times as high as the other. Wine is ordered, with the understanding that it will be regally removed and replaced when the customer tastes it and pronounces it unacceptable. Finally it is arranged that the customer will receive three important phone calls during the course of the meal.[3]

The Snowjob will probably succeed only as long as few people are aware of its existence, but similar gimmicks can be used to promote customer good will.

Telephone Selling

Telephone selling is used by retailers and service firms to generate additional business and smooth the work schedule of sales and service personnel. Service firms benefit by making a "reminder call" the day before an appointment is scheduled to assure a full schedule the next day. Reminder telephone calls made by firms selling merchandise or services that are purchased on a regular basis can stimulate additional sales from regular customers who should be ready to repurchase the item or service. For example, dentists can call regular customers after a proper interval has passed and the customer is ready to have his teeth cleaned and checked. The appointments can be scheduled for hours and days when the dentist is least busy. The same type of reminder system can be used by auto service stations that know the proper interval for oil and lube jobs, tune ups, and seasonal changeovers.

This process requires a detailed follow-up file of index cards that identify the consumer, the last date of purchase, and the type of item or service purchased. The solicitation is brief and friendly. The call should be made at a time when it is convenient for the consumer to talk. Housewives should not be called at hours when they may be preparing meals. Naturally, solicitations should be made from a telephone other than the one designated to receive the firm's incoming calls.

A special offer may be required to solicit a new customer, but the offer should be brief and easily understandable. Providing some extra free service may win the consumer's regular business if he believes the firm is really interested in him.

Personal Selling Outside the Store

Welcome Wagon, Howdy Pardner, and other organizations are engaged in acquainting newcomers with local retailers. These organizations send their representatives to the homes of new residents to give them free gifts from numerous local retailers. The cost of sending their representatives to consumers' homes is spread over all participating retailers. Providing free gift coupons to those consumers who are new in the trading area is a good way to introduce these people to a firm's location and its merchandise/service offering. It is important that the regular in-store clerks accept the gift coupons with a high degree of enthusiasm. A poor follow-through at the store level will negate any good will obtained by the initial contact.

Because store loyalties are frequently established soon after the newcomer has relocated, getting his attention during this crucial period can yield good results. Approximately 20 percent of the U.S. population moves during a year, so the size of this mobile market segment is substantial.

Another approach is to encourage non-employees to disseminate good word-of-mouth messages about the outlet. For example, a restaurant operator in suburban Cincinnati occasionally visits nearby gasoline service stations and asks the attendants if they know of a good place to eat. Those who recommend his restaurant receive up to $20. Those who recommend some other restaurant are invited to his restaurant for a free dinner and told that there will be future opportunities to win cash when they are next visited by a restaurant employee.

Training and Evaluating Sales People

Every store should have a continual training program for both new and experienced sales people. These programs are designed to increase sales by presenting sales people with information on the latest merchandise/service offerings and selling techniques. Many stores evaluate their sales people on each of the traits that are associated with successful sales persons. However, sales records may be a better overall indicator of sales people's performance. Dollar volume of sales, units sold, number of completed transactions, and gross margin contribution can all be used to indicate the sales performance of employees. In addition, the percentage of consumer contacts which resulted in purchases can be obtained by dividing the number of transactions by the number of customer contacts. A dollar per consumer contact figure can be calculated by dividing the dollar sales volume by the number of consumer contacts.

Regardless of the type of evaluation used, it is necessary that the evaluation procedure be thoroughly understood by each sales person. It is also important that the method of evaluation be objective and fair to all employees. This may be difficult because retail sales people do more than merely sell. They also provide customer service, handle complaints, accept merchandise returns, stock shelves, wrap merchandise, and perform other housekeeping duties.

Compensating Sales People

Retail sales people are usually paid a *straight salary,* which is either a pre-specified monthly salary or a pre-determined hourly wage. The straight salary approach allows the store manager to direct a sales person's activities more closely, and includes more shelf stocking, price marking, etc. However, it may not provide much incentive for the salesman to make sales.

The *straight commission* method of compensation rewards sales people only on the basis of their sales volume. At the end of a pay period, an employee's sales are multiplied by the pre-specified percentage commission rate to determine his or her earnings. This plan provides considerable incentive for the sales person because his earnings are solely dependent on making sales. The commission method also allows dollar selling expense to be more flexible from a retailer's point of view. Employee compensation is reduced when sales volume declines and increased when sales volume increases. The reduction in compensation during a period of slack sales is not desirable from the employee's point of view, as his income is uncertain. Thus he may ask to borrow (in a drawing account) on his anticipated commissions. In addition, it is difficult to encourage a sales person who is compensated on a straight commission basis to perform housekeeping duties that do not directly increase his sales.

Combination salary and commission or bonus plans are frequently used. The bonus or commission, added to a straight salary, provides an incentive to make sales and still maintains control over employee activities. The bonus may be a cash bonus or a premium bonus of merchandise or a service—anything from clocks, to a television set, to an automobile. The premium bonus is an especially attractive incentive for higher-paid employees, who may be influenced by members of their family who want to use the premium. The cash bonus may be more appealing to lower-income employees, as their need to purchase necessities may be quite high.

Fringe benefits are another way to compensate employees. Employee discounts on in-store purchases, medical and life insurance, savings plans, and profit-sharing plans may all be used to better compensate the employee. The use of fringe benefits can increase employee morale and encourage store loyalty. Deferred profit-sharing and savings plans, which allow the employee to get only his contribution back (not the retailer's matching contribution) if he leaves the firm, encourage good sales people to remain with the retail organization.

CUSTOMER SERVICES

Retailers should establish customer service policies and procedures under which services will be offered. These policies must reflect the fact that some services are required to meet those policies offered by the most competitive outlets. The type of merchandise carried influences the degree of service required in the offering. Bulky, high-value items that need to be installed and repaired by experts require more service than small, low-cost items that require little or no maintenance. Higher-quality merchandise is generally associated with higher prices and more service to appeal to the quality-oriented consumer group. On the other hand, bargain merchandise is usually sold with little service. Finally, the location of an outlet may dictate that it must provide services to meet the needs of its customers. For example, a furniture store that is located far from the residences of its target market may have to offer delivery service.

The retailer must choose his service offering from the consumer's point of view, as the objective of customer services must be to keep customers happy. Retail consumer services make it more convenient for the consumer to make the purchase. Free coffee in a small consumer lounge area, clean rest rooms, free minor alterations, free minor repairs, etc. cost little but generate much good will. Other services, such as packaging and gift wrapping, delivery, credit, and merchandise refunds and exchanges, represent larger monetary expenditures and thus require more detailed discussion.

Packaging and Gift Wrapping

A discussion of retail packaging cannot be confined to the product as it arrives from the manufacturer. In the long run, the retailer may have an important influence over the shape, size, color, and weight of the packaged product. However, in most cases he is relatively powerless to change the manufacturer's package. Thus the primary responsibility for branded product packaging rests directly upon the manufacturer. It is critical for manufacturers to understand the problems and complexities of retailing so that their package designs can meet these needs.

There are, however, two areas of packaging over which certain retailers can exercise substantial control: gift packaging and bulk in-store packaging. The department store, in particular, has discovered a rich opportunity for increased profits, customer good will, and image building through the use of these services.

The practice of offering free gift-wrapping service for purchases can help create a favorable image of the store through the color and style of the package, and may aid in establishing repeat sales or new customers. Nevertheless, this traditional approach to gift wrapping must be viewed as a cost center rather than profit generation. Many of the traditional gift wrapping centers also suffer from a lack of coordination as part of the store's total objective. They are simply areas of the store in which pretty wrappings are placed on merchandise.

Maximum benefits to a store can never be gained with this view of gift wrapping. Instead, gift wrapping must be viewed as a coordinated and integral part of the entire retailing system within a store. A coordinated and professional approach to gift wrapping can bring major rewards to retailers.

The package will become an integral part of the total image desired by a store. It can say much more than "I am a pretty package." By identifying the outlet tastefully on the wrapping, it can convey a store's total image of good taste, fashion, and styling—and to an audience far in excess of the buyer. Such packages will be seen by guests at showers, weddings, graduations, and dozens of other gift-giving occasions.

The package may be used as a part of the point-of-purchase display area. Wide lines of designs and materials are available to retailers from pre-designed package manufacturers. Retailers can now buy packages just as they do the merchandise to fill them. These are truly professional designs, which generally are sold to a retailer with the guarantee that his store will have exclusivity on this design within a particular market area. Yearly package designs are made, incorporating new trends and fashions. Professionally styled packages add to the point-of-purchase appeal of products and also help to differentiate departments or areas within departments.

The package itself can be sold at an excellent margin of profit. Thus what was once a cost center can become one of profit, while corporate goals are enhanced.

Bulk, in-store packaging is of growing importance to the department store retailer who is facing a serious problem of maintaining a unique image. With the growth of shopping centers, many retailers have tended to become more alike in appearance. In addition, manufacturers have altered or eliminated their policies of brand exclusivity. Moreover, it must be admitted that competing brands have taken on an appearance of similarity. Brand names which at one time meant exclusivity and uniqueness now are simply competing brands.

Several leading department stores have discovered that a new and unique package can be created in the store by packaging several items together in a box, bag, tote bag, or other container. As an example, selected brands and scents of toiletries may be placed together in a unique box and sold as a single item. In this way the retailer is able to sell multiple products at one time, and in a container that is unique. To top this off, the retailer is also able to incorporate the price of the box with full markup into the total package price. The obvious problem in this is the selection of the right merchandise for the package at the right price.

Delivery

Offering delivery service to customers can be a competitive tool that can be used to create a unique image for the retailer. Many customers do not like to carry large packages while they are moving from one store to another. Urban customers who depend on public transportation and older or physically disabled consumers are likely to respond favorably to a retailer's delivery service. Therefore delivery service can be an important part of the retailing effort in reaching these market segments. Delivery service can also expand a retailer's sales if the delivery person is alert and can recognize additional consumer needs.

Delivery service, on the other hand, can create new problems for the retailer. Preparing goods for delivery requires increased packaging, labor, and transportation costs. In addition, goods may be damaged because of improper handling during the delivery process. Some retailers recover these additional costs either by requiring a minimum purchase before free delivery is offered or by charging a small delivery fee to pay for most of the delivery costs. Retailers who sell heavy, fragile items (such as large appliances and furniture) and some service firms (such as interior decorating and plumbing) are forced to deliver because the customer usually considers delivery a part of the purchase.

Various delivery methods can be used to move the merchandise to the consumer. Bicycles, automobiles, trucks, commercial common carriers, and the U.S. Post Office are used by some retailers. The size and weight of the merchandise, the speed of delivery required by the consumer, the perishability of the merchandise, the distance covered, and the frequency and volume of deliveries all influence the choice of the delivery method. Stores that do not deliver much merchandise may use local common carriers or make cooperative delivery arrangements with other local retailers or wholesalers.

Regardless of the method used, delivery costs must be watched and controlled. Deliveries must be routed and scheduled to eliminate backtracking and duplication of service to a specific area. Unscheduled deliveries increase costs. Supervising the delivery person is important since nonproductive use of time is a large expense item. Relating dollars (or units) of merchandise delivered to man-hours worked and miles driven are methods for evaluating delivery costs.

Credit

Consumer credit in retail stores is now almost an institution. Barring serious social or economic disturbances, such as a depression, it is almost a permanent retailing tool. Although credit sales have grown tremendously since World War II, they are not new to retailing but, instead, have changed in form and amount. The folk songs and literature of mining and lumbering towns make frequent reference to the company store. "I owe my soul to the company store" was in many cases an all too true reality. Credit was extended to miners and families for almost all their daily needs by the company store. Pay checks were sent to the company store to settle accounts, only to discover that, according to company records, the entire pay check was insufficient to cover the charges.

In this way the company store excluded any chance of competitive retailing by independents and helped to create a near captive labor market for the mine operator. The history of retail credit also demonstrates that it was not a one-sided tool used solely by unfeeling, greedy exploiters. Without a grubstake from general stores, many prospectors for gold and silver would have found the pursuit of their dream impossible.

The depression of the 1930s found many retailers bankrupt and penniless due to an overextension of credit to their customers. This experience caused many retailers who survived the depression to institute conservative credit policies or to prohibit credit sales entirely. Some of the nation's best-known retailers did not institute a credit program until the late '50s and '60s. Retailers have discovered that credit can be a powerful, double-edged merchandising-corporate sword that can be used both as a merchandising tool and a source of profit.

Advantages of Using Credit

Customer convenience in paying for an item or service can be as important (or more important) a selling tool as advertising, personal selling, promotion, etc. Sometimes credit can be the major difference in influencing the decision to shop one store instead of a competitor's. More generous credit terms may make a prospective customer consider the retailer's "total product" more favorably.

The advantages of using credit are:

(1)   A more personal relationship can be maintained with credit customers, who feel they are part of the firm.

(2)   Credit customers are likely to be more loyal than cash customers who tend to go where bargains are the greatest.

(3)   Credit customers tend to be more interested in quality and service than in price.

(4)   Good will is built up and maintained more easily when credit is used.

(5)   Goods can be exchanged and adjustments made with greater ease and, if necessary, goods can also be sent out on approval.

(6)   Credit account records provide valuable market information which will allow the firm to:

a.   have a permanent mailing list for special sales promotions or research projects.

b.   discover opportunities for suggesting the purchase of certain items considered appropriate in the light of previous purchases, buying habits, etc.

c.   gather material concerning sales by department or by individual sales personnel, and

d.   detect any decline in purchases that might suggest a drifting away from the firm.

(7)   The firm's return on investment can increase if credit stimulates sales, because additional business can be secured and sometimes handled at practically no additional expense, thereby, reducing per unit costs.[4]

Whenever credit is extended by the retail outlet, it costs money. However, many retailers believe that credit extension is both necessary and attractive. Apparently, many target customers find immediate possession important enough to outweigh any extra costs.

Through the use of credit, individual retailers have demonstrated that demand for their products and services can be increased. In addition, total retail industry demand has increased through the use of credit. Whereas other promotional techniques, such as trading stamps, simply shift purchase patterns from one retailer to another, credit increases demand for goods and services in total.

Without credit, the demand for consumer durables such as refrigerators, boats, and automobiles would shrink markedly. The establishment of an installment credit department, General Motors Acceptance Corporation (GMAC), by General Motors played an important part in the tremendous marketing success of this firm.

If future consumer durables include such items as individual rocket ships, transistorized time machines, or any other futuristic product, one fact will remain constant. To buy new consumer durables, either cash or credit will be essential. As the cost of the item increases, the amount and payback period for credit will also increase.

Commercial bankers traditionally have been slow to finance new consumer durables, particularly when the payback period seemed long. It is doubtful that this attitude will change greatly during the working life of any reader of this book, or in the atomic-powered future.

This means that the experience of General Motors with GMAC is very likely to be as relevant 200 years from now as it is today. Retailers likely will be faced with the option of convincing commercial bankers of the profit opportunities in installment loans for these new products or establishing their own credit systems.

Recent retailing history has demonstrated that, sooner or later, most commercial banks eventually accept and encourage loans for consumer durables with long-term demand appeal and a "used" market.

A sales program aimed at acquainting bankers with the merits of a new consumer durable should be a first-step, combination effort of retailers, the trade association, distributors, and manufacturers of these products. This is of particular importance to independent retailers who operate without the benefit of a credit plan backed by the manufacturer. Retailers of mobile homes, campers, sail boats, and snow mobiles are examples.

Disadvantages of Using Credit

Over the past ten years, receivables have climbed 142 percent while sales rose 78 percent. In 1947 the average collection period was 34 days; by 1971 it had risen to 44 days.[5]

Credit policy is responsible for an increasing number of business failures. Dunn and Bradstreet has found that receivables difficulties rank first as a fundamental cause of business failures.[6] Poor credit and collection practices have contributed a disproportionate share to the unchecked upsurge in receivables. Proper evaluation of the credit policy is essential if it is to be used in a profitable manner.

Some other disadvantages of using credit are:

(1)   The firm's capital is tied up in merchandise bought by charge customers.

(2)   If the merchant has borrowed the extra money required when credit is granted, the interest is added to the cost.

(3)   Some losses from bad debts and customers with fraudulent intentions are bound to occur.

(4)   Credit customers feel more at liberty to abuse the privileges of returning goods and having goods sent out on approval.

(5)   Credit increases operation and overhead costs by adding to the expenses of investigation, bookkeeping, sending out statements and collecting payments.[7]

Deciding Whether to Offer Credit

Credit can be used to stimulate sales, but the profitability of credit usage is influenced by:

1.   How much sales are increased by using credit
2.   How large the gross profit margin is on the goods being sold
3.   How fast the money on credit sales is received by the retailer
4.   The cost of financing this credit balance
5.   The cost of maintaining the credit system
6.   The loss incurred by bad debts.[8]

One of the most significant factors that influences the decision to grant credit is the gross profit margin received on the store's merchandise. Other things being equal, the use of credit is more likely to be profitable if the profit margin is high. Thus credit must stimulate sales considerably if credit usage is going to be profitable in retail outlets that have a low profit margin.

Naturally, proper handling of accounts receivable is required to keep consumers current on their payments and to reduce bad debts. (Accounts receivable records are discussed in more detail in Chapter 15.) Screening applicants for credit by checking with the local retail credit bureau can also reduce the incidence of bad debts and result in faster recovery of the retailer's money.

Other factors, such as the amount of capital available to the retailer, the use of credit by direct competitors, and the general consumer insistence that credit be granted, also influence the retailer's decision of granting or not granting credit.

Kinds of Retail Credit

If the retailer decides to offer credit, he must evaluate the different types of credit available and choose the one that best meets his needs.

Bank credit plans, such as BankAmericard and Master Charge, allow retail customers to use a credit account they have established with one of the financial institutions. Customers can charge purchases at any participating outlet. The billing, recordkeeping, and collection activities are performed by the financial agency. This arrangement costs the retailer from 2 to 6 percent of the credit card sales volume. The exact rate depends upon the bargaining position of the retailer and the degree of competition between various bank credit card agencies. In return for this charge, a retailer transfers the work involved with offering credit and the responsibility for collecting unpaid bills to the financial institution. The retailer receives cash for bank credit card purchases when the charge slips are deposited in the participating bank.

The *30-day open account plan* is administered by the retailer who allows consumers to charge merchandise and pay the full amount within thirty days of the billing date. Interest is usually not charged unless a payment is not received when it is due.

The *revolving credit plan* divides the the unpaid account balance into equal monthly payments, but approximately 1½ percent per month interest charge is made on the remaining balance if the account is not paid in full by the stated due date. Each customer has a credit limit that he cannot exceed, but otherwise he can charge and make payments to meet his needs, providing a minimal payment is made each month.

Deferred payment plans allow purchasers of large items to make equal monthly payments for the value of the merchandise, plus a carrying charge. Because the agreement involves only the particular item purchased, a separate agreement must be made on each item. Installment contracts, which are one type of deferred payment agreement, let the title to the goods stay with the retailer until the provisions of the contract have been fulfilled. Under installment contracts, payments are scheduled so that the remaining balance due is always less than the current market value of the depreciated merchandise.

Who Uses Credit?

The use of credit is not limited to consumers from one social class or racial group. However, types of credit and the purposes of credit usage vary by class, and research on users of bank credit cards has demonstrated different use patterns among social classes.[9] Members of the lower classes were found to use their credit cards for installment purchases. Upper classes used theirs as a convenience tool in place of cash but not for installment loans.

Members of lower social classes also tend to look for stores that honor their cards. By comparison, upper-class members did not specifically seek out stores because they accept credit cards. Upper-class members did not feel their cards should be used to purchase most consumer durable goods. Members of this social class have more alternative sources of credit available to them, and also appear to be more conscious of interest charges than persons in lower classes.

There are also social class differences in attitude toward purchasing specific products by credit. Upper classes generally hold favorable attitudes toward using credit to purchase "luxury goods." Lower classes tend to restrict credit usage to durable and necessity goods.

Customer Complaints

The way complaints are handled affects the store image and either serves as a way to gain loyal customers or negates any good will built up by various promotional activities. Thus retailers should establish adjustment procedures that ensure that each dissatisfied customer receives understanding attention.

Complaints arise because of faulty merchandise, unsatisfactory installation or fit, delayed or incorrect delivery, damaged merchandise, errors in billing charge accounts, resentment with credit collection methods, and dissatisfaction with sales people.[10]

Naturally, a store is obliged to make satisfactory adjustment when the consumer has a legitimate complaint based on any of these reasons. Even if the consumer has no legitimate complaint, complaining consumers nearly always are convinced that they should receive adjustment. Therefore it is better for a retailer to let the complaining consumer have all the time he wants to explain his problem. The adjuster should not argue with the consumer, or blame him, but suggest that some sort of adjustment can be made.

It is better to give a generous adjustment to the customer than to irritate him. Customers who are dissatisfied with an adjustment generally inform their friends of their dissatisfaction, whereas satisfied customers recommend the store to their friends. If possible, many retailers try to satisfy customers with replacement items (which reduces the adjustment cost by the amount of the retail markup). However, the customer must be satisfied, so the adjustor should ask him if he thinks the adjustment is fair.

Most consumers try to be fair if they believe the adjustor understands their problem and is trying to solve it. A few consumers, of course, are habitual complainers who can never be satisfied. Adjustment records can reveal the identity of such individuals and they can be discouraged from trading at the outlet on the pretense of being out of stock on the items they request.

Retailers should keep good adjustment records, not only to identify habitual complainers but also to identify poor merchandise, poor delivery and credit procedures, and poor performance in sales people. For every reasonable complaining customer there are likely to be numerous customers who encountered the same problem but simply chose to discontinue trading at that store. Thus defective merchandise should be returned to the manufacturer and internal operations should be improved to reduce the occurrence of consumer complaints.

SUMMARY

Personal selling and customer services must be coordinated with the other elements of the promotional mix to ensure that a consistent message is communicated to consumers. Personal selling is unique in that it is the only promotional element that provides direct two-way feedback from the consumer.

The sales person's job is to identify the consumer's needs and emphasize the features of the retailer's product/service offering that will meet the consumer's needs. Thus the sales person's role involves the translation of the firm's offering into individualized consumer benefits.

Retail training programs, supervision, and compensation plans can encourage a sales person to use the techniques described in this chapter to generate customer satisfaction and close the sale.

Customer services are used to keep the customer satisfied, but services such as credit, delivery, and packaging are also sales-stimulating devices.

QUESTIONS

1. What characteristics do you think are most important for retail sales people?

2. In what types of retailing do you think the straight commission is the best form of compensation? What types of retailing positions would be best suited for straight salary?

3. What factors would you consider in designing a consumer service plan?

4. What is the effect of the availability of credit on total sales? How does credit availability affect the cash position of the store?

5. Has the recent use of bank credit cards been in the best interests of retailers and consumers, or do you think that the banks have enjoyed the largest benefit?

6. What factors determine whether a retailer can extend credit?

7. What factors should a small retailer consider in deciding whether to accept bank credit cards or set up his own credit department?

8. If a merchant is deciding whether to accept only the "free" bank cards (e.g., BankAmericard, Master Charge) or only the cards that members pay for (e.g., American Express, Diners Club, etc.), what factors must he consider?

9. Suggest several ways the average retailer can minimize customer complaints and outline a policy for handling complaints in a retail operation of your choice.

FOOTNOTES

[1] Karen R. Gillespie, "Revitalize Personal Selling in Your Store," *Small Marketers Aids Annual No. 9* (Washington, D.C.: Small Business Administration, 1967), pp. 82–89.

[2] C. A. Pederson and M. D. Wright, *Salesmanship: Principles and Methods* (4th ed.; Homewood, Ill.: Richard D. Irwin, 1966), pp. 481–516.

[3] Jack Phinney, "Restaurants Feed on Word-of-Mouth," *Denver Post*, April 8, 1973, p. 5E.

[4] John E. Payne, "What the Vice-President of Sales Wants from the Credit Department," *Credit and Financial Management* (January 1967), pp. 15–17; Pearce C. Kelley and Kenneth Lawyer, *How to Organize and Operate a Small Business* (Englewood Cliffs, N.J.: Prentice-Hall, 1961), pp. 491–521; and Wallace Reiff, "Capital Allocation in Credit Decision-Making," *Credit and Financial Management* (September 1967), pp. 20–23.

[5] "Collection period" is defined as accounts receivable in dollars divided by average

daily dollar sales. Frank Wey, "Keeping a Tight Rein on Receivables," *Credit and Financial Management* (September 1971), p. 21.

⁶ Merle Welshans, "Using Credit in Profit Making," *Credit and Financial Management* (February 1967), pp. 18–27.

⁷ Kelley and Lawyer, *How to Organize and Operate a Small Business*, pp. 491–521.

⁸ Raymond A. Marquardt and Anthony F. McGann, "Profit Analysis and the Firm's Credit Policy," *Business Ideas and Facts*, 6 (Winter 1973): 12–18.

⁹ Lee H. Matheus and John W. Slocum, Jr., "Social Class and Commercial Bank Credit Card Usage," *Journal of Marketing*, 33 (January 1969): 71–78.

¹⁰ Gerald D. Grosner, *Turning Complaints into Profits* (Washington, D.C.: Small Business Administration, 1959), p. 58.

LINDAL CEDAR HOMES
Exploring a New Retailing Technique and "Profit at Each Step" Marketing

Lindal Cedar Homes of Seattle is the largest manufacturer of pre-cut cedar homes in the world, with sales of over $15 million per year. The company has had a fivefold sales increase in the past four years.

Although it is an international company, in terms of retail distribution the top sales areas are the U.S. northeast, the U.S. west coast, Canada, and the U.S. midwest. Recent moves to offset sales seasonality and to expand company's operations have found Lindal Cedar Homes exerting more efforts in the south and southwest of the United States and in new international markets, such as Japan, Tahiti, and the Caribbean.

The company's primary product is a line of pre-cut cedar vacation homes, which are shipped by truck, rail, or boat, depending upon the distance involved. In all cases, a complete package—with the exception of wiring, plumbing, fixtures, and foundation—is shipped to the customer for erection by a local contractor.

The primary market segment for these products is the upper-income market. A recent survey demonstrated that the profile of a Lindal customer is changing more toward that of a high-income consumer (see Table 11–1). These individuals have property near lakes or ski resorts or in recreational developments.

Sales of the homes are made through four retail systems: independent franchised country dealers, independent franchised metropolitan dealers, company-owned metropolitan dealers, and telephone and direct-mail solicitation by the home office.

Franchised dealers are required to build a display home, to man it with

Table 11–1   Survey of Lindal Home Purchases

QUESTION	1971	1972
1. What is your profession or occupation?		
Professional	66%	76%
Blue collar	25	18
Retired	7	6
2. What age group are you in?		
20–35	24	31
35–50	42	39
Over 50	33	30
3. What income range are you in?		
Under $10,000	17	10
$10,000–$15,000	26	28
$15,000–$20,000	17	21
$20,000–$25,000	14	17
Over $25,000	23	24
4. Is your Lindal home used as a year-round residence or as a leisure home?		
Year round	49	49
Leisure	46	49
Rental	.01	
Office	—	2
Guest house	—	
5. Did you erect your Lindal home yourself or by contractor?		
Erected by self	26	20
Contractor	57	66
Owner and contractor	14	14
6. Where did you first hear of Lindal Cedar Homes?		
Magazine	25	37
Newspaper	17	10
Yellow Pages	.02	2
Friend	24	22
Display home	21	21
Miscellaneous	6	5
Direct mail	.004	1
Salesman	—	2
7. Did you purchase a set of plans before purchasing your home?		
Yes	44	49
No	54	51
8. Did you visit a Lindal Cedar Homes display court?		
Yes	79	79
No	19	21

sales personnel, and to pay a franchise fee to the company. Metropolitan dealers are required to build three model homes, rather than one, with a total investment ranging between $75,000 and $100,000. In turn, the retail margin for the metropolitan dealers is higher than that for the country dealers.

A strong system of metropolitan sales outlets is considered by Lindal Cedar Homes to be the key to success. It is the company's belief that the customer is more receptive to buying in the city than when he is in the country, since he is in a vacation- or leisure-oriented frame of mind in the latter case. Moreover, metropolitan dealers have more opportunity to follow through with prospects when they are located in the same area. This is difficult for a dealer several hundred miles away.

The business philosophy of Mr. Lindal and the entire company can be described as "profit at each step." Under this philosophy, dealers are taught not to give away anything. Instead of distributing catalogs and blueprints on a free basis, all of this material is sold at a profit to the company and the dealer.

The catalog is a beautiful four-color item that retails for $1 with a 50 percent margin built in for dealers. Photographs for the catalog come from customers, who are paid $1,000 for a photograph.

The concept of "profit at each step" does not exclude dealers, as they are required to pay for dealer training kits and other material. Unlike many franchisers, Lindal Cedar Homes does not distribute information to prospective dealers on a free basis but charges $10 for a basic information kit to those who send inquiries to the company concerning dealerships.

An example of the Lindal method of training new dealers is their instruction regarding the distribution of material at the grand opening. Dealers are instructed not to hire professional models to distribute free material but to hire high school students on a commission basis to sell catalogs to customers at the opening.

After a customer purchases a catalog, the next step is to sell him a book of blueprints for $35, and eventually the entire home. In this way, even if a prospect never moves beyond the catalog stage, the company and the dealer have made a small sale and profit.

In terms of total company sales, the greatest volume comes from franchised dealers. This is followed by company-owned displays, and lastly by telephone and direct sales from the home office. The telephone sales program yields yearly sales of $1 million or more.

This sales program is a direct result of the company's efforts to follow through on every lead generated by the $350,000 the company spends annually on mass media advertising.

The success of telephone sales from the Seattle office reflects both a problem and a tremendous marketing potential, according to Mr. Walter Lindal, president and founder. He believes that the reason telephone sales are successful is that dealers effectively follow up only about 60 percent of the leads sent to them.

After proving that sales can be made without a model home, the company decided to establish two showroom retail outlets under a franchised system. These were established in east coast cities, where the cost and availability of land for display homes is a limiting factor.

The system consists of utilizing a leased "showroom" where pictures and scale models of the homes are displayed. After several months of operation, this system had not produced the sales level desired by Lindal Cedar Homes or the franchised dealers.

The dealers complained that it was often impossible to close sales without having a display model to show prospects. They stated that only part of the AIDCA sales system (attention, interest, desire, conviction, and action) could be accomplished under this system. They also argued that the final and most important part (action) could not be accomplished without a display home.

While the home office was sympathetic, Mr. Lindal believed that the "showroom" sales force had fallen prey to negative thinking and convinced themselves that the task was impossible. He recognized that the sales effort would be more demanding, but continued to feel that the success of telephone sales from the home office had proved that high-volume sales are possible without a display home.

If the concept could be successfully implemented, it would be a powerful retail technique for Lindal Cedar Homes. In Mr. Lindal's opinion, the market for second homes was just beginning. He stated that literally millions of Americans had purchased land in developments throughout the United States at expensive prices on an installment basis and that many people were now completing their land payments. "When that happens, these people will want to build on that property. That will mean a fantastic market for second homes."

Mr. Lindal further feels that if the land developer can sell lots at expensive prices on a site-unseen basis, there is every reason to believe that the same customer can be sold a competitively priced vacation home through a retail showroom system without a model home.

DISCUSSION QUESTIONS

1. What is your opinion of the "profit at each step" concept of retailing? Do you believe it has application in other retailing situations, such as automobiles and boats? Is this a technique that traditional catalog merchandisers should initiate?

2. Read the ads in any magazine and see how many offer a catalog. List the companies and products associated with offers for a free catalog. Discuss the possibilities and potential problems associated with charging for these catalogs.

3. Why do you believe Lindal Cedar Homes has been successful in selling

homes over the phone from Seattle but relatively unsuccessful in establishing high volume through showrooms?

4.   What steps would you recommend to increase the sales productivity of the showroom retailers?

HAMILTON STORES INC.

"Part-Time Help Wanted!" Toward the middle of the tourist season in Yellowstone National Park, signs for part-time help begin appearing on the front of Hamilton Stores.

Hamilton Stores Inc. operates the grocery, souvenir, soda fountain, and general merchandise stores throughout Yellowstone National Park. This is not a new venture for Hamilton, as the company has continuously operated stores in the park since 1915. In fact, the management sometimes kids the Park Service about the fact that Hamilton was in Yellowstone before the ranger, since the U.S. Army had control of the park in the early years.

In addition to the stores in Yellowstone, a subsidiary company operates a resort at Stove Pipe Wells Village in Death Valley, California. Consequently, the company operates from winter corporate offices in Santa Monica, California, and from summer offices in West Yellowstone, Montana.

In Yellowstone, Hamilton operates stores at each major location throughout the park, such as Old Faithful, Fishing Bridge, etc.

Unlike most retailers, Hamilton Stores is faced with a short selling season. Although the company operates in Yellowstone from May 1 to October 30, the real sales period is even shorter—from mid-June to approximately Labor Day.

The limited sales season makes it impossible for Hamilton Stores to offer year-round employment for the majority of its in-store personnel. This means that each year the company must hire and train between 600 and 700 part-time employees. These employees perform the variety of tasks required in any retail store, such as stocking, clean up, and maintenance, but by far the greatest number are employed in behind-the-counter sales. This necessitates the use of reliable and intelligent personnel who comport themselves in a well-groomed manner. Women constitute the greatest number of the sales force.

Throughout the years the bulk of these employees has consisted of university and college students from all parts of the United States. As many as three generations have worked for Hamilton Stores in Yellowstone, and this employment has historically carried a tinge of romance.

Although Hamilton Stores tells every potential employee that this is not a paid vacation, there has always been a distinct aura of adventure and fun and a chance to meet people of all ages from all over the world. The management of Hamilton Stores is well aware of this, and helps to further it by open support of the employees' recreation organizations. Fish fries, dances, beauty contests, "Christian ministry," and even a miniature Christmas are parts of the Yellowstone employees' environment.

The pay scale for all employees begins with the Wyoming minimum wage. Higher hourly wages are paid to those who return for additional summers and to department heads.

Interested persons are told that it is unlikely their earnings from employment with Hamilton will enable them to pay for their college education, and each employee is required to sign an employment agreement for the season. The company also sees to it that the colleges and universities and the parents of the employees know the terms of the agreements.

Of the total work force, approximately 33 percent are returnees. Hamilton Stores has also found that these employees are good recruiters, as they often cause their friends or relatives to apply for employment.

In addition to the hourly pay, Hamilton Stores subsidizes, in part, the board and room of employees. The remainder, or $3.50 per day, is subtracted from the employee's pay check.

A recruiting program for college students is conducted each year by sending flyers to each university and college in the United States. Interested persons are then asked to write to corporate headquarters for more information. In the Los Angeles area, the company is able to conduct personal interviews since its winter headquarters are located there. However, the greatest number of employees are hired without such an interview.

As the selling season in Yellowstone begins, a full crew of employees is on hand and ready to work. In recent years, however, there has been an increase in the number who drop out before completing their employment. A few do so for health reasons, but the greatest number of dropouts is for reasons other than health. These range from old-fashioned homesickness to a desire to spend the rest of the summer bumming around the country.

These employees leave in spite of the fact they have signed a contract and given their word they would stay. When reminded of this, most of the dropouts seem unconcerned about it or about the bad work reference it may produce.

This situation puts Hamilton Stores under immediate pressure to find replacements. Since West Yellowstone is miles from centers of population, this is no easy task.

The large number of retired couples has presented the company with an excellent caliber but limited number of replacements. Signs are placed in storefronts advertising for a "trailer couple." Since trailer space is extremely limited in the park, it is necessary to recruit a couple. Otherwise, one employee would occupy one whole trailer space.

Even though retired couples have helped alleviate the problem of employee dropouts, they are not viewed as the ultimate answer.

Nor does the obvious solution of higher pay appear to be the ultimate answer. In the first place, Hamilton Stores is carefully regulated by the federal government as to the prices it can charge, and the management prides itself on keeping prices competitive with those in surrounding areas in spite of transportation costs.

In addition, retailing of all types has seldom been able to pay wages competitive with those in many other industries.

The result of a bonus program also demonstrates that higher pay may not be the only reason why employees are leaving. At the time this plan was in effect, during which employees were offered a bonus at the end of their contract season, dropouts continued at the same rate. For one thing, parents would often visit their sons or daughters in the park and encourage them to go home with them to save the transportation costs of returning separately.

The experience of Hamilton Stores with college students throughout the years has been so positive that management continues to believe they will be the backbone of the sales force in the future, as in the past. At the same time, there is no denying that the problem of dropouts has worsened in recent years and must be dealt with to ensure the smooth working of the entire operation.

DISCUSSION QUESTIONS

1. What do you believe are the major reasons why college students quit their jobs in violation of written agreements?
2. What new program do you believe Hamilton Stores should institute to reduce the dropout problem?
3. Is it possible that today's college student is different from those of past years in his attitude toward work and honoring contracts? If so, why?
4. Do you believe the problem of work dropouts is a temporary social phenomenon, or is it likely to continue and grow even worse? If you believe it is likely to increase, what should Hamilton Stores do?

MURRAY'S HARDWARE STORE
A Case on Personal Selling and Store Image

Mr. Murray is a hard-working and gruff but impeccably honest hardware retailer in an upper middle-class suburb of a major metropolis. He grew up on New York's East Side in grinding poverty and has worked all his life to establish himself in his own store in the suburbs.

Murray's store is conveniently located on a very busy street in the center of town, directly across the street from the railroad station. He considers his location fortunate for two reasons. First of all, trains stop every few minutes during the rush hours and pick up or discharge hundreds of commuters going to and from the city. Many of these commuters pass Murray's store on their walk home; they do not drive to the station because it is too difficult to park there. Secondly, a major bus line, which passes in front of Murray's store, also carries commuter traffic, and stops directly in front of the store. The buses carry so much traffic that they often travel in pairs, or even three at a time. Consequently, the bus stop is three bus-lengths long. This ensures Murray and his neighbors of good visibility from the street, because no cars can park in the bus stop.

Murray has always tried to promote a discount image while being careful to maintain an extensive inventory of hardware goods. Every item in the store is marked with two prices, and the higher one is crossed out. The lower price is sometimes competitive with the four other hardware stores in town. Murray's inventory is one of the most extensive in the area and his display shelves literally sag with merchandise. He handles every type of nut, bolt, washer, screw, and nail. He also handles all types of name brand hand tools, some power tools, paints, household goods, appliances, and garden hardware.

He carefully promotes his discount image by hanging signs in the window that say "Fantastic Savings," "Gigantic Sale," etc. He has done this even before the discount stores opened. In fact, he has used this technique so long that some of his signs have turned yellow.

Murray has two full-time employees and one part-time employee, all on straight salary. One of his full-time employees is a young man named Tony D'Italia, who is also a hard worker but not as smart as Murray. Tony often sells goods off the floor, and he always points out to customers that the store is a member of a hardware co-op and that this is why it is able to mark down the goods. The customers show a general lack of enthusiasm about the "competitive" price they are getting.

Murray's other full-time employee is a bookkeeper, who often waits on trade when the store is busy. She is very talkative and vivacious, and enjoys helping customers more than working on the books. She is generally untidy in looks, but Murray feels that her congeniality outweighs her often slovenly appearance. Her name is Loquacious Fiduciary.

Murray's part-time employee is an 18-year-old college student who works 2½ hours each afternoon and all day on Saturday. He diligently takes inventory of the display shelves and restocks them every afternoon. He also notifies Murray or Tony if they are low on some item so they can reorder before running out. Thus Murray is assured of a daily inventory check. The student also delivers merchandise to cash and credit customers daily, and he sweeps the floor before closing. Tony helps him deliver and install major appliances. The student also waits on trade when he has time and when customers are buying something he knows about and can find.

Murray buys most of his merchandise through the hardware co-op, but he also deals with hardware jobbers. Much of his business is done with Glib Hardware Wholesaling Company, and Murray's account is serviced by Harry Glib, vice-president and salesman. Harry Glib has a reputation in the trade for being able to sell anything to anyone, but Murray has dealt with Glib for many years and cannot be taken in by him. Harry has dealt with Murray so long that he knows Murray's merchandise as well as anyone in the store, and since he visits several times a week, he often waits on customers when the store is busy. Everyone appreciates his help, and although he does not have his own cash register drawer, he appears to outsell everyone else on the floor.

Murray has recently started a new line of plumbing and electrical supplies. He has introduced these lines cautiously, by carrying only a few of the items needed by plumbers and electricians, but he and Tony know the business well enough that they can direct plumbers and electricians to other sources if they cannot supply what is needed. Since Tony worked for a plumber after he dropped out of high school, and also wired his own garage, he was put in charge of the new departments. Murray had a shed constructed behind the store in which to keep long lengths of pipe and electrical conduits. If the alley is not too muddy, plumbers and electricians can pick up their supplies in back of the store, so that there is no need to carry these awkward pieces through the store. When it is wet, these pieces can be carried through the store and out the front door, if there are no buses at the curb.

Murray has recently been having trouble competing with the discount stores that have opened up in highway corridor locations. He has tried to compete by carrying low-price impulse items, using coupon sales, and advertising in suburban newspapers. These techniques have not been very successful and Murray is very disturbed. He often becomes belligerent when customers tell him they can get an item cheaper at a highway discount store, and he tells them to go there to buy it. He has other problems too. Tony is anxious to start his own hardware store, and Murray is afraid he will leave. Also, summer is coming and Murray's part-time helper is looking for full-time work for the summer.

As a retailing consultant, what would you suggest for Murray?

PART FOUR

Operating Policies,
Practices,
and Controls

CHAPTER 12

Photo courtesy of J. C. Penney Company, Inc.

Merchandise Management

Merchandise management, one of the most critical areas in retailing, is defined in this book as the activities involved in balancing inventories to meet expected consumer demands. The major merchandise policy decisions—those decisions relating to the question, "What products do we stock?"—were discussed in Chapter 4. This chapter concentrates on the other major merchandising issues—how much to buy, when to buy, and merchandise planning. Several techniques (such as the merchandise budget and stock turnover analysis) that can be used by retail management and buyers to plan and control inventory levels will be presented in this chapter. These techniques can simplify many of the activities associated with merchandise planning and control by establishing routine procedures. A discussion of the remaining buying issues—how to buy, organizing for buying, sources of merchandise, buying negotiations, and legal considerations—is presented in Chapter 13.

MERCHANDISE PLANNING

Retailers should recognize several factors that determine if their merchandise plans are providing a better balance between inventory levels and potential sales.

Planning and control methods are simply aids to the buyer's judgment. Such planning and control methods provide data which must be analyzed and interpreted in light of the buyer's previous experience and knowledge. Frequent review of the planning and control techniques must be made to ensure that such tools provide realistic information. Planning and control procedures are usually designed to provide information that is realistic only under a specific set of assumptions about the environment. Retail situations change quite frequently, so the planning and control procedures must be reviewed to be certain they are the most practical means of providing the desired information.

Planning and control procedures are effective only when information is analyzed and translated into action. The merchandise control process involves taking steps to bring actual results closer to stated retail objectives. The trend to larger retail organizations, combined with the tendency for the consumer environment to change more rapidly than ever, has made the use of some type of control process essential. However, changes in consumer preferences also have necessitated flexibility in allowing individual store managers to adjust their merchandise assortment to reflect the needs of their specific trade area more quickly.

Small owner-operated retail outlets have fewer formal control problems than large chain retail outlets. However, even the small retailer can make profitable use of such tools as merchandise budgets and stock turnover analysis to simplify his buying procedures and to meet the needs of his potential customers. Even the smallest retailers need to plan their sales, stocks, purchases, reductions, and margins by reviewing past records and observing inventory levels on a periodic basis.

BASIC MERCHANDISE INFORMATION PROCEDURES

Efficient merchandise management involves the use of the most detailed, accurate, and current information that is available. The merchandise budget is one management tool that can be used for both planning and controlling inventories.

Merchandise Budget

The merchandise budget can be used in planning and controlling sales efforts, markups, purchases, markdowns, and shortages. It usually consists of:

1. A forecast of sales for given periods
2. A plan for the stocks to be carried at the beginning of each period

3. Planned markup/reductions to be made on merchandise
4. Planned stock shortages and returns
5. Planned purchase quantities
6. Planned gross margin and
7. Anticipated stock turnover.

Such a budget enables the retailer to buy merchandise of the kind and in the quantity that better reflects the needs of his potential customers. By identifying fast-moving and/or highly profitable items, it provides information that the retailer can use to plan his promotional efforts more efficiently. The merchandise budget contains a record of both actual and predicted past sales which can be used to evaluate the performance of both the budget procedure itself and the store's merchandise buyers.

The budget can be constructed on a weekly, monthly, quarterly, semi-annual, or annual basis. However, the longer the time period covered by a budget, the more difficult it is to obtain accurate forecasts. Frequently the budget is made for six months or one year in advance and is revised each month. A normal sequence in merchandise budgeting is presented below. Deviations from the sequence of activities are both appropriate and common if other, relevant information is available.

Step 1:   Forecasting Sales

Either unit or dollar sales are forecast for each merchandise type for the specified time period. Past monthly (or weekly) sales performance should be recorded and analyzed to identify trends and seasonality patterns. The estimated sales volume is a critical element in the merchandise budget because an error in the estimated sales figures can cause a serious error in the projection of the firm's profitability.

Annual sales forecasts must consider such factors as past trends in store sales, as well as local changes in (1) population, (2) income, (3) employment, (4) competition (both in number and in action), (5) consumer preferences, (6) the general price level charged by the store, and (7) any of the other internal elements used by the store to attract customers.

Annual sales forecasts may be made simply by estimating a "reasonable" change from last year's sales or by using more complicated statistical forecasting techniques, such as multiple regression analysis (which is discussed in Chapter 17). Several pre-written computer programs are available at reasonable cost, so a commercial service bureau, such as Statistical Tabulating Corporation, may be able to provide annual forecasts less expensively than the individual retailer can.

Seasonality of sales differs by the type of merchandise being sold; so sales forecasts must be made for each different merchandise category on a monthly, weekly, or sometimes even a daily basis (Figure 12–1). In some cases an entire selling period, such as Christmas, Easter, etc., can be analyzed separately. Monthly sales indexes can be used to forecast monthly sales. Monthly sales can be forecast by dividing the estimated annual sales by 12

Figure 12–1   Seasonal Sales Patterns

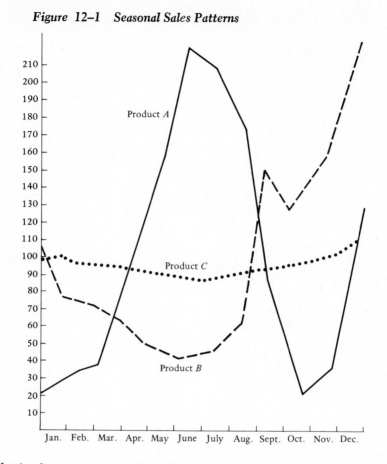

to obtain the *average* monthly sales estimate. Past monthly sales records can then be used to obtain a *monthly sales index* for each merchandise category. The monthly sales index is calculated by dividing each month's sales by an average month's sales and the result is multiplied by 100.

For example, suppose sales data for the past five years indicated average sales in January were $10,000 and the five-year annual average sales were $240,000. In this case the average previous monthly sales would be 240,000 divided by 12, or $20,000. The January sales index is ($10,000 / $20,000) 100, or 50.

Each monthly sales index is calculated in a similar manner, so an index of 100 represents sales made during an "average" month. The percentage that a monthly sales index deviates from 100 is the percentage deviation of that month's sales. From the sales of the average month in the above example, the 50 index for January indicates that January sales are 50 percent *below* average (because 50 is less than 100). An index of 110 for May would indicate that May sales are 10 percent *above* an average month's sales (because 110 is more than 100).

Once the value of the monthly sales index has been determined, it can be divided by 100 and the result multiplied by the average estimated monthly sales to provide an estimate of that month's sales for the upcoming year.

For example, suppose the forecast sales level for the upcoming year is $300,000 and the January sales index is 50. The forecast January sales is estimated average monthly sales, or $300,000 / 12 = $25,000 × [50 / 100], or $12,500.

Even the best estimates must be revised to account for unanticipated developments, such as *abnormally* severe weather, epidemics, etc. However, the seasonal index approach can be used to make accurate sales forecasts by making comparisons against similar pay periods, holidays, etc. Of course, the occurrence of a holiday in a different week (or month) from year to year must be accounted for in making weekly (or monthly) forecasts. This adjustment in forecast sales may consist of simply adding and subtracting the normal value of that holiday occurring or not occurring during the specified period. For example, forecasts should reflect the fact that Easter occurs during one week one year and another week the following year.

Step 2: Planning Inventory Levels

Inventory levels should be planned to maintain the necessary depth and breadth in merchandise assortment that will meet expected customer needs. However, the investment in inventory should also be held low enough to allow a sufficiently high inventory turnover.

Several methods are frequently used to plan needed inventories. The *basic stock method* involves ordering sufficient stock to begin the month (or any other specified selling period) with an inventory that exceeds estimated monthly sales by some "basic stock amount." The basic stock amount is really a basic inventory level or safety stock below which the retailer would not like to fall.

The *percentage deviation (variation) method* involves ordering stocks so that the beginning monthly inventory fluctuates from the planned average stock by 50 percent of the sales fluctuations from the average monthly sales. The beginning-of-the-month stock can be calculated by multiplying the averaging monthly stock by one-half (the deviation of the monthly sales index from 100). For example, if the January sales index is 50, the stock on January 1 is established at one-half (100 − 50), or 25 percent lower than the average annual retail stock.

Another technique, the *weeks' supply method*, consists of inventory being planned on the basis of a predetermined number of weeks' supply, with some stock turnover used as a goal. The planned inventory is usually specifically related to a desired stock turnover. For example, if inventory turns over six times a year, the 52 weeks would be divided by 6—to indicate that about a nine-week supply is to be stocked. The sales forecast for the next nine weeks then determines the amount of stock to be carried at the beginning of the period.

The *stock to sales ratio method* is also used to decide on inventory levels. This method involves multiplying the estimated sales volume for the month by the planned beginning-of-the-month stock-sales ratio to obtain the amount of inventory to be carried at the beginning of the month. In formula form, Estimated sales for the period × desired beginning-of-the-month stock-sales ratio = retail stock to be carried at the beginning of the month. For example, if a retailer wanted to maintain twice as much stock as the expected sales for June, and he estimates June sales to be $25,000, the retail stock at the beginning of June would be $25,000 × 2 = $50,000.

Retailers can analyze their past stock-sales ratios, or use the stock-sales ratios of similar retailers, to determine the desired stock-sales ratio. Stock-sales ratios are available from several trade publications, such as *Departmental Merchandising and Operating Results of Department and Specialty Stores*, published by the National Retail Merchants' Association in New York.

Each of the four methods provides a different solution to the inventory problem. The stock level indicated by the basic stock method is usually larger than the inventory level given by the stock-sales ratio method. Each method has the major disadvantage of not considering such serious factors as net margin contribution, perishability, fashion influences or style obsolescence, lead time needed before a new order can be received, and the effect that an out-of-stock condition can have upon regular consumers' store preference patterns.

DETERMINING INVENTORY LEVELS ON PERISHABLE AND FAD ITEMS   A relatively simple method, termed *marginal analysis*, can be used to determine the quantity of goods that should be stocked. This method is appropriate for goods that are either perishable (such as Christmas gift boxes of fresh fruits) or that are likely to become obsolete because of time (such as newspapers, magazines, or fad items). It can be used to examine the retail price, the wholesale cost, and the reduced price that can be obtained for perishable or out-of-date goods if they cannot be sold before they lose quality or become obsolete.[1] The marginal analysis method gives the retailer the minimum percentage chance he should have of selling the *additional* unit he adds to his inventory before he can profitably stock that unit.

Marginal analysis involves the calculation of *p*, which represents the minimum percent chance of selling at least an additional unit in order to justify the stocking of that unit. The value of *p* is found by using the formula

$$p = \frac{ML}{(MP + ML)} \times 100,$$

where *ML* is the marginal loss or the decrease in profit resulting from stocking an additional unit that is *not* sold at the retail price, and *MP* is the marginal profit or the increase in profit resulting from stocking an additional unit that *is* sold.

The use of marginal analysis can be illustrated in the following example. Suppose an item is purchased at wholesale for $4 per unit and is resold at retail for $10 per unit. If the product cannot be sold to a retail customer within a stated period of time, it can be sold to an industrial user for $1 per unit. The per unit profit obtained by stocking and selling the item is the marginal profit (MP), which is the retail price ($10) minus the wholesale cost ($4), or $6. The marginal loss ($ML$) is the per unit wholesale cost ($4) minus the reduced per unit price that the product can be sold for in the secondary market ($1), or $3. The calculation of p is $[3 / (6 + 3)]$ 100, or 33 percent. Thus a retailer would have to be at least 33 percent certain that he can sell the additional unit of stock before it will be profitable to purchase that additional unit. His previous sales records could be checked to determine at what stock quantity he is 33 percent sure of selling that additional unit.

For example, suppose the previous sales records follow the pattern in Table 12–1. The retailer would stock 16 units in this situation because he has a 39 percent chance of selling at least 16 units. It will not pay to stock the 17th unit because the percent chance of selling 17 or more units is 23 percent, which is less than the calculated 33 percent.

It is important to note that the retailer expects to sell about 15 units (the average weekly sale) but is stocking 16 units. He can justify stocking

Table 12–1 Illustration of the Marginal Analysis Approach to Determine Optimal Retail Inventory

LEVEL OF PAST WEEKLY SALES IN UNITS	NUMBER OF WEEKS WHEN SALES LEVEL OCCURRED*	PERCENT CHANCE OF SALES LEVEL OCCURRING†	CUMULATIVE PERCENT CHANCE THAT SALES WILL BE AT THIS LEVEL OR GREATER
10 or less	0	0	100
11	6	3	100
12	18	9	97
13	26	13	88
14	34	17	75
15	38	19	58
16	32	16	39
17	26	13	23
18	14	7	10
19	6	3	3
20 or more	0	0	0
Total	200	100	

Average weekly sales = 14.93
Median weekly sales = 15

* Weekly sales level may have to be analyzed as "adjusted weekly sales level," where a seasonality adjustment is used to increase the forecast accuracy for products whose demand fluctuates on a seasonal basis.

† Percent chance of sales level occurring is obtained by dividing total sales (200) into the frequency (6 for the 11-unit level) and multiplying the result by 100.

more units than he expects to sell because the per unit marginal profit ($6) exceeds the per unit marginal loss ($3). The retailer can afford to take more risk whenever marginal profit is greater than marginal loss. This is the case for items which carry a high markup on cost. The reverse also holds: if marginal profit is less than marginal loss, the retailer will want to stock less than he expects to sell if consumers do not become so dissatisfied with the outlet that they discontinue shopping in his store. If the marginal profit and marginal loss are equal, the retail outlet would stock exactly what it expects to sell (the average sales) because the calculated p value is equal to 50 percent.

This marginal analysis approach can be incorporated into computer programs which can rapidly indicate the proper inventory level for any item, *provided* its average sales and the variation in average sales are known.[2] This marginal approach is limited by the assumption that a customer will not become dissatisfied enough to refuse to trade with the retailer after that consumer finds an out-of-stock condition on a product he had intended to buy. This assumption is not too unrealistic in situations where close substitute items are available from the same store or where high buyer loyalty to the store has been developed.

DETERMINING INVENTORY LEVELS ON STAPLE ITEMS   Large retail outlets will reorder thousands of staple items regularly, so it is essential to develop a systematic method of reordering merchandise. Several kinds of data are needed to determine the appropriate stock level on staple items whose demand is not subject to wide fluctuations in preferences. The data needed are:

1. The level of sales expected before the next order can be received
2. The delivery period, which is the amount of time estimated to elapse between the time an order is placed and the time the merchandise is delivered and prepared for sale by the retailer
3. The reserve or safety stock needed to take care of deviations from expected sales
4. The level of stock currently on hand
5. The amount of merchandise currently on order but not yet received
6. The store's policy with regard to inventory review and reorder periods (where "review period" refers to the frequency with which inventories are checked to determine stock levels and "reorder period" is the time interval that normally elapses between orders).

Retailers need to order enough stock to meet the expected purchases during the combined delivery and reorder periods, *plus* an additional "safety stock" which is carried to prevent an out-of-stock condition if actual sales should exceed expected sales. The safety stock level may be determined by observing the sales fluctuations that have occurred in the past. A pre-specified level of confidence can be used to correspond to the desired inventory condition. If a merchant desires to create an image of not being out of stock on staple items, he can set a goal for a safety stock that is intended to accomplish this result nearly all (say 97 percent) of the time.

If sales of a staple item were distributed as indicated in Table 12–1, this would mean that a safety stock of 4 units (19 minus 15, which is the average) would be needed. If 90 percent protection is considered adequate, the safety stock would be 3 (18 minus average sales of 15 units), assuming immediate delivery can be obtained.

The order level on a *staple item* (following the sales distribution given in Table 12–1) for a firm which every two weeks reorders an item that requires three weeks for delivery and preparation for retail sale could be determined by a similar analysis of the distribution of sales over a *five-week* period of time—three weeks for the normal delivery period and two weeks for the reorder period. The usual minimum stock level would be the number of weeks (three) required for delivery and preparation times the average weekly sales, plus the desired safety stock. This is the point at which another order should be placed to prevent an out-of-stock condition before the newly ordered merchandise arrives.

Frequently, past sales information is not available on an item. Guidelines can be used to reveal the safety stock needed for these items and for items whose past sales have changed enough to make analysis of past sales records unreliable. Table 12–2 contains safety stock formulas which provide varying degrees of protection from running out of stock if average sales levels can be forecast with reasonable accuracy. The data in Table 12–2 indicate a general stocking rule that the level of safety stock needed is usually lower

Table 12–2 *Safety Stock Levels Needed to Obtain Varying Degrees of Protection against Running Out of Stock*

APPROXIMATE SAFETY STOCK LEVEL NEEDED TO OBTAIN STATED DEGREE OF PROTECTION AGAINST RUNNING OUT OF STOCK IF EXPECTED DELIVERY AND REORDER PERIOD SALES ARE:		RETAIL STOCK POLICY: APPROXIMATE % CHANCE OF NOT RUNNING OUT OF STOCK	SAFETY STOCK LEVEL NEEDED TO OBTAIN STATED DEGREE OF PROTECTION AGAINST RUNNING OUT OF STOCK
$\dfrac{25}{12}$	$\dfrac{400}{46}$	99	$2.3\sqrt{\text{Forecast Sales Level for Delivery and Reorder Periods}}$
8	32	95	$1.6\sqrt{\text{Forecast Sales Level for Delivery and Reorder Periods}}$
5	20	80	$\sqrt{\text{Forecast Sales Level for Delivery and Reorder Periods}}$

* This table is applicable to situations where average sales can be forecast with reasonable accuracy. In such cases, the Poisson probability distribution appears to appropriately describe variations in retail sales. See John W. Wingate, Elmer O. Schaller, and F. L. Miller, *Retail Merchandise Management* (Englewood Cliffs, N.J.: Prentice-Hall, 1972), pp. 342–343.

relative to sales on fast-moving merchandise than is the required safety stock on slow-moving items.

For example, the safety stock level of 12, when expected sales are 25, represents a safety stock of nearly 50 percent of expected sales to reach the 99 percent level of protection from running out of stock. When expected sales are 400, the safety stock required to provide 99 percent protection is 46 units, which is only 11.5 percent of the 400 units forecast to be sold.

DETERMINING INVENTORY LEVELS ON FASHION ITEMS   Fashion items such as apparel and home furnishings present the most complex and critical inventory problems because they are usually offered in many different styles, colors, sizes, materials, etc. The major characteristics of fashion goods are:

1. A short product life span
2. Relatively unpredictable sales level
3. Broad assortments, needed to create favorable store image
4. Extreme amount of consumer importance upon style and color
5. Consumer purchases made on impulse basis or only subjective evaluation of the item and its close substitutes.

Additional safety stock must be carried on fashion items, not only because of their wide fluctuations in sales but also because of a need to provide a broader merchandise assortment for fashion customers. The formulas in Table 12–2 can be used to determine the safety stock needed for fashion goods, but another reserve amount, called the "basic assortment reserve," must also be carried.[3] The amount of the basic assortment reserve is based upon the buyer's judgment of the level needed to provide the basic merchandise assortment demanded by consumers. Thus the total reserve stock of fashion goods will be larger than the safety stock level required of staple items.

There is some degree of predictability that can be used to estimate sales of fashion items. Because each retail outlet caters to a certain target market, the average-price merchandise sold within a merchandise line is not likely to change drastically over a short period of time. Thus an apparel merchandiser's total sales on all different price lines can be predicted with considerable accuracy. The distribution of sales by size is also fairly constant from year to year, as the distribution of human body sizes and shapes does not change suddenly for the population as a whole.

Seasonal patterns also exist in fashion merchandise, so monthly sales indexes can be used to forecast the sales distribution by color and type of material used. For example, black and white–colored clothing sells better during the summer months, pastel and light-background prints sell better in the spring, and green and rust are preferred in the fall.[4]

Step 3:   *Planning Retail Reductions*

Retail reductions can occur because of (1) markdowns and (2) stock shortages. Markdowns are price reductions that are used to stimulate sales of overstocked items and discounts that are given to employees or other specific customer groups, such as cash customers. Stock shortages are caused by pilferage, shoplifting, damaged merchandise, and the like.

Both markdowns and shortages are inevitable in retail outlets despite the efforts made to prevent them. Thus these items must be included in the merchandise budget. Markdowns reduce the *value* of retail inventory because the retail price is lowered on the same number of *physical* units. Shortages reduce both the value of the retail inventory and the number of physical units as well, because some portion of the physical stock is no longer available for sale.

Every effort should be made to minimize the value lost by markdowns and shortages. The discussions of markdowns in Chapter 8 indicate that good sales forecasting will reduce the volume of marked down items. (The effect that good management and control practices can have on reducing shortages is discussed in Chapter 13.) However, markdowns and shortages will occur in spite of even the most rigorous control methods. Therefore retailers should use their past experience, or that of similar stores, to provide an estimate of the value of the inventory loss. The reductions are usually estimated on a percentage-of-sales-dollar volume basis and entered as part of the store's merchandising budget.

Step 4:   Planning Purchases

The quantity to purchase is easily obtained if (1) sales have been forecast, (2) desirable inventory levels have been determined, and (3) retail reductions have been planned. If these data are available, the following formula can be applied to an entire store, department, or merchandise line:

Planned purchase quantity = desired inventory at end of period
+ estimated sales + estimated reductions
− inventory available at beginning of period.

The dollar amount of allowable purchases that the buyer can make during the remaining portion of the period under a merchandise budget system that establishes maximum inventory levels and planned purchasing figures is called the "open-to-buy amount." Thus the open-to-buy device assists the buyer in determining how much merchandise he is able to buy during the remainder of any merchandising period and still remain within the guidelines established in the merchandise budget.

Open-to-buy amounts are usually stated in retail-price dollars. The open-to-buy concept can be illustrated by an example of a buyer who is making purchases for the month of September. Suppose that the merchandise budget calls for a planned inventory of $20,000 on September 30, estimated September sales are $40,000, the beginning inventory on September 1 was $22,000, the planned markdowns and shortages are estimated at 10 percent of retail sales dollar volume, or $4,000, and the planned initial markup on cost is 30 percent. Also assume that during the first ten days of September net sales amount to $18,000, markdowns or shortages amount to $2,000, $12,000 worth of retail goods (valued at retail prices) are delivered, and goods already ordered during September are valued at $12,000. The open-to-buy amount may be calculated as illustrated in Table 12–3, which indicates that the buyer can still purchase goods costing $12,600 at wholesale prices during the remainder of September and remain within the merchandise budget.

The open-to-buy figure should not be a set quantity that cannot be exceeded. Consumer needs are the dominant consideration. If sales of a product line, department, or store exceed the forecast, additional quantities should be ordered above those scheduled for purchase according to the merchandise budget. Thus a buyer must have permission of the management to make occasional additional purchases of fast-moving goods whose demand has been underestimated. However, additional purchases of the same goods should not have to be made on a frequent basis. If this is the case, either the forecasting procedure is too conservative or the buyer is "overbuying" other goods that are not selling as well. Retail management should determine the causes of frequently overbought conditions and then take steps to prevent their recurrence.

*Table 12–3 Illustration of Open-to-Buy Amount**

INVENTORY REQUIREMENTS		AVAILABLE INVENTORY	
(a) Desired inventory level, September 30	$20,000	(e) Actual inventory, September 1	$22,000
(b) Estimated sales for remainder of September ($40,000–$18,000)	22,000	(f) Value of goods received during September 1–10	12,000
(c) Planned markdowns and shortages for remainder of September ($4,000–$2,000)	2,000	(g) Total inventory handled (e + f)	34,000
		Less deductions such as	
		(h) Markdowns and shortages during September 1–10	2,000
(d) Total Inventory Requirement (a + b + c)	$44,000	(i) Sales during September 1–10	18,000
		(j) Total Deductions (h + i)	20,000
		Plus	
		(k) Value of inventory already ordered for September delivery	12,000
		Equals	
		(l) Total Available Inventory (g + k − j)	$26,000

Total Inventory Requirement (item d or $44,000) minus Total Available Inventory (item l or $26,000) equals Open-to-Buy ($18,000) at Retail Prices.
Open-to-Buy at Cost equals Open-to-Buy at Retail times [(100 − markup percent)/100] or $18,000 [(100 − 30)/100] equals $12,600.

* All inventory, reductions, and sales are valued at *retail* prices.

Step 5:   Planning Profit Margins

It was indicated in Chapter 8 that the initial markup percentage should be adequate to cover expenses, reductions, and profits.[5] The initial markup percentage is usually planned on *all* the merchandise carried because detailed data on expenses and reductions are not available for each item.

The necessary markup percentage may be calculated by first forecasting the total sales for the store for the desired time period. Then expenses and price reductions needed to reach the sales goal can be estimated. And then a realistic profit goal can be established. These three components—expenses, reductions, and profits—are then added together and that sum is divided by the sum of sales plus reductions to give the required initial markup percentage needed to achieve the desired profit goals.

The calculation for initial markup percentage is:

$$\text{Required markup percent} = \frac{(\text{Expenses} + \text{profits} + \text{reductions})}{(\text{sales} + \text{reductions})}.$$

For example, suppose planned sales are $500,000 annually, with estimated operating expenses of $100,000, reductions of $70,000, and a profit goal of $50,000. The initial markup percentage would be:

$$\text{Required markup percent} = \frac{(\$100,000 + \$50,000 + \$70,000)}{(\$500,000 + \$70,000)},$$

or 38.6 percent.

This same equation can also be used when expenses, reductions, and profits are planned in percentage terms instead of dollars. Sales simply become 100 percent in the equation in this case. The remaining figures are expressed as percentages converted to decimals. In the previous example, expenses were estimated to 20 percent of sales, the profit goal was 10 percent of sales, and reductions were estimated to amount to 14 percent of sales. Thus the required initial markup percentage would be:

$$\frac{(0.20 + 0.10 + 0.14)}{(1.00 + 0.14)} = 38.6 \text{ percent.}$$

This equation can be used to determine what percentage markup a retailer must obtain on *all* his purchases if he is to cover all expected expenses, reductions, and markdowns and still make the desired planned profit. It should be reemphasized that this calculation yields the "overall" or "average" markup on all merchandise. The markup used on each item or in each department will deviate from this average markup depending upon consumer demand, competition, etc. However, the formula is a useful guide that shows the average markup needed to generate the desired profit level.

Gross margin is also sometimes calculated in the markup planning process. A calculation formula for gross margin is:

$$\text{Gross margin percent} = [\text{initial markup} \times (100 + \text{reductions})]$$
$$- \text{ reductions.}$$

Thus the calculated gross margin percent in the previous example is:

$$\text{Gross margin percent} = 0.386 \times (100 + 14) - 14$$
$$= 0.386 \times 114 - 14$$
$$= 44 - 14 = 30 \text{ percent.}$$

The percentage expenses (20 percent) may be subtracted from the gross margin percent (30 percent) to obtain the net profit percentage (10 percent). The retail buyer should strive to attain the planned markup goals. Expense percentages have been rising during recent years, and unless sales can be substantially increased by using lower prices, a higher initial markup is required to achieve the target net profit. Thus the basic merchandise budgeting problem consists of accurately forecasting a realistic initial markup percentage that will yield the desired net profit margin.

MERCHANDISE PLANNING AND CONTROL SYSTEMS

Merchandise planning and control techniques are related to both overall merchandise values (dollars) and to measurable quantities of goods or services (units). Unit controls are needed because the retail firm's buyer and the retail customer make their purchases in units. Dollar controls are needed because overall store sales, expenses, and financial reports require the use of dollars, as well as the quantity of physical units. Dollar control is the usual basis for establishing initial merchandise control systems.

However, the retail buyer must look beyond dollar figures to determine which sizes, colors, styles, and price lines are selling. This information is contained (both in dollar and unit terms) in the store's daily sales slips or records. In small stores, the sales data are likely to be recorded on sales slips or booklets. In large stores, cash registers are frequently linked to electronic computer systems which provide detailed information on inventories and sales for each item.

Sales and inventory information also is usually summarized and analyzed by classifying and categorizing the entire merchandise assortment into different subassortments, such as departments, merchandise lines, etc. Classification is needed in merchandise planning and control because it is easier to analyze smaller and similar types of products and services than the entire merchandise offering and then make inferences for the different merchandise lines. The split-total cash register, hooked up to a computer, is an efficient method of recording and analyzing data on large numbers of product categories. The categories may be defined by differences in color, price line, size, style, product content, etc., provided the appropriate key is pushed on the cash register. A more detailed discussion of the use of such systems will be presented in Chapter 15.

The main point for the current discussion is that stores using such systems obtain their classification totals at the end of the day as a by-product of their normal sales-registering procedure. These totals can easily be posted manually to merchandise control records from the cash register tape, or the computer can automatically print out the desired control records.

Dollar Planning and Control

Retail buyers plan and control dollar inventory values because they need to keep the stocks of each department or merchandise category in line with its sales. Proper dollar planning and control procedures allow the buyer to minimize both stock shortages and the markdown pricing that is required if the inventory is too large relative to sales. The dollar control process also allows the buyer to easily identify those merchandise items or lines that have the largest inventory investment and those that have the highest dollar sales.

Dollar control is initially concerned with determining the value of the firm's inventory at any point in time. Without the inventory valuation data, the buyer cannot plan or control any portion of the merchandise management process. Purchases, cost of goods sold, gross margins, and profit margins cannot be planned or determined until inventories are valued in dollar terms.

A periodic physical inventory count must be taken at least once a year to satisfy legal requirements. The counting of the actual physical inventory is a time-consuming process, so retailers use a technique called "perpetual inventory" to estimate inventory levels. The perpetual inventory results from recording the beginning inventory (counted at the start of the period), all purchases, and all sales in retail prices. The following formula is then used to estimate the retail value of the current inventory: Retail value of current inventory = retail value of beginning inventory + retail value of purchases made during the period — retail value of sales made during the period. The perpetual inventory method provides current, useful information, particularly if it involves the use of a computer-reported inventory system.

Reductions in inventory values resulting from pilferage, damaged merchandise, other forms of dishonesty, and price reductions do not appear on the perpetual inventory. Thus, despite the time required, retailers may decide to take a physical count more than once a year. Retailers of large items, such as automobiles, can afford to take physical counts quite frequently, compared to retailers of many small items, such as grocery stores that handle over 10,000 items at one time. Taking a physical inventory permits the buyer to determine the *overage* and *shortage* magnitudes by which the perpetual inventory deviates from the physical inventory.

Overage is the dollar amount by which the perpetual inventory exceeds the physical inventory value. Such a discrepancy is usually caused by clerical error, such as overcharging customers on sale merchandise or marking merchandise higher than it is supposed to be marked. Shortage is the dollar magnitude by which the physical inventory exceeds the perpetual inventory value. Such shortages can originate from both clerical error and retail reductions caused by markdowns and shrinkage.

The National Retail Merchants' Association has established electronic processing centers in New York and California to provide its member stores with a variety of reports for standard classification numbers.[6] Stores send in their sales, purchase, inventory, and markdown data and receive dollar and unit information on merchandise sold, received, and held in inventory, as well as stock to sales ratios and gross margin percentages for each category. A report similar to that in Figure 12–2 is sent to the participating stores on a monthly basis. The opening inventory figures in each category are reported semiannually or annually by the stores as they take a new physical inventory. The inventory for the intervening months represents estimated inventories calculated by the computer. A report such as the one in Figure 12–2 can indicate merchandise categories in which inventories appear to be out of balance relative to sales. If the present percent inventory distribution is much higher for a category than its percent of sales distribution, the merchandise described in this category may be overstocked.

On the other hand, if the percent of sales distribution for a product category greatly exceeds its present percent of inventory distribution, the category would probably be understocked; so inventories could be built up in this product line. Of course the gross margin and profitability ratios would also have to be considered to ensure that the retail outlet was not over-stocking a low-margin category.

A comparison of the perpetual and physical methods of obtaining merchandise data by merchandise classification indicates that when a computer is available, the perpetual inventory method can function accurately, and at a lower cost, to provide a more current source of data than the physical method. When the computer equipment is not available, the periodic physical inventory method can be used profitably in merchandise planning.

Unit Planning and Control

Unit merchandise control is used to maintain ideal merchandise assortments by recording and reporting quantities in inventory on order and the rate of sale of *individual* items. Unit control procedures are needed if the buyer is going to be able to (1) identify the items that are selling best, (2) invest properly in inventories, and (3) use good buying procedures, based upon the knowledge of what is needed and what has been selling well. Merchandise controls are valuable aids to the decision-making process the buyer must use in developing his purchasing strategy. Therefore unit control procedures should be designed to assist the buyer in his purchasing function.

Unit control involves the same general procedures as dollar control:

1. Implement some form of classification system.
2. Use either a perpetual or physical inventory system to provide unit inventory, order, and sales data.
3. Establish the ideal merchandise assortment to be carried and the unit levels of inventory needed to be stocked on each item.

Figure 12–2 Retail Inventory Management Report

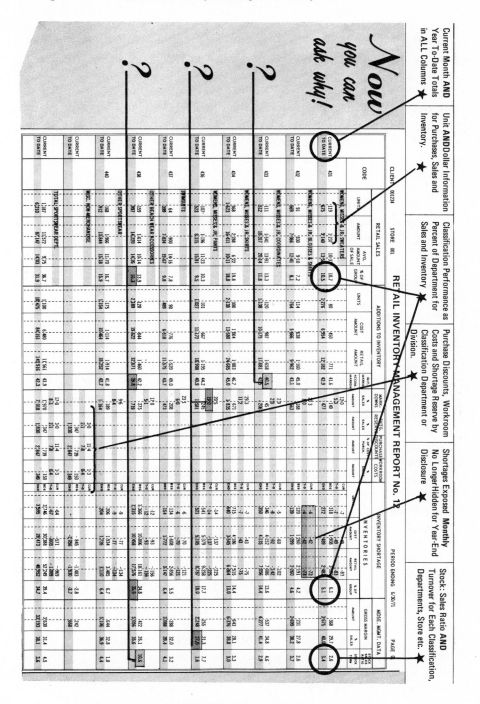

Item inventory requirements are established only after considering such factors as the item's rate of sale, the amount of time required to receive the item after it has been ordered, the markup obtained on the item, the effect an out-of-stock condition has on the retail customers, etc. Naturally, high inventory levels must be maintained on the faster-moving items if supplies are to satisfy consumer demand. Inventory levels will also be higher for items which require longer delivery periods because a store manager doesn't want to be out of stock on an item for a long period of time. Higher inventory levels should also be established for high-markup items because "lost" sales, caused by an out-of-stock condition on such items, decrease net profit considerably more than the same volume of lost sales on a low-margin item. A larger inventory level may be carried on unique items that the store stocks. If no close substitute products are sold by the store, other things being equal, management could justify a larger inventory on that item than on an item which is quite similar to several other items that are sold in the store.

Unit control systems are designed to minimize lost sales and consumer dissatisfaction caused by out-of-stock conditions and, at the same time, identify items or merchandise lines which are overstocked in relation to their consumer demand. In addition to periodic physical inventory counts and perpetual inventory methods, retail managers are also using unit control devices such as checklist systems, warehouse control systems, and requisition stock control.[7]

Cash register systems, hooked to electronic computers, are used to implement unit control procedures as well as cash control techniques. As the use of these types of systems spreads, the cost of implementing and using item control procedures will decrease. As a result, store managers will probably use even more unit control techniques as the basis for sounder merchandise management planning.

For example, COSMOS, a computer program, is used by a number of food chains to compute direct product profitability and projected rate of movement for *individual* items. The COSMOS program also calculates optimum selling space assignments, based on assigned-category space constraints and logistical considerations.[8] Chains that use COSMOS report that a significant profit improvement has been obtained by using the program. This may be attributable to (1) a reduction in out-of-stock conditions, (2) use of released "surplus" space for product line additions, or (3) increased sales obtained from products given more shelf space.

Another technique that can be used to implement unit control procedures involves perforated price tickets. Under this system, the sales person tears off part of the ticket when the item is sold and deposits the torn-off section in a container. At the end of the day these torn-off portions are sorted and totaled by classification on either a manual basis or by the use of a tag reader system that reads the tickets automatically, tabulates the data, and prepares a printed daily, weekly, and monthly summary report.

The more mechanical assistance provided by the system, the higher the initial cost of establishing the system. This higher installation cost must result in reduced manual operating costs or improved accuracy if the more mechanical systems are going to be a profitable investment. Large retail chains can usually spread the setup costs of a sophisticated electronic system over enough stores and/or sales volume to justify the installation. Smaller, independent outlets may be able to lease computer time, equipment, etc. to reduce the cost and still justify the use of electronic systems.

STOCK TURNOVER CONSIDERATIONS

Successful merchandise management involves the maintenance of adequate profit markups, combined with an acceptable level of merchandise turnover (the number of times during the year that the average amount of inventory is sold). The rate of stock turnover may be calculated for any period of time, but it is usually computed on an annual basis. Good buying practices are reflected by high turnover rates, which indicate that the consumers are buying the merchandise purchased by the retail buyer. Relatively low stock turnover rates indicate that consumers' preferences do not correspond with the purchases made by the store buyer, or that other elements of the retail marketing program are failing. A high stock turnover rate has other advantages, such as reducing the use of price markdowns to move stale or shopworn merchandise. Also, the return on investment capital is likely to rise in high turnover stores because fixed costs are spread over a higher sales volume.

Measuring Stock Turnover

There are three commonly used ways for calculating stock turnover:

1. On the basis of dollars in retail prices
2. On the basis of dollars valued at cost to the retailer
3. On the basis of units.

These calculation methods can be illustrated by the example of a grocer who begins the year with 30 cases of brand X canned peaches, which he sells for $10 per case and buys for $8 per case. If we assume no stolen or damaged merchandise and that no price reductions were necessary, his net sales of brand X peaches for the year consist of 560 cases, or $5,600. The grocer paid $4,800 for the 600 cases he purchased during the year. At the end of the year the grocer had 70 cases on hand, but the per case wholesale cost had just been increased to $9; so the grocer raised his retail price to $11 per case. The annual stock turnover rate, calculated by the three different techniques, is:

1. On the basis of dollars valued at retail prices:

    Opening inventory $ value at retail (30 cases @ $10) = $ 300
    Closing inventory $ value at retail (70 cases @ $11) = $ 770
    Average inventory $ value at retail (300 + 770)/2 = $ 535
    Net sales in retail dollars   = $5,600

Annual stock turnover rate

$$= \frac{\text{Net sales in retail dollars}}{\text{Average inventory at retail}} = \frac{\$5,600}{\$535} = 10.47.$$

2. On the basis of dollars valued at cost:

Opening inventory $ value at cost $30 cases @ $8) = $ 240
Closing inventory $ value at cost (70 cases @ $9) = $ 630
Average inventory $ value at cost ($240 + $630)/2 = $ 435
Cost of goods sold   = $4,800

Annual stock turnover rate

$$= \frac{\text{Cost of goods sold}}{\text{Average inventory at cost}} = \frac{\$4,800}{\$435} = 11.03.$$

3. On the basis of units:

Opening inventory in units   =   30
Closing inventory in units   =   70
Average inventory in units = (30 + 70)/2 =   50
Annual net unit sales   = 560

$$\text{Annual stock turnover rate} = \frac{\text{Annual unit sales}}{\text{Average unit inventory}} = \frac{560}{50} = 11.20.$$

Capital turnover is a ratio that is used to measure the number of times the cost of the average inventory investment is converted into sales.[9] Its value is calculated as follows:

$$\text{Capital turnover} = \frac{\text{Dollar sales at retail prices during a specified period}}{\text{Average inventory dollar value at cost}}.$$

Analysis of previous turnover ratios generated by a firm and comparison of these ratios with those of similar retail outlets provide a good basis for planning the inventory needed to meet consumer needs and still reduce inventory to a sufficiently low level that will generate a good profit. The *stock* turnover ratios should be interpreted with considerable caution: management should be certain that both the sales and the average stock figures used in the stock turnover ratio calculation cover the same operating period and that both are quoted in the same dollar terms—either in retail price or cost of merchandise.

Another factor that can lead to incorrect analysis is the use of an atypical inventory level as the average inventory level in the calculation procedure. The average inventory must reflect the average inventory level *for the period of time* covered by the calculation. For example, seasonal items or merchandise lines that sell well only during the summer months will show an abnormally high stock turnover ratio in an annual analysis that uses only the beginning-of-year and ending-of-year inventory levels to calculate average inventory level. This illustrates the necessity of conducting more frequent (monthly or quarterly) stock turnover analyses to obtain a more accurate performance measure.

The ratios of sales at retail prices to average inventory levels valued at cost, presented in Table 12–4, indicate that turnover varies according to the type of retail line offered. Several factors are usually responsible for fluctuations in turnover ratios. Frequent consumer purchases result in higher stock turnover rates, as reflected by the high turnover rate obtained in grocery stores versus the low rate experienced by farm equipment dealers and jewelry stores.

Stores that sell the same types of merchandise may experience lower stock turnover rates because the store is located in a small town or community where trade is limited. Such stores may have to maintain a fairly high level of inventory merely to provide an adequate merchandise assortment. In these cases, store management might not be able to increase sales enough

Table 12–4   Median Net Sales to Inventory Ratios for Selected Retail Outlets, 1970

RETAIL LINE	NET SALES TO INVENTORY RATIO*
Children and infants' wear stores	4.9
Clothing and furnishings, men's and boys'	4.0
Department stores	5.6
Discount stores	5.3
Discount stores, leased departments	4.9
Family clothing stores	4.5
Farm equipment dealers	2.9
Farm and garden supply stores	9.1
Furniture stores	4.6
Gasoline service stations	9.9
Grocery stores	16.8
Hardware stores	3.9
Household appliance stores	5.6
Jewelry stores	2.9
Lumber and other building materials dealers	5.4
Motor vehicle dealers	7.6
Paint, glass and wallpaper stores	6.3
Shoe stores	3.9
Tire, battery and accessory stores	6.1
Variety stores	4.5
Women's ready-to-wear stores	6.7

Source   *1970 Key Busniess Ratios* (New York: Dun and Bradstreet, 1971), p. 2.
    * "Net sales to inventory ratios are obtained by dividing annual net sales by merchandise inventory as carried on the balance sheet. This quotient does not yield an actual physical turnover. It provides a yardstick for comparing stock-to-sales ratios of one concern with another or with those for the industry" (*1970 Key Business Ratios*, p. 3).

to raise the stock turnover ratio significantly. On the other hand, stores in high customer traffic areas will probably show high stock turnover rates because the required inventory level needed to meet consumer needs is not likely to increase in proportion to the increase in sales volume.

Stock turnover rates can be increased by changes in merchandise policies, such as eliminating slow-selling items, handling fewer sizes, colors and styles, devoting more shelf space to fast-selling items, and maintaining only minimal inventory on slow-selling brands. Of course, stock turnover can also be accelerated by reducing the retail price charged customers or by using more advertising and price reduction promotions. However, turnover rates must increase considerably as a result of a price reduction or a promotion campaign if profit margins are to be maintained.

Manufacturers and wholesalers can also assist the retailer in achieving higher stock turnover ratios by reducing the delivery period needed to reach the retail outlet. Use of new production and/or distribution techniques that will allow more flexibility in producing merchandise required to meet the specific and immediate needs of an individual retailer with regard to sizes, colors, and styles can allow that retailer to reduce his stock level and still meet consumer demands for a wide selection of merchandise. The use of the laser beam to cut material at a very rapid rate is an example of a process that can benefit the retailer. Through the use of computers, conveyor belts, etc., material can be custom cut to meet the specifications of an individual clothing merchant. The considerable decrease in time required to deliver the items to the retailer allows both the manufacturer and the retailer to sell more merchandise by reducing out-of-stock conditions on items that "catch on" in the fashion world. Without this system, a large volume of the same item has to be ordered before the manufacturer can justify a rerun on the same fabric, color, style, size, etc.

Some manufacturers have also built shelf or free-standing displays which make better use of floor space and provide a clear view of the merchandise, arranged in an orderly manner. Other manufacturers provide merchandise guidelines that assist the retailer by setting up ideal stock levels in the pertinent category; they may also take inventory and offer to replace slow-selling items with fast-selling items. Small retailers may find such advice to be very worthwhile, providing the manufacturer and/or wholesaler does not try to overemphasize the importance of his products relative to those of other manufacturers or wholesalers.

SUMMARY

Merchandise management consists of the activities involved in balancing inventories to meet consumer needs. The merchandising department usually supervises these activities.

The merchandise budget is frequently utilized to plan and control sales efforts, markups, purchases, markdowns and shortages. It consists of:

1. A forecast of sales for given periods
2. A plan for the stocks to be carried at the beginning of each period
3. Planned markup/reductions to be made on merchandise
4. Planned stock shortages and returns
5. Planned purchase quantities
6. Planned gross margin, and
7. Anticipated stock turnover.

Merchandise planning and control techniques use both unit and dollar measures. Unit planning is needed because both the retail firm's buyer and the retail customer make their purchases in units. Dollar planning is required by the firm's accountants and financial planners, who work with overall sales dollars, expense dollars, and ratios between sales and expense dollars.

Electronic data processing equipment allows retailers to use more current retail inventory management reports (such as the report prepared by retail electronic systems) and direct product profitability calculations (exemplified by COSMOS) to increase profits.

QUESTIONS

1. December sales average $30,000 for product A, and the five-year annual sales average for A is $450,000. If next year's sales are estimated to be $500,000, what level of sales would you expect for product A in December of next year?
2. Briefly discuss the various methods of planning inventory levels and the shortcomings of each.
3. A college bookstore buys a certain book for $8 and sells it for $10. Assume it has a secondary market for unsold new books and can sell any number of them for $6 each. Using Table 12–1 as an expected demand schedule, how many of these books should the store stock? What gross profits can the store expect from the sale of this particular book?
4. What average markup must a retailer use to achieve a profit of 20 percent of gross sales if his sales are estimated to be $450,000, operating expenses are $120,000, and reductions amount to $80,000?
5. Find the gross margin percent for the retailer in problem 4.
6. Why are merchandise control systems usually established on a "dollar basis"? What else should be considered?
7. Why is the perpetual inventory method generally superior to the physical method?
8. Discuss the various functions of unit control, how each is used, and what type of retailer would use each.
9. What precautions should be taken in analyzing stock turnover ratios? What factors can be responsible for fluctuations in inventory ratios?
10. How can stock turnover rates be increased? Is it always desirable to increase these rates?

FOOTNOTES

[1] Richard I. Levin and C. A. Kirkpatrick, *Quantitative Approaches to Management* (New York: McGraw-Hill, 1965), pp. 96–111.

[2] Ibid., pp. 106–111.

[3] Ibid., p. 366.

[4] Ibid., p. 359.

[5] Reductions include price markdowns, discounts to employees, and stock shortages.

[6] Retail Electronic Systems, 100 Park Avenue, Staten Island, N.Y.   10302.

[7] J. L. Heskett, Robert M. Ivie, and Nicholas A. Glaskowsky, *Business Logistics: Management of Physical Supply and Distribution* (New York: Ronald Press, 1964), chap. 11.

[8] Ronald C. Curhan, "Shelf Space Allocation and Profit Maximization in Mass Retailing," *Journal of Marketing*, 37 (July 1973): 54–60.

[9] Capital turnover, as used here, measures only turnover in capital invested in merchandise inventory, not total capital used by the retailer.

COLLEGE BOOK STORES*
Survival May Dictate
a New Action Course

Dear Professor:

"Your College Store is in financial trouble whether or not you realize it. Even the major Bookstores and the big Co-ops are operating at substantial losses or near the breakeven point with the trend of decreased gross margin and increasing expenses causing everyone real concern."

What has happened?

Basically, costs of operation have gone up faster than the additional margins created by increased prices.

Both the university itself and the College Store have been hit hard by the effects of the minimum wage law from which the schools were exempt until the late sixties. Even with substantially higher sales, the salary cost in the text department alone has gone from 5 to 7 percent.

Freight-in—the cost of freight from publishers—has risen sharply and now amounts to 2 percent of the cost of a book on which the margin is 20 percent. Truck rates continue to increase and the Postal Service book rate will rise in the near future to the extent that a store will have to use other methods for the transportation of books. This will mean slower service.

SOURCE   Reprinted by special permission from *The College Store Journal* (April–May 1972), copyright 1972 by the National Association of College Stores, Oberlin, Ohio. Russell L. Reynolds, the author, is general manager of the National Association of College Stores and executive editor of *The College Store Journal*.

In addition, we must remind you that it costs twice as much to return a book as it does to order it. Even though returns can be made automatically, the freight in cost is doubled. With many stores returning 25 percent of the books purchased, this cost really is consequential.

Shrinkage, including pilferage by our customers, is nearly 2 percent as contrasted with a half percent a few years ago. Many stores are reporting substantial dollar losses due to theft by students and shrinkage in general book areas is running slightly above 4 percent.

Formerly stores paid 55 percent off the list price for books purchased on the open market from wholesalers. This margin is now down to 50 percent, the same price as paid to students when they sell to the store the books which will be used again.

Paying this high figure to students for their books represents an attempt by the store to pay the highest possible prices to students.

Markdowns—the loss on books which could not be returned to the publishers—average around 2 percent of the gross sales of books.

Although the general policy is for a publisher to permit returns, the days of unlimited returns are over. Publishers not showing willingness to grant additional discount to the store to assist in preventing losses have reduced sharply their returns policies during the past year.

Books which cannot be returned to publishers must be sold on the used book market, generally at a loss of at least 50 percent of the original value. Store purchases of used books, either from students or from wholesalers, are not returnable and must be sold at loss—the total loss being about 2 percent of the total volume.

All other expenses of a store average 10.5 percent of sales. Rent alone accounts for 3 percent. The other expenses include administrative salaries, fringe benefits, advertising, taxes, telephone, pension, insurance, depreciation and bad debts.

Telephone and other communications are about 0.5 percent, and this represents the store's efforts to get the books to the students on time.

It does not appear that it is economically feasible to sell short discount texts—20 percent—without subsidy from the institution or increased discount from the publisher. The selling of more profitable merchandise less subject to pilferage is another solution.

Appleton/Century/Crofts recognized this problem last year when that firm went to 27 percent off with a penalty on returns. Harcourt Brace Jovanovich, Inc. went to 23 and Collier Macmillan went to 25 on new titles.

A few other publishers made some modest changes in classification of paperbacks, but so far no others have followed the pattern set by the firms we have cited. Repeating—many did alter their returns policies.

The publishers know the problem. A year ago, the National Association of College Stores held a day-long symposium for them describing the problem. This year the Relations with Publishers Committee visited with most of the principal publishers in New York and Chicago.

What is going to happen if the situation does not change?

One alternative is for the store to turn its back on books and attempt to sell products which have larger profit margins and are less prone to pilferage and markdowns.

For the past twenty years the National Association of College Stores has told its members that the only way to gain recognition and stature on campus was to become a real bookstore by serving the needs of the students and faculty.

It is ironic that survival may dictate that this course be altered completely with books taking the back seat.

The general book department itself does not offer any real assistance for eliminating a deficit since the net profits are not substantial. And please note again the 4.1 percent shrinkage figure.

The school could decide to subsidize the operation, but with economic conditions as they are today, this does not seem possible. Besides, the administrations of the schools more and more are becoming insistent that the store operate in the black.

Another alternative would be for the store to cut its operation to the barest essentials. The elimination of special orders and a penalty on returns of books by students would be necessary in such a program.

A few publishers suggested that this was the solution.

Some way, somehow, our College Stores are going to have to find a solution to the dilemma. Hopefully, publishers will do something.

DISCUSSION QUESTIONS

1. As a student customer of college bookstores, what is your reaction to them? Does your college bookstore appear to be as well run as the off-campus bookstores?
2. What steps do you believe college bookstores should take to correct their problems?
3. Do you believe there is a need for an on-campus college bookstore? What are the pros and cons of doing away with the college bookstore completely or working out a contract with a firm to manage it?

HART SHOES

"We have one of the best locations in D.C., a good clientele, and a store that is popular with the customers. Unfortunately, we're only doing about a third of the potential that is here due to our lack of adequate merchandise. Our biggest problem has been, and continues to be, our inability to purchase enough inventory due to our capital short position."

As the owner of Hart Shoe Store, Mr. Reginald Hart, spoke of his store's operation, he concentrated on this area as a problem that has continually faced him throughout his nine years as a retailer.

The Hart shoe store is located in downtown Washington, D.C. in a popular retail section only one to two blocks on either side from two of the oldest department stores in Washington: Hecht's and Woodrup and Lothrup. The location on F Street places his store within walking distance of the Capitol and the White House and less than a block from the National Portrait Galleries.

Although there are seven other shoe shops in the same area, plus two clothing stores that also sell shoes, Mr. Hart does not feel that this amount of competition is bad. In fact, he stated that this is a fallacy in thinking on the part of many small retailers. "Competition doesn't drive out business, it attracts new customers for everyone."

In emphasizing this point, Mr. Hart cited the case of a shoe retailer in D.C. who had opened six competitive shoe stores under different names in the same location as his old store and had shown an increase in business in all. Mr. Hart also cited his experience as a black retailer in a ghetto area of D.C. At that time he was the only shoe retailer in the area, but that made little difference as the area simply was not a shopping area and customers didn't go there.

The area on F Street is the best location that Mr. Hart has ever had as an independent retailer, and he was determined to make the store prove its potential.

With the heavy population of blacks in D.C., it was not surprising that approximately 90 percent of his customers would be black. Many of them are downtown office workers and do their shopping during lunch hours. Consequently the store does its best business between noon and 2 p.m.

The decor of the store was designed to give a relaxed atmosphere, with living room furniture for customers and display cabinets made from breakfronts and other dining room–type furnishings. The walls consist of a barn board–type material and are decorated with pictures, including two nude oils toward the rear of the store. With carpeting, air conditioning, and piped-in soul music, the entire decor was designed to be first class.

This decor is in contrast to that of a friend of Mr. Hart, also a black retailer of shoes in D.C., who according to Mr. Hart runs an entirely different operation but earns a higher net. His friend operates in considerably more Spartan surroundings, sells less expensive shoes, and does all the selling himself—as opposed to the three full-time sales people employed by Hart Shoe Store (in addition to Mr. Hart).

In the Hart store, shoes for men and women are carried, but not children's shoes. Styles in stock are geared to fashion, as opposed to concentrating on heavily advertised brand names. In Mr. Hart's opinion, the black consumer of today has changed considerably from the black of ten years ago. Ten years ago, Mr. Hart feels, the black consumer was extremely conscious of shoes, regardless of the quality of the rest of his wardrobe, and was highly brand conscious. Today, he believes, the consumer wants a good-looking total wardrobe, and while he still demands quality and style, he is no longer willing to spend disproportionately for shoes.

Looking further at the profile of his customers, Mr. Hart related that about 50 percent are in the 18 to 26 age bracket and are very style conscious. The remainder are between the ages of 26 and 42 and are considered to be his steady, bread-and-butter customers. The younger ones are "gravy" customers, but are not as steady as the older group. With this kind of age breakdown, plus the need to serve both men and women, the need for greater selections and thus inventory is intensified.

The problem, according to Mr. Hart, is that he cannot find adequate financing to buy the needed merchandise. He has gone to banks in search of a 30-, 60-, 90-, or 120-day note but has consistently been refused. Wholesalers and other vendors of merchandise have extended credit, and have been more than fair, according to Mr. Hart, but there is a limit to how far they can go.

Although his store was established with the aid of an SBA loan, this primarily covered capital expenditures and left little for inventory. Thus inventory is paid for out of earnings, preventing a rapid buildup of lines and styles. By contrast, he would prefer to have 50 percent of the inventory paid for in this manner and the rest financed in another manner.

In speaking about the problem of obtaining adequate merchandise, Mr. Hart stated that it is a typical and persistent problem facing the black retailer. However, he also stated that he knows several small white retailers with the same problem.

With adequate financing, he felt that his store could be expanded by utilizing the rear of the store, which is presently used for storage. A basement area could be remodeled and utilized for inventory storage to allow the entire first floor to be used for selling. This would add considerably to the present 2,500 square feet of selling space. Consideration has also been given to remodeling the second floor into rental office space, but this would require at least $10,000.

There is also the very real possibility of urban renewal on his block within the next two years. The federal government has plans to remodel the storefronts and turn the block into a covered mall. Walkways would also be built to connect the second stories on either side of the street, but it would be the store owners' responsibility to do the interior work. Mr. Hart was uncertain how he would raise the capital to do the interior remodeling.

The owner of his building, and of most of the block, happened to be the Catholic church, which had acquired the property in the 1800s. A friend had told Mr. Hart that the church might be approached for the purpose of securing a commercial loan. Mr. Hart had also considered the possibility of a joint venture with a moneyed partner but had not yet located this individual. He had also been to a minority business aid organization and had received some valuable assistance, but not the working capital he felt was necessary.

The cash flow problem faced by Hart Shoe Store was intensified by the use of major credit cards and personal checks by established customers. In both cases there was a delay until the store received cash.

The accrual method of accounting required by the IRS also created problems since such a large percentage of his earnings had to go into merchandise—rather than into the bank as cash. Since the IRS would not accept shoes in payment of taxes, there was a yearly need to find cash to pay taxes.

In many ways the situation seemed to be a classic case of "the vicious circle" and the "chicken or the egg," all rolled into one. Somehow, an answer had to be found.

DISCUSSION QUESTIONS

1. What alternatives do you see for Mr. Hart in solving his problem? Which do you believe is preferable? Can it be confined to a single solution?
2. Explain the accrual method of accounting, as required by the IRS, and how it might affect the inventory level carried by a retailer. What effect (if any) might it have on a retailer's decision to hold a sale and to purchase new merchandise at particular times of the year?
3. Visit the commercial loan department of a local bank and ask for its policies on extending credit to purchase retail inventory. What suggestions does the banker give to correct a situation such as that faced by Mr. Hart?
4. Do you agree with Mr. Hart concerning his philosophy about competition in the area? Provide evidence to support your statement.
5. Since Mr. Hart's friend makes a higher net profit on sales, wouldn't it be a good idea for Mr. Hart to copy his style rather than persist in his present course?

CHAPTER 13

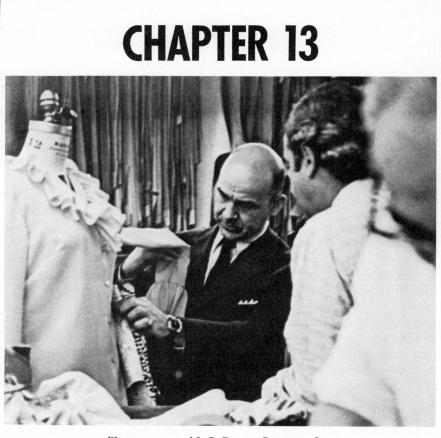

Photo courtesy of J. C. Penney Company, Inc.

Buying and Handling Merchandise

BUYING

The buying process consists of four phases: search, evaluation, selection, and review. *Search* activities involve determining what to buy and from whom it should be bought. Chapter 4 contained a discussion of procedures used to determine what to buy, and the remaining portion of the search process—determining how the desired merchandise can be obtained—will be presented in this chapter. The handling of merchandise will also be discussed.

    Evaluation involves the comparison of merchandise and vendor on the expected performance each is likely to yield in terms of quality and service. Naturally, the cost of the merchandise is also a prime consideration in the evaluation process, so alternatives are really evaluated on a benefit to cost basis.

    The *selection* phase consists of the actual purchase of the merchandise from the chosen vendor after all available alternatives have been evaluated.

Review, the final phase of the buying process, involves the buyer's reappraisal of the activities in the previous three buying phases. This reappraisal is designed to identify trouble areas in the buying process so that mistakes are not repeated. The review process may also yield suggestions that can reduce the amount of time the buyer spends on the more menial and routine tasks, thereby allowing the buyer to spend more time on the important buying considerations.

Determining the Reorder Period

One method of reducing the amount of work required to provide the merchandise continually needed to meet the ever-changing requirements of the consumer market is to establish a reorder period for all staple items that are bought from a single vendor. A reorder period is the time interval in which reorders are usually placed. The length of the reorder period usually depends upon the minimum quantity that a vendor is willing to ship and the length of time needed for the vendor to deliver the merchandise. Other things being equal, a short delivery period and a small minimum-order quantity will lengthen the reorder period because a buyer, when forced with a low-inventory rush order, can buy a small quantiy that will be delivered shortly and hence keep out-of-stock or low-stock conditions at a minimum even when sales levels are usually high.

The desired length of the reorder period also varies, due to the cost of carrying merchandise in inventory. Frequent deliveries of small quantities reduce the average stock level, which decreases the carrying costs on merchandise held in inventory. However, the increased cost and inconvenience associated with placing frequent orders and receiving and handling small-quantity shipments (instead of larger-quantity shipments) may overcome the reduction in inventory carrying costs. Combining orders for different items from the same vendor can reduce the order placement cost on small-volume purchases.

Similar items may be grouped together after the reorder period has been determined on each item. Fast-selling items, such as groceries, may be reordered weekly or even daily. Staple merchandise might be reordered on a four-week schedule, with the task of inventory counting and reordering spread over the four-week period on a rotating basis to balance the work load. Cash registers, when hooked to computer systems, can provide more current stock and sales data. Such systems also reduce the order placing cost and thereby make it economically possible to cut the reorder period. The computer system can also automatically prepare reorders and allow the buyer to *be* a buyer, not merely a reorder clerk.

Sufficient flexibility must be maintained, no matter what system is used, to allow the buyer to quickly identify items that are in a low or out-of-stock condition and to place rush orders to minimize out-of-stock occurrences.

Organizing for Buying

Every retailer, regardless of the size of the operation, must perform the buying functions efficiently if the firm is going to remain competitive in the marketplace. The merchandise or service provided must be of the appropriate *type*, *quality*, and *price* demanded by the consumers. In addition, the firm's offerings must be available in *quantities* that will parallel consumer needs at the *time* that customers want to shop for such goods or services. The offering must also be *placed* in the store in a way that customers can easily locate it. Both the manager of a small independent outlet and the merchandise division of a large retail organization usually perform the job of buying and maintaining merchandise that will satisfy these consumer demands.

The merchandise division of the *large independent store* does more than buy merchandise. Usually it is also responsible for selling, planning, and control activities. Buyers are generally appointed for each major merchandise line, so they buy, direct sales, plan, and control their activities in view of consumer demand and profit opportunities. Divisional merchandise managers supervise the activities of these buyers so that all departments reflect the image that top retail management is striving to achieve. This organizational plan allows the division merchandise managers to devote the majority of their time to activities that plan and control the merchandise assortment. The execution of these plans is left largely to the buyers.

Responsibility for buying and selling is usually separated in the *chain store organization*. Central buyers usually establish an approved buying list that contains new and regular items that the central buyers believe will enhance the chain's merchandise assortment. These same central buyers also make the decision of removing items from the approved buying list when they believe the items are no longer contributing to the overall merchandise assortment. The negotiation of terms is also handled by the central buyers. Individual store managers are then generally responsible for actually placing orders for specific quantities of each item and presenting the merchandise appropriately to stimulate sales.

The central organization in some chain systems may perform all of the buying and reorder activities. In this case, the store managers are responsible only for proper merchandise presentation, servicing consumers, and other selling-related activities. Merchandise planning is then performed by merchandise controllers, each of whom supervises one or more *central buyers*. These merchandise controllers plan stock assortment requirements for the entire chain after appropriate sales forecasts have been made. The central buyer(s) orders the specific items in the quantities required by the entire chain. The incoming merchandise is then allocated to the individual store units by *merchandise distributors*.

Branch store operations may follow a different approach in the buying process. A branch organization usually tailors its merchandise/service assortment to reflect differences in local market conditions. Chain organizations are more likely to provide a standardized merchandise/service assortment to all geographical areas. Variations in merchandise/service assortments are usually required to meet differences in consumer preferences for items such as better-quality jewelry, clothing, furniture, etc. that are fashionable, distinctive, and subject to regional peculiarities. Individual outlet managers in such branch operations are given the authority to deviate from the centrally devised purchasing plan because the demand for some merchandise differs from one area to another. The central buyers usually plan the initial merchandise assortment, establish the prices, select the new items that are added to the approved buying list, and decide which items are to be dropped from the list. Individual branch managers generally place the reorders in the quantities needed to meet the special requirements of that outlet.

A centralized buying committee is frequently used by both branch and chain store operations to allow regional representation in the buying process while maintaining the considerable buying power that is associated with volume purchases. A national buying committee may consist of approximately twenty persons, who are mostly the "better store" managers from various geographical locations. The centralized buying committee determines which products are "good" for the entire nation, and generally purchases the "bread and butter" items. The buying of specialty, fashion, or fad items may be done by the individual store managers, who are in a better position to know which specific items are likely to appeal to their customers. Allowing the individual store manager to buy specialty items which best reflect unique consumer differences can allow the store to set trends with its merchandise assortment. This kind of leadership can generate a progressive image that cannot be established with a buying organization that is not in tune with local consumer demand.

A disadvantage of the centralized buying committee is that an overestimated demand can quickly generate a massive overbought condition in some, if not all, geographical areas. Trading of inventory within the retail corporation is used to balance company inventory with consumer demand. The items that will not sell in one area or outlet frequently sell well in another (or even in a nearby outlet that serves a different type of customer).

Centralized buying of some type usually is used despite the disadvantages cited. The discounts given for large-volume purchases are generally large enough to make it economically attractive. In addition, individual central buyers may believe that they must justify their existence by buying all items. Such buyers may hesitate to relinquish any outright buying functions to the individual outlet managers for fear of losing "political" power in the retail organization.

No matter what organizational system is used, sufficient flexibility must be maintained to allow the buyer to quickly identify new items that are being requested by consumers. Individual outlet managers can inform their district sales manager of the consumer requests. The district sales manager can then check with other outlet managers to determine if it is a common demand.

The best ideas can then be passed on to the central buyer, who can check with other district sales managers to determine if the new item has appeal in other areas. If the item appears to have sufficient consumer demand, a manufacturer could be contacted to produce the item.

This "customer feedback" system can provide very useful new merchandise ideas for a retailer in fashion and other fast-changing merchandise lines. Use of the customer feedback system can result in a progressive or new merchandise image for retail outlets affiliated with such a retail organization. Smaller, independent retailers also have the opportunity to identify consumer needs. They have an additional advantage in being able to react to these needs without having to go through a large retail organization before the product can be ordered.

Resident Buying Offices

Resident buying offices provide both independent and chain retailers with current marketing information that can enable the retail buyers to achieve higher stock turnover and better stock assortments. Both local and central retail buyers need a great deal of information because a single buyer or store system can't keep up with changes in (1) types of new products being offered, (2) offerings of the numerous suppliers, (3) business levels, and (4) consumer preferences for different types of goods. The resident buying office usually makes such information available to retail buyers. The resident buying office is also a source of training for the local store buyers. Resident offices may conduct training workshops, and their personnel may even shop with the retailer's local buyers when the latter come to the wholesale market. Some resident buying offices check on orders, and even expedite deliveries on urgently needed merchandise. Resident buying offices may also provide assistance in planning promotional events.

The resident buying office may be either an *independent office* or a *store-owned office*. Independent offices can be either "salaried offices," which serve their clients on a contractual basis, or "merchandise brokers," who receive their payment (usually a 2 to 4 percent commission) from the vendor instead of the buyer. Hence local buyers can receive free buying assistance from merchandise brokers. However, the retail buyers should be aware that the merchandise broker is *also* trying to present—in the most favorable way—the products from which his commission is derived.

Store-owned offices may be "private offices," which are owned and operated by and for a single retailer, such as the Neiman Marcus New York City office, which assists only buyers in all Neiman Marcus stores. If several different retail groups own the resident buying office, it is called an "associated office." In this case the buying power and authority remains mostly with the individual buyers who use the service. The "syndicated office," on the other hand, represents the chain store system in the ownership group situation; so the syndicated office purchase recommendations are usually adopted by local personnel.

The wide range of services provided by all types of resident buying offices is very helpful to both large- and small-scale retailers. Therefore retail buyers should at least investigate the possibility of using a resident buying office to assist them in their buying procedure.

Trip Buying Plan

The merchandise manager and corporate retail management use dollars as the unit of measurement in the planning. The buyer must convert merchandising plans from dollars into units of merchandise. Actually, the buyer may first plan his unit sales and his unit assortment and then convert the figures into dollars to check against his merchandise manager's (or his own) dollar plan.

Buyers often develop a "trip buying plan," which indicates the specific quantity of each item they intend to buy on a forthcoming buying trip. Several different forms can be used to coordinate the buyers' purchases with the merchandise budget and their open-to-buy quantity. Figure 13–1 shows the trip buying plan form used by one retailer.

Sources of Merchandise

The trend toward "scrambled merchandising" has complicated an already enormous problem of retail buyers. Merchandising many nonrelated merchandise lines requires that many different sources of supply be used to meet consumer demands. The magnitude of the problem of evaluating different sources of supply is readily apparent for any large-scale retailer who handles well over 10,000 different items. However, even small-scale retailers make an important decision when they select their suppliers.

There are three major sources of supply available to the retailers: middlemen, manufacturers or producers, and foreign exporters.

The different types of middlemen, the product lines they normally carry, and the type of retail outlet for which they are especially well suited are described in Figure 13–2. Middlemen provide many services that are valuable to small and medium-size retailers who cannot afford to hire specialists in many different areas. However, retailers are themselves getting into the wholesale business by using many different retail-wholesale combinations in which a group of retail outlets either owns the wholesale organization, as in the case of "cooperative chain" operations, or performs the wholesaling functions of assembling and collecting goods in chain distribution centers. Retailers also enter into group buying arrangements to perform some (if not all) of the functions normally performed by middlemen.

Retailers purchase their merchandise directly from manufacturers or producers for several reasons. First, manufacturers' salesmen can cooperate in training the retailers' salesmen to use proper selling and display techniques for the specific merchandise purchased.

Second, direct buying *may* reduce the time required for delivery of the merchandise because the shipments can be made directly to the outlets or sent pre-packaged for each outlet to the chain's distribution center. This re-

Figure 13–1 Example of Trip Buying Plan Form

Department _____

Store _____

Date _____

Buying trip to _____

On order for next month delivery _____

Planned purchases next month _____

Estimated sales next month _____

Trip buying limit $ _____

Merchandise Code and Description	Units on Hand	Units on Order	Units Available for Sale	Forecast Sales until Delivery	Planned Stock at End of Month	Open to Buy This Month	Units Planned to Buy Now	Per Unit Cost	Planned Retail Price	Units Purchased	Dollar Amounts Purchases
(1)	(2)	(3)	(4) = (2) + (3)	(5)	(6)	(7)	(8)	(9)	(10)	(11)	(12)

Delivery date _____

Signed _____ (Buyer)

Approved _____ (Merchandise Manager)

344

Figure 13–2   Characteristic Types of Middlemen Serving Retailers

TYPE OF MIDDLEMAN	CHARACTERISTICS
Service (regular) wholesaler	Serves as the retailer's buying agent by assembling and collecting goods, storing goods, providing fast delivery, extending credit, and furnishing market information. These services appeal especially to small and medium-size retailers.
Limited function wholesaler	Charges less because he provides less service, as he generally does not grant credit or offer delivery service. Offers only fast-moving items; may do business only by mail.
Rack jobber	Supplies mainly non-food items to supermarkets, sets up displays, maintains merchandise assortment, and receives payment only on goods actually sold; thereby guarantees a pre-specified percent markup to the outlet.
Broker	Receives a commission to bring retail buyers and suppliers together; does not handle merchandise or take title to goods. Handles only a few lines—mainly grocery specialties, dry goods, fruits, vegetables, drugs, and hardware.
Commission agent	Similar to broker, except he handles merchandise, although he does not take title to it; supplies mainly large retailers with dry goods, grocery specialties, fruits and vegetables.
Manufacturer's agent (representative)	Renders services similar to those of a salesman; is restricted to a limited territory and by limited authority to negotiate price and terms of sale; sells only part of his client's output.
Selling agent	Similar to manufacturer's agent, except selling agent is responsible for disposing of entire output of his client.
Auctioneer	Product is placed on display and sold to highest bidder. Used mainly to sell livestock, fruits and vegetables to small restaurants, large chains, or other wholesalers.

duction in delivery time can be especially important for fad, fashion, or perishable items.

Third, retailers may buy direct because they can obtain lower net prices by not using the middleman. If some of the wholesalers' functions can be eliminated or absorbed by the retailer at a lower cost, direct buying offers an economic advantage.

Fourth, direct buying allows large retailers to purchase goods made according to *their* specifications. Consumer requests can be translated more easily into these specifications than in the case where the middleman is also involved in the communication process. Many large retailers, such as Sears Roebuck and Company, now specify the design of nearly all the items they handle.

Some large retailers have purchased manufacturing companies that produce sizable amounts of the merchandise they handle. Of course, this guarantees control over merchandise quality. In addition, it allows the retailer to reap more profits from the trend toward private label merchandise. Distribution costs frequently can be reduced because the products are placed in the mass market without incurring heavy advertising or sales costs. Per unit manufacturing costs may be reduced because high-volume sales allow spreading the fixed cost invested in machines, administration, etc. over the many units sold.

Foreign markets are becoming a more important source of merchandise supply as new trade agreements are made with nations such as Russia and China and as other countries, such as Japan, become more familiar with U.S. consumer needs. Foreign goods purchased by retailers pass through importers, who send catalogs and/or salesmen to retailers. Most importers are located in the New York area, the Pacific Coast area, Canadian and Mexican border towns, and several large metropolitan areas.

Some large retailers send their own buyers to foreign countries to negotiate purchases. An alternative is to make purchases from foreign buyers through resident buying offices. If a large retail firm buys large quantities of foreign merchandise, it may establish its own buying offices in the major foreign supply areas.

Evaluating Merchandise

Successful retail buyers must be able to judge the quality of merchandise to be certain that their purchases will meet the needs of their consumers. Hence buyers need considerable knowledge about raw materials, manufacturing methods, workmanship, and current fashion trends. Merchandise may be evaluated by personally inspecting all of the goods purchased. However, this can be a time-consuming process when volume purchases are made, so a sampling procedure (evaluating only a portion of the merchandise to be purchased) can be used to reduce the time devoted to inspecting goods.

Merchandise is also frequently purchased on the basis of a description of the item. U.S. government grades or standard industry definitions allow the buyer to make purchases on the basis of a description because the goods must meet prescribed quality standards to bear the label issued by the government or industry. The grading system used for beef is an example. Grocery outlets generally inform the meat suppliers of their needs in terms of both quantity and quality for a specified date. The quality description is merely a statement of which U.S. Department of Agriculture grade(s) a store desires to buy. The meat suppliers then respond with a bid price on the stated quantity and quality. Generally, the supplier who quotes the lowest price obtains the business for that specific period.

Testing bureaus are also used to assist the buyer in making his quality judgment. These bureaus may either be store-owned or independent commercial bureaus that charge a fee for evaluating goods. United States Testing

Company of Hoboken, New Jersey, is an example of an independent commercial testing bureau.

Buying Negotiations

The negotiation process begins when the retail buyer has determined the type of merchandise he needs and after he determines which suppliers appear to be acceptable. Price, of course, is one of the major elements to be negotiated. Figure 13–3 contains a description of the various discounts that may be deducted from the vendor's list price to arrive at the net purchase price. Retail buyers should attempt to purchase the desired merchandise at the lowest net cost, but should not expect unreasonable discounts or price concessions from the supplier. It is important to develop the respect of the vendors, who can aid the buyer by providing services, advice, and speedy delivery of the merchandise. Thus a long-run relationship, based upon mutual respect for one another, is desirable.

Retail buyers must be familiar with the prices and discounts generally allowed on each item. However, the buyer should realize that his bargaining position for small-volume purchases is not as great as for large-volume purchases. As a result, the large retailer may be able to purchase goods from the same vendor at a lower net price. Although the Robinson-Patman Act places limitations on the price bargaining that large retailers may use, it does not prevent the buyer from negotiating for the lowest lawful price that sellers are willing to accept.[1]

Another negotiation issue is "dating," which determines when cash discounts may be received and when payment is due if an interest penalty is to be avoided. The terminology for cash discounts under several frequently used "future dating" statements, such as 2/10–net 30 and 2/10 E.O.M., is explained in Figure 13–3.

Future-dating negotiations take many forms. The invoice date can be used as the *base date*, so that any cash discount and billing statement refers to the number of days after the invoice date. However, several other kinds of future dating are commonly used. End-of-month (E.O.M.) dating allows the cash discount and full-payment period to begin on the first day of the *following* month instead of on the invoice date. For example, 2/10, n/30, E.O.M. on an invoice dated any day in June indicates that a 2 percent cash discount may be received until July 10. The full amount of the invoice is due by July 31. If no net period is indicated, the full amount is usually due at the end of the next calendar month (July 31 if the purchase was made any time during June).

Under *receipt of goods (R.O.G.) dating*, the period begins on the date that the goods are received by the retailer. Thus payment on merchandise received on June 10 with a 2/10, n/30, R.O.G. dating must be made on or before June 20 to obtain the 2 percent cash discount and by July 10 to avoid possible payment of interest.

Advance or *seasonal dating* specifies a date in the future when the

Figure 13–3   Characteristics of Price Discounts Given to Retailers

TYPE OF DISCOUNT	DESCRIPTION
Quantity	Price reduction given from invoice price because purchases are made.
	Amount of discount must be justified by either a reduction in cost associated with handling a larger quantity or by meeting a competitor's equally low price if retail buyer is to avoid prosecution under Robinson-Patman Act.
Trade (functional)	Price reduction is based upon the marketing activities performed by the buyer. Discounts are deducted from list price in order stated, so a trade discount of 20, 10, 5 would be calculated as 20% off the list price, 10% off the balance, and 5% off the second balance, and the retailer would pay 100% − 20% (= 80%), −8% (= 72%), −3.6% or 68.4% of the list price.
	Trade discounts may be given in addition to quantity discounts.
Seasonal	Price reduction given to encourage ordering during "off" seasons.
Advertising allowances	Price reduction made to retailers who promote a product or service for the supplier. Amount of allowance must be justified by being a reasonable payment for such promotions and by similar offerings made by the seller to competitive dealers if retailer is to avoid prosecution under Robinson-Patman Act.
Cash	Price reduction given if retailer pays his bills promptly.
	Cash discounts are usually stated as 2/10, net 30 which means that a 2% discount is given if payment is received within 10 days of the date of the invoice, and interest charges will not be added unless bill is not paid during the 30 day period.
	Other forms of cash discounts are: 2/10 (2% discount if paid within 10 days, balance due in 30 days), 2/10–30 extra (2% discount is extended 10 days to 40 days), and 2/10 E.O.M. (2% discount runs for 10 days after end of month in which purchase was made).
	Retailers should use cash discounts because they are profitable (even if money must be borrowed) and they promote vendor good will.

terms become applicable. For example, an order placed July 20 and shipped on October 15 with a 2/10, n/30 as of November 1 dating would indicate that a 2 percent cash discount may be obtained if payment is made on or before November 11.

Future datings are advantageous from a retailer's point of view because they allow the firm to operate with a lower level of investment in merchandise. As a result, the retail buyer will benefit from, and negotiate for, the type of future dating that will delay the cash discount payment date as long as possible. Some suppliers will not accept future dating dealings but insist on immediate settlement. In this case the merchandise is sold on a C.O.D. (cash on delivery) basis and discounts must be taken and payment made when the goods are received. Cash-on-delivery shipments are not generally used unless the retailer has not established his credit standing with the particular vendor.

Retail buyers may also negotiate for an extra cash discount, called an *anticipation discount*, if the bill is paid before the expiration of the cash discount period. This extra discount is generally calculated on the basis of a pre-specified annual percentage rate, which is determined by the going commercial loan rate. Anticipation payments are normally calculated on the number of days remaining until the end of the cash discount period.

For example, suppose an invoice for $5,000, issued with terms of 2/10– 30 extra with a 9 percent pre-specified anticipation rate, is paid in 10 days. This invoice is anticipated 30 days ($40 - 10$) prior to the expiration of the cash discount period. In this case the buyer would be entitled to a 2 percent cash discount ($5,000 $\times$ .02), or $100, plus an anticipation reduction equal to 9 percent interest on the balance ($4,900) for 30/360 of a year (360 days), or $36.74.

Retailers can obtain external financing from vendors who do not allow either cash or anticipation discounts and who do not charge interest on the unpaid balance after a stated number of days. Retailers, in this case, intentionally delay the payment of bills for 30 to 60 days beyond the due date. The amount of money owed to vendors is used by the retailer at no interest charge, but long-term vendor relationships are likely to suffer by using this *delayed payment* approach. Large retailers, however, may be sufficiently important and their overall credit rating good enough to force the supplier to allow them to be continually behind in making their payments. The supplier will also be forced to maintain good service and speedy merchandise delivery to these retailers, or risk losing their business.

The delayed payment approach is not likely to be successful for smaller retailers. These firms, as individual accounts, do not represent a significant volume of business to the supplier. In addition, their credit rating is likely to decline rapidly if they attempt to use the delayed payment approach. Thus the supplier can reduce the level of service provided to the smaller retailers, or even cease to sell to them if they attempt to use the delayed payment approach.

The degree to which an individual retailer can successfully use the delayed payment approach is therefore dependent upon his bargaining position relative to that of the vendor. The use of this approach may also be restricted by the latest interpretation of the Robinson-Patman Act.

Transportation and physical handling considerations are still another set of items which need to be negotiated. Suppliers usually quote prices as:

1. *F.O.B. (free on board) factory*, which means the buyer pays all transportation costs from the supplier's delivery platform
2. *F.O.B. shipping point*, which means that the supplier bears the transportation charges to his local shipping point but the retailer pays all further transportation costs
3. *F.O.B. destination (or store)*, which means that the seller pays the freight.

The F.O.B. point determines the point of title transfer, which is the reason behind the assumption of responsibility for freight charges as stated in these three situations.

Buyers must be knowledgeable about freight and handling costs to make comparisons of prices quoted on different transportation terms. Extra physical handling services may also be provided by some vendors. Vendors who sort and package merchandise separately for each store in a chain (or branch) retail system are able to reduce the handling costs for that chain or branch store system. These and other vendor-provided services, such as prompt delivery of merchandise, making a small shipping error in the merchandise delivered, etc., are quickly reflected in the firm's net profit picture.

Retailers may negotiate for an *exclusive right* to handle the goods for a stated territory. This provision protects the retailer from direct price competition on identical or specified items. However, the vendor may change his policy at any time and in any way not covered by the agreement, so the "protection" may be of a relatively short duration.

Retail buyers may also want to negotiate a guaranty against future price changes. If such a *price guaranty* is granted, the retail buyer can benefit equally as well as current buyers if the supplier *lowers* his price after the order is placed. If the vendor raises his price after the order is placed, the buyer has the benefit of the originally stated price under the provisions of the price guaranty. Price guaranties are used frequently on orders for seasonal merchandise and for staple goods during periods of price uncertainty.

A final point for negotiation is the privilege of returning unsold goods. Of course, the privilege of returning merchandise reduces the retailer's risk of being "caught" with obsolete goods.

Purchase Procedures

The retail buyer usually completes a *purchase order* form when all the negotiations have been completed. This form may be supplied to its buyers by the retail firm itself (Figure 13–4 is an example of such a form) or a vendor's order form may be used. Large retail firms are likely to use their own, standard form because information can be printed in one location and

Figure 13–4 **Example of Purchase Order Form**

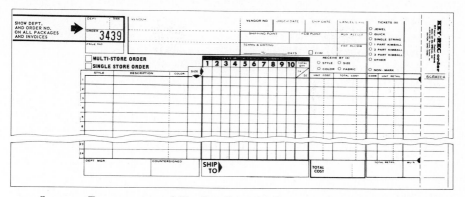

SOURCE Form courtesy of Key-Rec Systems, division of Allied/Egry Business Systems, Dayton, Ohio.

on as many copies as the firm needs to handle and control merchandise internally. These same forms are also used to give vendors shipping instructions. The written purchase order is issued by the purchasing department of the retail firm to the vendor. Upon acceptance by the vendor, it becomes a legal, binding contract.

The vendor sends an *invoice* to the buyer after the vendor has received the purchase order. The invoice is the itemized statement (or bill) containing the quantity, price, terms of sale, and other negotiated agreements on the merchandise being shipped. An example of an invoice form is presented in Figure 13–5.

Figure 13–5 **Example of Invoice Form**

NO.

DATE

YOUR
ORDER NO.

SOLD TO   SHIPPED TO

OUR ORDER NO.	SALESMAN	TERMS	F O.B.	DATE SHIPPED	SHIPPED VIA		
QUANTITY ORDERED	QUANTITY SHIPPED	STOCK NUMBER/DESCRIPTION			UNIT PRICE	UNIT	AMOUNT

The final major step in the buying process involves the *transfer of title*, which usually occurs when the supplier releases the goods to a common carrier for delivery. If the goods are damaged in transit, the buyer's recourse is *generally* against the transportation firm, not the vendor. But there are two variations from this procedure.

Goods may be bought on a *consignment* basis. In this case, title to the goods remains with the vendor until the goods are sold by the retailer. The supplier agrees to accept the return of any merchandise not sold; so the retailer does not take any risks caused by merchandise obsolescence or price declines. The retailer, however, is liable if the product is not properly cared for or is inadequately merchandised. Thus retailers should carefully evaluate the consignment merchandise and the vendor. New items are frequently introduced on a consignment basis because the retailer does not like to invest in a product that may not sell well.

Goods may also be purchased on a *memorandum buying* basis, which is a special form of future dating. In this case, the title to the goods passes to the retailer, who assumes all ownership risks but reserves the right to return any unsold portion of the goods to the supplier without payment. The retailer assumes little risk and is free to price the merchandise as he chooses. Memorandum billing is used frequently when goods are introduced on an experimental or "test market" basis.

It is quite common for large vendors to fill the orders of their large-volume, repeat customers first, and then, if there is stock and time left, fill the remaining orders from the merchandise on hand. Some large retailers have a standard cancellation policy for any order that is more than thirty days in processing and shipping. The merchandise is not opened but is automatically returned to the vendor, and he is charged the freight both ways. As a result of strict adherence to such policies by store managers, these large retailers usually get first choice of the merchandise and faster supplier support and service.

HANDLING MERCHANDISE

Additional activities must take place after the merchandise is purchased to ensure that the goods are properly assembled and presented to retail customers. First, the goods must be shipped from the supplier to the retail outlets. Then the goods must be examined to determine if the shipment contains merchandise that corresponds to the pre-specified quality and quantity stated on the purchase order. The merchandise is then marked, prepared for sale, and placed in the appropriate display area. However, close control activities are required to keep stock shortages, pilferage, and damaged goods to a minimum. The entire retail handling process must be planned to facilitate easy consumer pickup of merchandise or retail delivery to consumers. Finally, the merchandise that does not sell even after repeated sales promotion efforts may have to be disposed of by returning it to the supplier, by transferring or selling it to other retail outlets, or by throwing it away.

These activities will be discussed in more detail in the remainder of this chapter.

Moving Merchandise to the Store

Freight rate increases have tended to enhance the relative importance of activities that will allow merchandise to be moved to each retail outlet with minimum cost while maintaining a short delivery period. The activities involved in merchandise movement will be discussed under two topics: transportation and shipment consolidation.

Transportation Considerations

The retail manager or the retail traffic department of large retail organizations must select the desired carrier and routing of the incoming goods. The relative cost, the amount of time required to deliver goods, the care used in handling goods, the amount of packaging required for shipment, and the willingness and ability to deliver separate, small shipments to each outlet are major items that must be evaluated in making the routing and carrier decision. Cost may be the most important consideration for low-value, staple-type merchandise whose product life cycle is long and whose sales are fairly predictable. However, speed of delivery may be the dominant consideration for an order on out-of-stock or low-stock fashion merchandise.

Railroads and truck lines are the major carriers of full carload shipments of merchandise. Railroads usually offer the lowest freight rates on long hauls of more than 500 miles, but trucks provide more flexibility in getting merchandise directly to the retailer. The convenience of receiving merchandise by truck has made truck lines the major carrier of consumer merchandise. Piggy backing (hauling trailers on flat-bed rail cars) has reduced handling costs and speeded up delivery of railroad shipments, and is increasingly being used on intermediate and long-distance shipments.

Air freight offers the fastest method of delivery over long distances. For high-value, short-life merchandise (such as fashion or fad goods), the slightly higher rates can be justified. For example, a Denver department store receives 24-hour delivery via air on fashion clothing, which allows the store to offer a wider and more current merchandise assortment.

Retailers frequently encounter problems in transporting small shipments. Parcel post, air freight, United Parcel Service (UPS), REA Express, and Bus Package Express represent alternative ways of shipping freight weighing under 50 pounds. The four most attractive choices for shipments of merchandise weighing from 50 to 500 pounds are air freight, REA Express, freight forwarders, and shipper associations (cooperatives).[2] (The latter two methods represent shipment consolidation techniques.)

Freight bills must be carefully audited to detect clerical errors and overcharges caused by classifying goods in the incorrect freight category, by using a higher tariff rate when a lower rate could be utilized, or by calculating the freight rate over a longer route than is needed to deliver the merchandise.

Sizable savings can be obtained by audits conducted by a knowledgeable freight expert, as there are numerous "special" rates that can reduce the transportation costs considerably.

Prompt action should be taken when merchandise is delivered in a damaged condition or when the quantity of goods received does not agree with the quantity stated on the invoice. Retailers should make every attempt to determine who is responsible for the shortage and/or damage—the supplier or the carrier. Then the responsible party should be notified as soon as possible.

Shipment Consolidation

There are several methods that are frequently used to consolidate small shipments into large-volume shipments before the goods reach the individual outlet. Such consolidation is beneficial because a transportation cost reduction can be obtained by shipping large quantities, which may move on a carload rate basis. The *manufacturers* may provide a distribution center which receives different carload quantities of single products, stores these shipments, and sends large mixed-product shipments of ordered goods from the center to large retailers under carrier mixing privileges at truckload rates. Grocery product manufacturers, such as General Foods Corporation, have been using this type of distribution system effectively.

Consolidation may also be performed by commercial *freight forwarders*, which combine less than carload (L.T.C.) or truckload shipments from several manufacturers into full carload or truckload shipments.

Several independent commercial freight consolidation companies are expanding their services to include examination of merchandise for quantity and quality, marking merchandise with the stores' tickets, local distribution to retail outlets, maintenance of inventory control and sales data, and picking up merchandise returned by a store. These services can be especially helpful to the small retailer who cannot take advantage of quantity shipping rates or hire the expertise needed to analyze sales and inventory reports properly.

Numerous *shippers' cooperative associations* also perform consolidation services. These cooperatives, located in most major U.S. cities, consolidate the shipments, provide long-distance shipping, break down the shipments, and store the merchandise either in a local warehouse or at individual retail outlets.

Most large retail chain organizations have their own *chain store distribution centers*, which perform the same services as the other consolidation centers but may also check the merchandise, mark it, and provide inventory control services.

Managing Incoming Merchandise

Merchandise delivered to the retail outlet is unloaded at the store and moved to an area for unpacking. This procedure, commonly called *receiving*, involves certain inspection and recording activities. All merchandise containers should be inspected immediately upon delivery to determine if there is any apparent merchandise damage. If the receiving clerk finds no apparently damaged merchandise, he usually signs the carrier's receipt. If he detects damaged goods, he facilitates the filing of future damage claims by writing "DAMAGED" on the receipt and then signing it. Only the containers are examined at this point, unless there is apparent merchandise damage. The goods are then moved into the receiving room, the containers are opened, and the contents are checked for damage.

Incoming shipments must be recorded to provide data on the time of arrival, apparent condition of the shipment, delivery charges, vendor's name and address, carrier's name and address, name of the person making the delivery, number of containers, weight of goods, amount and number of invoices, and the department for which goods were ordered. A typical receiving record is presented in Figure 13–6. Such records may be analyzed by computer to assist and support the preparation of damage claims and vendor payments. Retailers can avoid paying for goods not yet received by comparing invoices against the receiving records.

The *checking* process begins after the receiving records are completed. The goods are usually moved into a separate checking and marking room to facilitate the checking procedure. This checking process begins with a comparison of the invoice and the purchase order. This allows the checker to determine if the description and quality of goods billed agree with the order. The dating and discount information is also compared at this time.

The merchandise is then removed from the shipping containers and sorted into similar categories. It is then advisable to immediately check the incoming merchandise against the invoice to determine if the correct amount and quality of merchandise has been received. Sometimes invoices are not available on goods which are needed on the selling floor. In this case, the purchase order can be compared against the shipment to determine if there are any discrepancies in quantity *or quality*. Making this check immediately allows the merchandise to reach the consumer quickly, but, even more important, discrepancies between the checker's count and the invoice count can be rechecked very easily. This recheck is usually made by the checker's supervisor, or by the proprietor in the case of a small store.

Merchandise is then *marked* by using tags, price tickets, gummed stickers, automatic imprinting systems, handwriting, and hand stamping. The mark should be legible, neat, and as permanent as possible without damaging the goods. If a price ticket is used, other necessary data, such as the cost of the item (coded), date received, department number, and size and color of goods, can be placed on the price ticket to assist in the merchandise management process.

There are many different systems of merchandise marking. Some large retailers reduce marking expense and speed the within-store merchandise preparation time by having the vendors mark the goods prior to shipment. This practice, called *source marking*, involves a standard tag code and format,

Figure 13–6   A Receiving Record

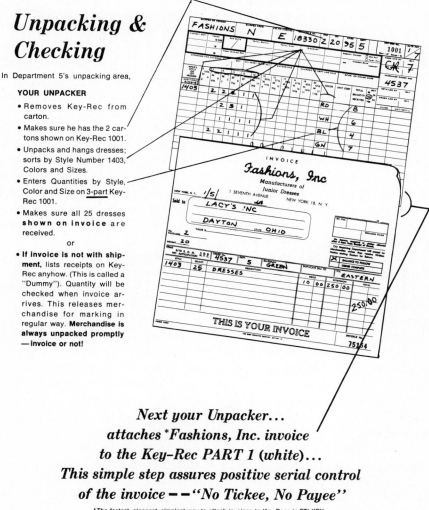

Unpacking & Checking

In Department 5's unpacking area,

YOUR UNPACKER

- Removes Key-Rec from carton.
- Makes sure he has the 2 cartons shown on Key-Rec 1001.
- Unpacks and hangs dresses; sorts by Style Number 1403, Colors and Sizes.
- Enters Quantities by Style, Color and Size on 3-part Key-Rec 1001.
- Makes sure all 25 dresses **shown on invoice** are received.

or

- **If invoice is not with shipment**, lists receipts on Key-Rec anyhow. (This is called a "Dummy"). Quantity will be checked when invoice arrives. This releases merchandise for marking in regular way. **Merchandise is always unpacked promptly —invoice or not!**

Next your Unpacker...
attaches *Fashions, Inc. invoice
to the Key–Rec PART 1 (white)...
This simple step assures positive serial control
of the invoice – –"No Tickee, No Payee"

*The fastest, cleanest, simplest way to attach invoices to Key-Recs is STI-KEY, a pressure sensitive strip at the bottom of Key-Rec 1. (Patented)

SOURCE   Form courtesy of Key-Rec Systems, division of Allied/Egry Business Systems, Dayton, Ohio.

so retailers can easily use electronic data processing (EDP) equipment to improve the flow of sales and inventory information. Other retailers require the buyer to place retail prices upon the store's copy of the purchase order at the time the order is placed. This practice, called *pre-retailing*, forces the retail buyer to consider the retail price when the purchase is made. This discourages purchases of items which do not appear capable of being sold at the retail price needed to provide the desired markup. Pre-retailing facilitates the marking procedure because the marking clerk merely refers to the purchase order to obtain the appropriate retail price.

Many different forms of price tickets are used in retailing. Several automated systems use precoded tags which can be read by electronic devices. (A description of a complete marking, checkout, and recording system will be presented shortly.)

Once the merchandise has been marked, it is ready to be moved to the selling floor. The retail buyer may give instructions (on the purchase order) indicating which department and area is to receive the merchandise. Otherwise the store manager of a chain store, the proprietor of a small retail store, or the department head may indicate where to move the goods. If the shelves are full, the merchandise may be placed temporarily in a reserve stockroom. (Generally, all of the store's shelf-stocking clerks are allowed in the stockroom to obtain goods as they are needed in the selling area. It is important to realize that merchandise in a reserve stockroom or in the checking or marking areas cannot be sold until it is displayed in the selling area; therefore these goods must be checked frequently and moved to the selling floor as quickly as possible.)

One suggested guideline for reducing merchandise handling costs through the processes discussed thus far is presented in Figure 13–7.

Figure 13–7   Guidelines for Reducing Merchandise Handling Costs

---

An order system designed to provide a complete record of merchandise movement can reduce labor requirements, over-ordering and merchandise "outs."

A separate door used only for receiving goods can reduce confusion and idle time.

Semi-permanent or permanent conveyors may speed up the receiving operation.

A well-designed storage area with multi-level bays can facilitate the segregation of merchandise as it is received, and utilize storage space more completely.

An intercom system between the selling and storage areas can increase productivity.

Properly designed stock carts can reduce travel time between storage and selling areas.

Competent, well-trained employees are necessary to make any system operate efficiently.

SOURCE   Earl H. Brown, "Reducing Grocery Handling Costs in Supermarkets," Miscellaneous Series, Circular E-20, Michigan State University Cooperative Extension Service (January 1962), p. 3.

Several automated retail systems involve the linking of store cash registers to computer processing units. One such system, the National Cash Register (NCR) 280 Retail System, will be described to illustrate how these systems are used in retail outlets in marking, checkout, and recording data.

All retail merchandise is ticketed with color-bar-coded tags that can be read by "wand readers" at the checkout stands. The "wands" eliminate manual keying-in on transaction data.

The terminals are linked to an NCR 723 data collector at the store to accumulate detailed sales transaction information on magnetic tape for nightly input to the retailer's central computer system. They are also linked to a magnetic disc storage unit alongside the collector for on-line credit authorization as part of each charge transaction.

Accuracy of the system is maintained under electronic control from start to finish. For example, the NCR 747 tag printer in the receiving room cannot produce a price tag with a wrong item number because it uses a check-digit verifier. This eliminates re-pricing costs due to errors. Yet price changing is made simple by way of pressure-sensitive color-bar-coded overlays also printed on the NCR 747. The tags include up to fifty-six digits of coded information, such as department, classification, stock-keeping unit (hereafter called SKU), and price. Tags are also imprinted in normal customer-readable characters.

Similarly, self-checking features in each wand reader ensure that it captures data with complete accuracy during checkout. When the cashier "reads" a tag with the wand, by passing it across the tag (which is still on the merchandise), the dollar amount appears on the indicator of the terminal, which is really a minicomputer, and the terminal automatically calculates the prices and taxes.

The tag can be read by moving the wand in either direction across its length and a "beep" response is given to the operator. Should the operator miss part of the tag, the system responds with a deeper-tone beep, and records no data. In this case, she simply passes the wand over the black, white, and green color-bar code again.

In a conventional retail system, fifteen to twenty people mark merchandise with various types of equipment and tags. The NCR system, with one tag printer operated by a trained person, practically eliminates ticket errors because, with the wand readers at the checkouts, virtually the only error possible is to put the wrong ticket on the wrong merchandise.

As a result, the NCR system reduces input errors in the merchandise reporting system. The speedy reporting system also reduces out-of-stock conditions and lost sales, while permitting reductions in inventory.

The speedy checkout facilitated by wands increases store sales because it permits a faster customer flow. One retail manager has taken this into account by establishing a new store with sixteen checkstands which are expected to handle at least the same volume that eighteen conventional registers could service in similar stores.[3]

The NCR data collector also indicates time intervals every 15 minutes on the same tape on which it records the sales information. From this, one can compare store traffic flow and cashier loads and improve the scheduling of cashiers to provide maximum service with minimum personnel.

The retail terminal also can accept information entered manually via its keys—the customer's credit card number, for instance. However, the retail outlet may issue color-bar-coded credit cards, which would speed the checkout procedure. This entire process is illustrated in Figures 13–8 to 13–11.

Reducing Stock Shortages, Pilferage, and Damaged Goods

Retailers encounter a continuous and growing problem in their efforts to reduce stock shortages. Theft of goods by employees, customers, shoplifters, and robbers has increased with the growth of self-service merchandise.

Reducing Internal Theft

Retail personnel offices have the task of screening applicants before they are hired. Careful evaluation of each applicant's work experience may reveal non-work periods, which can be checked to determine if the person was serving a jail sentence for theft. Retail personnel offices also keep records

Figure 13–8 Producing Color-Bar-Coded Tags in NCR System
Operator of the NCR 747 tag printer in the receiving room displays color-bar-coded tags produced under electronic control. Tags are produced ahead of need, then placed in envelopes and filed in the cabinets in background. Each tag contains up to 56 digits of information, including item price, department classification, and SKU numbers.

Source   National Cash Register Company, Dayton, Ohio.

Figure 13–9   *Ticketing and Reading Price Tags in NCR System*

Every item in the store is ticketed with a unique color-bar-coded tag (lower right), which the wand can read in a fraction of a second. The tags are also imprinted with customer-readable letters and numbers. When the cashier passes the wand across the tag, the item price appears on the indicator window of the terminal, just as it would on a conventional cash register.

SOURCE   National Cash Register Company, Dayton, Ohio.

on employees whom the organization has terminated because of theft. Most large retailers have a security department which works very closely with the personnel department to detect internal theft. Constant supervision of employees and informative, preventive communication programs presented to store employees must be used to combat internal theft.

Small retailers don't need to keep such detailed records on their employees who are terminated for theft, because the manager or proprietor is likely to know and recognize all employees personally. Large chain or branch retail organizations need to maintain detailed records (which contain fingerprints, photos, signatures, etc.) to prevent a terminated employee from being rehired at a different outlet without the knowledge of the personnel office.

Figure 13–10   Recording Credit Sales in NCR System
The cashier still uses the keys occasionally—in this case to enter a store credit card number on a charge sale. The system permits on-line credit authorization. Ultimately, the store may issue color-bar-coded credit cards, which the wand could read too.

SOURCE   National Cash Register Company, Dayton, Ohio.

Reducing Shoplifting

Shoplifting is reduced by many different techniques. Mechanical gadgets, such as two-way or "anti-pilferage" mirrors, closed-circuit television, one-way-glass observation posts, and completely automated detection systems, are used to detect shoplifting activities. However, store employees must be motivated to keep a sharp watch for shoplifting. Frequent meetings of employee groups, such as an employees' security committee that sets up rules and policy for both retail employees and customers, encourage all employees to keep alert to the problem. Using plainclothes security "floorwalkers" has also increased the detection of shoplifters. Unidentified floorwalkers might make

Figure 13–11   Checking Merchandise Report in NCR System
An NCR 723 data collector accumulates detailed sales transaction information
on magnetic tape nightly input to the central computer system.

SOURCE   National Cash Register Company, Dayton, Ohio.

only occasional appearances, or they might be regular in their observation
efforts. In any case, they are notified immediately when a known professional
shoplifter enters the store and they are constantly at that person's side. Store
employees also observe, from more distance, suspicious customers who loiter
without buying, who carry a large purse or shopping bag, or who wear a
topcoat in mild weather.

Detection and apprehension of shoplifters is only part of the process.
Many stores evaluate a person who has been apprehended to determine if
the case should be turned over to the law enforcement agencies or whether
some other treatment (such as having him clean up the parking lot) should
be used. Many local and state laws now allow the retailer more protection
from false arrest charges. The courts now are taking a more serious view of
shoplifting by placing larger monetary fines and/or imposing mandatory jail

sentences on convicted shoplifters. Everyone—retailers, employees, and law enforcement officials—must work together to curb shoplifting by letting it be known that shoplifters will be prosecuted by courts that impose meaningful penalties.

The importance of the pilferage problem is illustrated by looking at it from an economic point of view. Retail net profit may only be 2 percent of gross sales volume and pilferage may amount to 1 percent of sales volume. In this case, if pilferage can be reduced by 50 percent, net profit can be increased by 0.5 percent of sales, so net profit will increase by 0.5 divided by 2, or 25 percent (minus the additional cost needed to reduce pilferage). Hence the payoff generated by pilferage prevention systems is likely to be high.

Reducing Handling Errors

Employees are always going to make honest errors in marking goods, in counting inventory, in handling merchandise returns, in making change for customers, in recordkeeping, etc. Careful employee selection, training, and supervision can reduce the frequency of mistakes of this type. Internal auditing is being used increasingly by retailers to reduce the amount of shortages caused by both honest handling errors and employee theft. Less complex recording forms, less frequent label changes, and generally simple information-relaying systems can reduce the occurrence of honest errors. Systems need to be developed to ensure that employees understand why consistent marking, re-marking, recording, and accounting procedures are needed.

The system might also encourage employees to monitor the honesty of vendors. For example, Munford Inc., the nation's second largest chain of convenience food stores, offers its employees a $100 reward for reporting suppliers who steal or fail to deliver everything charged to its stores. Suppliers' agents are estimated to account for half of total losses and thefts at Munford's stores, while its employees cause 45 percent of the losses and shoplifting customers take the remaining 5 percent.[4]

Taking Physical Inventory

An actual count of all the goods in each outlet is usually conducted once or twice a year to provide financial and inventory control information. The physical inventory results in a listing of the types, quantities, and values of all the items in the store. These data are then used to classify merchandise by any desirable grouping—department, merchandise category, SKU size, etc. —so that the retail buyers can purchase merchandise intelligently and the amount of inventory overage or shortage can be determined.

The inventory-taking procedure must be carefully planned to provide accurate information. Several different approaches are used for taking the physical inventory, although it is usually valued only in retail prices. This allows retail management to measure the total value of merchandise on hand.

The value can then be compared to the book or "perpetual" value to determine the amount of shortage or overage.

Frequently, the store manager will carefully inspect his stock prior to counting each item. Slow-moving and out-of-season items are featured in advertising citing price reductions by using a "pre-inventory clearance sale" theme. Sales of this type can reduce some of the work associated with inventory counting. Employees are then instructed in inventory taking and the importance of accuracy. Standardized inventory forms (obtainable from trade associations or office supply houses) usually are used to record the desired information in a uniform method (Figure 13–12).

*Figure 13–12   **Example of Inventory-Recording Form***

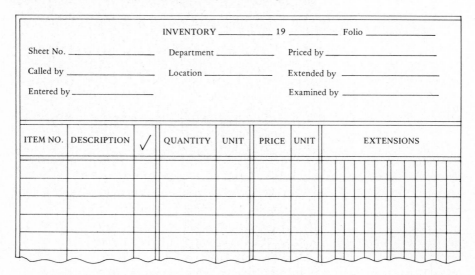

Some chain and branch retail organizations give no advance notice that an inventory is going to be taken. In this case an inventory crew arrives at the outlet unannounced and begins the stock-recording procedure. Each person may go through the stock, calling out the description of the items and giving the number of units of each price. This verbal information may be recorded either by a tape recorder or by an assistant. The detailed analysis of the data provided by the inventory is then conducted at retail headquarters. The unexpected element of the inventory-recording procedure can reduce internal theft in large organizations by detecting theft earlier and keeping employees informed that they will be caught if they steal.

Department stores and other outlets that merchandise fashion goods communicate with the retail buyer and merchandise manager to check the accuracy of their perpetual or ongoing records against the count obtained by the physical inventory method. The perpetual inventory records, the unit control records, and other essential forms are then adjusted to reflect the findings of the physical inventory. All information is shipped to the controller's office after counting and recording the data on a standardized form or recording sheet. The controller's office prepares the necessary financial reports (discussed in Chapter 15) and makes historical inventory comparisons. It also determines turnover ratios and stock levels, and calculates the amount of stock shortages or overages by departments.

Merchandise Returns

Merchandise is frequently returned to suppliers because goods may not conform to specifications, or they may be defective, or incorrect items or quantities were shipped, or the terms of the sale are different from what was communicated in the original negotiation.

A full explanation of the reason for returning goods should precede or accompany the returned goods to maintain good vendor relations. Of course, the merchandise should be returned promptly after it has been discovered to be defective or unsatisfactory. Vendors usually do not expect to receive goods back simply because they do not sell. Changes in price and consumer preferences are part of the risks that the retail firm assumes once it has accepted title to the goods. Suppliers' relations are likely to be strained by practices whereby the store benefits entirely at the vendors' expense. For example, refunds may be obtained for *some* consignment merchandise simply by proving that the goods did not sell. Vendors are not likely to appreciate retailers who re-package such goods and sell them at a considerably reduced price, although they have already claimed the refund from the vendor.

Re-marking Merchandise

Re-marking of merchandise can result from price changes, lost or mutilated tickets, and customer merchandise returns. Most retailers have such merchandise re-marked by the same employees who performed the original marking of the goods. Regardless of who performs the re-marking process, they must use standardized ticketing and accounting procedures. Any new tickets must contain the same information that the original label provided. A complete lack of inventory control will result from any system that allows department or sales personnel to make their own tickets or to make price changes without informing the appropriate supervisors.

Consumer Pickup and Delivery

One of the most important links in merchandise handling is consumer pickup and delivery. Since these functions are a major part of retail customer service, a detailed discussion was presented in Chapter 11.

SUMMARY

The purchase and handling of merchandise must be done efficiently if goods are to be offered in the form and at the time demanded by consumers.

The retail buying organization should be structured in a manner that purchases can be made as inexpensively as possible. Individual retailers have formed cooperative buying groups which make large-volume purchases, obtain quantity-price discounts, and thus reduce merchandise costs. Retail chain organizations use centralized buying committees that reduce their merchandise costs.

The negotiation process provides the retailer with many opportunities to maximize profit. Quantity, trade, seasonal, cash, and anticipation discounts can be used to reduce merchandise cost by lowering the "net price" paid by the retailer. In addition, advertising allowances can be obtained by promoting a manufacturer's brand name product. Other negotiations focus upon dating, transportation and handling considerations, price guaranties, the privilege of returning unsold goods, and the like.

Electronic equipment is being used to increase the efficiency of the receiving, checking, marking, and checkout processes. In addition, the electronic system generates data needed to keep management informed on sales, inventory levels, and profitability. The use of these computer-linked systems is likely to increase in the future as pressures mount to decrease operating costs.

QUESTIONS

1. How should a retailer determine his reorder time?
2. What is customer feedback, how can it be obtained, and of what use is it?
3. Write a job description for a buyer for a large department store.
4. Why do buyers often buy directly from manufacturers?
5. Why would a retailer want to delay his payments to suppliers as long as possible? What measures are used by suppliers to discourage this practice?
6. If you are a buyer and supplier A offers you terms of 2/10 n/60 and supplier B offers you terms of 3/10 n/30, which would you choose, assuming all other variables are the same? Suppose your subjective judgment indicates that you should deal with the supplier who is *not* offering the better deal. Which of the other variables would you try to negotiate in an attempt to make the two deals equal from a monetary point of view?
7. If a supplier comes to you wishing to introduce a new product in your retail outlet, what will be the negotiating position you will assume?
8. What is pre-retailing? If you were a buyer, would you consider it to be additional responsibility or would you consider it to be an "audit" to see that you are doing your job effectively?
9. How would a retail manager go about deciding whether to install an automated retail accounting system such as the NCR 280? What benefits are available and how would these benefits be evaluated?
10. A retailer is operating on a profit of 3 percent of gross sales of $100,000

per year and his pilferage allowance is 1 percent of this amount. If the retailer is sure that television cameras will reduce pilferage by one-half, how much can he afford to pay for the installation of these cameras? Assume that the mere presence of these cameras will produce the desired effect and neglect maintenance and monitoring expenses.

11. If the television surveillance in problem 10 offers a maintenance and monitoring service that will reduce pilferage by one-half (half the pilferage rate with unmonitored cameras), how much is this service worth to the retailer?

12. Is the expense of taking a physical inventory justifiable? Explain your answer.

FOOTNOTES

[1] Lawrence X. Tarpey, Sr., "Buyer Liability under the Robinson-Patman Act: A Current Appraisal," *Journal of Marketing* (January 1972), pp. 38–42.

[2] David R. Gourley "Transportation Alternatives for the Small Shipper," *Journal of Small Business Management*, 9 (October 1971): 32–34.

[3] A new Richway Discount store which uses this system was opened in Atlanta on July 13, 1972.

[4] *U.S. News and World Report*, July 23, 1973, pp. 67–68.

SANGER-HARRIS
Physical Distribution—Ordering and Receiving Systems

Sanger-Harris Department Stores was facing the problem of developing an improved system for merchandise ordering and receiving. Responsibility for this area fell under the vice-president for operations and management information. He stated that shipments from vendors often came to Sanger-Harris receiving stations in as many as eight different shipments. A buyer might order 4,000 dresses for the eight stores from a small manufacturer, only to find them delivered in groups of 1,000. If this was a new fashion, the trend might have declined or ended before the final delivery was made.

In addition, the shipping clerks at the factory might send the first 1,000 dresses to the first two or three suburban stores on the order form and none of the remainder, because the factory could not complete the order. If the vendor shipping clerk divided the partial shipment between the suburban stores, his judgment of sizes and selections to be sent to each store

Figure 13–13   Sanger-Harris Order Form

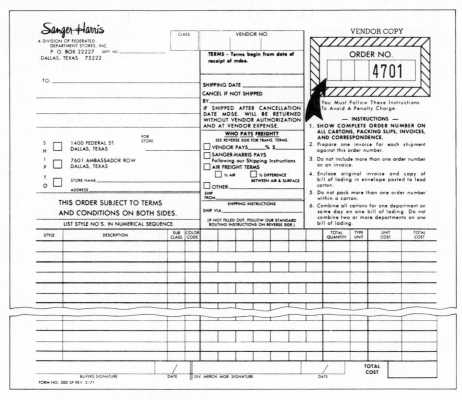

SOURCE   Sanger-Harris, Dallas, Texas.

often failed to match the buyer's intentions. In effect, a shipping clerk at the factory was making decisions that affected the merchandise assortment, customer relations, and overall profitability of all Sanger-Harris stores.

It was believed that part of the problem was in the complexity of the order form (see Figure 13–13). This form was considerably more complex than the single-store order form which Sanger-Harris had used before the last ten years' growth of this firm. The vice-president believed that the vendor's shipping clerks had a difficult time reading and completing the form, which led to delays and errors.

To correct the situation, he was seriously considering the adoption of a "post distribution" order system. Post distribution is a total vendor order by quantity, style, and color, with no distribution breakdown given to the vendor or manufacturer. Post distribution systems had been used by large chains for several years, but might present problems for medium- or small-size chains or department stores with branches.

There are many benefits derived from a post distribution system, as well as some drawbacks. The benefits are:

1. Lower freight
2. Fewer cartons to handle, therefore less trash
3. Higher productivity in checking and marking
4. Final distribution decision can be made closer to actual receipt of merchandise
5. Screening office can reject orders that don't show final distribution information
6. Earlier and more complete shipments from manufacturers, since manufacturers don't have to pack shipments for each branch.

A post distribution system would also relieve the vendor shipping clerks of the decision-making process regarding shipments and place it with the retailer.

Where shipping clerks at the manufacturing plant had formerly sent boxes marked for ultimate delivery to the branches, they would now send merchandise marked only for Sanger-Harris receiving stations. Distribution to the branches would then be accomplished by trained Sanger-Harris personnel.

This obviously meant that an increase in personnel would be needed to work in post distribution. It also meant that additional storage and sorting areas would be needed to handle this function. In addition, new order forms would be needed and buyers would have to learn a new system.

The proposed order form (see Figure 13–14) was designed with eight blocks in the right-hand corner. Each block represents a different Sanger-Harris store. This section of the order form was not used by the vendor's shipping clerks.

The buyers for Sanger-Harris would be expected to mark figures in code in each block. These figures would later be interpreted by personnel in the receiving section. The code would be designed to indicate the product mix the buyers had intended for each suburban store.

Both the buyer and the receiving station personnel would retain a copy of the order form. In the case of checking partial shipments of a style against an order, a photostat would be made of the order, showing new changes, and sent to the buyer. A second photostat would be attached to the original order in the receiving station, awaiting further shipment. This process would continue until the order had been filled or canceled.

The rapid growth of Sanger-Harris also created the possibility of future problems with the proposed system. Sanger-Harris presently owns eight stores and has plans on the drawing boards for two more. On the average, a new store a year had been added, and this trend seemed likely to continue.

Although management had studied the problem, it had been unable to derive a ratio or rule of thumb for the added personnel and storage space that a new store opening would create in the receiving area.

As new stores were added, the storage problems would continue to grow, which meant new construction or around-the-clock receiving. New construc-

Figure 13–14   Proposed Sanger-Harris Order Form

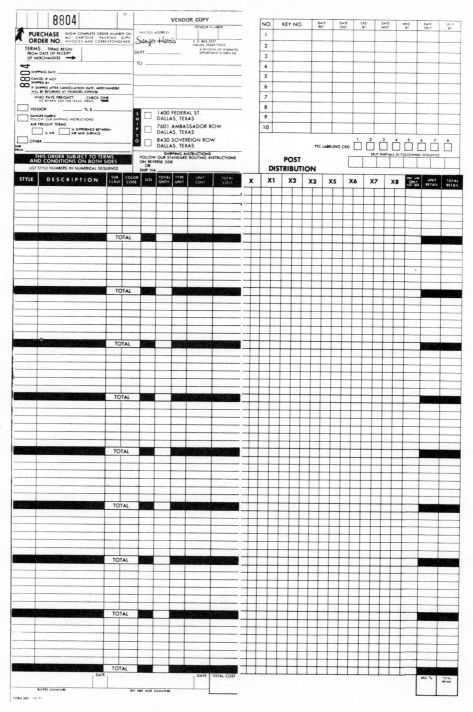

SOURCE   Sanger-Harris, Dallas, Texas.

tion costs and interest rates were high and retailers traditionally preferred to place expansion capital in retail stores rather than the back room.

Around-the-clock receiving would necessitate new and costly recruiting measures, as well as additional supervision. Also, security problems would increase.

There was also the question of just how many stores the buyers and receiving station personnel could efficiently handle.

The physical size of the proposed post distribution order form also presented filing and transportation problems, as it did not easily fit the file cabinets and attaché cases.

The vice-president stated that he believed the order form was the most important form in the store, and that any changes needed thorough and careful consideration.

DISCUSSION QUESTIONS

1. Do you believe Sanger-Harris should adopt the proposed post distribution order system? Why or why not?
2. Is post distribution the best answer to the problem? Could a workable system be developed that pushes this function back to the factory?
3. If Sanger-Harris adopts this system, can you see other problems than those mentioned in the case?
4. Check with a large chain store near your area. Is it using a post distribution system? If so, how does this vary from that proposed by Sanger-Harris?
5. What kind of a system should Sanger-Harris plan to use if it doubles the present number of stores?

THE PRICHARD COMPANY
International Buying

The foreign buying office of M. J. Prichard and Company was faced with the assignment of buying next season's shirts for pre-teen boys. These were to be sold through the basement shop of Prichard's in New York.

Mr. Dean Lynch was responsible for securing these contracts with clothing manufacturers in foreign countries. This assignment carried with it the

NOTE This case represents an actual experience of a large retailer, but the names have been changed; they do not purposely represent any existing retailer or retail firm.

responsibility of securing the right quantity of shirts at a quality and price consistent with Prichard's image and proven ability to meet consumer needs.

This task had become increasingly more difficult over the last few years due to increased competition from American discount operations. Buyers from discount houses could receive greater discounts from manufacturers due to the tremendous volumes in which they dealt. They could also effectively tie up the manufacturing capacity of many factories.

Mr. Lynch had developed contacts over the years with Korean manufacturers who could be depended upon for consistent quality, competitive prices, and meeting delivery deadlines.

In spite of Mr. Lynch's knowledge of Korean manufacturers and the reputation of Prichard, the situation suddenly changed.

The United States found itself faced with both a deficit in balance of payments and balance of trade. This pressure forced President Nixon to impose restrictions and heavier duties against foreign-made goods. Foreign governments were urged to impose export restrictions upon their own manufacturers or face losing massive amounts of trade with the United States.

As a result, the Korean government imposed export restrictions upon its own manufacturers, limiting their export production to 75 percent of the previous year. A manufacturer who had produced 100,000 dozen shirts the year before could now produce only 75,000 dozen for export to the United States.

This move eliminated a substantial part of the production of boys' shirts in Korea. The material and labor savings involved in manufacturing a boy's shirt versus a man's was not great enough to offset the difference in price. Thus Korean manufacturers either shifted entirely to men's shirts or charged substantially more for boys' wear.

To continue buying boys' shirts from Korea would have meant a marked increase in consumer prices in New York or a lowering of quality. Thus Mr. Lynch was forced to explore new markets in other foreign countries.

European goods were much too expensive, as were Japanese. Mexico and South America were developing these industries, but without enough strength to warrant a buying trip. After studying the alternatives, Taiwan was selected as the market area.

Several Taiwan manufacturers were contacted by Mr. Lynch, and for the most part their price quotes did not greatly vary. Although lower than Korean prices, they were still higher than last year's—meaning an inevitable retail price increase back in the States. Toward the end of his second week in Taiwan, Mr. Lynch received a price quote substantially lower than any of those he had already received. The quality of the goods and promised shipping dates were comparable. Only the price differed. Mr. Lynch had bargained long and hard with the manufacturer before receiving the price quote. This price would allow Prichard to maintain low prices in face of growing inflation and competition by discount operations.

None of the Taiwan manufacturers was known to Mr. Lynch but all had been recommended by resident buyers in Taiwan.

Even though the price quote was excellent, Mr. Lynch had serious reservations when he returned to his hotel room. His years of experience in the Far East had taught him that "saving face" is extremely important to the Asian vendor. He knew of cases where buyers had returned to the United States with excellent price quotes, only to receive a letter from the Asian vendor, shortly before shipping time, indicating that delivery was impossible for a multitude of reasons.

In these cases the buyer had bargained in a fashion that caused the vendor to "lose face." Consequently, the price quote was meaningless, as the manufacturer would not make delivery of goods.

Mr. Lynch believed he had conducted his business and bargaining with the Taiwan vendor in an acceptable manner, but could not be assured of this. If the price quote could be relied upon, it would be a "feather in his cap" and a real competitive advantage to Prichard. If it could not, he would have caused Prichard to have no boys' shirts for the basement, and his job could be in jeopardy.

DISCUSSION QUESTIONS

1. Do you believe Mr. Lynch should sign the contract with the lowest-price Taiwan vendor?
2. Is there anything Mr. Lynch might do in Taiwan to check on the reliability of the price quote?
3. What is "saving face"? How does it differ between an American and an Asian?

CHAPTER 14

SEARS PEOPLE

Photo courtesy of Sears, Roebuck and Company.

Management
of Human Resources

One of the least understood aspects of retail management is the effective utilization of the human resource. Without doubt, labor is the largest single contributor to a retailer's variable cost. A retailer can adhere rigidly to well-planned merchandise budgets, hold markdowns to a minimum, closely scrutinize transportation costs, and control shrinkage—and still suffer continuing poor performance due to inadequate manpower planning and utilization.

Much attention and interest is currently being focused on the problem of employee productivity. In short, in the last few years wages have accelerated at a faster rate than human output per man-hour. Over the last ten years, our annual rate of productivity increased about 3.2 percent per year nationally—compared with continental Europe's 5 to 6 percent and Japan's 11 percent.[1] Admittedly, these are national averages, that are heavily influenced by the manufacturing sectors of the economy, but this trend indicates that other nations of the world are closing the productivity gap.

HUMAN RESOURCE ROLE IN RETAILING

Retail managers may experience a wide variety of personnel responsibilities, depending on the amount of functional specialization in their organizations. For example, a small entrepreneur-retailer may carry the entire responsibility for the performance of the personnel functions. On the other hand, a department manager in a large retail chain may be charged only with the scheduling and supervision of his work force, while all other personnel decisions are made by a representative of a personnel department. In any case, and with whatever degree of responsibility the manager is charged, he should be aware of the entire personnel process. As the immediate representative of his staff, he is the one who relates its needs to higher management and, conversely, it is he who interprets company policy for employees.

The specific technical aspects of personnel administration could easily occupy volumes. It is not the intent of this discussion to make the reader a "personnel expert." Rather, the following presentation is designed to acquaint the individual with a broad overview of retail personnel functions that must be performed either formally or informally by a manager.

Retail Employment Opportunities

The trend toward large, multiunit retail and service outlets has resulted in an increased demand for professional retailers. The professional retailer is employed by these large retail organizations to sell, to manage their departments, outlets, and districts, and to make corporate decisions. There is an increasing demand for retailing professionals who have the ability to meet consumer needs at a profit. The recent availability of detailed sales and inventory information has increased the demand for people who can analyze these data and use them to make the retail unit a more efficient operation. Complex consumer buying motives and purchasing patterns require the interpretation of retailing professionals who can react to rapid, subtle changes in consumer preferences.

Beginning Salaries

Beginning salaries in retailing vary considerably due to the level of skill, knowledge, and experience required. Recently, chain organizations have begun to offer beginning salaries of $6,000 to $10,000 for mid-management store operations personnel. The starting salary is usually not large because employee turnover has been found to be high during the first two years of employment. In addition, the productivity of the employee is not likely to be high because of inexperience and the need to participate in training programs that may last up to two years.

Store support personnel are compensated in relation to their abilities and productivity. Sales people may be salaried or rewarded according to their sales performance. As a result, a good retail sales person can earn a fairly high income relatively soon after employment. Professional staff personnel such as accountants, promotion specialists, etc. generally receive a relatively high income as a beginning salary.

Advancement

Advancement opportunities are usually good in retailing because of the growth in the industry and because many part-time employees are not motivated toward advancement. In total, one management employee is required for every seven retail employees. As stores grow and new shopping centers are developed, the need for retail managers increases. Measurement of a retail employee's worth can be accomplished fairly quickly. Thus employees who have the ability and drive needed to perform well are likely to advance quite rapidly.

Advancement to manager of a large chain store can mean an increase in salary to $15,000 or $30,000. Continued good performance as a store manager can result in an annual income of $75,000 and up. Managers of medium-size chain stores and supermarkets receive annual salaries of $15,000 to $25,000 and up. Retail buyers are also rewarded in this general range.

It is becoming common for a well-motivated, knowledgeable, college-educated person to advance into corporate retail management within ten years of graduation. Some students are now being hired directly out of graduate school to fill vacancies on the corporate retail management team. The increased need for staff specialists such as lawyers, site evaluation experts, marketing researchers, promotion experts, computer programmers, etc. has caused this increase in the hiring of students directly from school. These employees are generally placed in some form of training program to acquaint them with the unique aspects of the specific retail firm.

A breakdown of male retail employee earnings is presented in Table 14-1, which indicates that 16 percent of male retail professionals and managers earned over $15,000 in 1970, and about 4 percent earned in excess of $25,000. Male professionals and managers of businesses and repair and professional services fared better, as about 25 percent of the individuals in each group earned in excess of $15,000 in 1970. The best-paid group was professional and managerial finance, insurance, and real estate employees, 30 percent of whom earned over $15,000 in 1970.

Employment opportunities for women are usually good in retailing. There are many women in high-level retail management positions, and a few are presidents of large retail organizations. Nearly half of the retail buyers are women, who frequently earn between $15,000 and $25,000 per year. Merchandisers of fashion goods prefer women buyers because they are more in tune with fashion trends and because women consumers are still more fashion conscious than men consumers. Women also occupy responsible positions in personnel, advertising, and various retail activities.

Table 14–1 *Distribution of Total Money Earnings for All U.S. Male Civilian Workers 14 Years Old and Over, 1970*

Group	Number (Thousands)	PERCENT DISTRIBUTION						Median Earnings $	Mean Earnings $
		$4,999 or Less	$5,000– $6,999	$7,000– $9,999	$10,000– $14,999	$15,000– $24,999	$25,000 and Over		
Total	56,265	34.4	14.3	23.1	18.9	7.2	2.2	7,152	7,685
Retail Trade, Total	8,060	51.0	13.6	18.3	11.5	4.2	1.4	4,849	5,780
Prof'l & Manag'l	2,278	23.9	13.1	26.0	20.9	11.6	4.4	8,334	9,505
Clerical & Sales	1,677	56.0	15.2	16.1	9.4	2.5	0.7	4,059	4,943
Finance, Insurance & Real Estate, Total	2,265	27.3	11.9	20.0	23.0	13.0	4.8	8,598	9,515
Prof'l & Manag'l	824	9.1	7.2	18.5	35.0	20.7	9.4	12,163	13,340
Clerical & Sales	1,129	31.4	12.7	23.3	19.2	10.7	2.7	7,809	8,187
Business & Repair Services, Total	1,885	40.6	17.7	18.5	14.1	6.9	2.3	6,001	6,993
Prof'l & Manag'l	571	19.4	14.0	18.3	23.6	18.8	6.1	9,713	10,893
Clerical & Sales	139	42.4	15.4	16.2	19.0	5.3	1.8	6,118	6,704
Personal Services, Total	1,595	66.7	13.7	12.8	6.0	2.1	0.7	2,058	3,849
Prof'l & Manag'l	280	39.6	10.1	21.0	18.0	8.4	2.8	7,029	7,809
Prof'l & Related Services, Total	5,594	32.6	12.7	19.2	18.5	10.7	6.5	7,629	9,582
Prof'l & Manag'l	3,714	19.4	9.4	20.6	25.1	15.8	9.7	10,112	12,272

SOURCE   U.S. Bureau of the Census, Washington, D.C., 1971.

Specific Personnel Functions

Personnel functions, in chronological order, include recruitment, selection, placement, performance appraisal, training and development, wage and salary administration, fringe benefit management, attending to the general occupational health and safety of employees, and constant effort to maintain and improve the firm's personnel system. This order of presentation represents a normal employment sequence, but in the real world of retailing the process is not this orderly. A manager may find that he is faced with a "no show" employee problem one minute and the next minute may have to switch his attention to a "suggestive" selling problem. This acknowledgment of the behavior required of a manager in the competitive situation need not be considered a hindrance as long as the manager remains consistent in his decisons on personnel matters. This reinforces the need for a manager to formulate his guiding personnel philosophies ahead of time, so that when crises arise he is adequately prepared to cope with the situation.

JOB EVALUATION: WHAT CONSTITUTES A JOB?

Effective human resource management begins with a successful attempt to achieve some degree of congruency between the skill needs of a job and a person's ability to perform those tasks. A job could be defined as a collection of related assigned duties that must be performed if a task is to be accomplished effectively.

Two points must be emphasized concerning job formulation. First, the quantity of activities and the quality of their performance (which are entailed in any job) will significantly affect the later staffing and compensation processes. Specifically, the more activities that must be performed or the higher the quality of performance, the more one narrows the range of appropriate human resources. For example, a fabric shop in a small rural town ideally may require sales personnel to be accomplished seamstresses; however, the store owner may settle for women who have had home economics in high school and experience in sewing for their families. Job formation should strike a balance between creating jobs that anyone can perform, and hence are likely to be boring and dissatisfying, and jobs that are so unique that only one person in 10,000 could perform them adequately.

The specific job tasks to be accomplished are found in the job descriptions while the specific skill and related attributes of a successful job performer are found in the job specifications. Many small firms do not formalize each job in this manner because the employees are in daily contact with each other and can make informal adjustments in the performance of assigned tasks to see that the jobs get done. Also, the owner-manager is present to give instructions and supervise the individual, which allows greater individual flexibility in the order and method of accomplishing the needed tasks.

Second, a job should have "elastic activities"; that is, the job should be expandable or contractable as a function of the person performing the assigned activities or it should be variable with the seasonality of sales volume. Admittedly, there are a certain, minimum number of activities and a level of quality of performance that any incumbent must meet, but as the job holder learns the job there should be opportunities for continuing challenge or job enlargement. It should be noted that not all individuals want to grow and develop in a job. They may simply want to perform the assigned activities at a minimum level of performance and seek their personal satisfaction elsewhere. There should be a place for both "upward mobiles" and "maintainers" in any retail organization.

JOB EVALUATION IN AN ONGOING ORGANIZATION

Most retail students will not have the opportunity to form their own retail firms but, rather, will enter an organization with the jobs already established. Job evaluation in this situation entails determining what activities each individual is performing and if these tasks are appropriate for the current situation. Such investigations usually disclose needless duplication of effort, overlapping responsibilities, and a host of inefficiencies that creep into any system over time if constant vigilance is not maintained.

The process of job evaluation involves reporting all the activities performed by a person holding a job or position. Such data may be gathered by a self-report based on a diary of daily activities or by a trained observer's recording both the activities performed and the amount of time spent in the performance of each activity. Daily activity schedules are condensed after some appropriate period, such as a week's observations, and the recurring activities are "filtered out." An intensive review of these activities should be made to identify appropriate and inappropriate activities and what changes in the job can be affected. The adjusted routine thus becomes the job description.

Job Description

The job description becomes a checklist of activities that must be performed by anyone occupying a particular position or job. More importantly, the job description serves as a guide for any new employee or promoted job holder by specifically detailing what he or she must do to meet the minimum performance levels of the job. It is important to stress that a job description should not be construed as a limiting classification; it is simply a compliance-level statement of minimum activity performance. While a job description may be biased by self-reporting in favor of the job holder, every effort must be made not to include personal biases in the job specifications.

Job Specifications

Job specifications state the specific personal attributes, abilities, knowledge, and skills necessary to perform a job satisfactorily. Under the provisions of the Equal Rights Act of 1964 (amended in 1972), management may be called upon to prove that job specifications are based solely on ability to perform the assigned tasks and in no way are associated with the race, age, creed, color, sex, religion, or national origin of the job seeker. Many firms in the past have attempted to use minimum educational levels, such as a high school or college diploma, as a screening device to reduce their selection effort. Recently some firms have been called upon by the Equal Employment Opportunity Commission to defend such discriminating criteria and prove their relationship to successful performance of the associated jobs. Failure to establish such task performance–personal ability relationships may result in costly back pay to applicants who were "unlawfully denied" employment or advancement within the firm. Job descriptions must be based on demonstrated ability to perform the jobs successfully.

MANPOWER PLANNING

Once the job evaluation process has been performed, the aggregate manpower or human resource that the store or chain needs must be determined. The retail manager must plan his human resource needs not only for tomorrow's sales coverage but for the entire week, month, and year, and in the case of large chain organizations, for the next five to ten years.

A firm's manpower needs are composed of those people being hired for new positions and those being replaced due to retirements, deaths, "quits," and firings. These latter elements comprise the replacement component that must be recruited, selected, and trained to fill job vacancies during the current planning period. Once these aggregate requirements have been estimated, the manager must identify specific persons who are ready for promotion and those who are promotable when given more time and appropriate training. Also, specific terminations must be determined and the timing of such managerial action must be established.

When these planned personnel changes have been identified and categorized, the manager must consider and plan for store growth and/or decline and determine what effects such changes will have on the quality and quantity of the human resource required. All too often, overly optimistic managers anticipate constant store growth and are caught short when temporary retrenchment is required. Accurate forecasting of the economic and competitive environment permits and encourages the manager to selectively eliminate the marginal producers in his department rather than take the crisis action of indiscriminate payoffs. Through such judicious pruning the entire human resource can be adapted to changing situations.

RECRUITMENT

"Where do you find good people?" This is the essence of the recruitment process. In the past, most organizations had three alternative strategies from which to choose: (1) actively go into the various labor markets and search for talent, (2) passively accept "walk ins" or those individuals who presented themselves for employment, or (3) combine the first two strategies.

Recently, due to the "new social awareness," large retail organizations have been encouraged to recruit potential employees throughout their metropolitan and local areas. Disadvantaged or underrepresented groups are being extended employment opportunities, special upgrading programs are being offered, and additional efforts are being made to bring all segments of the population into the employment mainstream of mass merchandising. "Can do" ability and associated self-confidence should be sought wherever it exists— ghetto, public employment agency, community college or university.

A Changing Personnel Mix

An interesting paradox seems to be developing in the recruitment of retail personnel. In the past, most large retail organizations sought out college graduates, or identified individuals within the organization who demonstrated personal initiative, to form their management trainee corps. In contrast, primarily due to their inability to offer competitive compensation, small- and medium-size retailers sought high school graduates and experienced non-college employees. Now the situation appears to be changing. Large retail organizations are turning to community college graduates and internally developed resources, with a very select few M.B.A. college graduates being sought for corporate-level decision making. Medium-size firms enjoy an influx of college graduates who appear willing to "trade" some salary and security for the personal challenge and risk of assuming more responsibility at an early point in their careers.

The changing recruitment process represents a healthy realization on the part of retail employers that they should attempt to match potential personal abilities and levels of aspiration and achievement with realistic job and career tracks. Not every management trainee will become a store manager or a member of the executive staff. Selection procedures and self-awareness cannot assure such finite discriminatory decisions at this point in the development of testing and evaluative techniques. While some individual profile screening is possible at the present time, much more research and development is needed to refine the man-job matching process.

More importantly, the retail recruitment process should seek individuals who could be called "maintainers." They learn the merchandise, the needs of their customers, and the strengths and weaknesses of their staff and turn their attention to "playing the game" or "tuning the system" to find and provide better retail products and services for "their customers." Each day holds a series of new challenges, even though they repeatedly perform the same set of activities. The personal attributes for a successful career in this kind of retail activity are markedly different from those necessary for a career that revolves around a constantly changing job, job environment, or client system. The overt recognition of such retail career differences in searching for human resources makes the following selection process potentially more effective.

Selection

Selection is the most crucial phase of the personnel process. By definition, the selection process is the exercise of discriminating among potential employees. Discrimination is not inherently bad; it is a fact of life. The basis for choice, or discrimination, is the point at issue. By law, such choice must be made on ability and nothing else.

Aside from the legal issues, selection serves an important function for potential employees that is often overlooked. All firms have a responsibility to each potential employee to assess his opportunities for personal growth and development as an employee. Through use of the latest bias-free psychological techniques, those persons can be identified who have a chance for a successful, personally rewarding work experience in retailing. This assessment should not be considered a guarantee of success.

Applicants who have successfully negotiated "successive hurdle" selective screenings, including interviewing and testing, are usually employed subject to any appropriate union agreement or state laws, such as basic health requirements for food retailers and the like.[2]

An alternate method of selection is "multiple correlation."[3] Instead of rejecting applicants at each evaluation point, the final hiring decision is reached after all the information—including the application form, the interview results, and the reference checks—is complete and any subsequent interviews or evaluation mechanisms have been executed. Some personnel specialists feel that this process is fairer to potential employees, even though such a process admittedly is more time consuming and costly. As the penalties for the use of improper selection systems become well known, more employers may begin to use the "whole man" selection process.

In many large retail firms the personnel specialists who use the selection process make the decision to hire an individual into the firm, but often the employee's specific placement is yet to be determined. Where does he begin his employment, at what time, in what department, for whom? The placement or orientation process is the critical link in employee acculturation into the firm's environment and assimilation into the work group. The new employee, in a large organization particularly, must become acquainted with the firm's operating policies and procedures, introduced to his superior and all members of his peer work group, and apprised of the merchandise in the assigned area. It is a good practice to designate an experienced employee to show the new member "the ropes," which will facilitate his acceptance by the work group as a member of the team.

The employee's personal satisfaction and effective task performance will be highly affected by his initial acceptance or rejection by his relevant work group. Therefore the placement and orientation process deserves the same attention to detail as the recruitment and selection procedures.

DIRECTION AND SUPERVISION OF THE HUMAN RESOURCE: GETTING THE JOB DONE EFFECTIVELY

"Direction in the form of leading, motivating, teaching, guiding, developing, praising, and criticizing is the catalyst which really jells the enterprise."[4] The manager-supervisor is the vital link between that abstraction called "the Establishment" and the staff. He is the facilitator, supporter-critic, father-confessor, representer-negotiator with the "higher powers" for all of his employees.

Effective supervision puts a heavy burden of responsibility on the manager to be "fair but firm" and "consistent but considerate." Supervision is much more than just giving orders and seeing that they are carried out. Supervision is a dynamic, never-ending personal interaction between the supervisor and each worker-colleague, not only on a formal job basis but also on an informal human basis.

Many managers who have been exposed to "human relations" feel that the supervising pattern should be based on sympathetic understanding of individual needs and problems. Unfortunately, this position only breeds individual dependence and, ultimately, a hostile backlash of animosity from the affected employees.

Effective supervision is based on empathetic or problem-oriented, problem-solving behavior. Sympathy simply reinforces negative attitudes that perpetuate an individual's problem. It is the supervisor's responsibility to guide a person in the direction of improvement and development; but one cannot make an individual improve unless the rewards of change outweigh the benefits derived from the current behavior.

Effective supervision stresses positive motivation, enthusiasm for living, and a positive attitude bordering on optimism. "Can't do" has no place in effective supervision. The supervisor must change an ability that is based on a "can do" individual attitude to one of "will do." The appropriate catalyst is proper motivation and rewards.

Unfortunately, many department managers do not have the delegated power to vary rewards among individuals to encourage their personal growth and development. The rewards given by the personnel department are based on cost-of-living adjustments, longevity, or other nonproduction-related criteria. This limitation, combined with various responsibilities, makes the department manager or assistant buyer's job of motivating his staff difficult.

Effective Supervision

Supervision and leadership are not necessarily the same phenomenon, although the terms have been frequently used synonymously. Ideally, one would like to have the leader also be the supervisor, but this is quite rare in practice. An effective supervisor is familiar with behavioral research and is aware of the problems associated with his position.

A supervisor-manager is an individual who has authority over organizational resources and some degree of responsibility for utilizing these resources for the profitable transfer of goods and services. Concurrent with these duties is his responsibility for employee need satisfaction. A supervisor's authority comes to him from the stockholders (or owners) down through the managerial chain, and when an individual accepts employment in an organization he implies consent to this authority. The employee and the employer form two contracts: a legal agreement to comply for a certain period in return for a package of compensation and a psychological contract that assumes equity and fairness to the employee and loyalty and best effort to the employer.[5] Thus the supervisor is charged with more duties and responsibilities than those associated with his formal position.

For centuries, great scholars have debated whether leaders are made or born. Various theories of leadership have been advanced and criticized, such as the trait theory, the "great man" theory, and, more recently, the situationalist theory.[6] The situationalist theory generally states that leadership is a function of the situation; the leader will be that individual who is best able to assess the group need by defining the situation in an ambiguous environment, assessing the talents and skills of his group and marshaling appropriate people to accomplish the group task and provide individual need satisfaction. It becomes apparent that the effective long-term leader must vary his leadership style to cope with a relatively wide range of situations until he has built a "bank account" of group trust and reliance on his personal abilities. When this occurs, he has considerable latitude in his direction and control of his followers.

At this point the potential for a supervisor–informal leader confrontation comes into play. As long as the supervisor-manager can provide his associates with personal need satisfaction, including higher-level need satisfaction, the leader and his informal group will be latent and inactive. However, if the supervisor, through his ineptness or by higher managerial edict, is unable to fulfill employee expectations, an informal leader may come forth, galvanize the employees into social solidarity, and challenge the supervisor for effective control of the group.

Usually, this type of situation is found where subordinates have little job mobility or considerable tenure within an organization. In the retailing field, these individuals may be found in career or professional groups of sales personnel which represent the full-time corps of the sales organization. This problem may not be as potentially great in retailing as in manufacturing because of the former's high turnover in part-time employees. However, if the problem arises, it can be just as dysfunctional in retailing as elsewhere.

In summary, the supervision of employees is a complex task requiring genuine concern for the growth, development, and general well-being of "your people." Leadership should precede supervision, relying on the latter only when all else fails. The effective supervisor, at all levels, translates abstract plans, policies, and procedures into reality through directing, coordinating, and supporting the "doers"—the goal-achieving, motivated employees he works with and through. People make things happen when the leader connects "can do" to "will do" and to "job well done."

Performance Appraisal

Performance appraisal is the process of comparing the current or recent performance of an individual with predetermined performance standards set forth in the job description. The conclusions drawn from this comparative process can be used in several fundamentally different ways, although the most common usage is for merit increases in wage and salary administration. Periodic performance appraisals can also be used to identify individuals who are ready for promotion, or, conversely, it can point out those individuals in need of further training or motivation in their current job.

Many attempts have been made to soften the image and impact of the evaluative process, but no matter how the activity is performed, the process is a potentially threatening situation for the employee. The managerial philosophy vis-à-vis its employees becomes extremely critical in determining how employees view and participate in the evaluative process. Most experts agree that performance appraisals should be made quarterly. The first and third evaluations should be directed primarily at identifying employee deficiencies and creating a systematic supportive program for improvement. These evaluations should review the behavior of the past six months in relation to mutually established, quantifiable goals. Such programs are oriented toward developing the individual's potential and helping him meet some of his higher-order needs for achievement. These reviews should be mutual, collaborative sessions between the individual and his superior, such as described in the management-by-objective approach.[7]

The second and fourth evaluations should be conducted for compensation considerations by the superior and the results should be conveyed to the employee with supporting rationale. Such evaluations should be based on some form of written record, such as production reports, a critical incidents diary, or other appropriate records of behavior.

Once the factual data are collected, the comparison process can be undertaken. Such techniques as the *forced distribution method, graphic rating-scale method, paired comparison method,* or the *forced choice-rating method* can be used to overcome some degree of supervisor bias, such as the "halo effect," "recency effect," and "central tendency effect."[8] In each evaluative situation the supervisor's emphasis must be objectively focused on the person's performance of the assigned and understood tasks. The employee can be expected to perform only the tasks that are contained in the job description and mutually agreed upon. Thus the importance of continually updating job descriptions to keep pace with the ever-changing job situation cannot be overemphasized.

A supplemental approach to performance appraisal has been developed and used more frequently in the last few years. In order to increase personal objectivity, *peer ratings, subordinate ratings, group or committee ratings,* and *field-review methods* have been selectively used.[9] The results of these evaluations can be compared with supervisory evaluations and any obvious discrepancies resolved.

Regardless of the combination of evaluative processes used, it is important to remember that the direct application of a generalized technique requires some specific modifications to deal with situations in a particular organization. In short, the appraisal system must be tested for validity and reliability. This is not only a good management practice but almost a necessity in future evaluations that may be subject to a court test by the Equal Employment Opportunity Commission (brought by an aggrieved employee or by the commission itself). Again, discrimination must take place, but only on the basis of ability.

Appraisal Interview

The appraisal process is not completed until the supervisor-manager discusses the results with the individual being evaluated and they jointly plan for his personal development. Although the concept of mutuality is critical to any behavioral change, it is important to note that not all appraisals result in negative or bad observations. For example, if the performance appraisal reveals that a department manager has met his quarterly sales goal, he should be congratulated and encouraged to apply his "winning game plan" to the next period, along with any needed modifications.

When communicating with the employee about his appraisal results, it is very important for the supervisor-manager to concentrate on problem identification and the generation of alternative solutions and to avoid any remarks that may be damaging to the employee's ego. Such supervisory thinking as "You're a lousy sales person" has no place in constructive performance appraisal. If the employee is not measuring up to agreed-upon standards, what is the reason for this failure? Poor health, personal indifference due to lack of motivation, or inappropriate rewards—any of these could be a contributory cause.

Find the cause, devise a plan of action to remedy the situation, and set specific time/money milestones to check progress. Behavioral change occurs slowly, and an effective supervisor should channel job-related behavior for the mutual benefit of the individual and the organization.

TRAINING AND DEVELOPMENT

Training and development programs vary widely in their scope and complexity. Some firms prefer to recruit trained, motivated employees, to utilize premium compensation packages to retain such individuals, and to leave personal development to each person's initiative and mode of learning, whether it be experience, night school, or other learning situations. On the other end of the spectrum, some organizations have in-house training and development programs specifically tailored for that retail firm and directed toward an individual's lifetime career development within the organization's many activities.

Regardless of the degree of a retailer's commitment to training and development programs, one fact is paramount: when such programs are properly designed, they will greatly facilitate a firm's adaptation to its environment. The benefits to the company are evident. Management must constantly recall that in order to change an organization one must first change the behavior of its people. People adapt, and organizations survive or perish on the basis of the appropriateness of their human adaptation.

Training

Many people in the retail industry tend to use the terms "training" and "development" interchangeably, which generates considerable confusion. Training and/or retraining refers to the acquisition of "basic skills and knowledge required in carrying out various specialized parts of the overall task of the enterprise."[10] Such skills as basic cash register procedure, posting invoices, constructing advertising layouts, or operating a pin-ticket machine all constitute basic skills needed in the operation of some retail operations. Obviously, whenever a procedural change is introduced to increase efficiency or the amount of the average customer sale, the affected employees need to be informed and given an opportunity to practice the new selling technique. Experience has demonstrated that simply telling people about a new technique is not enough; they must practice it until they can demonstrate an acceptable level of performance. For example, you may conduct a session on suggestive selling, but until the sales associates role-play such behavior in realistic situations, the behavior will not be changed. Thus training is primarily oriented toward improving productivity in the present position.

Training methods vary from firm to firm, but the most common include on-the-job training (OJT), conferences or discussion, classroom training, programmed instruction, and education-employer cooperative programs. Recently some government-sponsored programs under the Manpower Development and Training Act (MDTA) have been developed in cooperation with business, such as Job Opportunities in the Business Sector (JOBS) and Work Incentive Programs (WIN), to name just a few. Each program attempts to update the skill of the employee and to bring more individuals into the economic mainstream.[11]

Management Development

Management development, which has a broader scope than training, is directed toward the improvement of an individual's knowledge, skills, attitudes, perceptions, and personal characteristics in current and future managerial positions. Management development is increasingly extended not only to management trainees but to managers at all levels to improve their ability to cope with interpersonal relations. Interpersonal relations in retailing have become more important in recent years as more specialization has been required to keep pace with evolving markets. Cooperation and collaboration spell success, whereas individualism in large retail organizations is a relic of the past.

Management development may take the form of "understudy" assignments, such as an assistant buyer, job rotation, or lateral promotions, to gain an appreciation of different departmental operations and customer needs. Project or committee assignment, staff meetings, or simply coaching in an on-the-job assignment may also serve the same purpose. Many professional associations and consulting firms offer management development courses both on and off the company's premises. Such development activities may take the form of in-basket exercises, management games, role-playing situations, sensitivity training, or professional reading. Regardless of the mode of instruction, the objective is the same: to increase the individual's ability to cope with a wide variety of situations by recognizing his personal biases and to help him to see the "real world" more objectively.

In summary, training and development is an expensive, never-ending price that an organization must pay as part of its costs of remaining competitive. Without some realistic program of constructive innovation, a retail firm's days on the economic scene are numbered.

COMPENSATION

"How much should I pay 'em?" This question, for many, sums up the compensation situation. Today the actual hourly or monthly wage represents an increasingly smaller portion of the total compensation cost. In addition to the federal minimum wage or the union-negotiated wage or the salary determined in the labor market, the retail manager must consider:

1. Incentive sales programs
2. Federally required social security payments
3. Unemployment insurance and workmen's compensation payments
4. Fringe benefits of life, health, and accident insurance
5. Retirement plans
6. Supplemental unemployment benefits
7. Paid vacations, holidays, and sick leave
8. Time paid but not worked, such as coffee breaks, lunch periods, time off for deaths in the family, and voting
9. Costs of maintaining employee records
10. Merchandise discounts to employees.

Some retail organizations offer profit-sharing plans for certain qualified career professional personnel and the executive staff. The question is not, "How much should I pay 'em," but, "What set of rewards is appropriate for the sales associate, stockroom employee, or department manager?"

A new concept of "cafeteria compensation" is being introduced on the

American business scene.[12] Under this concept the employer determines his total compensation cost per employee within certain classifications, then subtracts the amount of legally liable charges for governmental programs, and allows the individual to determine how the rest of the compensation money will be allocated among the remaining alternative compensation components. For example, a young person without responsibilities may choose maximum wages, minimum life insurance coverage, moderate health insurance protection, and maximum paid time off. A person in his late fifties may choose minimum life insurance coverage, moderate wages, and maximum health protection. Although admittedly still in the experimental stage, this new concept of compensation shows promise of dealing with individual needs realistically, and may therefore improve employee motivation and productivity.

Viewing the compensation question from a broader perspective than day-to-day individual compensation issues, retail executives have come to the realization that they are well advised to compensate their human resources at a premium level and hence indirectly avoid the threat of unionization. As noted earlier, it has been shown that employees take collective action when they perceive that they are not being treated equitably. Consequently, if the employees are currently receiving total compensation benefits that are greater than a union can deliver through the process of collective bargaining, the employees are reluctant to join in union activity. Thus many managers see their alternative as beneficial to both the employees and the firm over the long term. Whether this strategy will continue to be successful in the future remains to be seen.

UNION—MANAGEMENT RELATIONS

A complete discussion of industrial relations is beyond the scope of this text. It is important, however, to note some philosophical and legal aspects of union-management relations. From a philosophical point of view, a retail manager can view a union as a threat in a situation in which what one party gains the other loses—the win-lose concept. The union movement is from such a viewpoint, the adversary to be resisted by all legal means.

An alternative perspective is that a union can be a constructive partner in the resolution of common or complementary interests.[13] Operating under this premise, each partner is not out to increase his share of the economic rewards at the cost of the other party; rather, each is vitally interested in increasing the absolute amount of economic reward possible. History has emphasized the win-lose strategy, while the international economic scene suggests that national unions and retail management may find it more appropriate to act as partners to maintain or increase this nation's competitiveness in the world marketplace.

A more particular concern to the retailer is the day-to-day relationship with the employees and the interpretation of a union contract. No matter how carefully the words of a labor agreement are chosen, no matter how well the negotiating representatives agree with each other on points in the contract, the provisions of the contract will be interpreted differently by both sides. If the supervisor and a union employee disagree, and that disagreement cannot be resolved by the union representative (the shop steward or his equivalent) and the supervisor's superior, the dispute becomes a formal grievance and must be settled by formal, agreed-upon procedures. Once grievance procedures are initiated, the supervisor-manager has lost control of the situation and must abide by the decision reached behind closed doors in a formal hearing. It becomes quite clear that when a retail firm becomes unionized the absolute formal authority of a supervisor-manager is markedly reduced, which means he cannot rely on an autocratic supervisory style to supervise his department effectively. Consultation and participation with employees in decision making, in a limited sense, becomes a practical necessity if the supervisor is going to be successful.

Another important implication of unionization is that the supervisor-manager loses much of his discretion in the use of his firm's reward and punishment mechanisms. In order to encourage, motivate, and channel his subordinates' behavior he must rely on informal methods of leadership such as persuasion, influence, and negotiation relationships. Often a supervisor's management style may be dictated by company policy toward union employees, such as "following the book," "dealing at arm's length," etc.—in which case, if a supervisor assumes an independent supervisory style, he risks higher management's wrath. As Professor Keith Davis remarks, "Truly the first line supervisor is the man in the middle."[14]

SUMMARY

This chapter has attempted to give the student of retailing a brief glimpse into the problems associated with the management of human resources in retailing. Entire courses are available to prepare the student to deal with the intricacies of the personnel management process, but only selected highlights have been presented to acquaint the student with the myriad problems that may require special knowledge and expertise. Today, the supervisor-manager should be mature enough to admit he may not have all the answers to such problems and that he should seek and accept the advice of personnel experts who are available either in the firm or in the local community. Ignorance is *not* bliss.

In the years ahead the management of human resources will demand increasing attention. Rising labor costs, reflecting—in part—rising levels of employee education, knowledge and skill, combined with rising levels of personal expectations of both the employee and the customer, will demand creative solutions to sales associate–customer-client problems. The management of human resources, today and tomorrow, constitutes a challenge worthy of the same major attention and concern given the other aspects of retailing—price, product, place, promotion, and competition.

QUESTIONS

1. What constitutes the personnel function? Who must bear the ultimate responsibility for its performance?
2. Why is retailing considered a "people" business? How does the merchandising policy affect the personnel function?
3. Many retailers, when asked to define their most difficult problem, say that personnel problems relating to retaining hourly paid employees is the most vexing. What specific suggestions might one make to deal with this problem?
4. What state and federal laws must the retailer observe when he or she performs the personnel function? (Hint: Library research may reveal other laws not presented in the chapter.)
5. What procedural ramifications does the Civil Rights Act Title VII (amended in 1972) have for the hiring policies of the large chain retailer? How is the small entrepreneur affected?
6. In what way does the Civil Rights Act of 1964 (amended in 1972) affect the performance of the personnel function in regard to current employees? Be specific.
7. Suppose you are a small retailer who is faced with the prospect of eventual unionization unless you take some affirmative action. Design a plan of action to deal effectively and legally with this problem.
8. What personal qualities are appropriate for supervising? Is it possible to develop such behavioral patterns or must one be born with them?
9. What part does compensation play in encouraging personnel to perform at the compliance level? At the motivated level? Be specific.
10. What specific steps can a retailer take to reduce his selling/non-selling costs and still remain competitive? What effect will such actions have on employee morale and satisfaction?

FOOTNOTES

[1] *Business Week,* September 1972, p. 112.

[2] Herbert J. Chruden and Arthur W. Sherman, Jr., *Personnel Management* (3d ed.; Cincinnati: South-Western Publishing Co., 1968), p. 161.

[3] Ibid.

[4] Arion Q. Sartain and Atlan W. Baker, *The Supervisor and His Job* (2d ed.; New York: McGraw-Hill, 1972), p. 14.

[5] Edgar H. Schein, *Organization Psychology* (Englewood Cliffs, N.J.: Prentice-Hall, 1965), p. 11.

[6] Fred E. Fiedler, *A Theory of Leadership Effectiveness* (New York: McGraw-Hill, 1967), p. 36.

[7] George S. Odiorne, *Personnel Administration by Objectives* (Homewood Ill.: Richard D. Irwin, 1971), p. 448.

[8] Wendell French, *The Personnel Management Process* (2d ed.; Boston: Houghton Mifflin, 1970), pp. 291–308.

[9] Chruden and Sherman, *Personnel Management,* p. 277.

[10] French, *The Personnel Management Process,* p. 481.

[11] Chruden and Sherman, *Personnel Management,* p. 221.

[12] George W. Hettenhouse, "Compensation Cafeteria for Top Executives," *Harvard Business Review* (September–October 1971), pp. 113–119.

[13] Richard E. Walton and Robert B. McKersie, *A Behavioral Theory of Labor Relations* (New York: McGraw-Hill, 1965), p. 4.
[14] Keith Davis, *Human Relations at Work: The Dynamics of Organizational Behavior* (New York: McGraw-Hill, 1967), p. 115.

SANGER-HARRIS
Personnel—Hiring Practices

The personnel department of Sanger-Harris Department Stores was faced with the need to find improved screening techniques to determine security risks among job applicants.

Sanger-Harris was concerned about this problem for each of its eight stores throughout the Dallas metropolitan area. As a member of Federated Department Stores, Sanger-Harris had access to information on what was being done by other department stores throughout the nation. The divisional manager of personnel for Sanger-Harris stated that the problem was industry-wide for retailers across the United States. She continually attended personnel seminars sponsored by Federated and other groups and kept up to date on the current literature. Although some solutions were discovered through these sources, the overall answer for a department store remained one of personally custom designing a system to meet local conditions.

A solution applicable in Chicago might not work in Dallas due to state and local regulations, a different population mix, and other regional differences.

The management of Sanger-Harris believed that shrinkage due to employee theft might account for more dollar losses than those from shoplifting.

A theft ring, involving company employees, had recently been uncovered. This and other industrywide examples underscored the need for improved applicant screening techniques.

The task of screening applicants had increased in complexity due to new federal regulations, particularly those from the Equal Employment Opportunity Commission (EEOC). The new regulations prohibited asking many of the questions which had formerly been asked of job applicants.

Questions dealing with dates of arrests and bonding refusals were examples of the types of questions which should no longer be asked.

Checking references and prior employers was not foolproof either. Former employers were often unwilling to divulge the true reason why an employee was discharged, even though it might have been for theft. This was particularly true in the case of phone calls to former employers and companies unknown by the Sanger-Harris personnel department.

Rather than press charges in court against employees charged with theft, a normal practice by employers was to discharge the employee and to write "No Rehire" on his files. Thus, for fear of libel suits, former employers were reluctant to tell an unfamiliar phone voice that an individual had been guilty of theft.

The polygraph was used by employers, but it was time consuming and cost around $25 per test. Although it had not been ruled illegal for use in employee hiring, there was a general feeling among employers that it would be one of the next practices to be prohibited.

To avoid the cost of administering the polygraph, some employers were asking, "Would you be willing to take a polygraph test?" Persons who said no were usually disqualified from further consideration. This also was a questionable future practice, in view of new regulations, and it had the dual problem of eliminating potentially good employees who simply did not wish to take the test.

Other scientific tests, such as a urinalysis, were also available but again were expensive. A urinalysis was used to determine if an individual was addicted to drugs. The close relationship between drug addiction and crime made it mandatory to determine the possibility of durg abuse before hiring an applicant. Urinalysis had been used, but the cost was $30 per test and special conditions were necessary, similar to those in a clinic.

With the increasing use of the computer in retailing, it was possible to check applicants' information against birth certificates, military numbers, social security numbers, and other identifying documents. This prevented rehires of bad risks but did not prevent hiring new high-risk employees.

To compound the problem, Sanger-Harris was faced with finding a better method for hiring temporary employees for the upcoming pre-Christmas season. With the tremendous number of part-time employees needed for this season, the procedure of following the slower security checks used for full-time applicants became impossible.

DISCUSSION QUESTIONS

1. Is Sanger-Harris fighting a losing battle? Should it continue to improve applicant screening techniques, or instead, improve security in the store and on the docks, possibly by one-way mirrors and other systems used by the U.S. Post Office to catch dishonest employees?

2. What should Sanger-Harris do if an employee is found with stolen merchandise? Is it worth the time, money, and potentially bad publicity to press charges, hoping for a conviction?

3. What do you think of the use of polygraphs, urinalyses, and other scientific tests to screen applicants?

4. Check the recent federal regulations affecting employment practices and then secure an employment application form from a local department store. Do you believe the store is in violation of these regulations? If so, what does the store need to change to comply with the regulations? How

will these changes affect the efficiency of its pre-employment security system?

5. Suppose that an employee was fired by Sanger-Harris for theft and five years later applies for employment with another store outside the city. What should the personnel department of Sanger-Harris tell the other store? To whom does Sanger-Harris have the greatest responsibility—
    a. The employee, who may have reformed?
    b. The other store?
    c. Themselves?
6. With the close relationship between drug addiction and crime, should Sanger-Harris ever hire an applicant with a drug record?

THE WIENER CORPORATION
Maintaining In-Store Personnel

The Wiener Corporation is a small, diversified chain of shoe stores, specialty leisure-wear shops, and men's wear stores.

These stores are located in an eight-state area surrounding the home office of New Orleans. Sales have tripled during the past five years—to $15,500,000—and the future is even more promising.

With locations in the booming south and southwest, plus a history of success and a young management team, Mr. Sidney Wiener, executive vice-president, was predicting sales of $30 million within two years. As an example of the planned growth, ten new leisure-wear shops, called "The Ranch," and three new Danny's Men's Wear shops were on the drawing boards.

Management realized that this growth would be possible only with the aid of highly motivated employees. This was one of the most difficult tasks facing the company. Buildings could be built rapidly, and merchandise could be acquired, but if the right in-store personnel were unavailable there would be no growth.

In commenting on this Mr. Wiener stated, "We are investing heavily in people, but retailing still faces a problem of attracting and keeping highly motivated people." He also stated that the company simply would not pursue its expansion plans without the right people.

The Wiener Corporation is known for its higher pay scale, relative to other retailers. A profit-sharing plan is also in use and open to all employees.

Other incentives include a stock option and bonus program on the basis of merit. The bonus is paid on a quarterly basis, with an accompanying letter of congratulations from the president which is sent to both the husband and wife.

The spouse of the employee is always included in such programs as it is felt that he or she could be a powerful behind-the-scenes motivator.

A $50 savings bond is sent to employees who send fresh ideas to the president. Sometimes the bond is sent even if the idea is not used, as management feels this serves as a motivating tool.

Under this program of salary plus incentives a store manager could earn $20,000 per year, not including the stock option or profit-sharing plans. With a record of stock splits and increasing market value, the regular acquisition of stock could provide an employee with a good-size "nest egg" over the years.

The company purposely made it possible for managers to attain excellent standards of living, since management believed that many life style aspects (such as travel) available in other professions were not available to store managers due to the time demands of their job. As a result it was felt that, with a higher income, store managers would seek peer groups with similar incomes and thus become acquainted with interesting people of more sophisticated tastes. The association with these peer groups and the improvement in life style would, hopefully, offset the disadvantages inherent in store management.

Although the company is a deep south firm, it is fully integrated, with multi-race hiring and promotion practices enforced throughout. Sex and age discrimination are also foreign to the company.

A man of seventy-two who serves as a full-time employee was told he could remain as long as he wishes, provided he could perform his tasks.

There is no formal program to attract college graduates, but neither are there policies against them. Mr. Wiener stated that he believes a college degree has never been necessary for most areas of retailing, and in many cases only contributes to employee boredom and job dissatisfaction.

Mr. Wiener also believes that one of the principal differences between his corporation and other retailers is that the telephone is an open link to any member of executive management. All employees are informed they may voice their problems, complaints, or suggestions to management at any time simply by picking up a phone—or by coming in to see them. It is not necessary to first "go through" their immediate supervisors.

Employees are also free to discuss personal problems with management. In some cases they have been referred to a mental health program at the cost of the company. The general feeling is that if an employee is the kind the company wants, that "extra step" will be taken to solve his problems. It is estimated that success with this approach has been about 50 percent.

The company depends largely upon word-of-mouth encouragement by its present employees to recruit new people. Limited use is made of classified ads, and personal- and executive-search agencies are never used.

Because of the planned growth, and the need to recruit, employees had to come from many other retailing firms.

The company experienced no difficulty in filling middle- or top-management positions. Executives from firms in large midwestern and eastern cities were continually inquiring about employment opportunities with Wiener Corporation. Instead, it was the acquisition and motivation of the store managers and personnel positions that created a problem.

Relative to many other retailing chains, the Wiener Corporation had experienced fewer problems in this area, but nevertheless recognized their existence. Symptoms were employee boredom, lack of company loyalty, and a don't-care attitude in terms of serving the customer. In addition, shrinkage from internal theft was beginning to be publicly admitted as a serious problem by retailers throughout the United States, and the Wiener Corporation was no exception. Mr. Wiener was one of the first top-level executives to publicly state that internal theft, not shoplifting, was the main cause of heavy shrinkage.

In addition, there seemed to be a prevalent and growing attitude of "instantism" among many employees and in society in general. These persons were unwilling to wait and work for advancements and higher positions; rather, they felt these things should come "now," regardless of training, experience, or seniority.

Management was also concerned that, as the company grew, many employees fall victim to the "Peter principle" (namely, that individuals are promoted to higher levels until they are no longer competent), although this was not considered to be a present problem.

Mr. Wiener stated that there also seemed to be a growing attitude among store-level employees of, "Go ahead, fire me—who cares?" He felt that perhaps this was some form of self-punishment, but really couldn't explain the reason.

In contrast to conventional wisdom, this attitude did not change during a recent recession.

In spite of company incentives, a highly competitive base pay, and other company policies, the fact remained that many employees did not seem to be motivated even though they faced family responsibilities and the possibility of more limited job opportunities.

DISCUSSION QUESTIONS

1. Do you agree with the Wiener Corporation in the philosophy of offering higher incomes for store managers to create different life styles? How much of a motivating role do you believe money plays?
2. Are there other programs the Wiener Corporation should initiate to ensure the motivation of employees? If so, what are they and how do they work?
3. What is the Peter principle? What, if anything, can management do to protect against this problem?
4. What do you think of the policies employed by the Wiener Corporation? Can they be used by all retailers?

CHAPTER 15

Financial Summary 1964-1972

J. C. Penney Company, Inc.
and Consolidated Subsidiaries

	1972	1971	1970	1969	1968	1967	1966	1965	1964
Results for year (In millions)									
Sales	$5,529.6	$4,812.2	$4,354.7	$3,912.7	$3,379.2	$2,927.0	$2,702.8	$2,407.9	$2,155.1
Per cent increase from prior year	14.9	10.5	11.3	15.8	15.5	8.3	12.2	11.7	14.1
Credit sales as per cent of sales*	38.7	36.8	36.9	37.4	35.5	35.4	33.2	31.4	29.2
Income before income taxes and other unconsolidated subsidiaries	311.2	265.6	219.9	231.3	237.3	177.5	156.5	152.1	133.2
Per cent of sales	5.6	5.5	5.1	5.9	7.0	6.1	5.8	6.3	6.2
Net income	162.6	135.7	114.1	114.3	111.5	94.3	82.4	80.7	69.2
Per cent increase (decrease) from prior year	19.8	18.9	(0.2)	2.5	18.3	14.4	2.1	16.6	23.8
Per cent of sales	2.9	2.8	2.6	2.9	3.3	3.2	3.0	3.4	3.2
Per cent of stockholders' equity	16.4	18.0	16.8	18.7	20.6	19.2	18.3	19.5	20.6
Dividends	59.5	55.3	52.9	52.6	46.3	45.8	43.8	43.5	37.8
Increase in reinvested earnings	103.2	80.4	61.2	61.8	65.2	48.5	38.6	37.4	36.9
Depreciation	52.5	45.5	38.4	34.9	28.8	27.0	24.0	20.1	17.3
Capital expenditures	185.5	237.2	213.4	175.8	127.7	111.0	71.4	46.4	40.5
Per share results									
Net income—primary	2.86	2.46	2.14	2.16	2.12	1.78	1.57	1.56	1.35
—fully diluted	2.86	2.43	2.08	2.10	2.08	1.78	1.57	1.56	1.35
Dividends	1.05	1.01	1.00	1.00	.90	.90	.86	.86	.75
Stockholders' equity	19.93	17.55	14.14	12.84	11.56	10.28	9.32	8.58	7.87
Financial position at year end (In millions)									
Assets	2,153.7	1,923.9	1,712.2	1,473.2	1,207.3	953.9	847.0	744.8	667.4
Working funds	732.7	554.7	492.0	407.7	422.1	277.0	297.3	295.7	273.0
Customer receivables—net									
J. C. Penney Financial Corporation . .	1,043.3	824.9	758.2	674.8	532.5	483.2	439.9	298.7	188.0
J. C. Penney Company, Inc.	67.7	46.5	29.4	25.7	56.7	13.8	12.7	63.0	101.1
Merchandise inventories	1,047.1	879.4	789.5	717.3	616.5	487.0	491.0	396.8	319.7
Long term debt	216.9	210.1	326.7	171.6	125.0	—	—	—	—
Stockholders' equity	1,138.0	989.6	753.3	680.6	611.0	540.7	490.0	451.3	413.8
Stockholders and employees									
Number of stockholders at year end	71,000	68,000	66,000	64,000	59,000	56,000	56,000	55,000	53,000
Average number of shares outstanding (millions)	56.7	54.9	53.1	53.0	52.8	52.6	52.6	52.6	52.6
Number of employees at year end	175,000	162,000	152,000	137,000	119,000	104,000	102,000	88,000	78,000

*Excludes sales of food supermarkets and European operations, which do not offer consumer credit.

Photo courtesy of J. C. Penney Company, Inc.

Obtaining and Conserving Money through Control

Adequate capital is a basic requirement for all retail operations. It is impossible to operate a retail outlet successfully unless sufficient funds are available, because the need for money is present in all phases of retailing. This chapter discusses sources of funds and the control concepts used in accounting, inventory evaluation, and finance. The cash flow analysis and financial ratios used in retailing also are presented.

The amount of capital required should be estimated before making a commitment to purchase, lease, or build. The estimate must include a reasonable safety margin that allows for unexpected demands for money not included in the original, carefully prepared estimate. The type and size of the retail outlet determine the capital requirement. It may require as little as a few thousand dollars to establish a small, limited-line outlet in leased facilities, while several million dollars may be needed to establish a large, fully stocked, wide-merchandise-line outlet in store-owned facilities. The purchaser of an established retail outlet can estimate the capital requirements by using company records. The purchase price for the outlet can be added to the estimated costs needed for remodeling, inventory changes, living expenses, additional working capital, and contingencies until the outlet is opened for business. Then a cash flow analysis can be performed to estimate ongoing capital requirements.

Estimating capital requirements for a new firm's outlet is considerably more difficult. Cost information may be obtained from comparable retail outlets in other communities. Trade associations, the Small Business Administration, university research bureaus, and other business organizations frequently prepare publications which contain cost estimates. Careful estimation procedures should also be used to ensure that inflation and unforeseen contingencies have been accounted for in the final estimation. Fixture and equipment costs should also be estimated, by obtaining bids from at least two different logical suppliers.

SOURCES AND APPLICATIONS OF FUNDS

The sources from which capital may be obtained can be evaluated after the estimated capital requirement is determined. Generally, the retailer's own capital is the most important source of retail funds. Financing may be difficult to obtain unless the owner's investment funds account for about half of the required funds.

Three different types of retail financing are required to ensure that adequate funds are available. "Short-term credit" consists of funds that are used mainly as operating capital for periods of less than one year. "Intermediate term credit" consists of loans needed to finance fixed assets, such as machines, fixtures, equipment, etc. These loans vary in length from one to ten years and are generally paid on a monthly basis. "Long-term financing" involves loans made primarily to purchase buildings and land. They are generally made for more than ten years.

Sources of Short-Term Funds

Several sources are available for obtaining the short-term funds. As discussed in Chapter 13, operating (short-term) capital may be obtained from vendors, who may make an inventory available on a 30-, 60-, or 90-day credit basis. These terms may allow the retailers to turn inventories over once before the invoice is due. It must be recalled, however, that considerable cash discounts can be obtained by paying bills before they are due. Thus firms may find it profitable not to use this source of funds unless it is a matter of financial necessity.

Commercial banks provide short-term loans that can be used for operating capital if the retailer can show (by a cash flow and/or net worth analysis) that the loan will be repaid within a specified period. Simple commercial loans, generally made for 30 to 120 days, are one of the most common methods of obtaining short-term financing. Commercial banks generally make this short-term loan for seasonal financing and/or the building up of retail inventories. These loans may be secured by requiring the retailer to pledge some type of collateral, such as inventory, accounts receivable, stock, etc. If the bank believes it can rely upon the retailer's credit reputation, it can make an unsecured loan (which doesn't require a pledge based upon physical collateral but upon a signature) for a specified credit purpose.

Floor-plan financing is an example of bank financing which requires the retailer to use inventories as collateral. Floor-inventory financing is most commonly used by retailers who do not have sufficient working capital to purchase an adequate inventory for their marketing needs. To be eligible for a loan in this case, the inventory must have unit value high enough to permit separate and positive identification by serial number.

The procedures for handling floor-plan financing begin when the supplier delivers the merchandise and prepares a draft on the retailer's bank for the full cost of the merchandise. The bank then contacts the retailer to determine if the merchandise is acceptable and if he wants to pay for the merchandise. If payment is to be made, the bank usually debits the retailer's account with 10 percent of the value of the merchandise plus freight costs. The remaining 90 percent of the cost is due in 90 days, but financing can be obtained on up to three additional 90-day periods, providing at least 10 percent of the balance is paid before each option is renewed. The bank sends the original payment made by the retailer, along with its check for the remaining 90 percent of the merchandise value, to the supplier. This payment is made as soon as the retailer indicates the merchandise has been accepted.

Banks that lend money under the floor-plan financing agreement usually inspect the inventory monthly on an unannounced basis. The retailers are also required to keep all merchandise insured. The interest rate charged on floor-plan financing is generally 1 to 2 percent above the prime interest rate.

Retailers can also sell their customers' notes (or installment promissory notes) to a commercial bank to obtain short-term funds. The bank then advances money to the retailer against the customer notes. Another alternative is to retain the retail customer notes and use them as collateral for obtaining short-term loans from other sources. The interest rate charged by banks will vary according to the going interest rate, the degree of risk associated with the retail firm involved, and the financial reputation of the borrower. The interest rate charged by commercial banks is usually lower than the savings the retail outlet could obtain by paying its bills promptly and getting a cash discount from its vendors. Not using vendor credit to the limit also provides a safety margin which could be used if unforeseen needs for funds occur.

Factoring offers yet another possibility for short-term financing. Factoring involves selling a retailer's accounts receivable to another party. If the accounts receivable are sold "without recourse," the buyer (or factor) assumes the loss resulting from any uncollected accounts. The relatively high commission—usually 1 to 3 percent of the total amount—is one disadvantage of this method of financing.

Sources of Intermediate Term Funds

Intermediate term credit, used to finance fixed assets (such as equipment, machines, fixtures, etc.), is generally granted for one to ten years. Such capital is needed as a means for small retailers to finance fixed assets which will depreciate over time. The primary difference between an intermediate term loan and a short-term loan is that a formal loan agreement is always needed. Many banks extend a *line of credit* to borrowers of intermediate term loans. The line of credit is a fixed amount, say $50,000, that a retail borrower can have outstanding at any one time. The retailer can borrow continually up to that specified amount on a permanent basis.

Frequently, suppliers of capital equipment that is required in retailing will lease their products to retailers. Equipment leasing can reduce the fixed-capital investment needed so that the retailer's funds can be used in other, hopefully better-yielding activities. Other liberalized trade credit techniques— such as lease with option to buy, buying equipment on installment terms, etc.—are also frequently used to provide a source of intermediate retail capital.

Sources of Long-Term Funds

Long-term loans can be used to construct a new building or to buy a store or warehouse. Long-term credit differs from intermediate credit in the type of security needed. The lender must have assurances that the retailer is stable and large enough to be in existence over a period of years. Mortgages make up the bulk of long-term debt owed by small retailers because they seldom have the resources for selling a bond issue. Small retailers frequently must invest their own savings in the firm to meet long-term credit needs.

Mortgage bankers and insurance companies may be used to finance real estate or construction capital requirements. Generally, these financial firms are interested only in financing large projects and hence are more likely to finance large retail outlets or entire shopping centers. Local savings and loan associations are good sources for long-term loans for small retailers who have a good credit reputation.

Other Financial Sources

The Small Business Administration (SBA), an agency of the federal government, provides short-, intermediate-, and long-term retail capital to small retailers. In addition to making cooperative loans with private lending firms and making direct loans to small retailers, the SBA also provides financial and management assistance. If borrowing appears to be the answer to a retail firm's problem, the SBA will help the retailer obtain a bank loan or will furnish part of the required capital itself, providing the bank cannot lend all of the money and SBA funds are available.

If the local bank cannot lend any of the money, the SBA will consider lending the entire amount as a *direct government loan*. In loaning money to small retail firms, the SBA is not in competition with private sources. The SBA steps in only when private financing cannot meet the needs of the small businessman. SBA loans vary in amount, from $500 to $350,000.

In addition to its general loan program, the SBA offers a small loan program which is designed to meet the needs of the very small or newly established retailer. The limited-loan participation plan is designed to help worthy firms which have only limited tangible collateral. Under this plan, private banks and the SBA cooperate in extending financing to the small retailer.

Another source of capital is the Small Business Investment Corporation, which is licensed and regulated by the SBA. It is designed to be a profit-making company, and may be either privately or publicly owned and operated. The SBIC is in business to furnish capital and consulting and advisory services to small businesses.

Numerous other federal loan sources are applicable to the small retailer in certain instances. A retailer who is a veteran could utilize the Veterans' Administration to acquire real estate, supplies, equipment, and working capital. Loans can also be obtained through the Bureau of Indian Affairs by Indians and Eskimos who have no other source of financing. Loans are also granted to citizens of other minority groups through the SBA.

A small retailer who has justifiable needs for additional capital, and a financial structure strong enough to offer reasonable assurance of success and repayment, should be able to obtain the necessary funds from one of the previously mentioned sources.

ACCOUNTING SYSTEMS

Sound recordkeeping and accounting practices are needed to conduct a successful retail business. The numbers and types of records needed depend upon management goals and needs. Small retailers may not need as much detailed data on each merchandise line or department as large retailers require. The small retailer or the branch manager may be able to "observe" sales and inventories on each line and make decisions (based upon merchandise movement) before any of the financial records are available. It is never-theless advisable to use accounting records to confirm his observation and to ensure that the firm's profitability corresponds to expectations.

A well-designed system of accounting should provide a record of all transactions which can be used to prepare periodic financial statements and reports. Properly prepared financial records can provide measurements of profitability and retail performance. An effective accounting system must also provide a basis for business planning. Only after a retailer can determine "where he has been" can he determine "where he is going." Thus complete and accurate financial records are needed, and must be used, to make retail decisions. Accounting records are also used to detect errors, theft, and fraud. Finally, retailers must have an accurate record of the availability and use of their assets because profits are maximized by making the most efficient use of these assets.

Several accounting terms and concepts make important contributions to the basic records used by retailers. An "asset" is anything *owned* by the retailer and a "liability" is anything *owed* by the retailer. Retail *assets* consist of land, buildings, equipment, furniture, fixtures, supplies, inventory, cash, and accounts receivable. Retail *liabilities* consist of accounts payable, notes payable, accrued wages, and accrued taxes.

The owner's "investment" or "equity" in the retail enterprise amounts to the difference between the total retail assets and total retail liabilities. All accounting systems are based on this concept: assets equal liabilities plus owner's equity.

Nearly all accounting records are based upon the "double entry" con-cept, which simply records the twofold effect every transaction has upon the equation, assets = liabilities + capital. For example, assume that a retailer pays $1,000 in cash for merchandise that has just been delivered to his store. In this case the value of one asset (inventory) will be increased by $1,000, but the value of another asset (cash) is reduced by $1,000, the total asset value remains unchanged, and the equation remains in balance.

In accounting terminology, every transaction involves a "debit entry" in one account and a "credit entry" in another account, so that total debits always equal total credits.

Basic Retail Records

The financial record of a retail outlet begins when merchandise is pur-chased by the retailer and the information is recorded. Most retailers bring this information together by recording daily transactions in one or more journals which provide a complete record of all transactions in chronological order. Many retailers transfer the journal-contained information to *ledger accounts*, which are records of the increases and decreases of one type of income, expense, asset, liability, or capital. Retailers use as many ledger accounts as they believe they need to observe their business activities.

Ledger accounts are used to organize the data in the journals so that the business transactions can be grouped. This grouping provides the information needed to prepare the two basic financial statements: the *balance sheet* and the *income statement*. Information contained in either the balance sheet or the income statement can be used to make nearly every analysis needed to measure the financial performance of the retail enterprise.

Balance Sheet

The balance sheet shows the financial condition of the firm on a given date. This report is called the balance sheet because it represents the equation, assets = liabilities + owner's equity, and thus summarizes the various assets, liabilities, and owner's equity accounts. The balance sheet also contains information on the relationship between creditors' claims on the assets and the percent of the assets held in the form of owner's equity in the firm. A comparison of a current balance sheet with balance sheets for previous periods allows the proprietor to conveniently observe changes in the firm's financial condition. The balance sheet is a good summary report which eliminates the necessity of examining many detailed records.

Figure 15–1 is a typical balance sheet, together with brief explanations of the terms contained in a balance sheet. Most of the terms are described in sufficient detail in Figure 15–1 so that they don't require further explanation. Those balance sheet concepts which require elaboration will now be discussed.

Current assets (cash, accounts receivable, inventories, and government securities) may be turned into cash quickly. *Retail inventories* comprise finished merchandise which is displayed in the store itself. Inventory values change as prices fluctuate, so retail inventories are usually valued at cost or current market price, whichever is lower. This method avoids overstatement of earnings and assets as a result of wholesale price increases.

Three methods are used to establish inventory values. The *first in–first out* (FIFO) method assumes that the "oldest" items are sold before later-purchased items are sold. This method allows "inventory profits" (caused by increased merchandise prices at the wholesale level) to be included as income. Such inventory profits are not realized profits if the rising wholesale prices are followed by a price decline.

Another method of determining inventory evaluation is the *last in–first out* (LIFO) method. This method is designed to cushion the impact of rapid price changes by matching current costs against current revenues. Sales are costed on the basis of inventory purchased most recently (last in) while first-in inventory is regarded as unsold merchandise. The LIFO method results in the application of a higher unit cost to items sold and a lower unit cost to inventory still unsold during a period of rising prices.

The *retail inventory method* is used in many chain stores to gain better control over store managers by charging goods to stores both at cost and retail prices. The retail method of inventory evaluation provides a procedure for determining the cost value of a closing inventory stated in retail price value. This method requires that both inventory and purchase figures be recorded and charged to each department in both retail prices and at cost.

Figure 15–1   Typical Balance Sheet

Assets, Liabilities, and Stockholders' Equity	Dec. 31 1974	Dec. 31 1973		The Company Owns
Assets	(Millions)			
Current assets:				Cash and U.S. government securities, the latter generally at either cost or market value, whichever is lower
Cash	$ 9.0	$ 6.2		
U.S. government securities		2.0		Amounts owed the company by its customers for goods or services rendered, less allowance for doubtful accounts
Accounts and notes receivable	12.4	11.4		
Inventories	27.0	24.6		
Total current assets	$ 48.4	$ 44.2		
				Merchandise on hand (usually valued at lower of cost or market)
Other assets:				
Surrender value of insurance	.2	.2		
Investments in subsidiaries	4.7	3.9		Miscellaneous assets and advance payments for insurance. Investments in nonconsolidated subsidiary companies
Prepaid insurance	.6	.5		
Total other assets	$ 5.5	$ 4.6		
				Land, buildings, and equipment and deductions for wear and tear on these properties (usually valued at cost)
Fixed Assets:				
Buildings, machinery, and equipment, at cost	104.3	92.7		
Less accumulated depreciation	27.6	25.0		
	$ 76.7	$ 67.7		*The Company Owes*
Land	.9	.7		
Total fixed assets	$ 77.6	$ 68.4		For merchandise, supplies, wages and salaries to employees, and such things as dividends declared, real estate, social security and income taxes, etc.
Total assets	$131.5	$117.2		
Liabilities and Stockholders' Equity				
Current Liabilities:				May be either a liability of a more or less definite nature, such as provision for possible inventory losses, or a part of earnings not available for dividends and segregated so as not to be included in surplus available for dividends
Accounts payable	$ 6.1	$ .5		
Accrued liabilities	3.6	3.3		
Current maturity of long-term debt	1.0	.8		
Federal income and other taxes	9.6	8.4		
Dividends payable	1.3	1.1		For money borrowed (excluding portion due in next 12 months, shown as a current liability)
Total current liabilities	$ 21.6	$ 18.6		
				Amount originally invested in the business by the stockholders. Additional capital received from sale of capital stock above par value
Reserves	3.6	2.5		
Long-Term Debt:				
5% sinking fund debentures, due July 31, 1986	26.0	20.0		Retained earnings reinvested in the business
Stockholders' Equity:				
5% cumulative preferred stock ($100 par)	$ 6.0	$ 6.0		
Common stock ($10 par)	18.3	18.3		
Capital surplus	9.6	9.6		
Earned surplus	46.4	42.2		
Total stockholders' investment	$ 80.3	$ 76.1		
Total liabilities and stockholders' investment	$131.5	$117.2		

SOURCE   Form and explanation obtained from *Understanding Financial Statements,* New York Stock Exchange (1965), pp. 6–7.

Complete records are maintained (in retail prices) on all additions to and reductions from stock. The markup percentage is determined, allowing one to calculate the cost percentage on the total merchandise handled. The closing retail book inventory (the retail value of the merchandise on hand in the closing inventory) is calculated from the records. The cost percentage is then applied to the retail book inventory and an annual physical inventory is taken (in retail prices) to check the accuracy of the method.

The closing physical inventory (in retail prices) can be converted to a cost valuation by using the formula, cost value of inventory = retail value of inventory × cost percentage. For example, suppose the closing physical inventory revealed $10,000 worth of merchandise is on hand in retail dollars, the total cost of merchandise handled (opening inventory plus purchases) over the last year was $140,000, and the total merchandise handled (opening inventory plus purchases) in retail prices was $200,000. The cost percentage is, cost of total merchandise handled / merchandise handled in retail dollars

× 100, or ($140,000 / $200,000) × 100 = 70 percent. The cost value of
the closing inventory is $10,000 × 70 percent, or $7,000.

The same formula can be used to calculate the cost value of book (or
perpetual) retail inventory. Suppose we have not taken a physical inventory
but that all other data are unchanged from the previous example. We know
the cost percentage (70 percent) but need to estimate the physical retail
inventory value. We can do this by subtracting from the total merchandise
handled in retail value ($200,000) all of the items that decreased the value
of this merchandise during the past year. Suppose sales were $150,000,
markdowns were $20,000, and estimated shortages are $20,000. In this case,
perpetual (or book) retail value = total merchandise handled − (sales +
markdowns + estimated shortages), or $200,000 − ($150,000 + $20,000
+ $20,000), or $10,000. The conversion formula given above could then be
used to obtain the cost value of the book inventory. In this case, cost value
of book inventory = retail value of book inventory × cost percentage, or
$10,000 × 70 percent = $7,000.

Fixed assets, with the exception of land, have a limited useful life, so
a provision is made for depreciation due to wear and tear. The depreciation
is subtracted from asset values so that the asset value is not overstated. The
depreciation reserve may also include an estimated amount for loss of value
in buildings, equipment, and land due to changes in technology, population
concentration, shopping habits, etc. It is important to note that the depreciated amount is not a cash expenditure of money but merely a decrease in
the value of company-owned assets.

Liabilities, which are on the "other side" of the assets equal liabilities
plus capital equation, are usually divided into two classes of debt. "Current
liabilities" are accounts due and payable within one year. "Long-term debt"
does not have to be paid until at least one year has elapsed.

Current liabilities are composed of:

Accounts payable, which are money that is owed to vendors and other
costs that are incurred in operating a retail business.

Accrued liabilities are items such as unpaid wages, salaries, and commissions.

Current maturity of long-term debt is the amount of long-term debt
due within the upcoming year.

Federal income and other taxes are all accrued taxes.

Dividends payable are dividends declared by the board of directors but
not yet paid.

Company *capital* comprises *all* sums (long-term debt, preferred stock,
common stock, and surplus) used in the business. The retail enterprise may
have raised funds through the sale of long-term debt (mortgage bonds or
debentures) or by selling ownership in the company by issuing *common*
and/or *preferred stock.* The amount included in the *long-term debt* caption
is the amount of the principal due at maturity less any amount that is payable in less than one year.

Income Statement

The income statement gives the retail manager a summary of the income and expenses over a period of time. Income statements are usually prepared monthly, quarterly, semiannually, and annually. Comparison of a current income statement with the corresponding statement for the previous year allows the proprietor to observe trends in income, expenses, and profits. In most retail operations, sales records are generally broken down by major departments. Such divisions more accurately show the response of sales and profits to changes in the retail mix. These breakdowns also allow the manager to continually identify the performance of each department. Figure 15–2 is a typical annual income statement, with an explanation of the terms used in this type of financial reporting.

Although Figure 15–2 adequately explains the meaning of the terms used in the income statement, the income statement depreciation concept may require additional explanation. The *depreciation* expenses differ from the other expenses in the income statement in that the provision for depreciation does not represent an actual cash outlay. Each piece of equipment and each retail fixture has a limited period of usefulness, so depreciation

Figure 15–2   Statement of Income

	Year Ended December 31		
	1974	1973	
	(Millions)		
Net Sales	$115.8	$110.0	Amount received or receivable from customers. Gross sales dollars less returns, allowances, and discounts
Less Costs and Expenses:			Part of income used for wages, salaries, merchandise, fuel and supplies, and certain taxes
Cost of goods sold	74.8	73.2	Part of income used for salesmen's commissions, advertising, officers' salaries, and other general expenses
Selling, general, and administrative expenses	14.2	13.0	
Depreciation	4.2	3.5	Provision from income for the reduction of the service life of equipment, fixtures, and buildings
	$ 93.2	$ 89.7	
Operating profit	$ 22.6	$ 20.3	The remainder after deducting the foregoing expenses from sales, but before providing for interest charges and taxes frequently called pre-tax profit
Interest charges	1.3	1.0	
Earnings before income taxes	21.3	19.3	
Provision for federal and state taxes on income	11.4	9.8	Amount required for interest on borrowed funds
Net income for the year	9.9	9.5	Amount paid or payable for taxes
Dividend on preferred stock	.3	.3	
Balance of net income available for common stock	$ 9.6	$ 9.2	This amount was earned for stockholders
			Amount paid to preferred stockholders
Statement of Earned Surplus			Amount remaining for common stockholders
	1974	1973	
Balance at beginning of year	$ 42.2	$ 37.6	Surplus or retained earnings reinvested in the business. Usually not all of the year's earnings can be paid out in dividends, a part being retained in the business for expansion or other purposes
Add net income for the year	9.9	9.5	
	52.1	47.1	
Less dividends paid on:			
preferred stock	.3	.3	
common stock	5.4	4.6	
Balance at end of year	$ 46.4	$ 42.2	

SOURCE   Form and explanation obtained from *Understanding Financial Statements,* New York Stock Exchange (1965), pp. 8–9.

makes a provision for using up the service life of each asset. Your firm's profit and net worth would be overstated if your statement did not provide for the wear and tear on equipment and fixtures.

Retailers need to observe more detailed monthly income statements to determine if any significant sales or cost changes are occurring. Figure 15–3 is an example of a monthly income statement which allows one to make comparisons with the same month last year and with the year-to-date performance. The performance of the XYZ store in June of 1974 and for the first six months of 1974 appears to be an improvement over corresponding periods in 1973. Not only have sales increased in 1974 but operating and net profits also have increased. The increase in net profits occurred despite a slight reduction in gross margin percentage. Better utilization of employees and the spreading of the fixed costs (such as rent, insurance, depreciation, taxes, etc.) over a larger sales volume allowed the store to reduce its total expenses on a percent-of-sales basis.

Other Retail Records

Retailers should also keep a detailed record of *accounts receivable* so customer billing can be handled accurately and good customer relations maintained. In addition, these records can be used to provide the detailed information needed to evaluate the firm's credit and collection policy. For example, the number and names of customers who are "slow payers" can easily be identified by examining the accounts receivable records.

Detailed information on *accounts payable* can help protect the financial reputation of the retail firm. Organized accounts payable records allow retailers to identify "due" accounts as well as invoices that allow cash discounts if payment is made promptly.

Most retailers also maintain separate and more detailed *inventory records,* which are essential to the control and security of retail stocks. Inventory records also provide the data needed for making buying decisions and for effective merchandise management.

Detailed *sales records* may be used to provide a basis for the compensation of retail sales personnel. These sales records may also provide information useful in marketing research activities, such as determining trading areas, identifying market targets, and the like.

Finally, accurate and detailed *tax records* must be maintained. These records should contain all the information needed to fill out the various tax forms requested by all levels of government.

Separate departmental records may be maintained on a monthly basis to allow retail management to identify changes in operating performance in each area. A monthly departmental operating statement, similar to that for the total store in Figure 15–3, can be used to identify performance changes within each department. Expense records on such items as salaries, wages, and supplies can be maintained on a departmental basis. Other expenses must be allocated to the various departments on the basis of time, space, or capital

Figure 15–3 Income Statement for Month of June, 1974, XYZ Store

ITEM	THIS MONTH				YEAR TO DATE			
	For This Year		For Last Year		For This Year		For Last Year	
	$	% of Sales	$	% of Sales	$	% of Sales	$	% of Sales
Net sales	102,900		90,300		610,800		570,000	
Less cost of goods sold:								
Beginning inventory	70,000	68.0	60,000	66.4	70,000	11.5	60,000	10.5
Merchandise purchases	70,000	68.0	70,000	77.5	410,000	67.1	390,000	68.4
Merchandise available for sales	140,000	136.1	130,000	144.0	480,000	78.6	450,000	78.9
Less ending inventory	70,000	68.0	70,000	77.5	70,000	11.5	70,000	12.3
Costs of goods sold	70,000	68.0	60,000	66.4	410,000	67.1	380,000	66.7
Gross margin	32,900	32.0	30,300	33.6	200,800	32.9	190,000	33.3
Less expenses:								
Salaries, wages, commissions	10,290	10.0	9,560	10.6	60,800	10.0	59,600	10.5
Rent	3,087	3.0	3,000	3.3	18,522	3.0	18,000	3.2
Utilities	515	0.5	510	0.6	3,118	0.5	3,120	0.5
Repairs and maintenance	3,087	3.0	3,100	3.4	15,200	2.5	14,700	2.6
Delivery expense	515	0.5	450	0.5	3,200	0.5	2,700	0.5
Supplies	515	0.5	510	0.6	3,150	0.5	3,020	0.5
Advertising	2,058	2.0	2,100	2.3	12,210	2.0	12,080	2.1
Depreciation	2,675	2.6	2,675	3.0	16,050	2.6	16,050	2.8
Bad debts	410	0.4	500	0.6	2,530	0.4	2,410	0.4
Taxes and licenses	1,545	1.5	1,500	1.7	9,210	1.5	9,020	1.6
Insurance	1,030	1.0	1,010	1.1	6,180	1.0	6,060	1.1
Interest	1,030	1.0	950	1.1	6,210	1.0	5,940	1.0
Other expenses	3,084	3.0	3,060	3.4	18,010	2.9	18,080	3.2
Total expenses	29,841	29.0	28,925	32.0	174,390	28.6	170,780	30.0
Operating profit (loss)	3,059	3.0	1,375	1.6	26,410	4.3	19,220	3.3
Other income	2,058	2.0	2,015	2.2	10,100	1.7	9,700	1.7
Net profit (loss)	5,117	5.0	3,390	3.8	36,510	6.0	28,920	5.0

requirements for each department. For example, total store rent could be allocated to each department on the basis of square footage occupied by that department. Cost accountants can provide valuable assistance in the allocation of these expenses to each department.

Operating a Retail Accounting System

The development and use of accounting records are essential because they allow retail managers to carry out more effective planning and control. Appropriate accounting records can reveal errors, employee fraud, and waste and can identify other sales and expense areas that may require changes if retail performance is to be improved.

Retail firms need a good accounting system to safeguard business assets and prevent errors. The accounting records must be accurately and honestly maintained for each of the many transactions that occur each day in a retail organization. A system of checks and balances should be used so no employee will have complete control of any business transaction. Cashiers or account collectors who handle cash should not maintain the accounting books. Where possible, record analyses and reports should be the responsibility of at least two people. Cash register tapes should be used to double check the amount of cash received by the cashier. Employee earnings and purchase expenditures should be computed by one person and then re-checked for accuracy and honesty by another individual.

The typical store manager is deeply involved in the operations of his business. Frequently he believes he would accomplish more by spending his time doing tasks within the store instead of sitting at a desk analyzing accounting records. If this is the case, he should consider using part-time outside accountants and financial consultants who can help develop and operate an effective program.

Frequent meetings with outside accountants may involve a comparison of performance in the previous month with that of a year ago, and then with the preceding month. Major performance deviations and current and future plans should be discussed. Regular discussions of this type allow many retailers to avoid making serious business errors.

Large retail organizations are likely to maintain their own accounting department, which performs nearly all of the firm's accounting services (except the independent audit). The functions of this internal accounting department are the same as those of an outside accounting service. The same honest, objective appraisals must be made to reduce errors, fraud, and waste.

Both internal and outside accounting systems are likely to make increased use of electronic data processing equipment. Such equipment speeds the processing of sales and expense data. Thus information is available for managerial review faster than under the manual system. In addition, electronic systems are able to make detailed calculations on ratios and percentages that are essential for more effective retail management.

FINANCIAL PLANNING

Financial management in a retail firm involves two objectives. First, an adequate *flow of cash* must be provided to meet current liabilities as they come due. Second, the retail firm must operate as *profitably* as possible in the long run.

Cash Flow Analysis

Cash flow analysis may be used to develop a plan that will ensure that adequate cash is available to pay bills as they come due. Retail cash receipts and cash disbursements fluctuate independently of each other. Thus, during certain periods of the year, cash inflows (sales receipts) exceed cash outflows and a surplus is created in cash reserves. During other seasons of the year, cash outflows exceed sales revenue. In this case an addition to the cash account is needed to prevent a deficit, unless a surplus has been accumulating in the cash account.

Effective cash flow management involves an analysis of the timing of cash receipts and disbursements to identify the periods when the working capital may be inadequate or excessive in terms of meeting current liabilities. Maintaining excessive amounts of surplus cash (as non-working dollars) violates the profit objective. These excessive cash reserves involve an *opportunity cost* equal to the amount they would bring if they were used in some other way, either within the retail store (advertising, reducing the amount of a mortgage, fixture improvements, etc.) or outside the retail store (investment in interest-bearing notes, etc.).

An inadequate cash level is also detrimental to the profit maximizing objective. Inadequate working capital may result in insufficient advertising, inventories, etc., resulting in consumer dissatisfaction and a loss in retail sales. It may also force the retailer to pass up trade discounts, or even cause a loss in the credit standing of the firm.

Cash flow analysis expresses future retail income and expenditures on a dollar basis, so it is simply a prediction of future cash flows based on an expected sales volume. The cash flow records the movement of cash into retail inventories, receivables, and back into cash. This analysis reveals future needs for short-term funds by indicating when cash inflows will exceed outflows and vice versa. A cash flow analysis is vitally important to a retailer as it identifies what the firm can do to reach its objective of maintaining adequate (but not excessive) cash balances.

The first step in a cash flow analysis is to *establish the period* covered by the plan. The analysis may be prepared on a monthly (or even weekly) basis to project the cash condition for the next six months or next year of business. The procedure is simply to record expected cash inflows and outflows and add (or subtract) the expected amount of the net increase (or decrease) to (or from) the original cash balance to obtain the expected cash balance at the end of the period.

The second step is the *estimation of sales.* Sales forecasting techniques are described in Chapters 12 and 17; however, it is important to note that both internal factors (such as changes in promotion, price policy, and productive personnel) and external factors (such as changes in competition, economic conditions, seasonality patterns, and consumer preferences) affect a retailer's sales level. Thus sales estimating procedures must use these variables to forecast sales volume accurately.

One cannot overemphasize the importance of sales forecasting. The accuracy of the entire cash flow analysis is highly dependent upon the accuracy of the sales forecast. Hence, every effort should be made to develop an accurate forecasting method. This usually requires a great deal of experience and good judgment. Historical data on past sales are usually analyzed to determine trends and seasonal sales patterns. Fortunately, it is usually easier to forecast sales for a store or group of stores than for an item or a specific merchandise line. Seasonal patterns on total store sales are not likely to change rapidly. Although the composition of the sales may change rapidly, the total volume is not likely to fluctuate widely unless the relative competitive position of the retail outlet(s) changes or unless the total industry sales are changing rapidly.

The third step entails *anticipation of future cash inflows* derived from the estimated sales level. The credit policy used by the firm will determine how closely cash inflows relate to sales, and this relationship should be identical if retail sales are made on a strictly cash basis. Of course, the handling of credit sales will also affect this cash-inflow-to-sales relationship. If most or all of the sales are made on a bank credit card basis (e.g., Master Charge or BankAmericard), the retailer will be reimbursed almost immediately after the handling charge (usually 2 to 6 percent of sales) has been deducted. Factoring of accounts receivable will accomplish the same result, namely, a close relationship of cash inflow to sales volume. Historical records, combined with an analysis of the firm's retail credit policy, can generally yield a highly reliable estimate of the relationship between sales volume and cash inflow.

The fourth step is an analysis of the *expected cash outflow* for the previously specified time period(s). Historical purchase and expenditure records, employee payroll data, contracts, negotiated purchase agreements, and other commitments can be analyzed to obtain an estimate of upcoming expenditures.

The fifth step involves the comparison of the estimated cash inflow against the estimated outflow to determine the *net cash gain or loss* for the period. This consists merely of subtracting the expected outflow (determined in step 4) from the expected inflow (determined in step 3) to obtain the net change in the cash balance.

Cash flow analysis also provides, in the sixth step, an *estimated cash balance* for the end of the specified period(s). The expected cash balance is obtained by adding the net gain (or subtracting the net loss) for the period—as calculated in step 5—to the cash balance at the beginning of the period.

These six steps, which constitute the cash flow analysis, provide all the information necessary to plan a retailer's needs for short-term capital. Figure 15–4 is an example of a cash flow analysis for a retail firm. Additions to working capital are required when the expected cash balance reaches a pre-specified minimum level. The additions to short-term funds may come from either internal or external sources.

The main internal sources of funds are the liquidation of inventories and short-term investments, cash sales, and a turnover of accounts receivable. Retail credit policies are not likely to be changed frequently simply to provide extra cash during a short-term period of cash deficiency. Consumers become committed to established retail credit policies and are likely to switch retailers if an outlet continually changes its credit rules. Promotions can be used to increase cash sales during periods when cash shortages are likely to exist; however, retail management must consider the overall effect such promotions may have upon future sales, store image, etc. Thus the stimulation of cash sales is not likely to be used as a solution to a short-term deficit cash balance problem.

Liquidation of short-term investments is frequently made to generate needed cash. Indeed, some money is sometimes put into liquid short-term investments not only to obtain a return on the money but also to provide a safety margin in case cash is needed internally at a later date.

External sources of funds (banks, trade credit, etc.) are required if internal sources cannot provide sufficient cash.

Ratio Analysis

Retailers not only attempt to meet current liabilities as their bills come due but also attempt to operate as profitably as possible. Thus retailers must have a way to measure the profitability and operating efficiency of their enterprises. Examination of selected ratios and relationships derived from data in the firm's balance sheet and income statement can provide helpful appraisals of the current and past performance of that firm. External financial sources, moreover, frequently require these data before they will grant loans to a firm.

A number of different ratios and relationships can be used by the retailer to measure the past and current performance of his firm. Ratios are generally compared both on a historical basis and against the industrial standards considered to be normal for that type of retailing. Several different standards are available from various trade sources and such sources as the Small Business Administration, the U.S. Department of Commerce, Dun and Bradstreet, National Cash Register, Robert Morris Associates, etc. The inexperienced retailer must rely heavily upon the standards developed by these sources. An experienced retailer is more likely to establish his own standards and make historical comparisons on each ratio.

Figure 15–4 Example of Cash Flow Analysis (for Three Months, Ending March 31)

	JANUARY Budget	JANUARY Actual	FEBRUARY Budget	FEBRUARY Actual	MARCH Budget	MARCH Actual
Expected cash receipts						
Cash sales	$12,000	$10,800	$13,000	$12,000	$20,000	$22,000
Collections on accounts receivable	10,000	10,000	10,000	9,500	10,000	10,000
Other income	300	200	300	200	300	400
Total cash receipts	22,300	21,000	23,300	21,700	30,300	32,400
Expected cash payments						
Raw materials, merchandise, and supplies	14,000	15,000	16,000	16,000	20,000	22,000
Payroll	2,500	2,600	2,500	2,400	3,000	3,200
Other expenses (including maintenance)	500	600	500	500	600	700
Advertising	300	300	300	300	500	500
Selling expense	1,200	1,000	1,200	1,000	1,200	1,200
Administrative expense (including salary of owner-manager)	1,500	1,500	1,500	1,500	1,500	1,500
New store facilities and equipment	2,500	2,500	1,000	1,500	1,000	600
Other payments (taxes, including estimated income tax; repayment of loans; interest; etc.)	300	400	300	300	500	700
Total cash payments	22,800	23,900	23,300	23,200	28,300	30,400
Expected cash balance at Beginning of Month	1,000	1,000	1,000	1,000	1,000	1,000
Cash increase or decrease	—500	—2,900	0	—1,500	2,000	2,000
Expected cash balance at end of month	500	—1,900	1,000	—500	3,000	3,000
Desired working cash balance	1,000	1,000	1,000	1,000	1,000	1,000
Loans needed						
Total amount of cash borrowed*	500	2,900	0	1,500	0	0
Loan repayment due	500	2,900	500	4,400	0	2,400
Cash available for owners, dividends, etc.	0	0	0	0	1,500	0

* Assuming no debt on Jan. 1 and that surplus cash is used for loan repayment.

413

Operating Ratios

Retail operating ratios express relationships among the items in the income statement to provide an evaluation of the firm's operating performance. Operating ratios yield a detailed understanding of the retail expenses involved in generating sales. These ratios can be used as tools to lower costs and improve efficiency within the retail firm.

A detailed breakdown of expenses is usually required to calculate the important operating ratios for a retailer. The operating ratios are calculated by dividing each item in a detailed income statement by the retailer's net sales figure and multiplying the result by 100. This procedure allows the ratios to relate each expense or income item to net sales by expressing each item on a percentage of net sales basis. These percentage figures are then studied to provide suggestions that will improve retail operating efficiency. Some retailers calculate and analyze some operating ratios each week on a department-by-department basis, which provides excellent control. Knowledge of current gross operating profit margins, inventory levels, and expense ratios can allow the retailer to spot a weakness before it gets to be a serious problem. Up-to-date ratio analysis can also let the retailer quickly determine the effects of changes in the retailing mix.

Thus a comparative analysis of operating ratio values over a period of time can be used to identify the cost of sales and expense trends. The operating ratios that are normally used to measure a retailer's performance are listed and explained in Figure 15–5. Of course, retailers like to observe declining values for the cost of goods sold and operating expense ratios described in the figure. On the other hand, they also like to observe increasing values for their net sales as a percentage of gross sales, gross profit, operating profit, and for both net income ratios.

New retailers can use average industry ratios to make an annual expense forecast. An example of the expenses encountered by appliance, radio, and television dealers is presented in Figure 15–6. Similar expense estimates for other types of retailers are available from trade associations.

Financial Ratios

A financial ratio may be used to express the relationship between two items on the firm's balance sheet or between one item on the income statement and one item on the balance sheet. These ratios can be analyzed to provide a basis for making comparisons on the historical performance of the firm. The financial ratios can also be used to make comparisons with similar retail operations and can thereby identify areas of relative financial weakness and strength. Thus financial ratio analysis provides guides for spotting trends toward better or poorer performance.

Average financial ratio values for numerous types of retail businesses are presented in Figure 15–7. Several ratios are used to measure a firm's *liquidity*. The *current ratio* indicates the ability of the firm to meet its current obligations and still maintain a safety margin to allow for possible shrinkage

Figure 15–5   *Operating Ratios Frequently Used to Measure Retailers' Operating Efficiency*

RATIO	CHARACTERISTICS
1. Net sales as % of gross sales	Measures percent shrinkage occurring from returns, allowances, estimated uncollectable accounts expected and cash discounts.
2. Cost of goods sold as % of net sales	Cost of goods sold may be defined to be beginning inventory valued at cost plus net purchases less ending inventory valued at cost to provide a ratio that measures the relative importance of inventory cost to net sales volume.
3. Gross profit as % of net sales	Gross profit may be defined to be the net sales minus cost of goods sold as defined in item 2, then this ratio will measure the relative performance of the firm before selling, general, administrative and interest expenses are deducted.
4. Operating expenses as % of net sales	Ratios may be calculated for each of the expense accounts (wages, supplies, maintenance, advertising, administrative salaries, bad debts, utilities, insurance, rent, taxes, depreciation) as well as an overall operating expense ratio. Expenses are often grouped into controllable or uncontrollable categories to provide a measure of the relative flexibility of the firm.
5. Operating profit as % of net sales	Operating profit is gross profit minus total operating expenses (listed in item 4); so ratio is pre-tax profit margin as % of net sales.
6. Net income before income taxes as % of net sales	Net income is operating profit minus the amount needed to meet interest payment on debt.
7. Net income after income taxes as % of net sales	Measure of after-tax profitability of retail firm stated as % of net sales.

in the value of its inventories and accounts receivable.[1] The current ratio (ratio 1 in Figure 15–7) is expressed in mathematical terms as, current ratio = current assets ÷ current liabilities.

High-volume, high-turnover outlets that handle merchandise whose demand is relatively stable do not require as much safety margin as low-volume, slow-turnover outlets that handle merchandise whose demand fluctuates widely. Thus chain grocery stories may have a current ratio of slightly less than 2:1 and still be very able to meet their current obligations. Less stable types of retail business generally attempt to maintain at least a 2:1 relationship, although an extremely high current ratio merely indicates that excess cash is lying idle or that excessive inventories are being maintained.

Figure 15–6 Expenses Encountered by Appliance & Radio-TV Dealers

ITEM	VOLUME OVER $500,000	VOLUME $250,000– $500,000	VOLUME UNDER $250,000	"MERCHAN- DISE ONLY" FIRMS*
Net sales	100.0	100.0	100.0	100.0
Cost of sales (Mdse. & Ser.)	68.7	66.2	65.7	75.7†
Gross margin	31.3	33.8	34.3	24.2
Total operating costs	28.3	30.8	31.5	23.4
Prop./part./exec. salaries	2.5	2.9	4.1	2.4
Office salaries	2.0	2.1	1.0	1.8
Salesmen's remuneration	5.0	4.6	3.8	5.6
Delivery wages	2.3	1.8	0.5	1.1
Other payroll	2.1	2.3	1.0	0.8
All payroll taxes	0.6	0.8	0.8	0.4
Other taxes (exc. inc.)	0.5	0.7	1.0	0.6
Occupancy	2.8	3.1	2.8	3.4
Advertising	2.3	2.1	2.0	2.8
Delivery truck expense	0.3	0.5	0.4	0.7
Service truck expense	2.9	4.1	3.7	—
Other auto, truck expense	0.1	0.7	1.3	0.1
Office supplies	0.4	0.5	0.4	0.4
Telephone & telegraph	0.4	0.3	0.4	0.2
Accounting & legal	0.1	0.2	0.2	0.7
Travel & entertainment	0.1	0.2	0.4	0.1
Dues & donations	0.1	0.1	0.2	0.0
Collection expense	0.0	0.0	0.2	—
Insurance	0.8	1.1	1.3	0.7
Other shop & service expense	0.5	0.3	1.0	0.3‡
Service warranty reserve	0.7	0.9	1.6	0.4
Miscellaneous expense	0.2	0.4	2.4	0.9
Net operating profit	3.0	3.0	2.8	0.8
Other income	1.8	2.0	0.7	3.3
Interest income	0.6	0.9	0.1	0.4
Suppliers rebates	0.4	0.4	0.1	2.3
Other	0.8	0.7	0.5	0.6
Total income	4.8	5.0	3.5	4.1
Other expense	1.1	1.6	0.8	2.2
Bad debt loss	0.2	0.4	0.1	0.6
Interest paid	0.5	1.0	0.6	1.2
Other	0.4	0.2	0.1	0.3
Total net profit before taxes	3.7	3.4	2.7	1.9
Federal & state income taxes	0.9	0.8	0.2	0.2
Net income after taxes	2.8	2.6	2.5	1.7

* Firms sell merchandise but do not provide service.
† Includes cost of merchandise and freight.
‡ Shop expense only.
Source NARDA's cost of doing business survey, National Appliance & Radio-TV Dealers Assn., 318 W. Randolph, Chicago, Ill. 60606.

The *liquidity ratio,* or "acid test," is calculated as (cash + marketable securities + accounts receivable) / current liabilities. This ratio also measures a retail organization's ability to meet its current obligations, but it is a more severe test because it concentrates on strictly liquid assets whose value is not likely to change radically. Inventories are not included in the numerator of the equation, so the liquidity ratio really evaluates the chance that a firm could pay its current obligations with readily convertible funds on hand. A liquidity ratio of less than 1:1 is a warning signal that a retail business would have to sell from inventory to meet current liabilities if the firm were pressured into paying its bills and could not borrow additional funds.

Several other ratios can be used to appraise the turnover relationships in retailing. The *collection period* (accounts receivable divided by daily sales), which is ratio 7 in Figure 15–7, is a rough measure of the overall quality of accounts receivable and of the credit policies used by the retailer. The collection period calculation can be compared to both the retailer's credit terms and to competitors' experience to determine if a collection problem exists.

A frequently used rule of thumb states that "the collection period should be no more than one-third greater than the net selling terms."[2] According to this rule, the collection period should not exceed 40 days for a retailer with selling terms of a 2 percent discount in 10 days, net 30 days. For retailers selling on an installment basis, "the collection period of the installment accounts, based on net sales after deducting the aggregate down payments, should be no more than ⅓ greater than ½ the average selling terms. If the average selling terms are 18 equal monthly installments, for example, ½ those terms would be 9 months, and ⅓ increase would give a standard of 12 months."[3] These rules of thumb have been designed to allow flexibility for a normal volume of "slow" but generally good accounts.

The *net-sales-to-inventory ratio* (no. 8 in Figure 15–7) expresses a rough measure of the frequency with which the average level of inventory investment was "turned over" on an annual basis. A higher turnover rate indicates that the business has managed to operate with a relatively small inventory investment, which indicates that the inventory is relatively current and contains little unusable stock. A high turnover ratio could also mean that inadequate inventories are being maintained. The latter could have a detrimental effect upon long-term profits if consumers are increasingly dissatisfied with out-of-stock conditions and *if* it is easy for them to buy these items at competing outlets.

Retail profitability may be examined in relation to sales volume or in relation to the investment required. There are several profit margin ratios that are used to describe the relationship of profits to sales volume. The *net-profits-on-net-sales ratio* (ratio 2 in Figure 15–7) merely expresses net retail dollar profits as a percentage of net retail sales dollars, or equals (net profit dollars / net sales dollars) × 100. This ratio is an indicator of the relative efficiency of the retail operation over time.

A more critical test of retail efficiency and profitability is provided by the *return-on-investment (or asset) ratio.* A high profit percentage on sales

Figure 15–7 Median Values of Financial Ratios for Selected Retail Businesses

LINE OF BUSINESS (AND NUMBER OF CONCERNS REPORTING)	CURRENT ASSETS TO CURRENT DEBT (1)	NET PROFITS ON NET SALES (2)	NET PROFITS ON TANGIBLE NET WORTH (3)	NET PROFITS ON NET WORKING CAPITAL (4)	NET SALES TO TANGIBLE NET WORTH (5)
	Times	Percent	Percent	Percent	Times
5641 Children's & infants' wear stores (50)	2.64	1.72	7.85	9.56	4.44
5611 Clothing & furnishings, men's & boys' (221)	2.75	2.35	6.68	7.70	3.11
5311 Department stores (259)	2.89	1.55	5.42	7.05	3.13
Discount stores (224)	1.88	1.49	9.97	13.29	6.28
Discount stores leased departments (53)	1.94	1.85	8.98	12.18	5.43
5651 Family clothing stores (93)	3.18	2.85	8.28	10.35	3.53
5252 Farm equipment dealers (91)	1.79	1.99	9.26	10.91	4.78
5969 Farm & garden supply stores (70)	2.79	1.90	7.01	14.45	3.18
5712 Furniture stores (186)	2.67	2.11	6.02	6.67	2.67
5541 Gasoline service stations (78)	1.79	2.97	9.75	28.26	4.07
5411 Grocery stores (138)	1.73	1.00	10.48	22.38	10.26
5251 Hardware stores (99)	3.58	2.64	6.91	8.41	2.51
5722 Household appliance stores (93)	1.95	1.54	8.54	9.36	4.74
5971 Jewelry stores (79)	3.16	2.66	5.73	6.68	2.05
5211 Lumber & other bldg. mtls. dealers (196)	2.80	2.07	7.03	9.78	3.27
5399 Miscellaneous general mdse. stores (84)	3.49	2.61	9.20	10.88	3.19
5511 Motor vehicle dealers (100)	1.50	1.35	10.63	18.18	9.71

NET SALES TO NET WORKING CAPITAL (6)	COLLEC-TION PERIOD (7)	NET SALES TO INVEN-TORY (8)	FIXED ASSETS TO TAN-GIBLE NET WORTH (9)	CURRENT DEBT TO TAN-GIBLE NET WORTH (10)	TOTAL DEBT TO TAN-GIBLE NET WORTH (11)	INVEN-TORY TO NET WORKING CAPITAL (12)	CUR-RENT DEBT TO INVEN-TORY (13)	FUNDED DEBTS TO NET WORKING CAPITAL (14)
Times	Days	Times	Percent	Percent	Percent	Percent	Percent	Percent
5.31	**	5.2	17.1	56.2	147.4	111.2	60.4	37.4
3.64	**	3.9	11.1	47.3	105.6	92.0	64.1	25.5
4.15	**	5.6	26.0	42.1	82.0	76.9	69.8	32.2
7.85	**	5.2	28.9	83.3	120.1	146.1	72.6	32.5
5.87	**	4.6	27.5	87.3	114.9	134.8	70.9	22.1
3.67	**	4.8	12.3	41.3	88.8	79.7	56.9	30.5
5.49	32	3.3	15.1	117.2	181.2	143.3	83.8	26.8
5.32	**	9.0	36.1	35.3	76.8	72.5	86.4	58.4
2.87	104	4.7	11.4	49.9	85.9	68.7	87.5	17.3
8.09	**	12.1	51.2	45.1	90.2	80.5	163.4	71.4
21.88	**	17.1	66.5	57.4	97.5	141.3	93.0	60.0
3.17	**	3.9	16.1	30.6	65.2	87.0	50.0	25.4
5.70	37	5.1	15.3	88.0	137.2	100.5	99.3	18.1
2.43	**	3.0	10.6	44.4	73.6	77.1	64.9	18.6
4.25	54	5.9	21.7	39.8	88.6	70.3	79.0	27.8
3.83	**	4.1	14.2	36.1	85.2	93.7	50.1	38.7
14.49	**	7.4	26.2	123.1	186.4	200.4	91.3	73.2

Figure 15–7 (Continued)

LINE OF BUSINESS (AND NUMBER OF CONCERNS REPORTING)	CURRENT ASSETS TO CURRENT DEBT (1)	NET PROFITS ON NET SALES (2)	NET PROFITS ON TANGIBLE NET WORTH (3)	NET PROFITS ON NET WORKING CAPITAL (4)	NET SALES TO TANGIBLE NET WORTH (5)
	Times	*Percent*	*Percent*	*Percent*	*Times*
5231 Paint, glass & wallpaper stores (31)	3.27	3.10	13.61	14.82	3.09
5661 Shoe stores (103)	3.20	1.67	5.24	5.86	3.30
5531 Tire, battery & accessory stores (69)	2.23	2.39	10.71	12.89	3.76
5331 Variety stores (71)	2.93	2.31	8.27	10.19	3.84
5621 Women's ready-to-wear stores (189)	2.51	1.81	6.68	8.64	3.95

Collection Period—The number of days that the total of trade accounts and notes receivable (including assigned accounts and discounted notes, if any), less reserves for bad debts, represents when compared with the annual net credit sales. Formula: Divide the annual net credit sales by 365 days to obtain the average credit sales per day. Then divide the total of accounts and notes receivable (plus any discounted notes receivable) by the average credit sales per day to obtain the average collection period.

Current Assets—Total of cash, accounts and notes receivable for the sales of merchandise in regular trade quarters, less any reserves for bad debts, advances on merchandise, inventory less any reserves, listed securities when not in excess of market, state and municipal bonds not in excess of market, and United States government securities.

Current Debt—Total of all liabilities due within one year from statement date including current payments on serial notes, mortgages, debentures, or other funded debts. This item also includes current reserves such as gross reserves for federal income and excess profit taxes, reserves for contingencies set up for specific purposes, but does not include reserves for depreciation.

Fixed Assets—The sum of the cost value of land and the depreciated book values of buildings, leasehold improvements, fixtures, furniture, machinery, tools and equipment.

Funded Debt—Mortgages, bonds, debentures, gold notes, serial notes, or other obligations with maturity of more than one year from the statement date.

SOURCE 1971 *Key Business Ratios*, published by Dun & Bradstreet, Inc.

NET SALES TO NET WORKING CAPITAL (6)	COLLECTION PERIOD (7)	NET SALES TO INVENTORY (8)	FIXED ASSETS TO TANGIBLE NET WORTH (9)	CURRENT DEBT TO TANGIBLE NET WORTH (10)	TOTAL DEBT TO TANGIBLE NET WORTH (11)	INVENTORY TO NET WORKING CAPITAL (12)	CURRENT DEBT TO INVENTORY (13)	FUNDED DEBTS TO NET WORKING CAPITAL (14)
Times	Days	Times	Percent	Percent	Percent	Percent	Percent	Percent
3.61	**	6.6	18.4	40.5	66.7	66.5	74.2	26.8
3.64	**	3.8	12.5	35.1	82.4	103.7	48.9	22.0
5.00	**	6.5	18.5	58.0	127.0	85.3	107.0	28.7
4.87	**	4.1	23.8	40.8	75.1	120.4	42.9	31.6
4.73	**	6.6	18.6	51.0	104.0	76.7	87.0	29.8

Inventory—The sum of raw material, material in process, and finished merchandise. It does not include supplies.

Net Profits—Profit after full depreciation on buildings, machinery, equipment, furniture, and other assets of a fixed nature; after reserves for federal income and excess profit taxes; after reduction in the value of inventory to cost or market, whichever is lower; after charge-offs for bad debts; after miscellaneous reserves and adjustments; but before dividends or withdrawals.

Net Sales—The dollar volume of business transacted for 365 days net after deductions for returns, allowances and discounts from gross sales.

Net Sales to Inventory—The quotient obtained by dividing the annual net sales by the statement inventory. This quotient does not represent the actual physical turnover, which would be determined by reducing the annual net sales to the cost of goods sold and then dividing the resulting figure by the statement inventory.

Net Working Capital—The excess of the current assets over the current debt.

Tangible Net Worth—The sum of all outstanding preferred or preference stocks (if any) and outstanding common stocks, surplus and undivided profits, less any intangible items in the assets, such as goodwill, trademarks, patents, copyrights, leaseholds, mailing list, treasury stock, organization expenses, and underwriting discounts and expenses.

Turnover of Net Working Capital—The quotient obtained by dividing annual net sales by net working capital.

Turnover of Tangible Net Worth—The quotient obtained by dividing annual net sales by tangible net worth.

may be obtained on a relatively low sales volume. The result will be a low profit percentage on retail investment.

The *net-profits-on-tangible-net-worth ratio* (ratio 3 in Figure 15–7) is one measure of return on investment that expresses net profit dollars as a percentage of tangible net worth. This ratio measures the return to the owners of the business after all taxes and interest have been paid. Hence it can be used to evaluate the earning power of the ownership investment in the retail enterprise.

The return-on-investment ratio is also used to describe profitability relative to investment in assets. This ratio is calculated as (net profit / total assets) $\times$ 100. This measure relates net profits to the firm's total assets (inventory, accounts receivable, cash, and fixed assets).

Return-on-Investment (Asset) Analysis

The return-on-assets analysis allows retail management to analyze most of the data in the previously discussed ratios in such a way that the firm's profitability can be determined. The return-on-assets chart in Figure 15–8

Figure 15–8   Return-on-Assets Chart

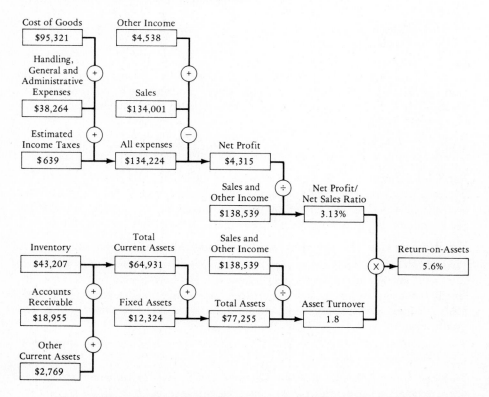

SOURCE   Reprinted with Special Permission from *Banking,* Journal of the American Bankers Association. Copyright 1970 by the American Bankers Association.

allows the retailer to establish goals in each segment in the chart. The top portion of the chart is used to determine net profit as a percentage of sales (ratio 2 in Figure 15–7). The lower part is used to calculate asset turnover (ratio 5 in Figure 15–7). The return-on-assets percentage is merely asset turnover times net profit percentage, so it equals the product of these two ratios. Since space has been provided for income taxes, the final return-on-assets percentage is an after-tax figure.

Retailers can improve their profitability by influencing the values of most of the factors in the return-on-assets chart. *Cost of goods* might be decreased by improved buying procedures. *Expenses* might be decreased by using better sales training. *Sales* might be increased by using better displays, improved promotion, and a better merchandise mix. *Other income* may be increased by taking advantages of cash discounts, placing excess cash in revenue-generating (but liquid) investments, and obtaining earnings from revolving credit programs. Managing these four factors properly can lead to an improvement in the profit-to-sales ratio.

The controllable factors in the bottom portion of the chart are inventory levels, accounts receivable levels, and other current assets. Inventory levels generally make up the largest portion of retail assets. Thus every effort should be made to increase the net-sales-to-inventory ratio by eliminating nonessential stocks. If accounts receivable become too high, a retailer may want to reevaluate his credit policy to see if the finance charge could be raised or the due date shortened. Accounts receivable management was discussed earlier in this chapter, but it is important to note the role it plays in determining return on retail assets. Other current assets consist mostly of cash, so placing excess funds in liquid investments improves the situation for both *other income* and *other current assets* categories.

The chief benefit of using the return-on-asset approach is that it demonstrates the interdependence of these controllable factors. Reducing inventory and accounts receivable levels will certainly improve the asset turnover, but if sales are decreased because of the reductions in these assets, then the profit-to-sales ratio is also reduced. The result might be a decline in the return on assets instead of the desired increase.

These interrelationships make it possible to design a system of management control that can monitor the effect of changes in a retail firm's performance as expressed in the various components of the ratios. Retail management can use the ratio dependencies shown in Figure 15–8 to provide a series of charts that reveal performance trends. The reader may trace the effect that a change in any of the components will have upon the firm's return-on-asset calculation.

Conclusions on Financial Analysis

The foregoing discussion acquaints the reader with the more important ratios and relationships that should be observed periodically. It is important to realize that rules of thumb and comparison of ratios with industry standards must be used with great caution. Each retail operation is unique, despite apparent similarities among competitive retailers.

Differences in accounting procedures can distort the comparative data. Thus ratio analysis provides only guides, not precise measurements, that the retailer can use to analyze his performance.

Retailers are concerned with the most efficient use of money. The tools of financial analysis presented above provide a way to evaluate the firm's management policies. Problems in money management may involve leaks (such as overbuying stocks relative to consumer demand) in the flow of funds. Another type of money management activity involves decreasing the number of slow and bad accounts which simply tie up excessive funds in receivables. Retail managers must also keep the firm in a liquid position so it is able to avoid late-payment charges and maintain a good credit standing. The ratios and the relationships discussed above should assist the manager in planning the need for funds and allow him to make more efficient and profitable use of the firm's resources.

RISK AND INSURANCE

Retail firms operate under risk of loss from many sources. Retail managers must learn how to use the various kinds of insurance to reduce the effects of these risks because unexpected losses can mean the difference between growth and failure. Insurance plays a vital role in forestalling the damage that the unexpected can do to the retail firm.

Retail organizations lack funds for total coverage against all types of risks. The retail manager must develop a planned approach to risk management by identifying the most crucial areas that require coverage. Figure 15–9 contains a list of the most common types of business risk and the types of insurance coverage available to retailers. *Periodic* reviews of the insurance program are needed to keep retail management abreast of changes in the type and size of risks that the firm faces. Replacement values of buildings, inventories, equipment, etc. are increasing rapidly due to inflationary pressures. Thus the coverage should reflect these higher values.

Once the risks have been recognized, retail managers can investigate the methods by which the costs of coverage can be reduced. The following considerations are important.

1. Determine which risks to insure against by estimating the amount of loss each peril could cause the firm.
2. Cover the largest loss exposure first, after considering premium costs and the funds available for protection. Be certain that coverage on all property and equipment is adequate to reflect its true current value. Conducting periodic, independent appraisals of property values can enhance the firm's ability to prove the amount of loss if a loss should occur.

Figure 15–9   Types of Business Risk and Insurance Protection Available

TYPE OF RISK	FORM OF PROTECTION
Loss of earning power	Business interruption insurance Profits insurance Rent insurance Life insurance on key personnel
Loss of property (destruction or damage)	Fire insurance Marine insurance Windstorm insurance Tornado insurance Explosion insurance Riot and insurrection insurance Automobile, fire and collision insurance Aircraft insurance Property depreciation insurance
Theft or infidelity	Auto theft insurance Burglary, theft insurance Forgery insurance Fidelity insurance
Failure of others	Credit insurance Surety bonding Title insurance
Loss of property (legal liability)	Workmen's compensation insurance Employers' liability insurance Contractual liability Public liability insurance Advertiser's liability Automobile liability insurance Power Plant insurance Elevator insurance Product liability insurance Sports liability insurance Physicians' insurance Aircraft insurance

SOURCE   Reprinted from Harvey C. Krentzman, *Managing for Profits* (Washington, D.C.: Small Business Administration, 1968), p. 155.

3. Use as high a deductible coverage as the firm can afford to carry. This will result in a considerable decrease in premium cost.
4. Buy insurance in as large a unit as possible to reduce premium costs. "Package" policies are frequently very suitable for the coverage needed by retail organizations.

5. Be aware of the firm's previous experience. Such knowledge can be used to get lower insurance rates or as a basis for changing to another form of insurance. Doing everything possible to minimize losses is essential to accomplish a reduced loss experience.

6. Develop a plan to implement good risk and insurance management. First, a clear statement of insurance objectives is needed. Second, select an insurance agent who is aware (or can become aware) of the firm's exposure to loss. Third, establish insurance responsibility with *one* individual or group. Finally, keep complete records of all insurance policies, premiums paid, losses, and loss recoveries to get better coverage at lower costs in the future.

SUMMARY

Retailers must use accounting records and control tools to evaluate their business activity. The balance sheet and income statement are the basic summary records that contain the data needed to chart the firm's financial performance.

Retail financial planning involves two objectives: providing an adequate flow of cash to meet current liabilities as they come due and operating as profitably as possible in the long run.

Cash flow analysis is used to plan monetary inflows and outflows so adequate cash is available to pay bills.

Trends in the value of the firm's financial ratios can be used to evaluate its profitability and the direction the firm's profits are headed.

The return-on-assets analysis is a useful method for tracing the interrelationships between the various financial ratios.

QUESTIONS

1. Why is factoring usually considered a "last resort" method of handling accounts receivable?
2. Of what use is a balance sheet? How does it differ from a profit and loss statement?
3. Why are inventories generally valued at cost and not at the price for which they are to be sold?
4. Since depreciation is a decrease in the value of company-owned assets, why is an accelerated depreciation rate considered desirable by most businessmen?
5. Sales departments often are interested in relaxing credit restrictions on store customers whereas financial and accounting departments sometimes want credit restrictions tightened. Explain this phenomenon.
6. Describe the difference between the LIFO and the FIFO inventory methods. In what instances would you use each?
7. Why is it unwise to allow one employee to handle all phases of a transaction?

8. What is the use of cash flow analysis in retailing? How is a cash flow analysis conducted?
9. What is the relationship between credit policy and cash inflows?
10. Why is the stimulation of cash sales an unlikely remedy for a short-term-deficit cash balance problem?
11. Distinguish between internal and external financing. How should a retailer go about determining which is his less costly source of capital?
12. Why are operating ratios expressed in terms of net sales? How do operating ratios differ from financial ratios?
13. What do the following financial ratios indicate about a firm—
    a. Current ratio?
    b. Acid-test ratio?
    c. Net-sales-to-inventory ratio?
    d. Net-profits-on-tangible-net-worth ratio?
14. Why would a retailer's creditors be especially interested in the retailer's acid-test ratio?
15. What is meant by a liquidity crisis in business and how may it be averted? Why not just maintain large cash balances?
16. How should the average retailer assess his risks in designing an insurance program? Consider two different types of retail outlets and suggest a method for assessing the risks faced by each.
17. Given the following data:

ASSETS		LIABILITIES AND NET WORTH	
Cash	$ 40,000	Bank loans	$ 40,000
Accounts receivable	40,000	Accounts payable	40,000
Inventory	40,000	Bonds	40,000
Fixed assets	80,000	Retained profit	40,000
	$200,000	Common stock	40,000
			$200,000

   a. Find the current ratio.
   b. Find the acid-test ratio.
   c. If profit is money that has been earned by the company, why is it in the liability column?
   d. Why does the total in the left-hand column equal that in the right-hand column?
   e. If the company suddenly made an unusually large return on its investment, would you expect assets to exceed liabilities and net worth? Why would you, or why would you not?

FOOTNOTES

[1] Erich A. Helfert, *Techniques of Financial Analysis* (Homewood, Ill.: Richard D. Irwin, 1967), pp. 58–73.
[2] *How to Control Accounts Receivable for Greater Profit* (New York: Dun & Bradstreet, 1966), p. 22.
[3] Ibid.

ALBERT HEIJN NV.
Combination of Promotion and Debt Financing

The Albert Heijn Company is a Dutch corporation that owns and operates the largest retail food chain in the Netherlands: 179 supermarkets and 204 other self-service stores. This makes Albert Heijn one of the largest supermarket chains in Europe.

In addition to supermarkets, the company is vertically integrated into food processing, and also owns a chain of restaurants, including the McDonald hamburger franchise in Holland.

The rapid growth of Albert Heijn created special promotional and capital acquisition needs similar to those faced by any rapidly growing retail chain.

Instead of being viewed as separate problem areas, they were faced in a coordinated approach. According to Mr. Fred Lachotzki, marketing service manager, the "marketing concept" was the guiding philosophy behind the program.

The management of Albert Heijn was familiar with the promotional games and the savings stamps used by retailers throughout the Western world.

It had been impressed with the short-run success and competitive advantage a retailer could gain through these promotional techniques. As a result, a program was devised whereby customers could obtain special stamps by shopping in Albert Heijn stores.

After saving the required number of stamps, the customer qualified to purchase a special corporate bond in the Albert Heijn Corporation.

These bonds were in the denomination of F100 ($33) and bore an 8½ percent interest rate, with a guaranteed 13 percent rate of interest at the end of twenty-five years.

This program proved to be so successful that its active promotion had to be stopped prior to the time planned, because otherwise the bond issue would have been sold out much too soon.

DISCUSSION QUESTIONS

1. Could a program similar to the bond promotion plan of Albert Heijn be successfully used by a retailer in the United States? Present a logical case for either side.
2. What types of retailers would likely be most successful with such a program?
3. What are the potential benefits and dangers in the use of such a plan?

MEMPHIS STATE UNIVERSITY BOOKSTORE

The manager of the Memphis State University bookstore, Mr. James Lippy, had just finished reading the article "Survival May Dictate a New Action Course" and he began to compare the operations described in the article to his own.

"In general," he said, "the article seems to sum up pretty well the problems facing our industry; however, our store has generally outperformed several of the industry ratios."

In commenting further on this, Mr. Lippy explained that the cost of freight for the Memphis bookstore was 1.7 percent, as opposed to 2 percent, but he added that this was due to the presence of a large manufacturer of notebooks and notebook covers in Memphis.

Pilferage rates were currently running 0.9 percent, as opposed to 4 percent or better for the industry. This was attributed to a number of factors, including six in-store closed-circuit TV monitors, special gates at the checkout counter, and heavy use of "blister" packs for merchandise. Mr. Lippy stated that ball-point pens could be purchased considerably cheaper in bulk, but trying to sell them in bulk bins was like putting out free gifts for the customers.

Even though his pilferage rate was below the industry averages, he was still beset by losses. That very day, a customer had entered the store and exchanged his old gym shoes for new ones, leaving the old ones behind in the box and not paying for the new pair. Price switching of merchandise was also common, especially in the soft goods area.

Although the industry average for markdown on books that cannot be returned to the publisher ran around 2 percent of gross sales, the Memphis store's average was 1.2 percent. This was attributed solely to keeping on top of return dates, so that excess books were returned before the expiration date.

The most significant difference in costs, according to Mr. Lippy, was in salary costs. At Memphis these were under 10 percent of gross sales, covering a work force of thirteen full-time employees and thirty students. A significant aid in the low cost was the college work/study program, in which the employer pays 20 percent of the wages and the federal government subsidizes the rest.

In terms of product mix, the Memphis bookstore was running approximately a 50-50 mix between books and non-books in terms of total selling space. Of the books sold, approximately 85 percent were textbooks and the remaining 15 percent were paperbacks and other trade books.

A very limited quantity of "gift" items, such as ash trays, maps, T shirts, etc., have M.S.U. insignias.

In commenting on the store's product mix, Mr. Lippy stated that only

7 percent of the 21,000-member student body are boarding students, with the remainder classified as commuters. As a result, he felt that the commuter students were in a position to shop other retailers in the area to a greater extent than non-commuters, thus affecting the product mix. Commuter students were generally believed to have less need to purchase non-book items on campus than boarders.

There was also very little walk-in traffic from non-students (other than university employees) due to parking problems on the campus. The university's 4,000 paid employees represented a market, but, like the community students, they had wide access to outside stores.

Nevertheless, Mr. Lippy believed that the 25,000 students and staff posed an excellent market for the correct blend of merchandise.

The fact that book sales were beginning to constitute a smaller portion of total sales demonstrated the possibility of increases in sales for non-book merchandise lines. Alumni offered a market potential for direct-mail advertising, and a full-page ad had been purchased in the next issue of the alumni magazine.

During recent years a new phenomenon had occurred on the M.S.U. campus, as well as on college campuses throughout the United States. Individual professors were being given increased autonomy over the type of books to be used in the classroom. This did not pose a particular problem in upper division courses but it was a huge inventory and ordering problem for basic courses. An example was that 159 titles were needed for six basic English courses. The problem increased almost proportionately to the number of professors teaching a basic course.

The most recent years had also witnessed fewer purchases of textbooks by students, although the last semester had completely contradicted this trend and all bookstores in the area had run out of books. It was not known whether students had suddenly become more serious—whether this was a quirk or the beginning of another trend. At any rate, it had become quite apparent in recent years that predicting consumer behavior—as related to textbooks to order—was no longer a simple matter of predicting the number of students in a course.

Summarizing the current situation of college bookstores, Mr. Lippy commented that the management task was becoming increasingly complex, and especially in states like Tennessee, where the state legislature specifically forbids the subsidization of bookstores.

He stated that the bookstore of the future was very likely to change considerably in appearance and in product mix. He felt that the trend toward more non-book items was almost certain to increase. Although this could have a positive effect upon the balance sheet of the bookstore, he expressed some concern as to what the increased stocking of non-book items would do to better serve the student, and stated, "Many bookstore managers forget why we are here and why we are called bookstores."

DISCUSSION QUESTIONS

1. What alternatives do you believe college bookstores have, other than diversify their product lines?
2. What product diversification moves would you suggest for a college bookstore? For example, boutique shops, record shops, tape recorders, expensive electronic equipment?
3. Are there new order systems that bookstores should consider in view of the expanded types of textbooks necessary?
4. Check with your campus bookstore and determine how its operations compare with the article in *The College Store Journal* (reprinted as a case problem in Chapter 12) and with the M.S.U. case. Outline a managerial approach for improving the efficiency and sales of your school's bookstore.
5. Discuss the operations of a college bookstore as compared to a drug store, a card and stationery shop, and another selected local retailer. Is there a similarity of problems in merchandise ordering, return merchandise policies, product mix considerations, and pilferage?
6. Assume you have been hired as manager of a bookstore serving a state university of 15,000 students. What questions will you need to ask as you begin this task, what research (if any) will you need to do, what problems would you expect to face? What additional information do you need to begin a managerial analysis?

PART FIVE

Retailing Services

CHAPTER 16

Photo courtesy of Sears, Roebuck and Company.

Consumer Service Firms

The field of retailing is much broader than simply selling goods to consumers, as it includes the marketing of services as well. This might appear to be too broad a definition for retailing—until one takes a closer look at the type of services offered today. A great number, if not the majority, of these services are in direct competition with traditional retailing. This chapter discusses the peculiarities encountered in the marketing of services.

The owner of a diaper service faces competition not only from other diaper service firms but also from retailers who sell disposable and nondisposable diapers. Innovations in retailing and in such retail products as low-cost disposable diapers may affect his business far more than any competitive efforts by other firms that offer a similar service.

When a homeowner needs a wheelbarrow, trailer, chain saw, plumber's snake, or a myriad of other products, he can borrow, rent, or buy these items. If he elects to rent a tool, it is obvious that a retail sale has been lost for the moment. Thus hardware stores, discount houses, department stores, plumbing supply outlets, and other retailers are in direct competition with the service industry. In addition, rental stores may also sell the product to the consumer. If a customer has enjoyed a successful day of cutting firewood with a rented chain saw, he may easily be in a receptive mood to purchase such a saw.

Many retailers have recognized the sales potential in the rental process and have added rental service to their line. It is common practice in many areas for paint stores to rent ladders, tarps, rollers, and other complementary equipment. Retailers with leisure-time-oriented products, such as motor bikes, canoes, and campers, have discovered substantial extra profits and sales potential in the rental business.

The service industry is not confined to a single market segment. It increasingly markets to all income and age groups and offers services from the day of birth through death. Weddings, Hanukkahs, showers, and other special occasions are serviced by this industry, with goods and services ranging from rented chairs to thousand-dollar ice carvings. To serve man in sickness and in injury, wheelchairs, crutches, special hospital beds, and oxygen respirators are some of the products offered for rent.

The potential for the application of modern marketing and management techniques in the service industry is scarcely confined to running a better "mom and pop" type operation. This is an industry that has formed huge national and multinational organizations.

This is true even in industries traditionally thought of as strictly the province for small independents. Service Corporation International of Houston, an example of the opportunity in these areas, during a four-year period acquired 101 funeral homes and 36 cemeteries in twelve states, Washington, D.C., and six Canadian provinces, making it the largest in the industry. Yet, impressive as this growth is, it represents less than 3 percent of total industry revenues in an industry composed of 20,000 U.S. funeral service firms and 10,000 nonprofit cemeteries reporting approximately $3.5 billion in gross receipts.[1]

GROWTH OF THE SERVICE INDUSTRY

The term "service industry" can be highly misleading, depending upon how the statistics are compiled. It is abundantly clear that a tremendous growth in the service industry sector has occurred in the last few decades. The United States is now described as the first service economy the world has ever seen, with over half the labor force involved in a service capacity. There have been estimates that this might reach 80 percent by 1990.[2]

It is a complex task to separate all the functions that can logically be classified as service retailing to form a dollar and cents value for the service industry. The fact is, however, that it is very large and obviously is growing. Consumer spending for services exceeded $300 billion in 1972, when service expenditures accounted for over 40 percent of the typical American family's budget.[3] In the early fifties, services claimed about 35 percent of the consumer's expenditures. Although prices for services have risen faster than prices for goods, there has been a trend for consumers to buy more services from a wider assortment of service offerings.

About half of the total consumer expenditures for services goes into housing and the cost of operating the home (Figure 16–1). Not only does this area account for the most important total service expenditure, it is also one of the fastest growing service areas (Table 16–1). Consumer expenditure for shelter and household operation services such as gas, electricity, telephone, and telegraph is increasing faster than increases in the consumer's income. This is illustrated by the income elasticity coefficient in excess of 1.0 in Table 16–1. The increased level of appliance ownership has resulted in increased power consumption. A large growth in the teenage population and emphasis upon color, style, and multiple connections are attributed to the rapid rise in telephone service.

Medical services accounted for about 15 percent of the consumer's service expenditures in 1970, but consumer spending for medical services also appears to be rising faster than the rise in consumer incomes. Other service areas that are expected to grow most rapidly in the 1970s are airline travel, foreign travel, higher education, and intercity travel (Table 16–1).

Figure 16–1 Total U.S. Family Dollar Expenditures for Selected Service Categories (Total Expenditures for Services in 1970 = 100%)

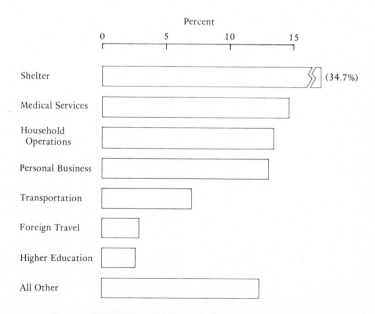

SOURCE   U.S. Department of Commerce, *The Conference Board Record* (May 1972), p. 50.

Table 16–1   Actual and Projected Annual Growth Rate for Consumer Service Expenditures, 1955–1980

		AVERAGE ANNUAL PERCENTAGE GROWTH RATE	
	*Income Elasticity 1955–1970**	*1955–1970*	*1970–1980 (Projected)*
Disposable personal income	1.00	4.2	4.4
All expenditures	0.97	4.1	4.3
Non-durables	0.76	3.2	3.4
Durables	1.41	5.9	6.2
Services	1.04	4.4	4.6
Shelter	1.16	4.9	5.1
Household operation	1.06	4.4	4.7
Gas and electricity	1.27	5.3	5.6
Telephone and telegraph	1.69	7.1	7.5
Domestic services	−0.34	−1.4	−1.5
Transportation	0.56	2.4	2.5
Automotive services	0.69	2.9	3.0
Local travel	−0.64	−2.7	−2.8
Intercity travel	1.30	5.4	5.7
Airlines	2.68	11.3	11.8
Medical services	1.16	4.9	5.1
Physicians	0.97	4.1	4.3
Dentists	0.81	3.4	3.6
Personal care	0.76	3.2	3.4
Foreign travel	1.61	6.7	7.1
Higher education	1.55	6.5	6.8

* Percentage increase in consumer spending for the indicated services for each 1% rise in real disposable personal income.

SOURCE   *The Conference Board Record* (May 1972), p. 51.

Consumer dollar expenditures are influenced by rising prices, so they may not appear to be the best unit of measurement in the service industry. However, it is questionable how service productivity should be measured inasmuch as quantity measurements are generally inadequate. Trades (beauticians, barbers, repair firms, etc.) depend upon the quality and uniqueness of their work, not upon the number of "look alikes" they can push out in one day. Nevertheless, as competition and chains of service firms grow, efforts to measure productivity and improve efficiency are bound to increase.

CLASSIFICATION OF CONSUMER SERVICE FIRMS

Although the service industry is highly fragmented, it can be grouped roughly into three main areas.[4]

Rented goods service. As the name implies, these firms rent products—

ranging from heavy-duty trucks to costumes for the Halloween dance. They may, however, engage in the sale of products at the same time.

Owned goods service. Firms in this category repair products, sell value (added to a product through custom work), or otherwise improve existing products. Upholstery shops, gun smiths, antique clock repair shops, ski repair shops, and many others are examples of such firms. In almost every case they also sell products at retail, such as gun oil, upholstery sprays and cleaners, keys to wind clocks, ski wax and bindings, and thousands of other products.

Non-goods service. The primary product for firms in this group is *not* a product but a service. Beauty salons, funeral parlors, poodle barber shops, travel agencies, and insurance and financial institutions are a few examples.

The previous classification of retail services by rental goods, owned goods, and non-goods should not be interpreted as meaning that a retailer must be one or the other type. In practice, the retail mix of a firm (such as Sears) includes each of these areas, plus the regular merchandising services.

In recent years traditional retailers have expanded into a variety of services. This has generally been accomplished in the following ways:

1. Acquisition or establishment of service. Under this system the retailer acquires majority interest in the service company and then offers it as a part of the store's total merchandising mix. Insurance and finance companies have been among the major services established in this way.
2. Leased department. Travel agencies, optical service, and shoe repair represent services that are commonly sold through an independent service retailer who simply leases space from another retailer. In addition to paying the lease, the lessee may agree to share a percentage of the gross.
3. Tie-in agreement. In these cases the retailer may do no more than agree to provide a signed order to the vendor of services, who then reimburses the retailer with a commission. Banks and car dealers often have such arrangements for car loans. In other cases the retailer may sell the entire package of services under his name but, in actuality, perform nothing more than the selling and bill-collecting functions. The service vendor then performs the actual service.

The mix of retail and service firms can be illustrated by the acquisition of financial and insurance services by retailers. This move has placed retailers in direct competition with insurance companies, banks, credit unions, and personal finance companies. In turn, members of the financial service industry, such as Beneficial Finance and Household Finance Corporation, have responded by entering into retailing. With the exception of financial institutions that are specifically prohibited by charter or law from engaging in such vertical integration, there is every reason to believe that many more will do so. The possibility for large banks to establish huge national and international retailing chains is quite foreseeable.[5]

Commercial banks already perform a host of important services for retailers and retail customers, such as letters of credit, floor planning, factoring, credit cards, and installment lending—to mention only a few. The acquisition of a retail chain could provide a bank with a built-in market for its services and a retailer with an excellent source of consumer credit.

Small, independent service firms generally specialize in one service area or in a few related areas. For example, most barbers confine their service offering to males who seek a haircut, shave, shampoo, or shoeshine. Movie theaters usually are used only to show movies. Increasing costs and shifts in consumer demand, however, may cause specialized service firms such as barber shops and movie theaters to change their service offering. Such changes would make better utilization of space and equipment by satisfying new consumer demands. Currently, most small service firms are built around the specialization-of-labor concept—the barber and shoeshine boy in the barber shop; the movie projector operator, usher, and ticket seller in the theater. Expanded service offerings might require the services of a fashion specialist for a barber shop and a day-care-center staff for the theater location near a residential area.

Thus the trends within both large and small service firms make the classification task difficult.

STEPS IN THE MARKETING OF SERVICES

Service marketing can benefit from considering the following marketing activities.

Defining the Offering

An accurate generic definition of the service offering is required if a service firm is going to keep pace with or ahead of changes made by competitors and benefit from changes in consumer wants. Creative thinking can be rewarded with a tremendous growth in business volume. For example, some financial institutions are expanding their offering by providing one-stop services, including real estate development, investment management, credit card services, leasing services, safety deposit facilities, insurance coverage, savings facilities, travel scheduling, accounting services, and other money-related activities.

Defining the Target Market

Segmenting the broad generic definition into similar subgroups of people who have common characteristics and then identifying and meeting the needs of the most attractive segments can be a very profitable strategy to follow. An accurate definition of the needs of a market segment can allow the service firm to tailor its service offering and the marketing of that offering to best satisfy the consumers in that segment.

The categorization of the population into different segments can be based not only on traditional demographic factors but also upon consumers' attitudes, activities, needs, and motivations. Indeed, in service marketing these four considerations may be the most profitable way to segment the market.

In addition to determining the market target groups, for some service firms it is equally important to determine which groups to avoid. Many professional service firms (such as market research firms, advertising agencies, lawyers, etc.) are restrained from entering certain businesses because of possible conflicts of interests. For example, marketing research firms and advertising agencies usually refuse to handle two competing products simultaneously. In some cases it may be possible to set up separate task groups for each account and work on competitive accounts, but both competitors should be made aware of the situation and agree to it before the second competitive client is added to the list of clientele.

Planning Differentiated Service Offerings

Selling to different market segments usually requires a different marketing approach to reach each group effectively. Each segment of a market for a given service will not respond to the same approach. The presentation of the service must be geared to the needs of the target market segments. Service firms can provide a differential advantage in their service offering if any part of that offering creates a special value in the minds of their customers.

For example, the manager of an auto repair shop in a suburb might cater to commuters who catch the train to work in the city. The auto service firm could drive the customer to the station when he arrives in the morning and meet him at the evening train. Other extras, such as washing and cleaning the car at no extra charge, may be provided on repair jobs over a certain amount.

The development of companion service offerings frequently is based upon the desire to use all of the firm's resources at near-capacity levels.[6] Near-capacity utilization in retailing firms generally allows overhead costs to be spread over a larger number of sales units and therefore results in a per unit reduction in selling costs. Service firms have a more important advantage in operating at full capacity because their offerings are generally so perishable that they cannot be stored. There is no way to market the rental car that went unused yesterday, or the unused time that an interior decorator or barber spent in waiting for customers to require his or her services. Thus it is important to develop a service offering that can reverse the underutilization of capacity and recapture labor and capital costs as regularly and as completely as possible.

Identifying and Evaluating New Service Offerings

The generation of new ideas that may be included in the service offering is likely to originate with the consumer. Service firms benefit from a relatively short channel of communication that extends from the consumer to the service personnel (employees or agents of the service retailer) to the firm's management. Consumer problems can be translated into business opportunities if service personnel are impressed with the importance of reporting these consumer problems (as well as their recommendations for a solution) to the firm's management. A service firm's management can then screen out the better ideas, rank them in priority, and perform a business analysis of the best ideas. The business analysis would focus on sales projections, cost considerations, evaluation of the company's resources (including managerial ability) to determine profitability and if compatible equipment and knowledge are available. The effect the new offering will have upon the satisfaction of current clients is also important.

One difficulty associated with the development of new service offerings is that they are seldom patentable and only a few are proprietary. Thus timing and resourcefulness are major ways that service firms can stay ahead of competitors. The need to search continually for new ideas and methods of better serving the consumer's desires is implied by the lack of protection provided by legal means. The progressive service firms must conduct continued service development programs if they are to keep ahead of the competitor who is simply copying old service offerings. The consequences of this competition through imitative action are evident by the ease of entry into many service industries and by the existence of many small service outlets.

Under the Lanham Act of 1946, the service industry has acquired the legal protection of "service marks," which are supposed to be the legal counterpart of the trademark.[7] The Lanham Act also made provisions for the legal use of the "certification mark" and the "collective mark" as service marks for the promotion of services. However, relatively few service outlets have used service marks to gain the advantages of market control, uniformity, and guarantee of quality that brand names appear to offer consumers. Perhaps future service marketing will make better use of the service mark to gain a competitive advantage over service-imitating competitors.

Packaging and Labeling

Except for very few cases—such as the wrapping that protects a piece of clothing on its return from the laundry or dry cleaners—services usually are not packaged or labeled in a manner that presents promotional possibilities.

Service Warranties

The provision of service warranties is another area in which service retailers can create a differentiated offering. The increasing importance of consumerism and the passage of new legislation must be recognized. Thus the service retailer who offers a good warranty policy may obtain consumer good will and may benefit from the resulting publicity by acting before his competition does and before it is a legal requirement.

By 1970 the Uniform Commercial Code had replaced the Uniform Sales Act in every state except Louisiana.[8] Under the Uniform Commercial Code, service warranties are included as "express warranties." An express warranty arises as part of the bargaining process between buyer and seller.

Case law since 1960 shows that service retailers create express warranties by their selling claims and their advertising. The growing number of warranty cases is influenced by class action possibilities against both the service firm and the manufacturer of the items being used and/or sold by the service firm.[9]

Thus it is likely that warranties will become an important issue to service retailers, and courts are likely to see an increase in the number of cases involving service retailers. A service firm that recognizes this trend can take steps not only to avoid possible court action but to turn the warranty into a promotable item by including a unique and clear statement of warranty as part of its service offering.

Establishing warranty standards that are higher than those set by the industry can be illustrated by a policy of guarantees on parts and labor in a repair shop. If sixty days is standard in the industry, the service firm could establish a *ninety*-day warranty policy. The extra thirty days provides an indication of the firm's good intentions and conveys to the customers an impression of high performance standards in the services performed. Making an exception for a good customer who experiences difficulties several days after the guarantee has expired can also generate consumer good will.

Guarantees of performance, however, may be more difficult to substantiate for a service than for goods because for many services there is no acceptable method of measuring quality. The end result of service activity is frequently identifiable only in intangible terms. However, the performance of many services can be evaluated in tangible terms, such as speed, accuracy, frequency of service, etc. If it is possible to substantiate claims, service firms benefit by using these claims because the buyer of services frequently may not feel comfortable in assessing the worth of a complex of activities that comprise the service offering. That is, the consumer frequently feels "helpless" because he is putting his fate in the hands of the service firm. Inclusion of a guarantee can reduce this feeling of uncertainty.

Many services (e.g., medical, accounting, insurance, interior decorating, beauty shops, etc.) do not offer their skills and resources *per se* but really offer the consumer "confidence," "hope," or "the reduction of uncertainty." In these cases the service firm promises the introduction of more certainty in an area in which customers feel unsure.

Displaying the industry code of ethics is one way to remind consumers of the quality service they can expect to receive from a service firm. However, merely displaying the code does little good unless service personnel live up to the code.

Reducing Consumer Uncertainty

It follows that the service firm will want to design a service offering that will minimize consumer uncertainty.[10]

Creating consumer awareness of the *need* for a service must be an objective of the firm's promotional effort. Frequently, the consumer will be aware that he has (or is likely to have) a *problem*. However, in many cases (making a will, obtaining a medical checkup, obtaining insurance, etc.) the consumer may not be aware of his need for the service. In these cases an awareness promotional campaign is essential for the industry or the individual firm.

Deciding what service is *applicable* for solving the consumer's problems is the next step. The successful performance of the service depends on a clear understanding of the customer's problems. Ideally, the potential service customer would approach the service firm with an objective description of his problem and request help in solving it. In reality, however, consumers infrequently take this approach. Thus it is the job of the service firm to determine the consumer's problems by questioning him. If the subtle questioning results in an "in depth" problem definition, the service offering can be tailored to meet the consumer's individual needs.

The consumer should be given an honest opinion, backed up by facts, on the worth of each purchase alternative. The objective is to gain customer confidence by giving an honest estimate. Even honest estimates are sometimes doubted by consumers, especially if the service outlet also sells new or replacement equipment. A consistent, honest approach, however, should win the trust of most consumers over the long run.

Selecting the employee who should render the service depends upon the person's demonstrable knowledge and skill in the claimed area of competence. Obviously demonstrable skill and knowledge will create consumer confidence. Many service retailers fail to recognize and acknowledge that they cannot do all things; that is, that there are limits to their skill and knowledge. In this case referrals to other people within the firm may be needed, or maybe it requires an honest admission that no one in the firm has the competence in that specialized area. Failure to admit incompetence in an area can cost a service firm longtime business if a customer loses confidence in the firm because of one bad experience.

However, admission of incompetence, if repeated several times, can point out new areas of expertise that could be included in the service offering.

How the service is performed is also important in establishing consumer confidence, and respecting the customer's time can gain consumer respect. People become distrustful of a service firm which always breaks promised service schedules, so every effort should be made to keep on schedule and not overcommit the service personnel. Service delays are sometimes unavoidable, and when this occurs the consumer should be informed that a repairman is going to be delayed. This allows the consumer to adjust his schedule. In the repair business, providing a replacement for the consumers to use while theirs is being repaired can lessen consumer aggravation when the service period is likely to be delayed.

Consumers also appreciate consideration and promptness in being informed when the estimated cost of service is changed because of unforeseen circumstances. In the repair business, the consumer may think that the revised cost is more than the item is worth and decide to purchase a new item.

Location

Location is another factor that the service firm can use to establish a differentiated service mix. For example, studies of consumer preference for airline service have shown that the most important reasons a consumer selects one airline over another are that the airline is going to the desired location at the desired time. Other factors, such as meal service, in-flight movies, stewardesses, magazine selection, etc., are much less important.

The same is true of other retail services. It is not likely that a consumer will travel across town to a muffler shop, brake repair garage, shoe repair store, or laundromat if there is a comparable shop in the neighborhood, even if the nearby shop is not the favorite one.

The large car-rental agencies have been faced with stiff price competition from industry newcomers in recent years. Even so, they have maintained their basic price policies due to their favorable image and the widespread availability of their rental counters. It is simply easier for a customer, particularly one on an expense account, to walk to the Hertz, Avis, or National counter than to call one of the competitive off-grounds firms and wait for a car to be delivered.

Studies have demonstrated the savings that can be realized by riding the bus rather than driving one's car to work. Yet, if an ample supply of gasoline is available, the real or imagined convenience of driving one's own car continues to win out over this service in most American cities. Motels must be located near a highway so that they are easily accessible to motorists. Laundry and cleaning firms must be conveniently available to their customers, even if the firm has to create the convenience by offering pickup and delivery service in the case of a poorly located firm. The list could go on and on, but it is generally true that location is an important consideration for all service firms that are visited personally by their customers. Unless very skilled personal expertise is involved, consumers are likely to patronize the service firm that requires the least effort to reach.

Services involving a considerable amount of personal skill (such as those of the medical doctor, lawyer, music instructor, etc.) and those service firms which are never visited by the customer can utilize relatively inconvenient locations. Examples of firms which are seldom visited by customers are window washing and television and radio repair services. These service firms can pay the lower rents generally associated with an inconvenient location and still satisfy their consumers' needs. The facilities do not have to be as elaborate for the seldom-visited service firms either, as the telephone is their primary method of communication with consumers.

Service firms requiring a customer visitation, on the other hand, depend upon a neat external appearance to draw the consumer inside. The interior must be neat, clean, and comfortable and offer a pleasant atmosphere, especially if consumers have to wait for service. The layout, equipment, and furniture should convey an appropriate impression, being both attractive and functional. The land, building layout, equipment, and furniture should generate the desired image for the firm—in the same manner that goods retailers use these factors to project a store image.

Planning the Promotional Mix

Aside from packaging, the communication channels available to service firms are identical to those available to merchandise retailers. Many promotional methods are rejected by service retailers as being too brash and costly without any real consideration of their relationship to the firms' service offering and the habits of their target markets. This unnatural shrinking of alternatives can result in uncreative promotional campaigns. For example, it can allow a more progressive promoting firm to be the first to offer a premium gift to consumers who deposit $5,000 in the firm's savings account.

Some services can effectively use more promotional expenditures than others, such as medical doctors, lawyers, and related professional service firms, which are restricted by their professional organizations in the type and amount of promotions they utilize. Besides advertising, personal selling, point-of-purchase promotions, and public relations, there are many types of sales promotion that service firms can use in making consumers aware of their offering and instilling consumer confidence in the quality of service offered. The main difficulty is selecting techniques that project the appropriate image.

Advertising

Service advertising differs from product advertising because it is more difficult (and sometimes impossible) to physically illustrate the use or benefits of a service. Thus service advertising is likely to depend more on image appeals. The differences in the use of advertising media are strongly influenced by the size of the service firm and by accepted practice within each service industry. Small service firms may be content with a listing in the Yellow Pages, while large service firms (such as H & R Block) may rely heavily upon television advertising. Yellow Page advertising and select forms of specialty and direct-mail advertising for small service firms can mean the crucial difference between a sale or an empty cash drawer.

Sign Media

The mobility of many services, such as Greyhound, U-Haul Trailer, or a brightly colored Braniff jet, gives certain service industries an extremely important advertising tool. In a period of twenty-four hours a jet may be seen by thousands of potential customers in a multiplicity of states and nations. The airlines and car rental industries also have learned that their personnel can serve as subtle public relations and advertising media. It is small wonder that such industries carefully regulate the social activities of uniformed employees.

Point-of-Purchase Promotion

Point-of-purchase advertising is critical to many service firms. Unlike products, the point of purchase may be in the customer's home or office rather than a store. Nevertheless, there is a "point of sale" for all services, just as for any product.

The often overlooked business card can be an effective medium at point of purchase. Business cards are retained by people, particularly businessmen, and since they are often held together with a rubber band or simply tossed into a desk drawer, it is important to give careful consideration to their design. Whenever possible, they should be distinctive and carry the service mark of the company.

It is equally important to plan carefully for the distribution of business cards and flyers in the service retail store. Service shops often fail to provide display racks or piles of cards and flyers for customers. Some service firms have found that a pleased customer will gladly distribute such items to his friends. Unless the retailer of goods has particularly distinctive merchandise or prices, it is unlikely he can share in this willingness of customers to cooperate gladly in advertising.

Word of Mouth

The success of a service retailer is probably much more dependent upon word-of-mouth advertising than goods retailing. "Bad mouthing" seems to be contagious. Airlines are particularly vulnerable to an infection of "bad mouthing," which sweeps through a population. While there is generally some substance to the bad imagery, it is apparent that a series of complex social and psychological variables is involved that causes both positive and negative image infection among a populace. The same phenomena witnessed in the sudden decline in popularity of an "in" restaurant or bar prevail throughout the service industry.

A high level of consumer satisfaction is the most crucial factor in obtaining good word-of-mouth advertising. Although much practical research is needed in this area, service retailers continually need to be aware of the "bad-mouth syndrome."[11]

Bumper Stickers

Bumper stickers can be used effectively to promote services, particularly if the sticker is designed to capture the curiosity of the reader. Service retailers of "glamor" or "in" places and events are able to capitalize on the use of bumper stickers in a method that most retailers would never dare attempt. It is difficult to imagine parking lot attendants at a Sears store suddenly descending upon all cars in the lot with bumper stickers advertising the store. Yet this is precisely what happens at a variety of recreational-service areas, ranging from Reptile Gardens to the newest 40-acre amusement park. One of the few examples in goods retailing is the name plate of the dealer that is attached to the back of new automobiles and recreational vehicles.

Perhaps a consumer's psychological need is met through bumper stickers, or else there would be far more objection to their use. Bumper stickers may meet many of the same needs as college and fraternity window stickers and the travel decals that were popular during the '50s. They may say to others

"I have visited unusual places" or "I am also a member of the group that enjoys 'in' things."

Other Specialty Advertising Forms

The service industry is particularly well suited to many forms of specialty advertising. A survey by the Specialty Advertising Association International showed that of the top ten groups of particular interest to specialty advertisers, seven were service-type industries.[12] Retail establishments such as camera and jewelry stores were given very low interest rankings by distributors of specialty advertising while banks and savings and loan associations ranked high.

The type of specialty item selected by a service retailer is only as good as the thought behind it and the application it has to the target market. In far too many cases a specialty gimmick has been used simply because it seemed clever and inexpensive. On the other hand, the success of Avis with its "We Try Harder" buttons in a variety of foreign languages is an example of the exposure that a good specialty item can give a service retailer.

Samples and Demonstrations

It is difficult for the service industry to give samples or demonstrations. How does a barber go about giving a sample of his service—by cutting only the front half of the head? Welcome Wagon and other greeting firms can distribute coupons which can be redeemed for a free haircut by newcomers to an area, but the alternatives are limited. Although free samples and demonstrations are normally not practical, special promotional cut rates can be given for services. This is true even in some regulated businesses, such as the airline industry. The introduction of the 747 was followed by low group rates for a half-hour ride in this plane. In many cases the revenue was donated to charity, and the ride became an effective demonstration or sample.

Promotion by Telephone

To many retailers the telephone is more of a hindrance to doing business than an aid. Many managers of supermarkets, discount houses, and other mass merchandising outlets believe that the telephone simply interrupts or intrudes on management and personnel time without adding to sales. This is scarcely the case with most service retailers, yet many treat the telephone as if it were a nuisance.

Generally, when a person calls a service retail establishment he or she is genuinely interested in learning more about the retailer's service, and should be regarded as a potential customer. A call from a potential customer should be viewed as the near culmination of all the efforts a firm has expended in advertising, public relations, location selection, and total imagery. It is the firm's chance to invite the customer to use its services, and may also be the moment to close the sale.

Thus the telephone should be considered the "hot line," and should not be left to indiscriminate answering by anyone who may or may not be handy. Programs should be established for the purpose of training personnel in the correct use of the phone. Order blanks and writing material should be placed near the phone, and a follow-through system should be implemented so that, when the customer arrives, she knows that she was expected and she is treated accordingly. The airlines are leaders in this field and may be viewed as models. The Bell Telephone System should also be contacted for help, as it has trained experts in this field to assist firms, as well as provide free educational films.

Customer Contact and Personal Selling

A large portion, if not the majority, of service retailers are highly dependent upon direct consumer contact. This has been found to be true even in the case of services originally based on the concept of "self-service." In some areas, the increasing rate of crimes of a personal nature, such as robbery and rape, plus vandalism, has created a need for attendants in—say—laundromats. Owners of these establishments have discovered that the attendant can act as more than a policewoman; she can greet customers, instruct them in the use of machines, and provide additional revenue through personal ironing of clothes.

To be successful, a service retailer must place primary emphasis on customer contact. This should begin before his business doors are even opened. In the case of service businesses that serve a local area, a key to success can be door-to-door calling on customers—at the same time that the contractor or remodeler is working on the service building.

The message is simple. After an introduction, the service retailer tells the consumer of his service and what it can do for him, asks for his future business, and asks him to tell his friends. An inexpensive specialty gift item, with the retailer's name, address, and phone number imprinted on it, should be left with the potential customer. Customer contact then continues every minute of the service retailer's day.

There is rarely such a thing as too much customer contact. Unless the importance of this message is continually transmitted to all personnel, it will soon be forgotten. The teller at a savings and loan firm who shows displeasure at opening piggy banks and counting loose change is a very weak link in the service chain. Unreturned phone calls from customers, an empty and unclean pot at the "free coffee" table, and halfhearted welcomes to customers who bring in "two for one" or other promotional coupons are examples of the negatives in customer contact. Correct customer contact must be a continuous philosophy that permeates all levels of a service retailer's organization.

Relatively less emphasis can be placed on personal selling by service firms which make most of their sales to customers who have already decided to buy when they make their initial contact with the service firm.[13] Such a service firm can advertise to attract new customers and then concentrate on building repeat business by providing prompt, efficient service. Radio and television repair shops, for example, receive a telephone call requesting repair service. The customer does not need to be sold on the fact that he needs help. In this case the role of a service person may not include any selling, or it may be limited to a suggestion that the consumer upgrade his purchase by replacing more parts, which will provide a longer, more productive life.

On the other hand, extensive use of personal selling may be required of service firms that contact customers who are not committed to buying at the time of the original contact with the firm. Good personal selling techniques are required in this case. These techniques begin with an understanding of the customer's problem and end with an explanation of how the firm's service offerings can satisfy those needs.

Personal selling plays a different role in the marketing of services than it does in the selling of products. Retailers of goods generally place more reliance on tangible product benefits to consumers in their advertising and selling. Service firms are, of necessity, likely to turn to images that communicate the benefits to the purchaser.[14]

Build Repeat Business

The success of many service firms is dependent upon obtaining repeat business from present and former customers. Repeat consumer business is based on satisfying the consumer with the service he has previously experienced. Satisfied consumers of services tend to show loyalty to the service firm and to return when they have a new problem that appears to fall within the area of the firm's expertise.

Established professional service firms such as doctors, lawyers, and accountants rely upon repeat business as the core—if not the entire source—of their business. In these cases, and in other service areas, additional business is fairly predictable and is forthcoming almost automatically, as long as a proper relationship is maintained with satisfied customers.[15]

Generating repeat sales from customers revolves mostly around the professional people who provide the services. Consumers become "tied" to personalities, particularly if they receive prompt, efficient service from the service person. The degree of loyalty may be affected by the amount of skill that the consumer perceives is required to solve his problems. For example, a consumer is likely to be more loyal to a doctor than to a barber. However, some customers change barber shops every time their favorite barber changes employment. Although no one is indispensable, these strong personal preferences must be recognized by service firms' management.

The importance of the service professional affects the firm's selling activity considerably. Technical service people are not as likely to want to develop selling techniques to the degree that goods salesmen may consider essential for their profession. As a result, the selling of former service customers is likely to be less organized and systematic than in product retail outlets. Instead, service selling is more centered on "opportunity selling," which consists of the technical service person's sensing an opportunity for future service and then communicating the benefits of using that service to his customer.

Undoubtedly, one of the best ways to build repeat business is to perform excellent service all of the time. A difficulty arises, however, because the customer is frequently unable to judge the quality of the service. Thus excellent service *alone* is not sufficient. It must be accompanied by an informal and discreet method of letting the customer become aware of the excellent service he receives.

Some scheduling of periodic contact is required if repeat business is to be maintained. As time passes from the date that the original service was performed, the less likely it is that the customer will return to the same service firm for future work.[16] Making periodic contact can remind the customer of the excellent service he received, and it can also remind him that time has passed more rapidly than he thought. For example, by the use of a good card-filing system, dentists, doctors, and the like can identify customers who are due for their periodic checkup.

Opportunities for suggesting the benefits of some further service should also be utilized to build repeat business. An accountant who is making a regular audit might suggest a way of improving the accounting practices or a way of making better managerial use of the data the firm already has. Many bowling firms help to build a permanent clientele by organizing and promoting bowling leagues, which use pressure from the team members to encourage each individual to be there at bowling time. Surely other service firms can use this competitive motivation to build repeat business.

Cooperative associations and chain organizations are also frequently used to build permanent patronage. For example, motels and restaurants benefit from association with one nationally advertised name. Generally the chain, franchise, or cooperative association establishes quality standards, inspects each establishment periodically, and extends the privilege of continued association only to those firms that meet the established standards. Their consumers, perceiving a more consistent type of service, tend to become loyal customers of the various associations' member firms. This consistent service concept is likely to grow in importance as people do more traveling and change their place of residence more frequently.

Customer relations—performing those activities that are designed to make the client personally attached to one of the firm's technical service people—is another method of stimulating repeat business. Providing special considerations, such as lunch, small gifts, etc., are methods used to varying degrees in attempts to build consumer loyalty.

Credit

Credit also can be used effectively by service firms to generate business. Service firms have too long restricted the granting of credit because they sold intangible offerings that could not be repossessed if the consumer refused to pay his debt. The fact that unused capacity in service firms cannot be sold later makes the granting of credit attractive even if there are occasional losses due to bad debts. Compared to goods retailers, the service firm with excess capacity certainly has less to lose by granting credit and risking losses due to increases in accounts receivable.

The use of banks' credit card plans has taken away most of the bad debt problem. The plans also make it easier and more economical for the service firm to make credit sales on small purchases.

In addition, surprising market segments can sometimes be discovered through research no more involved than examining company records. Many airlines found that their credit policies for unmarried young women were unduly restrictive. A policy of extending credit to married women or those over 25 did not take into account the number of gainfully employed career women. The number of people in this market segment is large, is growing, and is fully able to assume credit responsibility.

Planning Pricing Strategy

Developing good pricing strategies for service firms is an important activity. Most service firms use relatively little capital, so pricing and the use of time are the main factors used to generate profits. In addition, because of imperfect consumer knowledge about the quality of service performed, many services are less subject to the pressures and controls of the marketplace than goods retailers. As a result, these service firms have greater flexibility in their pricing activities.

Service firms can select many different pricing strategies, and the major alternatives will now be discussed.[17]

Cost Pricing

Cost pricing is a method of obtaining price by adding all of the chargeable costs. This method requires a reliable cost accounting system which identifies the costs and time used for each phase of the service. The allocatable costs are then assigned to each customer, and these costs are multiplied by a markup factor (2.5 is common for many professional service firms), which must cover profit, rent, utilities, insurance, taxes, and other nonallocatable fixed costs.

For example, a service firm performing a job which is estimated to cost $1,000 in wages and other allocatable costs would charge the customer $2,500 if the 2.5 markup factor is used. Only the value of service people's time used on this particular piece of work would be included in the $1,000 cost estimate. The time that these service people spend idle, in retraining, etc. would not be included in the allocatable costs, but would have to be recovered in the markup charge.

A major disadvantage of the cost pricing system is the difficulty of identifying and accurately allocating costs. For example, questions frequently arise on the ways to identify and allocate developmental costs, proposed costs, general administrative costs, etc. Good cost accounting systems can answer many of these questions, but all procedures are subject to the dedication of the management and service people. Cost pricing will not work unless everyone keeps records that indicate how much time is devoted to each activity and each service job. Frequently, because it is difficult to convince professional service people of this fact, many service firms cannot calculate the profit and loss contribution of individual types of services, individual jobs, customers, etc. Instead, they wonder why the overall profitability of the enterprise is low relative to what they think it should be.

Another disadvantage of the cost pricing method is that if costs are used as the sole basis for the establishment of price, there may be no incentive for controlling costs. However, competitive markets usually provide an indication, via decreased business, when this is occurring.

Contingency Payment Pricing

Contingency payment pricing is the term used when the price for the service is quoted as contingent upon the accomplishment of the task. It is similar to the commission fee for a salesman, as no charge is made unless the task is performed. This method is used by real estate agencies, employment agencies, and similar organizations.

The contingency system offers a great deal of motivation to successfully complete the work. The difficulty arises in defining what constitutes successful performance of the task.

Fixed Pricing

A fixed or uniform price is achieved by a controlling body such as a professional organization, or governmental regulation, or an informal agreement. Actually, this is a *result* of a pricing decision and not a *method* used to reach a decision. The service firm must abide by it, however, so its pricing strategy is predetermined by the controlling body. Transportation companies engaged in interstate commerce (moving companies, trucking firms, railroads, airlines), beauty shops, and barber shops are examples.

Value Pricing

Value pricing is based on the belief that buyers will respond to price in relation to the value that they associate with the service. One should recall that customers of most services have difficulty appraising the technical worth of the service offering because it is generally so intangible. The purchasing decision is likely to be based on the consumer's perception of the value of the service offering. Frequently, when consumers have difficulty appraising the worth of an offering, an association of poor quality is attached to "discount" prices. Thus value pricing may amount to a "what the market will bear" pricing policy, as the price is not based on cost but on the value the consumer attaches to the service.

Value pricing can be defended as "fair" despite the non-association of price with costs. Price, in this case, is associated with worth, so new ideas, new methods, and new knowledge that are valuable to the client are paid for in proportion to their value to the customer. Value pricing in small, local areas where there are no alternative sources of supply, or in cases of very essential services (such as brain surgery), may not be considered a "just" pricing policy by consumers.[18]

Planning Pricing Tactics

Service pricing strategy, no matter how it is determined, must guide shorter-term (or tactical) decisions to establish the actual quoted price. The same tactical pricing techniques that are used to sell goods can be modified effectively to sell services. The application of some of the major pricing tactics to the service area will now be discussed.

Loss Leader Pricing

Loss leader pricing is a deliberate reduction in price to establish initial contact with a customer. It is frequently used by service firms such as auto service stations or dancing studios, which give price reductions as "get acquainted" offers. One disadvantage of loss leader pricing is that a low price may tend to establish a price ceiling, above which the consumer may resist price increases if he knows he is getting the same service but paying a higher price.

Diversionary Pricing

Diversionary pricing is the practice of setting a low, basic price on selected services which, hopefully, will develop a "low price" image for the entire firm. It is generally effective if prices are lowered on all service items on which consumers are price conscious. If these price-sensitive offerings cannot be identified, or if all of the firm's offerings are price sensitive, diversionary pricing will not be an effective pricing tactic.

Discount Pricing

Discount pricing is a tactic which provides a price quotation that is subject to a discount on some predetermined basis, such as time schedule, volume of purchases over a stated time period, extent of commitment, etc. Discount pricing is widely used by leasing firms and many other service agencies. It provides an incentive for the consumer to remain loyal to the service firm because costs are reduced by purchasing all (or most) of the available services from one firm. The widespread use of discount pricing is explained by the fact that service firms are faced with a continuing problem because they are unable to inventory their particular service. If the goods inventory of a retailer does not sell, it can sometimes be returned to the vendor, or stored or placed on sale. This is not the case with a firm such as an airline or movie theater. Once the plane has left the ground, the empty seats are forever lost as revenue for that flight. As a result, service firms with this problem often turn to the practice of charging different customers different prices for only slightly different services.

Youth fares, tour packages, and Saturday afternoon matinees are examples of this type of pricing. Only rarely are these firms able to sell all their services without the aid of discount pricing. As a result, the concept of market segmentation is of paramount importance to firms in the service industry. It becomes a necessity to analyze market segments to determine new promotions and prices that might appeal to them. In the case of regulated and interstate firms, differentiated or discount pricing and promotion is automatically open to official debate and legal regulation.

Price Lining

Price lining is a tactic whereby prices are not varied, but the quality or extent of the service provided is adjusted to reflect changes in costs. This removes price as a major negotiating point, but the consumer may be able to perceive the change in the service offering and associate it with an "inferior" image of the firm in general. Leasing firms frequently use the price lining tactic when they make available, at different rental charges, different quality levels of the same item (garden Rototillers with various size engines, for example).

PROCUREMENT AND INVENTORY CONTROL

Procurement in most service firms is generally limited to buying equipment and supplies. The inventory control problem, therefore, is not large unless the service handles physical items as part of its consumer service business. Control of the work in process can be very important for small repair shops, laundries, photography developers, and the like. Accurate control is mandatory in these firms if consumer satisfaction is to be obtained and a permanent clientele maintained. The inventory costs for these firms are not likely to be large, but they cannot risk the loss of business associated with a consumer whose possession has been lost.

There are a few service firms that encounter large inventory costs as part of doing business. Auto repair garages, radio and television repair shops, etc. face the traditional retail problem of deciding how much inventory they can afford to keep on hand. In this case, the decision rules discussed in Chapter 12 can be used to evaluate inventory levels.

SCHEDULING WORK LOAD

Work scheduling is of considerable importance in service firms because of the "perishability" of the unused labor and the consumer ill will generated by not meeting a deadline. Work-scheduling tasks, similar to those in manufacturing companies, are faced by most service firms. Labor costs comprise such a large percentage of total costs for most service firms that management must consider all possibilities to improve the work flow.

Use of such techniques as critical path analysis, control boards, etc. can improve the overall labor performance by making better utilization of employee time.[19] Critical path analysis, which is simply a planning tool, provides a diagram that shows which jobs must be completed before other jobs can be started. It also uses estimated time requirements needed to perform each job so that they can be scheduled in an order that will minimize the time needed to complete the total job. This tool can be used to identify bottle-necks that limit the amount of work generated by a service firm.

Even small service firms can benefit from the type of thinking that critical path analysis requires. For example, parts can be ordered before they are needed so that they are available for use when needed by the service people. Repair and maintenance work can be done during idle time, so that equipment is in top shape and ready to operate at full speed during peak service hours. The list could continue indefinitely, but suffice it to say that proper planning, scheduling, and control procedures can result in increased profits for most service firms.

SUMMARY

The marketing of services differs from merchandise marketing in that:

1. Repeat customer business is absolutely required.
2. The firm's offering cannot be stored, so it is even more important to operate at near-capacity levels.
3. It is more difficult for the consumer to measure quality or the worth of services offered.
4. Service firms are particularly vulnerable to the "bad-mouth syndrome" because it is difficult for consumers to judge the value of a service.

Thus most of a service firm's marketing effort can be aimed at reducing consumer uncertainty. A consumer's confidence can be gained by analyzing his problem and providing an honest opinion, backed up by facts, on the worth of each alternative solution from the *consumer's* viewpoint. Competent employees should render the service, as demonstrable skill and knowledge will create consumer confidence. Warranties should reinforce the quality image.

Respecting the customer's time can gain his respect, as people become distrustful of a service firm that always breaks its promised service schedules. Some service delays are unavoidable, but the consumer should be informed that there is going to be a delay. Consumers also appreciate promptness in being informed when cost estimates are changed because of unforeseen circumstances.

QUESTIONS

1. How would you explain the trend toward vertical integration in the service industry?
2. Describe the steps you would use in marketing the following services:
   a. A travel agency in New York
   b. An insect extermination service in Des Moines
   c. A management consulting firm in Chicago
   d. A tourist guide service in Miami
   e. The only local computer service firm (the nearest competitor is 200 miles away).

3. How can a service retailer protect his market share? How can he increase it?

4. Service firms often encounter negative publicity through the warranty litigation difficulties of some members of the industry. Can you suggest any methods by which a service firm with a clean record could benefit from this situation?

5. Very few members of the service industry have a worse reputation with the public than the automobile service firms. If you accepted a position as service manager for a typical auto dealer, how would you go about marketing your services?

6. What types of service firms would you expect to be sensitive to location, and why? Why would other types of service firms be less sensitive to location? Give examples of each (other than those cited in the text).

7. Discuss the ethics of taxing "nonprofit" organizations which compete with private service firms. Assume a position, state your opinion, and defend it in a logical manner, using sound business principles and your own code of ethics.

8. The professional codes of the legal and medical professions discourage the use of promotion in the usual sense of the word. Does this mean that these services function without any form of promotion? Explain.

9. Independence and lack of tact are often considered to be admirable traits if they are accompanied by a high degree of technical competence. Discuss this phenomenon in terms of the market concept and the art of personal selling.

10. Discuss the advisability of physicians, lawyers, and dentists using bank cards to eliminate their bad debt problems.

11. Design a promotional mix for the following service firms:
    a. A small local flying service
    b. A print shop
    c. A real estate abstract service
    d. A professional photographer
    e. A psychological counseling service.

12. Suggest a pricing strategy or combination of strategies for each of the retail firms in question 11.

13. Suggest at least two types of service firms that might find each of the various pricing tactics (loss leader pricing plan, etc.) useful and explain why you think each tactic would be useful for the service firms you suggest.

14. Using another text, set up and solve a critical path problem involving a service firm of your own choosing.

FOOTNOTES

[1] Sam Weiner, "Monumental Undertaking," *Financial Trend*, 3 (January 28–February 3, 1973): 7, 10, 12, 15.

[2] E. B. Weiss, "Marketers: Don't Ignore Our Growing Service-Oriented Society," *Advertising Age*, May 5, 1969.

[3] "The Consumer Market in 1980: Services," *Conference Board Record* (May 1972), p. 50.

[4] John M. Rathmell, "What Is Meant by Service?" *Journal of Marketing*, 30 (October 1966): 32–36.

[5] E. B. Weiss, "Will Retailing Be a New Bank Service?" *Advertising Age*, September 4, 1967, p. 60.

[6] Robert C. Judd, "Similarities or Differences in Product and Service Retailing," *Journal of Retailing*, 43 (Winter 1968): 2.

[7] Ibid., p. 3.

[8] Commerce Clearing House, *1970 Products Liability Reporter* (Chicago: Commerce Clearing House, 1970), paragraph 1010.

[9] *Henningsen v. Bloomfield Motors*, 32 N.J. 358, 161 A.2d 69 (1960).

[10] Warren J. Wittreich, "How to Buy/Sell Professional Services," *Harvard Business Review* (March–April, 1966).

[11] Johan Arndt, "Word of Mouth Advertising and Informal Communications," in Donald F. Cox, ed., *Risk Taking and Information Handling in Consumer Behavior* (Boston: Howard University Graduate School of Business Administration, 1967), pp. 188–239.

[12] George Z. Herpel and Richard A. Collins, *Specialty Advertising in Marketing* (Homewood, Ill.: Dow Jones–Irwin, 1972), pp. 181–182.

[13] H. N. Broom and Justin G. Longenecker, *Small Business Management* (Cincinnati: South-Western Publishing Co., 1971), pp. 530–531.

[14] Judd, "Similarities or Differences," p. 6.

[15] Robert E. Sibson, *Managing Professional Service Enterprises* (New York: Pitman, 1971), p. 114.

[16] Ibid., p. 115.

[17] See also R. E. Sibson, "A Service," in E. Marting, ed., *Creative Pricing* (New York: American Management Association, 1968), pp. 14–152.

[18] Sibson, "A Service," p. 103.

[19] Philip Kotler, *Marketing Management, Analysis, Planning, and Control* (2d ed.; Englewood Cliffs, N.J.: Prentice-Hall, 1972), pp. 412–418.

THE BLESSINGS CORPORATION
General Diaper Service

One of the major divisions of the Blessings Corporation of New York is a door-to-door rental diaper service. This division accounted for more than $27 million during the last fiscal year, or 48 percent of the total gross sales for the company. The company owns and operates twenty-four diaper service firms from coast to coast throughout the United States. Most of these are identified as General Diaper Service but there are other names in use, such as Dy-Dee, Tidy Didy, Baby's Perfect, Baby's Valet, and Baby's Dy-Dee Service.

The collection of names resulted from acquisitions of established diaper service companies. Management had decided to retain the old, established names rather than change to General Diaper in all locations.

The Blessings Corporation also owns several other divisions, some of which complement and aid the diaper service. These include Baby Talk Magazine Publishing, a disposable products division, and a rental service of linen and uniforms to commercial businesses. Thus the company is quite highly integrated.

The diaper service consists of delivering a week's supply of clean diapers to the home and picking up the soiled diapers for laundering. Soiled diapers are stored by the mother in a plastic container that resembles a large trash receptable. A price of around $2.50 is charged to customers and $6 to non-customers for the plastic container.

Promotion of the service is handled several ways. Display tables are set up in the maternity and baby sections of department stores. These tables hold free copies of Baby Talk Magazine, with compliments of the particular department store marked on the outside cover. Stories of interest to mothers plus advertisements from baby-oriented companies appear in this magazine. In addition, large ads concerning the diaseptic process and General Diaper Service appear in each copy.

The tables also hold registration cards and a receptacle for a free gift pack from the Blessings Corporation. Once the cards are filled in, a representative from the local diaper service company either telephones or personally visits the potential customer. Sales representatives work on a commission basis. One of the newest offices found it difficult to hire good in-field representatives and was forced to rely for a period of time upon telephone sales people.

The Yellow Pages of the telephone directory also carry an ad which results in some call-in orders.

A program of calling on pediatricians and giving them free samples and a packet of information for their patients is also in use. Although this has resulted in some sales, it is difficult to initiate, due to the difficulties of calling on busy doctors and the reluctance of doctors to listen to laymen.

Route men are encouraged to call on other potential customers in their areas and are given a commission for new starts, but the success of this depends solely upon the nature and drive of the route man.

Gift certificates are available and have resulted in extra business; however, it is felt they would be more effective if they could be placed in the hands of "to-be grandparents." Unfortunately, lists of grandmothers are not in existence.

A contract has recently been signed with Sears Roebuck and Company to offer "Sears Diaper Service" in certain areas. Charges for Sears' service may be paid by cash or by a Sears charge account. Local Sears stores cooperate in obtaining customers, but General Diaper handles sales and all aspects of the service. Delivery and pickup may be made in company trucks plainly identified as General Diaper.

The cost of diaper service is surprisingly low, although it is management's belief that in new markets the general public is uninformed and believes it to be an expensive luxury. The cost of diaper service in a typical market for a supply of 90 per week amounts to $3.15, compared to approximately $5.50 per week for a well-known brand of disposables. The company has further determined that it costs a housewife approximately $3 to do home washing, not including her labor.

Disposable diapers have been gaining an increasing share of the total diaper market and Blessings Corporation has maintained its traditional share of the market. One school of thought was that the tremendous amount of publicity and advertising by disposable diaper manufacturers had caused women to shift from home laundry and had actually aided the sales of diaper service. About 70 percent of all diapers used today are cotton diapers washed at home; disposables have about 20 percent and diaper service 10 percent of the market.

General Diaper also carries and sells a line of disposables. These are priced between the well-known manufacturer brands and the private label brands. The addition of disposable diapers to the product line helped General Diaper even out the seasonality of diaper service during such times as summer vacation. Although birth rates remain fairly constant week by week, there is a seasonal pattern in diaper service usage.

Changes in society are soon reflected in the sales of diaper service. Declining birth rates per thousand is a negative factor, but the increased per capita discretionary income and the trend toward convenience are plus factors. The effects of core-city problems had recently been dramatically demonstrated in New York City. Before the company's withdrawal from ghetto areas, two men were required on each delivery truck to control thefts of diapers and robberies. Thus costs spiraled, resulting in the eventual withdrawal by General Diaper from much of that market.

Increasing awareness of ecology had begun to be an important sales point for General Diaper. Sales representatives often used "ecology" as a sales point to convince expectant mothers to use General's diaper service rather than disposables. This seemed particularly effective among young mothers.

General Diaper offers a special service of value for babies whose urine is highly acid and creates a rash called "acid scald." PH is a scale that measures the degree of acidity or alkalinity, and the skin of a normal baby has a pH of about 5.5. Most efficient soil removal occurs at a pH of about 11, and General Diaper uses alkali during processing to increase the pH of the wash water and fabric to that level. In the final rinse, souring agent is used to lower the pH of the fabric to 5.5 so that it will be compatible with the skin of a normal baby.

By reducing the amount of sour used, the pH of the diaper can be maintained at a level of 9 or 10 to produce an "alkaline diaper." Use of an alkaline diaper on a baby with a highly acid discharge can frequently neutralize the acid discharge and prevent rash. The technical knowledge required to control pH in this manner is normally not possessed by mothers who wash diapers at home, and disposable diapers have a fixed pH which cannot be altered.

Although a General Diaper representative will gladly visit the home and test a soiled diaper to determine if the acid condition exists, the availability of this service is not widely known. Pediatricians have on occasion recommended changing the diapering method when confronted with a rash case, without testing to determine if the acid condition exists. Thus the company faces the task of an educational program among mothers and doctors.

DISCUSSION QUESTIONS

1. How would you view the future for diaper service throughout the United States?
2. What additional promotional tools might General Diaper employ? For example, how could it put gift coupons in the hands of grandparents to-be?
3. Is there a danger in the association of General Diaper with Sears?
4. Do you believe the experience with the change in the core city of New York is indicative of what might happen throughout the United States?
5. Now that General Diaper is carrying a line of disposable diapers, would you recommend that it begin carrying other items, such as babies' sheets, blankets, dishware, etc.?
6. Do you believe that General Diaper should retain the different names for diaper service throughout the nation or change all of them to General Diaper? What advantages do you see either way?

BIG TOWN NURSING HOME

The Big Town Nursing Home is a modern home for the elderly, located in suburban Mesquite near Dallas. It is owned and operated by National Living Centers Inc. of Houston.

A total of 183 patients live in the home, 50 of whom are ambulatory (non-bedridden).

Although the home provides total care, many patients wish to purchase personal items such as greeting cards, cartons of cigarettes, antacid pills, cough drops, hair pins, and similar items.

Consequently, a small commissary was started and run by a 93-year-old man, Mr. Thomas, who resided in the nursing home. It was called The Country Store, and still retains that name.

Since Mr. Thomas became too ill to run the store, it has been run by three women residents and is open daily between 10:30 a.m. and 11 p.m. The Country Store is located in a storage-type room without windows, in which pine shelves have been built to hold the merchandise.

Although, it is agreed, the store serves a need for the patients, the total sales per month are only around $40 or $45. All items are purchased from a retail drug chain in Dallas that has agreed to sell at a discount to Big Town.

However, this necessitates driving to the chain store and requires as much as two hours' time. Since the elderly patients cannot drive to the store, supplies can be purchased only when one of the administrative staff has time to leave the nursing home. As a result, stocks become depleted.

In addition to The Country Store, there is another small retail area in Big Town Nursing Home where hand-crafted items made by the patients are displayed and sold. These are sold to the families and friends of the patients, who visit the home.

The administrator of Big Town, Mrs. Barbara Thomas, believes that both operations provide the patients with an outlet for their creative skills and available time and that both are definitely needed. She has also organized a yearly sale of surplus handicrafts in a nearby shopping center.

Mrs. Thomas also believes, from what she has seen of other nursing homes, that Big Town is an innovator in both retailing areas and that other nursing homes must have similar needs. Although it is generally agreed that both retail functions are needed, they are far less important than the other administrative details in running a successful nursing home. Consequently, they must of necessity take a back seat in order of priorities.

DISCUSSION QUESTIONS

1. Examine age distribution patterns for the United States and decide what the future of nursing homes will be in the next ten and twenty years. Would you expect to see more chains of nursing homes?
2. Is there a way that administrators of nursing homes can more efficiently establish and run small retail outlets within their institutions? Is there a possibility that the stocking of merchandise could be done by an outsider such as a wagon jobber?
3. Should the management of such nursing home chains as National Living Centers develop systems to control small internal retail outlets or should this be left to the individual nursing homes?
4. Do you visualize an opportunity for an enterprising individual to establish a wholesale business to service the "country stores" of nursing homes and to purchase and resell their handicrafts? Could this be done on a direct mail basis—by shipping packages of merchandise to nursing homes on a regular basis?
5. Investigate the way that small rural restaurants, bait shops, small marinas, and other isolated retailers receive their supplies.

PART SIX

Planning Future
Growth

CHAPTER 17

Photo courtesy of J. C. Penney Company, Inc.

Using Marketing Research to Plan Retail Changes

Only in recent years have retailers begun to recognize the importance of marketing research. The use of the marketing concept, which stresses the satisfaction of consumers at a profit, has increased the need for retailers to observe changing consumer demands. Marketing research can assist the retailer in observing consumers and making intelligent decisions. Retailers should have a basic understanding of research procedures, so they contract for outside research studies, conduct the studies themselves, and understand the results better. This chapter concentrates on the use of marketing research in a retail environment.

Research can be beneficial to the retailer whenever a decision must be made. The question then becomes one of establishing priorities on the types of problems that are considered important enough to warrant the use of marketing research. The level of expenditure on research should be related to the importance of the decision. Decisions involving significant costs or serious consequences for the retailer are likely to benefit considerably from the added information provided by research.

On the other hand, decisions that do not involve much added cost or do not have serious implications for the retailer's present business may not require the use of much, if any, research. The expected payoff from new sales resulting from a change in the retailing mix must, however, be considered as important as the added cost involved in making the change. This "opportunity cost" is frequently overlooked by retailers who view the importance of the decision only from the "What will it cost me?" approach. They do not consider the "What will it make for me if the idea works?" concept.

The strategic areas of retailing such as location, merchandise policy, pricing policy, promotional allocations, and allocation or performance of sales personnel usually account for the most important decisions that a retailer makes. Consequently, they may account for most of the firm's research activity.

RESEARCH AREAS

The major areas in which retailers can utilize the services of marketing research are location determination, shopping pattern behavior (including the study of parking needs and in-store layout), consumer profile analysis, advertising, image analysis, sales forecasting, physical distribution research, merchandising research, personnel research, and innovative research (long-range planning). A brief discussion of current research activity in each area will now be presented.

Location and Trade Area Research

Trade area research is conducted for both proposed and existing stores.[1] This research generally centers on the measurement and evaluation of the trade area. In addition, the flow of customers from one trading area to another may be studied to determine the size and characteristics of the outflow and inflow of consumers.[2] Identifying the types of consumers and the merchandise they buy from retailers doing business outside the trade area can indicate weaknesses in local retail assortments. The existence of such a weakness can reflect an opportunity for a new retailer or for existing retailers who can alter their offerings to meet the untapped market.

Trade area research may also be designed to measure the potential sales volume associated with the people residing within a defined geographic trade area.[3]

Finally, trade area research may be conducted to evaluate the change in trade area size and characteristics likely to be caused by a change in the retail environment. Such studies may attempt to determine the effect that a branch store will have upon the original downtown store. It may also estimate the effect that the opening of a competitive outlet (or a new shopping center) is likely to have upon the business of an existing outlet.[4]

Store location decisions have been approached by estimating the sales volume of a proposed site. Nelson has developed an estimating procedure which is especially applicable for retailers considering the establishment of "interceptor" stores in downtown areas.[5] Huff has developed a computer program which is designed to approximate the optimum location for a retail development.[6]

In-Store Traffic Shopping Pattern Studies

In-store consumer traffic pattern studies are frequently conducted to determine the effect that store layout has upon sales.[7] The procedure usually consists of observers' plotting the paths of a sample of consumers on a drawing of the store layout. This information is then used to determine the percentage of customers who pass by and make purchases from each merchandise group. Generally, merchandise groups having high passing and/or buying percentages are scattered throughout the store to maximize consumer exposure to the store's total merchandise assortment.

In-store traffic pattern studies measure association rather than causation, so the results must be interpreted carefully.[8] The estimated passing and/or buying percentage for a specific merchandise group may be influenced by its location relative to other products. For example, some items may have a higher percentage of consumers passing the section, but this may be due to its being near other products that draw the consumers to that area of the store. Conservative traffic estimates may be obtained on other merchandise groups that draw consumer traffic to their location. In this case the buying ratio may be independent of the location in the store as consumers will search for the product until they find it.

In addition, in-store traffic studies do not measure consumer pre-shopping purchase intentions, so it is difficult to interpret the passing and buying ratios.[9] A consumer may buy an item because the in-store stimuli remind him of a need or because he intended to buy it anyway. Thus traffic studies may need to be supplemented with attitude studies to be able to account for the effects of variables (such as pre-purchase intentions, consumer characteristics, and other store environmental characteristics) that influence the value of the estimated passing and/or buying percentages.

Farley and Ring have developed a method of predicting the likelihood that a shopper in any store area will move to adjacent areas.[10] They believe that this customer movement is determined by the "gravitational" pull of other departments and by shoppers' tendency to shop the perimeter of the store. Their model forecasts the traffic flows that result from alternative grocery store layouts. It has been found to predict quite accurately the actual flow of shoppers through five Pittsburgh supermarkets.

Consumer Profile Analysis

Consumer profile studies are conducted to identify the characteristics of the store's customers. Generally, the study consists of an interview of a sample of the store's consumers or an analysis of the retailer's credit records. Data on age, sex, income, social class, occupation, education, availability of transportation, ownership patterns for major items, general preference and purchase patterns, type and place of residence, etc. are collected in the interview. These data are then compared with those of the general population to determine any unique differences in the store's clientele.

Identifying the consumer through profile studies allows the retailer to anticipate his needs more carefully. It allows the retailer to spot opportunities for providing new products and services that will be consistent with his current customers' demands. Profile studies can also reveal the characteristics of innovative consumers who try new products first and who set fashion trends.[11] Groups that appear to be fashion and opinion leaders change over time, so profile studies are needed to keep "in tune" with these changes. Responding quickly to changes in the preferences of the innovative consumers can keep the inventory more current and generate a progressive, up-to-date store image.

Consumer Attitude Measurement and Store Image Studies

Attitude measurement studies generally involve a series of attitude scales consisting of attitude statements and questions that ask the consumer to express his degree of agreement or disagreement. Responses are then combined in a pre-specified manner to yield an overall indication of consumer beliefs.[12]

Many different attitude scales and approaches are available in retail attitude research. The more frequently used techniques will now be discussed briefly.

Likert Method of Summated Ratings

Likert scales involve the use of a list of statements related to the attitude being investigated.[13] Each respondent is asked to indicate his degree of agreement or disagreement with each statement. Each degree of agreement or disagreement is assigned a numerical value in the following manner: strongly approve—5, approve—4, undecided—3, disapprove—2, and strongly disapprove—1. The respondent's total score is computed by adding his scores on all of the statements relevant to the attitude being investigated.

Likert scales enable a researcher to rank attitudes because an individual's final score can be interpreted only in relation to the scores of the other respondents. In other words, Likert scales are *ordinal* measures only; they do not allow the researcher to measure the differences between attitudes.

Semantic Differential Scale

The frequently used semantic differential scales permit the development of descriptive profiles of consumer attitudes that facilitate the comparison of competitive stores.[14] This attitude-scaling technique consists of pairs of "polar" adjectives, with a 7-point scale separating the opposite descriptive terms.[15] Respondents are asked to select the point on each scale that best represents their attitude on the dimension in question. Usually an identical ordinal scale is used to obtain relative perceptions on several competitive stores. For example, the image of each of several competing stores might be measured on the characteristics in Figure 17–1.

The respondents are asked to rate several competitive stores on the same scales. The questionnaire is usually organized to measure consumer attitudes on one major dimension at a time—physical characteristics, convenience, merchandise offering, prices, personnel, advertising, etc. The semantic differential is a relatively simple technique to use and analyze. Consumer perceptions of the stores can be compared easily by plotting on the original questionnaire the median response (one-half of the respondents' ratings are higher and one-half are lower than the median rating) on each scale for each store. The differences in store images usually become readily apparent when these comparisons are made.

The semantic differential has the advantage of being easily replicated, so trends in consumers' attitudes can be detected. A disadvantage is the neutral midpoint in the 7-point scale, which seems to attract many respondents who are reluctant to score a store unusually good or bad.[16] For this reason some researchers use even-number scales which force the respondent to take a position.

Projective Techniques

Several projective techniques are used to measure store image. All of these projective techniques use an indirect questioning procedure which leads the respondent to believe that he is answering in a way that will not reveal his biases. These indirect approaches are used when customers appear to be unable or unwilling to specify their beliefs about some item.

Thematic apperception tests consist of presenting a series of pictures to the respondent, who is asked to tell a story about each picture. Questions such as, "What's happening in the picture? How did it come about? What will happen next?" are used to obtain the story. It is hoped that the respondent, in telling the story, indirectly reveals the factors that motivate him.

The "sentence completion" approach consists of presenting respondents with a number of incomplete sentences. The respondents are then asked to complete the sentences with the first thought that comes to their mind. The respondent is usually given a limited amount of time to complete each question. The questions may be worded in either the first or the third person so that the respondent's inner feelings are better revealed.

Figure 17–1 Example of the Use of the Semantic Differential in Obtaining a Store's Relative Rating on Different Characteristics

The following questions will permit you to express the level of your opinion for different characteristics about different stores. For example, if the store in question is extremely well known to you, then you would mark an X in the blank nearest "Well known generally"; and below the word "Extremely"; i.e., the blank on the extreme left. If, however, you do not know the store, then you would mark an X in the blank at the far right, beside "Unknown generally" and underneath the word "Extremely."

Please rate the following items for (store name) _____

General Characteristics of the Store

	Extremely	Quite	Slightly	Neither One nor the Other	Slightly	Quite	Extremely	
Well known generally	___	___	___	___	___	___	___	Unknown generally
Small number of stores operated by company	___	___	___	___	___	___	___	Large number of stores operated by company
Long time in community	___	___	___	___	___	___	___	Short time in community
Open during convenient shopping hours	___	___	___	___	___	___	___	Closed during convenient shopping hours
Open during convenient shopping days	___	___	___	___	___	___	___	Closed during convenient shopping days

Physical Characteristics of the Store

Dirty	___	___	___	___	___	___	___	Clean
Unattractive decor	___	___	___	___	___	___	___	Attractive decor
Easy to find items you want	___	___	___	___	___	___	___	Difficult to find items you want
Easy to move through store	___	___	___	___	___	___	___	Difficult to move through store
Fast checkout	___	___	___	___	___	___	___	Slow checkout

Convenience of Reaching the Store from Your Location

Nearby	___	___	___	___	___	___	___	Distant
Short time required to reach store	___	___	___	___	___	___	___	Long time required to reach store
Difficult drive	___	___	___	___	___	___	___	Easy drive
Difficult to find parking place	___	___	___	___	___	___	___	Easy to find parking place
Convenient to other stores I shop	___	___	___	___	___	___	___	Inconvenient to other stores I shop

Products Offered

Latest fashion or style is available	___	___	___	___	___	___	___	Latest fashion or style is not available
Wide selection of different kinds of products	___	___	___	___	___	___	___	Limited selection of different kinds of products
Fully stocked	___	___	___	___	___	___	___	Understocked

470

Undependable products	_____	Dependable products
High quality	_____	Low quality
Numerous brands	_____	Few brands
Unknown brands	_____	Well-known brands

Prices Charged by the Store

Low compared to other stores	_____	High compared to other stores
Low values for money spent	_____	High values for money spent
Large number of items specially priced	_____	Small number of items specially priced

Store Personnel

Courteous	_____	Discourteous
Cold	_____	Friendly
Unhelpful	_____	Helpful
Adequate number	_____	Inadequate number
Knowledgeable about product and service offering	_____	Not knowledgeable about product and service offering
Attractive appearance	_____	Unattractive appearance
Acceptable sales pressure	_____	Unacceptable sales pressure

Advertising by the Store

Uninformative	_____	Informative
Unhelpful in planning	_____	Helpful in planning purchases
Appealing	_____	Unappealing
Believable	_____	Misleading
Frequently seen by you	_____	Infrequently seen by you

Your Friends and the Store

Unknown to your friends	_____	Well known to your friends
Well liked by your friends	_____	Disliked by your friends
Poorly recommended by your friends	_____	Well recommended by your friends
Numerous friends shop there	_____	Few friends shop there

Customer Services

Easy credit policy	_____	Tight credit policy
Good layaway service	_____	Poor layaway service
Good delivery service	_____	Poor delivery service
Good product guarantees	_____	Poor product guarantees
Prompt repair service	_____	Slow repair service
Easy product-return policies	_____	Tight product-return policy
Satisfies customer complaints	_____	Does not satisfy customer complaints

The following questions have been used to identify components of store image: "When you think of *(store name)*, what is the first thing that comes to your mind?" "What do you like *most* about shopping at *(store name)*?" "What do you like *least* about shopping at *(store name)*?" "What are the major reasons why you think other people shop at *(store name)*?"[17] Using the last three questions, Berry [18] identified twelve components of department store image (Figure 17–2).

Figure 17–2   *Department Store Image Codes, Components, and Subcomponents Identified by Sentence Completion Approach*

01   Price of Merchandise
   a. Low prices
   b. Fair or competitive prices
   c. High or noncompetitive prices
   d. Values, except with specific regard to premiums, such as stamps, or quality of merchandise

02   Quality of Merchandise
   a. Good or poor quality of merchandise
   b. Good or poor department(s), except with respect to assortment, fashion, etc.
   c. Stock brand names

03   Assortment of Merchandise
   a. Breadth of merchandise
   b. Depth of merchandise
   c. Carries a brand I like

04   Fashion of Merchandise

05   Sales Personnel
   a. Attitude of sales personnel
   b. Knowledgeability of sales personnel
   c. Number of sales personnel
   d. Good or poor service

06   Locational Convenience
   a. Location from home
   b. Location from work
   c. Access
   d. Good or poor location without reference to home or work

07   Other Convenience Factors
   a. Parking
   b. Hours store is open
   c. Convenience with regard to other stores
   d. Store layout with respect to convenience
   e. Convenience (in general)

08   Services
   a. Credit
   b. Delivery

Figure 17–2 *(continued)*

---

    c. Restaurant facilities
    d. Other services (gift consultants, layaway plans, baby strollers, escalators, etc.)

09 Sales Promotions
    a. Special sales, including quality or assortment of sales merchandise
    b. Stamps and other premiums
    c. Fashion shows and other special events

10 Advertising
    a. Style and quality of advertising
    b. Media and vehicles used
    c. Reliability of advertising

11 Store Atmosphere
    a. Layout of store without respect to convenience
    b. External and internal decor of the store
    c. Merchandise display
    d. Customer type
    e. Congestion
    f. Good for gifts, except with respect to quality, assortment or fashion of merchandise
    g. "Prestige" store

12 Reputation on Adjustments
    a. Returns
    b. Exchanges
    c. Reputation for fairness

SOURCE Leonard L. Berry, "The Components of Department Store Image: A Theoretical and Empirical Analysis," *Journal of Retailing*, 45 (Spring 1969): 19–20.

Proponents of unstructured, open-end questions believe that by allowing the respondent to discuss only the concepts he remembers, only the critical reinforcing image components are identified.[19] The semantic differential approach, on the other hand, forces responses on all image components listed in the questionnaire. Thus the questionnaire should contain accompanying questions which allow the respondent to evaluate the importance of the attribute as well as his impression of the store's relative rating on that attribute. For example, a questionnaire such as the one in Figure 17–3 could precede the rating questions in Figure 17–1. This would allow the researcher to identify the most important components of store image and then determine consumers' perceptions on the important attributes of each store.

Promotional Evaluation Research

Although retailers use relatively few media in direct action appeals, they have (in credit and mail-order accounts) good customer records which allow estimation of the sales effect of a promotional expenditure. Sales response

Figure 17–3   Sample Questions That May Be Asked to Identify the Components of Store Image in a Semantic Differential Study

If you choose among several department stores, what factors would you consider important to the choice of shopping in a department store? Please score the importance of each of the following factors by circling the appropriate number. (For example, if the factor is one of your most important reasons for shopping in a department store, circle number 6; if it is of no importance, circle number 1, etc.)

	Most Important			Least Important		
General Characteristics of the Store						
Well-known store name	6	5	4	3	2	1
Small number of stores operated by company	6	5	4	3	2	1
Long time in community	6	5	4	3	2	1
Open during convenient shopping hours	6	5	4	3	2	1
Open during convenient shopping days	6	5	4	3	2	1
Physical Characteristics of the Store						
Clean	6	5	4	3	2	1
Attractive decor	6	5	4	3	2	1
Easy to find items you want	6	5	4	3	2	1
Easy to move through store	6	5	4	3	2	1
Fast checkout	6	5	4	3	2	1
Convenience of Reaching the Store from Your Location						
Nearby	6	5	4	3	2	1
Short time required to reach store	6	5	4	3	2	1
Easy drive	6	5	4	3	2	1
Easy to find parking place	6	5	4	3	2	1
Convenient to other stores I shop	6	5	4	3	2	1
Products Offered						
Availability of latest fashions and styles	6	5	4	3	2	1
Wide selection of different kinds of products	6	5	4	3	2	1
Fully stocked	6	5	4	3	2	1
Dependable products	6	5	4	3	2	1
High quality	6	5	4	3	2	1
Numerous brands	6	5	4	3	2	1
Known brands	6	5	4	3	2	1
Prices Charged by the Store						
Low compared to other stores	6	5	4	3	2	1
High values for money spent	6	5	4	3	2	1
Large number of items specially priced	6	5	4	3	2	1
Store Personnel						
Courteous	6	5	4	3	2	1
Friendly	6	5	4	3	2	1
Helpful	6	5	4	3	2	1

Figure 17–3   **(continued)**

Adequate number	6	5	4	3	2	1
Knowledgeable about product/service offering	6	5	4	3	2	1
Attractive appearance	6	5	4	3	2	1
Acceptable sales pressure	6	5	4	3	2	1

Advertising by the Store

Informative	6	5	4	3	2	1
Helpful in planning purchases	6	5	4	3	2	1
Appealing	6	5	4	3	2	1
Believable	6	5	4	3	2	1
Frequently seen by you	6	5	4	3	2	1

Your Friends and the Store

Well known to your friends	6	5	4	3	2	1
Well liked by your friends	6	5	4	3	2	1
Well recommended by your friends	6	5	4	3	2	1
Numerous friends shop there	6	5	4	3	2	1

Customer Services

Easy credit terms	6	5	4	3	2	1
Good layaway service	6	5	4	3	2	1
Good delivery service	6	5	4	3	2	1
Good product guarantees	6	5	4	3	2	1
Prompt repair service	6	5	4	3	2	1
Easy product-return policies	6	5	4	3	2	1
Satisfies customer complaints	6	5	4	3	2	1

functions can be developed for those firms where direct action appeals are made and customer records maintained. By associating sales response with cost, it is possible to develop fairly precise methods of budgeting promotional outlays.

Simon has developed such a method for direct-mail advertising by which the sales response can be estimated quite accurately.[20] The method uses the decision rule of mailing advertising messages to lists of increasingly unpromising prospects until the anticipated response rate is at the point where estimated net revenue (total revenue minus all costs except the advertising costs needed to reach the customer) is just inadequate to cover the costs of reaching that customer. His technique is practical in that it does not require unacceptable, simplifying assumptions but uses estimates of variables that many retail organizations can provide.

One of the most commonly used techniques to measure the success of a direct action appeal is the "offer response" method. This approach requires that the consumer present at the time of purchase some kind of evidence that he has read the advertisement. Advertisements that include a statement such as, "Bring this coupon to get a special prize (or discount)," generate sales, and the response rate indicates the relative strength of the advertisement. If the offer is buried deep in the copy, only those readers who read most of the advertisement will respond.

Some retail promotion is used not to make direct action appeals but to change customer attitudes toward the store or to make more people aware of the store's existence, location, and product/service offering. In such cases it is useful to measure the effect these promotional efforts have upon consumer attitudes and awareness. A "before and after" attitudinal test can measure the effect that the promotional efforts have had on consumer attitudes. The before-after test involves a survey of a sample of target market consumers *before* the promotional campaign is conducted and again *after* the campaign has been conducted. Any of the attitude measurement techniques (such as the semantic differential) can be used to determine if (and how much) attitudes have changed.

If the semantic differential is used, the median scale value for the two periods can be placed on the same scale to facilitate the comparison. The resulting measurement may be similar to Figure 17–4. In this case the promotional campaign did not alter consumers' perceptions of the time required to reach the store, but it improved consumers' perceptions of the store's merchandise assortment and the quality of the merchandise offered.

Another form of advertising research attempts to evaluate specific advertisements or advertising themes *before* they are introduced to the public. These techniques are used to identify the most effective advertisements, which are then presented to the consuming public.

Pre-testing of advertisements by a sample of consumers is usually accomplished by having the respondents rank in order of their preference several advertisements that are being considered. In addition, each consumer's attitude may be measured before and after exposure to each advertisement. Such a plan would call for the use of some type of experimental design. The design

Figure 17–4 *Illustration of Use of Semantic Differential to Measure Change in Attitudes Associated with a Promotional Campaign*

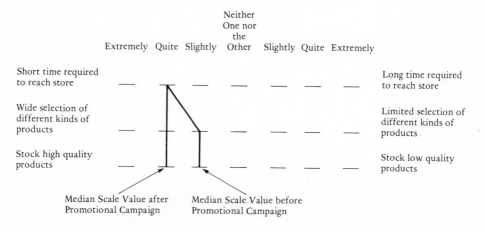

may be simply to present each advertisement to a different random sample of consumers and obtain before and after attitude measurements separately on each advertisement.

Direct action appeal advertising can also be pre-tested when advertisements can be mailed to charge customers.[21] In this case the store's charge customers can be randomly divided into equal numbers and a different advertisement can be mailed to each group with the monthly charge statement. This virtually assures the researcher that each advertisement will have a brief exposure to the customer. The number of customers exposed to each advertisement is identical and the identity of the advertisement is recorded for each customer. The charge records are then examined for the next several months to determine the rate of purchase of the products featured in the experimental advertisements.

This "closed circuit" technique allows the retailer to identify the advertisements which produce the greatest credit sales. It is then assumed that these advertisements will be the most effective in stimulating sales among the general public. This may be a valid assumption when the store's charge customers possess the same characteristics as its cash customers. This technique can also be used, effectively and economically, in stores where most of the sales are made on a charge basis.

The closed-circuit technique, if repeated several times, can also generate information on the type of promotional appeals that best stimulate sales among a store's charge account clientele.

Personal selling can be evaluated by sales effectiveness and time usage ratios. Calculations can be made on the volume of sales to the number of customers encountered, the percent of customers encountered who made a purchase, the number of customers encountered each day, the average value of a sale transaction, etc. Computer-linked cash registers can simplify the calculation task. Simply observing and recording which sales people are requested most frequently also can be a helpful evaluation technique.

Mock buying trips by employees who are not familiar to sales personnel can be used to evaluate the performance of sales people. One advantage of this technique is being able to observe the efforts of sales people to sell complementary products and to solve consumer problems. Consumers' preferences for particular sales people can be obtained by a survey if employees' photographs are included and if the number of employees is not too large. A more realistic approach consists of surveying consumers to determine their attitudinal preferences for characteristics of a specific type of retail sales person (but not specific individuals). Stafford and Greer, who have used the semantic differential to identify consumers' preferences for characteristics of a shoe salesman (Figure 17–5), concluded that he should be "friendly, courteous, pleasant, eager, attentive, prompt, aggressive, interested in being of service . . . although he should not be pushy, assertive, domineering or excitable."[22]

The problem of determining how many clerks to assign to selling activities has been approached by using queuing (or waiting line) models in numerous cases. Stokes and Mintz used a queuing model to determine the

Figure 17–5   *Profile of Consumer Attitudinal Preferences for Characteristics of a Shoe Salesman*

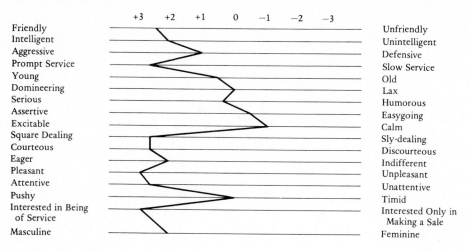

	+3	+2	+1	0	−1	−2	−3	
Friendly								Unfriendly
Intelligent								Unintelligent
Aggressive								Defensive
Prompt Service								Slow Service
Young								Old
Domineering								Lax
Serious								Humorous
Assertive								Easygoing
Excitable								Calm
Square Dealing								Sly-dealing
Courteous								Discourteous
Eager								Indifferent
Pleasant								Unpleasant
Attentive								Unattentive
Pushy								Timid
Interested in Being of Service								Interested Only in Making a Sale
Masculine								Feminine

Source   James E. Stafford and Tomas V. Greer, "Consumer Preference for Types of Salesmen: A Study of Independence-Dependence Characteristics," *Journal of Retailing,* 41 (Summer 1965): 33.

optimum number of sales clerks for a department store.[23] Schuchman reports that a large food chain used a queuing model to determine the number of checkout stations to use in each of its stores during various times of each day.[24] Queuing models have also been used to determine the optimum number of attendants and pumps for each of an oil company's gas stations.[25]

Queuing models are computerized, so they can be used to analyze many retail situations where people or physical facilities need to be serviced. Supermarkets must check out their customers, restaurants must seat people before they can be served, banks must service their depositors and other clientele, etc. In these and in most other retail situations, waiting lines may form. Queuing models analyze the costs associated with not servicing the people waiting in line and the labor and machine costs needed to service consumers more quickly. These two kinds of costs are inversely related (as one decreases, the other increases) because consumers do not like to wait in line and may go to a competitive outlet. On the other hand, using more service people and installing more machines to increase the service rate and thereby reduce the length of the waiting line results in additional store expenditures.[26]

Sales Forecasting

The success of retail planning depends upon the accuracy of the sales forecast. Merchandise budgeting, as discussed in Chapter 12, begins with a sales forecast. Inventory levels, purchases, reductions, and profit margins are then planned on the basis of the sales forecast. The forecasting procedure discussed in Chapter 12 mentioned the use of multiple regression analysis to obtain future annual sales estimates, and this type of analysis is frequently used to forecast annual retail sales because it can take into consideration several sales-influencing factors (including the annual sales trend) simultaneously.[27] The partial regression coefficients provide an estimate of the effect each factor has upon sales, which is helpful because such factors as annual advertising expenditures, annual expenditures for sales personnel salaries, etc. can be included in the forecasting model. This information can do more than provide an accurate sales forecast; it can guide management by indicating the estimated increase in sales associated with increases in advertising and personnel expenditures. Most multiple regression analyses also reveal the accuracy of the sales forecast for past years' sales data.

The multiple coefficient of determination (R^2), multiplied by 100, provides an estimate of the relative predictive power of the forecasting equation because this value is the percentage of variation in sales associated with changes in the other factors used in the predictive equation.

Step-wise multiple regression computer programs, such as BMDO 2R,[28] select the factor that explains the most variance in sales from all of the factors used in the prediction equation. Then another run is automatically made to select the next most important factor. This process is repeated until all factors are included in the analysis, or, if the researcher chooses, until no factors are left that add any explanation to the variation in sales.

Several problems can arise in interpreting the results obtained from multiple regression analysis. The predictive reliability of any regression equation depends upon the number of years of sales data that is used to establish the predictive equation. It is recommended that if no more than five observations are used, only one explanatory factor should be used in the prediction regression.[29] If twenty data units are used, about five explanatory factors are recommended as the maximum number for the predictive equation. The observations or units of sales data may consist of quarterly sales adjusted for seasonal differences. Step-wise regression can be used to select the most important explanatory factors and the others can be eliminated from the forecasting equation if they do not add any significant explanation of the variation in sales. However, the fundamental fact remains that many retailers do not have adequate records covering a very long time period.

Another concern involves the forecasting relevance of the prediction equation. Will the prediction equation apply to future conditions? Sales can be predicted far into the future by simply plugging new data into the predictive equation. However, the expected forecasting error increases as the sale estimate is projected further into the future. Thus the prediction equation may give a reliable estimate for next year's sales but not for sales five years from now. In addition, changes in environmental, competitive, or internal conditions (unless these variables are included in the regression equation) could create a new set of relationships that makes a prediction equation obsolete even for forecasting next year's sales.

Other more statistically complicated problems, such as the correlation of explanatory factors (multi-collinearity), the transformation of data into curvilinear forms, and the correlation of forecasting errors (auto-correlation of residuals), make it imperative that the forecaster be knowledgeable about the multiple regression analysis technique before he indiscriminately uses it as *the* forecasting tool.[30]

Monthly, weekly, or daily retail sales forecasts may require the use of time series analysis to incorporate the long-term (secular) trend forecast obtained by using multiple regression analysis with seasonal sales variations and cyclical sales fluctuations. Seasonal variations occur on regularly recurring intervals with the seasons of the year. Another periodic variation recurring with a fixed time pattern is fluctuation in daily sales each week. For example, about 60 percent of a supermarket's sales may occur on Thursday, Friday, and Saturday. In these cases, where a fixed time period is associated with sales fluctuations, seasonal indexes can be constructed and effectively used to forecast (as described in Chapter 12).

Cyclical fluctuations are more difficult to forecast because there is no constant time period between the peaks in each sales cycle. The cycles recur, but the length of time between cycles changes each time.

All three types of fluctuation—long-term trend, seasonal, and cyclical—can be incorporated into the sales forecast by using time series analysis.[31]

Physical Distribution Research

Most retail physical distribution research involves the use of time and motion studies to decrease handling, storage, and transportation costs. Time and motion studies consist of breaking each person's job down into separate activities and the amount of time needed to perform each activity is measured by a stopwatch and recorded. Changes in the layout of sales-facilitating equipment or in the equipment itself are then evaluated on the basis of the estimated time and cost reduction that is associated with the change.

Product Research

As retailers enter the private label business, their marketing research needs tend to mirror those of manufacturers. Consumer-taste tests, labeling research, test markets, and a variety of other tests in the spectrum of consumer research may be needed.

Costly errors can be prevented through this type of research. The Southland Corporation (7–11 Stores) was interested in the private labeling of beer for sale through its nationwide network of convenience stores. Before it entered this market in full scale it conducted market tests, which proved the concept was not economically feasible.

Many retailers still perform little or no marketing research on private label products. The philosophy seems to be, "Try it and see if it works." While this is easier for a retailer than a manufacturer, it can nevertheless be costly.

The tie-up of shelf space, the bad image which may result for the entire private label line, and the price reduction necessary to eventually move the merchandise are the costs of this practice. While research cannot entirely prevent these errors, it can reduce them. Good marketing research can also direct a retailer to the most likely candiates for private labeling, thus improving overall retailing efficiency.

Trial and error in the service industry can be even more harmful. In the case of regulated industries, the firm may be forced to continue the new service regardless of the results. A bad guess concerning merchandise can soon be eliminated in a sale, but an improper guess about a consumer service may result in years of unprofitable and undesired insurance policies, route structures, and the like.

Another area of retail research involves the products and assortments that a retailer should carry in the store's available floor space. A marketing research firm, SAMI, makes annual reports on the movement of major grocery product groups through about seventy of the largest distribution centers in the United States.[32]

The problem of establishing the merchandise assortment in regard to color, size, fabrics, widths, features, etc. when the possible choices are very large has been approached by using Bayesian decision theory, management's judgment on demand patterns, and the possibility of markdowns.[33] Guided by the criterion of obtaining highest expected profit, retail management's judgment and Bayesian statistics have been used to determine the optimum mix of sizes and widths to order for a women's fashion shoe department. In this case the Bayesian approach generated recommended merchandise assortments which corresponded closely with the assortments actually selected by the store's experienced buyers. Thus it appears that in complex situations Bayesian statistics and management judgment can facilitate the selection of assortments that are consistent with the merchandiser's marketing judgments and management's profit goals.[34]

Various statistical experimental designs have been used to determine the effect that shelf space allocation has upon retail sales.[35] An in-store audit of sales generated by varying allotments of shelf space to different supermarket items revealed that "the impact of changes in shelf space on unit sales is very small relative to the effects of other variables."[36] Although shelf conditions vary from store to store, this report suggests that more shelf-space research should be conducted to determine if the display area devoted to certain items can be reduced to provide room for the addition of new products.

Personnel Research

One phase of personnel research involes the study of selecting, training, compensating, motivating, and appraising all employees. This type of research evaluates specific aptitude and other psychological tests in selecting employees. It determines if these tests can be used to identify the more productive employees before they are hired. This type of research also investigates the relationship between test scores and employee turnover rates. Training methods, salary establishment procedures, and other motivation and reward systems are evaluated.

Innovative Research

Most of the retailing research currently being conducted consists of solving short-run or day-to-day problems. However, the payoff in solving long-run problems may be great. Retailers may benefit considerably by investigating how anticipated changes in the consumer of 1985 will affect retailing in 1985. Sociologists, psychologists, and consumer behavior specialists, by studying anticipated changes in consumer tastes, wants, satisfactions, life styles, etc., can make recommendations on how a retailer can be in a better position to meet the needs of the consumer of the future. Such advance planning can yield tremendous payoffs in the same way that acquiring prime suburban locations paid off for retailers who were quick to recognize the effect that the city-to-suburbs population movement would have upon retailing.

Analysis of the trends in retailing and communication may also indicate better opportunities to serve consumers at a profit before everyone else gets on the bandwagon. Communication and physical distribution systems that will reduce errors but increase the speed of consumer service are badly needed.

The trend toward increased consumer expenditures on services needs to be explored more fully. What implications does this trend have for the established retailer? Can profitable services be sold by using current mailing lists and making only small additions to the sales and service personnel?

QUESTIONNAIRE CONSTRUCTION

Questionnaires are frequently used to learn consumer attitudes, knowledge, and behavior. Questionnaire design should begin with the definitions of the problems that are being researched. Any questionnaire must be short in length or respondents will not take the time to answer all the questions or return it. Oral interviews should not exceed thirty minutes.[37] The response rate is increased and respondent fatigue decreased with shorter interviews. It is desirable to limit self-administered questionnaires to an even shorter length. Thus it is important to determine what information is needed to satisfy the objectives of the research project before the questionnaire is written.

Generally, the researcher develops a list of topics that must be covered and this list is then converted into questions. Each proposed question should be evaluated against the criterion, "What will be done with the information obtained from this question?" If the answer is, "Nothing," and the question does not contribute any information that can be used to satisfy the research objectives, it should be eliminated from the questionnaire.

Methods of Collecting Questionnaire Data

The way each question is worded will depend upon the method used to collect the responses from the consumers. Questionnaires can be obtained by personal interview, telephone interview, or by mail. The choice between these three methods is influenced by the type of information requested in the questionnaire, the type of respondents, and the cost of using each alternative.

Personal Interview Method

The personal interview consists of the interviewer obtaining the information from respondents in face-to-face meetings. This type of interview allows the interviewer to obtain answers to a great number of questions. It also can be used to obtain more detailed information and can probe to determine why the consumer believes or acts as he has said he does. Thus it is used when open-end, projective techniques are needed to determine the consumer's attitudes.

Personal interviews generally result in a higher percentage of completed questionnaires than is the case for telephone interviewing or the mail approach. This higher completion rate may cover a more representative group of respondents because many people will not respond to a mail survey and many people are not included in a sample from a telephone book.

On the other hand, more bias can creep into the interviewer's coding of consumers' responses unless trained interviewers are used. Responses to personal questions may also be more biased if the personal interview is used, because the respondent may be more embarrassed.[38] The interviewer should be given a list of specific people or houses to contact; if not, a bias toward selecting the better-appearing houses will result. Also, interviewers can cheat by filling out a questionnaire without making an interview.

These disadvantages of the personal interview technique can be reduced considerably by rechecking 10 to 20 percent of the responses and by using other good research methods. But the major disadvantage—substantially greater expense per completed interview—cannot be reduced by any significant degree.

Telephone Interview Method

Telephone interviewing is similar to personal interviewing except that communication occurs over the telephone instead of in person. The interviewer can still probe, check conflicting statements, and use unstructured questions—except, of course, those requiring responses to complex scaling techniques, drawings, or photographs. The major advantages of telephone interviewing are the short time required to obtain the data and a relatively low cost of data collection. The questionnaire, however, may have to be a little shorter in a telephone interview than in a personal interview as it is easier for the respondent to hang up the phone than throw the interviewer out of the house.[39] For personal questions, telephone interviewing may be better than personal interviewing because the respondent may talk more freely than he would in a face-to-face interview.

Telephone interviewing must be done when respondents will not be irritated by the call, but some evening re-calling is required to reach "no-answer numbers" of families where husband and wife both work. The same procedure is required for the personal interview, so there is no relative disadvantage to telephone interviewing because of the not-at-home problem.

Interviewer bias and cheating can also arise in telephone interviewing. However, if all interviews are made from a central location, the interviewer's technique can be controlled and checked with minimum effort.

The major difficulty in telephone surveys is drawing a representative sample of the target population. Unlisted numbers, families with a new telephone which is not yet listed, and families that do not have a telephone are excluded from the selection list and therefore are not represented in the sample unless random digit dialing can be used.

Mail Questionnaire Method

Mail questionnaires are given to the respondent through the mail, attached to products, placed in shopping bags, or placed in newspapers. Respondents generally return the questionnaire by the mail.

Mail questionnaires must usually be shorter than either the personal or telephone questionnaire or the consumers will not send them back.[40] Also, fewer probing and in-depth questions can be asked in mail questionnaires than in the personal interview. In addition, respondents tend to give briefer answers to open-end questions in mail surveys than in personal or telephone interviews.[41]

Mail questionnaires reach nearly everyone, so the not-at-home problem is reduced and families where both husband and wife work are reached. In addition, the mail method can be economical in reaching a sample of people who are widely scattered over a geographic area. However, the cost per completed interview depends upon the return rate. Frequently only 10 to 20 percent of the people who receive questionnaires by mail return them.

Thus a sample bias may occur as only the people who are interested in the topic respond, and the undereducated consumers may hesitate to write responses to open-end questions, or may not even return the questionnaire. Writing short, easy-to-answer questions on attractive questionnaire forms, which are accompanied by a cover letter, an incentive premium, and a self-addressed, pre-stamped return envelope, will increase the return rate and reduce some of this sample bias.

Robinson and Agisim report that by using these techniques and a good questionnaire construction it is possible to secure from 70 to 93 percent returns on mail surveys.[42] Their findings indicate that, with high-level returns, the differences between respondents and non-respondents were due to chance and not to inherent variations in characteristics. They concluded that when returns reach the level of 80 percent, reliability can be given to the findings because non-respondents would have little, if any, effect on the total.

The mail questionnaire approach has some disadvantages, however. First, the response to a mail survey is subject to a "sequence bias" in the questions asked: respondents can change their answers to early questions after they read the later questions. In addition, it is never quite certain whose response one is getting in a mail survey. The respondent can get aid in completing the questionnaire—or even have someone else fill it out for him.

One of the most important criteria affecting the method for reaching the respondent is cost per completed interview. Figure 17–6 contains a model that can be used to estimate the cost per completed interview for each technique. The calculations depend upon assumptions of wage rates, return percentages, etc.; so the cost estimates may not be realistic for current conditions. Thus prior experience in conducting a specific kind of survey may indicate that new figures need to be inserted in the model.

Determining the Content of Individual Questions

For the most part, questionnaire writing remains an art, so our discussion will be confined to some of the more important considerations.[43] The wording of each question must be simple and easy for each respondent to under-

Figure 17–6 Model for Estimating the Cost Per Interview via Personal, Telephone, and Mail Techniques

	ONE-TIME MAIL QUESTIONNAIRE WITH 1 FOLLOW-UP MAILING	TELEPHONE INTERVIEW WITH 3 CALLBACKS*	PERSONAL INTERVIEW WITH 3 CALLBACKS*
1. Number of people contacted	100	100	100
2. Not at home or undelivered	10	10	10
3. Number reached	90	90	90
4. Number refusing interview or failing to return questionnaire	70	30	20
5. Number of responses	20	60	70
6. Hours of interviewing time	0	30	70
7. Interviewing cost @ $2.50 per hour	0	$75	$175
8. Cost of reaching local respondents	$40†	0	$100
9. Total cost for interviewing and reaching respondents	$40	$75	$275
10. Cost per obtained response equals (9) / (5)	$2.00	$1.25	$3.93

* Callbacks made during different times of day and night to reach families where both husband and wife work outside the home.

† 100 mailings @ 40¢ because a self-addressed prestamped envelope is enclosed.

stand. The questions should be asked in terms that the respondent uses—and in clear, objective terms that do not lead the respondent to answer in a biased manner. For example, the question, "Do you like the delivery service offered by department store X?" will result in a larger percentage of respondents who are satisfied with X's delivery service than would the question, "What department stores offer free delivery services: store A? store B? store X? store Z?" In the second case, the question, "How do you rate the delivery service offered by each of the above stores?" is also asked. The better surveys do not identify the sponsor of the research in either the cover letter or the questions since this would introduce a bias. Instead, they obtain ratings on three or four primary competitors as well as for their own retail firm. The results allow the retailer to get a relative measurement of preferences or attitudes. This measurement, relative to competitors, is more meaningful to management than a mere rating on an attitude scale.

The writer of a questionnaire must evaluate each question to determine if the respondent (1) has the information requested and (2) will give the information if he has it. Has he the experience needed to answer the question? Maybe he doesn't even know that retail firm X exists, and he can't answer questions concerning the store's service, sales people, etc. Can he remember the information requested? Maybe a listing of the alternatives would aid his recall. Is the respondent likely to refuse to answer this question? If so, maybe some projective technique or other form of indirect question which asks for a response of what "other people" think will provide more information. Questions on personal matters such as age, annual family income, etc. are usually better received if they are presented in categories which allow the respondent to check or indicate to the interviewer the category in which he falls. The categories are usually large enough so that only a few responses will occur in the extremely low and extremely high groups.

Multiple choice questions that give a list of alternative answers should contain a list of all alternatives or there will be a bias against those not included on the list. Even the best pre-planning will result in an alternative's being omitted, so an "other—please specify" alternative is used to obtain at least a mention of factors that may be important to respondents but did not occur to the questionnaire writer. When listings are used, a bias can result from the order in which the alternatives are given. Therefore it is recommended that, if possible, the alternatives be rotated to allow each topic to be presented first, second, third, etc. an equal number of times.

Every questionnaire should be *pre-tested* on a small group of respondents who have the *same* characteristics as the group that will be surveyed. This practice, together with coding and analyzing the data obtained from this trial run, quickly points up any questions that are interpreted incorrectly by the respondents. It also provides new ideas that the questionnaire writer may want to include in the full-scale survey.

Question Sequence

The introduction to the questionnaire should include a brief and very general statement of the objectives of the survey without identifying the retail sponsor. A guarantee must usually be made that the respondents' comments will remain confidential and will not be revealed except in group summaries.

The first question must gain the respondent's interest and convince him that the survey is interested in his views on a "nonpersonal" basis. The remaining questions must be arranged in a manner that is psychologically sound. Simpler questions should be asked first, but the writer must consider the influence that each question has upon succeeding questions. The questions are usually placed in a logical order which obtains responses in one general subject area before going to another topic. Questions or topics which are likely to cause difficulty (such as requests for personal or embarrassing information) are generally placed in the later sections of the questionnaire. The more involved the respondent is, the more difficult it is for him to discontinue an oral interview or throw away a mail questionnaire. For this reason, questionnaires usually conclude with a request for the necessary demographic information, such as classifications by age and income.

Sampling

Seldom does a retailer have enough money to survey the entire population in his trading area. Therefore a sample of consumers is used to provide information about the population which the target consumers are supposed to represent. If the sample is selected properly and the survey is conducted appropriately, the sample should provide information which is representative of the data that would be found if the entire population were studied in a similar manner. Thus sampling is used to reduce research costs.

It is especially important for the retailer to carefully define the statistical population he wants to study. This should be done in precise terms which *describe his target market population in detail*. The researcher must then devise a plan for selecting a sample of consumers from the defined population. This design must allow generalizations about the population being studied. Ideally, the composition of the sample should be such that it gives a proportional sampling by family size, economic group, city size, sex, nationality group, education level, and age group. In short, what is desired is a sample that accurately reflects the characteristics of the market population to which the retailer merchandises his products and services.

Sampling Procedures

Simple random sampling is a method of choosing n people out of the defined statistical population (N) in such a way that every possible sample has an equal chance of being chosen.[44] In the most commonly used method of simple random sampling without replacement, the person who has been selected is not replaced in the population from which the next person will be selected. Thus no person can appear more than once in a sample drawn by this method.

Systematic sampling is somewhat different, as—first of all—every person in the population may be "numbered" 1 to N. To select a sample size of n, a number is selected at random from 1 to k, where k, the "skip factor," equals N / n. The sample then consists of the number selected at random and every subsequent kth number. Thus if the random number selected is r, the sample consists of r, $r + k$, $r + 2k$, $r + 3k$, etc. For example, if k is 25 and if the first unit drawn is number 13, the subsequent persons selected are numbers 38, 63, 88, etc. The selection of the first person determines the entire sample.[45] The chief advantage of this method is that it is easy to draw a sample. Systematic sampling can be used where the ordering of the population is essentially random.

In using systematic sampling it is crucial to recognize that the list from which the names are drawn should be random with respect to the characteristics investigated. In general, a telephone directory is not a random list of consumers; however, it may be reasonably random with respect to a retailer's potential customers.

One way to ensure that each consumer group is represented in proportion to the number of people in that group in the entire population is to select the final sample by stratified random sampling with proportional allocation. This selection may be based upon the information obtained in the preliminary questionnaire. Stratified sampling is the technique of dividing the population of N units into subpopulations (called strata) of N_1, N_2 ... N_L units. These strata are non-overlapping, and together they comprise the whole of the entire population. When the strata have been determined, a sample of a size which bears a proportional relationship between the stratum size and the size of other strata is drawn from each stratum. The selections are made independently in each different stratum. Stratified random sampling is the method of taking a single random sample in each stratum.[46]

Stratified random sampling has advantages over other methods because not all of the initial contacts will become sample members. This sampling method tends to compensate for the bias introduced by non-cooperation.[47]

While it is desirable to have as representative a sample as possible, it is not always economically feasible to achieve a purely representative sample. Preliminary surveys and screening are added expenses which are probably justifiable only to a certain point. An added problem is that for many retailers it is difficult to identify the exact, relevant consumer population. Thus the sample that is used in a particular test may be somewhat less than representative. However, it should be remembered that the more representative the sample, the more valid the results should be.

Sample Size

Other things being equal, large samples yield more reliable results than small samples, unless the smaller sample is likely to be selected and interviewed more carefully than the larger sample. On the other hand, the cost of conducting research increases as the size of the sample increases. Fortunately, relatively small samples, selected by the unbiased sampling procedures just discussed, will achieve satisfactory precision. In exploratory research, most information about attitudes and marketing processes can be obtained from a simple random sample of about 100 people.[48] Motivation research studies, designed to discover latent consumer attitudes, have been conducted by obtaining about thirty interviews.[49]

The approximate degree of confidence that one can expect with varying sample sizes when the sample is selected by a simple random sampling procedure is presented in Figure 17–7. This figure indicates that one can be about 95 percent confident that a reported sample of 50 percent does not differ from the true population percentage by more than approximately 4 percent if 500 completed responses are obtained. If 100 completed responses are obtained, one is about 95 percent confident that the 50 percent estimate obtained from the sample is within 10 percent of the true population value.

Getting More from Marketing Research

Although retailers are not expected to be experts in the field of research, it is wise to have a basic understanding of research procedures. This can

Figure 17–7   *Approximate Sampling Errors of Survey Findings*

Sampling errors of reported percentages: The chances are approximately 95 in 100 that the reported sample value does not differ from the population value by more than the percentage points shown below.*

	NUMBER OF INTERVIEWS ON WHICH THE PERCENTAGE IS BASED				
Reported Percentages	*500*	*300*	*200*	*100*	*50*
From 35% to 65%	4%	6%	7%	10%	14%
Near 20% or 80%	4	5	6	8	11
Near 10% or 90%	3	3	4	6	—
Near 5% or 95%	2	3	3	4	—

* Standard error of a percent $\times$ 1.96 gives the figures in the body of the table, where standard error $= \sqrt{PQ/n}$. P equals the reported sample percentage, Q equals 100 minus P, and n equals the sample size. The calculation is made under the assumption that the sample is selected from a large population where the sampling procedure will yield that stated degree of accuracy over the selection of many different samples.

prove to be very helpful when the retailer is contracting for research services or accepting the final results.

The costs of marketing research are high. It is common for major studies to cost $10,000 or more. If a retailer were going to purchase $10,000 worth of merchandise from a vendor, he would, as a basic step, check the merchandise to see that it conforms with the purchase order. Unfortunately, such a basic step is too often overlooked by clients who purchase marketing research work.

There are several steps which a retailer can take to ensure the best purchase and use of research data:

1. Hire research employees who indicate a research orientation. In other words, hire professionals for your company's marketing research department—people who are truly interested in the field and have demonstrated their interest through their training, writing, and experience. In far too many cases the marketing research department is a short-run training ground for middle management. Personnel are moved there from a variety of areas regardless of training.

2. Know from whom you are buying research. The same qualities that apply to a lawyer are equally valid for researchers: experience, education, general background, success with other clients, and the individual's specialty. It is well known that not all lawyers are qualified to do patent work, and the same thing is true with many areas of marketing research. It is essential to determine the individual's or the firm's areas of specialty, but all too often the answer from the researcher is, "We can do anything!" Seldom is this correct.

    It is equally important to determine what other products or services the researcher is selling, such as advertising, public relations, or image work. It is questionable how objective such firms can be if the sale of other services rests upon the research results.

3. Who will do the actual research? Don't buy the old story, "We have qualified interviewers." In far too many cases these interviewers are part-time workers or housewives who may or may not have been given more than a five-minute set of instructions. All interviewers should be checked to be certain they are conducting the interviews completely and according to instructions.

4. Come to a firm price agreement. Research is not a blank-check operation and should not be treated as such.

5. Require a written proposal and record major design changes in writing. Don't even consider anything like this all too typical agreement: "Dear Bob, Thanks for lunch and the invitation to work with you in the study we discussed. We will proceed soon." In the first place, poor old Bob doesn't even know who should pay for the lunch, and in the second place he's buying trouble.

    A good proposal should contain detailed statements on six major elements:

    a.   The problem. Often the researcher and the client don't agree on or understand the basic problem. Unless there is agreement here, there can be nothing but chaos.

    b.   Objectives. These should state, "To determine. . . . "

    c.   Methodology. This statement does not have to be long and involved, but it should give the client a basic idea of the data collection method to be used, the sampling procedure, and the sample size.

    d.   Definition of terms. Terms such as "the Chicago market" should be clearly defined, as the client may be thinking of the Chicago phone district and the researcher may be thinking of the Loop.

    e.   Time schedule.

    f.   Cost.

6. Demand an interim report. This report doesn't have to be lengthy (it can be a letter), but it should give the client an idea of the progress to date and the expected time of completion, plus an indication of any unusual problems which have been discovered.

7. Inspect the test market. Make sure the test market is well set up, and the only way to do this is to visit the area in person. It is not unusual to find that test markets have been established for the wrong retail outlets or shelf space.

8. Don't accept the word of experts as a substitute for objective research. This is especially true in international marketing research. Since income data and other statistics may be difficult to obtain in other countries, the researcher sometimes takes short cuts. The results from fifty government officials, ten bankers, and forty school teachers are not a substitute for a good sample of the potential users of a household product.

9. Examine the sampling technique from a logical standpoint. Don't worry about the hieroglyphics of statistics. The major questions are:

    a.   Is the size sufficient?

    b.   Who will be included in this sample?

    c.   Does the sample match the objectives?

10. Keep a diary of the outside environment. What important political, climatic, and social events took place during the time of the study that could easily affect the results?

11. Ask for a copy of the report before the presentation. Otherwise, the final presentation is simply a "dog and pony show." It is impossible for anyone to thoroughly understand the mass of results that will be thrown at him during a final, one-hour presentation. Come to that meeting prepared, by having read the report. The researcher won't like this, and will do his best to avoid giving a prior copy of the report, but it's to your advantage to demand one.

12. Don't accept unfinished work. It is easy to give the client a huge bulk of data, but what do they mean? A retailer wouldn't accept the work sheets of an accountant as the finished balance sheet, and the same is true for marketing research.

13.   Make sure the report is readable; if it is not, reject it. The report must be written in a style that can be read by a layman and that lends itself to decision making. If you can't read it, chances are the president can't either—and it will only gather dust and quickly grow useless.

14.   Ask for clarification of details. The details of a balance sheet are questioned, and so should the details of a research report.

15.   Don't let statistics throw you. Keep asking the researcher "What is the purpose of this test?" Ask until he explains in a manner that an ordinary, intelligent executive can understand. Basically, statistics serve these purposes:
   a.   To determine sample size
   b.   To test a hypothesis
   c.   To forecast.

16.   If necessary, ask the consultant to come back to further explain the data. If this wasn't agreed to in the original contract, pay him extra.

17.   Have the report checked and analyzed by others. If in-house capability exists, great! Use it! If not, pay a small consulting fee to an outsider to evaluate the report.

18.   Realize that the best research by the most qualified individual in the world is not 100 percent perfect. Any report can be picked apart in some area (trial lawyers long ago learned this). The point is not to be ridiculous about the depth of criticism but, instead, to look for gross errors and misinterpretation of data.

19.   Apply common sense. Don't completely disregard "gut feel" or forget past experiences.

Marketing research is an excellent aid in retail decision making when it is done well and used with thought. However, decision making is far too complex ever to let a research report replace all other considerations. In the final analysis, there is no substitute for sound management decision making by seasoned and knowledgeable executives who know how to use research as a useful tool.

SUMMARY

The expansion of retail organizations beyond a single location has increased the need for conducting research before making huge investments in land, buildings, and fixtures. The resulting growth in location and trade area research has provided the operational base from which other research activities have expanded.

Today, retail researchers are developing programs based on the firm's objectives. These programs assist the retailer in making improvements in the functions that propel the firm beyond its current levels of performance.

Research can be beneficial to the retailer whenever he must make an important decision. Priorities must be established and the level of research expenditures related to the financial consequences of the decision.

Retailers should be aware of the basic research procedures discussed in this chapter so they can spend their research dollar more wisely.

QUESTIONS

1. If you were a medium-price clothing retailer, what alterations would you make in your business in anticipation of a 20 percent increase in buying power by minority groups? Take a systems approach and assume the increase will occur over a period of about one year.
2. List the social and economic changes you expect by the end of this century and the implications for retailing of each of these changes.
3. How are in-store traffic shopping patterns used in a large department store? What difficulties can be encountered in their use? How would you suggest overcoming these difficulties or at least minimizing them?
4. How would you go about collecting the data for a consumer profile analysis? In what types of retailing would you expect such an analysis to be most useful? Why?
5. Unstructured, open-end questions allow the respondent to discuss only the concepts he remembers, but in doing so his answers are often obscured by verbiage. Consequently, the answers are difficult to evaluate and interpret. Can you suggest a method of obtaining the desired information without encountering this problem?
6. Many consumer attitude surveys and store image surveys require a considerable time for a customer to complete. Would you, as a retailer, feel that you could ask a customer to donate his time to improve your business and expect significant results? Discuss this problem and suggest possible solutions.
7. Frequently large department stores seem very anxious to enlarge their number of credit card holders. List several reasons why this policy is pursued.
8. How can future sales be predicted and what problems can be encountered in this type of prediction?
9. How can new product research and distribution research be useful to a retailer?
10. In what types of market research would you suggest using the telephone interview? The personal interview? The questionnaire? State your reasons.
11. Can you suggest a method of detecting a personal bias on the part of an interviewer?
12. Why should the firm that is sponsoring a survey not identify itself?
13. What is meant by pre-testing a questionnaire and why is this practice desirable?
14. If persons are selected at random from a population without replace-

[20] Julian L. Simon, "Expenditure Policy for Mail-Order Advertisers," *Journal of Marketing Research,* 4 (February 1967): 59–61.

[21] Darrell B. Lucas and Stewart H. Britt, *Measuring Advertising Effectiveness* (New York: McGraw-Hill, 1963), pp. 187–188.

[22] James E. Stafford and Thomas V. Greer, "Consumer Preference for Types of Salesmen: A Study of Independence-Dependence Characteristics," *Journal of Retailing,* 41 (Summer 1965): 32.

[23] Charles J. Stokes and Philip Mintz, "How Many Clerks on a Floor?" *Journal of Marketing Research,* 2 (November 1965): 338–393.

[24] Abe Schuchman, "Queue Tips for Managers," in Abe Schuchman, ed., *Scientific Decision Making in Business: Readings in Operations Research for Nonmathematicians* (New York: Holt, Rinehart and Winston, 1963), p. 300.

[25] James S. Cross, "Operations Research in Solving a Marketing Problem," *Journal of Marketing,* 25 (January 1961): 31–34.

[26] Marvin A. Jolson and Richard T. Hise, *Quantitative Techniques for Marketing Decisions* (New York: Macmillan, 1973), pp. 73–80, 86–90.

[27] Daniel B. Suits, *Statistics: An Introduction to Quantitative Economic Research* (Chicago: Rand McNally, 1963), pp. 155–225.

[28] W. J. Dixon, ed., *Biomedical Computer Programs* (Berkeley: University of California Press, 1971), pp. 258–275d.

[29] Philip Kotler, *Marketing Management: Analysis, Planning and Control* (Englewood Cliffs, N.J.: Prentice-Hall, 1972), p. 219.

[30] Ibid., pp. 219–220.

[31] John R. Stockton, *Introduction to Business and Economic Statistics* (Cincinnati, Ohio: South-Western Publishing Co., 1966), pp. 309–460.

[32] For a more complete description of the information provided by SAMI see "Fourth Annual Report on Grocery Product Movement" in *Progressive Grocer* (August 1971), pp. 38–47.

[33] Charles B. Riter, "The Merchandising Decision under Uncertainty," *Journal of Marketing,* 31 (January 1967): 44–47.

[34] Jolson and Hise, *Quantitative Techniques for Marketing Decisions,* pp. 29–69.

[35] Seymour Banks, *Experimentation in Marketing* (New York: McGraw-Hill, 1965); David K. Hardin and Raymond Marquardt, "Increasing Precision of Market Testing," *Journal of Marketing Research* (November 1967), pp. 396–399.

[36] Ronald Curhan, "The Relationship of Shelf Space to Unit Sales: A Review" (Marketing Science Institute working paper) (Cambridge, Mass.: Marketing Science Institute, 1972).

[37] William J. Goode and Paul K. Hatt, *Methods in Social Research* (New York: McGraw-Hill, 1952), p. 134.

[38] William F. O'Dell, "Personal Interviews or Mail Panels," *Journal of Marketing,* 26 (October 1962): 34–39.

[39] Glen H. Mitchell, *Telephone Interviewing* (Wooster: Ohio Agricultural Experiment Station, undated), p. 8.

[40] Two studies that showed that the return of mail questionnaires declined as the length of the questionnaires increased are Frank Stanton, "Notes on the Validity of Mail Questionnaire Returns," *Journal of Applied Psychology,* 23 (February 1939): 95–104, and W. Mitchell, "Factors Affecting the Rate of Return on Mail Questionnaires," *Journal of American Statistical Association,* 45 (1939): 683–692.

[41] O'Dell, "Personal Interviews or Mail Panels," p. 36.

[42] R. A. Robinson and Philip Agisim, "Making Mail Surveys More Reliable," *Journal of Marketing* (April 1951), pp. 415–424.

[43] See also Harper W. Boyd, Jr., and Ralph Westfall, *Marketing Research Text and Cases* (Homewood, Ill.: Richard D. Irwin, 1972), pp. 284–348.

[44] William G. Cochran, *Sampling Techniques* (New York: John Wiley & Sons, 1953), p. 11.

[45] Ibid., p. 160.

[46] Ibid., pp. 65–110.

[47] James D. Shaffer, "Methodological Bases for the Operation of a Consumer Purchase Panel" (Unpublished Ph.D. dissertation, Michigan State University, 1952), p. 194.

[48] Kotler, *Marketing Management,* p. 324.

[49] Ibid.

HERMAN'S GROCERY, INC.
A Case in Credit Management

Mr. Herman, owner-manager of Herman's Grocery, Inc., is evaluating his firm's credit policy. Herman's Grocery, Inc. is an independent outlet with annual sales of slightly over $1.5 million. The firm is one of two grocery outlets offering its own charge account system in a town of 25,000 residents. The other store, offering a similar plan, is on the other side of town.

Herman's trade area is concentrated in the surrounding neighborhood, but he draws 25 percent of his business from another neighborhood 25 blocks away. Herman operated another store in that neighborhood until it burned down nine months ago. Many of Herman's customers were then lost to competitive stores, but some remained loyal to Herman and drove to his remaining store. This store was built one year before his other store burned.

Herman operates his remaining store on a 21 percent gross margin. His net margin is 3 percent and his net sales to inventory ratio is 24. Credit sales now amount to 70 percent of Herman's total sales. Last year he lost $2,000 to bad debts. Last year's collection period varied from 33 to 36 days.

Mr. Herman is concerned about his bad debt loss, and he is also concerned about the high cost of maintaining credit records for each customer. He is considering dropping his credit plan entirely but does not know what effect this move would have on his customers. He does not know what his store's image is from his customers' point of view.

DISCUSSION QUESTIONS

1. What alternatives should Mr. Herman consider?
2. Design a research project that will help Mr. Herman make the correct decision on his credit problem and at the same time reveal his store's image.
3. What methods can be used to reduce bad debt losses? List these methods, their relative costs, and their effects on total sales and make a recommendation.

ARTS INTERNATIONAL INC.
Purchasing a Suitable Product Line

Arts International Inc. is the largest retail chain of low-cost original oil paintings, with thirty-one stores throughout the United States plus one in the Bahamas. The chain was started in 1962 by an attorney who is now president of the firm, Mr. Jack Solomon, Jr.

Mr. Solomon, who is knowledgeable in art, used to purchase original yet inexpensive oil paintings during his visits to Europe. Many friends would ask him to purchase paintings for them. As a result, he decided to purchase enough to have a weekend sale in his home. This produced sales of $15,000 and the beginning of Arts International.

The concept behind Arts International is to market good original art to the general public at a cost not to exceed $75. Frames are extra—between $3 and $50. The sales philosophy is to utilize the proven merchandising-marketing techniques successfully employed by retailers of other types of merchandise. The paintings are produced in standardized sizes and under a quality control program that carefully regulates the kind of canvas and paint to be used.

In organizing Arts International, Mr. Solomon believed that Americans were afraid to purchase art because it was high priced, and that they often felt embarrassed to enter traditional galleries. In addition, he believed that the quality and styles of many paintings simply did not meet American tastes. As an example, some European originals were painted with common house paint, which led to their rapid deterioration.

Unlike many galleries that procure works of art on a consignment basis, Arts International purchases the paintings. These paintings are purchased from a total of 400 artists, but the bulk is produced by 75 full-time artists who are located in enclaves in San Francisco, Chicago, and New York. They are paid per painting and on a weekly basis.

Each full-time artist is under contract to Arts International and cannot sell to any other gallery during the duration of his contract. However, the works of these artists sometimes become quite popular with the public and their prices tend to rise. When this happens, Arts International allows them to sell to higher-priced galleries.

In the long run, this has a very desirable effect for Arts International as customers sometimes find their paintings appreciating in value. This helps to spread word-of-mouth advertising.

Even though the concept behind Arts International is not to sell paintings for investment but, instead, for decorative-pleasure purposes, the appreciation of certain lines has helped to increase the image of the company.

New artists are required to work in a training program sponsored by

Arts International—much like the old European apprentice system. A new artist with a certain style is required to work under an older Arts International artist with a similar style.

The company does not have a recruiting program with talent scouts but it is continually on the outlook for new talent. Most of the new talent contacts the company after hearing about it from a friend or visiting a gallery. Each artist-applicant is carefully screened by experts in the Arts International organization who evaluate the quality of his work.

Executives of the company are continually on the lookout for new talent. As an example, Mr. Solomon spent many hours in Milan tracking down an artist after seeing his work in a gallery. Out of every fifty artists who approach Arts International, only one has the right talent.

Having enough paintings is the primary problem facing the company. In its entire history, only one store was closed for lack of sales, and that one broke even.

On average, over 2,000 paintings per week are sold through Arts International stores. However, Mr. Solomon expressed a belief that his company could open several new locations and could sell at least "twentyfold more" if paintings were available.

In the past, art schools had been solicited for artists, but this approach was not productive. For the most part, the type of training and the style of art produced in these schools do not match the needs of Arts International.

Geographically, most artists are found in the United States, South America, and Europe. A few paintings are purchased from other parts of the world; however, oil painting on canvas is largely a Western art form.

Gallery directors are asked to be continually on the lookout for new talent. Occasionally, an area such as Scottsdale, Arizona, will provide enough prospective artists to warrant an interview-showing at which the local talent can be inspected by company management.

In an effort to expand the product line, sculpture had been tried, but it was too expensive, and there were many problems in shipping. In addition, Mr. Solomon believes the American public is not sculpture oriented, although it has become quite conscious of original oil paintings.

The market for low-cost original art is excellent and is growing each year. Sales appear to be limited only by supply.

DISCUSSION QUESTIONS

1. Are there other methods or systems that Arts International should employ to recruit talented artists?
2. Do retailers of other goods, such as select fashion goods or ceramics, face a similar buying problem?
3. Obviously, Arts International has proved that original oil paintings can be sold through mass merchandising techniques. Are there other products

CHAPTER 18

Photo courtesy of Sears, Roebuck and Company.

The Retail Audit

The retail audit involves more than a financial audit, as the former consists of a review of the major ingredients used in the effective retail management process and a financial audit discloses the retail performance of the firm in dollars. The financial audit is a formal examination of the results of past practices, but it does not reveal current management practices that may lead to financial difficulties. The *inventory audit* is another audit that is frequently used to verify that the firm possesses stock valued at a stated level of dollars. This audit is needed not only to prevent and detect employee theft but also to determine the extent of damaged or out-of-date merchandise and record-keeping errors.

NATURE OF RETAILING AUDITS

There is no universally established definition of the term *retail audit*. As used in this book, a retail audit consists of a broad analysis which includes a systematic evaluation of all retail procedures and practices. The primary purpose of the retail audit is to develop an independent judgment of the quality of the firm's effort to improve the *future* performance of its retail outlet(s). Retail management is always seeking improvements. Frequently retail managers are so involved in their day-to-day activities that they cannot determine if the activities are being performed in an optimum manner. The retail audit, with its fresh, overall, independent evaluation of the effort, can stimulate a retailer to make needed changes before they are reflected in a poor financial performance.

There are two basic types of retail audit: *horizontal* and *vertical* audits. The horizontal (also called the systems-level) audit consists of an examination of all the elements that the retailer uses to market his goods and/or services.[1] Particular emphasis is placed upon the relative importance of each of these elements. It is designed to develop a total evaluation of the retailer's marketing effort. The appraisal deals not so much with particular marketing activities as with their relationships with one another. Horizontal audits, however, attempt to identify specific activities that appear to require closer investigation.[2]

The vertical (sometimes called the activity-level) audit examines and evaluates—in depth—certain functional elements of the retail operation. It is a closer, more detailed investigation into one or more of the specific retailing activities.

SYSTEMS-LEVEL (HORIZONTAL) RETAIL AUDITING

A comprehensive systems-level retail audit involves a periodic evaluation of both the basic framework used to generate retail activities and the performance of retail actions. The systems-level audit is comprehensive because it is an appraisal of all of the elements used in the retail effort, not merely an evaluation of the most problem-ridden activities. Confining the use of retail audits to occasions of company difficulties is likely to result in missed sales and/or lost cost-reduction opportunities. Successful retail organizations can benefit from retail auditing procedures by maintaining an objective view of changes occurring in both the outside marketing environment and the internal company operations.

Retail audits should be scheduled annually, so that the retail audit is a regular part of the periodic review of the long-range company plan. The retail audit comprises the first two steps in the business planning process, and the latter begins with the retailer's *diagnosis* of his market situation and the factors he believes are responsible for it.

marketing objectives must also be established to satisfy consumers' needs at a profit. If this is not done, retail outlets and organizations can become obsolete quite rapidly as shopping patterns and preferences change.

Continuous changes in the retailer's marketing environment necessitate a clear statement of the definition of the firm's business. Objectives must define which consumers' needs are to be satisfied by the firm's retailing efforts. The objectives should identify those market segments which appear to offer the most long-range profit potential and those segments in which the retailer believes he has the competitive advantage. The marketing and competitive environment changes at an increasingly faster rate, so it is now easier to identify and enter a market niche by "tuning into" these changes faster than competitors.

For example, a department store has used these concepts to clarify its marketing objectives. It recognized that the taste-making forces of American society have changed. The 20-year-olds of the 1970s are the first generation reflecting the impact of growing up under the influence of a constant bombardment of television commercials and programs that emphasize that you should "live life with real gusto because you only have one chance." Thus television's influence on the behavior of the young is probably more important than the traditional generators of values, namely, schools, churches, and parents. These factors, combined with the emphasis that all age groups placed on youth or on "looking young," were deemed to have an important impact upon the local clothing business.

The underlying desire in the United States is for consumers to buy goods and services that will make them appear to be at least ten years younger than they really are. The fashion-making forces have changed from the "trickle down" adoptions of merchandise by upper-class Europeans and Americans to adoption by the U.S. middle-class consumers to adoption by the U.S. lower class. Instead, the young "street people" have begun to generate fashion. Everybody else has followed this lead because of the basic desire to appear to be younger than he is.

These rapid changes in the environment allowed the department store to enter a market niche that was not being captured by competitors, who were still selling essentially the conservative style of clothing that did not reflect the fashion consciousness of a growing segment of the market. The market was segmented not only on the basis of demographic characteristics such as age, sex, social class, etc. but also on the basis of psycho-graphics of life style. The market segment that was fashion conscious was found to be growing and its preferences changing toward youth-generated styles. The department store adjusted its merchandise line to meet the needs of this market segment. It also promoted a whole new progressive retail image by generating a "making happiness happen" theme.

The image was carried over into non-clothing merchandise lines such as towels, bedding, and linens. In this case, the target customers were fashion-conscious women who were buying towels and bedding not merely for their functional uses but for their decorative purposes. Thus the consumer was willing to pay much higher prices for goods that would match her color-decoration scheme. Additionally, she was more likely to make more frequent repurchases of the item as she grew tired of a particular decorative theme. Most of these goods wouldn't wear out physically but they would be discarded early as they were no longer "in style." Of course, more frequent consumer repurchases tend to generate additional sales and to build store loyalty if the consumer is satisfied with his or her purchase. The slowness of competitors to recognize these changes allowed the department store to establish itself as the leader in catering to this most profitable market segment.

Establishing retail objectives involves more than the selection of the generic marketing objectives (such as satisfying the clothing needs of a growing segment of fashion-conscious, local consumers, as illustrated in the above example). Retail objectives also involve the establishment of specific sales and profit target objectives. These targets should be set on a realistic basis that reflects an unbiased evaluation of the retail firm's capabilities.

Figure 18–1 contains a form which auditors can use to analyze the present condition of stated company policy for any retail firm. The form contains a description of three classifications—outstanding, average, deficient —on each item. The auditor can objectively select the category which most accurately describes the situation in that specific retail firm. The auditor will be able to identify the areas requiring the most attention by reviewing all the category ratings for each area.

Figure 18–1   *Rating Form on Retail Policy*

✓	Outstanding Condition	✓	Average Condition	✓	Deficient Condition
	1. Company's policies and objectives clearly defined and understood by all.		1. Company's general policies not clearly defined nor understood.		1. No general policy except to carry on company's tradition.
	2. All current and potential economic factors recognized in overall company planning.		2. Sporadic consideration of potential economic factors in company planning.		2. Planning done under impulse.
	3. Agressive participation in trade and business associations.		3. Interest in trade and business associations limited.		3. Trade and business associations regarded as a necessary evil.
	4. Company kept currently informed on Federal, State and local regulations.		4. Government relationships determined by legal counsel but not passed along to company executives.		4. No policy on governmental matters. Local governmental office called when in doubt or in trouble.

Source   This form is a revised version of forms presented in Howard Ellsworth Sommer, *How to Analyze Your Own Business* (Management Aids No. 46) (Washington, D.C.: Small Business Administration, 1971).

Program

The efforts of retail auditors can then be focused upon the retailer's program that is used to achieve the objectives that have been established. The retailer's program consists of the decisions and policies on the level, allocation, and mix of his total marketing effort.

Initially, the auditor wants to examine the *level* of resources the retailer is using in his marketing effort, because this level must be adequate to meet the firm's stated objectives. This involves an objective look at the total sales-generating budget to determine if the budget is large enough to allow the firm to accomplish its objectives. The evaluation might consist of an analysis of the relationship of sales volume to the level of the market budget. This analysis can reveal if past additions to the marketing budget resulted in increased sales and profits.

The auditor can also appraise the desirability of changing the balance among the retailer's marketing activities. A retail firm's marketing allocations can become unduly influenced by particularly strong functional area executives. An independent, objective appraisal of the retailer's marketing allocations may reveal an excessive use of advertising, personal selling, merchandise styling, price reductions, etc. The more effective retail sales-generating programs offer a balance among all the available alternatives. It is not easy to identify when to shift money from one functional area to another, but analysis of past retail sales and expenditure data can guide this appraisal. Industry data can also be used to identify the functional areas which might be emphasized by the retailer. Larger emphasis upon a particular area (say advertising) does not, however, indicate that the firm uses too much advertising relative to its other marketing efforts. The sales response may increase faster than the increased advertising expenditure for this particular retailer because the outlet is situated in a "below average" location.

Finally, retail auditors also examine how the marketing expenditure is allocated to various target market segments. The appraisal would evaluate the retailer's efforts vis-à-vis geographical areas, merchandise lines, and consumer segments. The task is essentially that of determining whether the current allocation generates maximum sales and profits for the given budget level. This is not an easy task, but an analysis of customer trading areas, consumer image, and purchase patterns can provide the basis for recommending an increase or reduction in marketing effort toward each target market segment.

Figure 18–2 contains three categories which describe a retail firm's efforts to evaluate its sales and merchandising activities.

Implementation (Tactics)

Retail management may have designed an excellent program, but the firm's performance will depend upon proper execution of that program. Thus

Figure 18–2   Form to Evaluate Retail Sales and Promotion Activities

Outstanding Condition	Average Condition	Deficient Condition
1. Sound sales program—based on known customer needs, market research and analysis supported by good advertising and sales program.	1. Sales program based on past customer experience. Market potential not known. Advertising not selective.	1. Sales coverage incomplete. Knowledge of competition limited.
2. Sales budgets classified by products, customers, sales people, merchandise departments, geographic districts.	2. Sales total estimated but not budgeted by products to customers and geographic districts.	2. No sales budgets.
3. Sound pricing based on consumer demand and merchandise handling considerations.	3. Price structure rigid. Accurate product costs not used in setting sales prices.	3. Costs information not generally used in setting prices.
4. Profit or loss determined by sales people, customers' products, and geographic districts.	4. No attempt to analyze gross and net profit by sales people, products, customers.	4. No sales analyses.
5. Selective selling effort directed toward maximum profit possibilities.	5. Selling effort not directed toward best profit possibilities.	5. No selective selling program.
6. Trained sales people intelligently directed and compensated.	6. Sales people closely supervised but training program inadequate.	6. Sales people not well trained or supervised. Compensation not comparable to competitors'.
7. All sales records maintained currently.	7. Sales records not always maintained on a current basis.	7. No sales records beyond orders booked and sales billed.

Source   Form is revised version of forms in Sommer, *How to Analyze Your Own Business.*

the retail auditor turns his attention to both the *tactical means* and *procedures* used to accomplish the objectives. An examination of the alternatives available for each *tactical decision* can reveal if the reasoning behind each decision was logical. The auditor has an advantage in examining these decisions after they have been made as he can also observe the consequences of each decision. (Hindsight is much better than foresight.) If such a historical examination is not periodically made by an auditor, it is not likely to be made at all. Regular retail management can (and usually does) become so occupied with the day-to-day operating procedures that it does not have time for periodic analyses of this type.

Tactical retail decisions are needed in many areas, including the following:

Figure 18–3   Form to Evaluate Retail Personnel Policies

	Outstanding Condition		Average Condition		Deficient Condition
	1. An executive, vested with adequate authority, formulates sound industrial relations policies and represents the company in labor negotiations.		1. Value of industrial relations realized, but authority and responsibility not clearly defined.		1. The industrial relations function is one of employment only, also coupled with other unrelated functions.
	2. An industrial relations program minimizes labor turnover, builds employee morale and efficiency.		2. Industrial relations program not planned ahead, but ably administered; employee morale and efficiency average.		2. Little consideration given to industrial relations—employee turnover high.
	3. Program for effective selecting, testing, placing, and training of all personnel.		3. Employee selection not developed beyond separate formulas used by office manager for clerical help and by employment manager for all other help.		3. No uniform procedure for applicant screening, placement, and training. Original interviewing left to each department head.
	4. Salary and wage rates equitable and fair for each job classification from common labor to top management; established by sound job evaluation methods.		4. No job evaluation program. Wage rates increased under pressure. Top management and supervisory positions awarded largely on the bases of seniority.		4. Job rates fixed by personal opinion.
	5. Incentive plans for all levels of employees, based on an equitable measurement of performance.		5. Incentive plans for some employees only.		5. No incentive plan.
	6. Individual history and progress records for each employee; kept up to date for use as an inventory of qualifications.		6. Some records, but they are incomplete.		6. No records kept on individual employees beyond payroll requirements.

Source   Form is revised version of forms in Sommer, *How to Analyze Your Own Business.*

responsibility and the communication channels used to relay consumers' desires to the appropriate retail decision maker.

A major factor contributing to business failure is a lack of experience on the part of key retail personnel. A successful retail firm must use the talent of people who have a knowledge of (1) buying, (2) products in demand by consumers, (3) how to attract customers, and (4) handling finances.

The amount of experience required is dependent upon the size and type of the retail operation. A complex retail organization, formal manage-

Figure 18–4   Form to Evaluate Retail Merchandise Assortment

Outstanding Condition		Average Condition		Deficient Condition
1. Continuous search for improved products; for the development of new products and markets.	1.	Search effort spasmodic; objectives not definite.	1.	No search for new products or markets.
2. Merchandise and service offerings thoroughly planned and highly organized under expert supervision with qualified personnel.	2.	Merchandise search activities not well organized.	2.	No personnel qualified to conduct merchandise search activities.
3. Close cooperation with merchandising and sales personnel to insure market acceptance.	3.	The company has a program for merchandise search, but these activities are not carried out in cooperation with other retail divisions.	3.	Need for merchandise search ignored. No desire to add new products to assortment.

SOURCE   Form is revised version of forms in Sommer, *How to Analyze Your Own Business.*

ment practices, and established formal communications channels are required as different merchandise lines are offered and more outlets are opened. Single-unit operators especially should note the increased managerial effort required to open the second outlet. The business frequently runs smoothly until the new outlet is established; then the operator discovers that he can't communicate with the store employees unless he is continually present in the store.

The retail auditor cannot neglect any areas of the systems-level retail audit because all aspects affect retail performance. He must, however, place major emphasis upon the evaluation of retail objectives and programs. Establishment of effective retail objectives and programs provides the foundation for retail success. Poor store locations, merchandise lines, and store images cannot be overcome by making sudden changes in tactical or procedural areas. In other words, a retailer's strategy as reflected by objectives and programs is a long-run concept that cannot be changed in a short period of time. It takes time to locate and establish outlets on good retail sites or to establish the desired retail image in the minds of potential customers. Thus undetected errors made in establishing retailing strategy will have a severe effect on future performance for many years.

The consequences of poor tactical decisions and/or procedures will also adversely affect retail performance. However, they can usually be changed within a year after the mistake is recognized. The tendency for most people in retail management to spend most of their time dealing with problems of a tactical or procedural nature usually leads to identifying these problems more quickly than more strategical problems.

Figure 18–5 Evaluation Form for Retail Accounting Procedures

Outstanding Condition	Average Condition	Deficient Condition
1. Procedures, record forms, reports designed with a view to producing required information at lowest cost.	1. Accounting fairly comprehensive, accurate, prompt and well managed—some written procedures.	1. Accounting accurate from bookkeeping standpoint, but generally "old-fashioned" and incomplete.
2. Accounting data supplied promptly in a form best adapted to its use by management.	2. Accounting data not adequate in comparison with most modern control standards.	2. Accounting not highly regarded as a tool of management.
3. Modern accounting equipment used effectively in preparation of necessary information and reports.	3. Accounting machines used but not adaptable to modern methods.	3. Accounting equipment antiquated, cumbersome, and wasteful.
4. Cost system designed to reflect all variances between standard and actual costs.	4. Cost accounting fairly accurate but not organized to provide standard cost information.	4. No standard costs. Job costs inaccurate and uncontrolled.
5. Variances from standard performances supplied currently to management for corrective action.	5. Records and reports not best suited to control costs and expenses.	5. Cost information mostly estimated. Monthly profit and loss statements inaccurate.
6. Unnecessary accounting records eliminated—management control reports furnished as needed.	6. Many records, reports, and statistics maintained that are not useful as a tool of management.	6. Some records and reports prepared; have no practical advantage.
7. All control records and costs integrated with standard costs.	7. Records unrelated to control; therefore, of little assistance.	7. Production records required for suitable cost control not maintained.
8. All estimates for product pricing based on standard costs; loss of volume or profit is indicated.	8. Estimates not checked against actual cost.	8. Estimates determined by past performance and competition.
9. The effect that sales mixture and product selling prices have on the total company profits is known at all times.	9. No knowledge of the effect on total business profits of individual product or order pricing.	9. Profit or loss estimated monthly; verified and adjusted annually to inventory; no profit or loss known by product breakdown.

SOURCE   Form is revised version of forms in Sommer, *How to Analyze Your Own Business*.

Figure 18–6   Evaluation Form for Retail Financial and Budgetary Control Procedures

Outstanding Condition	Average Condition	Deficient Condition
Budgetary Control		
1. Budgetary control of all expenditures based on flexible performance standards equitably established by operating levels.	1. Budget structure rigid; ratios of expense to sales based on past performance, not on predetermined, flexible performance standards.	1. No attempt made to budget or forecast performance.
2. Sales budget by merchandise line, salesmen, customers and territories—based on market analyses.	2. Sales budget by merchandise line, salesmen, customers and territories—based on past sales performance only.	2. No sales budget. No "quotas" for salesmen. No program.
3. Knowledge and control of the effect of all selling price changes on budgeted amount of total net profits.	3. No centralized control of selling prices within limits of predetermined profit requirements.	3. No established pricing policy. Cost estimates ignored where considerable volume is involved. Effect of cutting prices to meet competition not projected in terms of lost profits.
4. Daily, weekly, or monthly reports on the performance of all departments controlled through: (a) standard or budgeted performance; and (b) variance from standard performance.	4. Divisional accounting reports periodically exhibited: (a) comparison of current with past periods; (b) no standards; therefore no comparison of actual results with what should have been accomplished.	4. No budgets; no broad long-term planning. Policies vacillating because not founded on complete comparative information and thorough analysis.
Finance		
1. Forecast of working capital and cash requirements for planned business volume and profits level.	1. No forecast of working capital or cash requirements. Funds not always obtained or employed.	1. Working capital and cash inadequate; credit policy lax. No forward planning.
2. Adequate reserves for replacement of obsolescent and depreciating assets—represented by earmarked liquid funds to the extent required.	2. Depreciation reserves conditioned on allowable deductions for tax purposes only; not properly planned from a capital asset replacement point of view.	2. Nominal reserves without due regard to actual value of assets; frequently used for purposes other than originally intended.
3. Dividend policy consistent with sound, long-term financial program.	3. No definite financial or dividend policy.	3. Financing dictated by immediate need for cash to meet pressing obligations.

Source   Form is revised version of forms in Sommer, *How to Analyze Your Own Business.*

Customer Analysis

Identifying the retailer's most profitable customers is one of the most important things to determine in a retail market analysis. Not all customers generate profits for the store they patronize, and retailers can use their resources in an inefficient way by catering to customers who buy only low-margin items on an infrequent basis but demand extra services. No retail outlet can be all things to all people, so the retail effort must be oriented to serve and satisfy profitable customers. Customers who do not pay their bills on time, or who habitually return purchases, add to the cost of conducting business. The low profit margins generally obtained in retailing may not be large enough to allow that kind of customer to be serviced at a profit. One way to determine if customers are paying their way is to estimate what it costs to serve different kinds of consumers and to sell different-size orders.

Retailers must be cautious in the way they identify unprofitable customers and in the way they treat them after they have been identified. Unprofitable consumers communicate with many potentially profitable customers. Bad word-of-mouth advertising can, of course, affect the purchase patterns of the profitable consumers.

Only the very largest stores can serve everyone. The retail audit must determine if management has adequately defined the group(s) of customers (market targets) that the store is going to serve. The audit should reflect the fact that small stores are more effective in catering to distinct groups, such as customers who have special tastes or interests, local residents, business people working nearby, etc. Larger retail organizations may cater to several different market targets by using boutiques, subdividing large departments, establishing bargain basements, and so on.

Customer Relations

Customer relations revolve around the type of store image that management seeks to implant in the minds of customers. The retail audit must determine if a clear definition of the desired store image has been made. First, is store management aware of the store's special features—the special kinds of merchandise and services it offers? Are these special features communicated to both present and potential customers?

Many outlets suffer because store personnel fumble their roles after the customer has been attracted to the store. Stores that cannot match the merchandise assortments and low prices offered by mass merchandising competitors must gain their strength from the use of special services. Is quick delivery service, personal customer attention, and the ability to help solve specific customer problems (such as garden care, interior decorating, clothing selection, etc.) being used to attract and retain customers? If not, why not?

The retail audit should also determine if sales people are treating each customer as an individual rather than as one of the crowd. Do they greet customers by name? Are sales people helping consumers by listening to their problems and offering solutions? Have campaigns been conducted to encourage employees to be considerate of customers' viewpoints? As a competitive advantage, courtesy, especially at the cash register or checkout counter, is a powerful attraction. The customer gets his last impression of the store in the checkout process, and a friendly and interested employee can make certain that it is a good impression.

Is service being provided on the merchandise after it has been sold? In some cases this consists of merely returning goods to the factory for repair. In other cases it involves on-the-spot maintenance. In either case, the service should be provided quickly and courteously.

Is retailing management aware of the consumer's need for convenience and shopping ease? A comfortable customer lounge can serve as both a meeting and a resting place. A "free" cup of coffee and other small extras can make a store a more enjoyable place to shop. Consumer convenience may also be provided by posting and maintaining regular store hours. This allows the consumer to depend on the store's being open and to adjust his purchasing and consumption patterns to the store hours. The small cost involved in providing such services frequently yields large returns in repeat business.

Location

A good location is essential for the successful operation of any retail firm. One of the most frequent mistakes is made by retailers who want to minimize the monthly rental payment needed to obtain a good location. These retailers suffer because they won't pay enough rent to secure a good location which could generate volume sales. As a result, they have to spend more money to promote the store, and still may not be able to attract convenience-oriented consumers.

The retail audit should determine if new outlets would increase the retailer's profits. If new outlets are being considered, is the firm's selection procedure an objective evaluation? The selection of a city or town which will contain the new outlet should be based upon characteristics such as population, area growth potential, consumer income and purchasing power, the purchasing habits of potential consumers, legislative restrictions, and competition. The index of retail saturation discussed in Chapter 5 may be used to measure the relative retail potential of an area.

Local trading area analysis of the most promising cities or towns can indicate if the firm's existing outlets are covering the market area that can be serviced profitably by the organization. New outlets may be required to serve areas in which few customers reside. This usually will be the case when each outlet's trading area is small, and when per outlet retailing costs do not decline rapidly as sales volume increases. Naturally, the firm should examine the characteristics of potential consumers residing in an area not currently being reached by the firm's existing retail outlets. A new outlet will not be warranted automatically unless the demographics and life styles of people residing in this untapped area are similar to those of the target market customers of the existing outlets. In untapped areas where residents' characteristics differ from those of current outlets, the firm could open a new outlet

the promotion activity include an evaluation of the consistency of the promotional activity. Small amounts of advertising on a frequent basis are generally more effective in creating the desired image than large amounts of advertising on an infrequent basis. Constant reminders that the store carries certain merchandise lines, that new products are now available, that expert service and advice is available at the store, and that the store offers specific advantages in specific areas are required to reinforce the consumer's image of the store. Stores that rely upon strictly "sale-price reduction" advertising do little to attain a favorable quality and service image. The level of expenditure for promotional activities should be related to the expected sales level for the store. Promotional activity should be increased *before* the sales peak is expected to occur. Large advertising expenditures just prior to pay day or normal shopping days are more likely to stimulate sales because consumers will have the ability to respond to the "message."

Tactical considerations can also be made during an audit. For example, advertisement can be improved by retaining copies of the advertisements previously used and evaluating their effectiveness. Successful advertisements frequently contain products and/or appeals that can be featured again to repeat the former success. Cost of the advertisement, media usage, weather conditions, and unusual competitors' activities should be recorded and analyzed in the process of identifying the effective advertisements.

Pricing

The retail audit should determine if prices are established to provide as much markup as possible without losing a substantial sales volume. Have price levels been raised and lowered on different items over a period of time? This will allow the retailer to identify those items whose demand is highly dependent upon price. Setting a lower markup on those items responsive to price changes can bring enough added sales to yield a larger total profit. The reduction in price on these key items, however, may disturb the public image of the store. Maintaining or raising prices on items whose sales do not respond to price changes can result in higher profits, provided this action does not damage the store image projected to consumers. Higher markups should be obtained on items whose risk and handling costs are high and/or whose turnover rate is relatively low. These higher markups will offset the low markups which are taken on competitive merchandise.

Has the outlet established price lines that provide good merchandise assortments at the price levels demanded by its target market consumers? This practice can be a profitable pricing strategy.

Temporary price markdowns can be used to cater to customer groups that do not respond to regular prices. This can result in increased sales, and may result in increased dollar margin.

However, the promotion must be truthful. The prices quoted in advertisements should reflect the store's intent to sell the merchandise at the stated price. Misleading promotions result in possible legal action and consumer ill will that, in the long run, far outweigh the temporary increase in store profits generated by the misleading promotions.

Buying

The retail audit may include an analysis to determine if the selection of merchandise assortments is meeting the needs of the retailer's target market consumers. Adequate stocking and quick reordering of new items that have been showing volume sales potential must be done to complement the buyer's original subjective judgment of consumers' needs. Can the firm that is being audited receive additional merchandise quickly? Why not? What can be done to improve speed of delivery?

Retail buyers should also be comparing new item offerings with the present merchandise assortment. Shelf space is not utilized efficiently if the new items are so similar that they merely represent a duplication of the current product offering.

Is central group buying being used advantageously on some items where individual store buyers cannot obtain style and price preferences? A central buying office may be able to act more quickly on new market offerings and developments as it has a broader picture of lines that are coming in and going out of style.

Is a written buying plan being used to guide the selections of the retail buyer who attends a particular market or trade show? The buying plan should be based upon such factors as price line, type, material, size, and color, and should not be left to chance. It does not normally specify style numbers but may include the number of different styles that the retailer wants to carry.

The audit should also contain an evaluation of the way the retailer increases his profits by taking advantage of available trade, quantity, seasonal, and cash discounts. Careful planning and proper timing of orders can result in substantial discounts not otherwise available. Transportation charges also can be reduced by proper planning. Placing orders too late for slower but cheaper delivery methods, ordering in uneconomical quantities (i.e., ordering 50-pound lots when the minimum charge is for 100 pounds), permitting the use of unnecessarily heavy packing materials, etc. result in excessive transportation costs. Procedures should be used to be certain that the order always specifies the method of transportation and the consolidator of the shipments.

Merchandise and Inventory Control

Merchandise control begins by checking the description and number of units of merchandise received against the description of the goods ordered. All orders must be followed to see that goods are shipped and received on time. Late delivery of ordered goods can result in consumer ill will and lost sales, which may necessitate price markdowns to eventually move the merchandise.

Organizing the store by departments allows retail management to deter-

buildings, and equipment. The coverage on public liability insurance should be evaluated at the same time. Inflation and greater awards on liability suits have caused many retailers to be underinsured when tragedy strikes.

A retail audit should contain an evaluation of the performance on these basic merchandise and inventory control factors.

Budgetary Control

Retail plans must be expressed in terms of a budget that establishes goals for sales, stocks, markups, and expenses. The audit should investigate the budgetary process used by the retailer. The budgetary period takes the form of both short-run and annual planning. The short-term budget must be prepared weekly or monthly to assure adequate control of current operations. The annual budget contains the expected cash flow for the upcoming year. It should include expected changes in costs and revenues resulting from implementing the retail plan.

Both kinds of budgets are more effective when the employees responsible for achieving the stated objectives have a chance to participate in the formulation of the goals. Previous company experience and published data on other firms engaged in a similar business provide a basis of comparison for determining the budget. The control process should also involve a comparison of actual company results against previous budget projections. Merchandising, promotion, and expense plans can then be adjusted as indicated by the deviation from the projections. Open-to-buy and open-to-spend control are needed to keep purchases consistent with previous plans. These plans must be revised as competitive and environmental changes occur if the retailer is to remain responsive to changes in consumer purchasing patterns.

Retail Organization and Personnel Management

Retail firms should be organized so that each employee takes orders from, and is under the direct supervision of, only one person. This type of organization can avoid the conflicts of divided responsibility. The retail audit should determine if the functions and lines of authority have been established in writing, and preferably on organization charts. This will assist each employee to understand his responsibility and the relationship of his work to that of others in the retailing organization.

Written job specifications are essential in selecting, training, and evaluating personnel. The "management by objective" approach can be used effectively by insisting that each person set specific objectives for himself. These objectives will guide his own activities and performance for the stated period of time. If the objectives that an employee first suggests for himself seem inadequate, they may be upgraded by mutual consent. Once agreed upon, these objectives become the basis of evaluation for his immediate supervisor.

The audit might also determine if top-level retail management is delegating as much authority as possible to those employees immediately responsible to it. The delegation of authority can free top management from using most of its time on unnecessary operating details. Top retail management and department managers can usually improve retail performance by allocating more of their time to planning, organization, coordination, supervision, and control activities.

Regular and consistent supervision of employees is more effective than sporadic criticism of poor performance. A retail audit will show whether this is being done.

Another factor that should be included in the activity audit in this area is the retailer's compensation policy. Wages and other forms of compensation must be competitive with wages paid by other firms. Wages must also be adjusted to the difficulties and responsibilities of each job. Most of the retail sales person's earnings generally come from a base salary, which is supplemented with a commission on sales. The more reliance that is placed on commission, the more incentive the sales people have to make sales. Other incentive plans give consideration to employees' needs for recognition, security, reasonable hours, congenial working conditions, and opportunities for advancement. Commission and quota bonus plans usually provide incentives for sales people, while seasonal bonus plans may provide more incentives for supervisors. Whatever pay plan is used, the pay policy (including overtime policy) should be clear to all employees.

Credit

A retail credit policy should be based on the costs of granting credit against the benefits obtained by granting credit. Bank credit card plans have advantages in that the store's cash is not tied up in accounts receivable. In addition, there are fewer problems in opening accounts and collecting overdue bills. Bank credit card plans, however, may weaken customer loyalty to the firm's outlets. The retailer's own credit card plan may encourage store loyalty because the card cannot be used in competing stores. If the retail firm uses its own credit plan, it must establish definite credit limits, explain the rules carefully to all applicants, and follow up promptly when customers do not make payments as agreed.

Periodical reviews should be made of the accounts receivable and revolving credit accounts to determine the collection period, the percentage of accounts that are current, overdue, etc. These regular reviews will be helpful when management sets up bad-debt reserves and establishes credit and collection policies. The firm's performance on bad debts, collection period, etc. can be compared with data for similar stores.

An audit of a retailer's credit policy should reflect these considerations.

Taxes and Legal Obligations

Important changes in tax and legal regulations occur frequently. The retail audit should determine if one specific individual or group is responsible for submitting the required taxes and various legal reports. Maintaining a calendar which shows when the various taxes and reports are due is a "must" as requirements and regulations become more numerous and more complex. Specialists in tax and other legal matters are required in order to keep up to date on the latest rulings. Laws on advertising, labeling, selling, and guarantee practices are changing rapidly, so periodic checks must be made to determine if the current practices satisfy the current laws and regulations. Wise retailers recognize legitimate consumer complaints. Through group action these retailers try to pass legislation that serves the consumer but does not add significant costs to the retailing effort.

IMPLEMENTING A RETAILING AUDIT

The success of the retail audit depends upon who conducts the audit and when it is scheduled. The retail audit can be conducted either internally, by an individual or group of individuals who are permanent members of the retail organization, or externally by outside consultants. The internal audit has the advantage that the auditors are intimately familiar with the operation and, as a result, the cost is reduced considerably. However, an objective, unbiased audit is not likely from an internal audit. Each member of the retail organization is likely to suppress any shortcomings in his operation. Even those internal auditors who try to remain objective may take a more narrow view of the firm's opportunities and shortcomings than will outside or external auditors.

The advantages of the external audit are derived from the consultants' broad experience in many different areas. Retailers are able to benefit from the experience of others by not duplicating their mistakes. The external auditors are also likely to be more objective, as they have no self-interest to preserve. Finally, external auditors are more likely to concentrate on the execution of the audit, as internal auditors can concentrate on the audit only if they are not concerned with time-consuming, day-to-day operating details.

The major disadvantage of using an external auditor is that the consultant must spend a lot of time becoming familiar with the internal aspects of the firm before he can make an appraisal. This disadvantage is not great when the company enters a long-term relationship with a consulting organization, under which the consultants become familiar with the retailer's operations as they audit first one and then another of the company's operations on a fairly continuous basis. Their contribution can be enhanced even more if they work with an internal task force which provides information, studies the auditor's reports, and implements the important recommendations in the consultant's reports.

Annual systems-level audits should be scheduled so that they can provide input into the retailer's annual planning efforts. Activity-level audits should be scheduled as determined in the systems-level audit. An activity-level audit should be scheduled whenever the annual systems-level audit or retail performance reveals that an activity is in great need of reform or supervision.

INTERPRETATION OF THE RETAIL AUDIT

It should not be concluded that positive findings in most of the areas covered by the systems-level and activity-level audits will assure the retail firm of a profitable future or that no further investigation is warranted. Even if the results of the audit seem to indicate that everything is well, it does not mean that management can afford to stop creating new approaches to reach the current or expanded target markets. The retail audit is only a tool which seeks to indicate information about the effectiveness of the organization. It can point out some crucial areas which warrant management's attention. When these weaknesses are revealed, the retail organization can rectify the situation sooner and more easily than if no systematic review process were used.

Financial audits and market research projects must be used in the retail audit to provide a truly creative approach to long-range retail planning. Creative changes should be made in an orderly manner by making only one change at a time, so its effectiveness can be measured. Continual changing of the *entire* program will generally allow management to evaluate only the success of the entire program, not each of the retail activities. When a reasonably successful plan has been developed, it is usually better to intensify it first and make only one major change at a time. All changes should be measured on a cost versus results basis. The evaluation then centers around the question, "Were the results worth the amount of time, talent, and money used to accomplish them?"

SUMMARY

Periodic systems-level and necessary activity-level auditing keep management's efforts concentrated on identifying trends, establishing objectives and policies, and acquiring and analyzing the data needed for objective decision making. It causes management to become more alert to needed changes caused by shifts in consumer shopping patterns and shifts in the competitive or legal environment.

QUESTIONS

1. Today the "geriatric set" is larger in numbers than ever before in history and it shows no signs of becoming smaller. Yet we see a continued emphasis on "young living" in all forms of merchandising. Discuss the marketing and especially the retailing implications of this situation.
2. How does a retail audit differ from an accounting audit? Do you think the average CPA would make a good retail auditor?

ASSOCIATED MERCHANDISING CORPORATION

Associated Merchandising Corporation is the world's largest retail service organization. It was started in 1916 by a group of leading department store owners to create the basis for an exchange of figures and operating information.

Since that time the role of AMC has markedly grown and changed. Today, AMC serves thirty major U.S. and ten foreign department stores in both the domestic and overseas markets (see Table 18–1). The major operations of AMC fall into two categories:

> To provide complete coverage, evaluation and reporting of world markets, and to assist the stores in using these markets with maximum effectiveness including the implementation of trend merchandising.

> To serve as a catalyst in the exchange and analysis of retail merchandising and operational information among its affiliated stores. Further, to interpret this information and initiate recommended action for the continual improvement of merchandising practices and operating methods in AMC stores.

In the domestic market, AMC merchants and fashion coordinators thoroughly research and evaluate the markets in which the stores purchase the merchandise requirement. They report their findings to the stores through various forms of communication. As a result of total market coverage by AMC personnel, the stores receive a continuous flow of fresh and specific information geared to support them in making merchandising decisions.

As an overseas buyer, AMC operates buying offices in twenty foreign cities and operates through commissionaires in nine others (Table 18–2). The corporate buying offices range in size from the Oporto, Portugal, office with three employees to the Florence office with ninety-five employees.

These offices are staffed with bilingual nationals who are first trained in the United States by AMC. Their responsibilities include seeking out local supplies of merchandise and new products and helping the buyers from each of the member department stores with the task of buying abroad. They are also responsible for gathering information of interest to the member stores. This includes best sellers, flash reports, fashion trends, and reports on the European retail scene. An extremely important report is the *European Figure and Resource Evaluation,* which reaches the stores on September 1 each year. It furnishes the stores with a guide of market strengths, key resources, stores' performance, and recommendations on scheduling European trips.

The responsibility for transacting financial arrangements between the buyer and seller in different nations in a smooth manner is also assumed by AMC. Consequently, it has established a computerized central payment office in Florence, Italy, to clear and handle all transactions.

Table 18–1   AMC Stores

Abraham & Straus, Brooklyn, N.Y.	Hutzler's, Baltimore, Md.
Bloomingdale's, New York, N.Y.	The F. & R. Lazarus Co., Columbus, O.
Brandeis, Omaha, Neb.	Levy's, Tucson, Ariz.
Bullock's, Los Angeles, Calif.	Liberty House, Honolulu, Hawaii
Burdine's, Miami, Fla.	Lipman Wolfe and Co., Portland, Ore.
The H. C. Capwell Company, Oakland, Calif.	Milwaukee Boston Store Co., Milwaukee, Wis.
Carson Pirie Scott & Co., Chicago, Ill.	H. C. Prange Co., Sheboygan, Wis.
Dayton's, Minneapolis, Minn.	Rich's, Inc., Atlanta, Ga.
Diamond's, Phoenix, Ariz.	Rike's, Dayton, O.
The Emporium, San Francisco, Calif.	Sanger-Harris, Dallas, Tex.
Wm. Filene's Sons Co., Boston, Mass.	Shillito's, Cincinnati, O.
Foley's, Houston, Tex.	Strawbridge & Clothier, Philadelphia, Pa.
B. Forman Company, Rochester, N.Y.	
Goldsmith's, Memphis, Tenn.	Thalhmer Brothers, Inc., Richmond, Va.
The Higbee Company, Cleveland, O.	
The J. L. Hudson Company, Detroit, Mich.	Woodward & Lothrop, Washington, D.C.

REPRESENTATIVES FOR

De Bijenkorf, Netherlands	Hudson's Bay Co. Retail Stores, Canada
C. B. O., Jelmoli, Ltd., Switzerland	Magasin du Nord, Denmark
A. S. Cooper & Sons, Ltd., Bermuda	Matsuzakaya Co., Ltd., Japan
Garlick, Ltd., South Africa	John Orr & Co., South Africa
Harrod's, Ltd., London	Panama Canal Company, Canal Zone

Table 18–2   Overseas Operations

EUROPEAN OFFICES

Alicante	Florence	Nuremburg
Athens	Helsinki	Paris
Barcelona	London	Oporto
Brussels	Milan	Tel Aviv
Copenhagen	Munich	Vienna
Dublin		Zurich

FAR EAST OFFICES

Hong Kong	Seoul	Taiwan	Tokyo

COMMISSIONAIRES

Bangkok	Bogota	Mexico City
Bombay	Istanbul	New Delhi
Buenos Aires	Manila	Rio de Janeiro

The home office of AMC—or "1440" as it is commonly known from its address at 1440 Broadway, New York—is also responsible for providing sales-supporting functions to retail members in addition to the merchandising activities previously mentioned. These are: Operations, Store Control, Personnel, Figure Exchange, Bureau of Standards, New York Overseas Office, and Publicity and Graphics.

"Operations" works with the stores' General Superintendents Division in the areas of receiving, marking, transportation, distribution, food management, and other store service functions. Examples of activities which have resulted in improved store operations are the detailed studies of merchandise handling for both furniture and major appliances. Assisted by outside consultants, AMC Operations sponsored the initial work on studies in telephone communications and food. Results of both indicate substantial savings for AMC stores that adopt the methods the studies propose.

"Store Control" acts as liaison to controllers and credit managers for information exchange and the formulation of operational procedures.

"AMC Store Personnel" is concerned with the training, employment, and other personnel functions of the stores. All of the special projects, meetings, and distribution of information for these functions are coordinated by the Store Personnel Division. One of the most useful store services developed by Store Personnel is the Employee Opinion Survey. The survey provides store management with a valuable tool for planning direct action to deal with the problems of general morale and employee turnover. Stores that avail themselves of this service pay a fee according to their usage. These charges are approximately half of what it would cost to obtain a comparable survey from the outside.

The "Publicity and Graphics Division," counterpart to the sales promotion areas in the stores, covers developments in advertising, merchandise presentation (display), and special events. It maintains contact with the many segments of the communications "market," interpreting information and exchanging it with the AMC stores.

"Figure Exchange" was the original reason for forming AMC. The various figure exchanges furnish AMC stores with the hard data on the state of business in every phase of store merchandising and operations. The exchanges go through a continuing evolution as various committees analyze and evaluate each exchange to make them most meaningful to the conduct of business in the current retail environment. For AMC and AMC stores, the value of the Figure Exchanges is in identifying weaknesses, pointing out strengths, spotting trends, etc.

The "Research Division" analyzes marketing and consumer buying trends and conducts specialized studies for use by AMC and the affiliated stores in the fields of retail distribution, merchandising, promotion, customer shopping trends, and store planning.

"Executive Placement" fulfills the executive needs of AMC and its member stores. This is the responsibility of the Executive Placement Division in those instances where promotion from within is not practical. Complete backgrounds on thousands of retail executives in almost 100 categories are continually kept up to date for the purpose of seeking and placing qualified executives.

The "Bureau of Standards" provides laboratory testing services for merchandise representatives, domestic and overseas, and AMC stores. It evaluates merchandise performance and safety characteristics, quality control, and merchandise specifications. The Bureau of Standards also issues bulletins outlining detailed analyses of action items or programs, along with recommendations to AMC stores for specific AMC policies and procedures covering product performance standards and legislative requirements. It researches and provides current information for the monthly *Consumer Affairs Newsletter*, which is sent to AMC management, domestic and overseas, and AMC stores as a summary of consumer and legislative activity.

"New York Overseas Operations" regularly advises and updates the AMC stores and overseas offices on matters pertaining to important shipping and maritime insurance and maintains a traffic department to process and distribute consolidated shipments for the stores. Overseas market trips for store and AMC personnel are planned, coordinated, and processed through this office. The Export Department is responsible for the order placing, shipping, and processing of purchases made by overseas department store affiliates.

In addition, AMC maintains a Washington, D.C., office to serve as an information post for existing and proposed legislation which will affect retailers. It has often been called on by congressional committees to supply data on retailing subjects, so in that sense it serves as a political arm.

In terms of consumer protection and consumerism, AMC's role is simply to help its retail members perform the kind of service that made them a success in the first place. AMC cites the example of a toy that was already in the members' stores prior to a federal finding that it was unsafe. The federal government did not tell retailers they could not sell the existing stock, nor were they told to brand it as unsafe. However, AMC suggested to its members that no more toys of this type be purchased and that any existing ones be tagged as potentially dangerous to children.

On a worldwide scale, AMC is continually faced with the need to evaluate new markets and to decide when to open a buying office. Again, this is not a decision to be made lightly, as it eventually involves all member stores and implies a continuing U.S. demand for goods from that geographical area. In addition, the distance and the problems associated with facilitating buying in large countries, such as Brazil or Argentina, are important considerations.

DISCUSSION QUESTIONS

1. Is the role of AMC likely to have greater or less importance to its member retailers in the future? Keep in mind the fact that several of its members are now multi-store chains with thousands of employees.
2. What new functions, if any, do you believe AMC will need to offer its members in the future? Are there any existing functions that are likely to deserve more importance?
3. What are the most important criteria you believe AMC should consider in opening new buying offices throughout the world?

4. Would a member retailer use the services of an independent importer of foreign goods, as well as AMC? If so, for what type of goods?
5. What forms of consumer research can an organization such as AMC employ to keep abreast of and forecast consumer trends? Is it possible to forecast the success or failure of trends, such as the midi skirt, before they occur in full boom or bust?
6. Discuss the factors that could cause AMC to open or close a foreign buying office. Include a discussion of consumer behavior, balance of trade, stability of a nation, currency exchange, and travel costs.

ABRAHAM AND STRAUS
BROOKLYN, NEW YORK
Delayed Billing

The management of Abraham and Straus constantly reviews the question of delayed billing programs. These are reviewed in terms of possible future action necessary to aid in-store sales and remain a leader in the field of retail credit promotion. Although delayed billing is not a new credit promotion concept within the retail industry, it has been given a new degree of importance as a merchandising tool by A&S.

In 1970 Abraham and Straus introduced a pre-Christmas delayed billing program called "Holiday Money." This program was repeated during the 1971 pre-Christmas season as a tool to increase total in-store sales.

A version of Holiday Money had been introduced by Broadway Department Stores, Los Angeles, and Gimbels New York prior to the A&S program, but not of the complexity of the one offered by A&S. No accurate information was available concerning either earlier plan, but it was believed that the Gimbels program accounted for between $8 and $9 million in sales per year.

The Abraham and Straus delayed billing program consisted of mailing packets of Holiday Money certificates to customers who had been selected from credit files as good credit risks. These packets contained either $300 or $400 worth of certificates in denominations including $50 and $100 certificates.

In October, packets of $300 were sent to revolving budget credit and revolving installment credit customers and packets of $400 were sent to 30-day charge customers.

The certificate denominations within each packet were of different colors and all contained the customer's name and account number. A letter from the president accompanied each packet.

After receiving these packets, the customers brought them into any A&S store. The customer then tore off a certificate or certificates for the amount she desired to spend, signed them, and redeemed them for a book of shopping coupons which served as in-store scrip. The customer was billed in February from the certificate(s) she had signed. The certificate was completed with a number corresponding to that on the scrip to reduce the possibility of fraud and as a check against actual purchases, should a customer ask for replacement scrip after losing those originally assigned.

Blank Holiday Money certificates were also available to credit customers from special display holders within the store. These certificates were unnumbered and unnamed. Anyone using them first had to take them to the credit office, where her credit status was checked. If it was found to be acceptable, the customer's name and a number were printed on the certificates.

Special change booths were set up in addition to the regular ones in the store. The special booths assembled the scrip and made change.

Scrip was redeemable in A&S stores only for merchandise, but was honored throughout the year.

After analyzing the results of this program, the management of A&S determined that the program had been a success in terms of "plus sales."

The effect of in-store impulse sales, good will, and other plus factors was not estimated.

After the first year of Holiday Money, several other New York area retailers adopted similar programs, and forecasts were for many more stores to adopt competitive versions in the coming pre-Christmas seasons. The idea had also spread to other outlets of Federated Department Stores, Inc., throughout the United States.

In many cases, other retailers changed the name but kept most other aspects of the program intact. Others eliminated the use of scrip by simply making a certain amount of new, delayed billings available to selected customers.

DISCUSSION QUESTIONS

1. Should A&S consider expanding the Holiday Money idea to other special seasons such as Easter, Mother's Day, and Father's Day?
2. Would it be a good idea to send Holiday Money certificates to non-A&S customers? If so, how would A&S develop a list of good credit risks?
3. With other competitors using a similar pre-Christmas delayed billing program, what competitive moves should A&S take, if any?
4. What is your opinion of delayed billing as a retail promotional tool, in the short run and in the long run? Is it a desirable technique for the retail industry in general?
5. Should A&S consider an approach to the Holiday Money idea that would eliminate the need for scrip and exchange booths? What problems do you foresee in such a change?

RIDGE VALLEY POULTRY
Promotion

After thirty-two years of business, Mr. Roxy Vendena has left active management of Ridge Valley Poultry and the store has begun to offer a somewhat different and expanded product line. Although the store still specializes in quality poultry and eggs, many new products have been added, such as Genoa salami, prosciutto ham, giant shrimp, lobster, and many other products (including milk and bread).

Ridge Valley Poultry was started in 1942 by Roxy Vendena. At that time there were twenty-five to thirty fresh-poultry retailers in the Denver area, but only Ridge Valley has survived. Not only has it survived, it has grown to the point where Roxy has retired from an active role in Ridge Valley to devote full time to the wholesale distribution of a product known as Permagreen, which previously had been simply a sideline. Now Roxy Jr. has taken over active management of Ridge Valley Poultry.

When Roxy Sr. began the business, he admits he knew very little about poultry. "That's why we didn't do things like other fresh-poultry retailers of that day," he recalls. "We prepared our products as if we were going to take them home and eat them ourselves; that meant no pinfeathers, clean eggs, and always the best quality. We learned from our customers. If they told us they wanted things a certain way, that is how we did it."

Roxy also stated that he learned early that consumers like change. At first, the little barn from which he originally operated was whitewashed every six months. Customers seemed to notice it and would comment on the change.

As a result, planned change remained a constant part of Roxy's promotional strategy. The building would be remodeled every four or five years, and signs in front told customers that progress was in process and that it would enable Ridge Valley to serve them better. This also extended to the signs used by Ridge Valley, which would be repainted or changed in some way after a period of time, even if that meant just tying a flag to the sign. Roxy found that otherwise people began to take them for granted and that they lost their effectiveness.

With a location in the then small Denver suburb of Wheat Ridge, there simply wasn't a large enough market in the area to support the kind of retail store Roxy wanted. As a result, he had to find ways to attract customers from Denver.

One of the ways that worked was to offer carton cigarettes at a savings, since there was no Denver tax in Wheat Ridge. Although this is still done, Roxy feels it has lost some of its effectiveness because of the new local, county, and city taxes that affect the cost advantage.

Roxy also observed that each day two or three funeral processions would slowly pass in front of his store on the way to the cemetery. As a result, he designed signs that could easily be seen from the slow-moving cars and slanted them in the direction of the processions. After the funerals it was not unusual for half the cars to stop for fresh poultry or eggs. The processions still pass, but now there are six or seven a day.

The first newspaper advertising by Ridge Valley was done in a free newspaper that was distributed once a week to area residents. Handbills were also tried but were never very successful.

The success of the newspaper ads led to a regular ad in both Denver papers. Instead of advertising cut-rate prices on poultry and trying to compete directly with supermarkets, Roxy decided to ask a premium for his products.

"We used the newspapers to brag about our products," commented Roxy. Once in a while promotions were used, such as a free can of charcoal starter with the purchase of six fryers, but the products themselves weren't cut in price.

In the early 1960s Roxy received national publicity for this. He had been selling his turkeys for 49 cents a pound, but then a surplus of turkey occurred and many supermarkets began selling them for 15 cents per pound. Instead of lowering his price, Roxy raised it to 59 cents a pound—and had better business than ever.

Roxy also stated that he took advantage of every promotional possibility. He once agreed to let the Heart Association place a collection box on his counter. After several weeks the container was full, and yet the Heart Association didn't come after the money, so he placed a milk carton alongside it. When that also filled up, he called the *Denver Post*. A reporter was sent out and pictures were taken of the full containers and of Ridge Valley Poultry.

At another time he became interested in midget auto racing and painted "Ridge Valley Poultry" on the hood of his car, even though chickens and race car drivers seemed to be an unlikely combination.

Early in his business career Roxy began to wear striped overalls, and he still does. This also seems to help his business, as people always recognize the man in the overalls and associate him with the poultry store outside of town.

He also called people's attention to his store by reminding them that the initials of his store were the same as his own: R. V.

To compete for the Thanksgiving and Christmas trade, Roxy would place ads in the Denver papers on the first of November to tell people that not all turkeys are alike and then tell them how his are superior.

Over the years, Ridge Valley began to attract a special group of customers that reads very much like the society section of the Denver papers. Roxy made special efforts to know his customers by name, and can recall the names of three generations that shop at Ridge Valley.

In recent years he has found that Ridge Valley is attracting a large number of doctors, osteopaths, and chiropractors from all over Denver, as well as many other types of professional people.

Roxy Jr. also noted this and decided that sales opportunities were being missed by not offering this market segment a greater variety of high-quality, premium-price foods. With the new products, sales have continued to increase. Roxy Jr. continues to stress high-quality poultry, but has shown that he also intends to expand the scope of operations.

Even though sales are strong, there is concern that the changes in product line may eventually force changes in the style and type of promotion that proved so effective in the past. Both Roxys agree that they will have to keep their eyes even wider open and be ready to adopt new promotional ideas to continue to make Ridge Valley grow.

DISCUSSION QUESTIONS

1. What effect do you believe the addition of new product lines will have on Ridge Valley?
2. Will Ridge Valley be able to continue to be known as a quality poultry and egg store as well as a store that sells many other products?
3. Can Ridge Valley make better use of its advertising dollars in the paper by advertising other products along with fresh poultry, or are the products mutually exclusive?
4. Considering the type of market segment that Ridge Valley has attracted over the years, what new forms of advertising and publicity do you believe might be successful?
5. How much influence do you feel the personality and image of Roxy Vendena Sr. had upon the success of Ridge Valley? Place yourself in the shoes of Roxy Jr. What would you do to ensure the growth of Ridge Valley now that Roxy Sr. is retired? For example, should he also be known as the man in striped overalls?

CHAPTER 19

Photo courtesy of EW Directions, Inc.

Epilogue—Afterthoughts on Retailing

In retrospect, after completing this detailed examination of retailing, it may appear that the reader is fully equipped to go forth and prosper in the field. Such is not the case because the retail environment is continually changing. As Professor McNair noted, "the wheel of retailing" continues to turn, always covering new ground. An unfortunate aspect of textbooks is their inherent failure to be up to the minute because of the twelve to eighteen months required for production. The reader has to extend the presentation to suit his own time and circumstances. This is the art of implementing the retail process.

IMPLEMENTATION: PROFITABLE PRACTICE OF KNOW-HOW

The bridge between intellectual knowledge ("knowing how") and successfully applying what one knows is experience. Personal failure, resulting from an individual's trial and error, can be significantly reduced by learning from the mistakes of others. Every entrepreneur-retailer feels optimistic about his personal venture in the beginning, but that attitude gradually changes as he approaches his third year of operation. Most retail failures can be categorized into a series of patterns that can be avoided with proper forewarning.

ANALYSIS OF RETAIL AND SERVICE FIRM FAILURES

The most dangerous period for retailers generally is the third year.[1] Over 20 percent of retail business failures occur during the third year, and 62.9 percent occur within the first six years. The major cause of retail failure seems to be inadequate sales (45.2 percent), followed by an inability to avoid conditions which result in competitive weakness (24.1 percent).[2]

When the statistics on retailing are examined, some interesting facts come to light. In 1970 the most failure-prone line of retailing (per 10,000 operating firms) was women's ready-to-wear (77), followed closely by furniture and furnishings (74) (Table 19–1). While the failure rate for automobile dealerships was relatively lower (28 per 10,000 operating concerns), they accounted for the most retail failures (1,029), resulting in losses of $75,075,000 (Table 19–2). One may infer that many unrealistic entrepreneurs open eating and drinking places but do not succeed. In 1970 alone, 940 such establishments failed, with total liabilities of $80,936,000—or a net loss of $86,102 per bankruptcy.

The most important lesson to be gained is that most failures of new retail efforts result from a combination of events: the usual managerial inexperience and undercapitalization. Both are directly related to entrepreneurial over-optimism. The best "preventive action" that can be taken is a two-year apprenticeship. Such employment experience with the best retailer in the aspiring retailer's chosen specialization is a virtual requirement to get the "feel" of the business. The potential entrepreneur gains valuable experience and accumulates some of the much needed capital.

FUTURE GROWTH IN RETAILING

Consider for a moment that the tremendous changes and growth of the retailing industry have occurred, for the most part, within the life span of the men who started such large companies. Entrepreneurs who literally began with a horse and wagon, a small, leased country store, or a neighborhood

Table 19–1   Failures in Specific Retail Lines, 1970

LINE OF BUSINESS	NUMBER OF FAILURES PER 10,000 OPERATING CONCERNS
Women's ready-to-wear	77
Furniture and furnishings	74
Cameras and photographic supplies	67
Infants' and children's wear	57
Books and stationery	57
Men's wear	52
Appliances, radio and television	45
Gifts	40
Sporting goods	40
Bakeries	32
Automobiles	28
Auto parts and accessories	27
Eating and drinking places	27
Toys and hobby crafts	26
Farm implements	25
Shoes	23
Drugs	21
Dry goods and general merchandise	21
Lumber and building materials	21
Jewelry	18
Hardware	16
Groceries, meat, and produce	15
Women's accessories	14

SOURCE   *The Failure Record through 1970,* Dun & Bradstreet, Inc., New York, 1971.

variety store have lived to see their corporations expand into empires employing thousands of people and annually selling more dollars of merchandise than the gross national product of many nations.

The truly astounding growth and changes in retailing could not have been predicted accurately by anyone. But has the period of unbelievable change finally reached a plateau? Will the future mean that retailers can relax and simply administer the daily needs of established empires? It is extremely doubtful that the answer to either of these questions is yes. The basic forces that create change are far too restless to allow stability.

FACTORS INFLUENCING CHANGE IN THE RETAIL ENVIRONMENT

Although it is impossible to list, or even know, all the forces that will create change, several can be identified from existing trends.

Table 19–2   Commercial and Industrial Failures, 1970

LINE OF INDUSTRY	NUMBER	LIABILITIES (000)
Retail Trade		
Food and liquor	533	$ 38,993
General merchandise	128	14,029
Apparel and accessories	525	29,105
Furniture, home furnishings	602	52,318
Lumber, building materials, hardware	200	19,961
Automotive group	1,029	75,075
Eating and drinking places	940	80,936
Drug stores	113	7,932
Miscellaneous	580	42,254
Total Retail Trade	4,650	360,603
Commercial Service		
Passenger and freight transportation	375	107,007
Miscellaneous public services	83	14,320
Hotels	40	9,952
Cleaning, dyeing, repairing	87	5,815
Laundries	35	3,721
Funeral services	6	166
Other personal services	140	5,568
Business services	463	146,148
Repair services	163	6,039
Total Commercial Service	1,392	298,736

SOURCE   *The Failure Record through 1970,* Dun & Bradstreet, Inc., New York, 1971.

National Mobility

The United States has truly become a nation of gypsies. Ask someone where he is from and the answer may be something such as, "You mean the last place, or the one before that?" More importantly, it is not simply the young career-minded individual who frequently moves. New communities of retired people have developed in California, Arizona, Texas, Florida, and other states. American settlements of retired people and artists have also mushroomed in places such as Cuernavaca and Guadalajara, Mexico.

This increased mobility forces the adoption of new life styles. Older modes of dress are shed in favor of new ones. Even long-acquired eating and drinking habits are modified and changed.

The desire for possession of true consumer durable goods, after many years of life, also changes. The difficulty and expense of transporting furniture and appliances has created a demand for cheaper products that last only a short time and can then be discarded.

A mobile society without roots is much less likely to be interested in "owning" and may, instead, be far more interested in leasing or renting. This undoubtedly causes much of the growth within a rental industry that accounts for nearly $2 billion in sales per year. According to U.S. Department of Commerce figures, the period 1969–71 showed a 45 percent increase in revenues from all franchised rental and leasing services.

Goods sold through many retail establishments may eventually be limited to short-lived consumer non-durables. The bulk of automobiles, appliances, boats, recreational vehicles, and many other items might one day be leased or rented, thus reversing the ratio between leased and purchased goods.

Many retailers might cease to exist except in small numbers. Already, many manufacturers of furniture, drapes, carpeting, and other household items have switched from selling to individual consumers through retail outlets to selling to industrial customers such as apartment complexes and institutions.

The trend has surely been toward "mobility," but is this likely to hold true for the future as well? In a day of low-cost jet travel, billions of acres of concrete strips called highways, automobiles everywhere, and a national fever for movement, the answer seems obvious. Yet there are counterforces at work.

An energy crisis is threatening to create serious shortages and higher prices for traditional fuels. The technology to produce and utilize alternate fuels, such as carbon dioxide, nuclear power, solar power, or anti-magnetic power, is not presently available on an economic basis. Without alternate energy sources, the recent increase in the cost of fossil fuels is likely to dampen the spirit of mobility, making it even more important for a retailer to be located near his target market consumers.

Lessening of Family Ties

Not many years ago it was the desire of parents to leave family heirlooms to their children. Furniture, jewelry, dishes, and silver were considered to be both a financial and sentimental treasure to be left to loved ones.

Today, the concept of leaving behind such sentimental items is much less prevalent. Parents often question the strength of the marriages of their sons and daughters, and tend to grow apart from them once they have left the home. The lonely and forgotten millions of aged people who wait out their final years in nursing homes were not all bachelors and spinsters without children or family. These are people whose children are still healthy and affluent but have grown apart from their parents.

Friendships outside the Neighborhood

It is growing increasingly rare to find neighborhoods in which neighbors are also close friends. Friendships now come from associates met at work, church, and through children's activities such as Scouts and Little League baseball. Keeping up with the Joneses is less likely to mean the next door neighbor than the "peer group" to which one belongs.

There is increasing evidence that the regional shopping center has replaced the neighborhood, and to a degree the church, as a social meeting ground. The need for social contact has not been eliminated but is, instead, being met by other places and activities than the older institutions.

Feelings of Restlessness

During the '50s and early '60s, high school teachers were warning students of the perils of a high school senior who had no idea what he wanted in life. Today, the high school senior has been joined by a league of dissatisfied and confused adults of all ages. It is not uncommon to hear a man of forty admit he still doesn't really know what he wants to be or do with his life.

A small trickle of urbanites has returned to small towns and farms, where new life styles are adopted. If the trickle becomes a stream, retailers of all types will need to adjust their thinking from centering on huge metropolitan areas to smaller stores, mail-order catalogs, telephone shopping facilities, and mini-size shopping centers.

Changing Institutions

Retailers of many goods and services are directly affected by a lack of interest and participation in traditional institutions. A lack of interest in lodges, fraternities, luncheon clubs, and other organizations affects the retail distribution of companies that manufacture and sell greeting cards, candy, uniforms, books, and many other products.

Changing Leisure-Time Activities

Perhaps no change has had a more dramatic effect than that in leisure-time activities. Entire new industries, such as the snowmobile and travel trailer, have developed in a span of only a few years. The camping and back-packing trend has created new retail stores, and undreamed of linear feet of retail space are now devoted to dehydrated foods, light-weight packs, and mountain-climbing equipment. A strong sportsman's service industry, selling "products" from hunting guides to dog training, has also grown in strength. Will the trend toward the sport of soccer (in many sections of the nation) replace football, and if so, what new retailing opportunities will it bring?

Growing International Awareness

The days of viewing Europe through pictures or waiting until one is 65 to visit other nations are past. International travel and education are becoming common occurrences.

Although there are exceptions, consumers generally are ready to accept new ideas and products from foreign countries. In addition, there is a growing feeling among youths of internationalism, rather than strict nationalistic pride.

Increasing Worldwide Competition and Consumption

In a period of only a few years, Japan has become a world merchant. Mexico has passed the "takeoff" point and is well on the way to becoming an industrialized nation. The "Green Revolution" in the Far East has helped to defuse Malthus' dismal prediction about population outstripping agriculture. At the same time, the United States has become a trading partner of Russia and China.

Like it or not, the United States cannot ignore the changes and growth in other parts of the world. As other nations grow economically, major changes will affect the United States. One of the earliest signs of international influence was the worldwide increase in beef consumption, which was reflected in the United States by shorter supplies and higher prices. The exports to the United States from traditional supplier nations were simply not available.

The United States uses a disproportionate share of the world's resources, but what will happen when nations such as India, China, or Russia begin to expand consumer consumption substantially? The availability of inexpensive raw materials for U.S. consumption is destined to become only a paragraph in a history book.

Higher prices, forced recycling, and disappearance of the philosophy of built-in obsolescence will surely be forced upon the American public. The effects upon retailing could easily produce undreamed-of changes. It is probably correct to think of the retailer of the future as a recycler of goods as well as a vendor. Corporations such as Coors and Budweiser brewing companies have already placed their distributors in the role of aluminum can recyclers.

If nations grow economically stronger, there will be increased marketing competition. If Sears and Woolworth can establish retail outlets in Mexico, what is to prevent Mexican retailers from eventually entering the United States? The Japanese have clearly demonstrated the competition that foreign nations can provide. The combination of Japanese and American marketing-retailing initiatives has produced such success stories as Toyota, Datson, and Honda. Japanese trading companies are among the largest and strongest marketing organizations in the world. Is it illogical to visualize a huge empire of Japanese-owned retail stores throughout the United States and Canada?

As these nations grow in economic importance, they represent an untapped market for U.S. suppliers of goods and services. For example, the movement to encourage foreign nationals to travel in the United States implies additional opportunities for American retailers. Lodging, eating, and recreational facilities that profitably cater specifically to these foreign tourists by introducing them to American customs and serving their needs may represent areas that deserve investigation.

Changing Role of Minorities

Many studies and several books have been written on the role of the minority market, particularly the blacks, in the U.S. economy. These have demonstrated the huge market that minorities represent. While this is true, it is also misleading if it is not viewed on a relative scale. The black and Mexican-American markets have many customers, and for many retailers constitute the primary source of customer income. Nevertheless, the gap that remains between the purchasing power of the average suburban white and the average ghetto black is tremendous.

At one time the world thought of wealth as being fixed. Thus one nation or group of people could increase its wealth only at the direct expense of another. This philosophy has been proved to be incorrect. Wealth is *not* a fixed sum, and can be increased overall. Thus an increase in wealth for minorities through economic growth within their minority groups could mean an increase for all. This does not imply a Robin Hood philosophy but, instead, means overall economic improvement through traditional means within minority and poverty-level groups.

Retailers should also recognize the possibility and implications of a forced income-redistribution program, regardless of their personal feelings. Such a program would surely result in increased spending by "income recipients" and thus in new markets for retailers. This might force them to establish branch outlets in new areas, such as Appalachia or the big-city ghettos. It would certainly create a need for a new merchandise and promotional mix to reach this market.

The history of income change by social class has demonstrated that a similar percentage increase in income for low-income groups results in a much sharper increase in spending as contrasted to the same percentage change for affluent individuals.[3] Thus a 20 percent increase in income for minority consumers could have far more dramatic effects for a retailer than the same increase for his present market among more affluent consumers.

There can be little doubt that, by and large, the rights and opportunities of minorities in the United States have markedly improved since World War II. Retailing has felt this change in both its customers and the persons it employs. The future will undoubtedly require even greater participation of minorities in all levels of retailing management.

Retailers will need to give increased thought to minority marketing. This may necessitate the development of new credit programs aimed at attracting the business of minorities, "personalized" store decors within minority areas, and individualized recruiting and training programs aimed at minorities.

It is illogical to assume that a black man, raised in a ghetto environment, will suddenly understand and appreciate the shopping behavior of middle-class whites when he is hired by a retail store. It is equally wrong to expect white managers, with a totally different cultural background, to automatically perform well in the management of ghetto area stores.

Increased Government Regulation

Like it or not, government regulation of retailing is a reality and appears as though it is here to stay. Government control, particularly by the federal government, directly affects *every phase* of retailing. Even medium-size chains have found it necessary to hire full-time legal staffs to keep management informed of what the company can and cannot do. Hiring and firing practices, pricing, buying, promotional programs, credit, packaging, and store location are some of the functions that come under direct control by a government agency at the local, state, or federal level.

Programs such as the Food Stamp Program also affect retailers. In only a few years this program grew from one designed to help feed the extremely poor to one that accounted for 5 percent of all retail food sales.

Other Factors

Many other variables are also likely to influence the shape and pattern of retailing, such as family formation (size and delay of), anti-culture or anti-materialism trends, increased longevity, changes in the age distribution of the population, mass geographical population shifts, and, of course, wars and economic cycles.

Obviously, an in-depth study of any of the previously mentioned factors is impossible for retailers, nor is this their province. It is in fact impossible for retailers to read even a portion of the data available on these subjects. Yet trends must be understood by the retailer and their information used to his advantage.

This awareness is possible from observation and from participation in the environment that surrounds him. Retailers who confine themselves to the isolation of the back room or plush offices are eventually destined to find their consumers seeking others who serve their needs better.

The old adage of "all work and no play" does in truth make Jack a dull retailer. The four walls of a store soon produce a myopic vision that can be corrected only by observing people as they live and play, by visiting new places, by observing new retailing trends, and by developing a "feel" for changing demands.

CONCLUSION

Retailing can provide a fascinating and satisfying career, or a comfortable living, for a retailer and his family. The choice is yours. Regardless of the path chosen, the successful retailer services a target market better than his competitors by constantly being attuned to it and anticipating its needs. The customer will cast his dollar votes with the candidate who offers the best value for the price. A retailer does not do the customer a favor just by being there; his success must be re-earned each day with each customer.

Profits, personal satisfaction, and store survival are the products of genuine consumer concern and dedicated, effective hard work.

FOOTNOTES

[1] *The Failure Record through 1970: A Comprehensive Study of Business Failures by Location, Industry, Age, Size and Cause* (New York: Dun & Bradstreet, 1971).

[2] Ibid.

[3] Paul A. Samuelson, *Economics: An Introductory Analysis* (New York: McGraw-Hill, 1964), pp. 209–213.

APPENDIX A:
How Retailers Say It

A

Accessories: women's fashion apparel worn with dresses, coats, suits, sportwear; includes fine and costume jewelry, neckwear, scarfs, handbags, and small leather goods, millinery, gloves, hosiery, shoes, handkerchiefs, watches, artificial flowers, ribbons.

Accessory Items: merchandise that "goes with" or is coordinated with larger items.

Accommodation Desk: a centrally located fixture in a smaller store where calls, gift wrapping, and other services are performed for customer convenience.

Added Gravy: "go with" sales. Example: in selling queen size or king size mattresses, larger sheets, blankets, comforters, bedspreads, are needed—added gravy for salesperson and store.

Advertising: any paid-for form of non-personal presentation of goods, services, or ideas to a group.

Airport-to-Airport Shipping: transportation of merchandise from one airport to another by an airline.

Anticipation: paying a bill before it is due, with benefit of extra discount, usually computed at 6% per annum (exception rather than rule).

Assocation of Buying Offices: organization of New York buying office executives to standardize and unify services available to stores; traditionally the manager of the NRMA merchandise division is ABO executive secretary.

Assortment Plan: complete range of merchandise in a category planned to various depths of inventory to meet customer demand.

Authorizing: approval of a charge transaction by credit personnel when the amount of the sale exceeds floor limits or when identification of the customer and account is required.

Automatic Reorder: reordering staple merchandise on the basis of a predetermined minimum quantity; when this minimum is reached, the quantity of the initial order is again purchased.

Autonomous Operation: achieved by branch stores as they grow larger, develop more autonomy in operation, and are treated on "equal stores" basis with downtown (flagship) store.

Average Gross Sale: dollar amount of gross sales divided by number of sales transactions or saleschecks which produced the gross sales.

B

Backup Stock: additional merchandise available in warehouse or in forward (in-store) stock room. Particularly important for runners or best selling staple staples.

Bargain Store: where everything is stocked, provided it can be sold in quantity at a sub-market price. Distress merchandise and job lots are often bought in huge quantities, but little or no attempt is made to maintain stock assortment.

SOURCE Compiled and edited by Ralf Shockey Associates Inc., Marketing Consultants, 295 Madison Ave., N.Y., N.Y. 10017

Balanced Stock: balanced stock and/or assortment makes available what the customers want throughout all price zones or price ranges in proportion to that demand.

Bargain Basement: the basement of downstairs store of a department store that specializes in price lines the upstairs store does not carry or of which the upstairs store duplicates only the top price line; the downstairs store emphasizes special values.

Basic Building: development of depth of staple-staples to insure neverouts.

Basic Stocks: items, numbers, or models that must be included in a line or classification. A basic stock is primarily an assortment of the bread-and-butter items that enjoy day-to-day customer demand. Basic stock is usually staples but non-staple items become basic when, for fashion or fad reasons, they enjoy temporarily increased customer demand. The best rule for basic stock is having what the customer wants when she wants it.

Big Ticket: usually big in physical size and size of price. Natural habitat: major appliances, furniture, and other hard goods. Often uses tick-tack-toe system of crossing through squares when item is sold, for read-and-run stock inventory.

Biller: personnel in the accounts receivable department whose responsibility is to prepare a bill for the customer for purchases made during the preceding month.

B/L (Bill of Lading): form used by the carrier denoting the consignor, consignee, number and weight of packages, description, shipping charges (sometimes, not always), date, and other information necessary for shipment and receipt of goods into the store.

Blank-check Buying: a retailer places an open order with a vendor generally prior to start of a season, with specific details following throughout season as needed.

Blanket Order: pre-season order to meet anticipated needs, placed before production has started; buyer orders against blanket order to meet needs as season arrives and progresses.

Bonus (P.M., Premium Money): additional bonus paid to sales-people for selling slow-moving, pre-season, or higher-priced merchandise, or for a special promotion; sometimes paid by vendor upon approval by store.

Book Inventory: amount of retail stock shown to be on hand by a perpetual inventory system wherein sales, markdowns, and discounts are statistically deducted from total purchases to date.

Boutique: small shop, especially one that sells fashionable clothes and accessories for women (recently department stores have expanded "boutique" to include just about everything from men's wear to home furnishings).

Branch Merchandising Power: increasing influence of branch store managers and their merchandising staffs in recommending or requesting items, lines, or brands from specific resources.

Branch Store: owned and operated by the parent or flagship store; generally located in a suburban area under the name of the flagship store.

Brand: is a word, letter, or group of words or letters composing a name or design or a combination of these which identifies the goods as services of one seller and/or distinguishes them from those of competitors. Brand is a more inclusive general term than trademark.

Brown Goods: radios, televisions electronics.

Budget Store: may be a section in flagship store or branch store specializing in price lines the regular upstairs store does not carry or of which the upstairs store duplicates only the top price lines; may also be called Bargain Basement or Downstairs Store.

Bulk Merchandise Delivery: large merchandise items such as major appliances, furniture, bedding, and rugs requiring at least two men to deliver, that cannot be handled by parcel delivery men. Some stores employ commercial trucking companies, or manufacturer's distributor (wholesaler) delivers directly to store's customer.

Buying by Specifications: where store submits definite specifications to manufacturer, rather than selecting from goods already on the market. Private or controlled brands are normally purchased by an individual store or through a RBO on specifications.

Buying Group (Buying Office, Resident Buying Office): organization representing group of noncompeting stores, formed primarily for buying merchandise; may be independent, store-owned, or own the stores (examples: Owns Stores: Allied Stores Corp., Associated Dry Goods Corp., Mercantile Stores Co.; Owned by Stores: Associated Merchandising Corp., Frederick Atkins, Inc.; Charges Stores Fee: Mutual Buying Syndicate, Inc., Felix Lilienthal & Co., Independent Retailers, Inc.

Buying off the Peg: where customers can buy merchandise, particularly ready-to-wear, for immediate "take-with" or delivery by store. This has not been true in European stores.

C

Call Credit: used when merchandise is picked up by store's delivery system from a customer, returned to store, and customer is credited for price of merchandise.

Call System: arrangement in some selling departments to give each salesperson, by numerical rotation, an equal opportunity to wait on customers; commonly used in men's clothing departments, major appliances, and furniture.

Call Tag: tag or form used by delivery driver to call for, and attach to, an article or package to be picked up at customer's address and return to store.

Carrier: a railroad, trucking firm, air line, express company, bus line, steamship, or river barge company that transports merchandise from vendor to store.

Carrier (Mechanical): cylinder used to contain saleschecks or media dispatched through pneumatic tube system; carriers are identified by color bands and numbers for type of media and dispatching station.

Carrier Transportation: transporting organization for shipment of goods (examples: Railway Express, National Car-loading, Shulman Air Freight).

Carry Outs: merchandise carried from store by customer, expediting delivery and saving delivery expense, particularly significant in branch stores. Also called "Take-Withs." Must be forward stock, immediately available.

Cash Discount: percentage off billed price; concession for paying bills within time period indicated on invoice. (Example: 2/10 means 2% deductible from bill, if paid within ten days of date of invoice.) Cash discounts include anticipation; cash discounts are merchandising gains, included in computing gross margin.

C.O.D. (**Cash on Delivery**): transaction whereby customer agrees to pay when goods are delivered.

Cash Receipts Report: form used by sales-people to list cash received from sale of merchandise at end of each day's business; the Change Fund is first deducted and placed in Change Fund bag; balance of cash is counted and listed and placed in Receipts bag together with the report.

Center City: the older city located within the original legal geographical area exclusive of suburbs.

Central Buying: buying activities of a group of centrally controlled or associated stores; generally for merchandise uniformly carried, where bulk purchases can influence the purchase price.

Central Control Office: office charged with responsibility for merchandise control system and accurate accumulation of pertinent statistics.

Central Information File: main data-storage memory in a computer system.

Centralized Buying: all buying done by merchandise staff located in flagship store or buying center, perhaps located in corporate headquarters or warehouse. Central buying increasingly influenced by requests, suggestions, opinions of branch store managers, and their merchandise staffs.

Chain Stores: two or more stores identical merchandise; owned and merchandised by one individual or one company.

Charge-a-Plate: copyrighted name of small identification plate showing customer has a charge account; plate is used to imprint saleschecks.

Charge-Authorizing Phone: telephone connecting selling department direct with credit-files section solely for credit authorization calls.

Check-Outs: stations where customers carry self-selected merchandise, pay cashier, and have merchandise wrapped.

Cherry Picking: buyer selection of only a few numbers from one vendor's line, other numbers from another line, failing to purchase a complete line or classification of merchandise from one resource (with rapid development of multi-unit stores, cherry picking from large number of resources becomes economically unsound).

Chislers: customers who attempt to get store to reduce regular prices for merchandise or services, particularly when buying multiple units, generally more successful with Mama & Papa stores. Also buyers and merchandise managers who try to force prices down from resources.

Chopped Ticket: that part of price ticket removed from sold merchandise and forwarded to vendor nightly as step in vendor's computerized stock-control for reorders.

Classification: all merchandise of given type or use, regardless of style, size, color model or price (i.e., men's dress shirts).

Classification Control: system of merchandise control wherein a classification is controlled by dollar inventory and sales rather than by units.

Classification Merchandising: classifying merchandise in groups that are interchangeable from customer's viewpoint.

Clerk Wrap: name applied to system in which salesperson disposes of entire transaction, including wrappings of "send" merchandise (a semi-clerk wrap is confined to "take-with" transactions).

Closed-Door Membership Store: discount-store operation requiring its customers to qualify as such by type of employment ("government employee," "public servant," "member of union," etc.) and by paying "initiation" fee or annual "dues" or both.

Club Stamp: rubber stamp used by cashiers for identification; has date inserts.

Cluster of Stores: that which will produce enough sales volume in a geographical area to bear cost of advertising, central warehousing, and distribution and provide a profitable operation.

COBOL: common business-oriented language—programming language for presenting business data-processing procedures.

COG: customer-owned goods, so identified when left for repair, trimming, engraving, etc.

Column Inch: one column wide by one inch deep; a print advertising term.

Commission: percentage of sales paid salespeople as all or part of their remuneration.

Commitment: unconfirmed order for merchandise which buyer has obligated store to accept.

Communication Efficiency: selection of fast-moving merchandise in immediate customer demand that will immediately bring customers into flagship or branch store. (In a 20-store study among 10,000 customers in flagship and branch stores, less than 6% come into store because of advertising for that day's business).

Community Shopping Center: usually defined in size as 20 to 40 stores, including one junior department store; on 20 to 25 acres; needing 5,000-family trading area; 100,000 to 200,000 square feet in store area.

Comparison Department: store department whose function is to compare prices, styles, quality, service, etc. with those of competitors.

Comparison Shopper: employee in comparison department charged with reporting competitor's activities and merchandise.

Compatible Personalities: two or more individuals who work cooperatively on problems and/or assignments.

Competing Against all Comers: policy of a store to meet all competition on quality, quantity, price line, payment terms, selling service, delivery.

Compliance Bureau: purpose is to collect, analyze, disseminate, and follow-up the various government regulations affecting the store, particularly in it's merchandising and personnel operations.

Consignee: shipping term applied to ultimate receiver of goods.

Consignment Purchase and Dating: purchase wherein title to merchandise does not pass at time of shipment but at expiration of specified period, when buyer is privileged to return to vendor any unsold goods.

Consignor: shipping term applied to originator of shipment.

Consolidated Delivery: delivery service of an independent organization which accumulates and delivers packages from various stores.

Consumer Cooperation: a retail store owned and directed by its own associated consumer membership.

Consumer Education: complete information on product performance and care to enable customer to make wiser buying decisions.

Consumerism: interest in the consumer's welfare, how honestly and how well the customer is served and informed, how accurate and how adequate that information is, how easily it can be understood.

Contingent: regular on-the-payroll member of sales or sales-supporting personnel or employee called in when needed to work part-time or full-time in whatever department assigned to.

Contract Account: customer account with stipulated periodic per cent payments.

Contract Division: sells to institutions such as schools, hospitals, hotels, motels, and large business firms, generally at lower markon than retail customers pay. Frequently merchandise is shipped direct from factory to purchaser, bypassing store's receiving, marking, merchandising, and delivery departments.

Co-op Money: Co-op: abbreviation for cooperative; money: what the vendor contributes toward helping promote his goods (sometimes abbreviated by FTC).

Co-operative Advertising: advertising in payment of which manufacturer, importer, or distributor cooperates with retailer.

Co-operative Display Fund: definite amount of money provided by vendor, generally matched by store, for development, construction, and installation by store's visual merchandising (display) department to support a specific promotion for vendor's products.

Co-ordinate Stuffing and Authorizing: combining of functions of authorizing and placing sales media in customer's files.

C & F (Cost and Freight): shipping term indicating seller will pay only freight charges to a destination, not insurance.

C.I.F. (Cost, Insurance, and Freight): shipping term signifying seller will pay all freight charges to destination.

Coupon Account: account wherein customer contracts for a certain number of coupons, for which he pays in weekly installments; the coupons can be used as cash throughout the store.

Creative Packaging: packaging that creates extra sales by virtue of eye appeal, informative labeling "fresh" appeal; aims to be protective, informative, revealing, easy to house and handle. (Creative packing is sharp modern competitive selling tool; buyers may beat a path to manufacturer's door for this better mousetrap.)

Credit Crunch: a severe tightening of credit influencing both vendors and retailers, due to government efforts to curb spiraling economy.

Credit History Card: record of customer's account indicating home address, employer, account activity, credit limit, delinquencies, past or present, other miscellaneous credit data.

Croque or Croqous: small, rough sketch from which an illustrative idea or ready-to-wear or home-furnishings number is designed or model developed.

Cross-Selling: term applied to salesperson's selling in more than one department.

Cumulative Markon %: in dollars, the difference between the delivered cost of merchandise including transportation costs and the cumulative selling prices originally set.

Customer Complaints: when customers state they are not satisfied with products sold by store—as to size, material content, length of service, color, fastness, cleaning instructions, warranties or guarantees.

Customer Demand: how much merchandise (how many items or how much in dollars at cost or retail prices) customers buy in a stated period of time.

COG (Customer's Own Goods), COM (Customer's Own Merchandise): customer-owned articles, so identified when left for repair, trimming, engraving, etc.

Customer Participation: encouraging customers to participate in sale by asking questions, making suggestions, and handling or operating merchandise.

Customer Surveys: positive efforts to determine what customers in a metromarket prefer.

Cut-Throat Competition: used when low prices on nationally known or nationally advertised products are used as "bait" to draw customers into a store and efforts are made to switch customer to higher-priced full-profit merchandise (as a rule, assortments of sizes, colors, models, and quantities of bait merchandise are very limited or quantity customer is permitted to purchase is limited.

Cycle Billing: correlation of alphabetical breakdowns to specific days of month to facilitate billing of customer's accounts; each breakdown is a cycle and billing for cycle occurs on same day each month.

D

Dating: "deadline" for paying for goods; to allow reasonable grace period for resale.

DECA: Distributive Clubs of America, where high school or other schools prepare students with skills in retailing.

Deep-Stocks of Key Items: popular merchandise carried in large quantities, in many sizes and colors: but variety of styles, patterns, types carried strictly limited to best-sellers.

De Luxe Goods: higher-priced, exclusive, advance styles or models that wealthiest customers can afford (store may handle de luxe trade without profit for reputation that comes with having this clientele).

Delivery Expenses: per cent of sales for cost of delivery, including expenses of packing, wrapping, delivery of merchandise to customer, picking up customer returns, postage, parcel post, and express charges.

Demonstration Sale: presented by vendor's representatives—territorial salesmen, demonstrators, or staff sales trainer, or by member of department's sales personnel, to arm departmental staff with facts, selling points and show better methods of presenting advantages, use, and care of a product.

Demonstrator: salesperson who devotes all his time to particular manufacturer's products.

Demurrage: detention of freight car or vessel beyond time allowed for loading or unloading, and subsequent charges for detention.

Department Manager: in both flagship and branch stores department managers are responsible for operation of selling department, freeing buyer to attend vendor meetings, working the market, planning and developing merchandising and advertising programs, devising new floor display ideas, scheduling and training departmental sales personnel.

D.O.S. (Department Operating Statements): monthly report of departments operation, including sales, stock on hand, markdown gross margin, expenses, all other pertinent factors.

Department Store Base: where resource works closely with a department store not only in producing volume sales in the flagship and branch stores but also to influence other stores in metropolitan area in purchasing and promoting the resources item, line, or brand.

Departmental Analysis: to analyze a department to determine 1) whether it is producing it's due share of sales volume in that line in store's metromarket, and 2) whether gross margin realized is adequate to cover expenses and contribute to store profits. When unsatisfactory condition is uncovered, detailed studies aimed at improving performance are made, including resources, markon, cash discount, styling, price lining, customer traffic, selling service, advertising, visual merchandising, departmental layout, workroom expense, customers returns and adjustments.

Departmentalizing: organization of related merchandise and subsequent identification as a department.

Depot Store: carries standard merchandise which customers buy because of store's convenient location.

Descriptive Billing: posting of customer's statement in which name of article purchased is written on statement (saleschecks retained by store for adjustment purposes).

Designer-Picked Fashions: high fashions selected and produced by big name manufacturers.

Detention Time: charge made by carriers due to lack of facilities and space on store's receiving docks for carrier to unload incoming shipment of merchandise.

Direct Mail: use of the mails to make announcements, sell merchandise, sell services, sell the store, its divisions, its departments, its character, and its ways of doing business. Personal approach to selective audiences.

Director of Personnel: executive responsible for development and activation of store's personnel policies and regulations, in employment, training, and performance reviews.

Discount Merchandising: low-margin retailing, generally self-service, selling goods at less than list price.

Discount Store: store operating on lower overall margin than conventional store selling same type of merchandise; generally offers less service.

Dispatcher: person or agent responsible for promptly routing and sending merchandise to its destination.

Display: presentation of merchandise, usually with signing (there are usually window displays, interior displays, and outpost displays in stores).

Distress Merchandise: merchandise which, for any reason, must be sold at a sacrifice (at either wholesale or retail level).

Divisional Merchandise Manager: middle management: executive responsibility for merchandising activities of related group of departments; transmits top management policy to line management; supervises department managers (buyers) and manager's assistants; influential decision-making supervisory executive.

Dock Areas: where incoming merchandise is unloaded, generally adjacent to receiving and marking area.

Document: paper denoting transaction or operation (invoice, markon list, salescheck, etc.).

Dollar Control: control of stock markdowns, markons, markups, and sales in terms of dollars rather than by units of percentage.

Dollar Sales per Square Foot: departmental results are derived by dividing each department's net sales by the average number of square feet of selling space occupied by the department. Increasing sales per square feet important objective.

Domestics: name originally applied to yard goods from which sheets, pillow cases, towels, etc., were cut; now broadly encompasses finished products in these classifications.

Don't Want: C.O.D. package which customer refuses to accept upon delivery.

Door-to-Door: shipping term denoting consignment of goods to be picked up at vendor's place of business and delivered directly to store's place of business.

Dress Regulations: store rules about what selling personnel can and cannot wear on selling floor (the most important thing to wear is a smile!).

Driver Accept: written instructions on C.O.D. salescheck for driver to accept an article of merchandise as an even exchange, additional C.O.D. charge, or refund to customer upon delivery of a new purchase.

Drop Ship: when buyer orders merchandise shipped directly to specific branch store, it is noted on order to "drop ship to ——— store." This procedure saves time and expense of vendor's shipping to central warehouse, store's trans-shipping to designated branch; it also means branch store will not be "out" for a long period; sometimes it is more expensive in terms of freight cost.

Dual Billing and Posting: posting customer's purchases to a ledger as separate operation from preparation of customer's bill.

E

E.D.P.: Electronic Data Processing, or work done or expected to be done by a computer.

Electronic Data Processing: putting programmed data through a computer.

Employee Discount: discount given employees on purchase of merchandise for their own use.

Enclosed Mall: shopping center where all stores face enclosed central mall with year-round air conditioning.

End-of-Aisle: spaces fronting on main traffic aisles, particularly important location for $4\frac{1}{2}$-second stopper displays to develop impulse sales.

E.O.M. Terms: End of Month: indicates time allowance for discount is reckoned from end of month during which goods were bought, not from date of invoice.

End Sizes: extreme sizes of an assortment, smallest and largest (which store seldom carries in depth).

Environmental Selling: displaying merchandise under conditions and settings similar to those of a customer's own home.

Equal Store Operation: company in which branch stores are operated on same (equal) basis as flagship or downtown store. (Buyer is not responsible for selling operation.)

Exclusive Merchandise: confined merchandise not available at other stores in that metromarket.

Executive Trainee: generally, a college graduate who works in various divisions of store while receiving on-the-job training for executive position.

Express Warranty: a subsidiary promise or a collateral agreement, breach of which does not entitle the buyer to make certain claims for damages against the vendor.

Extraneous Items: charges on saleschecks for gift wrap, parcel post, special delivery, etc., that must be culled when auditing sales to arrive at true net-sales figure.

F

Fat Budgets: adequate OTB (open-to-buy) approved for buyer by merchandise manager in anticipation of materially increasing sales potential. A very pleasing situation for buyer!

F.T.C. Guidelines: rules and regulations established by the Federal Trade Commission for vendor in granting advertising and other promotional allowances to retailers whether made direct to retailers or through wholesaler or distributors.

Feed Back: return of information; in retail control systems, return of information to vendor (after store's controller has analyzed operation of vendor's line at close of season, buyer and merchandise manager feed back results to vendor, especially in program in which store and vendor have agreed on specific goals).

Final Sort: last step in a sorting process, which leaves material in order desired.

Financing Consumer Purchases: stores provide merchandise for their customers whether the customer pays "cash on the barrelhead," uses a 30-day charge account, a time payment plan, or revolving credit plan.

Fixturing: layout and selection of fixtures to arrange merchandise for customer convenience; particularly important for self-selection.

Flagging an Account: temporarily identifying and suspending an account until brought up to date.

Flagship Division: downtown or central location where executive, merchandising, and promotional staffs are concentrated. Examples: Broadway Department stores, L.A., located next to central warehouse; May Co., L.A., located in flagship store.

Flash Report: total of daily gross sales by departments prepared at close of each business day.

Floating Displays: moved from location to location within flagship store or from branch store to branch store.

Flood Light: an artificial light so directed or diffused as to give a comparatively uniform illumination over rather large areas, as in a display window.

Floor Audit (Register Audit): accounting for sales transactions, in a department or section, by using local cash register.

Floor Limit: arbitrary amount established for floor approval of charge purchases without credit authorization when customer presents proper identification.

Fold-over Statement: customer's bill with address label pre-folded so that, when inserted, name and address will appear in transparent window of envelope.

Forward Stock: that stock which is carried in the selling department.

Four-Way Audit: daily sales audit by salesperson, department, kind of sale, and missing saleschecks.

Fraudulent Purchases: a) where store buyer writes orders to vendors that are not delivered to store but are paid for by store, b) where merchandise is stolen from store and returned for credit.

F.O.B. (Free on Board): shipping term signifying vendor or shipper retains title and pays all charges to F.O.B. point.

Full Line: stock of any given classification of goods which includes every variety of style, in every color, in every size, and in every material that a customer can reasonably expect to obtain a given price. A full line consists of four definite categories: 1) Staples, 2) Style merchandise, 3) Novelties, 4) Outsizes (for stock that have a size element).

Full-time Employees: all sales, sales supporting, and operating personal in a store employed on a year round basis.

G

Gazebo: a display fixture, frequently free-standing, upon which various types of fashion accessories are ensembled.

General Merchandise Stores: includes department stores, dry goods stores, most mail order houses, and variety stores.

Gift Certificate: certificate, suitably engraved, denoting value for which it may be used in lieu of cash throughout the store.

Glossies: prints of merchandise photographs supplied to store's advertising of display department for reproduction.

Gross Margin: difference between net sales and cost of goods sold; the "room to move around in" that determines net operating profit after subtracting operating expense. Shrinkage avoided by careful handling of initial markon, markdowns, discounts.

Guarantee: a promise or assurance, especially one in writing, that something is of specified quantity, quality, content, benefit, or that it will perform satisfactorily for a given length of time; a money-back guarantee.

H

Hard Goods: major appliances, including refrigerators, deep freezers, electric and gas ranges, washing machines, dryers, hot water-heaters, air conditioners.

Hold Slip: form used to identify merchandise that customer desires to purchase later.

Honor System: system wherein employees record their own working time on time sheets.

House Organ: publication for store's employees. Increasingly important with establishment of more branch stores in disseminating news from top management whom branch store employees seldom or ever see or hear from.

Housekeeping: presenting merchandise in neat, attractive, orderly manner; keeping stock in good condition in warehouse or forward stockrooms as well as on selling floor; physical maintenance (cleanliness) of entire store; also used to describe porter and maid service.

I

Image (Store Image): reputation of store; the feelings of customers toward store.

Impact Printer: data print out device that imprints by momentary pressure of raised type against paper, using ink or ribbon as a color medium, as opposed to photographs, electro-chemical, or other printing means.

Impulse Merchandise: articles of merchandise purchased on spur of moment by customer without predetermined consideration.

In Bond: merchandise shipped by manufacturer several months ahead of store's normal selling season is "held in bond" in store's warehouse until selling season; not charged against department's OTB until removed from warehouse to toward stock or selling floor.

In Transit: refers to merchandise that has left consignor's premises and is en route to its destination.

Incentive Pay: bonus or extra commission paid to salespeople for exceeding their production quota.

Increase in Merchandise Items: number of separate items required to meet customer demand in a single department.

In-Home Selling: selling in the home either from "cold canvas" or by appointment made by store earlier. Particularly applicable for major appliances, furniture, floor coverings, curtains, draperies and decorator upholstery fabrics, sewing machines, vacuum cleaners, television sets, wallpaper, paint.

Initial Markon: initial and/or first markon used when merchandise is originally offered for sale.

Installment Account: credit account in which customer contracts to pay specific amount by week or month.

Institutional Advertisement: advertisement to improve image of store or tell customers of a store service, policy or objective. (In one sense, all advertising is institutional because it creates a favorable or unfavorable impression of the store.)

Inter-Selling: system by which salespeople can consummate sales in various departments and which provides method for crediting each department with sale of its merchandise.

Interstore Transfer Forms: on which is listed merchandise to be shipped from central warehouse or flagship store to branch store or from one branch store to another branch.

Inter-Store Transfers: shipping goods from one store to another.

Internal Audit: plan of verification and control for checking store systems for accuracy, validity, and conformity to plan.

Intra-Store Transfer: buying goods from one selling department for another selling department within a store.

Inventory, Physical: determining by actual inspection the merchandise on hand in store, stock rooms, and warehouses; also recording of this information.

Inventory Shrinkage: takes form of theft, internal or external fraud, record distion, waste, sabotage, generally laxity, or careless operation.

Invoice: itemized statement showing merchandise sent to store by a supplier.

Item: a specific style, color, size, or price of merchandise.

Item History: record of the movement (sale) of a specific item, line, or assortment of merchandise.

J

Job Lot: miscellaneous group of assortment of style, sizes, colors, etc., purchased by store as a "lot" at a reduced price.

K

Kimball Tags: pre-punched tags attached to merchandise and containing size and style information, provided for high-speed processing and counting; used in inventory control reports recording, and restocking.

L

Labor Turnover: voluntary resignations of (experienced) employees, replacing them with inexperienced workers, particularly in lower salary classifications.

Lay-away: method of deferred payments in which merchandise is held by store for the customer until completely paid for.

Leased Department: department operated by outside organization, generally on percentage-of-sales basis. A lessor must abide by rules, regulations, operations, and objectives of lessee.

Ledger Card: record of customer's charge-account activity and bill payments, kept in accounts receivable files.

Liberal Return Policy: where store accepts returns by customer of merchandise for refund or exchange with minimum or no questions asked.

Loading: in reference to cash discounts is the building up of gross invoice price of merchandise and crediting cash discounts with amount of load.

Loading of Cash Discounts: building up gross invoice price of merchandise and crediting cash discounts with the amount of the load. It may be done by the resource through an adjustment of the invoice or, more often, by the store's through a bookkeeping entry.

Locker Stocks: a shipment by manufacturer or wholesaler of extra inventory assortment, which is held in store's central warehouse unopened (not consignment selling); as soon as buyer needs any item being held in locker stock, payment becomes due to vendor for entire shipment.

Loss Leader: merchandise advertised and sold at, near or even below cost by store to bring customers into store.

Low-Margin Retailing: discount or mass merchandising.

M

Maintained Markon: difference between net sales and gross cost of sold goods.

Management by Objectives: program of professional management techniques and merchandise as well as economic trend indicators to keep ahead of competition, strengthening management at store and corporate levels. These are geared to the goal of increasing sales per square foot—one of the key factors that measures earnings in retail business.

Manifest: shipping form used by carriers for consolidation purposes, listing all pertinent information (consignor, consignee, commodity classification, number and weight of packages, and sometimes cost); used by carriers internally to list contents of a particular vehicle, listing same information; also used by stores in transfer operations from central warehouse to branches.

Mannequin: a clothes model; a styled and three-dimensional representation of the human form used in display windows and on ready-to-wear selling floors to display apparel.

Manufacturer's Representative: selling agent, preferably retail-minded, capable of giving informative talks to selling personnel. (If loaded with selling ideas and merchandising information, rates as buyer's friend.)

Markdown: reduction in retail price of merchandise, primarily for clearance of broken assortments, end sizes, prior stock, for special sales events, and to meet competition.

Market Demography: science of vital statistics of population (households, marriages, births, age groups, incomes, sales by peak hours of the day, days of the week, and months of the year, etc.).

Market Penetrations: a store's share of a metromarket in a specific department or classification of merchandise. Within reason there is no limit on how deep a penetration successfully operated departments can make.

Market Representative: member of resident-buying-office staff whose major responsibilities are to act as market shopper, analyst, merchandise counsellor to merchandise managers and buyers of office's member stores; also expedites shipment of initial orders and reorders placed by member stores.

Marking: putting the correct price tag on new merchandise.

Markon: difference between cost price as billed (before deductions for cash discount) and retail price at which merchandise is originally offered.

Marketing: currently refers to everything connected with sales, advertising, sales promotion, public relations and publicity, merchandising, distribution, research.

Marriage: a merger or consolidation of two or more businesses or departments.

Mass Merchandising: self-service store displaying and selling all kinds of merchandise; displays tend to be massive, customers usually push wire carts to collect and carry their own selection of merchandise to cashier checkout counters.

Maximizing Space Productivity: arrangement of selling fixtures and display of merchandise to produce increased sales volume per square foot of selling space.

Media (1): evidence of transactions with customers (saleschecks, vouchers, return slips, etc.).

Media (2): as used in advertising: periodical (newspaper, magazine, shopper publications); direct (direct mail, catalogue, circular novelties, premiums); sign (outdoor or indoor poster, bulletin, sign, point-of-purchase, carcard, transit sign); sky-writing; motion pictures; program (theatre, menus, guides); broadcast (radio, television, public address, loud speaker systems).

Media Mix: planning use and coordination of advertising and promotional media, such as interior and exterior display, and newspaper, direct mail, radio, TV, magazine, transit, and outdoor advertising.

Media Representatives: sales and/or service representatives from newspapers, radio, TV, and direct mail media who service store accounts.

Memorandum and Consignment Selling: vendor agrees to take back goods if they are not sold in a specific period of time. Since the markdown risk is borne by the vendor, the buyer's maintainance is equal to his initial markon. Under the memorandum arrangement, title passes to the buyer, ordinarily, when goods are shipped, but vendor assumes contracted obligation of taking back unsold portion of goods at a specific time. On consignment purchase, title does not pass to store but instead passes directly from vendor to store's customers—store acts simply as an agent for vendor. Vendor can control retail price.

Merchandise Charge: extraneous costs, such as shipping charges, insurance, demurrage, etc., applicable to cost of merchandise prior to markon.

Merchandise Classification: applied to a merchandise group within a department and controlled by dollar volume rather than by units.

Merchandise Control: department that maintains accurate figures on purchases and sales merchandise, either by dollar or by units.

Merchandise Marts: buildings housing showrooms for manufacturers and importers where, under one room, store buyers and merchandise managers can inspect lines from resources in minimum time. The Merchandise Mart in Chicago is reported to be the largest in the world.

Middle Management: secondary layer of divisional managers, i.e., assistants.

Minimum Stock Control: method of reordering staple merchandise on basis of predetermined minimum quantity; when minimum is reached, quantity of initial order is again purchased.

Missing Salescheck: check which cannot be accounted for in sales audit (all salescheck books carry a serial number and saleschecks are numbered in sequence so a missing salescheck can quickly be detected).

Model Stock: "how much of what" to have, a stock which has the right goods at right time in right quantities at right price. A model stock in most classifications is three full lines and three price levels which move stock rapidly.

Mom and Pop Outlets: small stores generally operated by husband and wife with limited capital, in a restricted selling area composed of low income families. Very dependent on wholesaler and/or distributor for financial support.

Multiple Sales: encouraging customers to buy multiple rather than single items.

N

Neighborhood Shopping Center: or "strip center": 10 to 15 stores, including food, drug, sundry, and personal service stores; 5 to 10 acres; needs at least 1,000 families trading area for support; usually under 100,000 square feet.

Number of Stock Turns: stock turnover is calculated by dividing average inventory at retail into the net sales for the year. Average inventory is the sum of the retail inventories at the end of each month added to the initial opening inventory and divided by thirteen, the number of inventories used.

O

On Order: applied to merchandise purchased but not yet received.

On the Floor: time spent by buyer on the selling floor, to get the "personal touch" with customers; supervise sales personnel; be involved in selling function; devise new floor visual selling ideas. Unfortunately too many buyers are "married to the flagship store"; devoting little, if any time, to branch store floor supervision.

Open Order: order placed without price or delivery stipulation; order sent to market representative in resident buying office without specifying vendor.

Open Stock: additional and/or replacement pieces of merchandise (example— dinnerware) carried in bulk and kept in stock for several years. Open stock slows turnover materially.

OTB (Open-to-Buy): meaning buyer has money to spend. Buyer usually budgeted for month period; interim open-to-buy determined by subtracting cost figures (for goods received, in transit, unfilled orders) from alloted planned-purchase dollars. ("Open-to-buy" are sweetest words in retailing from vendor's viewpoint).

OTB by Classification: OTB for a specific line, number, or item, though department as whole is overbought (or, more factually, undersold).

Out of Stock: lack of merchandise in store in styles, colors, material content, price lines customers want when they want it.

Over or Short: resulting difference between established sales figure and actual audited figure, often caused by errors in change or missing saleschecks.

P

P.P. (Parcel Post): division of postal service that delivers packages and fourth-class literature. There are strict limitations on size, weight, and method of wrapping packages.

Part-Timer: employee who does not work full time but only on peak selling days.

Passer: Man, woman, or child who passes a store (important to remember that all passers are not prospective customers); also "hot" or bad check passer.

Peak Season: months or season in which an item or line of merchandise is in greatest customer demand. Examples: skis during major snow months.

P.B.A. (Perpetual Budget Account): account established for installment remittances to which cost of additional purchases may be added to extent previous purchases are paid for; system of revolving credit.

Perpetual Inventory: retail method of accounting whereby daily sales discounts and markdowns are deducted from book inventory, which also includes purchases and merchandise returns "today" and "to date."

Personal Care Items: hair dryers, electric shavers, saunas, electric hair curlers, hair setters, electric manicure and pedicure sets; merchandise to help improve customer's appearance.

P.O.P.: point-of-purchase display and signs.

Pre-Authorizing: obtaining credit authorization for charge-send transactions prior to package's or merchandise's leaving department.

Pre-Packaging: merchandise packaged by vendor for display, for "take-with" by customer or delivery by store. (Vendor can pre-package more economically via assembly line method than store.)

Pre-Marketing or Pre-Ticketing: marking of merchandise by manufacturer.

Prepay: payment of all shipping charges for merchandise by vendor, who rebills charges to purchaser on invoice for the merchandise.

Preprint: copy of an advertisement distributed to a store's customers and/or resources prior to publication in a general medium.

Pre-Retailing: system in which all merchandise is purchased to or carried at a pre-determined price, which is on record in the receiving and marking room. (Ready-to-wear is generally an exception due to desire to re-appraise value upon receipt in store.)

Pre-Ticketed: merchandise priced by vendor either on package or on price tickets or tags (often supplied by store to vendor with season letter, price, other necessary information) prior to packing for shipment to store. This saves store time, effort, and money in getting merchandise through receiving and marking room and onto selling floor.

Pre-Wrap: wrapping of merchandise before putting on sale (finding extensive use for types of merchandise of standard quality); also, merchandise wrapped or packaged by manufacturer for store "send" or customer "take-with."

Price Cutting: 1) cutting prices below a minimum resale price fixed (or suggested) by the vendor, and 2) selling below cost or below cost plus expenses of doing business; many discounters have developed a customer following by price cutting, particularly on nationally known brands.

Private Brand: controlled or private-label merchandise developed under store's own brand or developed under RBO's label exclusively for member stores.

Procurement Function: buying merchandise for resale to store's customers.

Purchasing Agent: executive who purchases products for store maintainance and operation—not for resale to customers.

Q

Quota: figure establishing goal of daily or weekly sales to be obtained by salespeople, individually or by department.

R

R.O.G. (Receipt of Goods) Terms: cash discount terms that begin when merchandise reaches store (designed to benefit retailers far from resource; also permits check of goods prior to due date for discount).

Receiving: process of accepting new merchandise at store or warehouse, includes initiating paper work to get merchandise "on the books" and processing incoming transportation bills.

Receiving Apron: form attached to store's purchase order contains information concerning status of vendor's shipment; forwarded by receiving department to invoice office, which audits all invoices before bills are paid.

Refund Check: form for refund of amount of purchase on a customer return; also, a bank check sent to customer as refund for merchandise returned.

Regional Shopping Center: 50 to 100 stores, including at least one major department store branch; 35 or more acres; requiring trading area of 100,000 people to support it, usually over 200,000 square feet in store area.

Regional Store: branch store generally situated at considerable distance from central downtown or flagship store, operating under name of parent store (its merchandise is frequently purchased by regional store's own merchandising staff), frequently operated on autonomous basis.

Remote Delivery: routing of merchandise from main metropolitan warehouse to distant customers by way of regional delivery stations in suburbs, or by trucks direct from store or warehouse.

Replenishment Orders: to fill-in (complete) assortments in a specific classification; usually referred to as a reorder.

Reprint: copy of an advertisement distributed to a store's customers and/or resources following publication in a general media.

Reps: individuals or wholesale companies representing a manufacturer or other vendors in specified sales territory, who solicit and accept orders that are shipped from vendor's factory or distributing point, but who do not actually own or stock merchandise.

Reserve Stock Control: method of earmarking sufficient amount of stock to maintain business while additional stock is purchased.

RBO (Resident Buying Office): office in a resource city to which non-competing stores belong; each store is exclusively served in its metromarket, the RBO is store's market representation and feeds it market information.

Retail Method Accounting: accounting method in which all percentages are relative to retail price instead of cost price. In cost method of accounting all percentages are relative to the cost. Example: Retail method—article purchased for $1 sells for $2, margin is $1 but only 50% of retail price. Cost method—article purchased for $1 sells for $2, margin is $1 but is 100% of cost price.

Retailing: basically, the business of buying for resale to the ultimate customer; also known as "acting as the customer's agent."

Return Policy: rules and regulations formulated by store's management covering merchandise returns by customers including exchange, credit, cash refunds, adjustments.

Returns to Vendor: shipments of merchandise returned by store to vendor because of errors in filling store's purchase order, substitutions in shipment, late delivery, defective materials or workmanship or fit, or other breaches of contract.

Routing Instructions: provided by store, to be attached by buyer to purchase order, informing vendor of routing and shipping instructions, specifying types of transportation store wants merchandise shipped by.

Rub Off: secondary benefit attained by a department from a promotion in another department. Example: opportunities for sales of oversize bed sheets, blankets, comforters, bedspreads because of sale of king or queen size mattresses and box springs.

Runner: item that sells and sells and sells (everybody's sweetheart); also used as for messenger.

S

Salescheck: form in triplicate listing customer's purchases, including price.

Sales Plan: department's promotional program for 6-month period, subject to monthly revision to take advantage of opportunistic purchases and other unpredictable merchandising opportunities.

Sales Slip: slip of paper from a roll on cash register showing only dollar and cents amount of purchase.

Salvage: applied to merchandise soiled beyond reclamation for salable purposes that must be disposed of through other channels; also refers to re-usable wrapping materials.

Selling Area: that part of sales floor devoted exclusively to selling (shoe and ready-to-wear stock rooms, ftting rooms and wrapping stations are considered part of selling area when sales could not be consummated without them.

Service Area: that part of sales floor devoted to servicing the selling area (such as escalators, elevators, stairways, freight landings, rest rooms, show windows).

Service Center: an area, frequently near small electrics department, however, may be located in warehouse where repairs or alterations are made.

Share of Market: per cent of a metromarket sales volume attained by a store, a department, or a classification within a department in the store.

Shoplifting: stealing of store's merchandise by customers. Of growing concern to all types of retailers.

Short Merchandise: merchandise purchased in limited quantities, generally in extreme sizes, to fill an assortment; also, items of purchase that through error were not included in customer's package or were missing in shipment from vendor.

Short SKU: system which permits full identification of an item, making possible the use of source-marked tickets either for backroom processing or cash register input, so that ultimately a store will be able to count sales, not stocks.

Short Supply Situation: merchandise where buyer has difficulty in maintaining adequate supply.

Showrooms: spaces maintained in various cities by vendors—manufacturers, importers, wholesalers, and distributors where merchandise is displayed for store buyers and merchandise managers to select styles and place orders.

Shrinkage: difference (on minus side) between merchandise on hand shown by physical inventory and that shown as "book value."

Side-Line Stores: stores run by organizations whose main activity is other than retailing.

Size Lining: method of organizing or grouping merchandise for selling by size. (Example: dress department set up with dresses of all colors, types, prices, and identified as "Size 10 to 20," "Size 38 to 44," etc.).

Skip: customer who moves from known address without paying his store bill.

Sleeper: potential "hot item" that, with aggressive promotion, may be developed into a runner.

Soft Goods: ready-to-wear for women, children, men; fashion accessories, piece goods, domestics.

Source Marking: pre-ticketing by resource before shipment. Very important in expediting arrival of merchandise on selling floor because not held up in receiving for price ticketing by store and also, less expensive because merchandise does not have to be opened in receiving, ticketed, then repackaged.

Specialty Stores: stores concentrating on specific classifications of merchandise. Examples: jewelry, furniture, books, men's clothing and furnishings, women's apparel and accessories, shoes, intimate apparel, sporting goods.

Split Ticket: price ticket perforated so portion can be removed for unit control purposes.

Spot Check: inspection and count of small, random amount of goods in large shipments.

Staple Stock: there is always the problem of overlap, in defining basic stock vs. staple stock. Essentially, the difference between basic and staple is assortments vs. single items. Staple stock is made up of items that are in practically continuous demand. Basic stock is an assortuent of items that are in current demand. Basic stock includes staple stock items.

Stock Book: record of purchases from orders and of sales from stubs of price tickets, usually maintained by buyer.

Stock Control: broad term for various systems and methods to control stock, i.e., keep it in line with customer demand, one step ahead when demand goes up; slowed up when demand falters.

SKU (Stock Keeping Unit): represents item of merchandise which is in stock.

Stub: in merchandise control, second part of price ticket, removed by salesperson at time of sale for unit merchandise-control.

Stub (Stubbing): extra copy of address label of salescheck which accompanies package to delivery depot, where it is removed and filed for use in adjustment of non-delivery complaints.

Stubber: sorter who removes extra copy of address label when placing package in route bin.

Stuffer: personnel in accounts receivable department who places original copy of salescheck in customer file.

Switching Customers: when a salesman cannot close a sale, he calls the buyer or department manager or even another salesman whom he introduces as a departmental supervisor, to take over the sale; more prevalent in men's clothing, furniture, or major appliance departments.

Synergism: the joint action of agents, which when taken together, increase each other's effectiveness.

T

"Take-Withs": merchandise carried from store by customer expediting delivery and saving delivery expense, particularly significant in branch stores.

Tally (Card or Envelope): form on which each salesperson records amount of each transaction; form is sometimes ruled for cash, C.O.D., and charge columns, has column for classification number.

Tight Money: high interest rates, which influence all facets of business.

To Pull: (verb) referring to advertising, e.g., "the ad pulled (produced sales) yesterday" or "that type of format doesn't pull."

Total Automatic Billing: exclusive use of machine in preparation and mailing store's customer bills.

Tracer: personnel in receiving and marking area and traffic department who trace delayed or lost shipments of incoming merchandise; also trace lost deliveries to customers. Also form used in these processes.

Trading area: surrounding area from which most of store's trade is drawn, varies by individual store location. Each store, main or branch, needs to know to what extent and from what directions it draws customers; checking automobile license plates in shopping-center parking lots, questioning customers who visit store, analyzing charge accounts, etc., will develop this information.

Traffic: number of persons, both prospective and actual customers, who enter store or department.

Transactions per Square Foot: number of transactions per square foot of selling space are obtained by dividing the number of gross transactions of sales checks of a department by the average number of square feet the department occupies for selling space.

Turnover: total number of times, within given period, that stock of goods is sold and replaced. (Whirling dervishes get top billing at retail level).

U

Unit Billing: customer receives single statement, list of articles purchased is posted on detachable strip which store retains for adjustment purposes.

Unit Control: system of recording vital statistics of stock on hand, on order, and sold for a given period; "control" is interpretation of statistics as barometer showing change in customer buying habits; works best when barometer readings are taken frequently and seriously.

Upgrading: increasing price lines by offering better quality and assortments plus improved visual merchandising in a specific classification of products.

V

Value-added Tax: a pyramiding form of assessment. At each level of manufacturing and distribution, from the raw material until the finished product is offered to the consumer, a tax on the increased value of the product is added.

Vendor: manufacturer, wholesaler (jobber), importer, or commission merchant from whom merchandise is purchased.

Vendor Chargebacks: where merchandise is returned to vendor store submits bill to vendor, frequently accompanied by proof of delivery to vendor.

Visual Merchandising: presentation of merchandise to best selling advantage and for maximum traffic exposure, plus projection of customer "ready-to-buy." Not a display technique but merchandising strategy.

Visual System Stock Control: method of arranging stock on shelves in piles of equal quantity for quick visual count.

Void: error which requires writing of new salescheck or re-ringing of amount on cash register; the wrong salescheck or cash register receipt is voided and must be returned to auditing department.

W

Walk-Outs: customers who enter store with acquisitive gleam in eye, walk out dull-eyed and empty-handed. Reasons why vary—absence of merchandise information at point-of-sale, lack of informative labeling, items out of stock due to non-existing basic stock plans, etc.—being fresh out of serpents in garden, i.e., buying temptations).

Want-Slips: a system where salesperson reorders customers request for merchandise not in stock and tells whether or not a substitute article is sold. The items added to stock on a basis of want slips may make the difference between profit and loss and play an important part in establishing a reputation for leadership and service. Sometimes store makes the form available to customers to fill out and deposit in a box.

Warehouse Stock: merchandise carried in bulk in a remote warehouse for reasons of economy. Some of these stocks are moved into store as department's supply is depleted, but generally saleschecks are filled out and delivery is made directly from warehouse to customer.

Warehousing Unit: a storage area devoted to specific classifications of merchandise, generally remote from flagship store.

Warranty: the act or an instance of warranting; assurance; guarantee authorization; an express warranty of the quality of goods made by the manufacturer.

Waybill: shipping form similar to manifest or bill of lading, stipulates names of vendor and consignee, shipping instructions, costs, etc.

White Goods: refrigerators, deep freezers, automatic dryers, washing machines, stoves, dish washers; all comparatively big ticket items.

Will Call: another name applied to lay-away; also applies to purchases which have been paid for in full but which customer will return and pick up.

Y

Youth Market: women, men under 25 years of age, including babies, children, subteens, teens, young men and women primarily interested in the new, different, unusual; often in contrast to the tastes of members of older generations, and sometimes in heated opposition!

APPENDIX B:
List of Retail Employers

FIRM	ADDRESS	NAME & TITLE OF PERSON TO CORRESPOND WITH	AFFILIATION	TYPE OF BUSINESS	NUMBER OF EMPLOYEES
Abraham & Straus	422 Fulton St., Brooklyn, N.Y. 11201	Olon Zager, Director of Executive Recruitment	Division of Federated Department Stores, Inc.	Retail department stores	9,000
Alexander's Inc.	Lexington Ave. at 59th St., New York, N.Y. 10022	Mrs. Dianne Leeds, Executive Placement Manager		Retail department stores	16,000
Allied Stores & Marketing Corp.	401 5th Ave., New York, N.Y. 10016	Mrs. Mary Audrain, Personnel Director	Allied Stores Corp.	Central executive & merchandising offices of national group of department stores	675
B. Altman & Co.	361 5th Ave., New York, N.Y. 10016	Doris Robsky, Director of Executive Development		Retail department stores	6,000
American Photograph Corp.	130 Steamboat Rd., Great Neck, N.Y. 11024	Mary McDermott, Training Director		Operation of portrait photograph studies in leading department stores in 44 states	1,900
Army–Air Force Exchange Service	3911 S. Walton Walker Blvd., Dallas, Tex. 75222	Lou Conde, Recruitment & Executive Development Section		Operation of retail stores, restaurants, snack bars, food processing plants, automotive service stations, personal service facilities	70,000

FIRM	ADDRESS	NAME & TITLE OF PERSON TO CORRESPOND WITH	AFFILIATION	TYPE OF BUSINESS	NUMBER OF EMPLOYEES
Associated Merchandising Corp.	1400 Broadway, New York, N.Y. 10018	Division Vice President, Personnel	Affiliated with 30 leading department stores throughout U.S.	Retail service organization	1,000
Bamberger's	131 Market St., Newark, N.J. 07101	R. Michael Rudman, Manager of Executive Recruitment	Division of R. H. Macy & Co., Inc.	Retail department store	10,500
Belk Stores, Inc.	308 E. 5th St., Charlotte, N.C. 28201	Ray A. Killian, Vice President, Personnel & Public Relations		Retail department store	17,000
Best Products Co., Inc.	P.O. Box 26303, Richmond, Va. 23260	J. Richard Bragg, Director of Personnel		Catalog distributor	800
Black, James, Co.	E. 4th & Sycamore St., Waterloo, Ia. 50704	Arthur B. Christman, Managing Director	Allied Stores Corp.	Complete department store	
Block, William H., Co.	50 N. Illinois St., Indianapolis, Ind. 46209	Richard Ross, Personnel Director	Allied Stores Corp.	Retail department store	3,100
Bloomingdale's	Lexington Ave. at 59th St., New York, N.Y. 10022	Robert Silver, Vice President, Personnel & Labor Relations	Division of Federated Department Stores, Inc.	Retail department store	7,200
Bon Marche Inc.—Massachusetts	Lowell, Mass. 01852	Mrs. Margaret E. Richards, Personnel Director	Allied Stores Corp.	Retail department store	200

Company	Address	Contact	Parent/Division	Business	No.
Bon Marche—Intermountain States	Boise, Ida. 83702	L. C. Stevens, Group Supervisor	Allied Stores Corp.	Operation of retail department store	1,200
Bon Marche Stores, Inc.	Seattle, Wash. 98101	W. A. Wilson, Executive Development Director	Allied Stores Corp.	Retail department store	4,500
Bonwit Teller	721 5th Ave., New York, N.Y. 10022	Mrs. Linda Whinery, Associate Personnel Director		Women's specialty store	1,000
Boston Store	331 W. Wisconsin Ave., Milwaukee, Wis. 53203	Robert Jewell, Executive Development Manager	Division of Federated Department Stores, Inc.	Retail department store	2,400
Brigham's Inc.	30 Mill St., Arlington, Mass. 02174	Irwin F. Gordon, Personnel Director	Subsidiary of Jewel Cos., Inc.	Chain of over 125 ice cream, sandwich shops & family restaurants	2,000
Broadway Department Stores	3880 N. Mission Rd., Los Angeles, Calif. 90031	Michael J. Munz, Manager of Executive Recruitment & Placement		Retail department store	12,000
Buffums'	Pine and Broadway, Long Beach, Calif. 90802	Mrs. Barbara Shanks, Director of Personnel		Retail department store	1,800
Bullock's	Seventh and Hill Sts., Los Angeles, Calif. 90055	Gene P. Ross, Director of Management Development	Division of Federated Department Stores, Inc.	Retail department store	7,200
Burdine's	22 E. Flagler St., Miami, Fla. 33130	Gary Piles, Manager of Junior Executive Recruitment	Division of Federated Department Stores, Inc.	Retail department store	4,300

FIRM	ADDRESS	NAME & TITLE OF PERSON TO CORRESPOND WITH	AFFILIATION	TYPE OF BUSINESS	NUMBER OF EMPLOYEES
Buttrey Foods, Inc.	601 Sixth St. S.W., Great Falls, Mont. 59401	Jim Pannell, Personnel Manager		36 supermarkets in Montana, Idaho, & Washington	
Cain-Sloan Co.	5th Ave. and Church St., Nashville, Tenn. 37219	Charles W. Fentress, Personnel Director		Retail department store	1,200
Capwell's	20th and Broadway, Oakland, Calif. 94612	Mrs. Joan Jensen, Assistant Personnel Superintendent	Division of Emporium-Capwell Co.	Retail department store	2,000
Carson Pirie Scott & Co.	1 S. State St., Chicago, Ill. 60603	Ruth Yohanan, Executive Placement Manager		Retail department store	8,000
Chevron Oil Co.—Eastern Division	1200 State St., Perth Amboy, N.J. 08861	H. A. Syring, Assistant Manager of Personnel	Subsidiary of Standard Oil Co. of California	Petroleum refining and marketing	1,900
Cook United-Discount	16501 Rockside Rd., Cleveland, O. 44137	Melvyn W. Labovitz, Director of Personnel	Subsidiary of Cook United, Inc.	National retail discount chain	14,000
Davison's	180 Peachtree St. N.W., Atlanta, Ga. 30303	M. A. Smiley, Vice President, Personnel	Division of R. H. Macy & Co., Inc.	Retail store	2,500
Dayton Hudson Corp.	777 Nicollet Mall, Minneapolis, Minn. 55402	Corporate Vice President, Personnel and Communications		Operation of department stores, discount stores, hard good stores, jewelry stores, bookstores, franchised electronics stores	40,000

Company	Address	Contact	Ownership	Business	Number
Dayton's	700 on the Mall, Minneapolis, Minn. 55402	Manager, Executive Placement	Subsidiary of Dayton Hudson Corp.	Retail department store	10,500
Denny's Restaurant, Inc.	14256 E. Firestone Blvd., La Mirada, Calif. 90638	F. C. Kostlan, Personnel & Industrial Relations		National chain of hotels, restaurants, coffee shops & fast-food units	5,000
Dey Brothers & Co.	401 S. Salina St., Syracuse, N.Y. 13201	Donald Shaffer, Personnel Director	Allied Stores Corp.	Retail department store	600
Economy Finance Corp.	108 E. Washington St., Indianapolis, Ind. 46204	Gerald D. Shoemaker, Vice President, Personnel	Subsidiaries are Shoppers Charge Service, Indianapolis Morris Plan, Transcontinental Credit Corp., National Public Life Insurance Co., Pioneer Finance Co.	Savings; consumer & commercial financing, incl. heavy equipment, cable TV, real estate; re-discount & retail charge account service	1,050
Eisner Food & Agency Stores	301 E. Wilbur Heights Rd., Champaign, Ill. 61823	Patrick Johnston, Personnel Director		35 supermarkets in central Illinois & Indiana	
Emporium	835 Market St., San Francisco, Calif. 94103	Mrs. Muriel Pearce, Manager, Executive Development		Retail department store	2,500
Famous-Barr Co.	6th and Olive Sts., St. Louis, Mo. 63101	Douglas J. Giles, Director, Training & Development	Subsidiary of May Department Stores Co.	Retail department store	8,000

FIRM	ADDRESS	NAME & TITLE OF PERSON TO CORRESPOND WITH	AFFILIATION	TYPE OF BUSINESS	NUMBER OF EMPLOYEES
Field, L. H., Co.	201 W. Michigan Ave., Jackson, Mich. 49201	Mark Tuttle, Personnel Director	Allied Stores Corp.	Retail department store	275
Filene's	426 Washington, Boston, Mass. 02101	Mrs. Jacqueline Sullivan, Director of Executive Recruitment & Development	Division of Federated Department Stores, Inc.	Retail department store	4,800
Firstmark Financial Corp.	110 E. Washington St., Indianapolis, Ind. 46204	Gerald D. Shoemaker, Vice President, Personnel	Subsidiary of CIC Corp. Subsidiary is: Indianapolis Morris Plan	Savings, consumer & commercial financing, incl. heavy equipment, cable TV, etc.	800
Florsheim Retail Division	Suite 200, 130 S. Canal St., Chicago, Ill. 60606	Paul R. Holmes, Director of Recruitment & Training	Subsidiary of Florsheim Shoe Co.	Marketing and related areas of retailing of shoes	
Foley's	1110 Main St., Houston, Tex. 77001	Bruce Krause, Manager of Training Department	Division of Federated Department Stores, Inc.	Department store	4,800
Fox, G., and Co.	960 Main St., Hartford, Conn. 06100	Mrs. Patricia Wilson, Executive Placement Director	Subsidiary of May Department Stores Co.	Retail department store	3,000
Friendly Ice Cream Corp.	1855 Boston Rd., North Wilbraham, Mass. 01067	D. R. Knight, Personnel Director		Manufacture of ice cream; operation of retail ice cream & sandwich shops	7,000

Company	Address	Contact	Notes	Description	Number
FS Services, Inc.	1701 Towanda Ave., Bloomington, Ill. 61701	R. P. Swan, Personnel Manager		Manufacture & distribution of agricultural supplies	5,200
General Tire & Rubber Co.	1 General St., Akron, O. 44309	College Recruiting Manager	Divisions are Acrojet-General, General Tire International, RKO-General, Chemicals/Plastics, Industrial Products; subsidiaries are A.M., Byers, Galis Mfg. Co., Frontier Airlines, Fleetwood Corp.	Worldwide operation includes manufacture of tires & rubber products, chemicals, plastics, rocket propulsion & space exploration, radio-TV electronics, aviation, athletic equipment, wrought iron and steel	45,000
Genesco Inc.	Genesco Park, Nashville, Tenn. 37202	William S. Montgomery, Director of Management Development		Manufacture and sale of apparel and shoes for men, women, and children	72,000
Gertz, B., Inc.	162–10 Jamaica Ave., Jamaica, N.Y. 11432	Kevin Tubridy, Personnel Director	Subsidiary of Allied Stores Corp.	Retail department store	3,600
Giant Food Inc.	6900 Sheriff Rd., Landover, Md. 20013	Personnel Officer		Retail food, general merchandise, and pharmacy chain	9,500
Giant Stores Corp.	9 Stuart Rd., Chelmsford, Ma. 01824	Percy E. Clemons, Employment Manager		Retail & wholesale marketing of consumer products	3,000

FIRM	ADDRESS	NAME & TITLE OF PERSON TO CORRESPOND WITH	AFFILIATION	TYPE OF BUSINESS	NUMBER OF EMPLOYEES
Gimbels, Midwest	101 W. Wisconsin Ave., Milwaukee, Wis. 53201	Eleanor Poss, Personnel Director	Subsidiary of Gimbel Brothers, Inc.	Retail department store	6,500
Gimbels, New York	Broadway at 33d St., New York, N.Y. 10001	Robert Siegel, Personnel Relations Director	Subsidiary of Gimbel Brothers, Inc.	Retail department store	7,000
Gimbels, Philadelphia	9th and Market Sts., Philadelphia, Pa. 19105	T. R. Amerman, Director, Executive Placement	Subsidiary of Gimbel Brothers, Inc.	Retail department store	6,500
Gimbels, Pittsburgh	6th Ave. and Smithfield St., Pittsburgh, Pa. 15222	David J. Wolfe, Director of Executive Development	Subsidiary of Gimbel Brothers, Inc.	Retail department store	6,500
Gold Circle	6121 Huntley Rd., Worthington, O. 43085	Charles Corthell, Vice President, Organization Development	Division of Federated Department Stores, Inc.	Apparel store	
Goldsmith's	Main at Gayoso, Memphis, Tenn. 38103	Fred Koch, Vice President & Personnel Director	Division of Federated Department Stores, Inc.	Department store	1,800
Goodrich	500 S. Main St., Akron, O. 44318	R. N. Sankovich Manager, Universal Relations		Manufacturer of rubber products, aviation products, plastics, chemicals, footware, sponge products, textiles, and basic research on all these products	47,000

Goodyear Tire & Rubber Co.	1144 E. Market St., Akron, O. 44316	R. W. Wheeler, Manager, Corporate College Relations (non-sales); J. T. Beckley, Manager, Sales Personnel (sales only)	Manufacturer of tires, industrial rubber products, foam rubber products, synthetic rubber, chemicals, plastics, aviation products, shoe products, textiles, metal products, atomic energy	136,000
Goudchaux's Department Store	1500 Main St., Baton Rouge, La. 70821	William R. Hamblin, Personnel Director	Retailing	500
Grand Union Co.	100 Broadway, East Paterson, N.J. 07407	V. J. Veninata, Vice President & Director of Personnel	Retail supermarket & general merchandise chain with related functions in purchasing, warehousing, distribution, real estate	26,000
Grant, W. T., Co.	1515 Broadway, New York, N.Y. 10036	D. R. McGeorge, Recruitment & Placement Manager; or Regional Personnel Managers — New England Region, Eastern Region, Pittsburgh Region, Central Region, Southern Region, Western Region.	Nationwide retail organization	66,000

FIRM	ADDRESS	NAME & TITLE OF PERSON TO CORRESPOND WITH	AFFILIATION	TYPE OF BUSINESS	NUMBER OF EMPLOYEES
Graybar Electric Co., Inc.	420 Lexington Ave., New York, N.Y. 10017	A. E. Picard, Manager, Personnel Development		Wholesale distribution & marketing of electrical products & appliances to industrial firms, contractors, commercial operations & export establishments, chain stores, universities, federal, state & municipal governments, retail dealers	5,300
Green Giant Co.	Le Sueur, Minn. 56058	Linda Wint, Personnel Supervisor		Food processing, restaurant operations, home & garden centers	4,500
Hardy-Herpolsheimer's	315 W. Western Ave., Muskegon, Mich. 49440	Mrs. Lora Coffel, Personnel Director	Allied Stores Corp.	Retail department store	2,600
Hartfield Zodys, Inc.	441 Ninth Ave., New York, N.Y.	Michael R. Stoler, Assistant Vice President, Director of Personnel		National chain of retail discount department stores	7,000
Hecht Co.—Baltimore	Howard and Lexington Sts., Baltimore, Md. 21201	Aldwin E. Jolly, Director of Personnel	Subsidiary of May Department Stores Co.	Retail department store	2,600
Hecht Co.—Washington	7th and F Sts. N.W., Washington, D.C. 20004	Stanley J. Mont, Director, Organization Development	Subsidiary of May Department Stores Co.	Retail department store	6,000
Heer's, Inc.	Public Square, Springfield, Mo. 65803	Miss Shirley Miller, Personnel Director	Allied Stores Corp.	Retail department store	6,000

Company	Address	Contact	Affiliation	Description	Number
Herpolsheimer Co.	1 Monroe N.W., Grand Rapids, Mich. 49502	Janet Fowler, Personnel Director	Allied Stores Corp.	Retail department store	400
Higbee Co.	100 Public Square, Cleveland, O. 44113	James M. Pfohl, Executive Development Manager		Retail department store	7,500
Hill Department Stores	210 South St., Boston, Mass. 02111	Robert W. Murphy, Recruitment Coordinator	Subsidiary of SCOA Industries, Inc.	Self-service department stores	2,500
Hochschild Kohn & Co.	Howard & Lexington Sts., Baltimore, Md. 21201	Ronald A. Cameron, Vice President, Personnel		Retail department store	3,600
Holiday Inns, Inc.	3742 Lamar Ave., Memphis, Tenn. 38118	Director of Personnel, Corporate Staff		International multi-diversified operations with 5 divisions: commercial services, transportation, sales, products, distribution	55,000
Holly's Inc.	245 Colrain St. SW, P.O. Box 8790, Grand Rapids, Mich. 49508	Edward Kulesza, Personnel		Operates motor inns & full-service steak house cafeteria restaurant	1,100
Host International, Inc.	Pico at 34th, Santa Monica, Calif. 90406	Paul Lucido, Employment Manager		Food services & airport terminal operations	9,000
Hudson, J. L., Co.	1206 Woodward Ave., Detroit, Mich. 48226	Ian C. Shaw, Management Development Director	Subsidiary of Dayton-Hudson Corp.	Retail department store chain	17,122

FIRM	ADDRESS	NAME & TITLE OF PERSON TO CORRESPOND WITH	AFFILIATION	TYPE OF BUSINESS	NUMBER OF EMPLOYEES
ITT Sheraton	470 Atlantic Ave., Boston, Mass. 02210	Thomas Fitzpatrick	Subsidiary of International Telephone & Telegraph	Transient and convention hotels	26,000
Jewel Box	Wachovia Bldg., P.O. Box 21768, Greensboro, N.C. 27420	Margaret Wright, Personnel Manager		Retail jewelry chain	1,200
Jewel Food Stores	1955 W. North Ave., Melrose Park, Ill. 60160	John McTigue, Manager, Management Development		260 supermarkets in Chicago metropolitan area; operations in 44 states	
Jones Store Co.	Main, Walnut, and 12 Sts., Kansas City, Mo. 64105	Mrs. R. A. Thompson, Personnel Director	Subsidiary of Mercantile Stores, Inc.	Retail merchandising	1,800
Jord-Inns of America, Inc.	303 Bassett Tower, El Paso, Tex. 79901	Manuel Lopez, Operations Manager		Restaurants	270
Jordon Marsh Co.	450 Washington St., Boston, Mass. 02107	Elwin H. Thomas, Manager of Employment and College Relations	Allied Stores Corp.	Retail department store	12,000
Jordon Marsh— Florida	1501 Biscayne Blvd., Miami, Fla. 33132	Durward E. Harrell, Personnel Director	Allied Stores Corp.	Retail department store	1,500
Joske's of Houston	4925 Westheimer, Houston, Tex. 77032	George Nelson, Personnel Director	Allied Stores Corp.	Retail department store	2,000

Company	Address	Contact	Affiliation	Business	Number
Joske's of Texas	P.O. Box 961, San Antonio, Tex. 78294	Mrs. Rex Johnson, Personnel Director	Allied Stores Corp.	Retail department store	1,400
Kaufmann's	400 5th Ave., Pittsburgh, Pa. 15219	George S. Wilson, Director of Personnel Management	Subsidiary of May Department Stores Co.	Retail department store	6,000
Kinney Shoe Corp.	Woolworth Bldg., 233 Broadway, New York, N.Y. 10007	Philip H. Cease, Corporate Personnel Director	Subsidiary of F. W. Woolworth Co.	Manufacturing and retail selling of shoes	15,097
Kresge, S. S., Co.	3100 W. Big Beaver, Troy, Mich. 48084	Regional Personnel Managers: Central Eastern, Midwestern, Southern, Western			
Kress, S. H. and Co.	114 5th Ave., New York, N.Y. 10011	Manager of Field Training, Manpower Division	Division of Genesco, Inc.	Retailing	8,000
Kroger Co.	1014 Vine St., Cincinnati, O. 45201	Coordinator, Campus Recruiting		Retailer in foods and drugs; food processor	53,000
Lazarus, F. & R., & Co.	High and Town Sts., Columbus, O. 43216	Dallas Tucker, Division Manager	Division of Federated Department Stores, Inc.	Retail department store	6,000
Levy's of Savannah, Inc.	201 E. Broughton St., Savannah, Ga. 31401	Mrs. Dorine Glass, Personnel Director	Allied Stores Corp.	Retail department store	200
Lord & Taylor	424 5th Ave., New York, N.Y. 10018	Miss Esther Bogart, Employment Director	Subsidiary of Associated Dry Goods Corp.	Retail specialty store	2,800

FIRM	ADDRESS	NAME & TITLE OF PERSON TO CORRESPOND WITH	AFFILIATION	TYPE OF BUSINESS	NUMBER OF EMPLOYEES
Maas Brothers, Inc.	P.O. Box 311, Tampa, Fla. 33601	William D. Davis, Personnel Director	Allied Stores Corp.	Retail department store	7,500
Mabley & Carew	Cincinnati, O. 45202	Mrs. Gladys Matthews, Personnel Director	Allied Stores Corp.	Retail department store	1,000
Maginn, J., & Co.	Union Square, San Francisco, Calif. 94108	Charles Gray, Vice President, Personnel	Division of Federated Department Stores, Inc.	Fine-apparel stores	2,300
May Cohens	117 W. Duval St., Jacksonville, Fla. 32202	Douglas J. Giles, Personnel Director	Subsidiary of May Department Stores Co.	Retail department store	1,000
May Co.— Cleveland	Euclid and Ontario Sts., Cleveland, O. 44144	Mrs. Ann Hupke, Personnel Development Director	Subsidiary of May Department Stores Co.	Retail department store	6,000
May-D & F	16th at Tremont St., Denver, Colo. 80202	Jack Collins, Vice President & Personnel Director	Subsidiary of May Department Stores Co.	Retail department store	2,500
Mercantile Stores Co., Inc.	128 W. 31st St., New York, N.Y. 10001	Gene Braham, Personnel Manager		Retail department store	250
Meyer's Co.	Drawer F-1, Greensboro, N.C. 27401	Miss Jenelle Miller, Personnel Director	Allied Stores Corp.	Retail department store	250
Mobile Home Industries, Inc.	1309 Thomasville Rd., Tallahassee, Fla. 32303	James S. Harvey, Personnel Director (P.O. Box 2253, Tallahassee)		Mobile home retail sales, manufacturing, parks & land development, insurance & finance agencies	1,500

Montgomery Ward & Co.	P.O. Box 8339, Chicago, Ill. 60680	P. D. Smith, College Relations Coordinator	Subsidiary of Marcor, Inc.	Retail stores, mail-order catalogs, catalog stores	100,000
Murphy, G. C., Co.	531 5th Ave., McKeesport, Pa. 15132	W. H. Sweet, Personnel Director		General merchandise chain	26,000
Nash Finch Co.	3381 Gorham Ave., Minneapolis, Minn. 55426	Frank L. Kitson, Director of Personnel		Retail and wholesale food distribution	3,600
Navy Resale System Office	830 3d Ave., Brooklyn, N.Y. 11232	R. L. Koch, Manager of Employment & Recruitment		Nonappropriated-fund government agency providing retail goods & services to Navy personnel & their families	32,000
Neiman-Marcus	Main & Ervay, Dallas, Tex. 75201	Manager of Supervisory Placement & Recruiting		Specialty store	3,500
Neisner Brothers, Inc.	49 East Ave., Rochester, N.Y. 14604	Donald M. Sabin, Manpower Development Manager		Retail chain of junior department & department stores	6,500
North Carolina National Bank	P.O. Box 120, Charlotte, N.C. 28201	Charles J. Cooley, Senior Vice President	Subsidiary of NCNB Corp.	Holding company; commercial banking, international banking, mortgage banking, investment management, factoring & consumer finance	4,200

FIRM	ADDRESS	NAME & TITLE OF PERSON TO CORRESPOND WITH	AFFILIATION	TYPE OF BUSINESS	NUMBER OF EMPLOYEES
Osco Drug, Inc.	3030 Cullerton Dr., Franklin Park, Ill. 60131	Dave Maher, Vice President, Personnel	Subsidiary of Jewel Companies, Inc.	180 self-service drug stores in Midwest, Idaho/Montana area & New England	
Peebles Department Stores	Lawrenceville, Va. 23868	John E. Keith, Jr., Director, Personnel & Training		Retailing–junior department store chain	550
Penney, J. C., Co., Inc.	1301 Ave. of the Americas, New York, N.Y. 10019	Charles R. Lops, Manager, Corporate College Relations		National retail distribution	160,000
Pet Inc.	400 S. 4th St., St. Louis, Mo. 63166	C. T. Canatsey, Management Employment		Processing & marketing of dairy products, frozen & gourmet foods, candy; specialty retailing & food service; merchandising equipment; warehousing & distribution services	20,000
Pogue, H. & S., Co.	4th & Race Sts., Cincinnati, O. 45202	Albert L. Schaefer, Personnel Director	Division of Associated Dry Goods Corp.	Department store	2,000
Popular Club Plan	128 Dayton Ave., Passaic, N.J. 07055	Anthony Zaldumbide, Personnel Director	Subsidiary of Popular Services, Inc.	Retail mail-order merchandising	1,800
Read, D. M., Inc.	Trumbull, Conn. 06611	Richard M. Winfrey, Personnel Director	Allied Stores Corp.	Retail department store	500

Company	Address	Contact	Affiliation	Type	Number
Rich's, Inc.	45 Broad St., Atlanta, Ga. 30302	Mrs. Jean Moss, Manager of Recruitment & Placement		Retail department store	10,000
Rike's	Secon and Main Sts., Dayton, O. 45401	Keith Maloney, Director of Executive Development	Division of Federated Department Stores, Inc.	Department store	3,000
Robert Hall Clothes	333 W. 34th St., New York, N.Y. 10001	Howard P. Korchin, Vice President	Subsidiary of United Merchants & Manufacturers, Inc.	Retail clothing chain	9,000
Rose's Stores, Inc.	Garnett St., Henderson, N.C. 27536	J. A. Roberts, Jr., Manager of Personnel		Variety retailing	11,000
Sanger-Harris	Akard and Pacific, Dallas, Tex. 75222	Miss Bette J. Smith, Divisional Manager of Personnel	Division of Federated Department Stores, Inc.	Retail department store	3,600
Sav-a-Stop Inc.	766 Gainesville Ave., Jacksonville, Fla. 32208	C. G. Bennett, Jr., Vice President of Employer Relations		Retail discount stores	5,000
Sears, Roebuck and Co.	925 S. Homan Ave., Chicago, Ill. 60607	W. W. Tudor, Vice President		General retail merchandising	375,000
Service Systems Corp.	8989 Sheridan Dr., Clarence, N.Y. 14031	David R. Henning, Manager of Wage and Salary Administration and Recruitment	Subsidiary of Del Monte Corp.	Contract food-service management, maintenance services, security & vending services	7,500

FIRM	ADDRESS	NAME & TITLE OF PERSON TO CORRESPOND WITH	AFFILIATION	TYPE OF BUSINESS	NUMBER OF EMPLOYEES
Shillito's	7th and Race Sts., Cincinnati, O. 45202	Richard Leibelt, Director of Executive Development	Subsidiary of Federated Department Stores, Inc.	Complete department store	4,200
Shopko Stores, Inc.	2800 S. Ashland Ave., Green Bay, Wis. 54303	James O. Harding, Personnel Supervisor-Training & Recruitment	Subsidiary of Super Value Stores, Inc.	Discount retail stores	1,200
Smith & Sons Foods, Inc.	2124 Riverside Dr., Macon, Ga. 31208	W. G. Moffat, Assistant to President		Commercial cafeterias, drive-ins; educational, institutional contract feeding; central commissaries & meat fabrication plants	2,800
Standard Oil Co. of Ohio	1422 CP Midland Bldg. Cleveland, O. 44115	Elwood G. Glass, Jr., Manager of Technical & Professional Recruitment		Integrated petroleum & chemical company; petroleum refining & marketing; manufacture & sale of consumer & industrial chemical & plastic products; research & engineering	20,000
Star Markets	625 Mt. Auburn St., Cambridge, Mass. 02138	E. F. Buron, Vice President, Human Resources	Subsidiary of Jewel Companies, Inc.	Supermarket	
Stern Brothers	Route 4, Bergen Mall, Paramus, N.J. 07652	Miss Ethel Eyre, Executive Placement Director	Subsidiary of Allied Stores Corp.	Retail department store	2,100

Company	Address	Contact	Affiliation	Description	Number
Stop & Shop Cos., Inc.	397 D St., South Boston, Mass. 02210	College Recruiting Manager		Retail corporation	20,000
Stouffer Restaurants & Inns	1375 Euclid Ave., Cleveland, O. 44115	James T. Kuczynski, Administration, Recruiting, Staffing & Training		Operation of restaurants and inns	8,000
Strouss-Hirshberg	Federal, Phelps & Commerce Sts., Youngstown, O. 44501	Michael J. Babcock, Vice President & Personnel Director	Subsidiary of May Department Stores Co.	Retail department store company	2,500
Thrifty Drug Stores Co., Inc.	5051 Rodeo Rd., Los Angeles, Calif. 90016	G. Bishop, Director of Personnel; G. Norton, Director of Management Training		Retail drug & discount stores	10,000
Titche Goettinger Co.	Main, Elm, and Paul Sts., Dallas, Tex. 75201	George W. Brickley, Personnel Director	Allied Stores Corp.	Retail department store	3,000
Top Value Enterprises	3085 Woodman Dr., Dayton, O. 45420	E. J. Gray, Personnel Manager		Sales promotion & business improvement through trading stamps; incentive, continuity & merchandising programs; operation of travel agencies	3,500
Turn-Style Family Centers	3030 Cullerton Dr., Franklin Park, Ill. 60131	J. E. Jannotta, Vice President, Personnel	Subsidiary of Jewel Companies, Inc.	18 self-service department stores in Midwest, New England	

FIRM	ADDRESS	NAME & TITLE OF PERSON TO CORRESPOND WITH	AFFILIATION	TYPE OF BUSINESS	NUMBER OF EMPLOYEES
Troutman, A. E., Co.	200 S. Main St., Greensburg, Pa. 15601	E. S. Lauffer	Allied Stores Corp.	Full-line department store	1,000
Union Camp Corp.	1600 Valley Rd., Wayne, N.J. 07470	Asa B. Johnson, Jr., Director of Organizational Planning & Development		Manufacture of paper & allied products; chemicals; building products; land development; retail building supply and home improvement centers	15,000
Union 76	200 E. Golf Rd., Palatine, Ill. 60067	Peter G. Harper, Recruitment & Employment Manager	Division of Union Oil Co. of California	Refining, transportation & marketing of petroleum products, incl. fuels, lubricants, petrochemicals	7,800
Ups 'n Downs Stores	461 Eighth Ave., New York, N.Y. 10001	Alex Lapina, Vice President, Store Operations		Junior sportswear for females	600
Venture Stores, Inc.	615 Northwest Plaza, St. Louis, Mo. 63074	Frank Tricamo, Director of Placement		Discount retail stores	4,200
Walgreen Co.	4300 Peterson Ave., Chicago, Ill. 60646	Roger D. Goldbach, Personnel Consultant		Nationwide retailer in restaurant & drug store operations	29,000
Western Auto	2107 Grand Ave., Kansas City, Mo. 64108	Jack Cooney, Manager of Selling & Training	Subsidiary of Beneficial Finance Co.	Retail and wholesale merchandising	10,000

Western International Hotels Co.	Olympic Hotel, 416 Seneca, Seattle, Wash. 98111	Gordon Schneider, Director of Personnel		Operation of hotels in principal cities on world-wide basis	15,000
Winn-Dixie Stores, Inc.	5050 Edgewood Court, Jacksonville, Fla. 32205	T. H. Moss, Personnel Director (Box B, Jacksonville 32203)		Retail food chain	35,000
Woolworth, F. W., Co.	233 Broadway, New York, N.Y. 10007	Management Training Director		Retail general merchandise & department stores	85,000
Wren, Edward, Store	14 E. Main St., Springfield, O. 45501	Margaret McDonough, Personnel Director	Allied Stores Corp.	Retail department store	230

NAME INDEX

SUBJECT INDEX